15⁰⁰ 2/24

THE

FOLKTALE

THE

FOLKTALE

by

STITH THOMPSON

UNIVERSITY OF CALIFORNIA PRESS
Berkeley • Los Angeles • London

University of California Press
Berkeley and Los Angeles, California
University of California Press, Ltd.
London, England
ISBN: 0-520-03537-2
Library of Congress Catalog Card Number: 76-48366
Copyright 1946 by Holt, Rinehart and Winston, Inc.
Reprinted 1977 by the University of California Press

2 3 4 5 6 7 8 9

TO THE MEMORY OF
ARTHUR BEATTY

WHO FIRST SHOWED THE WAY

PREFACE

THE past half century has seen an ever increasing interest in the folktale. Collectors have been busy in all parts of the world listening to story-tellers, and with better and better techniques recording and publishing what they hear. Some scholars have made classifications and local surveys so as to bring the enormous mass of material into order; others have evolved methods for the study of oral narrative; and still others have used these methods to plot out the history of many of the well-known stories.

All this activity has served to bring light into many places that were formerly dark and to correct early or premature theories. We begin to see the oral tale as the most universal of all narrative forms, and to understand its relation to the literary stories of our own civilization. We are learning of the function of the tale in the lives of those who tell and those who listen, and of the nature of this art in different lands and different times.

The very mass of the materials thus assembled is so overwhelming that it remains largely unknown except to a small group of specialists. Yet the subject is by its nature of great importance to all serious students of literature, of anthropology, of psychology, and of art in general. For these and for all those readers who find interest in man's attempt to bring enjoyment to his leisure through the art of story-telling there is now no work which can serve as a guide. To help supply this lack is the purpose of the present volume.

In the introductory section I have endeavored to show the importance of the folktale in society as the narrative form still used by the great majority of human beings, both among the so-called primitive peoples and among the unlettered of our own culture. This has led to a comparison of the oral tale with other forms of oral literature on the one hand and with written narrative on the other.

The second part of the book contains an account of all the well-known folktales now current in countries belonging to our western civilization, with a brief account of their history and dissemination. The recounting of these tales and the summary of the findings of folktale scholarship for each is sufficiently detailed to serve as a practical introduction to the field. This part of the work continues with an account of the folktale in the ancient classical world as we are able to learn of it from literary remains; and it closes with a study of the impact of the tales of Europe and Western Asia on those of far-flung primitive peoples.

The folktale in those cultures outside our own which we usually call primitive is the subject of Part Three. To cover the whole world has not been practicable, so that it has seemed wise rather to concentrate on one important group—the North American Indians—and thus afford sufficient comparison with the tales of Europe and Asia.

In the fourth part of the book I have attempted to see what students have thought about the folktale and to evaluate some of these theories. I have also detailed the methods employed by folktale scholars during the past half century and have suggested their further development. Such methods have involved the organization of scholars, on an international basis, for collecting, classifying, making local surveys, studying the life history of tales and considering the tale as an art and as a function of various societies. Much of this theoretical material and most of the practical procedures studied are difficult of access and too little known by students of related fields, in which work touching the folktale is often carried on in ignorance of the real accomplishments of folklorists in Europe and America.

The goal of this book is therefore (1) to present the folktale as an important art, vital to most of the race and underlying all literary narrative forms; (2) to acquaint the reader with most of the great folktales of the world, not only for their own interest as stories but also as important elements of culure; and (3) to indicate the goals of the student of the narratives and the methods by which he works.

STITH THOMPSON

Bloomington, Indiana

TABLE OF CONTENTS

ix

PART FOUR

Studying the Folktale

PART ONE

Nature and Forms of the Folktale

UNIVERSALITY
OF THE FOLKTALE

I

The teller of stories has everywhere and always found eager listeners. Whether his tale is the mere report of a recent happening, a legend of long ago, or an elaborately contrived fiction, men and women have hung upon his words and satisfied their yearnings for information or amusement, for incitement to heroic deeds, for religious edification, or for release from the overpowering monotony of their lives. In villages of central Africa, in outrigger boats on the Pacific, in the Australian bush, and within the shadow of Hawaiian volcanoes, tales of the present and of the mysterious past, of animals and gods and heroes, and of men and women like themselves, hold listeners in their spell or enrich the conversation of daily life. So it is also in Eskimo igloos under the light of seal-oil lamps, in the tropical jungles of Brazil, and by the totem poles of the British Columbian coast. In Japan too, and China and India, the priest and the scholar, the peasant and the artisan all join in their love of a good story and their honor for the man who tells it well.

When we confine our view to our own occidental world, we see that for at least three or four thousand years, and doubtless for ages before, the art of the story-teller has been cultivated in every rank of society. Odysseus entertains the court of Alcinous with the marvels of his adventures. Centuries later we find the long-haired page reading nightly from interminable chivalric romances to entertain his lady while her lord is absent on his crusade. Medieval priests illustrate sermons by anecdotes old and new, and only sometimes edifying. The old peasant, now as always, whiles away the winter evening with tales of wonder and adventure and the marvelous workings of fate. Nurses tell children of Goldilocks or the House that Jack Built.

3

Poets write epics and novelists novels. Even now the cinemas and theaters bring their stories direct to the ear and eye through the voices and gestures of actors. And in the smoking-rooms of sleeping cars and steamships and at the banquet table the oral anecdote flourishes in a new age.

In the present work we are confining our interest to a relatively narrow scope, the traditional prose tale—the story which has been handed down from generation to generation either in writing or by word of mouth. Such tales are, of course, only one of the many kinds of story material, for, in addition to them, narrative comes to us in verse as ballads and epics, and in prose as histories, novels, dramas, and short stories. We shall have little to do with the songs of bards, with the ballads of the people, or with poetic narrative in general, though stories themselves refuse to be confined exclusively to either prose or verse forms. But even with verse and all other forms of prose narrative put aside, we shall find that in treating the traditional prose tale— the folktale—our quest will be ambitious enough and will take us to all parts of the earth and to the very beginnings of history.

Although the term "folktale" is often used in English to refer to the "household tale" or "fairy tale" (the German *Märchen*), such as "Cinderella" or "Snow White," it is also legitimately employed in a much broader sense to include all forms of prose narrative, written or oral, which have come to be handed down through the years. In this usage the important fact is the traditional nature of the material. In contrast to the modern story writer's striving after originality of plot and treatment, the teller of a folktale is proud of his ability to hand on that which he has received. He usually desires to impress his readers or hearers with the fact that he is bringing them something that has the stamp of good authority, that the tale was heard from some great story-teller or from some aged person who remembered it from old days.

So it was until at least the end of the Middle Ages with writers like Chaucer, who carefully quoted authorities for their plots—and sometimes even invented originals so as to dispel the suspicion that some new and unwarranted story was being foisted on the public. Though the individual genius of such writers appears clearly enough, they always depended on authority, not only for their basic theological opinions but also for the plots of their stories. A study of the sources of Chaucer or Boccaccio takes one directly into the stream of traditional narrative.

The great written collections of stories characteristic of India, the Near East, the classical world, and Medieval Europe are almost entirely traditional. They copy and recopy. A tale which gains favor in one collection is taken over into others, sometimes intact and sometimes with changes of plot or characterization. The history of such a story, passing it may be from India to Persia and Arabia and Italy and France and finally to England, copied and changed from manuscript to manuscript, is often exceedingly complex. For it goes through the hands of both skilled and bungling narrators and improves or deteriorates at nearly every retelling. However well or poorly such a story may be written down, it always attempts to preserve a tradition, an old tale with the authority of antiquity to give it interest and importance.

If use of the term "folktale" to include such literary narratives seems somewhat broad, it can be justified on practical grounds if on no other, for it is impossible to make a complete separation of the written and the oral traditions. Often, indeed, their interrelation is so close and so inextricable as to present one of the most baffling problems the folklore scholar encounters. They differ somewhat in their behavior, it is true, but they are alike in their disregard of originality of plot and of pride of authorship.

Nor is complete separation of these two kinds of narrative tradition by any means necessary for their understanding. The study of the oral tale, which we undertake in this volume, will be valid so long as we realize that stories have frequently been taken down from the lips of unlettered taletellers and have entered the great literary collections. In contrary fashion, fables of Aesop, anecdotes from Homer, and saints' legends, not to speak of fairy tales read from Perrault or Grimm, have entered the oral stream and all their association with the written or printed page has been forgotten. Frequently a story is taken from the people, recorded in a literary document, carried across continents or preserved through centuries, and then retold to a humble entertainer who adds it to his repertory.

It is clear then that the oral story need not always have been oral. But when it once habituates itself to being passed on by word of mouth it undergoes the same treatment as all other tales at the command of the raconteur. It becomes something to tell to an audience, or at least to a listener, not something to read. Its effects are no longer produced indirectly by association with words written or printed on a page, but directly through facial expression and gesture and repetition and recurrent patterns that generations have tested and found effective.

This oral art of taletelling is far older than history, and it is not bounded by one continent or one civilization. Stories may differ in subject from place to place, the conditions and purposes of taletelling may change as we move from land to land or from century to century, and yet everywhere it ministers to the same basic social and individual needs. The call for entertainment to fill in the hours of leisure has found most peoples very limited in their resources, and except where modern urban civilization has penetrated deeply they have found the telling of stories one of the most satisfying of pastimes. Curiosity about the past has always brought eager listeners to tales of the long ago which supply the simple man with all he knows of the history of his folk. Legends grow with the telling, and often a great heroic past evolves to gratify vanity and tribal pride. Religion also has played a mighty role everywhere in the encouragement of the narrative art, for the religious mind has tried to understand beginnings and for ages has told stories of ancient days and sacred beings. Often whole cosmologies have unfolded themselves in these legends, and hierarchies of gods and heroes.

World-wide also are many of the structural forms which oral narrative has assumed. The hero tale, the explanatory legend, the animal anecdote—certainly these at least are present everywhere. Other fictional patterns are limited to particular areas of culture and act by their presence or absence as an effective index of the limit of the area concerned. The study of such limitations has not proceeded far, but it constitutes an interesting problem for the student of these oral narrative forms.

Even more tangible evidence of the ubiquity and antiquity of the folktale is the great similarity in the content of stories of the most varied peoples. The same tale types and narrative motifs are found scattered over the world in most puzzling fashion. A recognition of these resemblances and an attempt to account for them brings the scholar closer to an understanding of the nature of human culture. He must continually ask himself, "Why do some peoples borrow tales and some lend? How does the tale serve the needs of the social group?" When he adds to his task an appreciation of the aesthetic and practical urge toward story-telling, and some knowledge of the forms and devices, stylistic and histrionic, that belong to this ancient and widely practiced art, he finds that he must bring to his work more talents than one man can easily possess. Literary critics, anthropologists, historians, psychologists, and aestheticians are all needed if we are to hope to know why folktales are made, how they are invented, what art is used in their telling, how they grow and change and occasionally die.

FORMS OF THE FOLKTALE

‖

WITH the folktale as with all other products of man's artistic endeavor the scholar runs the risk of too subtle analysis. He may interest himself in studying the entire body of oral narrative of a people so as to divide it neatly into categories according to origin or form or content, but although such a close examination of the stories undoubtedly teaches him much, he must realize that the men and women who tell them neither know nor care about his distinctions. Much hair-splitting has taken place in the past and much useless effort devoted to the establishment of exact terms for the various kinds of folktale.

Yet some very general terms are not only helpful but necessary. The limitations of human life and the similarity of its basic situations necessarily produce tales everywhere which are much alike in all important structural respects. They have as definite form and substance in human culture as the pot, the hoe, or the bow and arrow, and several of these narrative forms are quite as generally employed. Others are confined to definite areas or belong to particular periods of time. But all of them, whenever they become so well recognized that they are continually referred to, have, in the course of time, been given names. Sometimes these are accurate and sometimes not, but from the very beginning anyone who discusses the folktale inevitably uses them and wishes his reader to be able to use them too.[1]

Perhaps the most frequent of all concepts to be met when one studies the folktale on a world-wide basis is that which the Germans call *Märchen*. We have nothing in English that is quite satisfactory, though the term is usually translated by "fairy tale," or "household tale." The French use *conte popu-*

[1] Several of these narrative forms are discussed in some detail farther on; see pp. 21, 234, and 303.

7

laire. What they are all trying to describe is such tales as "Cinderella," "Snow White," or "Hansel and Gretel." *Fairy tale* seems to imply the presence of fairies; but the great majority of such tales have no fairies. *Household tale* and *conte populaire* are so general that they might be applied to almost any kind of story. The German *Märchen* is better, and is fairly well agreed on. A *Märchen* is a tale of some length involving a succession of motifs or episodes. It moves in an unreal world without definite locality or definite characters and is filled with the marvelous. In this never-never land humble heroes kill adversaries, succeed to kingdoms, and marry princesses. Since *Märchen* deal with such a chimerical world, the name "chimerat" has been suggested for international usage, though it has not yet received wide adoption.

Near to the *Märchen* in general structure is the *novella.* Literary examples of this form may be seen in the *Arabian Nights* or Boccaccio, but such stories are also widely told by the unlettered, especially by the peoples of the Near East. The action occurs in a real world with definite time and place, and though marvels do appear, they are such as apparently call for the hearer's belief in a way that the *Märchen* does not. The adventures of Sinbad the Sailor form such a *novella.*

The distinction between *novella* and *Märchen* is not always drawn, the former being sometimes referred to as *Novellenmärchen.* In any case there is much overlapping between the two categories, so that some tales appear in one land with all the characteristics of a *novella,* in another with those of a *Märchen.*

Hero tale is a more inclusive term than either *Märchen* or *novella,* since a tale of this kind may move in the frankly fantastic world of the former or the pseudo-realistic world of the latter. Most *Märchen* and *novelle,* of course, have heroes, but would hardly be called hero tales unless they recounted a series of adventures of the same hero. Almost everywhere are found such clusters of tales relating the superhuman struggles of men like Hercules or Theseus against a world of adversaries. Stories of this kind are particularly popular with primitive peoples or with those belonging to a heroic age of civilization, like the early Greeks or the Germanic folk in the days of their great migrations.

For another general narrative pattern used all over the world, the German term *Sage* has been widely adopted. English and French attempts to express the same idea are *local tradition, local legend, migratory legend,* and *tradition populaire.* This form of tale purports to be an account of an extraordinary happening believed to have actually occurred. It may recount a legend of something which happened in ancient times at a particular place—a legend which has attached itself to that locality, but which will probably also be told with equal conviction of many other places, even in remote parts of the world. It may tell of an encounter with marvelous creatures which the folk still believe in—fairies, ghosts, water-spirits, the devil, and the like. And it may give what has been handed down as a memory—often fantastic or even absurd—of some historical character. The story of the Pied Piper of Hamelin, of the wild horseman encountered by Ichabod Crane, of old Barbarossa sleeping in the mountain, and the dozens of tales of Indian lovers' leaps from cliffs all over America—all these are *Sagen*. It will be observed that they are nearly always simple in structure, usually containing but a single narrative motif.

Very close to the local tradition is the *explanatory tale*. Other terms for it are *etiological tale, Natursage, pourquoi story*. The local legend often explains the existence of some hill or cliff or tells why a certain river meanders over the landscape. There are similar stories explaining the origins and characteristics of various animals and plants, the stars, and mankind and his institutions. Frequently this explanation seems to be the entire reason for the existence of the story, but more often than is usually recognized these explanations are merely added to a story to give an interesting ending. Such explanations may indeed be attached to almost any narrative form, such as the *Märchen* or the hero tale.

Of all the words used to distinguish the classes of prose narrative, *myth* is the most confusing. The difficulty is that it has been discussed too long and that it has been used in too many different senses. The history of such discussion is interesting but inconclusive. As used in this book myth will be taken to mean a tale laid in a world supposed to have preceded the present order. It tells of sacred beings and of semi-divine heroes and of the origins of all things, usually through the agency of these sacred beings. Myths are intimately connected with religious beliefs and practices of the people. They may be essentially hero legends or etiological stories, but they are systematized and given religious significance. The hero is somehow related to the rest of the pantheon and the origin story becomes an origin myth by attachment to the adventures of some god or demigod. Whether hero legend and origin story generally preceded myth or whether they became detached from it, the fundamental difference between these forms is reasonably clear.

Animals play a large role in all popular tales. They appear in myths, especially those of primitive peoples where the culture hero often has animal form, though he may be conceived of as acting and thinking like a man or even, on occasion, of having human shape. This tendency toward ascribing human qualities to animals also appears when the tale is clearly not in the mythical cycle. It is such non-mythological stories that we designate by the simple term *animal tales*. They are designed usually to show the cleverness of one animal and the stupidity of another, and their interest usually lies in the humor of the deceptions or the absurd predicaments the animal's stupidity leads him into. The American Indian series of stories of coyote and the popular European cycle of the fox and the wolf, best known in America as the tales of Uncle Remus, are outstanding examples of this form.

When the animal tale is told with an acknowledged moral purpose, it becomes a *fable*. The best known are the great literary collections, Aesop and the Panchatantra. They usually attach an actual maxim, though this is not necessary. But the moral purpose is the essential quality which distinguishes the fable from the other animal tales.

Short anecdotes told for humorous purposes are found everywhere. They are variously referred to as *jest, humorous anecdote, merry tale*, and (German) *Schwank*. Among some they are usually animal tales, but even where this is true the action is essentially that characteristic of men. Important themes producing these popular jests are the absurd acts of foolish persons (the *numskull tale*), deceptions of all kinds, and obscene situations. There is a tendency for jests to form cycles, since humorous adventures become attached to some character who thereafter attracts into his orbit all kinds of jests, appropriate and inappropriate. The same hero may be celebrated for his clever ruses, and for his utter stupidity, and obscene tales may often be told about him. But jests frequently detach themselves from cycles and may be encountered in the most unlikely places. They are easily remembered and universally liked, so that they travel with great ease. Some of the funny stories heard today have lived three or four thousand years and have been carried all over the earth.

Because of their possible confusion with terms we have already mentioned, two narrative forms primarily literary deserve a short notice. In some languages the term *legend*, which we have used above in discussing the local and the explanatory legend, can be used only in the special sense of the life of a saint. In English it is necessary to use the full expression *saint's legend* if that is meant. Such pious stories are normally handed down in literary collections, though a number have entered the stream of oral tradition, where they are sometimes not to be distinguished from the fairy tale, or *Märchen*.

Saga is also a misleading term. Its use should be restricted to the literary tales of the heroic age, particularly of Scandinavia and Ireland, and not employed loosely to mean "an experience" or "a story." And it should not be confused with the German *Sage*, which as we have seen has an entirely different meaning.

Other words for oral narrative forms have been suggested from time to time, but for the practical purpose of examining and discussing actual folktales as they appear over the world, these few which we have listed will be sufficient. We shall find these forms not so rigid as the theoretician might wish, for they will be blending into each other with amazing facility. Fairy tales become myths, or animal tales, or local legends. As stories transcend differences of age or of place and move from the ancient world to ours, or from ours to a primitive society, they often undergo protean transformations in style and narrative purpose. For the plot structure of the tale is much more stable and more persistent than its form.

PART TWO

The Folktale from Ireland to India

IRELAND TO INDIA: PEOPLES
AND LANDS

That the telling of tales is a constant activity everywhere seems clear enough. But this activity is by no means uniform in the various parts of the world, and as one moves over the continents, he finds extraordinary variability within the uniformity of the general practice. At first view this variety may seem merely kaleidoscopic and lawless. But only a little careful study is needed to show that, like all other elements of human culture, folktales are not mere creatures of chance. They exist in time and space, and they are affected by the nature of the land where they are current, by the linguistic and social contacts of its people, and by the lapse of the years and their accompanying historic changes. An approach to the understanding of the folktales of the world demands, therefore, that use be made of all possible resources furnished by the labors of historians, geographers, ethnographers, and psychologists.

This ideal for the study of the folktale is, of course, not easily reached. But it serves as a goal toward which all the efforts of folktale scholars are ultimately directed. Generations must perhaps pass before an adequate history of the world's folk narrative can be written, and many false starts will certainly be made and much time wasted in futile endeavors. Even so, with full appreciation of how fragmentary our present knowledge is and consequently of how fallible any conclusions will be, the folklorist must occasionally seek to obtain a view of the whole activity of folktales, and to chart, so far as possible, whatever may be certainly known, and even to suggest whatever may be plausibly hazarded about their history, their distribution, and their place in society. Such is the general purpose of the two

13

first major divisions of our study: "The Folktale from Ireland to India" and "The Folktale among a Primitive People."

Since there is an unmistakable historical connection among the traditional narratives of all the peoples extending from Ireland to India and of their descendants in newer lands, and an obvious common store of narrative motifs and even of formal elements, it will be convenient as our first task to bring together for special consideration the tales of this vast area—an area coextensive in its general boundaries with what we know as western cilivization.[1]

Few of the stories characteristic of this territory extend over its extreme limit, but a sufficient number of them do so extend that it is possible to define the area rather sharply. Normally, the tales characteristic of this European and west Asiatic region fade out in central Siberia and are not found farther east than India. Insofar as stories belonging to this tradition appear in China, Japan, or the Malayan countries, they are nearly always obvious borrowings from India. Buddhistic writings are largely responsible for these Indic tales in China and Japan, and further south this Buddhistic influence has been abetted by the carriers of Mohammedanism.

Eastern and southeastern Asia, then, lie quite outside this area we are discussing. There exist, quite certainly, very ancient strata of folk narrative in these countries, and much of it has become a part of the classical literature, especially of Japan and China. From neither of these far eastern lands have there been adequate attempts to recover the non-literary traditions.[2] For the lands farther south, Indo-China, Siam, the Malay peninsula, and the islands of Indonesia, a considerable amount of native story is now available. It is an interesting mixture of themes original in that region with obvious importations from India.[3] As one reaches the Philippines, the importations seem to increase, doubtless because of the Spanish occupation.

As we move westward from these countries and reach the eastern confines of India, we find ourselves unmistakably within that area of tradition which extends westward to the Atlantic and southward to the Sahara. Tales originating in any part of this area have been known to travel through the rest of it and become generally accepted. Throughout it all there is a free give and take of theme and motif that binds all these lands together by a multitude of common traditions.

This vast area is by no means uniform, and the peoples at its farthest extremes display the greatest of differences, not only in modes of life but even in their attitudes toward identical folk narratives. Any study of the tales of

[1] For the principal collections of folktales within this area and elsewhere, see pp. 467ff., below.

[2] Both Chinese and Japanese published collections have a tendency to keep reprinting the same tales, so that the student has a feeling, possibly unjustified, that folklore collecting has hardly more than begun in these countries.

[3] An excellent introduction to the folktales of the whole Indonesian area is Jan DeVries, *Volksverhalen uit Oost-Indië* (2 vols., Zutphen, 1925-28).

this large region must recognize the existence of many sub-areas which are necessary to distinguish if one is to understand the movements of tradition from one to the other.

Subdivision of Europe and eastern Asia from this point of view is neither easy nor exact. Some scholars would proceed almost exclusively on the principle of linguistic affinities, and would be interested in differentiating among Semitic, Indo-European, and Finno-Ugric, for example. Others are much more impressed by purely geographical considerations and are likely to use such terms as Baltic, Mediterranean, East European, etc., without regard to language or to ethnic classification. For the purpose of the folklorist, no such exclusive principle is possible, for affinities in language, consciousness of a common historic past as a recognized tribe or nation, religious unity, and association in a definite geographic territory, all have tended to produce within peoples of certain regions a psychological unity very important for its influence on their traditional lore.

1. *India.*—At the very eastern edge of the area is the immense subcontinent of India. It has had a long and varied history, and its peoples are of most diverse origins. Many of them are of Aryan stock and ethnically related to the Europeans. They have behind them a written literature going back centuries before Homer and an unbroken religious tradition changing but little in three thousand years. Superimposed upon the original religious pattern are many others, sometimes in conflict and sometimes supplementing one another—Buddhism, Jainism, Parseeism, Mohammedanism, and Christianity, to name but a few. Populations are found in all gradations from the fabulously wealthy princes to the abjectly poor peasants and the primitive hill tribes.

As might be expected, the folklore of India reflects this diversity of history and population. There are, first of all, a number of old literary collections of tales, some of them Brahmin, some Buddhistic, and some belonging to other cults. Much of the best folklore of India is imbedded in these collections. They have been known to the populace for centuries, and many of them have entered into the repertories of popular taletellers, so that it is not unusual to hear from an ignorant peasant a story which appeared two thousand years ago in the *Panchatantra* or in some of the *Jātakas*. In addition to this well-assimilated literary tradition, there exists in nearly all tribes of India a large store of purely oral tales. Just what the folklore repertory of a particular region may be depends upon many obscure historical and social facts. There is thus a vast difference among collections appearing in various parts of India. But in nearly all of them occur a considerable number of folktales already familiar to the student of European folklore.

The presence of these parallels with European tales in most parts of India and of still other parallels in the old literary collections caused a whole generation of older scholars to conclude that India is the great homeland of most of the European folk stories.[4] While this conclusion does not any longer seem convincing in its entirety, there can be little doubt that India has furnished rather more than its share to the great common stock of tales known in Europe and the Near East.

Whatever the relation of the tales of India to those of Europe, it is easy to see many important differences between the stories of these two great regions. With due regard for many exceptions, it is safe to say that the ordinary involved wonder tale is given as a piece of pure fiction in Europe but is expected to be believed in India. Such tales are nearly always definitely localized in India, so that the distinction between place legends and folktales breaks down entirely. There is a greater luxuriance in the supernatural trappings of the tales. They often depart so far from the realistic that it is hard for the western mind to follow them. But an almost opposite trait also appears in these stories from India, for these people are very fond of anecdotes based upon sharpness of wits. Tales of cleverness, as well as the fables with their lessons in wisdom and the cumulative tales with their joy in formulas, have come down, for the most part, from the older literature, but they are enjoyed by the people and have become an essential part of their folklore.

Stylistically there is considerable variation in the tales of different parts of India. Two general tendencies, however, can be noticed. The structure of the complicated tale is very loose, so that the plot is often very difficult to fit into the patterns determined by European analogues. Sometimes the story-teller seems to have a repertory consisting merely of single motifs which he strings together almost at will. Another characteristic observable among such tribes as the Kota is the extreme elaboration of psychological analysis. The reasons for every movement of the characters are discussed—sometimes *ad nauseam*—so that the story drags out interminably. Recent collections of these tales, carefully made in native text, show us how much we still have to learn about the tales of India and how desirable it is that they be conscientiously collected.

2. *The Moslem Countries.*—Though there is a large variety in the folklore of the Moslem peoples as they extend from Morocco to Persia, and even beyond, the folklorist frequently finds it illuminating to consider these populations as a unit. For tradition has moved with more than usual ease throughout this whole territory. Not only a common religion but the Arabic language has served to cement these people together. At the eastern and northern ends of the area, of course, there are large Turkish and Persian-speaking groups, and these differ somewhat both in the theme and style of their folktales from their Arabic co-religionists. Over the whole of these lands the work of the professional story-teller is of great importance. He is to be found in villages, but he flourishes principally in large cities and markets. Such great collections

---

[4] For a discussion of this point, see pp. 376ff., below.

as the *Thousand and One Nights* certainly go back in last resort to these humble authors. And these same tales continue to entertain the unlearned throughout the Moslem world. The task of separating literary from genuine popular tradition is extraordinarily difficult in these countries, and sometimes quite impossible.

3. *Jewish Tradition from Asia Minor.*—There still exist in various parts of Asia Minor and Syria Jewish traditions which come down in many instances from antiquity. These Jewish peoples played an important part in the transmission of tales between Europe and Asia. Many of their stories certainly became known to Jewish communities scattered throughout Europe, but an accurate understanding of their role in the dissemination of folktales has never been reached.

4. *The Slavic Countries.*—Intermediate between east and west stretch the enormous spaces of Russia. The folklorist finds enough distinction in the tales characteristic of Russia and, to a lesser extent, of neighboring Slavic peoples to justify their consideration as a single area. To the east, folktales of this general style extend to central Siberia, and with its opening up, ever farther and farther. Within European Russia appear the tales not only of the Great Russians, but also of the White Russians, near the Polish border and in Poland itself, and of the Little Russians or Ukrainians to the southwest. The South and West Slavic peoples—the Bulgarians, the Serbo-Croatians, the Czechs, Slovaks, and Poles—have tales resembling in many ways those of Russia, but also greatly influenced by their neighbors farther to the south and west. Bulgaria is thus marginal between Russia and Greece, and one finds plentiful Italian influence in Serbia, and many German elements in the tales of Bohemia and Poland.

5. *The East Baltic States.*—The four East Baltic states of Finland, Estonia, Latvia, and Lithuania are extremely important and interesting to the student of the tale. In the first place, their folklore has been collected with extraordinary thoroughness. For more than a century the Finns have been systematically recording their traditions, and the other Baltic countries have been busy building up their archives in recent years. In these countries the telling of folktales is not yet obsolete. This circumstance has made it possible to study certain of the tales current in these countries with a great wealth of documentation, so that we know a good deal about the movement of tradition in this whole area. To a greater or less degree, all these countries show in their folklore that they have been subjected to centuries of influence, now from the east and now from the west. Swedes and Russians have brought tales to Finland and taken others away, and in the small countries on the south shore of the Baltic Russians and Germans and Poles have been continual borrowers and lenders of folktales.

6. *Scandinavia.*—Occupying the whole of the Scandinavian peninsula, many of the islands in the Baltic, and the peninsula of Jutland are the Swedes,

Norwegians, and Danes. And on to the west peoples of this same Scandinavian stock are found in the Faroe Islands and in Iceland. These latter colonies are only about a thousand years old, but the Scandinavians in the homeland have been settled in their present positions since prehistoric times. In spite of important differences, both material and psychological, there is a strong community of tradition throughout this whole area. Essentially a common language, a common pagan religious background, and a marked resemblance in customs and beliefs—all these things are immediately apparent to the student of the folktale, and he is not surprised to find that he can usually recognize a Scandinavian tale wherever he finds it. Many folk stories show unmistakable signs of Scandinavian origin and many of such tales have not proceeded beyond Scandinavian borders. In all three of the countries the material has been well collected, and is systematically arranged in archives. Some of the best folktale texts have come from remote places in the north. Here the Scandinavians are in contact with the nomadic Lapps, whose stories they have profoundly influenced.

7. *German-Speaking Peoples.*—The prestige of the Brothers Grimm has been so great that many people are likely to think of the folktale as essentially a German product, but anyone realizing the international character of the popular tale will know that this is a mistake. In spite of the excellent collecting done in all parts of Germany and the German-speaking parts of Bohemia, Austria, and Switzerland it seems to be true that Germany has served primarily as transmitter rather than originator of folktales. It has touched the Slavic countries in the east, and the Low Germanic and Romance to the west and south. This has given it a wealth of tradition, and on this it has put its characteristic stamp. As we have already pointed out, the Baltic countries, Bohemia and Yugoslavia, and Hungary as well, show many unmistakably German traits in their folktales. To the west this is also true for Belgium and Holland.

8. *France.*—The importance of France in the general cultural life of Europe can hardly be overestimated. A great power of inventiveness seems to be characteristic even of unlettered story-tellers, for available evidence points to the development in France of some of our most important and widely accepted folktales. And where they have taken over stories from other cultures, they have imbued them with an unmistakably French style and spirit. The liking for popular tales persists with Frenchmen even after they have migrated, so that some of the best collections of such material have been made along the Saint Lawrence and in scattered settlements in Missouri and Louisiana. Unfortunately, the excellent scholarly work of the French folklorists of the nineteenth century has not been followed out in France itself in recent decades, and the good beginning recently made by a new group of folklorists was stopped by the Second World War.

9. *The Hispanic Peninsula.*—From the point of view of their traditional lore, the peoples of Spain and Portugal form a rather distinct unit. The domination during seven hundred years of a good part of Spain by the Moors and the consequent introduction of many elements of Moslem culture have left a permanent mark. The rigid orthodoxy of Spanish and Portuguese Catholicism is reflected in the great interest of the people in pietistic stories of all kinds, as well as in tales of miraculous manifestations. Nowhere does the ordinary folktale and the saint's legend approach each other as in these countries.

Even more interesting than the peninsula for the student of Spanish and Portuguese folklore is the larger Hispanic world in America. Only in recent years have the riches of the traditional lore of these countries begun to be properly explored. But we know even now that the Spanish and Portuguese colonizers brought to the new world not only their romances and folksongs, their beliefs and customs, their costumes and dances, but also a large number of their traditions and tales. We already have a good beginning of collections of this material from Mexico, the Dominican Republic, Chile, Argentina, and Brazil. And some progress has been made elsewhere. One of the interesting problems connected with this folklore concerns its relation to aboriginal tradition and, at least in some countries, to that of the Negroes. There is sometimes also a good opportunity for the study of a mixture of cultures through the tales of the *mestizos.*

10. *Italy.*—The first collections of European folktales appeared in Italy. Writers like Straparola in the sixteenth century and Basile in the seventeenth found the tales of the people of sufficient interest to adapt them to the prevailing literary fashions. We know from the work of these men that even in the early Renaissance a large proportion of the best known of our folktales was current in Italy and that, in spirit and style, they had already taken on those characteristics recognizable in Italian tales in our own day. These distinctly Italian stories are found not only in Italy itself, but in Sicily, Sardinia, and Corsica, and, to a degree, on the island of Malta.

11. *England.*—Folklorists have always remarked on the scarcity of the authentic folktale in England. Popular narrative has had a tendency to take the form of the ballad. But there are plenty of evidences, in literature and elsewhere, that some of our principal folktales have been current there in the past, and the collections made within the last century are not actually so meager as usually thought. Several tales have their most distinctive form in England—Jack and the Bean Stalk, Jack the Giant Killer, Tom-Tit-Tot, and the legend of Dick Whittington. The English seem to be particularly fond of the numskull tale, and have developed an interesting series called The Men of Gotham.

The English populations in America have brought over most of the tales they knew in the old country, and within the last few years these are beginning to be collected. There seems, in America, to have been practically no borrowing and lending of folklore between the British colonists and the Indians. On the other hand, we find a rather free exchange with the Negroes.

12. *Celtic Scotland and Ireland.*—The original Celtic populations of the British Isles are now found in the highlands and islands of Scotland, in Wales, and in Ireland. If there is any considerable body of folk narrative in Wales, it has never been collected. The highland Scottish tradition of the mid-nineteenth century was very competently reported by one of the world's great folklorists, Campbell of Islay, who published four volumes and left enough manuscript for many more. In Ireland, as has been recognized for at least a century, there still exists a tradition of folk narrative such as is to be seldom found in these days. Fortunately, the collecting and organizing of this material is being carried out with great thoroughness, and we already have available texts of folktales extending to many hundreds of thousands of pages.

A considerable part of material collected in the highlands of Scotland and in Ireland has been taken down in the original language, but much of it has been translated and a large amount is available to the reader who knows no Gaelic.

These twelve areas which we have indicated have been sketched with an extremely rough thumb, and they involve many contradictions. But the folklorist is continually aware that, nevertheless, each of these areas does have about it a certain unity which affects, favorably or unfavorably, the acceptance of folk traditions. From a practical point of view the divisions are useful and are not likely to be too misleading. Several countries, of course, have been left out, since they belong partly to one and partly to another area. This is true, for example, of Greece and Albania.

Other groupings than those proposed may well be valid. It is likely, for example, that the entire Mediterranean area, whether Christian or Moslem, has a sufficient resemblance in at least a large part of its folklore to justify a special study.

In the chapters that follow, covering the various kinds of folktales current in Europe and the Near East, the groupings just suggested—geographical, racial, linguistic, or merely cultural—will of necessity be continually referred to. As the life history of any tale is sketched, this charting of the area will furnish landmarks to clarify the course these tales take as they wander from land to land.

THE COMPLEX TALE

II

1. THE *MÄRCHEN* AND RELATED NARRATIVE FORMS

THE rough mapping out for the purposes of our study of the whole area from the Atlantic eastward to the farthest confines of India has suggested that large differences may be found in the attitude of story-tellers toward their traditional material. The clear-cut distinction made by the Irish between legends supposed to be true and purely fictional tales would be very rare, for example, in India. The student of the folktale therefore finds it very difficult to arrive at valid definitions of the various forms which the tale may assume. If he is dealing with the traditional fiction of a single country, it is usually possible to work out some rather exact definitions, but when he seeks to apply these to a distant area, all his sharp differentiations become blurred and in many cases disappear entirely.

In the English language little attempt has ever been made to arrive at sharp distinctions of this kind. The term "folktale" has always been used loosely to cover the whole range of traditional oral narrative. Sometimes the expression "wonder tale" or "fairy tale" is applied to stories filled with incredible marvels, in contrast to legends, which are presumably based upon fact. This general distinction between the legend[1] and the fictional tale holds good over a large part of this European-Asiatic area, but especially throughout Europe, and is therefore of great practical value.

The various expressions for "folktale" or "fairy tale" in other lands than England, though well established, are all vaguely and carelessly used. The French *conte populaire*, the German *Märchen*, the Norwegian *eventyr*, the Swedish *saga*, and the Russian *skazka* are certainly not always exactly the same thing. The Germans have made a very special attempt to achieve

---

[1] For a discussion of legends and traditions in this area, see pp. 234ff., below.

exactness in their use of the word *Märchen*, but they have succeeded only in arriving at what are essentially private definitions. The very laborious efforts of Albert Wesselski,[2] for example, have only shown that the usual German use of the word *Märchen* has been very loose and that such a collection as the Grimms' *Kinder- und Hausmärchen* contains not only stories like Cinderella (which he thinks of as having the only true *Märchen* style), but also legends of saints and of places, pious tales from the Middle Ages, and many jokes and anecdotes. Inaccuracy like this is painful to the student of literary forms, used as he is to the conscious development and growth of special styles in the various national literatures. Thus Wesselski, keeping his eye upon what he considers the typical *Märchen*—Snow White, Puss in Boots, Faithful John—and closely analyzing its particular stylistic effects, decides that this form is essentially a product of the Renaissance and that it probably does not go back before the sixteenth century.

Such a conclusion has its proper historic interest. But a student of any of the tales just mentioned soon realizes that even these may exist quite independently of this very special style popularized by Perrault and Grimm. In the life history of any of our most popular folktales, one must usually go farther back than the sixteenth century and much farther afield than western Europe. If the term *Märchen* is to be confined to the very special style suggested by Wesselski, we shall find that a large number of versions of our best known *Märchen* are not *Märchen* at all.

The number of folktales which in at least some of their versions are considered fictitious and which have some currency in Europe and western Asia is indicated fairly well by the list in the Aarne-Thompson *Types of the Folk-Tale* where are found some 700 stories, ranging from the simplest incident to the most complex wonder tale. Many of these stories, of course, have traveled a long distance to Africa or America, but there seems no doubt that their origin and principal history has been within the area we are considering.

For the practical grouping of tales, stylistic subtleties are of little value. The same tale in different lands takes on varying forms and is variously received by hearers and readers.[3] One distinction, however, is so common as to make it useful to anyone who tries to make a synopsis of the folklore activity of extensive areas. The simple anecdote, usually consisting of a single narrative motif, does not usually require any great skill or memory and seems nearly everywhere to be thought of as proper to particular social occasions different from those at which the longer complicated tale is enjoyed. There is, certainly, no absolute line to be drawn between these groups of tales, either in origin or function, and the distinction is often purely arbitrary.

---

[2] *Versuch einer Theorie des Märchens* (Reichenberg i. B., 1931).
[3] For some consideration of folktale style, telling, and reception, see pp. 449 ff., below.

It will, however, be convenient for our present purpose to make this distinction. We shall therefore postpone all notice of simple anecdotes[4] and first direct our attention entirely to those tales of Europe and western Asia which show complexity in their structure. Because these tales consist of a considerable series of motifs, they offer special difficulty in fitting into a satisfactory classification; and because most of them have existed over long periods of time and in many lands, their history is far from simple. For many of the tales these questions of classification and history have been seriously attempted by scholars, but the general results of such studies have never been brought together. In the pages which follow, we shall therefore pass in review not only the tales themselves, with their varieties of plot and treatment, but also whatever conclusions of folktale scholars now seem valid.[5]

2. SUPERNATURAL ADVERSARIES

IN nearly all complicated fairy tales there is some kind of conflict. The hero must overcome obstacles in order that he may at last win his reward. A large series of stories throughout the European and western Asiatic area confront the hero with some type of supernatural adversary. Frequently the exact nature of the opponent is not made clear or will vary from one version of the story to another. In those which we shall first consider this adversary is sometimes a dragon, a horrible animal, or simply an undefined monster.

In spite of the unstable character of the chief opponent, the tales relating to these adventures are well defined and are among the best known of all narratives current in this area.

[4] For animal stories, see p. 217, below; for jests and anecdotes, see p. 188 below; for formula tales, see p. 229, below; and for legends and traditions, see p. 234, below.

[5] In summarizing the conclusions of previous scholarship for the various tales to follow, no attempt has been made to furnish detailed bibliographical information. But those interested in assembling material for comparative study of any story can do so with relative ease and success.

Follow out the references given either in the Aarne-Thompson *Types of the Folk-Tale* or the Thompson *Motif-Index of Folk-Literature* under the proper numbers, giving especial attention to all works bearing one or two stars.

If there are references to Bolte-Polívka, they should by all means be consulted.

For pursuing the distribution in particular countries where the material has only recently become available, consult the following works:

Highland Scotland: McKay, *More West Highland Tales*
Indonesia: DeVries, *Volksverhalen*
China: Eberhard, *Typen chinesischer Märchen*
North Africa: Basset, *1001 Contes*
Lithuania: Balys, *Motif-Index*
Russia: Andrejev, *Ukazatel' Skazočnik*
      Afanasief, *Narodnie Russkie Skazki* (1936 edition, notes)
Puerto Rico: Boggs, *Index of Spanish Folktales*
Missouri French: Carrière, *Missouri*
Virginia: Chase, *Jack Tales* (especially notes)
For full titles of these and other works referred to, see p. 463.

If one wished to study the ways in which a tale in the course of centuries becomes scattered over the whole of Europe he could not do better than to direct his attention to the two closely related folktales, The Two Brothers (Type 303)[1] and The Dragon Slayer (Type 300). The Two Brothers, as a regular part of its construction, contains almost the whole of The Dragon Slayer, so that it is necessary to study the two tales together if one is to secure an accurate picture of their mutual relationships, and of the history of the two stories, both when they are merged together and when they exist separately. In his thorough study of these two types Ranke[2] has had available for analysis some 770 versions of The Two Brothers and 368 of The Dragon Slayer. When it is realized that practically all examples of the first story contain the second, and that since the appearance of Ranke's study more than a hundred additional variants of the two stories have been reported, it will be clear that about 1100 examples of The Dragon Slayer are now known, and new ones are being constantly collected.

It will be convenient to discuss The Dragon Slayer as an independent story before considering its relationship to other tales with which it has combined. As a result of his analytical study Ranke has arrived at a form of the tale which would seem to include all the original elements. From this form, or one very much like it, all the other thousand or more variants seem to have been derived. This reconstruction is as follows: A poor married couple have two children, a boy and a girl. When the parents die they leave behind them only a small house and three sheep. The girl inherits the house, and the boy the animals. He exchanges these animals for three marvelous dogs and sets out with them into the world. On the way he meets an old man (or a woman) from whom, in recognition of a courtesy which he has shown, he receives a magic sword or a magic stick. Everything that he strikes with it will fall dead.

He arrives at the royal city which he finds all hung with black cloth, and he learns at an inn of the cause of the mourning. He discovers that a seven-headed dragon who lives on a mountain in the neighborhood demands periodically a maiden as a sacrifice, else he will lay waste the entire country. The sacrifice has been agreed upon and the lot has fallen to the princess. The king promises that whoever saves her shall have her hand and half his kingdom.

The young man goes with his animals to the place where the dragon lives and reaches there at the same time as the princess, who has been brought by the king's coachman. He approaches her, comforts her, and promises to fight the dragon for her. The monster appears with a great roar, but the young man does not let himself be frightened. He goes against him and with his

---

[1] This and similar numbers in parentheses after the title of a tale refer to Aarne-Thompson, The Types of the Folk-Tale (hereafter referred to as "Types").

[2] Die zwei Brüder.

sword strikes off all his heads. In this action, the dogs help him by holding the dragon fast. The hero now cuts out the tongues from the dragon's heads and puts them into his pocket. The rescued princess wishes him to go back with her to her father to receive the promised reward, but the hero wants to wander about for a while and to experience adventures. They agree upon a definite time when they will see each other again. He bids her to preserve silence in spite of everything, and goes on his way.

The coachman, who has accompanied the princess and has remained near by so as to see what happens, comes now and threatens her with death if she will not agree, on oath, to tell the king that it is he who has slain the dragon. As further witness, he takes along the heads of the slain dragon. These he shows to the king and, supported by the declaration of the princess, demands the promised reward. The king is much pleased, and sets a time for the wedding. His daughter, however, is able to have it postponed until the time when she has agreed to meet her rescuer. But when at this time he still does not appear, the time for the wedding is definitely fixed.

On the very day of the wedding the young man arrives in the city which is now, in contrast to the first time, decorated in red. In the same inn he inquires about the rejoicing and learns of the wedding. The innkeeper expresses the wish that he may have food to eat from the royal table, and the young man sends his dogs several times with a basket and with a message written on a card tied to their necks. The princess recognizes the animals and fulfills the directions of her rescuer. She, or the king, orders him to be invited in and he appears at the castle. He immediately declares that he is the real dragon slayer and asks whether the dragon heads have tongues in them. The heads are brought forth and it appears that they have none. The young man takes them out of his pocket and lays each of them in that particular head where it fits. The king and all those present acknowledge him as the true rescuer of the princess and immediately carry out the marriage of the two. The impostor is punished.

The related story of The Two Brothers actually provides a larger number of examples of that part of the story given above containing the dragon slaying, the impostor, the dragon-tongue proof, and the marriage with the princess than does the form we have just discussed. Nearly 800 of these stories are known, and only a few lack the dragon fight. This story in outline is as follows:[3]

A fisherman who has no children catches the King of the Fishes, who begs to be let loose. In return for his freedom he promises the fisherman other fish or shows him the place where they can be caught. When the fisherman catches him the second time the Fish once more persuades him to let him swim away. When this happens a third time, the Fish advises the fisherman to cut him up into a certain number of pieces and to give one part each to his

[3] This reconstruction of the typical form of the tale is taken from Ranke, *op. cit.*, p. 341.

wife, to his mare, and to his dog, and to bury the rest in the garden under a tree. The wife bears two sons, and at the same time the mare and dog each give birth to two young ones, and in the garden there grow two swords and trees. The twin boys are nearly identical, as are also the animals.

When the boys grow up, the first of them wishes to go out into the world. If any misfortune should happen to him his particular tree will fade and the brother will come to his rescue.

He sets forth with his sword, horse, and dog, and after a while arrives at a royal city. *From this point on the story is identical with The Dragon Slayer tale given above, but after the marriage with the princess the narrative proceeds:*

On the marriage night the curiosity of the young king is aroused by an extraordinary sight, a fire in the woods or on a mountain. He asks his wife about the appearance of this fire, and she tells him that no one who has gone to the fire has ever returned. She warns him not to follow it. But he is overcome with the desire for adventure and decides to find out the cause of this mystery. He saddles his horse and rides with his dog and sword toward the light of the fire. He comes to a house in which lives an old woman who is a witch. She pretends to be afraid of his dog and bids him to lay one of her hairs on it so that the dog will be quiet and not harm her. The young man performs her bidding. The hair transforms itself into a chain. She now approaches and strikes him with a rod and turns him to stone.

Back home the tree fades, and the second brother sees from this that the first is in dire peril or possibly dead. He saddles his horse, takes his dog and sword, and sets forth. After a long wandering he comes to the city in which his brother has become king. The innkeeper with whom he first stops and the young queen to whom he then goes mistake him for her husband, since he looks exactly like his brother. He realizes immediately that people are mistaking him for his brother and he lets them believe this, so that he may more easily find out something about his brother's fate.

At night when he is to sleep with his sister-in-law, he lays the naked sword between her and him.

He also sees the curious light and asks about its occurrence. The queen is astonished at his question, which she remembers to have already answered once, and warns him a second time. But he rides away, since he realizes now where his brother has had his misfortune, and comes to the hut and finds the old woman. He does not obey her order to lay the hair on the dog, but he sets the dog on to the witch and threatens her with death. She gives him the rod with which she has enchanted the first brother, and he strikes the stone with it and in this way disenchants him. The old woman is killed, and both brothers return together to the city.

Such, in a general form, are these two well-known tales. It will be noticed that when the incident of the dragon slaying is used in the Two Brothers story the only modification necessary is that the hero be accompanied by only one dog instead of three. Several other possible introductions are to be found and some differences in detail, but the story as given above has a remarkable stability over the entire area where it is found.

Both forms, the longer Two Brothers tale and the simpler Dragon Rescue story, have approximately the same distribution. A definite indication of this distribution will be interesting as showing the relative importance of boundary lines, national, racial, cultural, or linguistic, for determining the dissemination of a widely-known tale which has been handed down by word of mouth for a long time. In the following list the number of reported versions of the Two Brothers story are given first and then those for the simpler Dragon Rescue tale. It will be noted that all of them contain the central core: the rescue from the dragon, the impostor, the dragon-tongue proof, and the marriage with the princess. The distribution is as follows:

German	65	57	Polish	11	5	Indic	6	2
Dutch	1	0	Great Russian	15	0	Cambodian	1	0
Flemish	14	9	White Russian	6	0	Malayan	2	2
Danish	66	129	Little Russian	13	0	Japanese	0	1
Swedish	11	8	Lithuanian	47	88	Arabian in		
Finnish-Swedish	8	13	Lettish	67	9	Africa	3	3
Norwegian	42	18	Estonian	31	1	Berber and		
Icelandic and			Livonian	3	0	Kabyle	8	2
Faroe	3	0	Finnish	141	2	Central		
French	14	2	Lappish	3	5	African	5	8
Rhaetian	3	2	Volga peoples			Madagascar	1	0
Italian	27	14	(Mordvinian)	1	0	North American		
Spanish	8	4	Votyak	1	0	Indian	8	8
Portuguese	5	3	Hungarian	15	0	Cape Verde		
Roumanian	21	2	Osman	3	0	Island	3	1
Breton	3	2	Chuvassian	7	0	French		
Scottish	3	1	Basque	2	4	Canadian	1	0
Irish	10	4	Albanian	4	0	Jamaican	2	1
Serbo-Croatian	15	1	Greek	5	4	Puerto Rican	5	3
Bulgarian	3	0	Gypsy	5	5	Haitian	0	1
Czech and			Jewish	2	0	Mexican	0	1
Slovak	38	23	Caucasian	11	1	Brazilian	2	2
Wend	0	2	Armenian	1	0			
Cashubian	5	0	Persian	2	0			

If certain countries in this list seem to be represented with a disproportionate number, it must be borne in mind that collecting has been much more thoroughly carried out in Germany, Denmark, Norway, Czechoslovakia, Lithuania, Latvia, and Finland than in most other countries. It seems quite certain, for example, that if French tales had been thoroughly collected during the last generation their showing would be much better. As it is, every French collection which we possess indicates the presence of these tales in the area which it covers.

The place where a folktale is most likely to suffer change is in its intro-duction, where a preliminary action really proper to another story but capable of being logically joined to the one in question is easily substituted. Such a substitution may very well be accepted and may set up a new tradition which, in a limited area, may live on side by side with the more regular form of the tale. This has happened with the two stories we are considering.

In The Two Brothers there has occurred confusion with the story of The Magic Bird-Heart (Type 567).[4] Since this is a tale of two brothers with magic objects, the confusion is not strange. This introduction generally appears as follows: A poor man comes into possession of a magic bird which lays golden eggs. The man sells the eggs and becomes rich. Once he goes on a journey and leaves the bird behind with his wife. She is persuaded to serve the bird to her lover for dinner. The bird possesses a marvelous charac-teristic—that whoever eats of its head will become ruler and whoever con-sumes the heart will have gold appear under his pillow while he sleeps. The bird is prepared, but by chance falls into the hands of the sons of the house-hold, and the young men, without knowing of the wonderful power of the bird, eat the head and the heart. From this point on in the story we usually have an account of the loss and recovery of the magic powers, but the narra-tive may also proceed with the parting of the brothers and the regular adventures proper to The Two Brothers.

Another story frequently amalgamated with The Two Brothers is the East European tale of The Three Brothers. This begins with the fishing episode of The Two Brothers, proceeds with adventures proper to supernaturally strong men (Type 650), then, with some variation, goes into The Two Brothers tale. The very nature of the story, however, makes it necessary to repeat many episodes. For example, the first two brothers fall into the hands of the witch, and the sleeping with the naked sword is repeated.

In some twenty percent of all versions of The Two Brothers occurs the motif of The Jealous Brother. In these tales the younger brother, having been resuscitated and having heard that his brother has slept with his wife, kills his rescuer. Then on hearing the truth he repents and resuscitates him. Ranke feels that this ending is hardly an original part of the story since it is far from uniform in its occurrence, and since the means of resuscitation is usually the same as that already used for disenchantment in the same tale. On the other hand, the motif is not a recent invention. It occurs in Basile's Pentamerone (1634-36) and also has a wide distribution, indicative of a rela-tively long history.

These are the most important variations of The Dragon Slayer and The Two Brothers. Ranke has attempted, on the basis of his huge collection and his careful analysis, to arrive at some conclusions as to the history of the stories. It seems clear that The Dragon Slayer is the older of the two stories,

[4] See p. 75, below.

and that The Two Brothers has simply taken over this old tale as a cluster
of motifs in its composition. Ranke's study is not concerned with any possible
earlier forms of The Dragon Slayer before it assumed its present definite
structure. He realizes that the concept of the dragon is old; he sees unmistakable resemblances between this story and the Greek myth of Perseus and
Andromeda, and with many older tales of rescues from monsters. He knows
also that, as Hartland has pointed out in his three-volume work on *The
Legend of Perseus*, many of the separate motifs in the story, such as the life-
token, the enchantment and disenchantment, and the magic birth, are found
in nearly all parts of the world, and may appear in a multitude of narrative
connections. But with more than a thousand examples of the fully developed
stories before him, he has confined his task to the establishment of a typical
form of the tale which would approximate the original from which all the
rest have been derived. These typical forms of the tale are those which we
have outlined here.

On the basis of the entire study, he is convinced that The Dragon Slayer
as we know it at present was developed in western Europe where the versions are closest to the typical form. As one goes east, greater and greater
variation occurs. Particular departures from type show special geographic
distribution, and are therefore to be listed as different redactions of the tale.
To illustrate once for all the way in which such a story develops new
forms, let us examine these redactions of The Dragon Slayer (and the Dragon
Rescue episode of The Two Brothers) as worked out by Ranke.

I. The Romance Cycle of Redactions
  (a) *French*. Like type except that in about half of versions impostor
       is a charcoal burner.
  (b) *French Colonial*. On the periphery of French, and in the colonies
       (Cambodia, North America, Malay peoples).
  (c) *Spanish*. Like French but not so regularly developed. Impostor a
       charcoal burner or Negro. In 63 percent of Type 303 no dragon
       fight. Spain, Puerto Rico, Jamaica.
  (d) *Portuguese*. Like French. But one Portuguese and Brazilian have
       introduction from Hansel and Gretel. Portugal, Cape Verde
       Islands, Brazil.
  (e) *Italian*. Near to original form. Basile's version (1634), recent
       Italian, Albanian.
  (f) *General Romance redaction*. Main characteristics: *periodic* sac-
       rifice to dragon. Change of details as one gets away from France.
       Found (in addition to Romance countries) in all parts of Europe.
       This form has apparently spread through Germany to Scan-
       dinavia, the Baltic Countries, and Russia and sporadically to
       Japan.

II. Central European. No periodic sacrifice to dragon. Sometimes this may be an unintentional omission. The spread is from Germany eastward and in a few cases northward. Some of these tales may be influenced directly by Grimm's version.

III. The *Murder* Redaction. The dragon slayer is killed by the impostor and later resuscitated. About half the Two Brothers tales in this group have The Magic Bird Heart (Type 567) as introduction, and thus show the influence of Grimm. It is a German reworking of the Romance redaction and then a dissemination (a) to Scandinavia and the Baltic, (b) to South Germany and the Balkans, and (c) to Czechoslovakia, Poland, and Little Russia.

IV. The Northern Redaction Cycle.

   (a) *General* Northern Redaction. Giant adventure precedes dragon fight. Red Knight attempts rescue but in fear climbs tree and witnesses fight, later to appear as impostor. Three dragons. Battle at sea side. Princess louses hero and leaves ring in his hair. Recognition by ring. This version is certainly Scandinavian, probably from Norway (1) to Denmark and North Germany, (2) to Sweden and the Baltic countries, (3) to Scotland.

   Of this Northern cycle, Ranke distinguishes a number of subgroups: (b) *Porter* (hero as porter for king; dragon knocks at door). Denmark to Schleswig-Holstein. (c, d, e) "Peril" redactions (no sacrifice, but king has promised daughter to monster to save his life). Denmark to rest of Scandinavia and Finland. (f) Danish *hesitation* redaction (dragon postpones sacrifice three days). (g) *Lillekort* ("little short"). Tiny hero. Dragon fight plus experience with sea troll. Recognition by costly garments of princess. Norway to all parts of Scandinavia. (h) Finnish *wake* redaction. Like Norwegian but princess awakens hero who sleeps with his head on her lap. (i) Glass mountain tradition. Continuation with Type 530. In Denmark and Holstein. (k) Swedish Dragon Slayer redaction (no examples of Two Brothers). Three trolls, three princesses. First two brothers successful. Third brother rescued by his dogs. Sweden (1) to Pomerania, Schleswig Holstein and Denmark, (2) to Finland. (l) *Troll* redactions. Miscellaneous adventures with trolls. Only in Denmark.

V. Binding redaction. Ogre magically bound. A mixture with Type 330. Seven German versions and scattered to Baltic countries, Denmark and as far southeast as Serbia. Only a few versions.

VI. Irish shoe redaction. Slipper recognition like Cinderella. Otherwise resembles Northern redaction.

VII. Spring redaction. Dragon guards spring and refuses to give people water. Arose in Balkans. Then (1) to Hungary, Russia, Poland, and

Baltic States, (2) to Greece and Turkey and around the Mediterranean to North and Central Africa and to Cape Verde Islands.

VIII. Baltic Impostor redaction. Like Central European (II) but hero places the dragon tongues under a stone which the impostor cannot lift. From Baltic to Finland, Poland, and Russia.

IX. Slavic Waking redaction. Hero sleeping with head in princess's lap is awakened by hot tears. Expansion of Central European (II). Great Russia to (1) Baltic lands, (2) Little Russia, Roumania, Greece, Arabia.

X. Baltic Wrestling redaction. Hero and dragon sink into ground as they struggle. Baltic countries and Denmark.

XI. Lettish Devil redaction. Like Central European (II) but devil or devils instead of dragon. From Latvia to other Baltic countries.

This investigation of the Dragon Rescue both in The Dragon Slayer (Type 300) and in The Two Brothers (Type 303) shows certain obvious facts about its history. The place in which the form characteristic of these two tale-types took shape would seem to be France, both because the French versions are nearer to the typical form and also because dissemination from France in all directions offers the best explanation of the distribution of the tale. From France it went to the Hispanic peninsula and thence to the New World. Eastward it spread to Germany and southeastward to Italy. Secondary centers of dissemination in these two places sent the tale, modified in many ways, into surrounding countries. From Germany it went to Scandinavia, the Baltic countries, Czechoslovakia, Poland, and the Balkans. In both Norway and Denmark new redactions arose and spread—the Norwegian to Denmark, Scotland, and Ireland, and the Danish to all the rest of Scandinavia, to North Germany and Finland. From Italy it traveled to the surrounding islands of Sicily and Malta and to Albania, Yugoslavia, and Czechoslovakia. Less important centers of dissemination are the Baltic States, Great Russia, and Yugoslavia.

The very few versions of this tale found outside of Europe are clearly the result of the telling of the story by travelers or colonists. The American Indian variants are all from the French or Spanish, and the Cape Verde Island from the Portuguese. The appearance in Cambodia, Sunda Island, and Japan is purely sporadic.

Careful analysis of the Dragon Slayer story indicates that literary versions have had very little, if any, influence on its development. It has apparently spread east over Europe and only slightly into countries beyond, where it has undoubtedly been carried long distances by travelers or colonists.

The Two Brothers (Type 303) seems likewise to have arisen in western Europe and very likely in northern France. From there it has traveled in all directions, and the farther it has gone from this center, the more changes have taken place in its structure. The redactions do not correspond exactly to those of the Dragon Slayer episode which forms a part of it, but the general picture of the dissemination shows a similar group of centers: France as primary and Germany, Italy, Spain, and Denmark as secondary.

It is impossible to tell just how old these two tales are. They have usually been placed as among the oldest stories belonging to the European tradition. As for The Dragon Slayer (Type 300), Ranke cites four reasons for believing that it is very old. (1) It has a great variety of redactions, each of which has taken time to develop and to spread far and in great numbers. (2) It is combined with other forms (especially Type 303) in spite of the fact that it has developed a form of its own which has a wide and active distribution. (3) Since it is possible to show special developments within particular redaction cycles, but often no *direct* connection between the various redactions, these fundamental differences must go far back. (4) Its presence in Type 303 shows that it is at least as old as that type.

As mentioned before, Ranke is not attempting a history of The Dragon Slayer before it assumed the typical form found in the modern folktale. What its connection with Perseus and Andromeda or with Saint George and the Dragon may be he does not consider. There may well have been such older dragon fight stories which served as a foundation for the present tale, but the special complex which seems to have spread outward from France had taken on all of its present characteristics before its dissemination began. And it is only with the history of this fully formed tale that he is concerned.

As to The Two Brothers (Type 303) Ranke considers it as distinctly younger than the Dragon Rescue episode which it contains. It appears in the Bjarka saga of the fourteenth century and in Basile in the seventeenth. Its distribution would indicate considerable age, though its logical and complex structure, Ranke thinks, prevent it from being placed too far back.

In the case of both these tales (Types 300 and 303) the conclusions about age are extremely vague. They both have old elements, but as well-formed tale-types they would not seem to go back to antiquity. A combination of the currents of population movements since the beginning of the Middle Ages and the natural slow spreading of tales from place to place offers sufficient explanation for the present phenomenal distribution of these two tales over Europe and their sporadic occurrence in other continents.

Although the two stories which we have just considered in detail are those usually associated with the dragon fight, the dragon may also figure as the supernatural adversary in several other well-known tales. There is a tendency in these other stories, however, to leave the nature of the ogre or monster very vague—sometimes with human form, sometimes as a giant, and sometimes as a frightful being in half animal form.

Probably the best known of this whole group of stories is John the Bear, or The Bear's Son (Type 301).[4a] In the most usual form of this tale, the hero has supernatural strength because of his marvelous birth. He has been supernaturally conceived or else he is the son of a bear who has stolen his mother. Even as a small boy he shows his extraordinary strength by breaking tools or by killing his playmates. He is eventually sent off from home and on his way he is joined by several extraordinary companions, a man of extraordinary sight, a keen hearer, and a great runner.[5] The three companions come to a house in the woods. They take turns in keeping house while the others are abroad. One after the other they are attacked by a monster who comes from an opening in the earth. On the third day the hero keeps house and chases the monster through the hole to his abode in the lower world. His two companions let him down after the monster by means of a long rope, and they await his return while he has adventures in the lower world. There he finds a marvelous sword and conquers several monsters and rescues three maidens. He returns to the rope and has his companions raise the girls to the upper world. They take the girls off with them and leave him to his fate below.

He eventually reaches the upper world through the help of a spirit or, more often, of an eagle who carries him on his back and who demands to be fed. The hero feeds the eagle with his own flesh. He arrives at the home of the rescued princesses on the wedding day and, just as in the Dragon Rescue story, he sends his dogs to steal from the wedding feast, presents tokens, unmasks his rivals, and marries the most beautiful of the princesses.

Most versions of the tale are fairly true to the outline just given. Frequently, however, an entirely different introduction appears. A monster comes in the night and steals from the king's orchard. One after the other, the king's sons guard the orchard and watch for the monster. The youngest son pursues the thief and follows him into the lower world. The elder brothers wait for the hero, expecting to pull him up on a rope. The treacherous abandonment, the theft of the girls, and the conclusion of the story are exactly alike, whether introduced by John the Bear or by the Watch for the Devastating Monster.

This story is one of the most popular in the world. It is scattered over the whole of Europe, being especially well known in the Baltic states and in Russia. It is found in the Near East and North Africa but seems to have traveled only in fragments as far east as India. It is very popular among the French and Spanish who have taken it to America, where it has been adopted by American Indian tribes and also is told by the French in Canada and in Missouri.

[4a] This story has never been thoroughly studied, though Panzer (*Beowulf*) has written a monograph pointing out the relations of this tale with the Beowulf epic. His conclusions are dubious.

[5] These extraordinary companions belong also to another story, Types 513, 514.

In the story of The Skillful Hunter (Type 304) the supernatural opponents are usually spoken of as giants. With his magic gun which he has received from a green-clad huntsman or from an old woman, the hero displays his skill as a marksman. Among other exhibitions is the shooting of meat from the hands of giants. With these giants he agrees to go to abduct a queen. He enters the palace and then calls the giants in. As they enter one by one, he cuts off their heads. In the palace he finds a sleeping princess and lies with her without waking her. When he leaves he takes from her a handkerchief, a ring, or the like to use as a token. As in the Dragon Rescue story, an impostor comes forth and this time claims to be the unknown father of the princess's child. She refuses to marry him, however, and is punished by being made to live in a house in the woods and cook for everyone, or else to stay at an inn where all comers must tell their life history. In due time the hero appears to her, tells his story, produces his token, and receives the princess in marriage.

This tale has some interesting motifs, especially the deception of the giants and the princess's recognition in the inn, but it has never achieved great popularity among taletellers. Although it is current through most of central Europe and as far east as the Caucasus, only a single version appears in France, and no other so far west. Even in Finland, where tales have been so well collected, there are but few variants, and in the huge Lithuanian collections it does not appear at all, nor has it been carried by travelers or colonists to other continents. In all, not more than seventy-five versions have thus far been reported.[6]

The tale of The Danced-out Shoes (Type 306) presents the supernatural opponent of the hero in human form and as the lover of the princess.[7] It is discovered that a princess absents herself at night and always returns with her shoes danced to pieces. She is offered in marriage to the man who can solve the mystery of her conduct. She has succeeded in giving a narcotic to all those who have tried to follow her, but the hero refuses to drink and accompanies her on a magic underground journey. He possesses the power of making himself invisible and is able to observe her when she dances with the supernatural being whom she visits every night. By means of tokens which he has brought from this subterranean realm, he is able to prove his story and to claim his reward.

This tale, like the last, seems to be primarily Central European with most frequent appearance in the area from Serbia north to Finland. It does not, so far as is now known, go east of Russia and is represented but once in France and Portugal. A single version is found in central Africa, and it has not thus

[6] This is to be compared with the 770 versions of The Two Brothers and more than a thousand versions of both The Dragon Rescue and The Bear's Son.

[7] For a series of other tales in which the heroine has a supernatural and usually monstrous lover, see Types 506-508.

far been reported in any other continents. Within its rather narrow geographical range it seems to be fairly popular, since somewhat more than a hundred variants are known.

The heroine in The Danced-out Shoes does not seem to be anxious to be rescued from her otherworld lover. In most tales, however, these supernatural lovers have forced themselves upon the princess and keep her in duress. One of the most popular tales of rescue from such an ogre lover is the story of The Monster with His Heart in the Egg (Type 302). The hero comes into possession of certain magic objects or powers which he finds useful in his adventures. He secures these magic aids in various ways: in some versions from grateful animals for whom he has made a just division of food, in some from giants whom he tricks into trading him their magic objects, in some from his animal brothers-in-law who give him the power of self-transformation. In any case, he hears that a princess has been carried off by an ogre and he goes to her rescue. He finds her and together they plot against the life of her unwelcome lover. She beguiles the ogre into telling her where he keeps his heart or what his life is bound up with. He tells her that his heart is to be found in a certain egg, very difficult of access or in a bird or insect which is guarded by dangerous beasts. The hero follows the instructions she gives him and finds the ogre's heart. When he destroys the heart, the ogre dies and the hero returns the princess to her home and receives his reward and takes the princess as his wife.

In the whole area from Ireland to India this tale has had a deserved popularity. It is frequently well told and the adventures of the hero and the princess in overcoming the monster lover have wide appeal to those who listen to tales of wonder. Within this area the tale has been reported some 250 times and seems to be well represented everywhere. In contrast to all the stories thus far mentioned it is popular in India. It has been pointed out that the versions in Asia place the ogre's heart in a bird or insect, whereas the typical European form has it in the egg. The story has been carried several times to Africa and to America, where it has taken its place in the traditions of the native Africans and the American Indians.

A. OGRES AND WITCHES

In the folktale generally known under the title of Bluebeard the evil creature who steals the maidens is usually conceived of as having human form and sometimes has no supernatural characteristics. To the literary world the story has become known through Perrault's famous collection of 1697, and wherever that version has exerted great influence it has determined the form of the story. The principal characteristic of the Perrault version is the fact that the sisters are rescued by a brother. In most countries independent of this tradition the rescue is done by the youngest sister.

In both these tales two sisters, one after the other, fall into the power of an ogre or frightful man, who carries them off to his castle (sometimes situated in the lower world). He gives them the run of the castle but forbids them to enter a particular room. When they disobey an egg or a key becomes bloody and betrays them. The ogre kills them and puts their bodies aside. When the youngest sister is stolen she discovers the bodies of the first two and succeeds in bringing them back to life and hiding them. The girls are put into sacks and the husband is persuaded to carry the sacks home without looking into them. The youngest sister escapes by leaving behind a skull dressed up as a bride and by disguising herself as a bird. The story ends with the punishment of the murderous husband.

The tale in approximately this form (Type 311) is known over most of Europe from Germany eastward. Its area of greatest popularity is found in the Baltic states and in Norway. In the north, it seems to go no further east than the Urals, but it is found in Palestine and has several versions in India. It has also been carried to the Eskimos and to Puerto Rico. The story has never been thoroughly studied, but a cursory examination of the variants suggests Norway as at least an important center of dissemination of this tale, if not its original home.

As indicated above, the rescue of the sisters may be accomplished by their brother (or brothers) (Type 312). Perrault has the husband give the wife a respite from death so she can say her prayers. In this way she delays matters until her brothers arrive and can rescue her. The influence of this Perrault version has been strong in France, Belgium, and Germany. But the tale does not always appear exactly as Perrault tells it. Outside the orbit of his tradition we find the rescue accomplished by the brother with the help of his marvelous dogs or other wild animals. This latter form is found especially in Norway. But the Bluebeard tale with the brother as rescuer has had no wide distribution and does not seem ever to have attained great popularity.

In an important series of tales about witches or ogres the principal part is played by children. Best known of these stories is Hansel and Gretel (Type 327A), one of the most frequently reprinted of the Grimm tales. To the musical public it is everywhere known through the remarkable operatic interpretation of Humperdinck. The two children sent by their poverty-stricken parents into the woods, the trail of grain eaten by the birds, the gingerbread house, the appearance of the terrible witch, the fattening of the boy in the pen, and the burning of the witch in her own oven are constantly recurring motifs in this tale. It is known over all of Europe and is especially popular in the Baltic countries. It is found in Asia as far east as India, where it has been reported several times. Travelers have carried it to the remotest parts of the earth, to all parts of Africa, to Japan, to the Negroes of the West Indies, and to American Indian tribes all over the continent.

In examining the versions in distant parts of the world one is frequently puzzled to know whether we are dealing with a borrowing or with an independent invention. The elements of the tale are so simple that their frequent combination does not offer great theoretical difficulties. Of all the African, Oceanic, Japanese, and American Indian tales of ogres who fatten children and who are themselves killed instead it is not quite certain which are derived from the European tale. Within the continent of Europe, however, the story has such uniformity and such continuous distribution that its history as a type should not be difficult to trace.[8]

So similar in its outlines to Hansel and Gretel that in many countries it is quite impossible to disentangle the two tales is the story popularized by Perrault under the title Le Petit Poucet (Type 327B).[9] In this tale the tiny hero (no bigger than a thumb) accompanied by his brothers comes to the house of the ogre (or giant). Realizing that the ogre intends to kill them in their beds as they sleep, the hero exchanges the nightcaps of his brothers and himself with the ogre's children so that their father cuts off their heads and lets the hero and his brothers escape.

The trick of the exchange of caps is by no means confined to tales with the Thumbling hero but may appear in any context where there are several children in the power of an ogre. The tale in very much the form Perrault tells it occurs in nearly all parts of Europe, though it is not generally so popular as Hansel and Gretel. It has been carried to the North American Indians of British Columbia, presumably by French Canadians, but apparently it has not been reported in other continents.

Especially popular in Norway and the Baltic states is the related tale (Type 327C) in which the ogre or witch carries the hero home in a sack. He usually escapes from her by substituting some animal or object in the sack. Eventually, however, he is confined and fattened for slaughter like Hansel and escapes by the same trick, burning the ogre in his own oven. This tale is so close to that of Hansel and Gretel that the two are seldom clearly differentiated. Indeed, the whole cycle of stories concerning the children and the ogre seems to form a definite tale type (327) which may appear with a considerable variety of incidents, the most usual of which are those which we have here recognized as 327A, 327B, and 327C. The whole complex seems to be European, though it is possible to find somewhat similar tales of children and ogres in other continents. There are, for example, tales among the Africans, the American Negroes, and the American Indians in which a person being carried in a sack by an ogre escapes by substituting an object

[8] The type has not been studied with any thoroughness. Its origin in India would seem highly problematical, though that is the assumption of Cosquin's article, "Le conte de la chaudière bouillante et la feinte maladresse dans l'Inde et hors de l'Inde," Revue des traditions populaires, XXV, 1, 65, 126.

[9] In English it is sometimes known as Tom Thumb, though that title is also applied to the tale relating the many adventures of the tiny hero which constitute Type 700. For this reason it is less confusing to use the recognized French title for the story here under consideration.

or animal.[10] Actual borrowing of this incident from the European tale is highly problematical. The incident is so simple that it may well have been independently invented by the American Indians and by African tribes from whom it was brought to America in the days of slavery.

In the stories of children and ogres just mentioned the hero and his companion fall into the power of the ogre by an unlucky chance. But sometimes the adventure with the ogre is deliberately sought, since the hero wishes to steal his magic objects. Such is true in the tale known to English readers as Jack the Giant Killer (Type 328). The reason for the theft from the giant is the principal point in which the tale varies from version to version. One introduction especially characteristic of British tradition is Jack and the Beanstalk.[11] As a result of a foolish bargain Jack acquires some beans which his mother throws away. Overnight a beanstalk grows to the sky and the next day Jack climbs up on this stalk and finds himself in the upper world. In his wanderings above he finds an old woman who tells him about a giant and his magic possessions. Jack goes to the giant's house and is hidden in the oven by the giant's wife. He sees the giant get treasure from his hen who lays golden eggs. While the giant is asleep Jack steals the hen, descends the beanstalk, and brings riches to himself and his mother. In like manner he steals from the giant purses filled with gold and silver, and escapes, in spite of the barking of the giant's magic dog. Finally he steals the giant's magic harp and escapes down the beanstalk. The giant tries to follow, Jack cuts down the beanstalk, and he falls to his death.

This particular form is one of the most popular of English folktales. It differs in many respects from the story as told in other countries. The undertaking to steal from the giant is sometimes for the purpose of revenge for former ill treatment, sometimes to help a friendly king, and sometimes it is a task assigned by the king at the suggestion of jealous rivals. The tricks the hero uses to defeat the giant are many. Sometimes he makes him think that a great army is approaching and locks him up to protect him. Sometimes he oversalts the giant's food and steals the objects when he goes out for water, and sometimes he distracts the giant's attention by fishing through the chimney. The objects stolen also vary: a magic light, a marvelous horse, a self-playing violin or harp occur most frequently. To aid in his escape the hero tricks the giant into giving him certain magic objects such as a cap of knowledge, an invincible sword, a cloak of invisibility, or the giant's seven-league boots. The giant is sometimes enticed into a cage and taken to court, though usually he is tricked into killing himself. The experiences at the giant's house are frequently like those of Hansel with the witch. The fattening of the hero and the burning of the giant in his own oven may occur

---

[10] See motif K526, with bibliography there given. (Citations of motifs like the present refer to Thompson, *Motif-Index*.)

[11] See Bolte-Polívka, II, 511.

in either story, and likewise in either story there may appear the incident of the magic flight. Either the hero (and his companions) are transformed into objects or other persons so as to deceive the pursuer (Transformation Flight, D671), or else the fugitives throw behind them magic objects which become obstacles in the giant's path (Obstacle Flight, D672).

This story of the theft from the giant seems from the versions thus far reported to be primarily a north-central European tale. It is very popular in Finland and Norway and has been collected as far south as Spain and Roumania, but it apparently does not exist in Russia or anywhere east of it. The French tell it in eastern Canada and have taught it to American Indian tribes from Nova Scotia to British Columbia.[12]

In two closely related tales the "ogre" is a fierce animal, usually a wolf. To English readers, these stories are known as Little Red Ridinghood (Type 333) and The Three Little Pigs (Type 123). The essential difference is that in the former the wolf deceives a child and in the latter, small animals. In many versions of both tales the conclusions are identical. Little Red Ridinghood (Le Petit Chaperon Rouge, Rotkäppchen) has become one of the best known "fairy tales" for those who depend upon the printed page for the stories they tell their children. The version usually read in books is that of Perrault (1697) or, less frequently, that of Grimm. The little girl, going through the woods to see her grandmother, is accosted by the wolf who reaches the grandmother's house ahead of her. The wolf kills the grandmother and takes her place in bed. When the little girl arrives, she is astonished at the "grandmother's" large ears, large eyes, etc. ("Grandmother, what makes your ears so large?—To hear the better, my child," etc.) until finally she inquiries about the long teeth. From this point on, there are two different endings to the story. In one of them the little girl is rescued at the last moment by someone who chances to come to the house. But this ending seems to be designed for the nursery on the theory that children would be shocked unless the little girl were rescued. The other ending permits the wolf to devour not only the grandmother, but also the little girl. When the rescuers arrive, the wolf is cut open and his victims rescued alive.

This tale of Little Red Ridinghood has never had wide circulation where folktales are learned by word of mouth. Even in France and Germany, where the largest number is reported, practically all are based upon Perrault or Grimm. It does not extend east beyond the Russian border. The frequent African versions belong partly to this type and partly to the Three Little Pigs: The child is human, but the rest of the story is essentially an animal tale.

The Three Little Pigs (Type 123) tells of the adventures of the young animals—seven goats, three pigs, or the like—who are left at home by their mother in their house and are warned not to open the door to the wolf.

---

[12] Those versions of this tale in which the tasks are assigned through the machinations of a jealous rival merge imperceptibly into the tale of The Master Thief (Type 1525).

Several times they succeed in keeping the wolf off but he finally makes them believe that he is their mother. In order to do this, he paints himself or puts flour on his paws, or else he has his voice changed by an operation such as swallowing hot iron or having it filed down by a goldsmith or silversmith. At any rate, the wolf succeeds in entering and devouring the young animals. When the mother returns, the wolf is cut open and the animals rescued.

This story has had a long history. In a simple form it appears in some of the early collections of Aesop's Fables, and was frequently retold from that source throughout the Middle Ages. No comparative study of the tale has been made, so that the geographical limitations of the various incidents have not been determined. The story as a whole, however, is popular over all of Europe and well out into Siberia. It appears all over China and is known in Japan. An interesting feature in the dissemination of the tale is its frequent and widespread African occurrence in contrast to the sparcity of variants in America. The African and Russian versions apparently come from the same tradition, since they all have the operations on the voice of the wolf. It is impossible without a serious investigation to say more with certainty about the development and history of the Three Little Pigs.

Within the last few years it has become known to millions through the delightful cinema treatment by Walt Disney and by the catchy song "Who's Afraid of the Big Bad Wolf?"

B. VAMPIRES AND REVENANTS

Almost universal, except among the most sophisticated groups, is the fear of the dead. This fact is shown by scores of world-wide practices designed to keep the dead from coming forth from their graves and molesting the living.[13] Traditions of experiences with such wanderers are common to all countries, but they are usually so connected with definite places that they are considered as local legends. Several widely distributed folktales, however, are based upon this belief. In some the dead is considered definitely as a vampire, who comes forth from the grave and lives on the blood of the living. In others it is a less malevolent ghost.

The tale of The Princess in the Shroud (Type 307) is very popular in eastern Europe, particularly Estonia, Lithuania, Russia, and the Balkans. This is not surprising since the vampire belief is so strong among just these peoples. It is known but not popular in western Europe and has not been reported farther than Armenia. African versions sometimes cited show so little real resemblance as to indicate that they certainly belong to a different tradition.

Parents who are childless make a solemn wish for a child even though it may be a devil. The daughter born in response to this wish proves to be

---

[13] For an excellent discussion of the importance of the belief in the "living dead man," see Naumann, *Primitive Gemeinschaftskultur*, pp. 18-60.

diabolical, and at her death she wanders as a vampire. All the soldiers who watch her grave in the church at night are killed. The hero of the story receives the advice of an old man and succeeds in bringing her back to life and overcoming her enchantment by following the old man's directions. For three nights he prays, once kneeling before the altar, once prone before the altar, and once in her grave. All this time he endures her severe punishments. At the end all the watchers are restored to life and the hero and the girl are happily married.

In a story almost entirely confined to the shores of the Baltic and to Norway (Type 363), the vampire is a man. A strange man appears and marries a girl without her knowing much about him. As they are driving at night in a wagon toward his home, he stops before a church and tells her to wait for him. She becomes impatient and slips in to see what he is doing. He has a burning lamp and a dead body before him and is eating the corpse. She returns to the wagon without being discovered. The same thing happens at the second and the third church, except that there are two and then three corpses. They eventually reach his home, where she lives in fair content. One day he tells her that members of her family will visit her but that she is not to tell them what she knows about him. This happens and she refuses to talk freely to her brother and her mother, but eventually tells her sister the secret. The husband has merely taken on the form of the members of the family to test her. He now assumes his own form and devours her.

Much better known to the tradition of western Europe, largely because the theme has been used so much in ballads, is the Lenore story (Type 365). No comparative study of the relation of the folktale to the ballad has been made which would indicate whether verse or prose would seem to be the original form. In verse it achieved an enormous popularity at the end of the 18th century after it had been used by Bürger in his "Lenore." The tradition is usually given in prose form in the Baltic states, where in Lithuania not fewer than 42 versions have been reported and in Finland, 174. But the prose versions hardly appear in other parts of Europe. A few Hungarian and Roumanian variants form the only exception. The story itself is very simple in structure. A girl's lover appears to her at night and invites her to ride with him on his horse. He has been away and she has had no news of him. As they ride she realizes that he has returned from the dead and becomes frightened. He takes her to his grave and disappears as the cock crows. Sometimes she is pulled into the grave and sometimes she is found dead outside.

The three stories which we have just given are the only ones of dead lovers which have acquired great popularity in Europe. There are many local stories, particularly in eastern Europe, with these basic situations but with the details considerably changed.[14]

[14] See, for example, Balys, *Motif-Index of Lithuanian Narrative Folklore*, p. 33 and Schullerus, *Verzeichnis der rumänischen Märchen*, pp. 37f.

Ghost stories have a tendency to be localized and to vary a great deal from place to place. A whole series of such local legends has to do with a person who returns from the dead to claim some object which has been stolen from him. One such tale is so widely known that it has lost any definite attachment to place and is told as an ordinary folktale. This story of The Man from the Gallows (Type 366) is well known in western Europe. Its greatest popularity seems to be in Denmark, though it is told in England and as far south as Spain. There are frequent German variants, but it fades out as soon as one moves east of the German border. Versions have been carried by travelers to the Malay peninsula and to the Hausa in Africa. A poor man, desperately in need of meat for his family, finds a thief hanging from the gallows. He cuts meat from the legs of the thief, takes it home, and has it served at a feast. The dead man comes and demands the return of his flesh. In most versions the man who stole the flesh is carried off. Some variation is made in the story from place to place. Sometimes it is the heart, or even a piece of clothing of the hanged man which is stolen.

C. DEVILS AND DEMONS

The people who tell folktales are not always clear in their conception of the supernatural creatures whom their heroes must meet in combat. In the stories of the return from the dead which have just been considered, the gruesome opponent is certainly no mere spectre, but has enough solidity to be dangerous and often unconquerable in combat. But just what these vampires or wandering dead men look like is never clearly stated. The same situation is found in tales about the devil.

Three or four different concepts seem to be thoroughly confused when the term "devil" is used by the teller of tales. In Germany and Scandinavian countries, it frequently means nothing more than the vague word "ogre." Thus when they speak of the "stupid devil" they may equally well say "the stupid ogre" or "the stupid giant." Again the term "devil" is frequently equivalent to the Oriental "demon," or even the "djinn" of the *Arabian Nights*. The English usage is likely to be somewhat narrower than those just suggested. "Devil" is likely to have some connection with Satan, the devil of Christian theology, and to have the outward appearances made familiar by long centuries of medieval writers and artists. Indispensable as part of his equipment are his cloven hoofs, his tail, and usually his pointed ears—the whole possibly a reminiscence of Pan and the satyrs of old Greek legend.[15]

Except when conceived of as an ogre, the devil does not usually engage his opponent in open combat. The power which he exerts is normally supernatural.

Most "devil" stories consist of a single incident. Such, for example, is The

[15] For literature on the subject of the devil, see motif G303.

Snares of the Evil One (Type 810), in which the man who is promised to the devil is permitted by the priest to spend the night when the devil should come for him in the church. The priest draws about the man a ring which the devil may not enter. The man resists the devil's temptation to come out and in this way saves himself. This little story is hardly known outside of Scandinavia and the Baltic states, but is very popular there.

Entirely confined to the Baltic states are two other simple tales of adventures with the devil. In one of these he takes service as a mower and works under an evil overseer. The devil has a magic sickle and mows so fast that when the overseer tries to keep up with him he dies of exhaustion (Type 820). In the other (Type 815) a rich man's money is buried in his grave within the church. When the devil comes to get the money, the cobbler draws a circle about him and keeps him away. The cobbler himself steals the money and nails the devil fast.

Though most of these stories of the devil as an adversary are short and simple, they are not always so. The Devil's Riddle (Type 812), a tale especially popular in Germany and the Baltic states and sometimes heard in southern and western Europe, has a complex plot and frequently an elaborate treatment. It begins with the well-known devil's contract, by the terms of which the hero (sometimes three heroes) promises himself to the devil at the end of a certain time if he cannot solve the riddles which the devil propounds. The devil has various objects which appear to be different from what they really are. The hero must guess their real nature. For example, what really seems to be a horse is a he-goat. Some of the other illusions are a piece of cloth (a goat-skin), a gold cup (a cup of pitch), roast meat (a dead dog), a spoon (a whale rib), a wine glass (a horse's hoof), and the like. Sometimes the devil asks seemingly impossible questions such as What is sweeter than honey? What is softer than swan's down? or What is harder than stone? Sometimes he asks for symbolic interpretations of the numbers one to seven. Or he may set the hero a series of impossible tasks. It will be seen that this part of the tale offers opportunity for large variation. The methods whereby the hero learns the solution are much more uniform, for most of them depend upon the fact that in some way the hero overhears the devil. Sometimes he masks and sometimes he hides with the help of the devil's grandmother. If it is tasks he must perform, the hero gets the help of some supernatural being. In all cases he succeeds in outwitting the devil and escaping from the fulfillment of the contract.

Certain of the details of this story appear elsewhere. The contract in which the hero, like Faust, promises himself to the devil forms the introduction to several other well-known complex tales.[16] Besides these there is to be found a considerable number of short anecdotes, consisting of only a single motif, in which the man who sells his soul to the devil saves it by deceit, usually

[16] See Types 330, 360, and 756B. For this motif, see M211.

by imposing some impossible task (Types 1170-1199). The devil in these stories is stupid and the principal point of these tales is the contrast between him and the clever hero. All these stories are popular in Scandinavia and the Baltic countries, though most of them are not unknown in the rest of Europe. Such is the tale of the man who is to belong to the devil as soon as he has sold all his goods, but if he has any goods that no one will buy he is to go free. He puts an evil old woman in a glass case and offers her for sale. When the devil sees her, he realizes that no one will buy her, and releases the man (Type 1170).

Among the impossible tasks assigned the devil in stories of this kind are catching rabbits in nets set out in high trees (Type 1171), collecting all stones from the brook or field, making knots from drops of spilled brandy, making a rope from sand, straightening curly hair, catching a man's broken wind, pumping out water from the whole sea, or catching water in a sieve (Types 1171-1180). Other kinds of cheats are perpetrated on the devil. Having agreed to give the devil a part of his body, the man gives him a paring from his fingernail (Type 1181).

Three other deceptive bargains are The Level Bushel, The Last Leaf, and The First Crop (Types 1182, 1184, and 1185). In the first, the student is to come into the devil's power if, at the end of a year, he does not at least return for the heaping bushel of gold a level one. The student immediately hands back the level bushel and keeps the surplus. In the second the man is to pay the devil when the last leaf falls from the tree. It is an oak tree and the leaf never falls. The oak also figures in the third of these stories. The man is to pay the devil as soon as he harvests his first crop, but he plants acorns and the devil must wait long. These three tales are widely distributed and popular over most of Europe.

Frequently the escape from the devil takes place at the last minute. The hero asks for a delay while he repeats a prayer for the last time (Type 1199). The man arranges never to finish the prayer and the devil is cheated. Sometimes other last requests are made, to be allowed to finish dressing or the like.[17]

Most of these short anecdotes about escape from the devil belong primarily to the oral tradition, but the tale of The Devil and the Advocate (Type 1186) has received first-rate literary treatment. Chaucer uses it as his "Friar's Tale," but it had already appeared more than a century before in Der Stricker's *Pfaffe Amis*. In spite of its primary literary association, the anecdote is also handed around by word of mouth and has been so reported from Scandinavian countries. The devil refuses to take anything which is not offered him with the whole heart. He hears the advocate cursed for fraud ("The devil take you!") with such sincerity that he carries him off.

The tales about the devil thus far mentioned have assumed that the devil

[17] For a discussion of this motif in its many varieties, see K551.

was wandering about upon the face of the earth. We shall find several stories, treated later in other connections, in which the devil is found in hell.[18] One short anecdote of this kind tells how the devil is deceived into putting on "the chains of Solomon." He is thus bound and must stay in hell.[19]

We shall find the devil in two other connections. As mentioned once before, he is sometimes conceived of as a stupid ogre,[20] as in some of the tales we have already met. Sometimes, however, the devil is by no means stupid and turns out to be a very valuable ally and helper of the hero. In such stories[21] the devil's cleverness is emphasized and not, as in the tales we have just discussed, his malevolence or stupidity.

D. DEATH IN PERSON

In his malevolent character, the devil is sometimes thought of as the equivalent of Death, or even its personification. This confusion is particularly apparent in the tale generally known as The Smith and the Devil or The Smith and Death (Type 330).

This story has been told in so many forms, both literary and oral, that a clear history of it would be very difficult to trace. Motifs are added or omitted with the greatest freedom, though a central core serves to maintain its identity. The following generalized statement of the tale contains most of the incidents which occur with any frequency. The smith has made a contract with the devil that in return for becoming a master-smith he is to belong to the devil after a certain time. In some way, occasionally from the Lord or Saint Peter, who is wandering on the earth, he receives three objects: a tree and a bench that cause people to stick to them, and a knapsack that draws persons into it. In the course of his adventures he causes the devil (or Death) to stick to the tree or the bench. Sometimes Death is put in the knapsack and pounded on the anvil until he gives up his claim on the smith. At last the smith goes to hell, but he is not admitted, since the devil has lost power over him. He therefore goes to heaven, but he is unknown there and is refused admittance. But he gets permission to throw his knapsack inside and the knapsack pulls him after it.

Though the versions are confused and the motifs freely interchanged, there is a tendency for the adventures with the Lord and Saint Peter to appear in connection with Death sticking to the tree (Type 330A). The magic knapsack is naturally found where the smith enters into heaven by a trick (Type 330B). In the course of his experiences with the Lord and Saint Peter, the

[18] See pp. 66, 131, and 252, below.
[19] Type 803. See also J. Balys, "Lithuanian Legends of the Devil in Chains," *Tautosakos Darbai* (Publication of the Lithuanian Folklore Archives), III (1937), 321-333 (25 Lithuanian variants).
[20] See p. 35, above.
[21] See p. 66, below.

story may tell of how he unsuccessfully attempts to imitate a miracle by which the Lord rejuvenates an old woman or shoes a horse by cutting off his leg and later putting it back (Type 753).

The idea of Death sticking to the tree or to a stool can be traced back to antiquity, where it is found in both Greek and Hebrew originals. The story with most of the motifs mentioned above appeared in literary form in Italian as early as 1525 and became the subject of a very popular French chapbook, "Histoire nouvelle et divertissante du bonhomme Misère, par le sieur de La Rivière" (Rouen, 1719). This was often reprinted and has been the basis of many literary treatments. The most striking part of the story, Death on the Tree, was recently used as the central motif of the cinema production "On Borrowed Time."[22]

The story has had considerable popularity as an oral tale, whether or not the tradition may eventually go back to a written form. It is known literally all over Europe and as far east as the Caucasus and Palestine. It is found in Iceland, Scotland, Spain, and Italy, but its greatest popularity is in central and northern Europe—Germany, Lithuania, Estonia, and Finland. At least 25 versions are found in Russia.

An adequate study of the history of this tale remains to be made. Even a superficial glance at the material indicates that such a study, while extremely exacting on the scholar who undertakes it, would show many interesting results. Such problems as the looseness or stability of a folktale type, and the mutual relations of written and oral versions would be ever present. One problem, however, the scholar would escape: the story does not seem to have been carried and transplanted into remote parts of the earth.

Also the subject of frequent literary handlings from at least as early as the year 1300 is the story of Godfather Death (Type 332). The tale begins with the well-known motif of the search for a godfather. For this office a poor man chooses Death, since he considers him more just than either God or the Devil. As godfather, Death gives to him (or sometimes to his son) the power of seeing Death standing at the head or the foot of a sick bed, and thus forecasting the progress of sickness. By using this power, the man becomes a famous doctor. When the man himself sees Death approaching he escapes by a trick. In some versions he turns the bed around and thus confuses Death; in others he asks for time to finish the Lord's Prayer, but never gets to the end.[23] At last, however, Death gets his revenge. In some way he tricks the man into finishing the prayer, or else he takes the man to the lower world, where all the living are represented by life-lights. When he comes to the man's own light, he puts it out.[24] The history and distribution of this tale

---

[22] For a discussion of the literary forms of this tale, see Bolte-Polívka, II, 186ff.

[23] We have already seen this motif (K551.1) in another connection (Type 312).

[24] This tale has been studied by R. Th. Christiansen in *Danske Studier* (1915), pp. 72-78. His study is based upon 124 variants.

is almost identical with the one we have just discussed, The Smith and Death. Though it appears frequently in medieval literature and has continued to be a subject for artistic and literary treatments,[25] it is widely known by tellers of oral folktales in all parts of Europe and as far afield as Iceland and Palestine. Its greatest popularity is in the Baltic countries, Scandinavia, and Germany. It is also well established in the folklore of France, Spain, and Italy. The interrelation of the oral and the written versions is not easy to untangle.

While we are discussing stories concerning Death mention should be made of a literary tale, "Death's Messengers" (Type 335), popular with such collectors of exempla and moralistic tales as Bromyard, Johannes Pauli, and Hans Sachs, and having its ultimate origins in Buddhistic literature. Death promises a man to give him warning of his approach. He gives the man a blow, blindness, white hairs, etc. In spite of these messengers of Death, the man fails to understand the signs and lives happily on. This tale cannot be said to have found a place in folklore, since it has been so rarely reported by collectors.

Finally, before leaving those stories which concern supernatural adversaries, there remains the tale of The Spirit in the Bottle (Type 331) or The Bottle Imp. Though its treatment in the *Arabian Nights* is undoubtedly most familiar to the literary world, it has been frequently told in every century since the Middle Ages, and the experiences have been attributed variously to such worthies as Paracelsus (Theophrastus) or Virgil. Oral versions are only occasionally encountered and these are likely to be closely related to some literary retelling. The essential point in all versions is that a man frees an evil spirit from a bottle and in return receives some magic power. Finally he succeeds in tricking the spirit back into the bottle.

What kind of spirit is meant in this tale of the bottle is never clearly defined. He is apparently a demon of some kind, but is seldom or never to be identified with the devil. This indeterminate quality has been observed also in many of the other stories of supernatural adversaries which we have now considered. In the next group of tales, where we shall encounter a group of extraordinary helpers, a similar confusion in the exact nature of the helpers will be observed.

3. SUPERNATURAL HELPERS

A. SUPERNATURAL SPINNERS

The first important folktale study made by the distinguished Swede, C. W. von Sydow,[1] concerned two tales of miraculous spinners. The first of these

---

[25] For these, see Bolte-Polívka, I, 382.
[1] *Två Spinnsagor.*

is known over most of the continent as Titeliture or Rumpelstilzchen, but in England as Tom-Tit-Tot (Type 500). The principal traits of the story are rather constant. A woman is compelled on account of her foolish boasting to give her daughter in marriage to a prince. She has actually made some silly remark about her daughter: "My daughter ate five pies today." But when the prince asks her what she said she misreports her remark as, "My daughter has spun five skeins today." The prince, anxious to have so skillful a wife, marries the girl and then commands her to carry out her mother's boast and spin an impossible amount in a single day. Sometimes the spinning is to be of yarn, but frequently she must spin gold. A tiny creature appears and agrees to help the girl, but she must promise to give herself (sometimes, her child) if within a certain time she fails to guess his name. The creature spins the required amount, but eventually the time is near when she must guess his name. In one way or another she discovers his secret. Usually he is over-heard repeating a rhyme. In the English version it is:

> Nimmy nimmy not,
> My name's Tom-Tit-Tot.

When it comes time for her to guess his name, she deliberately guesses wrong the first two times, but at last she repeats the rhyme, pronounces his name, and saves herself. The story is well known in Germany and Scandinavia and all around the Baltic, but it is also told throughout the British Isles and as far south as Spain and Italy. It seems to have penetrated little, if at all, into Russia, and except for an obvious borrowing from the Spanish in Puerto Rico, has not been reported outside Europe. Von Sydow was convinced that the story developed in Sweden, and the distribution does give some grounds for such a conclusion. Recently he has announced his belief that his earlier conclusions were erroneous and that the tale has moved from the British Isles to Scandinavia.[2] A widespread legend concerning the making of a great building has the same motif of the supernatural helper whose name must be guessed,[3] but direct relation between the legend and the tale seems improbable.

The other tale handled in this study by von Sydow is that of The Three Old Women Helpers (Type 501). The opening of the story is almost the same as that of the one just treated. The girl is to marry the prince if she can spin the impossible amount which she has been assigned, either because of her mother's boasting or her own, or because of the false reports of jealous servants. In this tale she receives the help of three old women spinners. They have become terribly deformed on account of their excessive spinning. In return for their help the girl promises to invite them to her wedding. She is true to her promise and the old women appear at the wedding, so deformed

[2] Von Sydow, "Finsk metod och modern sagoforskning," reprint from *Rig* (Lund, 1943).
[3] See Bolte-Polívka, I, 495.

that the prince cries out in disgust. They tell him that their evil shape has come from doing too much spinning. He thereupon decrees that his wife shall never have to spin.

These two tales are so much alike in their earlier parts that it is natural that there should be some mixing of the two. The Three Old Women Helpers received literary treatment in Germany as early as 1669 and has been well known in Germany at least since that time. Its distribution is almost the same as Titeliture, viz. all of Europe west of Russia, but particularly Finland, Germany, and Scandinavia. Von Sydow is undecided as to whether it may have first developed in Sweden or in Germany.

B. HELPFUL DWARFS OR FAIRIES

In spite of the fact that in English we are likely to speak of all tales of wonder as fairy tales, the truth is that fairies appear rarely in such stories. Occasionally in some literary reworking of a tale, one hears of a fairy god-mother, but most accounts of fairies appear as legends or traditions. In one well-known tale, however (Type 503), the central incident does concern fairies. Sometimes they are spoken of as "the little folk" and sometimes they are called dwarfs. A hunchback comes across the fairies as they are dancing. He gains their favor by joining in their dance or by making music for them. Sometimes in their song they are trying to name the days of the week, but can never get beyond a certain point: he supplies the names of the missing days. Sometimes he submits peacefully while they cut his hair or shave him. The fairies reward him by taking off his hump and sometimes by giving him gold. He has an avaricious companion who thinks he will imitate the hero's good fortune. But the angry fairies give him the hump they have taken from the other, and where he had expected to get gold they give him some worthless coals.

In much its present form, this tale appeared in the 17th century in the literature of both Italy and Ireland. Earlier there had been an Arabic literary story dating from the 14th century in which a demon (afrit) removes the hump and puts it on the second man.[4] Within a relatively small area the story is very popular in folk tradition. In France it is one of the most frequently told of all folktales, and it is well known in Ireland, Belgium, Italy, and Germany. It does not, however, seem to have reached Scandinavia, the Baltic states, or Russia except sporadically. In spite of the assiduous collection in Lithuania and Finland, where most folktales are reported by the scores, there appear only five versions for Lithuania and none for Finland. By some accident of long-distance transmission, the story appears with fair faithful-ness in a Japanese collection. Otherwise it seems to be confined to western Europe. The relations of the oral and the literary forms should make an

[4] For a discussion of these literary forms, see Bolte-Polívka, III, 324, 328.

interesting study, but this has not been undertaken except by Joseph Bédier, who does little more than suggest the problem and scoff at those who would seriously undertake its solution.[5]

In some other versions the helpful little folk are dwarfs, whom we shall meet again when we discuss the tale of Snow White (Type 709). The envious companion who is punished for attempting to imitate the hero's good luck (N471) appears in several other popular European stories (Types 461, 503, 613, 676).

C. THE GRATEFUL DEAD

The helper in a notable group of European and Asiatic tales is a mysterious person known as the grateful dead man. The chain of circumstances by which this helper joins the hero and certain details of his later experience are so uniform and well articulated as to form an easily recognizable motif, or rather cluster of motifs. This fact has caused some confusion to scholars who have not sufficiently distinguished between such a motif and the entire tale of which it forms only an important part.[6]

Though this group of motifs appears sporadically in a considerable number of tales where it may replace other helpers,[7] there are about a half-dozen tales, some of them obviously varying forms of the same story, in which the grateful dead man always plays the leading role.

In all these tales we learn of a hero who finds that creditors are refusing to permit the burial of a corpse until the dead man's debts have been paid. The hero spends his last penny to ransom the dead man's body and to secure his burial. Later, in the course of his adventures, he is joined by a mysterious stranger who agrees to help him in all his endeavors. This stranger is the grateful dead man (E341). The only condition which the dead man makes when he agrees to help the hero is that all winnings which the latter makes shall be equally divided. In all the stories the hero eventually wins a wife and the helper demands his half. Usually the dead man interferes in time to prevent the actual cutting in two of the woman.

It will be seen that this train of events is actually only a framework for the adventures of the hero. The various tales relating these adventures have been studied with some thoroughness by Sven Liljeblad.[8]

Two of these tales, obviously related, refer to a rescued princess. In the first of these (Type 506A) the hero ransoms a princess who has been held in

---

[5] *Les Fabliaux*, p. 276.

[6] An example of such a study is G. H. Gerould's *The Grateful Dead*.

[7] For example, a variant form of Puss in Boots told exclusively in Denmark (Type 505) uses a grateful dead man instead of a helpful cat.

[8] *Die Tobiasgeschichte und andere Märchen mit toten Helfern*. His conclusions have been discussed by Walter Anderson (*Hessische Blätter für Volkskunde*, XXVII, 1928, 241ff.) and Kaarle Krohn (*Übersicht*, p. 89).

slavery. He has been sent for her by the king who has learned her whereabouts by means of a cloth or a flag which she has sewed, and on which he recognizes the characteristics of her fine needlework. On the way home with the princess the hero is thrown overboard by a rival, but he is rescued by his dead helper and is finally brought to the princess, where he is identified by a ring thrown into a cup, by recounting his life history, or by means of a picture. The tale then proceeds to the point where the grateful dead man asks for his half of the winnings. In some cases this demand is not made until long after the hero's marriage, when the dead man calls for the dividing of the infant child.

In the other tale of the rescued princess (Type 506B) the hero saves her from a den of robbers and flees with her to her father's home. In all other respects—the grateful dead man, the casting of the hero overboard, the recognition by the princess, and the dividing in half—the two stories are alike. The rescue from slavery is much the more popular of the two stories: it appeared in a French collection of exempla as early as the fourteenth century and is known in all parts of Europe, in Indonesia, in North Africa, and in North America, not only among the Indians, but also among the Portuguese settlers in Massachusetts coming from the Cape Verde Islands. On the other hand, the tale involving the robbers seems to be confined to Northern Europe and to have Scandinavia as its primary center of distribution.

The second group of tales concerning the grateful dead man is the one which, because of its embodiment in the story of Tobit, most people think of when the grateful dead is mentioned. The tales in this group have so many identical traits that it seems unreasonable to suppose that they do not represent a threefold development from some common original. All three of the types begin with the regular incident of the ransomed corpse and the joining of the hero by the grateful dead man. And they all end, in one way or another, with the motif of the dividing in half of the bride. In the first of these tales, The Monster's Bride (Type 507A), the hero wooes a princess whose former suitors have all come to misfortune and whose heads he sees stuck upon poles as a warning to him. He may win the princess only if he finds certain objects which she hides and if he succeeds in killing the monster of whom she is enamored. His friend, the grateful dead man, has acquired certain magic powers and comes to his aid. He kills the monster lover and, usually by means of beating, burning, or bathing her, takes away from the princess her remaining magic power.

In the second tale, The Monster in the Bridal Chamber (Type 507B), the hero finds that all the bridegrooms of the princess have perished during the bridal night. His helper, the grateful dead man, advises him to marry her, and keeps watch. When the dragon (or serpent) comes into the chamber to kill the bridegroom, the helper slays him. It turns out that the princess is enchanted and has serpents in her body. When the dead man demands his half of the winnings, they cut her in two and thus break the enchantment. The third tale, The Serpent Maiden (Type 507C), seems hardly more than a variant of the second. All the bridegrooms of the princess have perished during the bridal night. The hero marries het, nevertheless, and the helper saves his life by killing the serpent which creeps from her mouth to strangle the bridegroom. She may be ridded of the serpents by cutting her in two, or by hanging her head downward so that they come out of her mouth.

One interesting thing about this group of three tales is that we have a form of the story as early as the beginning of the Christian era in the book of Tobit. This early redaction of the story is so thoroughly adapted to the Hebrew literature of which it forms a part that it would surely seem to represent the results of a long period of change and adjustment. In this apocryphal story the ransoming of the corpse is done by the pious old Tobit, whereas the romantic adventures are assigned to his son. An angel appears in place of the grateful dead man. In the form closest to the Tobit story (Type 507B) this tale is still best known in eastern Europe and the Near East. The very closely related Serpent Maiden (Type 507C) also has its greatest popularity in southeastern Europe. On the other hand, The Monster's Bride (Type 507A) is popular over northern and western Europe and has been known there in literary form from the sixteenth century. Its general acceptance was greatly increased through the influence of Hans Christian Andersen's "Rejsekammeraten" (The Fellow Traveler). A mapping of the three types in which the bride is rendered harmless by the dead man makes clear that two of these tales are primarily eastern and one of them an essentially western development.

There remains one story of a grateful dead man which seems not to be clearly related to the three which we have just discussed. In this tale (Type 508), after the usual joining of the hero and the dead helper, we have a tournament in which the dead man furnishes his companion with a magic horse and with wonderful weapons. After the princess is won in the tournament there follows the usual incident of the dividing in half. This story is obviously a result of the chivalric romance tradition. It appears as early as the twelfth century in a French romance, an Italian novella, and a German poem, and in the thirteenth century in an English romance and a Swedish prose tale. It is also included in the Italian literary folktale collection of Straparola in the sixteenth century. The tale hardly exists in oral tradition at all.

In spite of the attention devoted to this group of tales by men like Gerould and Liljeblad, the whole group needs a thorough restudy. It is impossible to get at the truth about these tales without subjecting each of the types to an independent investigation. It would seem that we have at least three different tales within the framework of the grateful dead motifs. Nowhere is the problem of the relation of tale type and motif more baffling than in this

group. Without such definitive study, it is impossible to say more than that
we have here a very old tale which seems to have come into Europe from
the Near East. This old tale, represented by the book of Tobit, contained
the striking sequence of motifs which we know as The Grateful Dead Man.
In some way or other this exact sequence of motifs seems to have been
adopted by the two tales of the rescued princess and by the story of the
winning of the bride in the tournament. Just how these changes took place
and just what relation these stories may have to one another cannot be safely
declared without more study.

D. THE EXTRAORDINARY COMPANIONS

In the story of The Bear's Son (Type 301) we have already met the next
group of helpers to be considered, the extraordinary companions who are
each endowed with some remarkable power. This motif (F601ff.) is by no
means a necessary part of that tale, but it may well have been taken over
from the two stories we are now to consider in which these helpers play a
leading role. Both of these stories have the same beginning, but show considerable variation in the body of the narrative. The first story especially is
very widespread, and an examination of the variants shows that the story-
tellers have used a considerable freedom in the way in which they have
combined motifs. The tales have never been adequately analyzed and studied,
but a superficial examination of them indicates that both tales and both of
the main varieties of the first tale are current in the same areas. The types
are certainly not always kept clearly apart.

The youngest of three brothers, unlike the two elder, has been kind to an
old man who helps him provide a ship that goes both on land and water.
For the building of such a ship the king has promised to give his daughter
in marriage. On his way to the court with the ship the hero encounters, one
after another, six extraordinary men. One of them is so strong that he pulls
up trees. One can shoot out the left eye of a fly two miles away. One can blow
hard enough to turn a windmill. One can hear grass grow, or the wool on
the back of a sheep. One can run around the world in a moment, and one
can eat or drink enough for an army. A number of other strangely endowed
men appear in the hundreds of variants of this tale.

With his marvelous ship and these strange friends who have joined him,
the hero reaches the castle, shows his ship, and demands the princess in
marriage. The king puts him off and will fulfill the bargain only when the
youth has performed certain tasks—deeds which the king knows are quite
impossible. With the help of his companions, the hero succeeds in performing all the tasks assigned and in winning the princess.

The tasks assigned in this tale are always fitted to the special endowments
of the companions. With this limitation, they show a wide variety. Most

usual are: eating a tremendous amount, fetching water from the end of the world, enduring extreme heat or cold, defeating an opposing army, or rescuing the princess. Sometimes the task takes the combined efforts of two of the helpers. When the water must be brought from the world's end, the runner goes for it, but he sleeps on the way and the shooter has to wake him.

As one looks over the versions of this tale, it is clear that a large number do not have the incident of the land and water ship. The simpler version is usually called, after Grimm, How Six Travel Through the World (Type 513A); that with the marvelous boat, The Ship that Went on Sea and Land (Type 513B). Both varieties of the tale are found all over Europe, but it is only the first which has gone farther, and The Ship seems to be a special development which has taken place on European soil and has not traveled elsewhere.

The most striking part of this tale is undoubtedly the specially endowed companions and the way in which they perform the tasks set for the hero. This nucleus of the story is very old. It has interesting parallels in the literature of ancient India.[9] Similar characters were found among the Argonauts, though they were not used exactly as in our story. The most striking resemblance to our tale in the older literature is the old Welsh story of Kylhwch and Olwen which is found in the Mabinogion of the eleventh century. It is interesting that in this Welsh tale the companions are at the court of King Arthur and that some of them bear names which in the later development of the Arthurian story are given to certain knights of the Round Table.

We do not, of course, know how long this story has been told by taletellers in Europe. None except the Mabinogion have exalted the companions into Arthurian knights, but have kept the adventures on the usual folktale level. The tale has been fortunate enough to be reworked by several composers of literary stories, Sercambi in fourteenth century and Basile in seventeenth century Italy, and Madame d'Aulnoy in France at the end of the seventeenth century.

The whole story, in its various modifications, shows evidence of having come into Europe from India. It is found not only in older Buddhistic writings, but also in the modern oral collections of tales of India. It is also reported frequently in the folklore of the peoples of western Asia and eastern Europe. In Europe itself, the distribution is remarkably uniform, and indicates a long period of development. The tale of the remarkable helpers has also been carried to distant places by travelers and settlers: to China, to Indonesia, to Africa, and to America, where it is found not only among the French of Canada and Missouri, but also among the American Indians of Nova Scotia and of the central plains.

With its wide ramifications of plot, its obviously long history, its great

---

[9] This aspect of the history of the story is developed by Theodor Benfey in his "Menschen mit den wunderbaren Eigenschaften" (*Kleinere Schriften.* III. 94-156).

popularity as a folktale, and its frequent use in literary tale collections, an adequate investigation of this story would bring the scholar face to face with practically all the difficult problems of folktale scholarship.

Before leaving the extraordinary companions, mention should be made of a story which was developed by literary writers of the seventeenth and eighteenth centuries, and which has been collected in a few countries from oral raconteurs (Type 514). A maiden disguised as a man goes to the wars in place of her brother (or father). The complications that arise are not consistent in all versions. In some she marries the princess, who keeps her secret. In others the queen attempts to seduce the "hero," and then when unsuccessful, demands that the king send him on a dangerous expedition. Whether expelled for marrying the princess or because of the anger of the king, the heroine secures the help of extraordinary companions and performs the tasks necessary. In some versions she disrobes and brings about the discomfiture and execution of the queen, and later marries the king. In others she secures magic help whereby she actually does change her sex and then returns to be reunited with the princess.

E. HELPFUL ANIMALS

In some of the versions of the tales of extraordinary companions, particularly in North Africa, these peculiar helpers are animals. Though no one has ever taken the trouble to count all the occurrences, it is likely that, considering folktales all over the world, an even more important part is played by animal helpers than by human or supernatural. Such animals appear as actors in a large number of tales everywhere and they are substituted by story-tellers for human helpers with considerable freedom. In some tales, the role played by these animals is so important as to form the actual center of interest.

Such is true of The Animal Brothers-in-Law (Type 552), a story made popular in literary circles in the seventeenth century by Basile and carried on in the eighteenth by Musäus in his sophisticated retelling of folktales. A bankrupt man, in return for safety and money, promises his three daughters in marriage to three animals. Frequently these animals are a bear, an eagle, and a whale. Or it may be that the three girls themselves, despairing of marriage, say that they will marry anyone, even if it is an animal. In either case the animals take the girls as wives and leave with them. The brother of the girls visits his sisters, and he discovers that the animals periodically become men. The brothers-in-law, out of kindness, give him a part of their bodies, the eagle a feather, the bear a hair, and the whale a scale. These he can use to call on them for help. The brother now goes on his adventures and succeeds, by calling, at the proper moment, on his animal brothers-in-law.

The story up to this point is well integrated and justifies its being thought of as an independent tale. But from here on we may enter into any one of several adventure stories where the timely aid of the animal helpers is appropriate. The hero may use them in saving a princess from a monster, as in the Dragon Rescue tale, or in defeating the ogre with his life in an egg (Types 300, 302, 303), or occasionally in recovering the castle, wife, and magic objects which have been stolen from him (Type 560). Essentially, then, the story of The Animal Brothers-in-Law serves as an elaborate introduction which may be attached rather freely to suitable adventure stories.

Aside from those versions obviously dependent upon the literary work of Musäus or Basile, this tale is known in the more distinctly oral tradition of every part of Europe, though its occurrence is strangely inconsistent. It seems most popular in the Baltic states and in Russia. Its distribution is continuous from Ireland to the Caucasus and Palestine. At least one version has been carried by the French to America, where it is told among the Micmac Indians of Nova Scotia.

A special form of this tale, popular in Norway but hardly known outside (Type 552B),[10] has the father of the girls visit them. He sees the animals produce food by magic. When he attempts to imitate them, he not only fails but gets into trouble and is sometimes killed.[11]

Another tale of very limited distribution in Norway and the Baltic states, and rather rare even there, is The Raven Helper (Type 553). When the hero shoots a raven, the latter gives him a feather and with this feather the hero receives magic objects and treasure from the raven's three sisters. In his later adventures the hero makes use of this help in rescuing a princess from a sea monster. This latter part of the tale merges into the Dragon Rescue story (Type 300) in such a way that this whole type might well be considered merely one variety of that story.

The best known of stories, or episodes, which tell how the hero got the help of animals is that usually called The Grateful Animals (Type 554). As in most other tales of gratitude, the hero is the youngest of three brothers. Going on his adventures, he performs kind deeds for animals and wins their gratitude. In some cases he rescues the animals from danger or starvation, and in some he makes a satisfactory division of booty for three animals who are quarreling over it. As in The Animal Brothers-in-Law, the animals usually give the hero a part of their body so that he can summon them if he ever needs their help. Most frequently the animals are ants, ducks, and bees, or a raven, a fish, and a fox. The hero then proceeds, and the animals, called upon in his hour of need, perform his tasks for him and bring him success. In his choice of adventures for the hero at this point, the story-teller has considerable freedom, for his introduction may

[10] A similar story in Russian is listed by Andrejev (*Ukazatel' Skazočnik*) as Type No. 299*.
[11] This motif of the unsuccessful imitation of the production of food by magic seems to have been invented independently in this tale and in a group of American Indian stories (see J2425).

lead him almost anywhere. In practice, however, the episode is used as an introduction to a relatively small number of rather well-known stories. He may win a beautiful princess by performing certain difficult tasks, such as the sorting out of a large quantity of scattered seeds or beads, or the bringing of a ring or key from the bottom of the sea. The ants and the fish help with these two tasks. This would seem to be the normal course of the story of The Grateful Animals, for these tasks are seldom found in other connections. But the animals may help the hero bring back the water of life and death from the end of the world (Type 551); they may help him choose the princess from her identically clad sisters (Type 313); or they may help him hide from the princess, and thus win her hand rather than lose his life (Type 329).

Although the story is known in the Persian *Tuti-Nameh* of the fourteenth century, its principal use seems to have been in oral folktales. It has been in Europe long enough to be told in every country, except possibly the British Isles. There are oral versions from India, Indonesia, and Ceylon, and from the Turks, Armenians, and Tartars. It is known in Africa in at least a dozen versions from Madagascar to the Guinea Coast, and has been carried by the French to Missouri.

None of the three tales of helpful animals which we have discussed has received adequate study. They should undoubtedly be handled as a group because of their frequent interrelation. It would be almost necessary to study the various tales for which these stories serve as introductory episodes. How independent a life can such merely introductory types have? These questions and the relation of written to oral versions, not to speak of the obvious Oriental affinities, should afford many interesting problems for future research.

In a special variety of The Grateful Animals tale the animals give the hero a part of their body so that he may use it to transform himself into that animal when he wishes to. This introduction is sometimes used as a part of The Dragon Rescue or any other tale where it is appropriate.[12] It is widely but thinly distributed over continental Europe and has been carried, presumably by the French, to the island of Mauritius.

This power of transforming himself to animals is a regular part of a rather complicated story (Type 665) told in the Baltic countries and to some extent in Hungary and Russia. The hero does not always receive this power from helpful animals, but in some versions is thus rewarded by an old man with whom he divides his last penny, or by a grateful dead man. While the hero is serving in the war, his king, about to be defeated, sends him to secure from the princess his magic sword (or his ring). By swimming as a fish, flying as a bird, and running as a hare he reaches the castle and secures the sword. As he leaves in his bird form, the princess cuts off one of his

[12] See Bolte-Polívka, II, 22, n. 1.

feathers. Later, as he is returning in the form of a hare, he is shot by a man who takes the sword to the king and claims the reward—which includes marriage to the princess. The hero is restored to life by his helper and, in the form of a dove, flies to the castle in time to forestall the wedding. The princess recognizes him by the feather which she has cut off.

This tale of self-transformation has its greatest popularity in Estonia, Lithuania, and Finland; it appears never to have been recorded in Germany or western Europe. The other tale in which this motif is most frequently used (Type 316) displays a distribution almost exactly the opposite. Its principal occurrence is in Germany and it is known (though it has never attained any great circulation) in France, the British Isles, and Norway. One version has been reported from the Negroes of Jamaica. But, in spite of the enormous collections made there, the tale does not appear in the Baltic countries. In this story, best known from the Grimm collection, a boy has been unwittingly promised to a water nix and tries to avoid carrying out the promise. From grateful animals he receives the ability to transform himself into their shapes. He does fall into the water nix's power, but is finally rescued partly by the help of his wife, who has received advice from an old woman, and partly through his ability to transform himself. The story goes on to tell how after a long time the hero succeeds in being recognized by his wife and finally reunited with her.

Largely because of the influence of Perrault's collection of fairy tales, one of the best known of all stories of helpful animals is Puss in Boots. Though the story is generally concerned with a hero who is helped by a cat (Type 545B), a considerable number of versions (Type 545A) have a girl as the central figure. A difference is also made in the animal helper. Instead of a cat, very frequently there appears a fox, and sometimes even other animals.

The hero (or heroine) inherits nothing but a cat, who turns out to have miraculous powers. The cat takes the youth to the palace and proclaims to the king that the boy is a dispossessed prince. He also wooes the princess in behalf of his master. Obeying the cat's instructions, the boy is not abashed at the luxury he sees about him, but always remarks that he has better things at home. When the king is to visit the boy's castle, the cat goes ahead and succeeds in making the peasants tell the king that they are working for his master. The cat also goes to the castle of a giant, whom he kills through trickery. He takes possession of the castle for his master and brings about a happy marriage with the princess. At the end, the cat's head is cut off and thus the enchantment is broken, so that he returns to his original form as a prince.

Among the writers of literary folktales this has been one of the most popular stories. It appears in the Italian collections of Straparola and Basile in the sixteenth and seventeenth centuries. Perrault's French version at the end of the seventeenth century has been of primary influence on the tradition of this tale. No systematic investigation has been made, but it seems clear that this is primarily a folktale which lives in books and is more at home in the nursery than in an adult gathering. Nevertheless, the story has maintained a real oral tradition. It is found not only in all parts of Europe, but clear across Siberia; and in southern Asia it is well known in India, whence it has traveled to Indonesia and the Philippines. Colonists and travelers have carried it to the American Indians and to Africa, though sometimes it is difficult to be sure whether a particular helpful animal story actually belongs to this tradition or not. As one gets away from central Europe, the greater variations one finds from the literary version of Perrault. It is in such more purely oral tales that we find the girl as central actor. In some of these the helper may not be an animal at all, but, instead, a grateful dead man (Type 505). All these complications would make the story of Puss in Boots an interesting study in the mutual relationships of literary and folk tradition.

F. HELPFUL HORSES

Of all helpful animals, none has been so popular with taletellers as the horse. In not fewer than five well-known folk stories he plays a role almost as important as the hero himself.

The most popular of these stories is undoubtedly that known by the Germans as the *Goldener Märchen*, from the hair of real gold which the hero acquires in the course of his adventures (Type 314). The tale usually begins with telling how the young man came into the service of the devil. Sometimes, in return for the devil's services as godfather, his parents have agreed that the child shall come into his possession on his twenty-first birthday.[13] For whatever reason the bargain has been made (and sometimes even by pure accident), the boy arrives at the devil's house and becomes a servant. The devil gives him the run of the house, but forbids him to enter a certain chamber. As in the Bluebeard story, he breaks the prohibition and sees horrible sights. As a mark of disobedience his hair turns to gold. He placates the devil temporarily and remains in service. He is commanded to take good care of certain horses, but to beat and starve a particular horse which he finds in the stable. The abused horse, who is an enchanted prince, speaks to the youth and warns him to flee.

The boy mounts the magic horse but is followed closely by the devil, who almost overtakes him. At the horse's advice, the boy has provided himself with three magic objects, a stone, a comb, and a flint. When he throws the stone behind him, a mountain rises in the devil's path and delays him. Later the comb produces a forest and the flint a great fire. At last the youth escapes.

He arrives in the neighborhood of the king's court, hides his magic horse, and covers his golden hair with a cloth, pretending to have the scald head.

[13] For similar bargains with the devil, see Types 400, 502, 756B, 810.

He is employed as gardener to the king and as such is seen one day by the princess as he combs his golden hair. She falls in love with him and insists upon marrying him. The king consents, but puts them into the pigsty to live.

Much despised by his haughty brothers-in-law, he goes to his magic horse for help. Whatever the task may be that the hero needs to carry out, the horse brings it about, so that his young master is honored and the brothers-in-law put to shame. In some versions the hero slays a dragon or brings a magic remedy for the king.[14] The usual adventure, however, is participating in a tournament. When the hero leaves for the tournament his horse has the appearance of a broken-down nag, so that when, three days in succession, he and his wonderful steed are the victors, no one recognizes him. By means of various tokens—centers from the captured flags, the point of a sword which his brother-in-law has broken off in his leg, and the hoof marks which the vanquished brothers-in-law have permitted him to place on them—he proves his identity and is accepted by the king as his favorite son-in-law.

This complicated story appears without much variation over a large area and in many versions. It is particularly popular in Germany, Scandinavia, and the Baltic countries. But it is also well represented in Ireland and France, and has been carried by the French to America, where it is told by American Indians in at least fifteen versions, as well as by the Missouri French. Eastward it is popular in Bohemia, Poland, and all parts of Russia, and is told throughout the Caucasus, south Siberia, and the Near East. In south Asia three versions have been reported from India and three from Indonesia. It is also known in diverse parts of Africa.

The tale contains within it one incident which is literally world wide, The Obstacle Flight (Motif D672).[15] Though this incident is a standard part of our tale, it can be used wherever a pursuer needs to be delayed.[16] That tales with this general motive of pursuit are found everywhere is no cause for wonder, but when one finds the obstacle flight with its characteristic form of three or four magic objects which produce mountains, forests, fire, and water in South Africa and in North and South America, not only sporadically but in scores of versions, he is faced with one of the most difficult problems of folklore.

One whole group of tales about the golden-haired hero and his horse (Type 502) is represented by Grimm's tale of The Iron Man (No. 136). A magic man of iron is found in a lake and is confined by the king in a cage. The king's son is playing and lets his ball roll into the cage of the wild man. In exchange for the ball, the boy releases the man from the cage. The wild man thereupon puts the boy on his shoulders and carries him off. He treats

---

[14] The dragon slaying belongs properly to Type 300. For the magic remedy, see Type 551.

[15] This motif (or really cluster of motifs) was the last subject to which the distinguished folklorist, Antti Aarne, gave his attention. See his *Magische Flucht*.

[16] It is almost a regular part of the Hansel and Gretel story (Type 327) and of Type 313, in which the youth's supernatural wife helps him escape.

the boy well and promises that if he obeys him he will always be the boy's helper. He leaves the boy, but forbids him to put his finger in a certain pool. The boy disobeys, and his finger turns to gold. The third time he disobeys, his hair is turned to gold. The youth binds his hair and the story proceeds as in the *Goldener Märchen*. There has been no horse in the story up to this point. But when the boy must go to the tournament (or perform his other tasks), the wild man appears and furnishes him with a magic horse. The ending of the two stories is identical.

While this story of the wild man is by no means so popular as the other, it is spread over almost exactly the same territory in Europe, but it hardly goes outside that continent. It has been carried to Siam, to Missouri, and to Brazil. Both of these two tales which we have just treated appeared in literary form as early as the sixteenth century in the work of Straparola. No attempt, however, has been made to investigate the influence of this literary form on the very strong and far-flung oral tradition.

Confined, so far as now appears, to a very limited section of eastern Europe is the story of the hero called "I Don't Know." It is hard to tell whether this should be considered as a distinct tale type (Type 532), or merely as a variety of the Goldener story. The hero is driven from home by a cruel step-mother (or, in some versions, he is simply the laziest of three brothers), and, in the course of his adventures, gains possession of a magic horse, who advises him to answer all questions with "I don't know." His peculiar behavior attracts the attention of the princess, who marries him. From this point on the story is the same as in the Goldener tale. Sometimes the hero must make a rescue from a sea monster, but more often he has to help in a war brought on by jealous suitors incensed because the princess has chosen him. In any case, the horse helps him to success.

This seems to be essentially a Russian development which has achieved some popularity in Finland and Hungary. It is known in the Baltic countries, but not popular, and is not found further west.

The tales of helpful horses have a tendency to merge into one another in many of their details, sometimes in the way in which the magic horse is acquired, sometimes in the remarkable deeds accomplished. Nevertheless, the separate tales are unmistakable entities. This confusion of parts is seen with especial clearness in the tale of the Princess on the Glass Mountain (Type 530). In its best known form the tale is about a poor peasant who has three sons of whom the youngest is considered a good for nothing. Every morning the peasant finds that his meadow has been grazed bare by horses. He sends his sons out to keep watch. The two elder go to sleep, and the grass continues to be eaten down. The youngest remains awake and succeeds in catching the horse. He hides the horse, cares for it, and rides it.

The king offers his daughter in marriage to the man who can ride up to her on top of a glass mountain. Although all suitors have failed to do so, the hero succeeds and receives from the princess at the summit a token which he later presents and by means of which he receives her in marriage.[17]

This story is clearly divided into the two parts mentioned above, the acquisition of the horse and the marvelous deed. Sometimes instead of the watching for the devastating animal, the hero may take care of his flocks at night so as to keep them from wandering over into the possessions of an ogre or troll. The animals do so in spite of his watching, and he overcomes the troll when he goes after the animals. He finds the magic horses among the troll's possessions. This introduction would seem to have been borrowed from the tale of The Dragon Fighter (Type 300). In a third type of introduction the sons must keep watch over the body of their dead father.

The second part of the tale also displays considerable variety. Instead of to the glass mountain the riding may be to the top of a tall building, three-storied or four-storied. Sometimes the magic horse must jump over a wide excavation or ditch; sometimes, as in the last two stories we have noticed, he helps his master to victory in a tournament; and sometimes he wins a race, it may be with the princess herself.

The tale is well distributed over Europe, particularly northern and eastern, and it is found in the Caucasus and the Near East. One version is reported from Burma. The last word on this tale has certainly not been written. Dr. Boberg's study is far from adequate, since it is based upon less than half of the available material. Her analysis of the story into "oikotypes," each characteristic of a certain linguistic area, is unconvincing, as Professor Krohn clearly shows. On the other hand, Krohn's conclusion that the tale originated in India and reached Europe at a relatively late period by way of Asia Minor is at least problematical, in view of the fact that only one version has been reported from India.

In the Grimms' tale of Ferdinand the Faithful and Ferdinand the Unfaithful (Type 531) the magic horse is assisted by other helpers, animals and giants. In most tales of this type the hero receives a magic key, sometimes from a beggar at his christening. With this key he obtains a marvelous horse which speaks and gives advice. The hero also finds a pen, and from a thankful fish he obtains a fin. Thus equipped, he takes service, along with a companion, at the king's court. At the suggestion of the treacherous companion, he is assigned various dangerous tasks. Among other things the hero is to fetch a beautiful princess for the king. On advice of his horse, he demands as a condition from the king a supply of meat and bread. With this food he obtains help from certain giants and birds, and secures the princess and, later, certain writings of hers. The fish returns his pen which has fallen into the water. On the return to the court, the princess beheads him and then re-

---

[17] See Inger Margrethe Boberg, "Prinsessen på Glasbjærget," *Danske Studier,* 1928, pp. 16-53. Discussed by Krohn, *Übersicht,* pp. 96-99. For a later study by Dr. Boberg see *Handwörterbuch des deutschen Märchens,* II, 627. For a very ancient analogue of the idea of reaching the princess on a height, see p. 274, below.

places his head to make him handsomer. The king has the same thing done to himself with fatal results. As for the magic horse, he changes himself at last into his proper form as a prince.

As a general thing the quest for the princess in this tale is caused by the sight of a beautiful hair which has been found floating down a stream and which is shown to the king, who will not rest until the faraway princess to whom the hair belongs has been found. This motif, combined with the tasks assigned at the suggestion of a treacherous rival, is very old. It is found in the Egyptian story of The Two Brothers in the thirteenth century B.C.[18] It also occurs frequently in literary tales since that time, for instance in the story of Tristram and Isolt. Nevertheless, the combination into the tale as we have it does not seem to go back to antiquity, though it must have been developed by the twelfth century after Christ and in several parts of Europe. In its oral form it is distributed with remarkable uniformity over the whole of Europe. It is found in an unbroken line through the Caucasus, the Near East, India, Cambodia, and the Philippines. Five versions have been reported from the Arabic population of Egypt, and three from Central Africa. The French have carried it to Missouri and to the Menomini Indians of Wisconsin; the Spanish to the San Carlos Apache of New Mexico. The story has never been thoroughly investigated, but a superficial view of its distribution suggests that it may have come to Europe from the East, probably from India. The tradition is not always coherent and the tellers of the tale apparently do not always understand the significance of what they are telling. The place of the pen in the story is an example of such confusion, for it is seldom clear why the hero should have a pen and what good it is to serve in the tale.

In one story at least, the horse renders his most efficient service after his death. This tale is best known from the German version of Grimm, The Goose Girl (Type 533). A princess is accompanied on her way to marry a prince by a servant girl. Before setting out, the princess has received from her mother some costly gifts, including the wonderful speaking horse Falada and certain magic objects. On her way the princess becomes thirsty and asks for a drink, but the servant girl makes her get down and drink from the brook. The horse speaks and says, "If your mother knew about this, her heart would break." And the magic objects also speak. Three times the princess stops for water, and finally the servant girl compels her to exchange clothes with her and to swear to keep the matter secret. The servant girl mounts the princess's horse and, when she reaches the palace, claims to be the princess. The heroine herself is made to watch the geese. Meantime, the false princess, fearing that the speaking horse may betray her, has it killed and has its head set up over the castle gate. The little goose girl has miraculous power over animals and over the weather and wind. One day she is combing

[18] See p. 275, below.

her hair and the servant boy who is with her sees that it is of gold. He tries to take some of the golden strands from her, but she asks the wind to carry off the boy's hat, so that he runs away after it. In the evening as she drives her geese home, she sees the head of her slaughtered horse. She weeps, and the horse answers, "If your mother knew about this, her heart would break." When all of this happens a second day, the boy goes to the king and tells him what he has seen and heard. The next day the king follows the boy, overhears everything, and learns the true state of affairs. The treacherous servant girl is executed and the princess marries the prince.

In some versions the princess is blinded, and it is later necessary to buy back her eyes from the person who has blinded her. In addition to the speaking horse-head, other means are sometimes employed for bringing the truth to light. Her magic objects may speak, or she may sing a song into a stove which she must take care of.

This tale has not been found in any great multitude of versions. Liungman's study[19] is based upon fourteen variants, all of them European, extending from France to Russia, except a single one among the Kabyle of North Africa. Besides this list, he cites several central African tales with a similar plot but lacking some of the principal characteristics. It is problematical whether all tales in which a servant girl replaces a princess on the way to marry a prince should be thought of as having any organic connection with this story of The Goose Girl.

Liungman's conclusion as to its origin and dissemination is that it seems to have developed somewhere on the upper Danube, but that the German versions have been of greatest influence in its subsequent distribution. This tale has so much in common with several other stories of false brides that it has frequently become confused with them, particularly with The Black and The White Bride (Type 403).

The tales of helpful animals which we have just reviewed are those best known in Europe and western Asia, but there are, of course, many other stories in which animals aid their human masters and mistresses. Some of these are legends, such as that of Llewellyn and His Dog, and some of them are more elaborate folktales much like the European stories we have been studying, but current entirely among some primitive group such as the American Indians.[20] Although scholars of two generations ago tended to find connection between the stories of helpful beasts and the Hindu attitude toward animals,[21] stories with this motif have been found in so many parts of the world as to show that it is a natural development in story-telling which may take place anywhere.

[19] *Två Folkminnesundersökningar.*
[20] For Llewellyn and His Dog, see Motif B331.2.
[21] See A. Marx, *Griechische Märchen von dankbaren Tieren* (Stuttgart, 1889).

G. HELPFUL DEVIL OR DEMON

Although most treatments of the devil picture him as an adversary of man,[22] several folktales tell of heroes who enlist the aid of the devil in one way or another and are thus able to succeed in their enterprises. The four tales which we shall cite seem to have no organic relationship with one another, in spite of the fact that the area of their popularity is much the same: Germany, the Baltic states, and Russia.

The first of these stories, well known through Grimms' The Three Journeymen (Type 360), consists of three motifs which are often found independently or in other connections. The combination shown in the Grimm version is sufficiently stable, however, to have considerable distribution. The three journeymen make a bargain with the devil, who gives them money, in return for which they are to be in his power. In one way or another they gain the good will of the devil, and he becomes their helper. In the course of their adventures the boys take a pledge that they will always answer everything with the same words: "We three," "For gold," "That was right." They stay at an inn where the host commits a murder. They are accused and, since they will speak no words except those agreed upon, they seem to confess the murder. When they are to be hanged the devil rescues them from the gallows and brings it about that the host is hanged in their place. The devil, having received the soul of the host, is satisfied with his bargain and releases the boys from their obligation to him. The tale as a whole is known over most of Europe, but has not been reported elsewhere. The second part of the tale, concerning the men who speak only a single phrase, goes back at least to the fourteenth century, where it appears in the *Summa Predicantium* of John Bromyard. The story as told by Bromyard omits the relationship with the devil and puts its emphasis upon the troubles caused by the limited vocabulary; for his boys go to a foreign land, and each knows only a single phrase of the language. They are not able to defend themselves when accused. This anecdote (Type 1697) is told side by side with the longer tale and over much the same area. It seems to be a literary invention which has become established in European folklore only during the last three or four centuries. The last part of The Three Journeymen, in which the devil rescues the condemned boys, seems likewise to belong to literature rather than folklore.[23]

Another bargain with the devil which turns out successfully for the hero is found in the story of Bearskin (Type 361). A soldier, discharged after years of service, finds himself unwelcome at home and is in distress. The devil appears to him and makes a bargain. The man must take a bearskin

---

[22] For stories in which the devil appears as a supernatural adversary, see p. 42, above.

[23] For a discussion of the literary history of the two motifs just mentioned, see Bolte-Polívka, II, 563-6.

coat and live in it for seven years without washing or combing himself; otherwise he is to belong to the devil. In return for these hard conditions it turns out that the coat has an inexhaustible pocket from which he can secure all the money he wishes. As time goes on he comes to look more and more like a beast, but he pays his way. Of the three daughters of an impoverished man whom he helps, the two elder treat him shamefully, but the youngest is kind to him in spite of his disgusting appearance. At the end of seven years the devil appears and rewards him for fulfilling his bargain. Cleaned and made handsome by the devil, he comes to the home of the three sisters and makes himself known by the broken ring which he has divided with the youngest. The two elder sisters are so chagrined that they hang themselves. The devil disappears, calling out to the hero, "I got two, you only one."

This tale has been told frequently in literature since the seventeenth century, but a strong oral tradition has also preserved the story. It is extraordinarily popular in the folklore of the Baltic states, of Sweden, Denmark, and Germany; and it is known over all parts of Europe. It has not thus far been reported from Asia, and would not seem to be Oriental.

Very closely related in idea to Bearskin is a story in which the hero heats the kettles in hell (Type 475). The two tales begin alike, with the devil's bargain by which the hero is to go seven years without washing or combing. In this case he must actively serve the devil during those years. Part of his duty is to heat the kettles in hell in which are languishing his former masters. In payment for his services he receives the sweepings of hell, which turn into gold. Later the host at an inn robs him of his gold, but the devil helps him recover it. The area of popularity of this tale is the same as for the two which we have just discussed. In contrast to them, however, it does not seem to have appealed to the writers of literary stories.

In a fourth example of help from the devil, the emphasis is on his appearance as an advocate in the courtroom. The details of the bargain may differ, but, in any case, the hero is the subject of an unjust accusation. Instead of rescuing the falsely accused from the gallows, as in The Three Journeymen, the devil carries the judge from the courtroom (Type 821). In one form of the tale (Type 821A), the judge is confuted and in his chagrin cries out, "May the devil take me if—." The devil does. In the other type of the story he demonstrates the judge's absurdity before carrying him out (Type 821B). Usually the host has demanded an enormous sum for twelve boiled eggs which he claims that his guest has eaten many years before, since, by this time, they must have hatched out chickens which in turn have laid eggs, etc. The devil as advocate comes in and demands that the host cook his peas before planting them. The absurdity of the claim being made clear, the devil reveals himself and carries off the unjust judge.

The Devil as Advocate was one of the popular stories in the literary jestbooks of the sixteenth century.[24] In these the first form—"May the devil take me if—"—is the favorite, but in the oral tradition both forms of the tale maintain about equal popularity. This is the only one of the stories of help from the devil which has been reported from Asia. It appears in Turkish jestbooks and in the tradition of south Siberia. It has also been told by Cape Verde Island Negroes in Massachusetts.

In the tales of supernatural adversaries and of extraordinary helpers we have given our principal attention to persons, animals, or other creatures who have assisted or opposed the hero in his adventures. The part these secondary characters have played is so important in these tales as to be the object of primary interest. The enlisting of their aid or the overcoming of their opposition is usually the motivating force in the action of the tale. They are not merely accessories to the plot but are so necessary to it that their absence is almost unthinkable. The same kind of fundamental importance of a seemingly subsidiary part of the plot holds true with those tales concerned with extraordinary objects, qualities, and powers which we shall now examine. The acquisition, possession, loss, or recovery of these powers or qualities is always the center of narrative interest.

4. MAGIC AND MARVELS

A. MAGIC POWERS

IN A very large proportion of folktales wherever they may be found magic plays a considerable part, and it is almost universal in some form in all those stories we know as wonder tales. In an important group of these stories the possession of such powers and objects serves as the crucial point in the narrative.

A good example of such a tale is that known as The Lazy Boy (Type 675). Just as in the story of The Two Brothers (Type 303), the hero catches a large fish, usually a salmon, and when he agrees to throw the salmon back into the water the latter gives him the power of making all his wishes come true. He has but to say, "By the word of the Salmon." Among his other accomplishments he makes a saw that cuts wood of itself and a self-moving boat or wagon. His arrival in the royal city in his strange conveyance and the sight of his marvelous saw at work causes the princess to laugh at him. In his anger, he wishes her pregnant. When in due time she has a child an inquiry is made as to who the unknown father may be and all the probable men are gathered together. The child picks the hero out as his father, and the parents

---

[24] For the literary variants, see Bolte, *Pauli's Schimpf und Ernst*, II, 432, No. 807; for the oral variants, see Bolte-Polívka, II, 368, n. 1.

are then joined in marriage. In his anger, the king has the hero and princess abandoned in a glass box in the sea or in a cask in the mountains. The hero still has his magic power, which he uses to make a great castle next to the king's. He then invites and humbles his father-in-law.

This is one of the few very well-known European tales which do not appear in the great collection of Grimm. It has been known, however, for a long time, since it is found in the *Nights* of Straparola in sixteenth century Italy and a hundred years later in the *Pentamerone* of Basile. It is disseminated rather evenly over the whole of Europe and extends eastward far into Siberia. It does not appear to be known in India or Africa, but two versions have been reported from Annam, and it has been carried to New Guinea and to America. The Cape Verde Island version told in Massachusetts is obviously from Portugal, and the Missouri French and the American Indian tales told by the Maliseets of New Brunswick and the Ojibwas of Michigan are clearly from France.

I am not a collector of folktales, but this happens to be one of the few which I have taken down in the field. The story in question is such a good example of the way in which a tale entering an alien culture may be changed that I cannot forbear making special mention of the story as told me by an Ojibwa Indian on Sugar Island, Michigan, in the summer of 1941. He had been telling us stories of the Ojibwa culture hero. Suddenly he asked, "Did you ever hear the tale about Rummy and his little Ford car?" He proceeded then to tell what is undoubtedly the present story, though confused with some other French tales. Rummy was clearly the hero of these French tales, René, and the little Ford car was Mr. Joseph's idea of the self-moving wagon. The automatic saw played its part, and the experience with the princess was exactly as we have outlined it above. From other tales he brought in the story of the magic tablecloth which produced food of itself and the tabu against looking backwards, which he repeated frequently but apparently did not understand or actually make use of in the story.

No one has investigated this tale systematically, but a casual listing of the versions country by country suggests the strong probability of origin in southern Europe and of the predominant influence of the literary treatments of the two famous Italian taletellers of the Renaissance.

If the literary origin of The Lazy Boy appears not to be certain, there can be no doubt that the story of Open Sesame (Type 676) has been learned by those who tell it either from a copy of the *Arabian Nights* itself or eventually, perhaps through many intermediaries, from the same source. It seems likely that this tale has entered the oral tradition of nearly every European country since the time of Galland's translation of the *Thousand and One Nights* into French at the beginning of the eighteenth century. Whether the versions current in central Africa have come more directly from the Arabic versions of the work has not been determined, but seems probable.

The fact that the story is now an authentic part of the folklore of a good part of Europe, whatever its actual origin may have been, justifies its inclusion in the canon of oral folktales. It is known to almost everyone. The poor brother observes robbers entering a mountain and overhears the magic words "Open Sesame," which gives them admittance. He secures much gold from the mountain and takes it home. He borrows money scales from his rich brother and a piece of the money remains in the scale and thus betrays the secret. The rich brother tries to imitate, but forgets the formula for opening the mountain and is caught inside. Though the magic words vary as the tale passes from country to country, they always seem to be at least a reminiscence of the phrase "Open Sesame."

Another tale of magic powers which surely comes from the Orient, but this time from India, is that of The Magician and His Pupil (Type 325). The fact that it is well known in India and also throughout Europe has served to bring it to the attention of those folklorists interested in the problem of the Indian origin of the European folktales. In 1859 Theodor Benfey in the Prolegomena to his *Pantschatantra* uses this story as an illustration of the way in which tales from India are taken over into the Mongolian literature (in this case, as part of the collection of Kalmuck tales known as *Siddhi-Kür*) and carried through this intermediary into Europe. More than fifty years later his disciple, Emmanuel Cosquin,[1] while accepting the main thesis of Indic origin for European tales, made exception to the importance of the Mongols and uses the present tale as the foundation for his case. He shows clearly enough that the European tales are like the purely Indian ones and are considerably different from the Mongolian form.

The main fact that this tale is originally from India seems never to have been disputed, though it has become so well known in Europe that it must be ranked among the most popular of oral stories. It is told in the sixteenth century by Straparola. It appears in nearly all the collections of the Near East and of southern Siberia. Beyond India, where it has been frequently reported, it is told in the Dutch East Indies and in the Philippines. It is popular in North Africa, and has been brought to Missouri by the French and to Massachusetts by Portuguese-speaking Cape Verde Island Negroes.

The details of the story remain remarkably constant wherever it is told. A father sends his son to school to a magician. The father may have the son back if, at the end of one year, he can recognize the son in the animal form to which the magician will have transformed him. The boy learns magic secretly, and he escapes from the magician by means of a magic flight. He either transforms himself frequently, or else he casts behind him magic obstacles.[2] He thus returns to his father and helps his father make money by

---

[1] "Les Mongols et leur prétendu rôle dans la transmission des contes indiens vers l'Occident Européen," *Revue des traditions populaires*, XXVII (1912) = *Etudes folkloriques*, pp. 497-612.

[2] This motif appears in many tales; cf. Motifs D671 and D672.

selling him as a dog, an ox, or a horse. At last he is sold as a horse to the magician. Contrary to his instructions, the father gives the bridle along with the horse and this brings the youth into the magician's power. The boy succeeds in stripping off the bridle and then he conquers the magician in a transformation combat. He changes to various animals and the magician likewise changes himself. The details of these changes vary somewhat. One of the most popular varieties of this motif is that in which the youth (or prince) has flown to a princess in the form of a bird and is hidden by her after he has transformed himself to a ring. As the princess throws the ring, a great number of grains of corn fall on the ground. When the magician as cock is about to eat the corn, the boy becomes a fox and bites off the cock's head.

In this tale, as in the two treated immediately before it, the magic powers are thought of as inherent in the hero. Much more common in folktales is the use of objects whose intrinsic magic power does not depend upon any special quality in the person who uses them.

B. MAGIC OBJECTS

A general pattern is found in nearly all stories of magic objects. There is the extraordinary manner in which the objects are acquired, the use of the objects by the hero, the loss (usually by theft), and the final recovery. Of these tales, we shall first examine The Magic Ring (Type 560). This story was one of the first to receive exhaustive treatment by the so-called Finnish method. After a close examination and analysis of several hundred versions, Aarne[3] constructs an "archetype," somewhat as follows:

A poor (or impoverished) young man spends the little money he has in order to rescue a dog and later a cat who are about to be killed. With the help of these animals he also rescues a serpent who is in danger of being burned. The thankful serpent takes him to his home, where his father gives him a stone (sometimes with a hole in it). By means of this magic object the young man constructs a beautiful castle and wins a princess for a wife. The stone, however, is stolen from him by a stranger, and through the magic power of the stone the castle and the wife are likewise removed far away. The helpful animals now set forth to recover the magic object. The dog swims, carrying the cat on his back, and succeeds in crossing the river to the opposite bank where the thief dwells. In front of the castle the cat catches a mouse and threatens it with death if it will not get for her the stone which the thief is holding in his mouth. In the night, the mouse tickles the lips of the sleeping thief with its tail. The thief must spit the stone up onto the floor. The cat receives it and carries it away in its mouth. On the way home as they are crossing the river the dog demands the stone so that he can carry it. But he lets it fall out of his mouth, and a fish swallows it. Later they are

[3] *Vergleichende Märchenforschungen*, pp. 3-82.

able to catch the fish, to recover the stone, and to bring it to their master. He immediately has his castle returned and joins his wife, with whom he lives happily ever after.

In most of the European versions, of course, we deal with a magic ring rather than a stone. But Aarne is convinced that the stone represents the older form of the story. Although he did not have available nearly so large a collection of versions as it would be possible to assemble today, his dis· cussion shows that there can be little doubt that the tale was made up in Asia, probably in India, and that it has moved from there into Europe. It was certainly well established there before the seventeenth century, when it was apparently heard in Italy by Basile, who tells the story in his *Pentamerone*. While the tale is undoubtedly more popular in eastern Europe than in western, it is told, at least sometimes, in almost every country or province on the Continent. It has been reported from the Highland Scottish, and the Irish, but seems not to be known in Iceland. It is popular through North Africa and the Near East and has penetrated as far south as Madagascar and the Hottentot country. Eastward of India the tale has been recorded several times in farther India, the Dutch East Indies, and the Philippines. A clear enough version is also current in Japan. The French have brought the story to the Indians of the Maritime Provinces and to Missouri. There are Portuguese versions (from the Cape Verde Islands) in Massachusetts, and Spanish in Argentina. If, as Aarne contends, the story started in India, it has gone a long way and has made itself thoroughly at home in the western world.

The same general pattern is, of course, familiar in the tale of Aladdin and His Wonderful Lamp (Type 561). The finding of the lamp in the underground chamber and the magic effects of rubbing it, the acquisition of castle and wife, the theft of the lamp and loss of all his fortune, and the final restoration of the stolen lamp by means of another magic object is known to all readers of the *Arabian Nights*, even of the most juvenile collections. Though this tale has entered somewhat into the folklore of most European countries, it has never become a truly oral tale. Its life has been dependent upon the popularity of the *Arabian Nights*, especially since their translation by Galland a little over two hundred years ago. There was, indeed, doubt for a good while as to whether the Aladdin story really belonged to the canon of the *Arabian Nights*, and it was suggested that it was a concoction of Galland himself. But the authenticity of the story as a part of the *Thousand and One Nights* has now been sufficiently proved. It is doubtful, however, whether the story has ever been a part of the actual folklore of any country.

Much the same relationship between written and oral versions is to be seen in the closely related tale, The Spirit in the Blue Light (Type 562). The form in which it is now told over a considerable part of Europe has undoubtedly been influenced, and in most cases is the direct result of its artistic telling by Hans Christian Andersen in his Fyrtøjet (The Tinder Box). As in the Aladdin story, a fire steel, or tinder box, is found in an underground room. With this the hero makes a light, in response to which a spirit comes to serve him. Among other adventures, he has his servant bring the princess to him three nights in succession. He is discovered and in his confusion loses his tinder box. As he is about to be executed he asks permission to light his pipe. A comrade has brought back his tinder box to him and given it to him in prison. As he lights his pipe, his spirit helper appears and rescues him.

In spite of the fact that this tale was carefully studied by Aarne,[4] he has not very clearly distinguished this tradition from that of Aladdin and, indeed, the two are almost inextricably mixed up. The essential difference is that in this tale the magic object is lost through accident rather than through the plot of an enemy. Though the tale is not unknown in southeastern Europe, its greatest popularity is in the Baltic states and Scandinavia. Not all these versions have been analyzed, but it would seem probable that Hans Christian Andersen has had a predominant influence in the dissemination of this story.

Three other tales of the loss and recovery of magic objects have been studied together by Antti Aarne.[5] The magic objects they treat of are, respectively, three, two, and one. By far the most popular of the three is The Table, the Ass, and the Stick (Type 563), and indeed it seems likely that the other two are little more than special developments of this type.

A poor man receives from a benefactor a table, a tablecloth, or sack which supplies itself with food. This is stolen from him by the host at the inn where he stays and an object identical in appearance is substituted for it. When the poor man goes home and tries to produce food, he fails. When he goes again to his benefactor he is given a marvelous ass or horse which will drop all the gold he may desire. The host at the inn plays the same trick a second time, and the man finds himself possessed of a worthless animal. The third time the benefactor gives him a magic cudgel and with this he compels the host to return the magic objects he has stolen.

This tale has a very extensive distribution, and is present in almost every collection of stories in Europe and Asia. It is told almost throughout Africa and has been carried frequently to both North and South America. Aside from the present day oral forms in India, there is indication that a tale with most of its essentials was current at least as early as the sixth century after Christ, since it appears in a collection of Chinese Buddhistic legends.[6] After all his extensive study of the versions of this tale, Aarne is undecided as to whether it has moved from Asia into Europe or vice versa.[7]

---

[4] As a part of his study of The Magic Ring (*Vergleichende Märchenforschung*, pp. 3-82).
[5] *Die Zaubergaben* (Journal de la Société Finno-Ougrienne, XXVII, Helsinki, 1911, pp. 1-96).
[6] Chavannes, *500 Contes*, III, 256, No. 468.
[7] For a discussion of this question, see Krohn, *Übersicht*, pp. 51-2.

In the same study Aarne has handled the related story which involves only two magic objects. This is usually known as The Magic Providing Purse and "Out, Boy, Out of the Sack!" (Type 564). Aarne is surely right in thinking of it as a special development of the story just treated. The magic objects are received in the same way. The first of these, usually a purse, is stolen by a neighbor and it is recovered by the use of a magic sack which either draws the enemy into it or contains a manikin which beats him until called off. There is a rather free exchange in the kinds of magic objects between this tale and that of the magic tablecloth. It may well be that we have here nothing more than an abbreviated form of the latter in which the number of objects is reduced from three to two. At any rate, this particular form appears in a very limited area around the eastern end of the Baltic Sea. The single versions reported for Norway and for Flanders are quite isolated from the main area in which this type has developed.

Of somewhat wider distribution is the third of these stories treated in Aarne's study. In this there is only one object, a magic mill or pot (Type 565). The hero receives a magic mill which grinds meal or salt, and which only the owner can command to stop. Sometimes it is a girl who is given a magic pot which fills with porridge and which will obey no one but its owner. The tale may proceed in any one of three ways. In one, the girl's mother commands the pot to work, but the house overflows with porridge before the daughter can return and stop it. Or the man who steals the mill sets it to grinding meal and must call the owner to the rescue. The third ending is more tragic: A sea-captain steals the salt mill and takes it aboard ship, where he commands it to grind salt. He is unable to stop the mill, which keeps on grinding even after the ship sinks under the weight of the salt. This is the reason why the sea is salt.

Aarne comes to the conclusion that this tale, extending from Norway through central Europe to Greece, is a special development of the story with two magic objects which we have just discussed. A particular subgroup, that concerning the salt mill, he thinks has been developed by a mixture with an old seaman tradition about why the sea is salt.

A tale of magic objects known to the literary world through the Fortunatus legend is The Three Magic Objects and the Wonderful Fruits (Type 566). This story resembles the other handling of magic objects in that it involves their loss and recovery. Three men each receive a magic object from some supernatural being, a manikin, an enchanted princess, or the like. One of them is given a self-filling purse or a mantle with an inexhaustible pocket, another a traveling cap that will take him wherever he wants to go, and the third a horn (or a whistle) that furnishes soldiers. Two of the objects are stolen by a princess with whom the hero plays cards. By means of the traveling cap they transport the princess to a distant place, usually an island, but she succeeds in using the cap to wish herself back home. The hero now being deserted happens to eat an apple which causes horns to grow on his head, but later he finds another apple, or another kind of fruit, which removes the horns. With both kinds of apples in his possession he returns to the court and succeeds in enticing the princess into eating one of the apples. Horns grow on her head. In payment for curing her with the other apple, he receives back the magic objects.

The story is not always satisfactorily motivated. The three companions soon drop out of sight, and the hero is left alone to complete his adventures. In those versions in which the objects are received from enchanted princesses, the hearer expects to learn more about these women and vainly imagines that they are going to end as wives for the three companions. In spite of these inconsistencies, however, this is, as far as Europe is concerned, one of the most popular of all the tales of magic objects. It is distributed rather evenly over the whole continent, but does not extend any appreciable distance into Asia. Though some features of the narrative are to be found in the Persian *Tuti-Nameh*, and more remotely in the Indic collection *Sukasaptati*, the fully developed story seems to be essentially oral and west European.[8] It has been carried by the French into America, where it is told by the Penobscot Indians in Maine, and by the Portuguese from Cape Verde Islands to Massachusetts.

Another story in which three magic objects regularly appear is that of The Knapsack, the Hat, and the Horn (Type 569). This tale is not generally so popular as the one concerning the marvelous fruits, but it has a much wider distribution. It seems to be about as well known in Indonesia and India as it is in Ireland. It has never been systematically studied, and a cursory examination of its distribution does not throw much light on its history. It appeared in Germany in literary form as early as 1554 and has been frequently used by later writers. Its popularity in the old tradition of such countries as Germany, Flanders, Ireland, and Russia would indicate that it has had a vigorous life quite aside from the literary tradition.

The details of the transactions in this story differ a good deal from version to version, though the general outline is clear enough. The youngest of three brothers finds a magic object, exchanges it for another, and by means of the second gets hold of the first again. By such trick exchanges he comes into possession of the three magic objects which give the tale its title, and with these he is able to produce an indefinite amount of food and a huge army. He makes war against the king and succeeds in all his enterprises.

This tale differs from the other stories of magic objects in that there is no loss or recovery. The simplicity of the plot makes it natural that it has attached itself to other stories with ease.

Considerable resemblance to the tale of the wonderful fruits is also found

---

[8] This conclusion has been reached by Aarne's thoroughgoing analysis of the tale (*Vergleichende Märchenforschungen*, pp. 85-142).

in The Magic Bird-Heart (Type 567).[9] On the basis of his careful analysis, Aarne has reconstructed the probable form of the original tale:

Fate has brought into the possession of a poor man a magic bird which lays golden eggs. The man sells the precious eggs and becomes rich. Once he goes on a trip and leaves the bird with his wife to take care of. In his absence the man who has bought the eggs (sometimes another) comes to the wife and engages in a love affair with her and persuades her to prepare and serve the marvelous bird for his meal. The bird possesses a wonderful trait, that whoever shall eat its head will become ruler and whoever swallows its heart will find gold under his pillow when he has been sleeping. The bird is killed and prepared, but by chance falls into the hands of the two sons of the man wh is absent on his journey. Knowing nothing of the wonderful characteristics of the bird, they eat the head and the heart. The lover does not yet give up his plan, for he knows that a roast which is prepared from the eaters of the bird will have the same effect as the bird itself, and he demands that the boys shall be killed, and finally persuades the mother to agree. The boys suspect the plot, and flee. The one who has eaten the head arrives in a kingdom where the old ruler has just died and the new one must be chosen. Through some type of marvelous manifestation the young man is chosen ruler. The other boy receives all the gold he wishes. In the course of his adventures he is betrayed by a girl and an old woman. He punishes the girl by using his magic power to turn her into an ass so that she will be severely beaten. But at last he restores her to her human form. In most versions the boys eventually punish their mother.

The story of the magic bird-heart has been cited in the older literature as an illustration of a tale which has travelled from India into Europe. Aarne's exhaustive study, however, while indicating an Asiatic origin, concludes that the most plausible home for the story is western Asia, perhaps Persia. It is well known in eastern Europe, especially in Russia and around the Baltic, but it is to be found in western and southern Europe as well. It is frequently found in North Africa and is reported once from much farther south in that continent. The French have taken it to Canada, where they still tell it, and from them it has doubtless been learned by the Ojibwas of southern Ontario. Though it is found in the Persian *Tuti-Nameh* of around 1300 A.D., Aarne demonstrates clearly that its life has been primarily oral and practically uninfluenced by literary retellings.

In a considerable number of the stories about the ownership of magic objects the hero comes into possession of these objects by means of a trick which he plays upon certain devils or giants. He finds them quarreling over the possession of three magic objects (or it may be that three heirs to the property are quarreling), and he undertakes to settle the quarrel. He must

---

[9] See the extensive study by Aarne (*Vergleichende Märchenforschungen*, pp. 143-200). For the opening of this tale as an introduction to The Two Brothers (Type 303), see p. 28, above.

hold the object, but as soon as he gets hold of it, he uses it to get possession of the other objects. He then goes on his adventures, which may consist of the performance of tasks assigned to the suitors of a princess, or the freeing of the princess from an enchantment. But this method of acquiring the magic objects is by no means confined to any particular folk story, and it is a real question whether one is justified in considering that we have here a real folktale. It is, perhaps, convenient for cataloguing purposes to list it with an appropriate number (Type 518), but it is essentially an introductory motif (D832) which may lead into almost any story in which magic objects can be used for the performance of tasks, for effecting rescues, or for acquiring wealth.[10]

Considered as a motif, it has a long history. It appears in unmistakable form in a Chinese Buddhistic collection of the sixth century after Christ, in the *Ocean of Story* (eleventh century), and in the *Thousand and One Nights*. Aside from its subordinate role in connection with other tales, there are a considerable number of versions in which the principal interest seems to be in this trick. In one way or another, the motif has a very extensive distribution throughout Europe and Asia. It is common in North Africa and appears occasionally much further south. Because of its wide distribution, of its association with so many different folktales, and of its easily ascertainable antiquity, this story (or tale motif, if you like) affords many interesting problems for anyone who may undertake to write its history.

An interesting variation on the story of the hero with his three magic objects is that known from the Grimm collection as The Jew Among Thorns (Type 592). The tale is widely distributed over every part of Europe, but, except for single and apparently sporadic appearances in Indonesia and among the Kabyle of North Africa, it has not traveled east or south. It has been reported in English tradition in Virginia, among the Missouri French and the Jamaica Negroes. It has been so frequently treated in literature, especially in Germany and England, ever since the fifteenth century, that these literary forms have undoubtedly affected the oral tradition. For whatever reason, the story appears with unusual variation of detail. Perhaps a thorough comparative study of the relationship of the more than two hundred and fifty reported versions with the many literary treatments would clarify its complicated history.

The story has many points in common with several we have been examining. The hero is driven from home by an evil stepmother or he is dismissed from service with a pittance after many years of labor. He gives the small amount of money he has to a poor man, and in return he is granted the fulfillment of three wishes. Most important of these is for a magic fiddle which compels people to dance. Usually he asks for a never-failing crossbow

[10] Bolte-Polívka (II, 331) point out that this introduction appears in Types 302, 306, 313B, 400, 401, 507A, 552, and 569.

and for the power of having all his desires obeyed. Other magic objects or powers besides these frequently appear in this story. In the course of his adventures he meets a monk, or more frequently a Jew, and they shoot at a bird on a wager. As the loser of the contest, the Jew must go into the thorns naked and get the bird. With his magic fiddle the hero compels the Jew to dance in the thorns. In some versions this whole episode of the dancing in the thorns is replaced by a story of the defeat of a giant by making him dance. Eventually the boy is brought to court for his misdeeds and is condemned to be hanged. As a last request he secures permission to play on his fiddle, and he compels the judge and all the assembly to dance until he is released.

Anyone acquainted with European folktales will recognize a number of motifs in this story which he has already encountered in other tales. Its central unifying idea seems to be the magic fiddle and the dancing it compels. The evil stepmother, the dismissal from service with a pittance, the helping of the poor man with the last penny, and the escape from execution by an illusory last request show affinities with many other tales. A consequence of this abundance of folktale commonplaces is the fact that there are many points at which this story may lead imperceptibly into other well-known plots.[11]

We have already encountered several magic animals, aside from the many helpful beasts which assist in the action of folktales. The hen that lays golden eggs, in Jack and the Beanstalk, and the horse or donkey which drops gold for its master are but two of these. Perhaps most surprising of all magic animals is the half-chick. Because he appears so frequently in French tales, he is usually known by his French title, Demi-coq (Type 715). The very fact of his being only a half animal has caused the tellers of this tale to permit themselves the greatest extravagances of invention. Two children are left a cock as their only inheritance. They divide it by cutting it in two. One of them receives the help of a fairy godmother who makes the half-cock magic. Demi-coq now sets out on his adventures. He first wishes to recover some borrowed money. Under his wings, or elsewhere in his body, he takes with him some robbers, two foxes, and a stream of water. When he goes to the castle and demands the money, he is imprisoned with the hens, but the foxes eat them up. Likewise in the stable, the robbers steal the horses. When he is to be burned, the stream puts out the fire. He is finally given the money. The story usually ends with the discomfiting of the king. When, in spite of all his tricks, Demi-coq is eaten by the king, he keeps crowing from the king's body.

This story has been studied, as far as the western European versions are concerned, by Ralph S. Boggs.[12] His conclusion is that the center of the development is Castile and that the tale spread from there throughout France and was carried to various parts of South America—Brazil, Chili, and Argen-

---

[11] For a list of the most usual of these combinations see analysis for Type 592.
[12] *The Halfchick Tale in Spain and France.*

tina—by Portuguese and Spanish settlers, and to the Cochiti Indians of New Mexico and to Missouri by the Spanish and French, respectively. In the literature of the eighteenth and nineteenth centuries the story appeared twice, once in France and once in Spain. It is referred to in a play published in France in 1759. Boggs is of the opinion that the Spanish tale given literary treatment in the early nineteenth century by Fernán Caballero has been of primary importance in the development of this story in southwest Europe. This tale is, however, not confined to that area, but, with some variations, is found throughout most of the continent and as far east as India. It is very unevenly distributed. No versions have been reported from the British Isles, from Germany, or Czechoslovakia. On the other hand, the Finns possess nearly a hundred, and it is popular in Estonia and Russia. As a supplement to Boggs's study, a treatment of the tale in the other areas would be illuminating.

Seldom in folktales does any thought seem to be given to the processes by which marvelous objects may be constructed: their existence is merely taken for granted. One exception to this statement is the tale of The Prince's Wings (Type 575). It usually begins with a contest in the construction of a marvelous object. A skillful workman makes wings (or sometimes a magic horse) that will carry one through the air. A prince buys the wings from the workman and flies to a tower in which a princess is confined. They fly away together and when the father of the princess offers half his kingdom as a reward for her return, the prince flies back with her and enforces the bargain.

The essential part of this story, the journey on the flying horse or with the wings, appears in several Oriental tales, notably in the *Thousand and One Nights* and in the *Ocean of Story*, and it is familiar to the readers of medieval romance through the adventures of Cléomadès. It does not appear to be known in oral tradition outside of northern and eastern Europe.

Of three tales of magic objects known only in Scandinavia and the Baltic countries, the most popular is the story of the young man who has power to make all women love him (Beloved of Women, Type 580). By means of this power he secures magic objects and eventually marries a queen. Not more than a half dozen versions have been reported of the other two tales. One of these is Fiddevav (Type 593) in which an old woman gives the hero a magic stone and advises him to go to a peasant's house at night, to say nothing but "Thanks," and to lay the stone in the ashes. The stone prevents fire from being made, and all who poke in the ashes, the daughter, the housewife, the preacher, etc. must keep saying "Fiddevav" until they are released from the magic. This happens only when the hero receives the peasant's daughter. The second tale, The Thieving Pot (Type 591), tells how a peasant exchanges his cow for a magic pot which goes out and steals food and money from the peasant's rich neighbors.

These last two tales are good examples of stories known in a relatively small area. If other parts of the world had been as thoroughly explored for tales as Scandinavia and the countries of the eastern Baltic, there would doubtless be hundreds of other such stories which have never wandered far from the place where they were originally told.

C. MAGIC REMEDIES

A special kind of magic object which appears very frequently in tales is magic remedies. The belief in things endowed with such healing powers is practically universal and plays a minor role in a large number of folktales,[13] some of which we have already noticed. At times the acquisition and use of these potent agencies constitutes the central motivation of the tale. It cannot be said of such stories that they form a group for, excepting this central motif, they have little, if anything, in common.

One of them is really little more than an introduction which may be attached to several other tales.[14] In this story of The Healing Fruits (Type 610) the hero, in contrast to his elder brothers, has been kind to an old woman. As a reward, she gives healing power to the fruits which he has. In the course of his adventures he is able to cure a sick princess who has been offered to anyone who can restore her to health. As is true in many stories of this general pattern, the hero does not immediately receive his reward, but is compelled to undertake dangerous tasks or quests. At this point the story may go off into any one of several well-known folktales: The Rabbit-Herd (Type 570), in which the hero must bring together a large flock of rabbits; The Land and Water Ship (Type 513B); or The Three Hairs from the Devil's Beard (Type 461), in which he must fetch a feather from a magic bird.

It is really impossible to study this tale without at the same time investigating those which are usually joined with it. As an introduction to one or other of these stories it is found in all parts of western Europe, but has never achieved any great popularity except perhaps in France, where seven versions have been noted. It does not seem to have gone as far east as Russia nor to have been reported outside of Europe.

Even more restricted geographically is The Gifts of the Dwarfs (Type 611), which seems to be primarily Norwegian and Finnish, with only isolated Danish and Livonian variants. The hero, son of a merchant and betrothed to the daughter of another merchant, goes to sea. As the reward for rescuing a child he receives certain magic objects, among them a healing salve. He is able to heal the sick princess and to overcome a hostile army with his magic sword. Having achieved great wealth, he returns home and marries his first love.

[13] For example, Types 551 and 612.
[14] For an example of a similar introductory tale, see the story of the devils who fight over magic objects (Type 518).

This same general pattern—acquisition of the magic medicines, healing of a princess, and reward—is also found in the very common story of The Two Travelers (Type 613). This tale has had such a long history and is spread over such immense areas that several ways of handling its main incidents have developed. The essential point of the first part of the story is that one of the companions is blinded. There are three ways of accounting for this mutilation. Two travelers (often brothers) dispute as to whether truth or falsehood is the better (or in some cases, which of their religions is the better), and they call on someone else, who is in league with the first, to act as judge. As a result of the loss of the wager, the second man permits himself to be blinded. The other openings of the tale are simpler. One traveler has the food and will not give any to his starving companion unless he permits himself to be blinded. In still other tales a traveler is robbed and blinded by his covetous companion.

In any case, the blinded man wanders about and settles himself down for the night, often in a tree where he can be safe from molestation. During the night he overhears a meeting of spirits or animals, and learns from them many valuable secrets. By using the secrets which he has heard, he first of all restores his own sight, cures a princess (sometimes a king), opens a dried-up well, brings a withered fruit tree to bearing, unearths a treasure, or performs other tasks for which he is richly rewarded. When his wicked companion hears of his good fortune and learns how he has acquired it, he himself attempts to deceive the spirits or animals in the same way. But instead they tear him to pieces, and the ends of justice are served.

As a literary story, this tale is not less than fifteen hundred years old. It is found in Chinese Buddhistic literature, in both Hindu and Jaina writings, and in Hebrew collections, all antedating the ninth century after Christ and some of them much earlier. It has appeared in such medieval collections as the *Thousand and One Nights* and the *Libro de los Gatos* and in novellistic tales of Basile in his *Pentamerone*. In spite of this very considerable literary history, which shows clearly enough the popularity and long standing of the tale throughout the Near East and even as far afield as China and Tibet, the story seems to have been accepted long ago into European and Asiatic folklore. As an oral story, it enjoys great popularity throughout the whole of Europe and Asia. Eleven modern oral versions have been reported from India, and it is known in Ceylon, Annam, and Korea. It appears not only in North Africa, but in practically every area of central Africa. In America variants have been recorded from the Canadian and Missouri French, from the Micmac Indians of Nova Scotia and the Tepecanos of Mexico. A good Negro version, perhaps from Africa, has been taken down in Jamaica.

A tale of such wide acceptance naturally presents many problems to the scholar who attempts to unravel its history. Its rather remote and Oriental origin seems clear, and the general lines of development of the oral versions as worked out by Christiansen[15] are plausible. Some of the questions involved are, for example, whether the original tale concerned a dispute over religion or over good and evil, whether the secrets were learned from devils or animals, whether the travelers were originally brothers or not. Whatever be the final conclusion about these matters, the story does illustrate nearly every problem that concerns the student of a tale. It is a long road from The Two Travelers as it appears in the ancient literature of the Orient to the utterly unsophisticated story-telling of the Jamaica Negro.

D. MARVELOUS SKILL

It is not always easy to tell, in tales of the marvelous, whether we are dealing with magic or with mere exaggerations of actual qualities. Particularly confusing in this respect is a small group of stories of men who are endowed with extraordinary skills.[16] The first of these tales, The Four Skillful Brothers (Type 653), is by far the best known. The father of the four brothers sends them away to learn skillful trades. When they return home he puts their skills to a test and bids them display their accomplishments. The star-gazer sees how many eggs are in a bird's nest on a distant tree; the thief steals the eggs; the huntsman shoots them, although they are scattered about upon a table. Finally, the tailor sews them up so that they can be returned to the nest: only a red line is around the necks of the birds when they are hatched. This is only a preliminary test for the brothers, who now hear of a princess who is offered in marriage to her rescuer. The astronomer finds her on a rock in a distant sea; the thief steals her; the huntsman shoots the dragon guardian; and the tailor sews together the shattered planks on the boat on which they are returning.

This dragon rescue story with its four rescuers does not lead to the neat conclusion possible with a single rescuer. Each of the brothers claims that he played the most important role in the rescue and should receive the princess. The versions offer three possible solutions of the quandary. The tale may be left with the dispute still unsettled. Or it may be proposed that she be divided, and in this manner, reminiscent of King Solomon, the true lover is discovered. A third solution is to give the brothers half the kingdom instead of the princess.

The tale has a long literary history, with its origin apparently in India, where it is told in the *Vetālanpañcavimçati*, or *Twenty-Five Tales of a Vampire*. Later stages are represented by the Mongolian *Siddhi Kür*, the Persian *Tuti-Nameh*, and an Italian novella of Morlini. From the sixteenth

[15] R. Th. Christiansen, *The Tale of the Two Travellers, or the Blinded Man*; see also: A. Wesselski, *Märchen des Mittelalters*, 202, No. 14; K. Krohn, *Neuphilologische Mitteilungen*, XXVI (1925), 111ff.; M. Gaster, *Studies and Texts in Folklore*, II, 908ff.

[16] We have already encountered a series of these men in the story of The Extraordinary Companions (Type 513).

century down it has appeared frequently in literature, notably in the famous tale collections of Straparola and Basile. But though its literary origin seems clearly established, the tale has been taken over into the oral folklore of a good part of the world. It is well represented in every part of Europe and is unusually popular in Asia, where it is known from the Mediterranean to Japan and from India to Malaysia, Farther India, and Indonesia. It is scattered over much of Africa and has been carried, apparently by Negroes, to North America. On the other hand, it has not been reported on the American continent from American Indian, French, Spanish, or English tradition. We may well expect at some time to hear of the tale from Spanish America, since three versions are known in Spain.

A story so similar to some aspects of The Four Skillful Brothers as to suggest the possibility that it is a mere outgrowth of that tale is the one known as The Three Skillful Brothers (Type 654). The beginning of the tale is identical with the other. The brothers having been sent out for training return and display their accomplishments. The fighting master swings his sword so fast that he does not become wet in a heavy rain; the barber shaves a running rabbit; and the blacksmith shoes a horse while it is galloping. The action usually goes no further than this simple anecdote, though we may hear of further adventures of the brothers. A version of this story somewhat different from that current today is found in the *Scala Celi* of Johannes Gobii, Junior, composed in France at the beginning of the fourteenth century. It has been used in jestbooks from the sixteenth century and has been collected orally, though not frequently, from most parts of the European continent. It does not seem to have traveled beyond.

A third tale of skill recounts the accomplishments of The Three Doctors (Type 660), who show their extraordinary ability in surgery. One of them removes one of his eyes, another removes his heart, and the third a hand. They are to replace these members without injury the next morning. The story does not turn out as happily as the other tales of skill, for during the night the severed members are eaten and animal members are brought in to act as substitutes. In this way one of the doctors acquires a cat's eye which sees best at night, another one is given a thief's hand which makes him want to steal, and the third is given a hog's heart, so that he is impelled to root in the ground. This tale likewise is apparently literary in origin, since it is told in the Middle Ages in the *Gesta Romanorum* and was reworked in the sixteenth century by Hans Sachs. As an oral anecdote it is popular in the Baltic states and is told throughout Scandinavia, in Ireland, Flanders, Germany, Russia, and Hungary. It seems not to be known in the Romance countries nor to have traveled outside of Europe.

All three of these tales of marvelous skill appear to belong to literature rather than to folklore, though all of them have been taken over by the tellers of oral tales. One story which is suggested by these three is purely literary, having a place in most of the important collections of artistic tales, both of the Orient and of Europe,[17] but being reported orally only from Norway, Denmark, Estonia and Russia, though rarely even in these countries.[18] This is the tale of The Wise Brothers (Type 655), who are asked by the king to speak three wise words. They declare, among other things, that the king is a bastard, or that the roast they are eating is dog meat, or that the wine tastes of a corpse.[19] It turns out upon investigation that all of these statements are true, but could not have been known to anyone who was not almost supernatural either in his fineness of perception or unusual powers of deduction.

E. KNOWLEDGE OF ANIMAL SPEECH

A skill which proves convenient to the heroes of a number of tales is that of speaking and understanding the language of animals. This trait is old and widespread in folklore and mythology. Siegfried in Norse myth and Melampus in Greek possessed this power, and they both received it from a serpent[20] or dragon. This motif in all its details forms the introduction to one of the best known traditional stories of Asia and Europe, The Animal Languages (Type 670). As reconstructed by Aarne,[21] the generalized form of the tale is as follows:

A snake who wishes to repay a man for a favor teaches him the language of animals, but does so under the condition that he shall never say anything to anyone about it: if he should do so, he must die. In his home one day the man hears two animals talking together and their conversation amuses him so that he laughs at it. When his wife sees him laughing when there is apparently nothing to laugh at, she demands to know the cause. The man hesitates to tell her, and says that he must die if he should ever tell anybody the reason. The wife, however, insists upon her demand. Finally the man makes up his mind to satisfy the curiosity of his wife, and prepares to die. But just then he chances to hear another animal conversation. The male animal (usually a cock) speaks words of warning about a man who can maintain no discipline in his house, but who is thinking about dying for the sake of his wife. The man takes these words to heart and refuses to betray the secret.

[17] For a comparative study of the tale see Fischer and Bolte, *Die Reise der Söhne Giaffers* (Bibliothek des Litterarischen Vereins in Stuttgart, No. 208), pp. 198-202.

[18] Two versions have been reported from the Sudan and one from Indonesia.

[19] For a considerable list of these proofs of marvelous sensitiveness, see Motif F647 with all the literature there cited.

[20] This motif is found in Grimm's tale, The White Serpent (Type 673) and in an Estonian and three Finnish analogues. By the use of the knowledge of animal languages the hero discovers the queen's necklace or prevents an accident. These folktales apparently go back to medieval literary sources. For a good discussion of them, see Bolte-Polívka, I, 131-34. The trait seems to belong quite as much to local tradition and mythology as to folktale. For another story of animal languages, see Type 781.

[21] *Der tiersprachenkundige Mann.*

Both on account of the frequent appearance of this story in the older literary texts of India and because of the stability of the oral variants of India and surrounding countries, there seems little doubt that the tale has been brought into Europe from the East. It appears in such notable Oriental collections as the *Ramayana*, the *Jātaka* (both the Indian and the Chinese forms), the *Twenty-Five Tales of a Vampire*, the Persian *Tuti-Nameh*, and the *Thousand and One Nights*. Its presence in medieval Europe is indicated by its appearance in the *Gesta Romanorum*, in a novella of Morlini, and in Straparola's collection of tales. But in spite of this literary background the story has been adopted by the people and has become a part of the repertory of oral tales in almost every country of Europe. It is especially common in Finland and the Baltic states. In the Near East and in present-day India it is well established, and beyond India it is known at least in Annam and Java. It is one of the most popular of all foreign tales which have been taken over by African tribes, not fewer than twenty-five versions having been reported, from every quarter of the continent. The tale has, however, hardly entered the western hemisphere; at least none have been noted except from Jamaica and from a Cape Verde Island tradition in Massachusetts.

In some stories the knowledge of animal languages serves to promote the success of the hero in much the same way as Aladdin's lamp did his. In the tale known from the Grimms' title as The Three Languages (Type 671), the father sends his stupid son off to school, but all he learns is the language of dogs, birds, and frogs. His father is disgusted at his stupidity and orders him killed. But a compassionate servant substitutes an animal's heart, and lets him escape.[22] By means of his knowledge of animal languages, he cures a sick princess or discovers a treasure, and eventually he marries the princess. Later a bird indicates his election as pope (or king) (Motif H171.2). This tale is so frequently confused with another containing this same power to understand the animal languages, namely, The Boy Who Learned Many Things (Type 517), that any consideration of their origin and distribution will be postponed until the latter tale is taken up in a more appropriate place.[23]

Special virtues in connection with the learning of language are ascribed to a serpent's crown, though its efficacy is by no means confined to this function. In one story of this kind (Type 672A) a man steals a serpent's crown and when the serpent pursues he throws a garment behind him and escapes. The cook now cooks the crown and learns, in place of his master, the language of animals. In some versions he receives instead, or in addition, a considerable sum of money. A second tale of a serpent's crown (Type 672B) tells how a little girl takes away the gold crown which the serpent has laid

[22] For the appearance of this motif in other tales, see Motif K512.2 and the literature there cited.
[23] See p. 138, below.

down. As a result, the serpent dies. A third tale (Type 672C) is one of gratitude. The maiden feeds the serpent milk[24] and as a result he appears at her wedding and leaves a crown of gold and silver. All three of these small tales of serpents' crowns are frequently told as local legends. They seem to be confined largely to central Europe, primarily Germany.

F. EXTRAORDINARY STRENGTH

In the story of The Bear's Son (Type 301) we have already encountered the supernaturally strong hero. The same introduction that leads to the train of events in that story is very frequently used as an opening of an entirely different tale. A very common designation for this story is Strong John (Type 650). It begins in the same way as The Bear's Son by accounting for the hero's origin. Frequently he is actually a son of a bear and a woman, though sometimes he may simply have the strength of a bear because his mother had been carried off and was still in captivity to the bear at the time of his birth. Other extraordinary origins are ascribed to him: he may be the son of a woman of the sea or of a kind of wood-nymph, or of a troll woman and a man who has merely dreamed a connection with her. Finally, he may be said to be struck from iron by a smith. Whatever may be his marvelous birth, he is usually precocious. His mother suckles him until he is well grown, and even before his weaning he practices his strength by uprooting trees. He is finally sent from home on account of his enormous appetite. For his journey he takes along a giant cane (sometimes said to hold fifty cattle). He undertakes to work for a smith, but he drives the anvil into the ground and he throws trees onto the roof of the smithy and breaks it.

Thus far the tale is identical with The Bear's Son. Instead of meeting the extraordinary companions and having adventures in the lower world, the hero in this story goes to work for a man with whom he enters into a strange contract. The stories differ among themselves as to the details. The three most popular are these. As payment for his year's labor he is to be allowed to give his master a single blow: the stroke sends the man to the sky; or he is to receive in payment all the grain he can carry off: he makes away with the whole crop. The third bargain is known as the anger bargain (Motif K172). Severe punishment shall be given to the first of the bargainers to become angry. The youth heaps all kinds of indignities on the master to provoke his anger and finally annoys him beyond endurance, so that in the end when his anger explodes the boy gives him a great blow or even some-times cuts off his ears. The interest in the story largely consists in these tricks which the hero plays on the master. When he is asked to thresh grain, he breaks the flail and makes a new one of the stable roof beams. Similarly,

[24] In a similar incident well known in Germany and surrounding countries (Type 285) the child not only feeds the serpent milk but says, "Have some bread, too."

when he is to clear land or to dig ditches or to plow, he breaks the tools or kills or injures the work animals.[25] The master tries his best to kill the youth, but the latter always turns things to his own advantage.[26] The boy is sent to the devil's mill, but he drives the devils to his master's house. Likewise when he is sent for a wild horse or demons in hell, he brings them back with him. The master commands him to dig a well. While he is down below, the master throws a millstone on him, but the strong boy puts it around his neck as a collar and asks that chickens stop scratching sand on him.

Many other separate incidents in this story also appear elsewhere. Such, for example, are the long nursing of the strong hero (Motif F611.2.3), and the supernatural birth from an object (Motifs F611.1.11, T540). The setting out of the hero, especially his adventures at the smithy, are strongly reminiscent of the Siegfried myth. In other respects even the casual reader is reminded of the story of Hercules, not only because of the strength of the hero, but particularly because some of the tasks, such as bringing the devils from hell, are practically identical.

In spite of all these connections with ancient myth or with separate anecdotes or with the folktale of The Bear's Son, Strong John, as a modern oral tradition is a very definite entity, well constructed by the Scandinavians and Baltic peoples. Nearly four hundred versions have been reported in Finland and Estonia alone. It is also known in nearly every European country, but seems to extend very little into Asia. The French have brought it to Canada where it is still told, not only by their descendants, but by Indians both in Nova Scotia and in British Columbia. A Portuguese version has come by way of the Cape Verde Islands to Massachusetts.

Any distribution study of Strong John is made difficult because of its close relation with The Bear's Son. One is not always quite sure whether cataloguers have been careful to discriminate between the two types. It seems fair to say, however, that the special development of the strong man motif seen in this story has been essentially European. Some kinds of tales of powerful men are found nearly everywhere, and it is natural that some of the incidents should be similar.

G. EXTRAORDINARY SMALLNESS

Though gigantic persons are very frequent in local tradition, they have played little part in the regular folktale. It is quite different with the tiny hero. In ancient literature we frequently hear of impossibly small men[27] and

---

[25] For details of these impudent or destructive acts, see the whole series of types numbered from 1000 to 1029. These sometimes appear independently or in small groups. Some of them are widespread, but others are confined to the Baltic and Scandinavian countries, where they have received vigorous development.

[26] Many incidents which appear in this section of the tales are found separately or in other connections. See Types 1115 to 1122.

[27] For a discussion of such ancient stories, see Bolte-Polívka, I, 395.

this theme has retained its popularity, not only in the literary account of the travels of Lemuel Gulliver, but also in the widely told popular story of Tom Thumb (Type 700).

This tale of a boy the size of a thumb and his adventures goes back at least to the period of the Renaissance. It seems to have given the name, Le Petit Poucet, to Perrault's hero of the story usually known as Hansel and Gretel (Type 327), and it undoubtedly suggested Fielding's satirical play of Tom Thumb the Great. As a nursery tale it is very popular and has doubtless been propagated very largely through children's books. A glance at its distribution indicates that it is a European story, well established over the whole continent, which has been carried to the nearer parts of Asia, to scattered points in Africa and the Cape Verde Islands, and thence to Jamaica, the Bahamas, the American Negroes of the southern states, and to one tribe of Indians in the Plains.

There is no great variety in the telling. A childless couple wish for a child, however small he may be, and as a result they have a boy who is only as large as a thumb. He drives a wagon by sitting in a horse's ear; lets himself be sold and then runs away; is carried up the chimney by the steam of food; helps thieves in their robbery but betrays them by his cries; is swallowed by a cow and mystifies everyone by crying out from within, so that the cow is slaughtered and he is rescued. Finally he is eaten by a fox or a wolf, whom he persuades to go to his father's chicken-house or pantry for food: when he arrives, he calls for help and is rescued. A few variations, but not very many, are to be found in the details of the thumbling's marvelous adventures. It would seem to be a story whose history would repay a thorough investigation such as it has never received.

5. LOVERS AND MARRIED COUPLES

A. SUPERNATURAL WIFE

MANY of the tales of supernatural adversaries and helpers and of marvelous objects and powers which we have been noticing deal also with the hero or heroine's success or misadventures in love. We see the lowly hero or heroine win a royal mate so frequently in folktales that this revolution of fortune has come to seem the most characteristic sign of the "fairy tale." In the stories thus far examined, the union of hero and heroine has been incidental to other motifs which have occupied the center of attention. In a very considerable number of stories, however, the winning of the wife or husband or the recovery of the mate after some disaster forms the central motivation of the whole. If magic objects or powerful helpers and adversaries appear, they are entirely subordinate to the love interest which lies at the heart of the narration.

Many of such tales are on a supernatural level and the action moves in a world far from reality. A particularly interesting group of these deals with the experiences of the hero and his supernatural wife.

The story of the Swan Maiden forms a part of three well-known folktales. All three may exist without the swan maiden, so that classifiers have difficulty in working out a satisfactory scheme for an accurate listing of these three tales. The hero in his travels comes to a body of water and sees girls bathing. On the shore he finds their swan coverings which show him that the girls are really transformed swans.[1] He seizes one of the swan coats and will not return it to the maiden unless she agrees to marry him. She does so, and, as a swan, takes him to her father's house where she again becomes human. From this point on the story may go in either one of two directions. The hero may be set difficult tasks by the girl's father and may solve them with her help. This may serve as introduction to Type 313, The Girl as Helper in the Hero's Flight. In other tales of the swan maiden the hero is careful to hide her swan coat, so as to keep her in her human form. Once when he is absent, she accidentally finds the wings and feathers, puts them on and disappears. The main part of tales containing this motif is concerned with the disappearance and painful recovery of the wife. This series of motifs is frequently found in Type 400, The Man on a Quest for his Lost Wife, and Type 465A, The Quest for the Unknown.

This sequence of events, either in its shorter or more extended form, has had a long history and is found nearly all over the world. It is in such Oriental collections as the *Thousand and One Nights* and the *Ocean of Story*. It constitutes one of the poems of the Old Norse *Edda*.[2] As an oral tale it is worldwide. It is evenly, and thickly, distributed over Europe and Asia, and versions are found in almost every area of Africa, in every quarter of Oceania, and in practically every culture area of the North American Indians. Scattering versions are reported from Jamaica, Yucatan, and the Guiana Indians.

In the great majority of these occurrences of the Swan Maiden we have the discovery of the wings and the disappearance of the supernatural wife, but sometimes only the marriage to the swan maiden. It is strange to find this familiar tale of the bathing maidens among the Smith Sound Eskimo only a few hundred miles from the North Pole.[3]

In its shorter form the swan maiden incident usually serves to introduce the tale of The Girl as Helper in the Hero's Flight (Type 313). In all versions

[1] Or the swan maidens may appear to the hero in a meadow where he has been sent to keep watch all night.

[2] The *Völundarkvida*. For a discussion of these literary treatments, see Bolte-Polívka, III, 416.

[3] For a good discussion of the whole Swan Maiden cycle, see Helge Holmström, *Studier över Svanjungfrumotivet*.

of this story the hero comes into the power of an ogre. Sometimes he has sold himself to the ogre in settlement of a gambling debt. Sometimes he simply pursues a bird to the ogre's house. But most often he is brought by the swan maiden to the house of her father, who turns out to be a cruel ogre. In any event, the hero is put to severe trials. Sometimes he is forbidden to open a box containing a magic castle (Type 313B). But most often he must perform impossible tasks on pain of death. Some of the most frequent of these tasks are the planting of a vineyard overnight, the cleaning of a stable which has been neglected for years, the cutting down of a whole forest, the catching of a magic horse, the sorting of large numbers of grains, or the making of a huge pond. Whatever the tasks may be, the ogre's daughter performs them for the hero and plans to escape with him. In many versions the hero is compelled to choose his wife from among her sisters who look magically like her. He has killed and resuscitated her, and in the process she has lost a finger. He is thus able to pick her out, and temporarily placate the ogre.

The young people prepare for flight and leave behind themselves some magic objects which speak in their place when the ogre talks to them. This ruse does not delay him very long, however, and he sets out in pursuit. Sometimes we hear of how the couple transform themselves into various objects or persons so as to deceive the girl's father. He sometimes finds only a rose and a thornbush, or a priest and a church, when he thinks to overtake them. Or they may escape by means of an obstacle flight. That is, they may throw behind themselves magic objects such as a comb, a stone, or a flint which become obstacles—a forest, a mountain, or a fire—in the path of the pursuer.[4] Or they may escape over a magic bridge which folds up behind them. The story may very well end here (Type 313A). But it is usually followed by the episode of the Forgotten Fiancée (Type 313C). In such case, after the young people have escaped, the hero tells his fiancée, or bride, that he must leave her for a short visit to his own family. She warns him against certain specific acts which will bring on magic forgetfulness: kissing his mother, fondling his dog, or tasting food while at home. He breaks the prohibition, and loses all memory of his bride. She realizes what has happened and undertakes to overcome the magic forgetfulness. Frequently this does not occur until after the hero is about to marry again or even until after his marriage. In one series of tales she bribes the new bride to let her sleep beside her husband. He awakens on the third night and recovers. Or, in some cases, the forgotten bride may simply attract attention in some unusual fashion. For example, she places three lovers in embarrassing positions and arouses gossip. Or she magically stops the wedding carriage of her husband and his new bride. Or she may carry on a conversation with objects or animals and thus call attention to the situation. In one way or another she always succeeds in the end, and the hero chooses her instead of his new bride,

[4] A worldwide motif. For extensive literature, see Motif D672.

sometimes remarking that the old key which has been found again is better than a new one.

This tale is immensely complicated, and offers many possibilities for variations. Some of its motifs it shares in common with many other tales: The Swan Maiden (Motif D361.1), The Transformation Flight (Motif D671), The Obstacle Flight (Motif D672), and the Son-in-Law Tasks (Motif H310). The heart of the story would seem to be this last motif, but there are tales of son-in-law tasks which do not seem to have any organic relation with this story.[5]

Aside from the fact that it contains several very popular motifs, the whole tale complex is widely distributed over the earth, though not nearly so uniformly as either the Swan Maiden or the Obstacle Flight motifs. It is known throughout Europe and is one of the most popular among the stories which have been brought to America. At least twenty-five versions have been noted from American Indian tribes scattered over the entire North American continent. It is also found in English, French, and Negro traditions in Virginia, Canada, Missouri, and the West Indies. On the other hand, it seems to be almost, but not completely, absent from central and east Asiatic folklore, and but two parallels, neither of them very close, have been noticed in Africa.

With this tale it is extremely difficult to be quite sure when we are dealing with a remote parallel and when with an actual occurrence of the type. The combination Supernatural Wife + Son-in-Law Tasks + Magic Flight can be found in widely scattered parts of the world without seeming to have any organic connection with this European tale. Stories of this kind, for example, are met in Japan and on the island of Mauritius. Likewise an analogous tale in the *Ocean of Story* may be merely similar rather than identical.[6]

As a story unmistakably of this type, it begins to appear in literary tale collections of the Renaissance such as Bello's *Mambriano* and Basile's *Pentamerone*. In oral European tradition, though there is considerable freedom of combination, three forms of the tale are most popular: Swan Maiden (or other supernatural wife) + Son-in-Law Tasks + Flight (Type 313A); same + Forbidden Chamber motif (Type 313B); and either of these followed by the Forgotten Fiancée (Type 313C).

The Swan Maiden, it will be recalled, sometimes recovers her wings and leaves her husband. When the motif is handled in this fashion it belongs to an entirely different tale, the central interest of which is the loss and recovery of the supernatural wife. The first half of this tale shows so many variations that it presents a difficult problem to the classifier. But once having furnished the hero with his unusual wife—in any one of a half dozen ways—the taleteller arrives at his central motif, The Man on a Quest for his Lost Wife

[5] For an interesting tale of this kind, see Thompson, *Tales of the North American Indians*, p. 79, No. 39, "The Sun Tests his Son-in-Law," and notes 111-126. This group of stories has a wide distribution among the North American Indians. See pp. 329ff., below.

[6] For a discussion of these parallels, see Bolte-Polívka, II, 524ff.

(Type 400), and from that point on the development of the story is uniform, irrespective of its introduction. One of the introductions tells of the swan maiden and of her discovery of her wings in the absence of her husband and her flight as a swan. Sometimes she succeeds in sending her husband an enigmatic message as to where he will find her. There are several other introductions important enough to deserve mentioning. In one, the hero has been unwittingly promised by his father to a giant or ogre. When the ogre comes for him, he cannot take the boy because of the Bible the young man carries under his arm. Eventually this hero goes to the ogre's home and marries his daughter. In another opening, the hero and his brothers must keep watch in a meadow which is being destroyed by a monster. The younger brother alone keeps awake. Sometimes the monster comes and leads him to further adventures, but more often swan maidens appear to him. Occasionally we are merely told that a prince is on a hunt and encounters the supernatural woman. A somewhat more complicated introduction tells of the hero's voyage in a self-moving boat to a foreign castle, where he finds the heroine. Sometimes he finds a bewitched princess in a castle and succeeds in disenchanting her, either by enduring silence three frightful nights[7] in the castle or else by sleeping by the princess three nights without looking at or disturbing her.

In any case, the hero marries the supernatural woman and lives happily with her. On one occasion he wishes to go home on a visit. She consents, and gives him a magic object, usually a wishing ring, or else the power to make three wishes come true. But she warns him in the strongest terms against breaking certain prohibitions. He must not call for her to come to him or utter her name. Sometimes he is forbidden to sleep or eat or drink while on the journey.

When he goes home he tells of his adventures and is induced to boast of his wife. He calls upon her to come, so that they may all see how beautiful she is. Sometimes it is another one of the prohibitions which he breaks, but in any event she does come, takes the ring, and disappears, giving him a pair of iron shoes which he must wear out before he can find her again. In addition to this manner in which the supernatural wife may be lost, there is (besides the swan maiden disappearing with her wings) a third motif which appears in some versions. The wife has promised to meet the hero but an enemy uses a magic pin and causes him to sleep when she comes.

In whatever way the wife is lost, the narrative now proceeds with his adventures while he seeks for and eventually recovers her. In this part of the tale the versions are relatively uniform, regardless of what type of introductory action has been used. He meets people who rule over the wild animals, the birds, and the fish. He receives advice from an old eagle. He inquires his way successively of the sun and the moon: they know nothing,

[7] For this motif, see Types 307, 401.

but the wind shows him his road. He meets one old woman who sends him on to her older sister, who in turn sends him to the third still older, who gives him final directions for reaching his wife. Among these is the climbing of a high and slippery mountain without looking back. Sometimes he meets people fighting over magic objects and gets these objects by trickery.[8] The objects most frequently mentioned are a saddle, a hat, a mantle, a pair of boots, and a sword. With the help of the north wind and by means of his magic objects he reaches the castle and finds his wife. Sometimes she is about to be married to another man. A ring hidden in a cake, or some other device, brings about recognition, and the couple are reunited. Some versions proceed from this point into the story of The Girl as Helper in the Hero's Flight (Type 313), in which he must perform tasks and in which eventually the couple flee from her father.

With all the many variations in the earlier part of the story, and with the wealth of detail possible in the central action, it is remarkable that the tale should retain a definite enough quality to be considered a real entity. And yet the characteristic incidents of the quest are so constant that it is not difficult to recognize this tale type in spite of the almost kaleidoscopic variations it has assumed.[9] Three stories of Grimm's famous collection (Nos. 92, 93, and 193) deal with this material, each handling it in a different fashion. Sometimes it appears as part of a local legend, and sometimes has received elaborate literary treatment.

At least three of the tales in the *Thousand and One Nights* are close analogues. The narrative pattern also appears to have been familiar to writers of chivalric romances.[10] Perhaps best known of these are the lays of *Graelent* and *Lanval*. In addition to these literary associations of the tale, it has had a vigorous life in the repertories of unlettered story-tellers in many parts of the world. There is hardly a section of Europe where it is not popular, and it also exists in western Asia. At least twelve oral versions are known from India, though not all of them may be really related. It is found across Siberia, even to the most northeasterly point. Whether these Chuckchee variants represent the carrying over of a tale from Asia to North America or vice versa is not clear. The American Indian versions seem much more like borrowings which came to them in one fashion or another across the Atlantic. Most are certainly taken from the French Canadians.

[8] For this motif, see Type 518.

[9] The best treatment of this tale (or rather, small cycle of tales) is by Holmström, *Studier över Svanjungfrumotivet*. On pages 15 to 20 is an excellent analysis of the various combinations of motifs usually found. The study is important for arranging the material, but the student is disappointed that Holmström does not give a more satisfactory discussion of his material that would throw more light on probable origins and routes of dissemination.

[10] For a discussion of its use in the medieval romance, see L. Hibbard, *Mediaeval Romance in England* (New York, 1924), pp. 200ff., and W. H. Schofield, "The lays of Graelent and Lanval and the story of Wayland," *Publications of the Modern Language Association of America*, XV (1900), 121.

A re-examination of all the material relating to this story is necessary before any conclusions as to its history can be reached. Many of the things written about it in the past are clearly antiquated. Some of these studies fail to distinguish between this tale and others of supernatural and offended wives, such as the legend of Mélusine. Others interest themselves in the situation because it seems to have some relation to primitive totemism or to a primitive matriarchy.[11] It is, of course, possible that some such ideas lie behind the motifs in this story. But these older investigators were purely theoretical and unrealistic in their approach. They did not actually attempt to answer the question as to just when and just how this particular tale was composed and in just what manner it has been propagated.

In addition to the two stories last discussed, the swan maiden episode frequently serves to introduce the tale of The Man Persecuted Because of his Beautiful Wife (Type 465). The main lines of this story are familiar from its being told in the Bible concerning David and Bathsheba, whether or not that literary treatment has had a part in the origin and propagation of this tale. In one way or another the hero comes into possession of a supernatural wife—a swan maiden, an animal with the power of transformation, or a wife received directly at the hands of God. In any case, the envious king conceives a great desire for the wife and plots to get rid of the husband. He assigns him a series of impossible tasks, but the husband, sometimes by securing supernatural aid, but always with the help of his wife, succeeds in performing these tasks and thus defeating the king's purpose.

According to whether the wife is a swan maiden or a transformed animal or a gift from God, there is a rather consistent variation made in the nature of the tasks. This fact has made it possible, with some consistency, to divide the versions into three groups. But a cursory examination of the distribution of these groups does not show that this division is of great significance in working out the history of the story. It is clear that the tale is essentially east European. It does not appear in central, western, or southern Europe, but is most at home in Russia, the Near East, the Baltic and Scandinavian countries. Sporadic versions appear in India and Korea. It has not been reported from Africa or the western hemisphere.[12]

B. ENCHANTED WIFE (SWEETHEART) DISENCHANTED

In the Swan Maiden episode it will be recalled that the hero, by means of taking away from the swan her wings and feathers while she is temporarily in human form, brings it about that she can keep this human form as long

[11] See, for example, J. Kohler, Der Ursprung der Melusinensage (Leipzig, 1895); Lang, Custom and Myth (London, 1904), pp. 64ff.; J. A. MacCulloch, Childhood of Fiction, pp. 272, 341ff.; Frazer, Golden Bough, IV, 125ff.; and Hartland, Science of Fairy Tales, pp. 255ff.

[12] For help in assembling the data on this tale, I am indebted to Professor Thelma G. James of Wayne University, who has in preparation a definitive study of the type.

as her bird covering is not available to her. This is but one of the ways in which human lovers disenchant wives or sweethearts who may have been so unfortunate as to have been turned into animals or objects, or have been placed under an enchantment.

One such tale is little more than a variation of the story about The Man on a Quest for His Lost Wife (Type 400), and is frequently referred to as being a sub-type of that tale. The emphasis in the story of The Princess Transformed into Deer (Type 401), however, is on the method of disenchantment rather than on the recovery of the wife, which may or may not appear in the story. A prince and his companion are hunting, and are enticed into a deserted castle by a deer who is really a transformed princess. The hero is able to disenchant her by spending three frightful nights in the castle and enduring in silence all the horrible things which happen to him. The story normally continues with the loss, search, and eventual recovery of the wife thus acquired.

As compared with some of the tales we have considered, this is not really well known. In no part of the world does it seem to be a favorite, but there can be no doubt of its validity as a well-recognized story. It seems to be most popular in Italy, among the south Slavic peoples, the Czechs, and the Flemish. But it is also told in Iceland, in Scotland, in France, and in Turkey. Apparently it has not traveled outside of Europe.[13]

Much more popular where it is known, but confined almost exclusively to southern and southeastern Europe, is The Three Oranges (Type 408). A casual examination of its distribution suggests the probability of Italian origin. Practically every tale collection from Italy, Spain, Portugal, and Greece has at least one version of this story. It is also very common in Hungary and Turkey, but it does not appear in any northern country except Norway, where it was recorded from an Italian fruitwoman. It is found in Persia and in India, but not frequently enough to indicate Oriental origin. The numerous versions reported in Latin America are obvious importations from Spain and Portugal. From the latter country it has been taken to Massachusetts through the medium of Cape Verde Island settlers.

The plot of The Three Oranges is rather constant wherever the story is told and follows the general lines of the literary reworking in Basile's *Pentamerone*.[14] For one reason or another, a young man sets out in search of a faraway princess. Sometimes this happens at the suggestion of his false elder brothers, and sometimes it is because he angers an old woman who puts a curse on him which sends him on the quest. On his way he is kind to an old woman, or to an animal or bird, and receives help. Eventually he arrives at a

---

[13] This tale does not appear in the Grimms' collection, though it resembles in many ways their No. 92. A good example of the type is Gonzenbach's *Sicilianische Märchen*, No. 60.

[14] The tale has never been thoroughly studied. A good list of versions appears in Bolte-Polívka, II, 125, n. 2, and IV, 257, n. 1. All of these and a number of additional references are found in Penzer, *Pentamerone*, II, 158ff.

castle, where he finds the three oranges which he has been told to look for. These oranges are enchanted maidens, and he succeeds in rescuing the youngest from her spell. A kitchenmaid later tries to replace her mistress. She sees the reflection of the princess in a pond or stream and throws her in, thinking to drown her. The kitchenmaid succeeds for a time in passing herself off for the princess. Meantime the heroine has been transformed into a silver fish and she subsequently assumes various other shapes and finally her own form. The tale ends with the recognition and reinstatement of the princess and the punishment of the false servant girl.

Although the Grimm collection does not contain The Three Oranges, it does have two stories in which girls are transformed to flowers. One of them is very simple, since it merely tells that the hero disenchants her by breaking a stalk of the flower. They thereupon marry and live without further adventures. It is really handled as a riddle, and the romantic story is only incidental.[15]

The other tale, The Prince Whose Wishes Always Came True (Type 652), has a good deal of complication, and it is only after we are half through the story that we encounter the carnation-girl. The story opens with an incident rather common in folktales, the choice of a godfather for the king's son. This is done by chance, and the first person to arrive is given the high office. After a few years the old man who has been chosen as godfather takes the boy secretly to a church, gives him his blessing, and along with it the power to make all his wishes come true. A treacherous servant has concealed himself and overhears what has happened. He steals the boy, smears blood on the queen's mouth, and accuses her of killing and eating him. She is walled up in a tower.

The boy is reared by a forester. He falls in love with the forester's daughter, who tells him who he is. When the treacherous servant comes to take him away, the prince uses his powers and transforms the servant into a dog and his sweetheart into a carnation. He now takes the dog and the carnation to his father's court, where he enters service as a huntsman. He always gets his food by wishing and changes the carnation to her human form whenever he desires. When the king asks him for the carnation, the boy tells him everything. The queen is thereupon released, the servant imprisoned, and the prince and his sweetheart are married.

Neither of these two tales of girls transformed into flowers is widely known. The first has been reported only five times outside the Grimm collection and can hardly be said to have established a real oral tradition. As for the second of these tales, it is well known and fairly popular in the Baltic states, Germany, and Scandinavia, as well as in southeastern Europe. Analogues have been noted in Turkey, India, and Farther India, but the tale has not traveled to other continents. It is closely related and frequently confused

[15] Grimm No. 160, A Riddle Tale; Type 407, The Girl as Flower.

with a common legend of southeast Europe, The Devil's Bride, in which a prince plucks a flower from the grave of a maiden who has turned into a vampire. Thereupon she assumes her human form.[16] The handing down of this tale has also been somewhat confused by a very similar story given currency through Basile's *Pentamerone* (Day 1, No. 2) in which a woman, through a curse, gives birth to a plant which she puts in a pot and keeps in her room. The prince buys the pot and takes it into his own room, where the plant assumes the form of a maiden. The prince and the girl live happily together until her envious rival enters the room in the prince's absence and tears up the plant. The versions of the story of the carnation girl cited above as coming from southeastern Europe and Asia may belong more properly to the tradition of Basile's story than to that contained in the Grimms' collection.

Largely because it has a place in Grimm, the story of Jorinde and Joringel (Type 405) should be mentioned here. The heroine, turned into a bird by a witch, is restored to her former shape by the hero through the help of his magic objects. The story is entirely without complication and, except as taken directly from Grimm, is not known outside of Germany.

A somewhat similar story of transformation of a woman from an animal (Type 409) has wide currency in Estonia and Livonia, but is entirely unknown elsewhere. The woman who has been transformed into a wolf suckles her child on top of a stove. On the advice of a magician the stove is made hot and when the woman lays her wolf clothing on the stove, she is restored to human form.[17]

In some folktales the form from which the woman must be disenchanted is neither plant nor animal, but may be merely some monstrous deformation or even a magic spell which has been cast over her. One such story, The Beautiful and the Ugly Twin (Type 711), begins with the common motif of the barren mother who longs for a child. She gets advice from a witch, but breaks one of the conditions, and as a result has twins, one of them beautiful, but the other hideously deformed, sometimes with an animal head. The ugly sister always helps the beautiful one. At last a prince is to marry the ugly twin. On her wedding day she is transformed, and becomes as beautiful as her sister. This story is popular in Norway and Iceland, and seems to be quite unknown elsewhere.

Of tales of enchanted brides there remains one of the most familiar of all stories for those who learn their folktales through children's books. This is Sleeping Beauty, La Belle au Boix Dormante (Type 410). The story is best known as told by Perrault, whose version has been widely translated and forms the basis of the story as it appears in our nursery books. A fairy who has not been invited to the princess's christening celebration makes a wish

---

[16] For the distribution of this legend, see Bolte-Polívka, II, 126.
[17] For another tale of disenchantment of a woman from animal form, see Type 402.

that the princess shall die from a spindle wound. Another fairy changes the curse from death into a hundred-year sleep. In accordance with the prophecy, the maiden and all the dwellers in the castle fall into a magic sleep and all about the castle there grows up a thick hedge of thorns. At the end of a hundred years a prince breaks through the hedge and awakens the princess with a kiss.

Stories with slight variations from Sleeping Beauty occur in Basile's Pentamerone and in the Grimms' collection. Even as early as the fifteenth century the main outlines are found in the French prose romance of *Perceforest*. But the tale has never become a real part of oral folklore. The single versions reported from Greece or Russia or Arabia are obviously mere retellings of one or other of these printed variants.

C. ENCHANTED HUSBAND (LOVER) DISENCHANTED

The presence of the supernatural wife in folktales—whether she be a transformed animal, an inhabitant of another world, or some kind of fairy or elf—has long interested those who like to speculate about the ultimate origins of folktales and other human institutions. Each generation of scholars has had its favorite theory. A century ago these scholars were talking with the utmost certainty and dogmatism of these supernatural spouses, telling us that they represented now this, now that phenomenon of sky or cloud or seasonal change. A generation later these creatures were dogmatically described as always essentially animals and as related to primitive totemistic ideas. Still later the ritualistic school had its inning and all these stories became embodiments of ancient rites. And even today there remain some scholars who assert that they have the key that unlocks this mystery. This key they find in the interpretation of dreams.[18]

No matter whether one is convinced by such general theories of origin or, like the present writer, is skeptical of them all, it is clear enough that to the teller of tales the supernatural wife is no more important than her male counterpart. Fairy lovers, animals who are really transformed men, and even demigods marry human maidens and eventually take on human form themselves so as to live happily with their faithful wives.

Most of the problems connected with this group of tales come to light when we examine the story of Cupid and Psyche. This tale receives its name from the treatment given it by Apuleius in the second century after Christ.[19] This classical form of the tale certainly does not represent the original from which the modern European versions are derived. It belongs to a widely-diffused tradition which has a considerable variation from place to place.

[18] For some considerations of this dream theory in connection with the story of Cupid and Psyche, see p. 99, below.

[19] This tale is inserted in a larger narrative known as *The Golden Ass*. It has been frequently translated, never more charmingly than by Walter Pater in his *Marius the Epicurean*.

These variations can best be clarified by means of a generalized summary of the story (Type 425). In one way or another a girl is married to a monster husband. This introductory part of the story has many variations. Sometimes the monster is born as a result of a hasty wish of the parents. Usually he is a man at night and a monster or animal by day. Frequently the father of the girl promises his daughter in marriage to the monster, either because he has fallen into the power of the evil creature and thus buys his freedom or else in order to secure an unusual present which his youngest daughter has asked him to bring back from his journey. In some cases the father and daughter make unsuccessful attempts to evade their bargain. Usually, however, the girl goes willingly and joins the supernatural husband.

At this point, no matter what the introduction to the story may have been, the manifold versions of the tale begin to converge. In spite of the fact that the girl has been really forced into this marriage and that the husband is thought of in the earlier part of the story as a monster or a disagreeable animal, the heroine is not only complacent about the marriage but almost immediately comes to love her unusual mate. Frequently the life of the pair together is described as taking place in the midst of the greatest luxury. The chief desire of the girl is now to disenchant her husband, so that they can continue their joyful existence as normal human beings. In some of the related tales the girl succeeds in disenchanting the monster from his animal or supernatural form by means of a kiss or tears, or by burning the animal skin, or sometimes by cutting off his head. But in Cupid and Psyche she always loses her supernatural husband because she fails in some way to obey instructions. It may be that she burns his animal skin too soon, but more frequently she learns and reveals the secret of his unusual form.

As soon as she disobeys, the husband leaves her, sometimes giving her vague instructions as to where she may find him. She sets out immediately on a long and sorrowful wandering. Sometimes she wears iron shoes which must be worn out before she reaches the end of her journey. She gets magic objects from an old woman (or frequently from three in succession); she asks her direction from the wind and stars; she climbs a steep glass mountain at the top of which she finds her husband. Before being reunited she still has to win him from the wife that he is about to marry and especially to cause him to recognize her, since he has forgotten all about her. To do this she sometimes takes service as a maid and buys with three jewels the privilege of sleeping with her husband three nights. The story always ends with the reunion of the couple and a happy marriage.

In both the introductory part and in the last section which describes the search for the husband, this tale has much in common with a great many related stories. We have seen daughters promised to animals by bankrupt fathers in the tale of the Animal Brothers-in-law (Type 552), and we shall shortly mention a number of other stories of marriages to animal husbands.

The quest for the lost husband corresponds in a great number of details with the similar quest for the lost supernatural wife (Type 400). The adventures at the very end of the story are frequently the same as those in the tale of the Forgotten Fiancée (Type 313C).

The most complete study of this story is that of Ernst Tegethoff.[20] He considers the kernel of the tale to be the interruption of the happy life of the heroine and her supernatural husband because of the disobedience of the wife. In his consideration of the distribution of the versions of the tale he finds that the nature of the prohibition which the wife violates is an important indication of the direction in which dissemination has taken place. In spite of the great detail with which the material for Tegethoff's study has been assembled, he has not made adequate analysis so as to show clearly the probable relationships of the widely scattered versions. The tale has been known in literary circles for nearly two thousand years and has been frequently the subject of artistic treatment since. But Tegethoff is inclined to think that, except for Italy, the literary treatments have had little influence on the oral.

Where and when the first Cupid and Psyche tale was told is certainly not known, but it would be possible by close analysis to find much more than we now know about that probable time and place and something of the form of the story which has given rise to such a long and vigorous folk tradition. It is told in every part of Europe, but it is especially popular in the western half, where several countries have already reported more than fifty versions. The sixty-one Italian oral variants are of especial interest in connection with the appearance of the tale in Apuleius and Basile. There are a few examples of the story in the Near East and in India. Among primitive peoples it does not seem to be told except by the Zuñi of New Mexico. It has been recorded from the French in Missouri, and the Negroes of Jamaica. In all, several hundred oral variants are available to the student of this tale.

Instead of making such an investigation, Tegethoff chooses to speculate as to the psychological condition which might conceivably produce this story. It would seem to the reader that he decided upon his theory first and interpreted all of his facts in the light of that theory. Since he wishes to show that the story is the result of a dream experience, he first sloughs off all motifs that appear in other tales. There is left, then, only the bare fact of a girl who is married to a monster husband and whose happiness is interrupted by some transgression of hers. Though the story never appears in this particular form, the author presumably imagines that it was first told in this elemental fashion as a result of somebody's dream. Whose? Presumably of a girl who dreams of a lover and is rudely awakened by someone entering the room with a

---

[20] *Amor und Psyche.* See also: G. Huet, "Le roman d'Apulée: était-il connu au moyen âge," *Le Moyen Age*, XXII (1909), 22, XXIX (1917), 44; B. Stumfall, *Das Märchen vom Amor und Psyche*, 1907; Maurits de Meyer, "Amor et Psyche," *Folkliv*, 1938, pp. 197-210.

light. This may be the explanation for this story, and I should not wish to deprive anyone of the privilege of believing so. But even in the search for the ultimate origins of a folktale, there is no reason to be absurd. It would be much fairer and honester to say that we have no idea, and probably never will have, as to the original form of this tale and as to who made it up. And we certainly have no way of finding out what was the particular psychological state of the unknown and unknowable person who invented this story.[21]

Tegethoff is convinced that the story of the animal husband who is disenchanted has a different origin from that which we have just mentioned, but if so it has become so thoroughly amalgamated with the other Cupid and Psyche stories that it is impossible now to separate them.[22]

It is true that the motif of the disenchanted animal husband appears frequently in other tales than Cupid and Psyche. These stories are all rather simple in structure leading to the disenchantment as the climax of the action. In one of these, The Two Girls, the Bear, and the Dwarf (Type 426), the girls let a bear into their hut in the woods. They also rescue an ungrateful dwarf from death. It turns out that the bear has been enchanted by the dwarf. When the bear kills the dwarf, he changes into a prince. This story is a literary concoction which appeared in a German folktale collection in 1818 and was retold by Grimm. It has not been reported outside of a very small area in central Europe.

In an Italian tale known as The Wolf (Type 428), which is probably a mere variation of Cupid and Psyche, a girl is assigned seemingly impossible tasks by a witch. Eventually she is sent to another witch with a letter giving instructions that the girl is to be killed. The wolf who helps the girl escape is thereby disenchanted and becomes a prince who marries her. This story is well known through its appearance in Gonzenbach's Sicilian collection. It has been recorded orally in Italy, Spain, Portugal, Norway, Sweden, Denmark, Finland, and Russia.

Even less a part of the oral tradition of Europe is the story of The Ass (Type 430). It is really a retelling by the brothers Grimm of a fourteenth century Latin poem, *Asinarius*. The prince who has been transformed to an ass plays a lyre and is entertained at the king's court. A princess disenchants him and becomes his wife.

Somewhat more of the folk flavor is found in Grimm's tale of The House in the Wood (Type 431). It has at least a large number of motifs found in well-recognized folktales. Three sisters, one after the other, are sent out into the woods. Like Hansel and Gretel, they leave a clue of grain, but this is eaten by birds. Each in turn comes to a house where they find an old man,

---

[21] For some further considerations about the dream theory of folktale origins, especially in its Freudian aspects, see pp. 385f., below.

[22] It is convenient to designate the story when the hero is animal as Type 425C.

a cock, a hen, and a cow. The elder sisters are discourteous to these animals and are thrown into the cellar. The youngest feeds them and in this way disenchants them all. The old man turns out to be a prince and the animals his servants. He marries his rescuer. Only nine versions of this tale have been noted, and all of them seem likely to be mere retellings of the Grimm story.

Belonging to this same group of tales are two about serpents. In one of them (Type 433A), a huge serpent carries a princess into its castle. She kisses it and disenchants it. In the other (Type 433B), a childless queen bears a son who has the form of a serpent and who stays far away from home. He is disenchanted by a maiden, usually by bathing him. Both of these serpent stories are most popular in Scandinavia, though the first has also been reported in the Baltic countries and in Hungary. The second tale, known in Danish as Kung Lindorm, was given a thorough study a generation ago by Axel Olrik. This has been recently elaborated in the light of newly available material by Anna Birgitta Waldemarson.[23] The peculiar distribution of the versions—some simple legends in India and complicated tales of exactly the same pattern in the Near East and in Denmark and southern Sweden—shows upon analysis that there can be little doubt of the origin of the tale in the East, of its development into a story of the disenchanted serpent husband, followed by the adventures of the cast off wife (either Type 451 or 707). This secondary development was accomplished in the Near East, and the tale, with both parts, seems to have been carried to Scandinavia without having left any important traces on the way.

Another tale which may be nothing more than a truncated Cupid and Psyche story is Hans My Hedgehog (Type 441) which has been given some popularity through its appearance in Grimm. It does not seem to be known outside of Germany and the countries to its immediate east. A childless woman gives birth to a hedgehog. Years later the king unwittingly promises his daughter to the hedgehog in return for showing him the way out of the forest. The hedgehog is eventually disenchanted by the girl and changes into a handsome youth.

Finally, in this group of supernatural husbands should be mentioned The Frog King (Type 440), sometimes also known as Iron Henry. This tale goes back to a Latin story written in Germany in the thirteenth century. It also received literary treatment in Scotland in the sixteenth century. But in spite of this literary background, it seems to be fairly well known to story-tellers in Germany and eastward well into Russia, and it has been reported sporadically from nearly all countries in Europe, though not from any other continent. It has achieved a certain fortuitous fame because it appears as number one of the celebrated Grimm collection. The youngest of three sisters throws a ball into a spring. A frog promises to give her back the ball (in some versions, to make the spring run clear) if she will promise to marry him. The girl proceeds to forget her promise. But the frog duly appears at her door and requests entrance. He sleeps at the door, later on the table, and finally in her bed. He is disenchanted and becomes a prince. This may happen in any number of ways: by being allowed to sleep in the girl's bed, by a kiss, by having his head cut off or his frog skin burned, or by being thrown against the wall. A picturesque trait is added to this story by the experiences of the frog king's servant, Iron Henry. He has grieved so at his master's misfortune that he has three iron bands around his heart to keep it from breaking. As his master is disenchanted the bands snap one by one.

D. WOUNDED LOVER HEALED

Two common European folktales concern the wounding of the heroine's lover or husband by an enemy. The climax of the action in both cases deals with the healing of his wounds by the heroine and their happy reunion. The first of these, The Maiden in the Tower (Type 310), is usually known as Rapunzel from the name of the heroine in the Grimm version. The tale was apparently a favorite in Italy as early as the seventeenth century, since Basile uses it with slight variations twice in his *Pentamerone*. Whether because of the influence of Basile or because of the Mediterranean origin of the story, it has its greatest popularity in Italy and adjacent countries. A French literary version of the early eighteenth century doubtless aided in spreading it to northern Europe. It has appeared in German collections since 1790. It does not seem to be known in Russia or among any of the Finno-Ugric peoples, and except for a Massachusetts version originating in the Cape Verde Islands, it has not gone outside of Europe.

The tale begins with a motif which we have frequently met in other folktales: in order to appease a witch whom he has offended, a man promises her his child when it is born. The witch keeps the girl imprisoned in a windowless tower which the witch enters by using her long hair as a ladder. The king's son observes this and does likewise. The witch eventually discovers the deceit and cuts off the girl's hair and abandons her in a desert. When the prince comes he saves himself by jumping from the tower and is blinded. After various adventures the heroine finds him. Her tears falling on his eyes heal his blindness and they are happily reunited.

The confinement of the maiden in the tower, reminiscent of the futile imprisonment of Danaë, also usually forms a part of the story of The Prince as Bird (Type 432). In its best known European form the tale concerns a prince who takes on the form of a bird in order to fly to a beautiful maiden who lives in a tower. When in her presence he becomes a man. When her stepmother (or sister) discovers the mysterious lover, she wounds him, either by cutting him with a knife, piercing him with a thorn, or strewing glass on the window ledge where he lights when he arrives as a bird. The heroine now sets out to find her lover and minister unto his wounds. On the way she overhears animals (or sometimes witches) talking and learns from them how to heal him. By following their directions she succeeds.

The tale of the bird-lover appears several times in medieval literature, notably in Marie de France's *Yonec*. Details vary somewhat in the medieval stories from those in the modern folktale but it seems likely that they belong to the same tradition.[24] The story was probably current in Italy in the Renaissance: it appears in Basile's *Pentamerone* and it is especially popular in the Mediterranean countries today. Madame d'Aulnoy published the tale in France in 1702 and apparently from her version it has become popular in Scandinavia. On the other hand, there are interesting gaps in the tradition; it has apparently not been collected in Germany or the rest of northwest Europe, the British Isles, or the western Slavic countries. There are, however, five known Russian versions, and two particularly well-told variants from India. An African tale from the Hausa of the Western Sudan is an obvious borrowing of this story from India. The tale has never been thoroughly studied, and the relationship of the versions in India and in Europe is such that the question of its origin is extremely puzzling.

E. SHREWISH WIFE REFORMED

Most of the favorite folktales involving lovers and married couples are laid in a world of unreality and are filled with the supernatural. But at least two large groups of stories treat this subject without entering into the never-never land of swan maidens and bear lovers. On the one hand there are the humorous or scurrilous anecdotes of married life so popular in the fabliaux and the novella. These move in an unreal world, it is true, the world—in Charles Lamb's words—"of cuckoldry, the Utopia of gallantry," but the events are conceivably true and within the range of possibility. The same may be said of the romantic tales in which, after astonishing but not impossible adventures, the lovers are united and live on in a timeless happiness as if they had come direct from the heart of fairyland. These romantic tales, having sloughed off the supernatural, are the direct ancestors of the romantic novella and of the modern love story.

In a considerable number of these romantic tales we find a faithful wife who goes on a long search for her husband—a thoroughly realistic search filled with high adventure instead of magic and mystery.[25] There are also stories in which a princess is won by cleverness, but the interest there is in the keenness of wit rather than in the romantic conclusion. Two realistic

---

[24] For a discussion of the literary treatments of this story, see Bolte-Polívka, II, 451.
[25] For these tales, see p. 109. below.

tales, however, have their main interest in bringing about a happy marriage, even though the means adopted may seem to the modern sophisticated reader unnecessarily violent. In both of them a shrewish wife is reformed.

The first of these stories is King Thrushbeard (Type 900). In its main lines it seems to have developed in the Middle Ages, probably in Italy. It has been popular with literary taletellers since its appearance in a German poem of about 1260.[26] It is in the Icelandic *Clarussaga* of about 1330. In Italy, in addition to its appearance in earlier novelle, it is told as one of the numbers of Basile's *Pentamerone*. Within a definitely limited area the tale has been rather popular in oral tradition. It is known from Iceland to the western borders of Russia but apparently has not been carried to any other continent. Philippson, in his definitive monograph on the tale, comes to the conclusion that it was probably invented in Germany. On the other hand, Kaarle Krohn, after reviewing all of the evidence, feels sure that the homeland must have been Italy.[27]

A king sends out invitations for suitors to woo his daughter. Either as a reply to this invitation or because he has seen a picture of the princess (sometimes in a forbidden chamber), a prince falls in love with her and appears as her suitor. The princess has no mind to get married and treats her suitors shamefully. Among other things she calls them by ugly names. She repulses the prince and calls him King Thrushbeard. In spite of her unwillingness, the princess is forced to marry. Sometimes her father in anger compels her to marry the first man who comes along, and this turns out to be a beggar. Sometimes the seeming beggar is really the disguised prince, who wins the princess by solving riddles or by gaining admission to her room, or, in some cases, really winning her love. After the princess and the beggar are married, her father banishes them. She is then compelled to endure great hardship—poverty, menial work, begging, peddling, and eventually service as a maid in the king's kitchen. As a climax to her shame, she attends the wedding of the prince. But he reveals himself in good time as the man who has masked as her beggar husband, and they celebrate their wedding together.

This story inevitably calls to mind Shakespeare's *Taming of the Shrew*. And, indeed, that tale has had some popularity as an oral story (Type 901).[28] The dramatist has kept very close to the main outlines of the folktale. It will be recalled that the husbands of three sisters wager as to whose wife is the most obedient. The youngest of the sisters is a shrew. The husband proceeds to bring her to submissiveness by his own outrageous conduct:

---

[26] "Diu halbe bir" by Konrad von Würzburg; see von der Hagen, *Gesamtabenteuer*, No. 10.

[27] Ernst Philippson, *König Drosselbart*; Kaarle Krohn, *Übersicht*. See also: E. Gigas, "Et eventyres vandring," *Literatur og Historie*, 3 saml. (København, 1902); A. H. Krappe, *Etudes italiennes*, II, 141-153.

[28] See Wesselski, *Märchen des Mittelalters*, p. 216, No. 24; Köhler, *Kleinere Schriften*, I, 137, III, 40.

shooting his horse and his dog and treating her to all kinds of indignities. The tale goes back to the Exemplum literature of the Middle Ages, where it appears in Juan Manuel's *El Conde Lucanor*. It was also retold by Straparola in the sixteenth century. Whether from these literary forms or otherwise, it is popular in the folklore of the Baltic states and Scandinavia. It has also been reported from Scotland, Ireland, Spain, and Russia, and has been heard from a Zuñi Indian in New Mexico. It would seem most reasonable to suppose that we have here a literary tale which has become a real part of the folklore of northern Europe.

6. TASKS AND QUESTS

PROMINENT in the action of a very large number of folk stories is the performance of difficult, and sometimes impossible, tasks and quests. Frequently such compulsory labors form only a subordinate part of the story,[1] the principal interest of which is an extensive plot in which these tasks are of only incidental importance. In contrast to such tales there are some half a dozen in which the performance of tasks or the accomplishment of quests is the most important event of the entire action.

The quests on which the heroes of folktales set forth are frequently impossible or strange, but none stranger than those undertaken by The Youth Who Wanted to Learn What Fear Is (Type 326). The hero has heard of fear but does not know what it is. He goes out on a search for it and tries various frightful experiences which have been suggested to him. He plays cards with the devil in a church; he steals clothes from a ghost; he spends the night under a gallows, and another in a cemetery; he stays in a haunted house where dead men's limbs fall down the chimney; he overcomes ghostlike cats; he plays ninepins with a dead man whose members have been reassembled; he cuts the devil's fingernails; or, lastly, he has himself shaved by a ghostly barber. In spite of all his efforts he fails to discover fear. Later, after his marriage, he learns what fear is when cold water is thrown on him or when eels are put down his back while he is asleep.

In exactly this form the story does not have any early literary treatments. Straparola in the sixteenth century wrote a story about a boy who went on a

---

[1] Among such stories already discussed are the following: Jack the Giant Killer (Type 328), The Devil's Riddle (Type 812), Tom-Tit-Tot (Type 500), The Three Old Women Helpers (Type 501), The Monster's Bride (Type 507A), Ferdinand the Faithful and Ferdinand the Unfaithful (Type 531), The Devil as Advocate (Type 821B), The Healing Fruits (Type 610), The Gifts of the Dwarfs (Type 611), The Two Travelers (Type 613), The Three Oranges (Type 408), and The Wolf (Type 428). Still to be discussed are the following: The Prince and the Armbands (Type 590), The Spinning-Women by the Spring (Type 408), The Journey to God to Receive Reward (Type 460A), The Journey in Search of Fortune (Type 460B), The Prophecy (Type 930), The Dream (Type 725), Three Hairs from the Devil's Beard (Type 461), The Clever Peasant Girl (Type 875), The Son of the King and of the Smith (Type 920), and The Master Thief (Type 1525).

quest for death, and one of the Icelandic sagas tells of a similar journey to find out what anger is.[2] As an oral tale in very much the form we have outlined it is present throughout the European continent, in the British Isles, and in Iceland. It seems to be popular in all parts of this area, and only a special investigation could determine the part of Europe where the tale may have originated. For it is certainly European: it does not occur in Asia or Africa, and where it appears in the New World it has obviously been carried by European settlers.[3]

The assignment of tasks to suitors by the father of the prospective bride is a prominent motif in several well-known stories (Motifs H310-H359). Much less usual is the imposition of tasks by the maiden herself, but this is the central motif of Grimm's tale of The Sea-Hare (Type 329). A princess is possessed of magic windows which give her the power of seeing everything. She assigns her suitors the task of hiding themselves from her. Those who fail have their heads placed on stakes before the palace.[4] After his elder brothers have lost their lives in this attempt, the youngest undertakes the task. He receives the help of grateful animals or, in some versions, of an old man. With their aid he hides himself in a raven's egg and in the belly of a fish, but the princess discovers him even there. As a last resort he has himself transformed into an insect under the princess's hair. In her anger she breaks her magic windows and thus loses her power. The youth is eventually disenchanted and marries the princess.

The tale is made up of a great many motifs which are mere folktale commonplaces: the suitor tasks, the helpful animals, the successful youngest son, transformation and disenchantment, and the final happy marriage. Nevertheless, the outlines of the tale are distinct enough wherever it is known. Nowhere can it be said to be popular, but some versions occur in most countries from Iceland to the Caucasus. It does not seem to have had any literary treatment, nor to have been carried to other continents. Its distribution would suggest that it is essentially eastern European.

Certain elements of the tale just discussed are found in a story which is popular in Norway but is apparently confined to that country. In this tale of The King's Tasks (Type 577) it is the king who imposes tasks on his daughter's suitors. The youngest son, through his kindness to an old woman, receives magic objects and information, and with these succeeds where his elder brothers have failed.

The assigner of tasks in folk narratives is sometimes the hero's father. In a story made popular through its literary handling by Madame d'Aulnoy

[2] For these literary references, see Bolte-Polívka, I, 32 and 37.

[3] It has been reported from the Zuñi Indians and from the Spanish-speaking peoples of New Mexico, from the Missouri French, from the Cape Verde Islanders in Massachusetts, and from British tradition in Virginia.

[4] An old and familiar motif, appearing both in Greek mythology and in medieval romance; see Motif H901.1.

in 1710 under the title The White Cat (La Chatte Blanche [Type 402]), the youngest of the three brothers succeeds best in the quests set by his father. The youths are sent out to bring back the best of various things— the most beautiful bouquet, the finest of chains, the best of bread, the smallest of dogs, the finest of horses, and finally the most beautiful bride. The hero is helped by an animal, frequently a cat, but sometimes a mouse or frog. She eventually changes herself into a beautiful maiden and marries him.

The Grimms use this plot for two of their stories, one with a frog and the other with a cat as the transformed heroine. Except for this inconsistency in the kind of animal who acts as the hero's helper, the story maintains a clear and vigorous tradition in the folklore of all of Europe. Somewhat more than 300 versions have been recorded. Two variants are known from Armenia and one from North Africa; otherwise it seems to have remained in Europe.

Two tales of quests are so much alike that it is convenient to consider them at the same time. In both stories a king sends his sons out on a quest; in both the youngest succeeds and eventually overcomes the treachery of his elder brothers. The first of these tales is The Bird, the Horse, and the Princess (Type 550). At night a bird steals golden apples from the king's orchard, but while doing so drops a golden feather. The king orders his sons to find the bird. As in so many tales of this kind, the two elder boys are discourteous to animals or to an old woman and fail, but the youngest, because of his kindness, receives their help. As the brothers leave, they find a place where three roads part and where inscriptions on each tell what will happen if that road is chosen. Each brother chooses a different road. The hero reaches the tree of the golden bird, but he finds that he may not have the bird until he undertakes further quests. He succeeds in accomplishing these, receives a magic horse, wins a princess, and, along with the magic bird, reaches home. His elder brothers rob him and throw him into a well or a den. He is helped out by a friendly fox or wolf to which he feeds meat. The fox is decapitated and becomes a prince. The hero is restored to his wife and possessions.

This story has a considerable literary history. With slight variations it is known in the Thousand and One Nights and has appeared since that time frequently in literary reworkings.[5] The story is, however, so well established in the oral repertory of taletellers in practically every country of Europe, and fits in so well with the general spirit of many other common oral tales that its essentially popular nature seems unmistakable. It is quite as well known in Scandinavia as it is in Italy and Russia and the Baltic states, and, indeed, all the rest of Europe. It is almost equally popular in western and southern Asia, where it appears in a number of versions in Armenia, India, Indonesia, and central Africa, and is told by the French in Missouri. With so many Asiatic versions balanced against so many European, it is quite impossible,

[5] For a discussion of the literary history of the tale, see Bolte-Polívka, I, 511.

without exhaustive study, to hazard a guess as to where this tale may have originated.

From the general likeress of plot, the identity of many details, and the similarity of the geographical pattern of their occurrences in folklore, it seems reasonable to suppose that this tale and that one which the Grimms called The Water of Life (Type 551) have had much the same history. A mere hasty comparison of the several hundred versions of each of the tales is not sufficient to determine which of these gave rise to the other or whether two stories with the same basic outline have, in the course of time, converged into something like twin types. Future research will doubtless clarify the mutual relation of these stories. It would seem that the first has much the older literary history and is known in Asia. The second has no Asiatic distribution, but has been carried to both North and South American continents.

The plot of The Water of Life, as its name indicates, concerns a quest for a magic healing water or for some other marvelous remedy. The sick or blind king sends his three sons out on this quest. As in the other tale, the two elder brothers are unkind and the youngest kind to animals or an old person. With their aid he succeeds where his brothers have failed. He not only secures the water of life (or of youth), but he also reaches a magic garden where he sees a princess asleep. He lies by the princess and on his departure, writes his name, leaves it with her, and returns home.[6] As in the other tale, his treacherous brothers rob him and throw him into a well or den and he is helped by the fox or wolf. The princess comes seeking the father of her child. After overcoming the treachery of the elder brothers she finds the hero and marries him.

7. FAITHFULNESS

WHETHER in the oral folktale or in the most highly developed literary narrative, the interest of reader or hearer is always carried along by the interplay of contrasting forces, the good and the evil, the clever and the stupid, hero and villain, the faithful and the unfaithful. Every serious tale with any complication of plot has characters whose fortunes we follow with sympathetic concern in their conflict with others whom we do not like and whom we consider as enemies not only of the hero, but of ourselves.

Of the qualities which bring about universal admiration for a character in fiction, none is more compelling than faithfulness. Usually the folktale deals with a faithful relative—a wife or sister or sweetheart. We have already found Psyche and women of her kind going on long wanderings or enduring

---

[6] It will be noticed that the entire episode with the sleeping princess appears also in quite another connection in the story of The Hunter (Type 304).

hardships in order finally to restore their husbands or lovers.[1] Or it may be that the interest is in the faithfulness of a man to a woman,[2] one friend to another (Type 470), or a servant to a master (Type 516), or a sister to a brother (Types 450, 451).

A. FAITHFUL WIFE SEEKS HER HUSBAND

A favorite theme in the romantic literature of the Middle Ages was that of the wife who, in spite of misunderstandiugs and often of hardship and abuse, seeks her husband and at last finds him after many adventures. The tales vary only in the nature of the undeserved sufferings of the wife and of the circumstances under which the husband is recovered. They appear not only in medieval literature, but in that of the Renaissance as well; not only in the romances, but in the novelle and later in the drama. Eventually these literary tales were adapted to the purposes of the oral story-teller, though they have never become popular and cannot in any sense be thought of as a product of folklore.

Two of them are interesting because Shakespeare has written plays about them. In *Cymbeline* he tells the story of The Wager on the Wife's Chastity (Type 882). The merchant who wagers with the ship captain that he can seduce the captain's wife secures through treachery a token of her unfaithfulness. When the captain, believing her false, leaves home, she follows him, disguised as a man, and is eventually able to show him his mistake. This story, more than the others of this group, is known in the folklore of a number of European countries. Sporadic examples have been also picked up in Sumatra, in the Philippines, and from Cape Verde Islanders in Massachusetts.

The other Shakespearean play which uses this general motif is *The Merchant of Venice*, but the dramatist has actually used only the Pound of Flesh incident which gives title to the tale (Type 890). Though the literary history of the story is interesting, it is not to our purpose here.[3] In oral form, however, it seems to be current in the folklore of Norway and Iceland and not to be dependent upon Shakespeare's treatment. As told in Norway, it concerns a merchant who buys a bride in Turkey for her weight in gold. In order to get the money, he gives as security a pound of his own flesh. After they are married he is away from home and three merchants seek the love

---

[1] These faithful women appear in Cupid and Psyche (Type 425); The Two Girls, the Bear and the Dwarf (Type 426); Hans my Hedgehog (Type 441); The Maiden in the Tower (Type 310); and The Prince as Bird (Type 432).

[2] We have already seen examples of fidelity in husbands or lovers who have sought to recover or to disenchant their wives or sweethearts. Such tales have been: The Man on a Quest for His Lost Wife (Type 400); The Man Persecuted because of His Beautiful Wife (Type 465); The Princess Transformed into Deer (Type 401); The Three Oranges (Type 408); and The Prince Whose Wishes Always Came True (Type 652).

[3] For a discussion of these matters, see Köhler, *Kleinere Schriften*, I, 211f.; Bolte-Polívka, III, 517ff., Cosquin, *Etudes folkloriques*, pp. 456ff.

of his wife. She deceives them all and gets much money for keeping the matter secret. She decorates the house for her husband's homecoming, but he misinterprets her act and casts her out, either into the sea or onto an island from which she is rescued by a ship. She clothes herself in men's clothing and arrives in Turkey where she finds her husband in prison and brings about his release. His creditor demands the pound of flesh, but she appears as a judge and frees him.

The other tales[4] of this group belong so definitely to the literary tradition and their appearance in folklore is so restricted that they can hardly be thought of as folktales at all. For some reason the only peoples who have admitted such stories into their oral repertories are the Finns, the Lithuanians, and the Russians.

B. FAITHFUL SISTER

Of tales concerned primarily with the experiences of faithful sisters, the best known are undoubtedly Little Brother and Little Sister (Type 450)[5] and The Maiden Who Seeks Her Brothers (Type 451). The latter story forms the basis of three of the tales in the Grimm collection.[6] In spite of the minor variations of treatment thus indicated, the tale-type is well defined in all its major incidents. A number of brothers (sometimes seven, sometimes twelve) have a younger sister. The boys are compelled to flee from home. In some versions the parents have promised to kill the sons if a daughter is born to them; the brothers discover this and when the mother lets them know by a sign that a girl has been born, they leave home. Sometimes the reason for the flight from home is the fear the boys have for their father or stepmother. The next stage of the story is the transformation of the brothers into ravens. This occurs sometimes because of a wish of the father or stepmother and sometimes because their younger sister has plucked twelve (seven) flowers from an enchanted garden. The sister knows of the transformation and undertakes to find them. She asks her direction of the sun, moon, and stars, and finds the brothers on a glass mountain.[7] In some versions she succeeds in disenchanting them there, but in others she is compelled to remain speechless for a certain number of years and to make shirts. In these latter versions the speechless girl is seen by a king, who marries her. On the birth of her children, they are stolen, and she is accused of killing them.[8] The conclusion

[4] For these other tales, see The Man Boasts of His Wife (Type 880); Oft-Proved Fidelity (Type 881); The Innocent Slandered Maiden (Type 883A); The Punished Seducer (Type 883 B); The Forgotten Fiancée (Type 884); and The Faithful Wife (Type 888).

[5] For a discussion of this story, see p. 118, below.

[6] The Twelve Brothers (No. 9), The Seven Ravens (No. 25), and The Six Swans (No. 49).

[7] This quest is almost identical with that undergone by Psyche (Type 425) and by The Man on a Quest for His Lost Wife (Type 400).

[8] For this experience with the king and for the wife accused of killing her children, see The Maiden Without Hands (Type 706).

of the story is perhaps its most characteristic part: as she is about to be executed, her period of silence elapses; the raven brothers fly down and are disenchanted and all is cleared up. Sometimes the disenchantment of the brothers takes place when she throws over the head of each of them the shirt she has been making for him.

The story has a long literary history. It was used as early as 1190 in the *Dolopathos* of Johannes de Alta Silva and it became connected with the legend of the Swan Knight.[9] It appears in Basile's *Pentamerone*, and this may indicate the presence of an oral Italian version in the early seventeenth century. However that may be, the tale is included in folktale collections from all parts of Europe, in considerably more than two hundred versions in all. Except for one Armenian variant and a borrowing from the French by the Thompson River Indians of British Columbia, the tale has not been reported outside of Europe.[10]

C. FAITHFUL SERVANT

One of the most interesting of all folktales, Faithful John (Type 516), is concerned with the fidelity of a servant, though sometimes instead of the servant some versions may tell of a brother, a foster brother, or a faithful friend.[11] The tale, which has been given definite study by Rösch,[12] is about a prince who is reared with the servant who is to be his later helper, a boy of nearly the same age but of lower social standing. In the absence of his father the hero disregards the advice of his helper and enters a forbidden chamber. There he sees the portrait of a beautiful maiden, his future bride, and he is overcome with love for her and resolves to win her. Through the cleverness of his helper he succeeds, either by enticing her aboard a merchant ship, by stealing into her presence in women's clothes, or by securing access to her through an underground passage; or the servant may woo her on behalf of the prince. On the return journey the prince and his bride undergo three perils which have been contrived either by the father of the princess or by the hero's own father or stepmother. A considerable variety exists in the nature of the perils mentioned in the different versions of the tale. The couple may undergo danger because of poisoned food or clothing, or when they meet robbers or encounter a drowning person, or when they cross a stream or pass through a certain door. The last of the perils is the entrance of a snake into the bedchamber of the bridal pair. The faithful servant learns of

---

[9] For a discussion of these literary treatments, see Bolte-Polívka, I, 432.

[10] At this point may be mentioned a tale, current only in Norway, The Children of the King (Type 892), of a sister who is slandered but who succeeds eventually in proving her innocence to her brother.

[11] The faithful friend, sometimes a "blood brother," appears in The Two Brothers (Type 303); see also Motifs P311, P312.

[12] *Der getreue Johannes.*

these perils, usually through the conversation of birds, and strives to prevent them. In warding off the danger from the snake he touches the prince's sleeping wife and he is immediately accused of treachery toward his master. Since those who told him about the perils forbade him absolutely to speak of them, he must either maintain silence or disobey them. He explains the situation to his master and justifies his conduct, but he is immediately turned to stone because of his disobedience. The only way the faithful servant can be restored to life is through the blood of the prince's own children. This sacrifice is eventually made and the servant is restored. The children are then resuscitated.

This story is of rather frequent occurrence in all countries from Portugal to India. Rösch considers that the kernel of the story is the attempt on the part of the servant to save his master and the misunderstanding that results. Stories of this kind have been recorded in India for the last two thousand years. In this connection Rösch considers significant such tales as that of the faithful but misunderstood dog who is killed when he tries to save his master's child from a snake.[13] There are also stories of a faithful but misunderstood minister of state. More fully developed forms of the tale appear also in India, especially in the *Ocean of Story*, of the late eleventh century, and in some recent oral versions. Rösch studies in some detail the relationship of this story with the romance of *Amis and Amiloun,* which has the turning to stone and the disenchantment by the blood of the children. He concludes that the story of Faithful John was developed from material coming originally from India and from the Amis and Amiloun motifs, and that this composition took place in Hungary. He explains the striking similarity in the Portuguese and Hindu tales by supposing that they were carried directly by Portuguese colonists from India to Portugal.

Kaarle Krohn,[14] after examination of the same material, comes to radically different conclusions. He obviously thinks of the tale as very old in its relatively complete form. He suggests that it spread westward all the way from India to Portugal throughout all the intervening countries and that the form found in India and in Portugal (but not between) represents the original form of the story as it spread over the whole area. Variants in between are to be explained as later developments. The Amis and Amiloun tale he thinks of as a specialized literary treatment of Faithful John and not as a source of the folktale. Krohn's conclusions seem much more reasonable than Rösch's, since it assumes a greater age for the fully developed tale and adequate time for its dissemination and special developments.

In the tales of the Grateful Dead Man (Types 505-508) we have seen that the hero is rewarded by securing the services of a faithful servant who is none other than the grateful dead man himself. In nearly all of these tales one of

[13] For a discussion of this incident and others relating to it, see Motif B331.
[14] *Übersicht,* pp. 82ff.

the chief of these services of this faithful servant is the overcoming of difficulties in the way of the hero's successful marriage. One of these tales, not hitherto mentioned, seems to have developed in Russia, from which a few versions have spread to countries immediately adjacent. Because of the resemblance to the Germanic story of Brunhilde it is sometimes called by that name. In this tale of The Strong Woman as Bride (Type 519) a prince and his faithful and extraordinary companion woo a bride who is beautiful, strong, and warlike, and who will have as a husband no man who is not her equal in strength. The prince must wield her gigantic weapons and ride her untamed steed. By substitution of his companion, this is accomplished. On the bridal night she lays her feet and hands on the prince and almost stifles him. He asks permission to go outside and in the darkness the helper substitutes himself and overcomes the princess. The rest of the story concerns the princess's revenge after she discovers the betrayal. She cuts off the feet of the helper and drives forth the prince, who becomes a swineherd. The lamed helper joins a blind man and they assist each other. They overcome a giant and compel him to show healing water. The helper, with his feet restored, returns and compels the restoration of his master.[15]

8. GOOD AND BAD RELATIVES

These tales of faithful servants and faithful relatives nearly always imply the presence, and sometimes active machinations, of their opponents. In a considerable number of folktales the deeds of the wicked are far more than incidental; they constitute the central interest in the story. Already we have seen dozens of such tales in which the adversary of the hero is supernatural.[1] But even his own relatives may have their hands against him. Mothers may plot against sons, sisters against sisters, and even wives against husbands. For some reason, to the composer of folktales, it is the woman in the family who is nearly always chosen for the part of the villain.

A. FAITHLESS MOTHER, SISTER, OR WIFE

A small group of tales, with a tendency to fade into one another and thus obscure their identity, concern the evil deeds of a faithless sister or mother. The main action in these stories is nearly always the same, the differences being found in the introductions. In The Faithless Sister (Type 315) a brother and sister have been promised to a water spirit (or some other kind of monster). After they enter the services of the monster, the sister marries him and plots against her brother. In The Prince and the Arm Bands (Type 590) a boy who is traveling with his mother finds an arm band (or a blue

[15] See A. von Löwis of Menar, *Die Brünhildsage in Russland* (Leipzig, 1923).
[1] Pp. 23 ff., above.

belt) which gives him supernatural strength. They find lodgings with a giant, who persuades the mother to marry him. Later the mother joins the giant in his plot against the boy. Whether the young man's opponent be his mother or his sister, a succession of attempts is made against his life. Because of his strength, he defeats the giant. The mother or sister feigns sickness, and sends the boy on a quest for lion's milk. Because of his great strength he succeeds, not only in getting the milk, but in bringing the lions along with him and turning them loose on the giant. Likewise, he is sent for magic apples which grow in the garden of the giant's brother. These apples will cause him to sleep, so that the brothers may kill him, but the lions protect him. On awakening from his magic sleep, he rescues a princess from the giant's castle, marries her, and lives in the castle until she leaves to go to her father, a distant king. He now returns to his mother and she beguiles him into telling the secret of his strength. She steals the belt, blinds the boy, and sets him adrift in a boat. He is rescued from his peril by the helpful lions, who restore his sight with magic water which they have seen animals use for that purpose. He eventually recovers his belt, avenges himself, and brings back his wife.

Where the sister is involved as the faithless relative, practically the same train of events may occur, though there is a good deal of variety in the details. The sending for the dangerous animals because of feigned sickness is the most characteristic trait of these two stories. This cycle of tales has not been analyzed so as to see whether that about the faithless mother is really anything more than a variant of the one about the faithless sister. They would certainly have to be studied together, because if they are not really variations of one tale, they have influenced each other profoundly.

They would seem to be primarily east European. They are found in abundance in the Baltic countries, Russia, and the Balkans (particularly Roumania),[2] and are rather well established in North Africa and the Near East. On the other hand, they are scarce in western Europe. A particularly good version of The Prince and the Arm Bands is found in Norway, and this Norwegian version is apparently responsible for the presence of this tale in almost identical form among the Chipewyan Indians of western Canada.[3]

The Faithless Sister occurs not only in the tale we have just discussed (Type 315) but also in a considerable number of versions of The Dragon Slayer

[2] Schullerus, in his survey of Roumanian tales, lists all his 22 versions of The Prince and the Arm Bands (Type 590) under 315A, where it might well belong.

[3] It was a study of the relation of this Norwegian and Chipewyan tale which helped mark the beginning of my interest in the North American Indian tales, and which eventually led to my study, *European Tales Among the North American Indians* (1919) and *Tales of the North American Indians* (1929). Dr. Pliny Earl Goddard had sent this Chipewyan tale to the late Professor Kittredge for his opinion as to where it may have come from. Professor Kittredge happened at the moment to be working over some Roumanian variants of the same tale. He read the letter to a seminar of which I was a member and discussed the interest of the problem and later encouraged me to study it. I have never learned whether he went further with the study of this story in southeastern Europe.

(Type 300). In that story the hero is often a shepherd with a sister who later joins his enemies and plots against him.[4]

A story much resembling these two of the faithless mother and faithless sister is found in eastern Europe, where it is usually known as The Faithless Wife (Type 315B*).[5] This story begins with the well-known rescue of a princess from a dragon. The hero marries the princess, but she falls in love with another man. She deceives her husband into giving up his magic weapons and plots against his life. A magician teaches him how to take the form of a horse, a tree, and a duck.[6] The wife always recognizes him and orders the horse to be killed, the tree to be cut down, etc. Through the help of a servant girl the husband regains the magic weapons, avenges himself on his wife and her lover, and marries the servant girl.

Another tale of a faithless wife which is especially popular in eastern Europe is The Tsar's Dog (Type 449*), a modification and perhaps an adaptation of the story of Sidi Numan from the *Thousand and One Nights*. The central point of the story concerns the untrue wife who turns her husband into a dog in order that she may more easily desert him and go with her lover.[7]

If there is any doubt as to the Oriental and literary origin of The Tsar's Dog, there can certainly be none of another faithless wife story, The Three Snake Leaves (Type 612). That tale appeared in the Buddhistic legends of both India and China and became a part of the repertory of medieval monks in their collections of exempla.[8] Nevertheless, it has frequently been recorded as an oral folktale in all sections of Europe, as well as in India and Indonesia. This story begins with the hero's promise to his bride that if she dies before him he will be buried with her. Shortly after the wedding this happens, and in the grave he sees a snake revive another with leaves. By imitating the snake, he resuscitates his wife. In some other forms of the tale the wife is restored to life in reply to a prayer on condition that the husband give up twenty years of his own life. Sometimes the tale closes at this point, but frequently it proceeds as follows: the wife falls in love with a shipmaster and the two of them throw the husband into the sea. He is drowned, but is

[4] For a list of these versions, see Ranke, *Zwei Brüder*, p. 381. He lists 52 versions ranging from Brazil to the Caucasus.

[5] For references, see Balys, *Motif-Index*, p. 26 (37 Lithuanian); Schullerus, *Verzeichnis der rumänischen Märchen*, p. 35 (3 Roumanian); Afanasief, *Narodnie Russkie Skazki* (1938 ed.), II, 606, Nos. 208-209 (3 Russian).

[6] This whole incident is strongly reminiscent of the Egyptian story of The Two Brothers; see p. 275, below.

[7] The obvious resemblance of this story to *The Golden Ass* of Apuleius and indeed all other relationships of this story are discussed in Walter Anderson's *Roman Apuleya i Narodnaya Skazka* (Kazan, 1914), I, 376-487, 612-633; see also Afanasief, *Narodnie Russkie Skazki* (1938 ed.), II, 627, Nos. 254, 255; Bolte-Polívka, III, 122.

[8] For a discussion of the tale, see Gaston Paris, *Zeitschrift des Vereins für Volkskunde*, XIII, 1-24, 129-150; Polívka, *ibid.*, XIII, 399; Bolte-Polívka, I, 126; Wesselski, *Märchen des Mittelalters*, p. 188.

resuscitated by a faithful servant, who uses the snake leaves. The guilty pair are suitably punished. There is considerable difference in the motivation of the variants of this story. In some, the story-teller is obviously most interested in the marvelous cure and its discovery; in some the central point is the willingness of the husband to give up twenty years of his own life in order to recover his wife. But whether it is the central point or not, all of them emphasize the ingratitude of the wife.

Of cruel relatives in folktales the stepmother appears more often than any other.[9] We have already found her as an incidental part of several stories, and she will appear later on in the Cinderella cycle and elsewhere. In one story at least the stepmother's cruelty is the very center of the interest. The Juniper Tree (Type 720), with its bird song, is best known to the world as a German tale, not only because Faust's Marguerite sings it in prison, but because in the Grimm collection it is told in a dialect which has caught the attention of most readers of that collection. As in a number of folk stories, the father takes a second wife against the advice of his child. In this story the stepmother is very cruel to his little boy. Her own daughter, little Mary Ann, however, is fond of the boy and helps him all she can. One day while the father is away the stepmother closes the lid of a chest on the boy and kills him. She cooks him and serves him to his father, who eats him unknowingly. Little Mary Ann gathers up the bones from under the table where the father has thrown them and buries them under the juniper tree. The next day a bird comes forth from the grave. The bird goes to various places and sings a song about the murder.[10] He receives presents, which he takes back to the juniper tree. He drops a ring for his sister, slippers for his father, and, at last, a millstone on the stepmother. At her death the bird becomes a boy again.

The song seems to be the most persistent part of this tradition. There are a relatively small number of European tales in which songs are an essential element, and their relation to the popular ballad is obvious. As for this story, it does not appear in any of the literary collections and it would hardly seem to have any connections with literature except its use by Goethe. As an oral tale, it is popular in all parts of Europe, and sporadic versions, certainly the result of travelers or colonists, are found in North Africa, South Africa, and Australia, and among the Louisiana Negroes. The almost purely oral nature of this tradition, along with the interesting combination of prose and verse, should make this tale a very profitable subject for comparative study.

The fact that the stories just treated are concerned entirely with the cruelty of women[11] does not mean that fathers and brothers are always kind. But the interest in such tales is most frequently in the way these cruel relatives

[9] See Motif S31 for a list of tales including cruel stepmothers, and also a bibliography.

[10] For other stories about the way in which murder comes to light, see pp. 137, below.

[11] A sufficient number of examples of cruel mothers-in-law will be found in the tales of substituted brides and banished wives, the next subject of our discussion. See Motif S51 for references.

are defeated, rather than in the cruelty itself. Elder brothers are particularly wont to plot against the youngest in the family, and frequently a woman finds that she is married to an ogre or a cruel husband.[12]

B. SUBSTITUTED BRIDE

Though the story of the substituted bride[13] sometimes concerns the treachery of a servant girl[14] or some other rival of the heroine, its most characteristic form is that in which a sister or stepsister, usually aided by her mother, takes a wife's place without the knowledge of the husband and banishes the wife. This substitution by the sister occurs in two of the most widely known of folktales, The Black and the White Bride (Type 403) and Little Brother and Little Sister (Type 450). Because of their similarity the tales have influenced each other so that although the plot is clear enough for the most characteristic forms of each, many versions lie on the border line between the two.

A very common opening for The Black and the White Bride is the Kind and Unkind motif (Q2). The stepdaughter, hated by her stepmother, is sent to perform an impossible task, usually the gathering of strawberries in the middle of winter. She is kind to the dwarfs[15] she meets and in gratitude they bestow on her the gift of great beauty and the power of dropping gold or jewels from her mouth. The woman's own daughter is unkind under these conditions and is cursed with hideousness and made to drop toads from her mouth. In some versions the help does not come from dwarfs but from a witch, or even from the Lord. The heroine is seen in all her beauty by a king (prince), who marries her. After the marriage the stepmother plots against her and, on the birth of her child, throws her and the child into the water. The woman's own ugly daughter is substituted for the bride without detection. The heroine is transformed to a goose (or other animal). The child is cared for by animals or sometimes is kept in the court.[16] The mother, in her form as fowl or animal, comes to the king's court three times, frequently in order to suckle her child. On the third appearance the king awakes[17] and succeeds in disenchanting her by cutting her finger and draw-

---

[12] For this whole subject of cruel relatives in folktales, see Motifs S0 to S99, and K2210 to K2219.

[13] For the literature of the subject and an analysis of the various forms in which the motif appears, see Motif K1911 and all its subdivisions. The definitive treatment is P. Arfert's *Motif von der unterschobenen Braut.*

[14] The servant girl as substitute bride we have already met in The Goose Girl (Type 533) and in The Three Oranges (Type 408).

[15] We shall find these same helpful dwarfs taking care of little Snow White (Type 709).

[16] As to the treatment of the child, there is sometimes confusion with the tale of The Three Golden Sons (Type 707).

[17] For the awakening of the husband from a magic sleep on the third appearance of his wife who has sometimes purchased the privilege of sleeping with him, see Motifs D1971 and D1978.4 with all the references there given. In addition, it sometimes appears in Cupid and Psyche (Type 425) and in The Three Oranges (Type 408).

ing blood, or by holding her while she changes form. At the end always occurs the reinstatement of the true bride and the punishment of the villains.

In a considerable number of the variants, a brother takes a prominent part in the story. He is in the service of the king, who sees a picture of his beautiful sister. Sometimes the girl is summoned to the court and a substitution takes place on the way, where the girl is thrown overboard from a ship. The tale with this introduction (Type 403A) would seem to be influenced by the story of Little Brother and Little Sister, and the episode of the picture is at least similar to the introduction to Faithful John (Type 516). In a form of the tale very popular in Estonia (Type 403C), but apparently not known elsewhere, the husband recognizes the deception and throws the false bride under a bridge. From the girl's navel grows a reed in which her mother recognizes her own daughter.

Much more frequently the tale appears without the brother, with the quest for strawberries, the helpful dwarfs, the substituted bride, and the eventual recovery and reinstatement (Type 403B, or simply Type 403). It is this form that is known over a large part of the world. Not only are several hundred versions found in all parts of Europe, but it has gone to almost every part of central and southern Africa, and to widely scattered tribes of North American Indians. It is told in India and the Philippines and has been carried by the French to Canada, by the Spanish to Mexico, by Cape Verde Islanders to Massachusetts, and by Negroes to Jamaica. Among both the Africans and the American Indians there exist tales with somewhat similar plots, so that some confusion has arisen by those who have discussed these borrowed stories.[18] In spite of many points in common, the most reasonable explanation of these primitive tales is an independent development from particular centers on the two continents.

In some ways the story of Little Brother and Little Sister (Type 450) may be thought of as a mere variant of the tale just discussed. The brother and sister are turned out into the woods by their stepmother, who is a witch. The experience of the children in the woods is vaguely reminiscent of Hansel and Gretel (Type 327). The boy is overcome with thirst and, in spite of the warning of his sister, drinks from a small pool of water. This pool has been enchanted by the stepmother, so that the boy is turned into a roe. The sister remains with the enchanted boy in the forest. She is eventually seen by a king, who marries her.[19] The tale now proceeds with the substitution of the stepsister in the young wife's place, the disenchantment of the wife, punishment of the impostor, and eventual disenchantment of the brother.

The relation of this story to The Black and the White Bride is obvious,

[18] For these North American Indian tales, see Thompson, *Tales of the North American Indians*, p. 350, notes 262 to 265. Many of these contain the incident of the return by the dead mother to suckle the child. See p. 362, below.

[19] This incident occurs not only in this tale, and The Black and the White Bride, but also in Our Lady's Child (Type 710).

especially to Type 403A, but the tradition seems to be very well recognized in just this form, so that the tale must be considered as more than a mere variant of that story. It was told in Italy as early as the seventeenth century, since it appears in Basile's *Pentamerone* (1634-36). It is well represented today in Italy, the Balkans, Russia, the Baltic countries, and Germany. It also appears in the Near East, and as far away as India. Several versions have been reported from North Africa and three from central Africa. It does not appear to have been brought to the New World.

Though both of these tales of substituted brides are very popular in oral folklore, neither seems to have entered into the earlier literary collections of tales. Only in Basile are they found, and they have all the appearance of being oral Italian stories which he has reworked. A thorough investigation of these two tales should prove very interesting because of the seeming independence from the literary tradition, the close relation of detail between the two stories, and the wide geographical range of the versions.

The motif of the substituted bride also forms the central action of two stories, closely related to each other, in which the impostor is not a sister, but merely a rival. One of these tales, The Princess Confined in the Mound (Type 870), seems to be essentially Scandinavian, for the versions are plentiful in all the Scandinavian countries, including Iceland. It also occurs, though not frequently, in the folklore of Finland and Germany.[20]

Because of her faithfulness to her betrothed, a princess, along with her maid, is confined by her father in an underground prison or mound. After many years, she escapes and takes service as a maid in the king's castle, where she finds that her lover is about to be married. The woman who is to be the bride forces the heroine to take her place at the wedding. This may be because she wishes to conceal her pregnancy or merely because of her hideousness. The heroine has agreed not to reveal the truth to the prince, but on the way to the church she does reveal it by some subterfuge. Sometimes she talks to her horse, or to the bridge they are crossing, or to the church door, and thus reminds the prince of his first love. That evening when the bride, who has resumed her own clothes, comes to the prince, she is unable to recall the conversation which has taken place on the way to church, and she must always consult with the maid. When the prince asks to see the necklace which he had given her immediately after the wedding, the truth comes to light. He drives her away, and marries his faithful sweetheart.

The Little Goose Girl (Type 870A)[21] is very much like this tale. A little girl who is herding geese accosts a prince who is passing by and tells him that she is going to be married to him. She hears of his approaching wedding and

---

[20] The tale has been studied in great detail and with a very elaborate set of maps by Waldemar Liungman (*Prinsessan i Jordkulan*). He favors Denmark as the place of origin.

[21] See Liungman, *Två Folkminnesundersökningar*. The tale seems certainly of Scandinavian origin.

attends. As in the other story, the bride persuades her to act as substitute. But the substitution takes place in the marriage bed, since the prince has a magic stone by his bed that indicates the bride's chastity. The recognition the next day is brought about by means of the ornaments which he has given his bed partner.

This second story as a folktale is confined to the Scandinavian peninsula. But it appears also in ballad form not only in Scandinavia, but also in France and in Scotland. In the latter country, at least eight versions have been recorded.

C. BANISHED WIFE OR MAIDEN

The same hostile forces which frequently bring about the replacement of the true bride by the false are often responsible for the invention of slanders or for other machinations which result in the banishment of an innocent wife or maiden. Four popular and widely distributed tales have this central motivation, and still others have developed in particular areas.[22] This theme of the banished wife was popular in the literature of the Middle Ages, and sometimes appeared in forms very close to those found in oral tradition today.[23]

Most closely related to the tragic story of Constance, as Chaucer has made it known to the literary world, are The Maiden Without Hands (Type 706) and The Three Golden Sons (Type 707). These two tales have in common the motif of the wife who is accused of giving birth to animals or monsters. The Maiden Without Hands always begins by telling how the heroine has her hands cut off and is abandoned to her fate. The reasons for this cruel punishment differ widely as the tale is followed from one area to another. It may be because she refuses to marry her father,[24] or because her father has sold her to the devil (S211), or because, in spite of his commands, she has persisted in praying, or because of the jealousies and slanders of her mother-in-law or sister-in-law. Whether she is abandoned in the woods or on the sea, she is observed by a king[25] who takes her home and marries her in spite of her mutilation. For the second time, she is cast forth with her newborn chil-

---

[22] The whole subject of the outcast child, including both banished daughters and banished sons, has been discussed in some detail by E. S. Hartland (Folk-Lore Journal, IV, 308). He makes the following divisions: (1) the King Lear type, dealing with the adventures of the king's three daughters; (2) the value of salt type, concerned only with the adventures of the youngest daughter; (3) the Joseph type, in which a boy or girl is banished because of dreams of future greatness. The fourth and fifth types record the career of an only son who has fallen without reasonable cause under his father's anger. Of these types, the third will be discussed in section IX, p. 138, below. The fourth and fifth are represented by Types 671 and 517.

[23] An excellent discussion of this whole cycle of literary tales is found in Margaret Schlauch's Chaucer's Constance and Accused Queens (New York, 1927).

[24] An incident which we shall find in Type 510B.

[25] See Motif N711 and all its subdivisions for references to other tales in which this incident appears.

dren because one of her relatives has changed a letter announcing their birth, so as to make the message announce the birth of monsters. This central incident will be familiar to all readers of *The Man of Law's Tale*. The way in which the heroine has her hands restored and is eventually reunited to her husband is handled with considerable variety, both in written and oral versions. Sometimes also, as in Chaucer, there is reduplication of the banishment.

The literary treatment of this general theme begins as early as the year 1200 in southern England. Between that time and the seventeenth century it received not fewer than seventeen distinct literary handlings,[26] including those in Chaucer and Gower and in the romance of *Emare*. With slight variations, it appears in the *Thousand and One Nights* from which it has entered the Arabic oral tradition. Basile tells the story in his *Pentamerone* and it forms the subject of a special group of south Slavic folksongs.[27] Whatever may be the relation of the oral tale to the well-known literary treatments, there can be no doubt as to the popularity of the theme among unlettered storytellers. Few collections of any extent in all of Europe from Ireland to eastern Russia fail to have this story. It is known in the Near East and in central Africa, but has not been noted in the tales of India or lands beyond. In America it has not only been taken over by the Micmac and Wyandot Indians but has been carried by the French to Missouri and by Cape Verde Islanders to Massachusetts. It has reached Brazil and Chile in South America. The oral tale is so popular and so widely distributed that it deserves more study than it has yet received.

Even more popular is the other tale of the calumniated wife, The Three Golden Sons (Type 707). Though no adequate investigation has been given to this story, it is clear that it is one of the eight or ten best known plots in the world. A cursory examination of easily available reference works shows 414 versions, an indication that a thorough search might bring to light several hundred more. These are found in practically every European tale collection. In Asia they have been reported from almost every quarter of Siberia, from the Near East, and from India. It is well established in all parts of Africa. In America three traditions are represented: the French among the French Canadians and the Thompson River Indians, the Portuguese in Brazil and among the Cape Verde Islanders in Massachusetts, and the Spanish among the Tepecano Indians of Mexico and in the white tradition of Chile.[28] It does not seem to have a long literary history, since the oldest version appeared in the six-

---

[26] For a listing of these, see Bolte-Polívka, I, 298ff. The whole tale has been studied by Däumling (*Studie über den Typus des Mädchens ohne Hände*, München, 1912) and the Comte du Puymaigre (*Revue d'histoire des religions*, Sept.-Oct., 1884; summarized in *Mélusine*, II, 309).

[27] For these, see Bolte-Polívka, I, 306.

[28] For a study of the Chilean versions of the tale, see Rodolfo Lenz, "Un Grupo de Consejas Chilenas, Estudio de Novelística comparada" (Santiago, 1912); see also Espinosa, *Journal of American Folklore*, XXVII, 230.

teenth century in Straparola's *Nights*. In the early eighteenth, Madame d'Aulnoy and Galland both published it, the former using a tale based upon Straparola and the latter reporting one which he had heard in Arabic. The story would seem to belong almost entirely to folklore rather than to litera-ture. Its distribution would suggest European origin, though a thorough study might conceivably show that the dissemination was in the other direc-tion.

Over the entire area the story appears with considerable uniformity. As in The Maiden Without Hands, the king marries a girl whom he happens to meet. Here, however, we usually have three girls who make their boasts as to what would happen if they should marry the king. The king over-hears the youngest of the girls say that if she were the queen she would bear triplets with golden hair, a chain around their necks, and a star on their fore-heads. After the king has taken her as wife her sisters plot against her. They substitute a dog for the newborn children and accuse the wife of giving birth to the dog. The children are thrown into a stream, but they are rescued, sometimes by a miller or a fisherman. The wife is imprisoned,[29] or banished. After the children have grown up, the eldest one sets out on a quest. The reason for his undertaking the quest varies much in the different versions. He may go out to try to find his father or to seek the speaking bird, the singing tree, and the water of life.[30] On his quest the eldest brother fails and is trans-formed into a marble column. The second brother has the same experience, and it remains for the youngest (sometimes a sister) to rescue them. The kindness and consideration of the latter secures the help of an old woman, and eventually the disenchantment of the brothers and the possession of the magic bird and the magic objects. When all have returned from the quest, the king's attention is attracted by means of the magic objects, and the bird of truth reveals to him the whole story. The children and wife are restored and the sisters-in-law punished.

Another tale which has many points in common with The Maiden With-out Hands (Type 706) is Our Lady's Child (Type 710).[31] In one way or an-other the heroine of this story secures the ill will of some powerful person. In some forms of the tale she is under the special protection of the Blessed Virgin, whose enmity she incurs by falsely denying that she has looked into a forbidden room. As a punishment, the girl loses her power of speech. In other variants, instead of Our Lady, the opponent is a witch or some naturally malevolent woman; occasionally even a man appears in this role. In any event, the maiden becomes the wife of the king. But when she gives birth

[29] In some versions the wife may be thrown into a stream and transformed, as in The Black and the White Bride (Type 403).

[30] In connection with the quest, the story frequently shows the influence of The Three Hairs from the Devil's Beard (Type 461).

[31] The oldest known version of this story, that in Straparola's *Nights*, is a thorough amalga-mation of the two tales.

to children, she is punished by having them stolen one by one. Only when she finally acknowledges her guilt are they returned to her.

This tale shows so much variation from the time it appeared in Straparola in the sixteenth century and a hundred years later in Basile that its history might be difficult to work out. It shows frequent contamination with other tales, especially The Maiden Without Hands, and the uncertainty of whether we are dealing with a pious legend of the Blessed Virgin or with a story of a cruel witch has introduced many inconsistencies into the tradition. It is known in all parts of Europe, the Near East, North Africa, and Jamaica, but seems nowhere to have achieved great popularity. On the whole, the witch as the foster mother seems to be better known than the Blessed Virgin. The central incident of the loss of the children, as well as the marriage of the king to a girl who has been mutilated or disabled, makes understandable the confusion of this tale with the two just discussed.

Before leaving the tales of slandered wives, mention should be made of a story which has been reported only from the Scandinavian peninsula, Born from a Fish (Type 705). As in the tale of The Two Brothers (Type 303), a man catches a magic fish which he is to feed to his wife. Instead, he eats it himself and becomes pregnant. A girl child is cut out of his knee. The child is carried off by birds and lives in a bird-nest. The story now proceeds like others of this group: she is seen by the king who marries her; her children are stolen away and she is driven forth. The ending is unusual. The king, realizing his mistake, seeks for his banished wife. She is found by means of a riddle which could apply only to her: a fish was my father, a man was my mother.

The main action of the four tales which we have just examined—the discovery of the persecuted maiden in the woods or a tree, her marriage to the king, the slander concerning the birth of her children, the loss of the children, the abandonment of the queen, the eventual discovery of the truth, and the reunion of the family—is so uniform that there has been much transfer from one tale to the other, if, indeed, they are all essentially different stories. In the brief summary of the plots, a number of widespread motifs, found now in one and now in another, have escaped our notice. Among these are the casting off of the wife and child in an open boat (S431.1) and the accusation of murder supported by the evidence of a bloody knife left in the queen's bed (K2155.1.1).[32]

The banished girl in our European folktales is frequently a young maiden, like Snow White.[33] The motivation in this story (Type 709)[34] is the jealousy of the stepmother who learns from her speaking mirror that Snow White is

[32] For other motifs belonging here, see cross references assembled at Motifs S400, S410, and S431.

[33] Aside from Snow White and The Maiden Without Hands, we shall find Cap o' Rushes and others of the Cinderella cycle being cast out. See also Motif S301 with all its references.

[34] See Böklen, *Sneewittchenstudien*.

even more beautiful than she. The hunter who has been ordered to kill her substitutes an animal's heart and lets her go.[35] Or sometimes she is sent directly to the house of dwarfs or robbers where the stepmother expects her to be killed. She is kindly received by the dwarfs, who adopt her as a sister. The stepmother learns Snow White's whereabouts from her magic mirror and succeeds, often after several trials, in poisoning the girl. Sometimes this is by means of poisoned lace and a poisoned comb; finally, after the dwarfs have revived her from her first two poisonings, the stepmother succeeds by means of an apple. The dwarfs lay the maiden out in a glass coffin. A prince sees her and orders his men to carry the coffin. They stumble and thus dislodge the apple, so that the girl revives. She marries the prince, who sees to it that the stepmother is given a horrible punishment.

The version just outlined is essentially that given by Grimm. The tale appears without great variation over a considerable area—from Ireland to Asia Minor and well down into central Africa. Except for one Portuguese version in Brazil, it does not seem to have come to America. The story appears in two variations in Basile's *Pentamerone*, and it is likely that the oral tradition has been greatly influenced by this literary treatment. Böklen also shows that there has been extraordinary borrowing from other tales with similar motifs. There are also many resemblances to older mythical stories, but how significant these are in the actual history of the tale may be doubted. In spite of Böklen's detailed analysis of the stories, he has made little attempt to reach conclusions about its origin and history.

In the last few years this story has come to the attention of millions of children and adults through the remarkable treatment in the cinema version of Walt Disney. This was based directly upon the Grimm text.

Much less well known than Snow White is the tale of The Wonder Child (Type 708). It seems to be most popular in Scandinavia, though there are scattered versions as far away as Hungary and Brittany. Through the magic power of a witch stepmother, sometimes merely by a curse and sometimes by being fed a magic apple—a princess gives birth to a monster son. She is driven forth into the forest or abandoned in a boat on the sea. The monster son develops miraculous powers. He helps his mother in her work of spinning at a castle. He accompanies a prince in search of a bride, or on a hunt. When they are cast in prison together, the boy promises to rescue the prince if the latter will marry his mother. Though the prince imagines that the mother must be a monster also, he consents. He rejoices to find her like other people. At the wedding, the monster is disenchanted when his mother calls him her son. In some versions the disenchantment occurs when his head is cut off.

---

[35] The compassionate executioner appears in a number of stories from the time of Joseph on down; see Motif K512 with all its subdivisions. We have already met it in the tale of The Three Languages (Type 671).

A study of this last tale might show some very interesting results. Though its area of distribution is relatively small and though it is nowhere especially popular, the tale seems well enough recognized to constitute a real tradition. No literary versions have been noticed, so that we are apparently dealing with something which is essentially, if not entirely, oral.

D. SUCCESSFUL YOUNGEST CHILD

In a large proportion of the stories of substituted brides and of persecuted wives or maidens the heroine who undergoes these sufferings and who finally triumphs is the youngest sister who is brought into contrast with her cruel or haughty elder sisters.[36] Likewise, in a whole group of the tales which we have noticed, the youngest son plays a similar role.[37]

This contrast between elder and younger child does not always play a subordinate role in folktales, but in one of the most famous of all groups is all-important in the action of the story. The whole group is sometimes known as the Cinderella cycle, even when we are dealing with a hero.[38] It is normally true that in all tales of this kind the youngest child is also especially unpromising, either because of appearance, shiftless habits, or habitual bad treatment by others. But even though such qualities are emphasized in the narrative, it is never forgotten that the distinguishing quality of these heroes and heroines is the fact that they are the youngest.

The tale known in the Grimm collection as Frau Holle (Type 480) tells how the despised youngest daughter[39] sits spinning by a well and loses her shuttle in the water. Being scolded by her mother, she jumps into the well to recover it. She loses her senses and awakes in the lower world. In reply to various appeals, she milks a cow, shakes an apple tree, takes bread out of an oven, and the like. At last she takes service with a witch, and she is so industrious that she pleases the witch, for she performs all tasks assigned her with the help of the animals and objects which she has obeyed. As a reward, she is given a large amount of gold (sometimes in a casket) and is allowed to return home. The ungracious sister wishes to imitate, but she refuses to help the animals and objects. Instead of a casket of gold, they cause her to choose a casket filled with fire, or in some versions kill her as a punishment.

This general theme of the two daughters, one kind and the other unkind, has already appeared prominently in the story of The Black and the White

---

[36] In cases where the contrast is not with elder sisters it is usually with stepsisters.

[37] For the victorious youngest daughter, see Motif L50, where a list of the tales containing this trait is given. Similarly for the victorious youngest son, see L10.

[38] Some authors have used the term "male Cinderella" for such younger and unpromising sons.

[39] In many versions she is the stepdaughter and is made to contrast with the stepmother's real daughter.

Bride.[40] There it was merely the introduction to the story of the substituted bride. But in Frau Holle the contrasting action of the two girls in the lower world and their appropriate rewards is the whole story, and there is every tendency to elaborate the details. Basile told the tale in two different forms in his *Pentamerone*, and it received further literary treatment by Perrault. All of these authors added to the wealth of detail, and it has received much independent elaboration wherever it has been told.

It is one of the most popular of oral tales, being distributed over nearly the whole world. It is found in almost all collections from every part of Europe, from southern and eastern Asia, from northern and central Africa, and from North and South America. In the western hemisphere it occurs in three widely separated American Indian tribes; in the French folklore of Louisiana, Canada, the West Indies, and French Guiana; and in the Spanish tradition of Peru and the Portuguese of Brazil. A cursory examination of appropriate bibliographical works shows nearly six hundred versions. A serious study, which we hope may sometime be undertaken, would probably bring to light many hundreds more.

One special development of this tale, found only in eastern Europe, tells how the devil demands entrance into the house. But, on advice of the helpful animals, the girl demands that he bring her various things until the night has worn away and he must depart.[41]

Possibly to be considered as a special variation of Frau Holle is a tale of which only six versions have been noted—Basque, French, Danish, and Swedish. In this story, The Presents (Type 620), the haughty sister is the one who goes forth first. She succeeds, by means of the old woman's help, in being given a castle and becoming queen. Because of her haughtiness she is driven forth. The other sister makes better use of her presents, which bring her all good fortune.

Probably the best known of all folktales is Cinderella (Type 510A), particularly if we include its special development known as Cap o' Rushes (Type 510B). These tales were not only included in the influential collections of Basile and Perrault, but they both have an even older literary history. A good Chinese literary version of Cinderella has been reported from the ninth century after Christ,[42] and Cap o' Rushes has appeared in both French and

---

[40] Type 403. This motif (Q2) is usually known as "Kind and Unkind." Among other tales in which it is found are: Bearskin (Type 361); The House in the Wood (Type 431); The Frog King (Type 440); How Six Travel Through the World (Type 513A); The Bird, the Horse, and the Princess (Type 550); The Water of Life (Type 551); The Grateful Animals (Type 554); All Stick Together (Type 571); The King's Tasks (Type 577); The Healing Fruits (Type 610); The Presents (Type 620); and The Three Golden Sons (Type 707).

[41] See Bolte-Polívka, I, 221ff. for a list of these versions. Though some seventy are mentioned, they are all from countries between Bohemia and the Caucasus. See Motif K555 and its various subdivisions.

[42] For a discussion of this version, see R. D. Jameson, *Three Lectures on Chinese Folklore*, pp. 45ff.

Italian literary treatment from the beginning of the sixteenth century. This pair of tales was the subject of Miss Cox's *Cinderella* which appeared in 1893 and was the first extensive investigation ever made of a folktale.

In Cinderella the heroine is abused by her stepmother and stepsisters. Her name is always connected in some way with ashes (Cendrillon, Aschenputtel, or the like), indicating her lowly position in the household. The poor girl receives supernatural aid, sometimes from her dead mother, or from a tree on the mother's grave, or from an animal (often a reincarnation of the mother), or from a fairy godmother. In some versions the helpful animal is killed, and a tree springs up which magically provides beautiful clothes for the girl. As in the familiar Perrault telling, she may dance three successive nights with the prince and escape just before the forbidden hour. Some versions tell how the prince sees the girl in church. At any rate, she flees from the prince and a search for her is necessary. It is not always the lost slipper which brings about identification, but she may be found by any of the approved methods known to readers of fairy tales—a ring thrown into the prince's cup or baked in his bread, or the special favor shown her when the tree bows before her so that she can pluck its golden apple.

The version of Perrault is so familiar through two hundred and fifty years' use as a nursery tale that we are likely to think that all the details which he mentions are essential. Some of them, as a matter of fact, are practically unknown elsewhere; for example, the glass slipper. A vast majority of the versions do have a slipper, but not of glass. It has been suggested that Perrault's glass slipper comes from a confusion between the French words *verre* and *vaire*, and this may possibly be true. The fairy godmother is a relatively rare occurrence in the tale. On the other hand, traits not found in Perrault assume importance as we trace the tale around the world: the help of the dead mother, usually reincarnated as an animal, the clothes colored like the sun, moon, and stars, and the appearance of the heroine as a herder of turkeys.

This story of Cinderella appears in not fewer than five hundred versions in Europe alone. It seems to be popular in India and Farther India and has been taken without change by Europeans to the Philippines and elsewhere in Indonesia. It is found among the North African Arabs, in the Western Sudan, in Madagascar and on the island of Mauritius. It has also been well received in America. The French have brought it to Missouri and Canada, and the isle of Martinique. It has also been reported from Brazil and Chile. Especially interesting are the modifications of this story by the North American Indians, the Piegans of the Glacier Park area, the Ojibwa of the Great Lakes, and the Zuñi of New Mexico. In the latter version an almost complete adaptation to the Zuñi environment has been made. The abused daughter is a turkey herd (as in some European versions). Her turkeys take pity on her and furnish magic clothes. She attends the tribal dance and attracts the chief's son, but she disobeys her turkeys and overstays her time. They punish her by taking away all her beautiful clothes. A reader who was not familiar with the Cinderella story might well imagine that this is a native Zuñi tale. Its actual Spanish origin is unmistakable.

As Miss Cox's analysis of this cycle shows, there is very considerable mutual influence exerted between Cinderella and the related tale of Cap o' Rushes (Type 510B). This story begins with the flight of the heroine from home, or with her banishment, because her father wishes to marry her (as in the tale of The Maiden Without Hands [Type 706]). Or it may be that, like Cordelia in *King Lear*, she does not reply as her father wishes when he asks her how much she loves him. She says that her love is like salt, in contrast to her sisters who have compared theirs to sugar.[43] In either case, the heroine assumes a peculiar disguise, indicated by the various titles of the stories, not only the two mentioned here, but others like Katie Woodencoat, Allerleirauh, etc. She takes service among strangers and is accidentally seen by the prince in her own beautiful clothes. The story then proceeds much like Cinderella. Frequently there is the thrice repeated flight from the prince and the elaborate recognition after the search for the girl. This latter is usually brought about by means of a ring placed in his food or drink, rather than by fitting the slipper. In those stories where it is appropriate, the heroine shows her father how much more valuable salt really is than sugar. The interesting way in which all these motifs shift as we go from version to version and yet maintain the essential plot is skillfully displayed in Miss Cox's detailed analysis.

This tale has been made popular in the world of readers by treatment in every important literary collection of stories since the sixteenth century— Straparola, Basile, and Perrault. But its wide acceptance in the folklore of the whole area from Scandinavia to India would seem, for the most part, to be independent of these literary treatments. While not so universally told as its companion story, Cinderella, well over two hundred oral versions have been noted by folktale students. But only a single variant each from Africa and the two Americas have thus far come to light.

So closely related in detail to Cinderella and Cap o' Rushes that it is frequently considered a variant form is the story of One-Eye, Two-Eyes, Three-Eyes (Type 511). Of the three sisters, the heroine is the only one with the normal two eyes. Her monstrous sisters, One-Eye and Three-Eyes, are in league with their mother against her. She is compelled to herd goats and to go hungry. She secures the aid of an old woman who provides her with a food-supplying table which she can use with the aid of one of her goats which has magic power. In the course of time, her sisters spy upon her and kill the goat. On the advice of her old woman helper she has the goat's entrails buried and from them there grows a magic tree with golden apples. The tree

---

[43] This motif, "Love like Salt," sometimes appears as a separate tale (Type 923), and, with a slight variation, in another (Type 923A). See Motif H592.1 and literature there cited.

will yield its fruit only to Two-Eyes, into whose hands the apples come of themselves. When a prince asks for some of the apples the sisters fail and only Two-Eyes can give them to him. The tale naturally ends with her marriage to the prince.

It seems unlikely, in spite of Dr. Krappe's contention,[44] that this modern European folktale has any organic connection with the old Greek myth of Phrixos and Helle. There are, however, literary versions of our story in Germany and Sweden from the sixteenth century down. Though it is by no means as popular as either Cinderella or Cap o' Rushes, it is distributed rather evenly over the whole of Europe. It is also known in India, Indonesia, North Africa, and Madagascar. A version from English tradition has recently been reported from Virginia.

What may be considered a variation of this story is the tale of The Little Red Bull (Type 511*).[45] In this tale there is always a youth instead of a girl as the principal actor. He is helped by a magic bull (sometimes a horse) which provides food for him. When his enemies kill the animal he follows his helper's last instructions and keeps some part of the animal's body, through which he receives magic aid in all his adventures. Sometimes these adventures are the same as those of the hero of the *Goldener Märchen* (Type 314), and some folktale students have considered The Little Red Bull as a variant of that tale. Its wide distribution, however, and its relative uniformity would seem to indicate that we have here an autonomous tale and not a mere variation of some more popular story. Though in small numbers, it is scattered over the entire continent of Europe and is found in India, North and Central Africa, and among the Wyandot Indians of North America. Its peculiar distribution and its relationship to the two tales here indicated should make this story worth further investigation.

Although many examples of the fortunate youngest son have appeared in other connections in some of the tales we have already examined and in those to come later,[46] one story of a "male Cinderella" deserves special mention here. In The Prodigal's Return (Type 935) the youngest of the three brothers is a spendthrift, but clever. He goes abroad as a soldier and swindles his father into sending him money. Through cleverness he makes his fortune and marries a princess. He visits his parents' home in humble disguise and is mistreated by his brothers. At the end, the princess arrives and puts the jealous brothers to shame.

[44] A. H. Krappe, *Folk-Lore*, XXXIV (1923), 141ff.

[45] For discussion see: Bolte-Polívka, III, 65; *Béaloideas*, II, 268, 273.

[46] Among other places, the favorite youngest son is found in the following tales: The White Cat (Type 402); The Bridge to the Other World (Type 471); How Six Travel Through the World (Type 513); The Bird, the Horse, and the Princess (Type 550); The Water of Life (Type 551); The Grateful Animals (Type 554); The Knapsack, the Hat, and the Horn (Type 569); All Stick Together (Type 571); The King's Tasks (Type 577); Beloved of Women (Type 580); The Healing Fruits (Type 610); and The Three Lucky Brothers (Type 1650).

In Europe this story seems to be entirely confined to the Baltic states and Denmark, where it has been collected in large numbers. But its presence in America among the Micmac Indians and among the Missouri French gives every indication that it was brought across the ocean by Frenchmen. In Missouri it has been skilfully combined with the tale of The Youth Who Wanted to Learn What Fear Is (Type 326).

9. THE HIGHER POWERS

A. JUSTICE

ESSENTIAL in the action of nearly all the folktales which we have been reviewing is the contrast between the evil deeds of malevolent persons and the commendable activity of the heroes or heroines of the tale. For the whole area of Europe and the Near East it seems to be a well established characteristic of the folktale that in such conflicts good shall eventually triumph and wickedness receive a fitting punishment.[1] These punishments are often horrible enough, but they are always justified for the teller of the folktale by the reflection that the villain was planning just such punishments himself and that he is getting exactly what he deserves.

1. God's Justice

But villains and wicked persons in general are subject not only to the revenge of those whom they have plotted against. There is also a higher justice. From his seat in the heavens, God looks down and bestows his blessings on the righteous and metes out stern justice on all trespassers of the Divine Will. The ways of the Almighty often seem dark, but a real insight into his activities will always show perfect justice. So it is in The Angel and the Hermit (Type 759), where the angel takes the hermit along with him and does many seemingly unjust things. He repays hospitality by stealing a cup, inhospitality by giving a cup, hospitality again by throwing his host's servant from a bridge and by killing the host's son. Later the angel demonstrates to the hermit how, in the light of a full knowledge of each case, all these acts were just. This was one of the most popular of the exemplary tales used by the priests in the Middle Ages, and it is still frequently told as a folk story, particularly in Ireland, Spain, and the Baltic states.

Such mysterious divine punishments are sometimes manifested in a dream. In a tale known in the Baltic countries and in Russia, The Punishments of Men (Type 840),[2] a man and his son pass the night in a strange house. The

[1] For a detailed account of such punishments, see Motifs Q200-Q599.

[2] A good example of this tale may be found in L. A. Magnus, *Russian Folktales* (London, 1915), pp. 151-3.

son is unable to sleep and observes queer things happening all about him. A snake creeps from the sleeping man's mouth into his wife's mouth. Or a snake is lying between the man and his wife. The details of these mysterious manifestations vary considerably, and sometimes they are seen in a dream rather than in a waking state. In any case, the master of the house explains the next morning the justice of each of the appearances.

The literature of the medieval exemplum is filled with stories of people punished in hell. Only a few of these have become known to folktale tellers. The Estonians and Finns tell a story of a cruel rich man who has to serve as the devil's horse (Type 761). He sends his son a letter warning him against a similar fate.

This story is seldom heard, but another tale of punishments meted out by the devil in hell has great popularity with European story-tellers and has been used as a subject by a number of writers of Russian short stories. This tale, which we may call The Three Green Twigs (Type 756), appears in three special forms. The first of these is The Self-righteous Hermit (Type 756A), known, but not very popular, in various parts of Europe. As a man is being taken to the gallows a hermit remarks that he has been punished justly. For his self-righteousness the hermit is assigned penance: he must wander as a beggar until three twigs appear on a dry branch. In the course of his wanderings he tells the story of his misfortunes to a band of robbers and so impresses them that they are converted. Thereupon the green twigs appear, and his penance is over. This is the least well-known of the three forms of the story.

With the second tale of this group, The Devil's Contract (Type 756B), sometimes called The Legend of the Robber Madej, we pass to one of the most popular tales of eastern Europe. It has been reported in not fewer than twenty-five versions from Germany, fifty-four from Poland, sixty from Russia, forty-eight from Lithuania, and twenty-one from Bohemia, not to speak of scattering occurrences far out into Siberia and as far west as Ireland and Spain. The general outline of the tale is as follows: A boy has been sold to the devil before his birth. When he grows up he takes a journey to hell in order to recover the contract. On his way he sees a hermit from whom he inquires as to the direction to hell. The hermit sends him on to his brother, who is a famous robber. The robber takes the boy down to hell. There the young man obtains his contract and observes the fiery bed or chair already waiting for the robber. On his return the boy tells the robber what he has seen. His brother the hermit now assigns the robber penance, which he must continue until his staff puts forth fresh blooms and fruit. Eventually this happens, and the robber, assured of forgiveness, dies happy. His brother the hermit is astonished at this manifestation of God's justice. In some versions he reconciles himself, but in others he blasphemes God and is damned.

In his investigation of this story, Andrejev[3] considers that we have here a combination of three different stories of the kinds which were popular in legendary literature of the Middle Ages: a tale of the boy who is given over to the devil, a story of a miraculous penance, and a tale of a self-righteous hermit. In the self-righteousness of the hermit this story resembles the first tale of this group. In spite of the fact that the principal distribution of The Robber Madej is nowadays in eastern Europe, Andrejev is convinced that it was constructed in the late Middle Ages in western Europe and spread from there. It has interested the eastern Europeans so much that today it has the appearance of belonging primarily in that area.

The third tale of this group, which we may call The Greater Sinner (Type 756C), also deals with a severe penance. In some versions the sinner has murdered ninety-nine men, in some he has killed his parents, and in some he has shot at a consecrated wafer. He vainly seeks a confessor and only after a long wandering does he succeed in getting penance assigned. He must plant a firebrand and water it daily with water brought from a distance in his mouth. And he must plant a garden and offer free hospitality to everybody. In some versions he must carry a bag of stones on his back, a stone for each murder. Or he must wear an iron hoop on his head till it falls off. Or he must pasture black sheep until they become white. After many years of penance he intercepts a man who is about to commit a great crime. To prevent this greater crime, he kills the man. Thereupon he is shown divine favor, for his firebrand blooms, or the stones or the hoop fall off, or the sheep turn white. His confessor tells him that in payment for the last murder all his sins have been forgiven.

Andrejev has also studied this tale,[4] which has an entirely different distribution from The Robber Madej. In spite of the resemblance of the two stories, the author is convinced that they have no organic relationship and that the analogies are purely casual. Especially noteworthy is the fact that The Robber Madej is entirely unknown in the Balkan countries, whereas Andrejev's evidence points to the south Slavic countries as the original home of The Greater Sinner. The tale seems to be essentially oral, though it has received frequent modern literary treatment in Russia.

The pious literature of the Middle Ages is filled with cases of mysterious punishment, but these have not generally entered into folklore. Where they have, the Baltic states have seemed most receptive. For example, the Legend of Polycarp (Type 836), who boasts that God has not power to make him poor and who returns home from church to find that his house has burned and that he is reduced to poverty, has become a legendary tale in Estonia, Lithuania, and Finland. Apparently confined to Estonia is a story of retribution, How the Wicked Lord was Punished (Type 837). The lord puts

---

[3] *Die Legende vom Räuber Madej.*
[4] *Die Legende von den zwei Erzsündern.* In 1928 he decided on a Moslem origin.

poison into the beggar's bread. As the beggar is spending the night at an inn, a traveler arrives and since no other bread is convenient, the beggar gives the stranger his bread. The traveler is the lord's son. He dies of the poison.

Several other tales of mysterious punishment are also found in the Baltic states, where story-tellers seem to be fond of such moralistic legends.[5] One such story, The Punishment of a Bad Woman (Type 473), tells how the man is kind to a beggar but the wife unkind. The beggar later invites the man to him and shows him many mysterious things, among them his wife transformed into a cow. Another tale is The Dishonest Priest (Type 831) in which a priest tries to frighten a poor man out of his money by masking in a goatskin. When he gets home the skin has grown to him. Something like Polycarp is The Boastful Deer-slayer (Type 830) who shoots a stag but denies that God has given it to him and insists that he shot it himself. The wounded stag jumps up and flees. Finally, in this small group of tales, is one which preaches against greed, The Disappointed Fisher (Type 832). The fisher, his wife, and his child always catch three fishes. From greed, they kill the child in order to have more fish for themselves. But from then on they never catch more than two.

Similarly popular in the Baltic states, but known also in most other parts of Europe, is the story of The Rose from the Stone Table (Type 755).[6] The preacher's wife magically prevents the birth of her children. Since she therefore throws no shadow, her husband casts her forth as a sinner until a rose shall grow from a stone table. Another churchman takes the woman at night into a church. The children appear and forgive their mother. They go back home and the rose springs forth.[7]

In the eyes of the story-teller, the woman who prevents the birth of her children is looked upon as wicked and joins the ranks of the other evil mothers in fairy tales. Of such, we have had sufficient example in a number of complex stories.[8] One simple tale in which this is the principal motif appears among the Estonians, the Finns, and the Lapps, The Mother Who Wants to Kill Her Children (Type 765). The father succeeds in rescuing them, and hides them away, though the mother thinks that they have been killed. After many years they come forth and the mother dies of fright.

Such are some of the tales of divine justice which have appealed to oral story-tellers enough to become a part of folklore. It is certain that if all col-

---

[5] That these stories are found only in Estonia, Lithuania, and Finland may have no significance other than the fact that collectors took them down when they heard them. It is probable that at least some of them exist elsewhere, but that they seem so different from the ordinary folktale that collectors have neglected them. 831 is also Russian and Czech.

[6] In his study of this tale (*Euphorion*, IV, 323-333), Bolte cites many Norwegian, Celtic, Romance, German, Czech, and Little Russian versions. The tale has received literary treatment in Lenau's *Anna*.

[7] The resemblance of this sign of forgiveness to The Three Green Twigs (Type 756) is obvious.

[8] For some examples, see pp. 113., above.

lectors had been interested in recording this kind of material, the number of such stories would be much greater. While in Ireland several years ago I heard a story recorded by a Connemara peasant on phonographic records. The telling consumed more than half an hour and consisted entirely of an account of the unfortunate results of losing one's rosary. So far as I know, this story has not been published, but is in the archives of the Irish Folklore Commission.

2. *Wishes Rewarded and Punished*

One of the purposes of the good teller of folktales is to see that wickedness is properly punished. It is not always easy to discover the unworthy or the evil-doing. But, as all story-tellers know, one of the best ways to search the heart is to see what use one will make of unlimited power. If a person is naturally modest and kind, such power will be only a strength; but if he is overbearing and unkind, it will certainly bring about his downfall. So it happened in the amusing old story of The Fisher and His Wife (Type 555). As it is told in the German-speaking and Slavic countries, and occasionally in France and Spain, a poor fisher catches a fish who is really a transformed monster. He heeds the pleas of the fish to be put back in the water and is rewarded by the promise that all the wishes of the fisherman's wife shall be granted. In the Italian versions, and sometimes in the French, the granting of these wishes is secured in another fashion: the husband climbs a beanstalk to heaven,[9] and there secures this concession either from God or from the doorkeeper of Paradise. In any case, the wife begins to use her wishes. The principal point of the story consists in a description of the increasing extravagance of the wife's wishes and their amazing consequences. She wishes to be a duke, then king, then pope. When at the end she aspires to be God himself, she loses all her good fortune.

As we have indicated, this story is well known in both eastern and western Europe. It has been carried by the Spanish to Puerto Rico and by the Dutch to the East Indies. In Indonesia it is told alongside of similar tales, presumably native, but parallel to a story current in Japan.[10] In this tradition it is also brought into close relation with a cumulative story known as Stronger and Strongest (Motif Z41.2). A peculiar development of The Fisher and His Wife in a few variants among the Russians and Letts has the man as the maker of the foolish wishes.

Whereas The Fisher and His Wife would seem to be essentially an oral tale, the story of The Wishes (Type 750A), which the Grimms call The Poor Man and the Rich Man, has a long and somewhat complicated literary background. As usually told by the peasants of Europe, it belongs to the

---

[9] Like Jack with his beanstalk; see Type 328.
[10] For discussion, see DeVries, *Volksverhalen*, I, 356, No. 1; II, 356, No. 100.

series of tales about the wanderings of Christ and the saints on earth,[11] a theme frequently treated in medieval literature. The other part of the story, the foolish wishes, was likewise popular in the writings of the Middle Ages, but belongs primarily to the literature of fabliaux and jestbooks.

Christ and Saint Peter are wandering on the earth as simple travelers. When they ask hospitality, they are sometimes refused and sometimes gladly entertained. In either case, the hosts are rewarded by being given the power of fulfilling three wishes. The story is very little concerned with the wise and successful wishing of the hospitable peasant. But the story-teller lingers on the foolish use made of the three wishes, and the consequent discomfiture of the man who has been unkind in his treatment of strangers. Three general types of foolish wishes appear in these stories. In his anger the man may make two extreme wishes (that his horse may have his neck broken, or his wife may stick to the saddle, or the like), and he must use the third wish to undo the first two. Or, frequently, he transfers his first wish to his wife, who wastes it on some trifle. In his anger, he wishes the trifle in her body, and then must use his third wish to remove it. In a third group of these tales, only one wish is given to each of the peasants, usually to keep on doing all day what one begins. The hospitable peasant begins some profitable action (getting good linen), whereas the other thoughtlessly throws water on his pig and must keep on doing it all day long.[12]

The details of these wise and foolish wishes vary a good deal, but the idea is always the same, rewards and punishments, based upon magic, for treatment accorded to holy or supernatural persons. In spite of the saints' legend atmosphere, the whole intent of the tale is facetious. It is therefore interesting as a combination of three traditions—the wonder tale (filled with magic), the pious legend, and the humorous story. It has entered into the folklore of nearly all countries of Europe. But in its complete form it does not seem to be known elsewhere. The three foolish wishes, not connected with the saints' legend, is also found over practically all of Europe and has analogues in Indonesia and Korea.

A very similar tale of Hospitality Rewarded (Type 750B) tells how the pious beggar is refused hospitality at a house where a wedding or other festival is going on, but he is graciously received in the home of a peasant, who kills his only cow to entertain his guest. The peasant finds that his cow has been brought back to life, or that in its place a number of new cows have appeared. This story is known over a good part of Europe, but the details differ considerably. Von Sydow has shown[13] that this goes back to a legend of Saint Germanus, which is found in Nennius as early as the eighth century,

---

[11] For other tales of this kind, see p. 150, below.
[12] For the literary history of the foolish wishes, see Bolte-Polívka, II, 213; Bédier, *Fabliaux*, pp. 212ff. and 471. See also Motif J2071 with references there given.
[13] *Danske Studier*, 1910, pp. 91ff.

and which he considers to be of Welsh origin. A similar legend is well known in Scandinavian mythology in connection with Thor's journey to Utgard.

3. *Truth Comes to Light*

If the rewards and punishments given by our mysterious strangers are filled with magic and miracles, even more marvelous are the ways of divine justice in uncovering hidden crime. Even an idea usually so foreign to the peoples of western Europe as reincarnation is used to reveal a murder in the story of The Singing Bone (Type 780), which not only appears as a popular folktale but is sung as a ballad throughout northern and western Europe and the United States.[14] The details of these stories show considerable variation. Usually in the prose form we have the murder of one brother by another, whereas in the ballad we are dealing with two sisters. In any case, the murdered person is either buried or left in the water where he has been drowned. Sometimes a harp is made from various parts of the body, or a flute from a bone, or some other instrument from a tree which has grown over the murdered person's grave. The musical instrument is played in public and sings out the accusation of the murder.

How widespread this story is considered to be will depend upon the investigator's definition of the tale-type.[15] Accounts of murders revealed by some reincarnation of the victim are to be found in all parts of the world. But this motif is so simple that there would seem to be no necessary connection between primitive tales of this kind and the European tradition. Thus, the many stories cited from central Africa may well represent an independent tradition.[16] The prose tale, as told throughout Europe, does seem to have a sufficient number of common details to constitute a definite narrative entity. Mackensen feels that this prose story probably originated in Belgium, but he recognizes the great difficulty of reaching conclusions that will give proper weight to the ballad tradition and to analogous tales which may have independently arisen in remote parts of the earth.

Some of the African versions mentioned above are more properly analogous to another story of revealed murder, The Princess Who Murdered Her Child (Type 781). The hero of this tale, who understands the language of birds,[17] hears a bird above him sing, "The bones lie under the tree."[18] The murder is

[14] The ballad tradition is discussed in F. J. Child, *English and Scottish Popular Ballads*, I, 118ff. Since Child's day, many more have been collected. In the British tradition of the United States and Canada not fewer than 120 have been noted. In the ballad it is nearly always a musical instrument which betrays the murder.

[15] The most important study of this type is that of Mackensen, *Der singende Knochen.*

[16] For these African versions, see Mackensen, pp. 164ff.; also Bolte-Polívka, I, 275.

[17] For other tales in which a person is endowed with a knowledge of animal speech, see pp. 83ff., above.

[18] The singing of the little bird in The Juniper Tree (Type 720) will be recalled. He was a reincarnation of the murdered boy and sang a song about his murder.

thus brought to light. As for the European tale, it seems to be confined to Estonia and Finland, where it is well known. The African story of the revelation of the murder by the bird is certainly independent of this Baltic tradition.

There are also other European tales of murders betrayed by birds which may or may not be dependent upon the Baltic story.[19] Psychologically much more striking than any of these supernatural revelations of murder are those stories in which the slayer himself is induced, in one way or another, to betray the murder. A good representative of this group of tales is the Grimms' story, The Sun Brings All to Light (Type 960). The dying man has declared, "The bright sun will bring it all to light." On one occasion the sun shines brightly on the murderer's food and he thoughtlessly addresses the sun, "You would like to bring it to light, but cannot." His remark is investigated and the murder revealed. This form of the tale is current in Germany, the Baltic countries, and Serbia. About as frequently, the object which causes the revelation is some plant, instead of the rays of the sun. This variation is found all the way from Spain to Russia.

Perhaps more common than the betrayal by either the sun or a plant are stories in which some kind of bird causes the murderer to betray himself. Such tales have received literary treatment by many authors since classical times. They all follow in general lines the Greek myth of The Cranes of Ibycus. In this story the murdered man calls upon the cranes, the only witnesses of the murder, to avenge him. The cranes follow the murderer and point him out.[20] Though the tale appears in many literary versions, it is well established in oral tradition, especially of the romance countries and Germany. There is no doubt that these tales of The Cranes of Ibycus and The Sun Brings All to Light have been of so much mutual influence that they may properly be considered as two forms of a single folk story. In it may be found a good instance of a theme so well grounded in the belief in a higher justice that it has appealed to the essential optimism of both the learned and the illiterate and has therefore become a part not only of the European literary tradition but also, in many countries, of the native folklore.

B. PROPHECIES

A particularly important idea in the stories of murder brought to light is the power which the prophecy of the dying man exerts on the murderer. It is but one example of the strong hold which the belief in forecasting the future

[19] Most of these are definitely literary; for a listing and comparison, see Bolte-Polívka, II, 532ff.

[20] For this tale, see Motif N271.3 and the studies there listed. A large number of versions from Europe and the Orient are assembled in Bolte-Polívka, II, 532ff. and in R. Basset, 1001 Contes. For an additional Brazilian version, recently reported, see Luis da Camara Cascudo, As testemunhas de Valdivino (see Diario de Noticias, Rio de Janeiro, Jan. 15, 1939, p. 3).

continues, even in our own day, to exert on all except the most rational thinkers. That certain persons are endowed with supernatural power to look into the days to come; that the Goddess of Fortune, or at least good luck, keeps watch over some and neglects others; that the stars or the flight of birds or the condition of a slaughtered animal's liver foretells the issue of future events—all these are a part of folk faith, and when they appear in a popular story seem so natural and so worthy of belief that they are never questioned. Rather, they are cited as certain proof of the very marvels which they illustrate. For these prophesyings are never the result of logical considerations. They are never given by a person whose good sense or judgment we would trust in ordinary business affairs. And the conditions under which they are produced are those which we would recognize as least conducive to judgment and clear thinking. We shall find that the prophecies given most weight come from half-demented old men or women, from the dying, or from those who have weakened themselves by long fasting or by narcotics, and from those notorious as cheats and rascals, as well as from truly holy men who have sincerely sought to penetrate the veil of the unknown.

Even animals are valued as prophets. One old tale popular with both priests and rabbis of the Middle Ages[21] is about The Boy Who Learned Many Things (Type 517). The hero understands the language of birds.[22] One day he hears them prophesy that his parents shall humble themselves before him. He repeats the prophecy, and his parents drive him away. The boy has many adventures and becomes a great man. He returns unknown to his parents and the prophecy is fulfilled.

Though this tale has been collected orally, at least once, in practically every country of Europe, it is essentially a literary story and cannot be thought of as a product of folk imagination. We recognize clearly enough something of the biblical account of Joseph, though several other stories which we shall now look at are even closer to that legend in general outline and in detail. Such is the tale which we may call The Dream (Type 725) in which the hero, like Joseph, dreams that his parents shall serve him and that the king shall pour water on his hands. Unlike Joseph, the hero is loath to tell his dream and persistently refuses to. He has a long series of adventures. He successfully solves riddles; he performs difficult tasks suggested by a hostile prince; he overcomes his enemies and wins a princess. As in the other tale, the prophecy is fulfilled and the parents humble themselves before their successful son.

The general outline of this story is old. Whether the literary versions of the Middle Ages, such as the accounts of the life of Pope Sylvester II and of

---

[21] Among other places, the tale appears in the *Seven Sages*, in the *Scala Celi*, and some Jewish exempla collections. There are Czech and Armenian chapbooks relating this tale. For a discussion of its literary history, see Bolte-Polívka, I, 323.

[22] For several other stories about men who understand the language of birds and other animals, see pp. 83ff., above.

Pope Innocent III, are based eventually upon the Joseph tale, it has certainly long been popular.[23] As an oral legend, it seems to be told mostly in eastern Europe, especially in Hungary and the Baltic states.

By far the best known of all stories prophesying future greatness for the hero is the tale studied by Aarne under the title of The Rich Man and His Son-in-Law (Type 930).[24] At the birth of a poor boy it is prophesied that one day he will become the son-in-law of a great and powerful man—in some versions, the king; in some, a very rich man. The rich man hears about the prophecy and buys the baby from his parents, so that he can get rid of him. He makes various attempts to put the boy out of the way. He sometimes abandons him in a box on a river, or exposes him in the forest or in the mountains. The child is rescued and adopted by some humble man such as a miller, a shepherd, a hunter, or the like. When the boy is grown up, the king discovers him and again plots against him. He sends him with a letter to the queen with instructions to have him killed. On the way robbers change the letter so that the queen is instructed to give the princess to the boy in marriage. The king orders his servants to throw the first comer into a hot oven or kiln, but this time also the boy is interrupted on his way, and the king's own son arrives first and is thrown into the oven.

The tale in the form just given is very old and has an extensive literary history.[25] As Tille shows, the literary texts consist of four groups, the Indic, the Ethiopic, the west European, and the Turkish. The Indic group has the oldest texts, which go back to the third century after Christ. There is a considerable number of these versions in the literature of India, extending down to recent times. They are very true to the form outlined above, which, according to Aarne's very careful analysis, seems to be the original plot of the story. It seems plausible to conclude that the story has traveled from India to Europe. The literary Ethiopic texts are clearly based upon Greek sources. This tale began to appear in literary collections of western Europe in the thirteenth century, associated with the legendary histories of the Emperor Henry III and of the Emperor Constantine. Finally, an interesting combination of the Indic and Ethiopic traditions is found in a Turkish romance by Suhaili, written in the seventeenth century.

All of these literary versions correspond with each other in considerable detail, and are unmistakably part of the same tradition. Tille cites a Latin work going back to the first century of our era which has most of the features of this story except the initial prophecy. He is inclined to think that this form represents an earlier stage in the development of the tale than the more elaborate versions found in India.

---

[23] See Bolte-Polívka, I, 324f.

[24] *Der Reiche Mann und sein Schwiegersohn.*

[25] For an excellent discussion of this literary history, see Tille, "Das Märchen vom Schicksalskind," *Zeitschrift des Vereins für Volkskunde,* XXIX (1919), 22ff.

Alongside of literary retellings of this tale, it appears in the folk tradition of most parts of Europe, especially of the countries east of Germany. But usually the European folktale combines the story of The Rich Man and His Son-in-Law with another, in which the hero is sent on a quest to a far-off realm, usually the other world. This tale is the one which Grimm calls The Three Hairs from the Devil's Beard (Type 461). When not combined with The Rich Man and His Son-in-Law, as given above, that tale may have any one of a number of introductions, but in any case, the hero is sent by his prospective father-in-law (or by some other powerful person) on a quest to hell to bring back three hairs from the devil's beard. In all these stories, the other world is conceived of as lying beyond a great body of water. On his way, the hero is asked various questions which he shall find the answer to before he returns. He must seek to find why a certain tree does not flourish, how a certain water animal can be freed from an annoyance, how a sick princess can be cured, why a certain spring has gone dry, how to find a lost princess, where the lost key can be found, how a girl thus far avoided by suitors can marry, why certain livestock die. Finally, the ferryman to the other world wants to know how he can be freed from his duties.

When the youth arrives at the home of the devil, he is aided by the devil's wife, or sometimes his mother,[26] who assists the youth in securing not only the three hairs which he desires but also the answers to the questions. On his homeward journey he receives a large award for the answers to the questions. The envious king attempts to imitate the youth's success. He does not, of course, realize that the way in which the ferryman can be released from his tedious task is to have someone else take the oar into his hands. When the king reaches the farthest shore, the ferryman hands him the oar, and he must keep the ferry until he succeeds in turning it over to someone else.

As an independent tale, this quest to the other world is known in all parts of Europe in more than three hundred versions. It has practically no literary history, unless we consider an episode from the cuneiform fragments of the Assyrian myth of Izdubar, which, as Tille points out,[27] shows not only a general resemblance, but some striking common details.

In Europe there is a very frequent combination of The Rich Man and His Son-in-Law with The Three Hairs from the Devil's Beard. In these combinations the quest to the other world is assigned to the youth after the rich man, or the king, realizes that the youth has survived all earlier attempts to get rid of him. This combined tale is found all over Europe and as far east as China. Sporadic versions appear in northern and central Africa, among the Thompson River Indians of British Columbia, and among the Cape Verde Island Portuguese of Massachusetts. The frequency of the combined versions makes it impossible to study either of these tales alone. Both Aarne and Tille

---

[26] A common motif in ogre tales. See Motif G532.
[27] See Tille, loc. cit.

are convinced that originally the two tales had nothing to do with each other and that the combination was made in the oral tradition of Europe.

The contention that the tale of the quest to the other world is really an independent story is strengthened by the existence of two other tales of this kind which sometimes combine with The Rich Man and his Son-in-Law and sometimes appear alone. The first of these, The Journey to God to Receive Reward (Type 460A), has a peculiar introduction: A young man has heard that God returns tenfold the alms given to a poor man (Motif K366.1.1; Type 1735). He sets out on his journey to God and receives his reward. On the way he is given the questions to which he receives the answers in the other world. The related tale, The Journey in Search of Fortune (Type 460B), is much like this. A poor man who has never had good luck goes on a quest for Fortune. The questions and answers appear here just as in the tales of the journey to God and to the devil.

As independent stories these three quest tales are found in various parts of Europe, but outside of that continent they seem always to be combined with the tale of The Rich Man and His Son-in-Law. Except for this very usual amalgamation, these tales would belong properly with a group of otherworld journeys later to be discussed,[28] and not, as here, with accounts of the marvelous fulfillment of prophecies.

In our discussion of the literary background of The Rich Man and His Son-in-Law, the tales mentioned were all quite clearly a part of an unbroken tradition. Certain remoter parallels to this story are well known, both from ancient legendary history and from literature. The Hebrew legend of Joseph and the Persian of Cyrus both tell of such prophecies of greatness carried out. Except insofar as they are paralleled in the folk stories we have just studied, these legends have remained purely literary. On the other hand, one famous story coming from Greek drama keeps being repeated as an oral tale, the myth of Oedipus (Type 931). The essential points always remembered are the prophecy that the youth shall kill his father and marry his mother. He is saved after exposure and reared by another king. The prophecy is fulfilled with tragic results. This story seems to be particularly popular among the Finns and has been collected several times in Hungary and Roumania, and sporadically in Lithuania, Lapland, and from the Cape Verde Islanders in Massachusetts. The fact that it is still told as a traditional story testifies to the close affinity of this old myth with real folk tradition.

C. LUCK

In the face of so much that remains unexplained in the life of man, of so many rewards that come to the undeserving, and of so much unmerited

[28] P. 146, below.

trouble and disaster, it is no wonder that folktales should concern themselves with the working of luck. Sometimes they are interested in examples of persons pursued by misfortune and sometimes of those whose lucky star saves them from every effort of adversity. In such tales the story-teller usually seems to conceive of Luck as a personal force for good or evil, like the goddess Fortuna and sometimes like the Eumenides. But Luck has not always been treated in a mystical or even serious mood. Taletellers have rejoiced in lucky accidents in which a fool, usually also a rascal, out of mere bravado, chances into unexpected and astonishing success.

The tales of the mysterious ways in which Luck accompanies some men and refuses to follow others consist usually of a single simple anecdote. Such, for example, is the one popular in Russia, Estonia, and Lithuania, but not reported elsewhere, of The Rich Man's and the Poor Man's Fortune (Type 735). The Fortune of the rich brother gives the poor brother the advice to seek his luck under a bush. The poor man goes there and Fortune tells him to become a merchant. He does so, and gains a fortune.

Deserving of mention here are also two stories, both literary, and belonging to the *Arabian Nights* and medieval European tradition, and both occasionally told as a folktale in the Baltic countries. The first of these, Luck and Wealth (Type 736), tells of a poor man who gives a fisherman a piece of tin or other valuable which he has acquired by accident. The fisherman agrees to repay him with his first catch of fish. In the net is found a fish with a precious stone in its body.[29] The other tale, sometimes called Hatch-penny (Type 745), relates the unsuccessful attempt of the owner to get rid of a coin. The tale is told in various ways. For example, a miser being told that his hoard is to go to a poor man hides it in a trunk and throws it into the sea. It drifts to the house of the poor man, who tries in vain to restore it. Sometimes the coin is eaten by a cow which the owner happens to buy and slaughter. The center of interest in this story is the succession of unavailing attempts to avoid good fortune which persists in staying with one. This tale has received frequent handling in recent literature.

The capriciousness of luck also appears in a tale current in the Baltic countries and in Iceland, and which has also been reported from the Pochulata of Mexico, obviously from Spanish tradition. In this story, One Beggar Trusts God, the Other the King (Type 841), the two beggars are given loaves of bread by the king, who sees to it that the loaf of the one who trusts him is filled with gold. Ignorant of this, the beggars exchange their loaves and thus show that luck attends the man who trusts God. This tale has

---

[29] Much better known, of course, is the story of the Ring of Polycrates (Motif N211.1) in which a ring is thrown into the sea but is found next day in a fish which has been caught. This story comes from the third book of Herodotus and has been retold in many literary works since. It has been reported from the Gold Coast of Africa and from the Philippines. It also occurs in many versions of the European folktale of grateful animals (Type 554).

hardly a proper place in folklore at all: it was one of the most popular exemplary tales of medieval and Oriental literature.[30]

That the oral story-tellers of the Baltic countries frequently use old literary tales is immediately apparent to anyone who investigates their collections. One more good example of such use is found in the tale of The Luck-bringing Shirt (Type 844), best known to the modern world through Hans Christian Andersen's The Shoes of Happiness (Lykkens Galosher). The story appears with some slight variation. The king is to become lucky whenever he puts on a shirt which belongs to a lucky man. The only man who admits that he is lucky is so poor that he has no shirt. The story is sometimes told about shoes and, in the older forms of the tale, the search is made for a person who has never had sorrow. The resemblance between the older tales and the modern is striking in detail, however, and there seems to be little doubt that all the known versions go back for their ultimate source to a legend of Alexander as it appears in the *Pseudo-callisthenes*.[31] From this Greek legend, not only the medieval Latin stories, but also the literary Oriental tales, seem to have come. The modern versions, however, all appear to depend upon a Renaissance Italian collection of novelle, the *Pecorone* of Ser Giovanni. The story has appeared frequently in literature, perhaps most recently in Edwin Markham's poem "The Shoes of Happiness."

Disputes similar to those we have just recounted about whether luck comes from God or the king are much enjoyed by tellers of traditional stories. A good example is the tale of Luck and Intelligence (Type 945) in which a test is made as to which of these qualities is most powerful. To carry out the test, a simple gardener is endowed with intelligence. The details of the test vary somewhat. Usually, however, a princess who never breaks silence is offered to the man who can make her speak.[32] The gardener makes up a story which he tells his dog in the presence of the princess about a wood-carver who carves a beautiful wooden doll, a tailor who clothes her, and himself, the gardener, who gives her the power of speech. He asks, "To whom does she belong?"[33] The princess breaks silence, and intelligence would seem to have conquered. But the king refuses to carry out his bargain, and condemns the gardener to death. He is saved by luck.

Though this tale occurs sparingly in the folklore of eastern Europe, it clearly belongs to the Orient. Not only is it in the *Panchatantra*, an indication that it was known in India by the sixth century after Christ, but it is also

[30] See Bolte, *Pauli's Schimpf und Ernst*, II, 333, No. 326 for an exhaustive listing of these literary versions.

[31] For a discussion of this version, in relation to the whole tradition, see Köhler, *Aufsätze über Märchen*, p. 129.

[32] More usual in folktales is the task to make the sad-faced princess laugh. See Types 559 and 571.

[33] This is like the dispute of The Four Skillful Brothers (Type 653) who have cooperated in rescuing a princess.

known in the folklore of modern India, of Indonesia, and of practically every country in the Near East. Through the Arabs, it has been taken to North Africa. In many of these versions the initial dispute between luck and intelligence is not found, though it is usually implied.

The interest in the tales of luck thus far noticed has been concerned with the principle of Luck itself and its dealings with mankind. But the teller of folktales recognizes well enough that usually Luck may be assisted by cleverness or rascality. Particularly beloved are the adventures of an impostor—a well-meaning and harmless impostor, of course—who meets with an astonishing series of lucky accidents. Perhaps the story that occurs to everyone first is that of The Brave Little Tailor (Type 1640). It has a wide distribution and occurs in most countries in many variants—over 350 in all—most of them very close in general outline to the well-known version of Grimm. Some of the episodes occur independently or may be omitted from some abbreviated tellings of the tale.

The story is usually told about a tailor, but this feature is by no means necessary, since substitution of trade is very easy to the story-teller. He kills seven flies with a single stroke of his hand and in his pride puts up an inscription "Seven with One Stroke." The audacious placard comes to the attention of the king, who submits the tailor to various tests.[34] By his cleverness and audacity, he always succeeds. The king then orders him to kill two giants: he strikes them from ambush so that they fight and kill each other. He catches a unicorn by tricking it into running its horn into a tree. He also captures a wild boar by driving him into an empty church. When he is married to the princess, he forgets and betrays his calling by asking for thread. But when the soldiers are sent to take him away, he intimidates them with his boasting. Finally he goes to war for the king and when his horse runs away with him, he grasps a cross from the graveyard (or a limb of a tree) and waves it so that the enemy flee in terror.

This form of the story, popular in oral tradition all over Europe and the Near East, and known in many parts of both North and South America, seems to come from a jestbook of Montanus[35] published in 1592, though the tale was mentioned several times in the century preceding. The story is probably of Oriental origin, for a fairly close analogue is found in the Buddhistic literature of China dating from about the third century after Christ. It is probable that the many modern Oriental versions belong to this tradition.

Oriental also in origin is Doctor Know-All (Type 1641), a story of even greater popularity in all parts of Europe and Asia. It is also found in Africa and among the Negroes of Jamaica and Georgia, and the French of Louisiana. In all, more than four hundred variants are known. A peasant

[34] Some of these tests will be discussed in other places: see K18.2; K18.3; K71; K72, K1112
[35] For a discussion of the literary history of this tale, see Bolte-Polívka, I, 164f.

with an extraordinary name, Crab (or Cricket or Rat), buys the clothes of a doctor and puts himself forward as "Doctor Know-All." The king agrees to test the wise man's powers and employs him to detect a theft. Crab demands that first he must be given a feast. At the entrance of the first servant into the dining room, he remarks to his wife, "That is the first one." So, with the second and third. The servants, believing that they have been detected, confess the theft. As a second test of his powers, the wise man is to tell what is in a covered dish which will be served him. When he sees it coming, he realizes that he cannot pass the test. He calls out in despair to himself, "Poor Crab!" It happens that the dish is full of crabs. His third test is to find a lost horse. Sometimes he has previously hidden this horse so that finding it is no difficulty. In other stories the "doctor" gives his host a purgative, and thus brings about the accidental discovery of the horse.

The entire story of Doctor Know-All is found in most of the older literary tale collections of India and it is frequent in the European jestbooks of the Renaissance. Sometimes the separate incidents appear as independent stories, particularly the discovery of something which the rascal has already hidden, the episode with the covered dish, and the accidental discovery by casual remarks like "That is the first." The importance of this witty tale in Oriental and Renaissance literature and its popularity in folklore should make it very interesting for comparative study.

Finally, in this group of tales of lucky accidents, there may be mentioned three so closely related that they can best be considered together. The first of these is the most comprehensive: as a matter of fact, it frequently contains both of the others. This we may call The Three Lucky Brothers (Type 1650). The story usually begins with an account of their inheritance. The eldest brother sometimes inherits a cock, the second a scythe, and the youngest a cat. In other versions the inheritances are respectively a millstone, a musical instrument, and a reel. Two sequels appear, each represented by a tale to be considered presently. (1) The brothers reach countries in which the objects or animals which they have inherited are unknown, and they sell them for a fortune; or (2) the eldest brother lets his millstone fall on robbers who are counting their money (Motif K335.1.1), the second calls wolves together by means of his musical instrument (Type 1652), and the third threatens to draw the lake together with his reel and thus intimidates his master (Motif K1744).

As for this complete tale, it seems to go back to a French collection of Nicolas de Troyes, which appeared in 1535. As an oral tale it is especially popular in the Baltic countries and in France and Belgium, and is occasionally told elsewhere in Europe. The sale of the cat alone, known from its English version as Whittington's Cat (Type 1651), is found as a literary tale as early as the twelfth century. About the year 1600, it was attached to the legend of Sir Richard Whittington, Lord Mayor of London, who lived at the beginning of the fifteenth century. This tale may simply tell the story of how the hero is left a cat as his only inheritance and how he sells it for a fortune in a mouse-infested land where cats are unknown. A peculiar variation in the introduction relates that the hero earns or finds four coins which he tests by throwing them into a stream. Only one of them floats: the rest are counterfeit. With this coin he buys the cat which later brings him fortune.

Another episode of The Three Lucky Brothers which appears independently is that concerning The Wolves in the Stable (Type 1652). Here the youth who has acquired the musical instrument plays music and entices wolves out of a stable and makes them dance. He receives much money from the guardian of the wolves, who has let them out. As an independent tale, this seems to be confined to Finland and Estonia. Whittington's adventures with his cat, on the other hand, are told all over Europe and as far east as Indonesia and well down into Africa.

There are, of course, many other stories of luck in the folklore of Europe and Asia. But, as in the tale of Whittington's cat, many of them are essentially legends, rather than folktales. Such, for example, are the frequent accounts of the discovery of hidden treasure or of the chance acquisition of money. Sometimes tales of luck are mere exaggerations designed to be humorous. Tales of unbelievable success in hunting or fishing are usually meant to inspire laughter rather than wonder. It will be seen, therefore, that the concept of Luck is very broad, that it has many shades of meaning, so that it produces tales of wonder, stories made up of a series of clever accidents, jests, and local legends. As an incidental feature, it enters into many of the stories already considered, especially those having to do with supernatural helpers and with prophecies of future greatness.

10. THE THREE WORLDS

A. JOURNEY TO THE OTHER WORLD

IF ONE considers the multiform origins of the European and Asiatic folktale—the basic traditions going back perhaps to prehistoric times, the older Oriental tale collections with their reflections of ancient religions, the Celtic and Norse mythological stories, and the legends of the medieval Church—he will not be surprised to find that beliefs in other worlds than this in which we live are not only to be taken for granted as a part of the imaginative background of folktales but constitute the real focus of interest in a number of stories. We have already noticed tales in which the hero makes a journey to the other world. Sometimes this is thought of as the lower world, like Dante's Hell. Such it was in The Devil's Contract (Type 756B) and in The Man as Heater of Hell's Kettle (Type 475), to mention only two. In other tales the concept of an upper world, the Christian Heaven, is clear. We have already seen the smith who tries unsuccessfully to get into both Hell and Heaven (Type 330). Sometimes the direction in which the journey to the other world is made is very vaguely indicated. It is not unusual to find this realm across a body of water,[1] but it must be remembered that Charon's boat seemed to carry Greek souls across a lake or stream, but nevertheless into a lower world. Celtic tradition has been particularly interested in terrestrial other worlds lying across mountains or on distant islands.

It is all but impossible to come to any understanding of the way in which a story-teller visualizes his other world. For most of the European folktales, it seems fair to assume a belief in three worlds: the earth on which one lives in his normal state of being; the upper world, or the Christian Heaven, but sometimes merely another realm where extraordinary things happen; thirdly, a lower world compounded of ideas from vision literature as illustrated in Dante, of old Greek conceptions of Hades, and perhaps of even more ancient beliefs in a hierarchy of worlds. These upper and lower worlds are not alway far removed, for trees may grow to the upper world in a single night[2] and a rope may be sufficient to let one down into the lower.[3]

In the two somewhat related stories which we shall now notice, the other world seems very vaguely imagined. The first of these, Friends in Life and Death (Type 470), is known in literature through the legend of Don Juan.[4] The tale frequently begins with the pledge of two friends never to part. When one of them dies, the living friend invites the dead man to visit him on Christmas, and he goes with him when he returns to the other world. The other opening of the story is that peculiar to the Don Juan legend: a man in a churchyard invites a skull, or a memorial statue, to dinner, and then is compelled to go off with the skull. In any case, the living man makes the journey to the other world. On the way he sees many strange sights. Among them are fat and lean kine (as in the story of Joseph), a broad and narrow road, people and things that continually strike one another, and the like. The living man goes to sleep by a stream of water and when he wakes he finds that he is covered with moss. He also sees in the other world houses of feast and of mourning. When he returns to this world he finds that he has been away for many centuries. All is changed and he knows no one. The ending of the tale varies. Sometimes he dies the next day by falling from a tree or from a high place. Other versions report that he vanished after prayer.

This story has appeared in Europe in literary form since the beginning of

---

[1] Such is usually true in the stories of The Three Hairs from the Devil's Beard (Type 461).
[2] See Jack and the Beanstalk, Type 328.
[3] See The Bear's Son, Type 301.
[4] For a discussion of the relation of the Don Juan legend to this tale, see Bolte, *Zeitschrift für vergleichende Litteraturgeschichte*, XIII, 389.

the thirteenth century[5] and it was popular in the collections of exempla used by the priesthood. But its oral history is by no means confined to Roman Catholic countries. An excellent Tartar version is reported from Siberia, and it is also popular in Scandinavia and the Baltic countries.

Closely related to this in many of its motifs is The Bridge to the Other World (Type 471). As far as its introduction is concerned, the action is already familiar to us.[6] Three brothers, one after the other, set out on a quest. Sometimes this is to find their lost sister, but it may be any kind of quest to a distant land. On the way, the boys are appointed to herd seven foals (or oxen) and at the end of the day they are to bring back a sample of the animals' food. The elder brothers get into trouble. Sometimes they are lured away by a bird, or they yield to the suggestions of an old woman that they rest. In any event, they turn aside from a certain bridge which they should have crossed and are consequently turned into stone. The youngest brother, on the other hand, crosses the bridge which leads over into another world. In this world most unusual things happen. Animals pass in and out of a church and become human beings. Stones continually strike on each other. Wild boars fight. And the hero sees fat and lean kine and many another strange sight. From the altar in the church he takes bread and wine to carry back with him. The animals follow him back and he cuts off their heads and disenchants them. A religious explanation is given of everything that he has seen. The story ends with the disenchantment of his brothers.

The relation of certain parts of this tale with the one immediately preceding is obvious. The strange sights in the other world are frequently the same in the two stories, and in both cases constitute the center of interest. There may be some connection between these tales and the story of The Angel and the Hermit, already noticed (Type 759), in which we have peculiar events which are later explained and made reasonable.

But the story of The Bridge to the Other World is well known as an independent tale. There are early literary parallels in India, and the tale appears as we know it in Europe in the Seven Sages tradition.[7] Orally, it does not seem to have become really popular except in Norway, Iceland, and Russia, though excellent versions are reported from Brittany, Mexico, North Africa, and especially from the Tartars of Siberia.

B. AT THE GATE OF HEAVEN

The other world in these two stories of extraordinary sights has no striking counterpart in the teachings of the Christian Church and, though they

[5] For its use in literature, see Köhler, *Kleinere Schriften*, II, 224ff. A recent definitive study is Dorothy Epplen MacKay, *The Double Invitation in the Legend of Don Juan*, Stanford University, 1943.

[6] See, for example, a number of the tales discussed on pages 105ff., above, under the heading "Tasks and Quests."

[7] For these Oriental relationships, see: Oertel, *Studien zur vergleichenden Litteraturgeschichte*, VIII, 123, and Chauvin, *Bibliographie*, VIII, 160, No. 168.

were beloved of the medieval clergy, it is likely that concepts from other systems of thought have entered in. In the stories about Heaven, however, and especially those which picture Saint Peter as acting as the doorman of Paradise,[8] no such exotic influence is probable. It is entirely in line with traditions current in all Christian countries.

Already, in the tale of The Smith and The Devil (Type 330), we have seen the rascally smith getting permission from Saint Peter to throw his magic knapsack inside the door of heaven and then successfully wishing himself in it. This is but one of the many tricks employed to get by the heavenly porter.[9] Not all the tales of the gate of heaven, however, are concerned with merely deceiving the gateman. Of those which develop this basic situation otherwise, there are four which have acquired some popularity in folklore.

First may be mentioned The Tailor in Heaven (Type 800). One day, when God is absent, Peter admits an unworthy tailor into heaven. Thereupon the tailor becomes censorious of behavior on earth and finally throws God's footstool at an old woman thief in the world below. For his presumption, he is expelled from heaven. This story was a favorite among the writers of jestbooks in the Renaissance. Presumably from these written accounts it has been taken over by story-tellers in various parts of Europe and as far east in Asia as the Buryat in Siberia.[10]

Another grumbler to be admitted into heaven is Master Pfriem (Type 801). He has been warned by Saint Peter that he must never find fault with what he sees. When he enters, he sees so many absurd things happening that he cannot keep from complaining and is eventually expelled. A considerable part of the story is concerned with a description of the absurd things the cobbler sees: men carrying a beam crosswise through a narrow gate; others putting water in a tub full of holes, and the like. He is able to remain silent for a long time, but his resolution is broken down when he sees horses hitched both before and behind a wagon and pulling against each other. We have really two traditions in this folktale. The first is the admission to heaven, provided no fault be found. The tale in this simple form appears in both the fabliaux and the jestbook literature, and was known orally as early as the sixteenth century in Germany. As to the illogical and absurd events used to test Master Pfriem's restraint, these have a much older history. Some of them go back to Greek myths and some are found in the saints' legends of the Middle Ages.[11] In modern folklore, the tale of Master Pfriem has a very limited popularity. It is probable that the few versions reported from France and Scandinavia and sporadically elsewhere are really only retellings of the version in Grimm or in one of the older jestbooks.

[8] For this whole series of tales, see Köhler, "Sanct Petrus, der Himmelspförtner," *Aufsätze*, pp. 48-78.
[9] See Motif K2371.1 and all its subdivisions.
[10] For the Buryat tale, see Holmberg, *Siberian Mythology*, p. 441.
[11] For a discussion of these motifs, see Bolte-Polívka, III, 302f.

Much better established as an oral narrative is the tale of Saint Peter's Mother (Type 804). Though she has been sent to hell for her uncharitableness, the Saint receives permission to pull her out of hell on a stalk and thus raise her to heaven. When the other dead catch hold of her feet, she kicks them off and, as punishment, falls back into hell herself. This story has been traced back to a German poem of the fifteenth century, but it has existed primarily on the lips of illiterate story-tellers in eastern and southern Europe, where more than a hundred versions have been recorded. It has also traveled far into Siberia, where it is told by the Mongols.

The Grimms also told the story of The Peasant in Heaven (Type 802), though it seems to be very little known elsewhere.[12] The peasant is received in silence because the entrance of peasants into heaven is not unusual. But when at length a rich man comes in, there is song and dance and great festivity in celebration of the rare event.

C. SAINTS WANDER ON EARTH

In pious legends everywhere a popular theme is the incognito wanderings of saints or other holy men, or even of gods themselves, in the world of mortals. Ovid's tale of the appearance of Jupiter and Mercury at the home of Philemon and Baucis and of the hospitable treatment of the unknown guests is one of the most attractive ancient stories. In Christian lands such adventures are usually ascribed to Christ and Saint Peter. Of such tales there is a considerable number scattered through the collections of saints' legends and exempla of the Middle Ages. Several have established themselves in popular tradition and are frequently picked up by folklorists. In another connection we have already noticed the tale in which these mysterious strangers reward hospitality by granting wishes, some of which are foolishly wasted.[13]

Christ and Peter are not always received hospitably. In one story, The Greedy Peasant Woman (Type 751), although her cake is made to grow magically larger, she gives the holy visitors only a morsel. As a result she is punished, usually by being transformed into a bird.[14] In a peculiar variation known only in the Baltic countries, she must take two snakes as foster children.

Sometimes the unknown holy men are lodged, but the host, not realizing who they are, mistreats them. In the tale of Christ and Peter in the Barn (Type 752A), they are not allowed to sleep in the house, and the peasant forces them to rise early and help with the threshing in order to pay for their lodging. Christ separates the grain miraculously by means of fire. When the

[12] For the scattering German, Danish, Catalonian, Serbian, and Lithuanian versions, see Bolte-Polívka, III, 274.

[13] See Types 750A and 750B.

[14] For a detailed discussion of the transformations of this greedy woman in the several versions of the tale, see Dähnhardt, *Natursagen*, II, 123ff.

peasant tries to imitate, he burns his barn down. This tale was retold by Hans Sachs in the sixteenth century; as an oral tradition it seems to be confined almost entirely to the Baltic area. It has been reported, but only sporadically, from Flanders, Denmark, and Roumania.

The two elements in this tale are paralleled elsewhere. The boorish treatment of the guests by the host is found in another poem of Hans Sachs', the Story of The Savior and Peter in Night Lodgings (Type 791). Here Christ and Peter are sleeping in the same bed. The drunken host returns home and beats Peter, who persuades Christ to change places with him. The host then comes in to beat the other lodger, and Peter again receives the blows.[15]

The unsuccessful imitation of the miracle is best known in the tale of Christ and the Smith (Type 753). This is essentially a saints' legend, but is told by the people all over Europe. It was used by Hans Sachs and is frequently employed as an etiological tale accounting for the origin of apes. In this story Christ performs two miracles: he takes off a horse's foot in order to shoe him and then replaces it without harm; and he rejuvenates an old woman by putting her on the fire. The smith tries disastrously to do the same thing. In some versions of the tale a happy ending is given by bringing in a second smith who succeeds in undoing the damage.

Among the stories of the adventures of these two sacred persons with the keepers of inns is one somewhat reminiscent of the tale in which the wishes are foolishly wasted. In this story of The Forgotten Wind (Type 752B) Christ permits the innkeeper, who is continually complaining about the weather, to order the sunshine and the rain as he will. The corn grows well, but all the ears are empty because the innkeeper forgot to include the wind. This is probably not a well-known tale, since it has been noticed only in Denmark and Livonia. It has some analogies to the story in which various people are allowed to order the weather as they will. It is a very unsatisfactory arrangement, for no one is happy except the person who orders it, and finally the control of the weather is left to the higher powers.[16]

The holy wanderers are not always looking for food or lodging, but they sometimes interest themselves in general social life. This is shown in the story of The Lazy Boy and the Industrious Girl (Type 822), a legend appearing both in the collections of exempla and in the Renaissance jestbooks, and known, not only in most of Europe, but also in the Near East. The Lord and Peter come across a boy so lazy that he only points with his foot when they inquire their direction. Later, they find a most industrious girl. Much to Peter's astonishment, the Lord decrees that the two shall marry, so that her industry will balance his indolence.

---

[15] This tale is more popular than the one about threshing the grain. It is found, either as a wonder tale or a legend, in most countries of Europe.

[16] See, for example, John Heywood's "Play of the Weather."

Most of the tales of this group are very simple and consist of nothing more than an anecdote. Somewhat more complex and much freer in entering into combinations with other material is the tale, Who Ate the Lamb's Heart? (Type 785), well known all over Europe. It is usually told of Peter and a companion who are traveling together. The companion stealthily eats the heart of the lamb and denies having done so. He declares that the lamb had no heart. Later, it chances that the companions heal a princess and receive money in reward. When the money is to be divided, the third part is assigned to the man who has eaten the lamb's heart. In order to get his part, the companion confesses.

For the story of a stolen heart, or other member, and the contention that the animal had none, there are a legion of parallels from all over the world.[17]

11. REALISTIC TALES

A. CLEVERNESS

UP TO this point, as we have passed in review the more complicated of the European and Asiatic folktales, the element of the supernatural has usually played a considerable role. Ogres and other supernatural monsters, helpful creatures like dwarfs and fairies, ghosts and grateful dead men, magic and enchantments—these all come from the world of wonder that gives to this class of tales the general name of wonder stories. But even in tales not primarily concerned with the marvelous it frequently lurks in the background of the story-teller's thoughts and he assumes a faith in his hearers which will carry them with him into a world of fancy far removed from the actual world of their everyday life. Though such tales may contain no motifs from the realm of faery or magic, they do not hesitate at the most extravagant exaggeration of the physical qualities of the characters, of the nature of the deeds accomplished, and of the astonishing coincidences which are ascribed to the power of prophecy or to luck, or to the inevitable course of divine justice. There is real validity not only for these presuppositions of a taleteller about the frame of mind of his hearers but also for the ease with which these hearers move about from one world to another and range from familiar scenes of everyday to heaven or to hell or to fairyland.

But those who tell and those who listen to fairy tales live a practical life and even in their taletelling they have their realistic moods in which they are particularly interested in stories of deception, cheats, swindles, and clever thefts. They enjoy instances of stupidity, where they can see an amusing contrast with their own sane and well-advised behavior. Many of these anecdotes

[17] See Motif K402 and all its subdivisions for the literature of this subject.

are extremely simple, having only a single point, and are best studied along with series of others like them.[1]

In contrast to these simple anecdotes, a number of stories of cleverness, of cheats, and of robberies are as complicated in their structure as many a wonder tale. Sometimes the central point—essentially an interest in the workings of a keen mind—is combined with all sorts of other material. For this reason the behavior of tales of this kind as they are handed about or travel from country to country is of the same order as that of other stories with complicated plots. Though some parts may drop out, and though substitutions may be made, the tale as a whole maintains its identity.

1. *Princess Won by Cleverness*

One of the most usual situations in folktales is the contest for the hand of a princess. In the wonder tales the hero normally succeeds in this competition through some marvelous help or through some supernatural power of his own.[2] But quite as interesting are those stories in which his success depends upon his quickness of wit. We have already noticed the tale in which the princess is to be given to the man who can make her speak (Type 945) and in which the hero so cleverly propounds a question that she is brought to speech in spite of herself. The silent princess is relatively rare in folktales; it is much more usual to find one who has never laughed. To cause such a woman to burst out in laughter will bring the hero not only her hand, but wealth and a share of the kingdom. Two of the stories involving this incident have several points in common and are occasionally confused, though the main action in each is clear.

The first of these is the tale of Dungbeetle (Type 559). It is so named because the help of this humble insect appears in nearly all versions of the narrative. When he hears that the princess has been offered to the man who can make her laugh, the hero sets out and, in the usual way of folktales, secures the help of grateful animals, or sometimes acquires magic objects, particularly a rope that binds and tightens and a magic fiddle which compels people to dance.[3] By employing these animals or objects, he succeeds in bringing the princess to laughter. But, instead of receiving her in marriage, he is thrown into a lions' den. By use of his magic or his helpers, he escapes. When again he has been refused the princess, he causes wasps to attack and drive out successive rivals on the bridal night. Eventually the princess recognizes his power and marries him.

[1] These simple jests and anecdotes are discussed in the next chapter, pp. 188ff., where they are arranged in a logical series.

[2] For a detailed discussion of such suitor contests, see Motifs H331 and H335.

[3] All these motifs have been met before. For the help of the three animals, see Type 554. For the binding rope, see Types 564 and 569. For the magic fiddle, see Type 592. Two other tales containing it will be presently studied, Types 851 and 853.

This story appeared in Basile's *Pentamerone* and most versions conform rather closely to his telling of the tale. It seems to be known in all parts of Europe, but is not popular in any. It has also been reported from the Nuba of east Africa.

The closely related story, "All Stick Together" (Type 571), is much more popular. Though it is sometimes impossible to make a clear-cut distinction between the two stories, the center of interest in the latter is the sticking together of people and objects. The youngest of three brothers is the only one who divides food and drink with a hungry man, and, as a reward, he receives a golden goose with the power to make everything stick to it. Sometimes the goose is acquired through a lucky bargain. He takes the goose to an inn where the innkeeper's daughter tries to steal one of the golden feathers. He compels her to stick fast to the goose and later those who try to help her— the parson, the sexton, and others. It is usually through this absurd parade of people stuck to the goose that the princess is brought to laughter. But sometimes, as in the last tale, it is occasioned by the sight of three small animals which the hero owns, and sometimes by the foolish actions of the hero. As in the other tale, he is not immediately given his reward, but is assigned preliminary tasks: drinking a cellar full of wine, eating up a mountain of bread, or making a land and water ship. These he accomplishes, sometimes with the help of extraordinary companions.[4]

The tale has a way of adapting motifs from other stories, so that all kinds of contacts with material familiar elsewhere are noticeable as one moves from version to version.[5] The sticking together of the people as punishment for meddling appears in many other connections, particularly in a fifteenth century English poem, "The Tale of the Basyn."[6] As for the folktale, it is popular all over Europe, and several versions are known from the Near East. The French have brought it to Canada and from them it has passed on to at least four of the eastern American Indian tribes.

Several of the tales already reviewed have shown the hero winning the princess through the help of his magic objects. The story known as The Rabbit-herd (Type 570) combines such magic means with cleverness and trickery. The king has offered the princess as a prize to the man who is able to herd all his rabbits. The king has a magic pipe which always calls the animals back. The hero, unlike his elder brothers, is kind to an old woman and from her he also receives a pipe, stronger in its magic than the king's,

---

[4] Versions having this latter trait have suffered confusion with The Extraordinary Companions (Type 513).

[5] For a good discussion of these relationships, see Bolte-Polívka, II, 40f. The material on this tale is well summarized there, where, presumably, the results of Polívka's special study are given. Unfortunately, I have not been able to consult this work: G. Polívka, *Pohádkoslovné studie* (Praha, 1904), pp. 67-106.

[6] See Hazlitt, *Remains of Early Popular Poetry* (London, 1866), IV, 42. The poem has been frequently reprinted.

with which he is able to call all the animals together. The success of the hero with his magic pipe causes great envy on the part of the king, the princess, or the queen. The versions differ as to which of them tries to obtain the pipe. In some, the queen bribes him by kissing him; in some, the princess lies with him; and in some, the king kisses a horse. In any case, the youth now knows a disgraceful story to tell. Before finally granting the princess to him, the king orders the boy to tell a sack of lies. He begins to tell great lies until the king or the queen sees that he is going to betray their disgrace. They make him stop, and give him the princess.

The characteristic trait in this story seems not to be the magic pipe so much as the hero's use of blackmail to gain his point at the end. For that reason, the story is frequently known as The Sack of Lies, or something similar. It is rather popular all the way from Iceland to the Caucasus, more than two hundred versions having already been noted. Sporadic variants have been collected on the Gold Coast of Africa, in the Philippines, from Cape Verde Islanders in Massachusetts, and very recently from persons of English stock in Virginia. Its general distribution would seem to indicate that it is essentially a European, rather than an Oriental tale.

The princess as a prize for correct guessing is the principal feature of The Louse-Skin (Type 621). She has had a louse fattened until it becomes as big as a calf and at its death has had a dress made from its skin. She agrees to marry the man who can guess what the dress is made from. The hero learns by trickery, and thus wins her. The major interest in this tale is concerned with the tricks whereby the puzzle is solved.[7]

As an autonomous story, we find it here and there all over Europe, whence it has been carried to Indonesia and the Philippines. Within Europe, the overwhelming majority of the variants are from four east Baltic countries. In other parts of Europe, the tale is more likely to serve merely as an introduction to Cupid and Psyche (Type 425B), King Thrushbeard (Type 900), and The Robber Bridegroom (Type 955). In some cases our story proceeds, like the next one we shall consider, with the giving of the princess to the suitor to whom she turns in the night.

A tale very closely related to the last two, since in part it is like one, and in part like the other, is The Birthmarks of the Princess (Type 850). The hero here, like the rabbit-herd, has a magic pipe which causes hogs to dance. The princess covets his dancing hogs, and he sells them to her in return for seeing her naked. By using his knowledge of her birthmarks thus acquired as a basis for blackmail, he wins her as his wife. As a further test, the princess is to be given to the suitor to whom she turns in the night. The hero and a rival suitor are put to bed with her. They each strive to entice her and finally she turns to the hero.

[7] For the guessing or finding out of the nature or cause of a mystery, see The Danced-out Shoes (Type 306) and Tom-Tit-Tot (Type 500).

In spite of its appearance as being a mere concoction of two other tales, this narrative as a whole is told all over Europe and has been carried to Virginia. There seem to be no older literary versions, so that its development probably belongs to the authentic folklore of the European continent.

Three of the tales concerned with the winning of a princess place her in an open contest of wits with the hero.[8] The first is The Princess who Cannot Solve the Riddle (Type 851). Here she is offered to the man who can propose a riddle too hard for her. On the way to the contest, the hero is given a clue which he develops later into a riddle. He sees a horse poisoned and then eaten by ravens, who in turn fall dead. The ravens are then eaten by twelve men, who die of the poison. In case the story has this introduction, the riddle which the hero propounds is "One killed none, and yet killed twelve." Other riddles are sometimes substituted, particularly that of the murdered lover and of the unborn. The first of these is generally given: With what thinks, I drink; what sees, I carry; with what eats, I walk. (The queen has a cup made from the skull of her murdered lover and a ring from one of his eyes, and she carries two of his teeth in her boots.) The riddle of the unborn is: I am unborn; my horse is unborn; I carry my mother on my hands. (A boy who has been taken from his dead mother's body digs up her body and makes gloves of her skin. He rides a colt which has been taken from a dead mare's body.) Whichever of these riddles he uses, the princess is greatly puzzled and tries to learn the answer by trickery. She slips into his room at night, hoping that she can learn it from his dreams. He knows about her visit, however, and keeps a token. When he uses this to prove her visit, she surrenders.

In comparison to the other stories of wit contests with the princess, this has the widest distribution as an oral narrative and the most extensive literary history. The general theme of the winning of a bride through the giving or solving of a riddle goes back at least to the Greek romances and recurs in medieval collections. As a part of folklore, the tale is current from Iceland and the British Isles to Russia, and it has been carried abroad frequently: to central Africa and to North and South America, through Spanish, Portuguese, French, and Negro settlers. The tale may well have intimate Oriental relations, because of the great interest eastern story-tellers have in all kinds of riddles and other displays of wit.[9]

In another tale of this group, The Hero Forces the Princess to Say "That is a Lie" (Type 852), he accomplishes the task indicated by the telling of impossible tales, usually gross exaggerations. The interest of the story is primarily in these "tall tales." They may be mere exaggerations of size about an enormous animal or building (a type of story familiar in America in the

[8] For direct contests between the princess and her suitor (racing, wrestling, overcoming in strength), see Motif H332.1 and all references there given.

[9] For a discussion of these relationships, see Bolte-Polívka, I, 197.

legends of Paul Bunyan), or they may be about impossible happenings: a tree growing to the skies overnight, like Jack's beanstalk, or the ascent or descent from the skies on a rope of chaff, or of a man who cuts off his head and replaces it.[10] Usually he is not able to bring her to the desired words until he makes up shameful slanders about her.

Though this tale appears to have no literary history, it is scattered rather evenly over Europe as an oral story, and it is found in single versions in Indonesia, North and Central Africa, and in the British tradition of Virginia and the French of Missouri. The distribution in Europe shows the tale unusually popular in Ireland and Scandinavia, though only a detailed analysis of the versions would indicate where the story originated and what has been its history.

In The Hero Catches the Princess with her Own Words (Type 853) we see resemblances to several of the tales just discussed, and indeed to many others farther afield. The princess is offered in marriage to the man who can outwit her in repartee. On the way to the contest the hero picks up various objects, a dead crow, an egg, and the like. In his contest with the princess he always reduces her words to scorn by producing these objects at the proper time. This part of the tale is often very obscene. As usual, the successful hero is put off and is thrown into prison. By means of his magic tablecloth, purse, and fiddle he escapes. Then, by means of his fiddle, he captures the princess and refuses to release her unless she answers "No" to all his questions. By properly phrasing the questions, he gets her into his bed and marries her.

The last half of this tale frequently appears independently, namely, the play upon the word "No."[11] The whole story appears in a Middle High German poem and later was used both in French poetry and in the English ballads. As a part of folklore, it is most popular in states around the Baltic, though it is known in all parts of Europe. In America it has been brought by the French to the Ojibwa Indians, by the Spanish to the Zuñi, to Massachusetts by Cape Verde Island Portuguese-speaking Negroes, and to Jamaica by Negroes from Africa. The tale does not appear to be known in Asia.

There are, of course, other tricks by which story-tellers have imagined their lowly heroes as winners of the much desired princess.[12] One of them, The Golden Ram (Type 854), reminds us of a scene in Shakespeare's *Cymbeline*. The hero has made a boast that if he had only one thing, he could marry the princess. The king challenges him to make good his words. He says that the desired thing is money. When the king gives him all the gold he needs, he has a hollow golden ram constructed. He hides himself in the ram and has

---

[10] For exaggerations of this kind, see Motifs X900 to X1045.

[11] For a good discussion of this motif, see K. Nyrop, *Nej: et Motivs Historie* (København, 1891).

[12] Some of these have only local distribution, though they may be very popular in a single area. An example is the tale listed as Type 555 in Andrejev's Russian survey, *Ukazatel' Skazočnich*.

it left where the princess will see it. She insists upon having it carried into her room. Of course, the hero eventually comes out and wins her.

In spite of the suggestion of the Trojan horse and of boxes and trunks hiding lovers familiar to literary stories of the Middle Ages, this tale in its present form seems to be an oral development. Its distribution is by no means uniform in Europe, where ninety percent of the versions have been found within Finland, either among the Finnish or the Swedish inhabitants. It seems to have some popularity in Italy and it has been learned, presumably from the French, by the Maliseet Indians of New Brunswick.

In this whole group of tales in which the princess is won by cleverness there is a mixture of motivation. Sometimes the taleteller seems really interested in the romantic aspects of the story, the lowly youth winning the lady of his desire, but most often this is subordinated to the desire to see a sharp contest of wits won by a man against what seems to be overwhelming odds.

2. *Clever Riddle Solvers*

A small group of widely known folk stories receives its interest from the clever solving of riddles and other enigmatic statements. No matter what the ultimate origin of these various tales—and they all are certainly literary in the first instance—once they have been taken up by oral story-tellers, they have attained a great popularity and have become an authentic part of folk tradition.

Three of these tales are so close to one another in many of their traits, and their traditions have sometimes become so confused, that it is impossible to make a clear-cut separation.[13]

Most popular of this group is The Clever Peasant Girl (Type 875). The tale always begins with showing how it happens that the king summons the clever girl into his presence. The most usual handling of this part of the tale is as follows: a peasant finds in his field a golden mortar and tells his daughter that he plans to take it to the king. She advises very strongly against this, because she says the king will demand the pestle also. It turns out as she has predicted, and the peasant in his distress bemoans the fact that he did not obey his daughter. The king inquires about what he means, and hears the whole story, whereupon he insists upon having the daughter come to court. Another opening of the story begins at the court itself, where two peasants must give answers to questions propounded by the judge. One of them answers correctly as his daughter had advised him. This comes to the attention of the king, who wants to see her.[14] When the clever girl arrives at the

[13] The definitive study of this whole series is that of Jan DeVries, *Die Märchen von klugen Rätsellösern*. A later study, taking issue in some respects with DeVries, is Albert Wesselski's *Der Knabenkönig und das kluge Mädchen*.

[14] The questions asked the peasant are sometimes found in all the stories here treated together. They are: What is most beautiful? (Spring); What is the strongest? (The earth); What is the richest thing on earth? (Autumn).

court, he assigns her various tasks and propounds various questions. She must come to him neither naked nor clad, neither by day nor by night, neither washed nor unwashed, or the like.[15] She comes wrapped in a cloth, or at twilight, or with only part of her body washed, or otherwise carries out the paradoxical order. She answers questions—usually the same ones which the Abbot must answer in the jest of The Emperor and the Abbot (Type 922). She weaves a cloth with two threads, hatches out boiled eggs, or carves a fowl so as to give the appropriate pieces to all members of her family.[16] After she has successfully passed all the tests, she marries the king. One day as she sees him make a manifestly unjust decision about the possession of a colt, she advises the owner how to act so as to show the king the absurdity of his decision.[17] The king is incensed at her meddling with his affairs and casts her out with the permission to take with her only that one thing which she holds dearest. She takes with her the sleeping husband, who is so moved by this touch of affection that he forgives her.

Before considering the distribution and probable history of this story, it will be wise to look at the plots of the other two tales which contain much common material.

The Son of the King and of the Smith (Type 920) is frequently connected with the name of Solomon. The king decides to get rid of his son and exchanges him for the son of a smith. The reason for this exchange is variously explained. It may be that the boy has uttered a slanderous truth about his mother or that he has reduced to an absurdity a decision of his father's, just as the clever peasant girl did. In any case, the young prince grows up at the home of the smith and manifests in many ways his cleverness and his superiority to his companions. In the child's game of playing king, he is miraculously chosen to take the part. And where he and the smith's son are brought together, they each show their low and high origins. In this tale there occurs a similar series of paradoxical tasks which the boy succeeds in performing. At the end, of course, he is received by his father and inherits the kingdom.

The third of these tales is The King and the Peasant's Son (Type 921). Here there is very little plot. The king rides up to the peasant's hut and looks into the hut. The king asks the boy (a) "What do you see?"—"One and a half men and a horse's head" (himself, the legs of the king who is horseback in the doorway, and the horse's head). (b) "What are you doing?"—"I boil those coming and going" (beans that keep rising and falling in the water). (c) "What is your father doing?"—"He is in the vineyard and is doing good

---

[15] For this whole series, see Motifs H1050 to H1073.

[16] The wise carving of the fowl is by no means confined to this tale. See Motif H601 for the literature.

[17] For this *reductio ad absurdum* of the decision, see Motif J1191 and all its subdivisions. The owner of the colt, whose opponent has claimed that it was the wagon rather than the mare which bore the colt, fishes in the street, and when the king asks about it, tells him that this is more reasonable than the king's decision.

and bad" (he prunes vines, but sometimes cuts good ones and leaves the bad). (d) "What is your mother doing?"—"At daybreak she baked the bread we ate last week; in the morning she cut off the heads of the well to cure the sick; now she is striking the hungry and compelling the satiated to eat" (she bakes bread to repay that borrowed from neighbors last week; she cuts off a chicken's head so as to feed her sick mother; she drives away the hungry hens and stuffs the geese). (e) "What is your brother doing?"—"He hunts. He throws away what he catches, and what he does not catch, he carries with him" (hunts for lice on his body). The number of these questions can be multiplied, and the whole interest of this tale is in the questions and answers.

DeVries's study of this group of three tales shows clearly that they have been of great influence on one another. His investigation brings out the fact that The Clever Peasant Girl is essentially a European development. He feels that the other two stories about male characters are made up of Oriental material coming ultimately from India. He shows that in India nearly all of the separate motifs of these tales are well known and go far back into literary history; they also occur in contemporary oral stories, presumably derived from the older literary monuments. He draws a sharp distinction between the narrative method in the folktales of the Orient and that used in Europe. As illustrated by the tales he is studying, he finds that the European storyteller works with a closely knit plot which he can vary only in small details. He feels that this method, in contrast to the chaotic nature of Oriental narrative, is a result of the influence of western literature, which has always been more logically constructed than the Oriental. DeVries therefore feels that these tales are constructed of Oriental material, but that the plot structure has been imposed upon this material in the process of its migration to the west, or at least, shortly after its arrival.

Specifically, he feels that the story of The Son of the King is based upon an ancient literary original from India and that it was eventually received by Jewish story-tellers who made it a part of the legend of Solomon and thus unified its plot. The story of The King and the Peasant's Son is also connected with this legend. The Clever Peasant Girl is a European development in which the story is adapted to a female character. DeVries shows that there is an utter freedom of exchange between the stories of the peasant girl and the peasant boy.

In the matter of actual distribution in Europe the story of the peasant girl is the most popular of the three and it is rather evenly spread over the continent, as well as in the Near East and North Africa. An early form of the tale appears in the Icelandic saga of Ragnar Lodbrok. The clever responses of the peasant boy are not quite so generally popular in Europe, but where they are well known, they appear in a phenomenally large number of versions. For example, seventy German variants have been noted and one hundred seventy-seven Finnish. This tale has also received literary treatment in several European languages from the twelfth century on. In contrast to the wide European distribution of the stories of the boy and the girl, that of The King's Son is confined to the Baltic states and Russia and is therefore essentially an east European story, perhaps Oriental, in any event connected with the legend of Solomon.[18]

Touching these three tales of riddle solvers in many places is the jest of The Emperor and the Abbot (Type 922), known primarily to the English-speaking world through the old ballad of King John and the Bishop. To students of folktale research this story is of extraordinary interest because of the exhaustive treatment which it has received by Walter Anderson, an investigation so thorough that it has come to serve as a model for all scholars attempting to study a tale by means of the historic-geographic method.[19] The plot of the story is relatively simple. The emperor tells the abbot that if, within a certain time, he does not answer correctly the three questions he is given, the emperor will order his execution. A humble man, a miller or a shepherd, masks as the abbot and answers the questions correctly. Within the framework of this simple train of action a very great variety may be displayed, not only in the persons involved—the questioner, the questioned, and the answer-giver—but in the riddles and their answers. It is in the latter, of course, that similarity to The Clever Peasant Girl and to The King and the Peasant's Son is seen. The favorite riddles (or enigmatic questions) in the present tale sometimes appear in these others. The emperor nearly always propounds just three questions, but when all versions of the tale are considered, there are not fewer than eighteen of these riddles which must be considered by the investigator of the tale. The most popular are the following: (1) how high is heaven? (a day's journey, since Christ went there in one day—or any one of twenty-five other answers); (2) how much is a golden plow worth? (a good rain in May); (3) how much am I worth? (twenty-nine pieces of silver, since Our Lord was sold for thirty, and you are worth at least one piece less). Of the last question there are two distinct types which come to the same result in the answer. The first of these is "What is God doing?" The answer may be either "He maketh poor, and maketh rich; he bringeth low, and lifteth up" (referring to the poor man's

---

[18] Wesselski, in his study *Der Knabenkönig*, takes issue with DeVries about the origin of this part of the Solomon legend. He is convinced that it is taken directly from the legend of Cyrus and is therefore not connected with the literature of India. I do not have sufficient competence in the literary traditions discussed to make any attempt at judging between these two positions. Both of the scholars agree: (1) That all three tales are ultimately Oriental and literary; (2) that the literary tales have been taken over by oral story-tellers; (3) that the movement of this tradition has been rather consistently from east to west. Their point of difference concerns particularly the importance of the role played by Jewish tradition in the literary relationships of Orient and Occident.

[19] *Kaiser und Abt.* For a discussion of this method, with some illustrations from Anderson's employment of it, see pp. 430ff., below.

disguise) or else "God is astonished that a poor miller should answer in place of the abbot." The other question which may bring the jest to a proper conclusion is "What do I think?" The answer is "You think I am the abbot. As a matter of fact. . . ." The jest usually ends with the king delighted at the wit and ready to forgive the abbot. Sometimes the poor man is offered the abbot's place, but he realizes his incompetence and declines.

By an extremely close analysis of almost six hundred versions, written and oral, Anderson divides his tale into eighteen different redactions and traces out a plausible history whereby these various redactions are derived from an original form. This original, he feels, developed in some Jewish community of the Near East, possibly in Egypt, perhaps about the seventh century after Christ. This is not the place to go into the detailed history which he presents in some sixty-three stages. One point, however, of great interest to folklorists, is the fact that this tale seems to be fitted both to the prose tale form and to the ballad. In English and American tradition it is nearly always sung. Its attachment to the name of King John continues even among illiterate singers utterly ignorant of English history.

Not only does this tale permit interesting comparison between ballad and prose story, but also it demands a close study of the mutual relationships of the literary and the oral versions. For Anderson deals with 151 literary versions, dating all the way from the ninth century. He is extremely careful to weigh the evidence presented by these literary documents, and he thus adequately meets the criticism that those who, like him, employ the historic-geographic method are neglectful of the importance of the written document.

The abbot saves his life by seeing that the riddles proposed by the king are answered. Exactly the opposite situation appears in another story of enigmas, Out-riddling the Judge (Type 927). Here the accused person is to be set free if he can propound a riddle which the judge is unable to solve. He always does this from some peculiar circumstance which he has recently observed. Most commonly the riddle is "What has seven tongues in one head?" The judge, of course, cannot guess. The condemned man then tells how he found the skull of a horse with a bird's nest and seven young birds in it. The student of this tale has two things to consider. There is, first, the general dramatic situation where almost any kind of riddle would be appropriate. It happens, however, that this particular riddle is nearly always the one used. The interest of the student may therefore be in the riddle itself. It is frequently given without the story at all, and sometimes the story is added as a commentary or afterthought. The tale is known in northern Europe and has been reported from Spain; but it seems to have its greatest popularity in England and in the British tradition in America. Seven variants in America including both the situation and the riddle show that the tale is known in Nova Scotia, New England, Pennsylvania, New Jersey, Maryland, North Carolina, and Mississippi. The Pennsylvania tradition is clearly German, but all the rest seem to be British. In addition, the riddle by itself is widely known, both by Negroes and whites, in the southern states and the West Indies.[20]

The framework of the five tales we have just considered affords room for the display of a large number of riddles. Those mentioned in connection with each of the tales are only the most popular, but if we consider all those which are used, we shall find that several score of them appear at one place or another. Even so, however, the folktale makes use of a relatively small number of the riddles available in the repertory of most story-tellers. That this group of stories involving the solution of enigmas has almost universal popularity is only natural considering the extremely widespread interest all over Europe and Asia in the riddle for its own sake.[21]

3. Clever Counsels

Not less popular than the riddle and even more nearly universal is the proverb. From whatever source they may ultimately come, proverbs eventually attain the status of unimpeachable wisdom. They are thought to embody the best results of the experience of a race, and a large proportion of mankind is governed by them in the activities of daily life. Their exact formulation assumes an importance almost as great as the essential wisdom contained. Sometimes they are uttered by shamans or priests, or by oracles, such as that at Delphi. And even if no specific religious origin is ascribed to them, they may come from the lips of a well-known sage or leader among men.

Often these aphorisms are so precious that they are bought, like a prescription from a doctor. When this is true, the formulation of the wise saying is nearly always mysterious, and it is only by later experience that the soundness of the proverb is made manifest. A group of tales is devoted to illustrations of this fact: seemingly senseless or foolish counsels are proved through experience to be wise.

Two of these stories have so much in common that they are best looked at together. In both Wise Through Experience (Type 910A) and The Servant's Good Counsels (Type 910B) the hero receives, in one way or another, a series of such precepts. Usually he buys them. In the first of these tales the

[20] Bibliographical material upon this type is widely scattered. Some important references are: Köhler, Kleinere Schriften, I, 46; Feilberg, Ordbog, I, 602b, s. v. "hestehoved"; Herbert Halpert, "The Cante Fable in Decay," Southern Folklore Quarterly, V, 199, n. 22; E. E. Gardner, Folklore from the Schoharie Hills, New York, p. 252.

[21] For a rather detailed listing of the riddles which appear in connection with folktales, see Motifs H530 to H899 and all the literature there cited. For the independent riddle, see Aarne, Vergleichende Rätselforschungen (FF Communications Nos. 26, 27, and 28, Helsinki, 1918-20). Professor Archer Taylor of the University of California has been giving much of his attention recently to riddles. His forthcoming study promises to be of great interest.

precepts most frequently found are: (1) Do not marry a girl from abroad; (2) Do not visit your friends often; (3) Do not lend out your horse. The story then proceeds to give the man's distressing experiences with the foreign wife; to show how the frequent visitor eventually becomes a nuisance and is treated shamefully; and, similarly, to illustrate the evil consequences of lending the horse. The related story, The Servant's Good Counsels, is handled with somewhat more variety. One of the precepts is, Do not leave the highway. The hero forgets the advice and falls into the clutches of robbers. Likewise, he disregards the counsel not to cross the bridge without dismounting his horse. As a result, he breaks his leg. The other counsels in this story have to do with domestic relations. For example, the hero is told not to walk half a mile with a man without asking his name. The hero unwittingly makes a wager with his wife's paramour and loses her to him. He is also told, "Do not go where an old man has a young wife." The hero narrowly escapes becoming involved in a murder at an inn. Finally, he is counseled never to act when angry (or sometimes to say his paternoster when he is impelled to act in anger). He returns home and sees someone sleeping with his wife. Though he thinks it is a paramour, he restrains himself, and finds that it is a new-born son.[22]

These two tales are certainly Oriental. They appear in the older literary collections from India, in Arabic and Persian reworkings, and in most of the books of exempla and jests in the Middle Ages and Renaissance.[23] In the course of time, both of these stories have been adopted into the oral folklore of many European countries, as well as in the Near East and India. Generally, the second of the tales has been better received than the first. Especially well known is the incident of the return home and the finding of the child in the mother's arms.

The other two stories in this group are each concerned with a single precept. The first is primarily an exemplary story of Oriental origin. It appears in both Jewish and Christian tradition. The precept in this tale is Think Carefully Before You Begin a Task (Type 910C). A barber has been hired to cut the king's throat. He sees on the bottom of a basin which he is using the words, "Whatsoever you do, do wisely, and think of the consequences." He drops the razor and confesses the plot. Also belonging to an almost purely literary tradition is The Treasure of the Hanging Man (Type 910D), known in England as a ballad, "The Heir of Lynne." The dying father tells his son to hang himself in a certain place if he ever loses his property. The

[22] In a tale popular in Finland and also known in Estonia and Russia (Iron is More Precious than Gold [Type 677]), the counsel, indicated by the title of the story, is essentially a magic formula. By its use the hero, who has let himself fall from a ship to the bottom of the sea, acquires much gold.

[23] For a good discussion of the literary history of these two tales, see: Cosquin, *Etudes folkloriques*, pp. 100ff.; Chauvin, *Bibliographie*, VIII, 138, Nos. 116 and 136; Köhler, *Zeitschrift für Volkskunde*, VI, 169-171.

son runs through with everything and at last is about to hang himself, when the roof falls down with the money which the father has hidden there.

Of tales concerning precepts, these are about the only ones which seem to have become known to the oral story-teller. On the other hand, the books of exempla and the novelle of the Middle Ages and Renaissance multiplied these stories very freely.[24]

B. CHEATS

In "Big Claus and Little Claus" Hans Christian Andersen succeeded in writing one of the most popular of his stories without making any significant changes in the tradition as he had learned it. The material itself is so diverting that it has pleased not only the literary audience which he addressed but also the listeners to tales in all parts of the world. We need not inquire too curiously as to why men of all countries and stations delight in the successful accomplishment of a swindle, but the truth seems to be that if the terms of the transaction are clearly understood, a story of clever cheating receives a universal response. This tale of The Rich and the Poor Peasant (Type 1535) has been told in European literature since its appearance in the Latin poem *Unibos* in the tenth century and has seldom been omitted from any collection where it was at all appropriate. But it is also immensely popular as an oral tale. A hasty survey of easily available versions shows 875. It appears in nearly every collection of stories over the whole of Europe and Asia; it is among the most popular stories in Iceland and Ireland, in Finland and in Russia, in India and the Dutch East Indies. It is well known not only on the North African coast but is also found in many parts of central and south Africa. In the western hemisphere it has been reported all the way from Greenland to Peru. Eleven North American Indian versions show borrowings from the Scandinavians, the French, and the Spanish. It appears in the French tradition of Missouri, Louisiana, and Canada; in the English of Virginia, the Spanish of Puerto Rico and Peru, the Portuguese of Brazil and Massachusetts, and the Negro of Jamaica and the Bahamas.

It is natural that in these hundreds of occurrences considerable variation should appear, both in the order and the nature of the details. But all versions conform sufficiently well to a norm to make identification easy and unmistakable. The story frequently begins with a piece of blackmail. A man is set to watch a chest which is falsely said to be full of money, or he is asked to guard a wooden cow which is supposed to be a real cow. The rascal brings it about that the object is stolen and demands damages. The cheater next takes along a supply of lime or ashes and succeeds in selling this under the pretext that it is gold. Another trick is the sale of some pseudo-magic object—a cow-

[24] See, for example, all the various subdivisions of Motif J21. See also the additions to these in Rotunda, *Italian Novella*, J21.23 to J21.31.

hide or a bird-skin that is alleged to accomplish marvels. Sometimes this object is exchanged for a chest in which an adulteress has hidden her paramour. The rascal is usually given a large sum of money by the frightened lover in payment for his freedom. These adventures with the adulteress and her lover sometimes occur independently (Motif K1574). The next cheat, the unsuccessful imitation, we have met before in stories of magic or the miraculous.[25] Here, however, there is no magic, but only a pretense of it. The rascal claims to have a flute (or a fiddle or knife, or the like) which will bring people back to life. His confederate, a woman, plays dead, and he apparently revives her. The rich peasant buys the magic object, kills his own wife so as to use it, and then is unable to bring her back to life. Sometimes before and sometimes after this adventure the poor peasant reports the large price that he has received for his cow-hide. The rich peasant is therefore induced to kill all his cows in order to sell their hides. He finds, of course, that it was only the frightened lover in the chest who would pay an exorbitant price for a cow-hide. Eventually the cheater is caught and is placed in a sack or a chest where he must await execution of his sentence. A shepherd finds him there and asks what he is doing. The cheater says that he is the angel Gabriel on the way to heaven or that he has been put in the sack because he will not marry the princess. The shepherd is only too glad to take his place so as to receive the good things he tells about.[26] The rich peasant now sees the escaped cheater and asks him where he came from. He tells him that he has been down in the river where he has acquired many sheep, that the way to get them is to dive down after them. The rich peasant dives off the bridge and kills himself.

As indicated, several of these traits occur independently and may constitute complete anecdotes in themselves. The order in which the incidents occur is also treated with great freedom. Particularly is there a frequent mixture of the elements of this tale with that of Cleverness and Gullibility (Type 1539), if, indeed, the two are actually to be thought of as independent stories. In the latter tale much is made of the sale of worthless animals and objects under the pretense that they are either magic or marvelous. Sometimes a cow is sold as a goat, a rabbit as a letter-carrier, or it may be a magic hat which is supposed to pay all bills, a wand that revives the dead, or a pot that cooks of itself. He also has a horse that is alleged to drop gold. By means of placing a gold coin in the horse's dung, he is able to persuade the buyer. After many such tricks the young man has himself buried alive and when his enemy comes to where he is, stabs him with a knife from out of the ground.

Most reporters of folktales have not distinguished this latter type from

[25] See, for example, Type 531 and Type 753.
[26] This incident of the exchange of places in the sack occurs as a separate story, The Parson in the Sack to Heaven (Type 1737).

the more familiar story of The Rich and the Poor Peasant. It is clear, however, that this particular type is very well known all around the Baltic and in Russia. The tradition seems to center in Finland, where 253 versions are listed.

One difficulty in a comparative study of tales like the two we have just noticed is the fact that they are little more than a loose series of single anecdotes. Types of this kind have a natural instability very baffling to the investigator of folktale origins and dissemination.

A story represented by the old French romance of *Trubert* of the thirteenth century has some elements in common with The Rich and the Poor Peasant. The Youth Cheated in Selling Oxen (Type 1538) concerns itself with the revenge which the hero takes on his enemies. He masks as a carpenter and persuades the man who has cheated him to go to the woods to look at trees. He gives him a good beating and exacts a large sum of money before he will stop. Later he masks as a doctor and again beats his enemy. In some versions he also avenges himself on the purchaser's wife. Eventually he is arrested and condemned to be hanged. But he persuades a miller to take his place by the old trick of lying about the good things awaiting him.[27] In some versions the story ends with the youth having himself buried and stabbing his enemy from the ground.[28]

Although this tale has never attained extraordinary popularity in any country, it has been collected orally in every part of Europe. No comparative study of the tale seems to have been made, but it would seem probable that we have here a literary invention which has been taken over into the repertory of oral story-tellers.

The material handled in the tale of The Rich and the Poor Peasant and in the two other related stories just examined has been freely drawn upon to make other combinations. One of these has attained some currency in northern and eastern Europe—The Clever Boy (Type 1542). It will be noted that almost every incident belongs in one of these tales, though the story of The Master Thief (Type 1525) has furnished at least two traits. A brother and sister live together but are poor, and the brother goes out to make a living by fooling people. He reports to the king that he has some marvelous "fooling sticks," and he gets the king's horse by borrowing it to ride home for them. In other versions he sells the king a wolf to guard his fowls and a bear to keep watch over his cows. He sells the king what he says is a self-cooking kettle and a marvelous staff to hang it on. He feigns to kill and resuscitate his sister with a magic pipe, which the king buys and experiments with disastrously. The hero now puts on his sister's clothes and is taken into the palace as a companion of the princess. A prince comes as a suitor to the supposed maiden, who leaves just in time, but not before the princess is with

[27] See Types 1535 and 1737.
[28] Cf. the tale immediately preceding this (Type 1539).

child. The story may end in several ways: he may be caught and put in a cask or sack, where he exchanges places with a shepherd; he may be condemned to be hanged but again persuades someone to take his place; or the king may be so impressed with his cleverness that he takes him as son-in-law.

We have here about as clear a case of a folktale concocted out of others as it is possible to find. When the incidents from other stories are eliminated, there seems to remain nothing but the brother and sister as confederates in their swindles, and the access to the princess through masking as a girl. Even these motifs can easily be found elsewhere.[29]

A very diverting story which seems to be rather well known in Scandinavia and Finland[30] is The Man Who Got a Night's Lodging (Type 1544). In this tale the rascal feigns deafness and always accepts hospitality before it is offered. He deliberately misunderstands everything. For example, he takes the host's horse out of the stable and puts his own in. He is supposed to pay for his lodging with a goat skin: he takes one of the man's own goats. At the table they put poor food before him but he always manages to get the best. At night he succeeds in sleeping with the wife or the daughter. He eats the food which the wife has put out in the night for her husband. Having seduced the women, he now threatens to tell about it, and they confess. The husband becomes very angry and is going to kill the trickster's horse, but kills his own instead.

The tale of the rascal who seduces his host's wife and then tells on her has many variations in the literature of jests, especially those of the Renaissance. One told by Hans Sachs and by Johannes Pauli, The Parson's Stupid Wife (Type 1750), has received some oral currency in northern and eastern Europe. A mercenary lover makes the parson's wife believe that chickens can be taught to talk. At her request, he undertakes to hatch out hens' eggs, and he receives a large amount of corn to feed the chickens. When the chickens do hatch, he declares that they sing, "The peasant has slept with the parson's wife." He is allowed to keep the corn.

The four tales of tricksters just considered are all of relatively limited popularity and serve as good examples of the fact that tales of this nature may often be well known in one area without spreading to neighboring countries. But the extreme popularity of The Rich and the Poor Peasant shows that sometimes these stories may be almost universal in currency.

Another trickster tale which is well known both in the Orient and the Occident is The Student from Paradise (Paris) (Type 1540). As told in most of Europe, it begins with a wandering student who tells a woman that he is just back from Paris. She thinks he has said "from Paradise" and she immediately gathers together a sum of money and a quantity of goods for him to take to her late husband. The student has hardly gone with the mis-

---

[29] For seduction by masking as a girl, see Motif K1321.1.

[30] A single version each has been reported for Russia, Spain, and Flanders.

appropriated goods when the woman's son returns home. He realizes the cheat and sets out to overtake the student and recover the goods. He finds the student, who tells him that the thief has just escaped through the woods. They are too thick to ride through, so that the man leaves his horse, which the student rides away. In other versions the student tells him that the thief has gone to heaven by way of a tree. The man lies on his back to look for the ascending thief and meantime the student steals the horse.

This jest is popular in the joke collections of the Renaissance, and as an oral tale it is related not only in all parts of Europe but in Asia as far east as Indonesia. Antti Aarne has accorded the tale a thorough study based upon more than 300 oral versions. He finds that the play upon words (Paris, Paradise) is essentially a European trait and is absent from the Oriental. In the eastern stories the deceased to whom a present is sent is the woman's son rather than her husband, as in the European. In the latter part of the tale the report that the thief has escaped up a tree is Oriental; the escape through the woods European. Aarne is uncertain as to which of these forms is the earlier. In his discussion of Aarne's work, Kaarle Krohn[31] concludes that an origin in India is very likely. It must be said, however, that the evidence as to the direction in which this tale has moved is inconclusive.

One of the most important elements in many trickster tales is the use made by these rascals of the desire most people have to avoid scandal. Almost as strong is the fear of being haled into a law court. In a story whose oral distribution extends from the British Isles to the Philippines—The Profitable Exchange (Type 1655)—both these fears are played upon to the enrichment of the cheater. He has asked hospitality, since he has only one grain of corn left. The corn is eaten by the cock and when he threatens suit, he is allowed to keep the cock as damages. Later he has the same experience when the hog eats the cock, and when an ox eats the hog. The story may very well end at this point, but it frequently proceeds with further profitable exchanges.[32] He barters his ox for an old woman's corpse, which he sets up so that the princess knocks her over (Motif K2152). In order to avoid the scandal that will come from the accusation of murder, she marries the rascal. The ending of the story is often not well integrated with the main plot. Sometimes it is said that he and the princess have a son who surpasses even his father in cunning. In others, he places the princess whom he has won in a bag, but he is at last outwitted, for someone substitutes a worthless object or an animal and lets the princess escape.

In his thorough monograph on this tale, Christiansen,[33] who has started with a discussion of a story from the Scottish island of Barra and one from County Kerry in Ireland, concludes: "So far some main lines in the dis-

---

[31] See Aarne, *Der Mann aus dem Paradiese*; Krohn, *Übersicht*, pp. 155ff.

[32] For a similar story told of animals, see Type 170.

[33] R. Th. Christiansen, "Bodach an T-Sílein," *Béaloideas*, III (1931), 107-120.

tribution of the tale emerge. The versions from Kerry and from Barra belong to a chain of tradition running through France to Italy. It is, however, difficult to discern how the further development went. Perhaps the tale is a combination, made in Italy (?) or somewhere in Southern Europe, from those two motifs, the lucky exchanges, and the girl in the bag. Outside of Europe both these incidents occur as separate stories, as some brief references will show." The lucky exchange by itself occurs frequently in African tales, and the substitution of an animal or object in the bag is practically worldwide.[34]

The humor of the folk does not always make close discrimination between stupidity and cleverness. Sometimes a story begins with a series of absurd actions where we are amused at their utter foolishness. But later the fool turns out to be really clever. This pattern is well enough known in romantic stories of the Male Cinderella type;[35] but the mixture is also found in tales designed for humor.[36] Such a tale of mixed motifs is The Good Bargain (Type 1642). It appears in Basile's *Pentamerone* in the seventeenth century and is known throughout central Europe, both north and south, but has not been reported from either the east or the west of the continent. Many of the separate motifs appear by themselves, so that the tale has no well-integrated plot. A numskull throws money to frogs so that they can count it,[37] or he sells meat to dogs or butter to a signpost. He complains of his losses to the king and thus makes the princess laugh for the first time. Though the king offers her to the boy as a reward, he does not want to marry her. The king therefore tells him to return later for his reward. When he does so, he promises the doorkeeper to share the reward with him. It turns out that the boy is to be rewarded with a beating, which the doorkeeper receives instead. At the end of the tale the boy is summoned before the king on the complaint of a certain Jew. He borrows the Jew's coat and then discredits his testimony by predicting successfully that the Jew would even claim the coat which the boy is wearing.

Tales both of clever tricks and of stupid action are very likely to have extremely loose plots and to be susceptible of easy addition and subtraction. Indeed, for a whole series of such relatively unstable stories, it is much more convenient to examine anecdotes separately with only incidental attention to some of the ways in which they are occasionally combined. Thus a considerable number of incidents listed by Aarne in his type index as having to do with stupid people or with clever tricksters[38] are not mentioned here but will be noticed along with other similar motifs in a later chapter.[39]

[34] See Motif K526 and references; cf. Type 327C.

[35] See pp. 125ff., above.

[36] This peculiar combination is especially popular in the stories of certain primitive peoples. See pp. 319ff., below.

[37] This motif has been reported from persons of English tradition in Virginia.

[38] Here belong most of the types from No. 1030 to 1335, as well as many more listed between No. 1350 and 2000.

[39] See pp. 188ff., below.

C. ROBBERS

The final group of stories which we shall notice in our survey of the complex tale in Europe and Asia is concerned with robbers and their adventures. Many stories with this general theme consist of a single incident or motif. But since these incidents frequently form a part of one of the longer complex tales, it will be convenient to notice them in connection with these longer stories with which they have affinity and of which they are frequently an organic part.[40]

One of these complex robber tales has a very long known history. Herodotus, in the fifth century before Christ, tells the story of the treasure house of Rhampsinitus (Type 950).[41] Some of the parts of this tale were apparently known in Greece before his time. But there seems little doubt that all subsequent versions of the story go back eventually to Herodotus. It appears not only in the literary collections of the European Middle Ages and Renaissance, but also in the Buddhistic writings of the early Christian era and in the *Ocean of Story* from India of the twelfth century. Moreover, the tale has had a wide acceptance in oral tradition all the way from Iceland across Europe and Asia to Indonesia and the Philippines. It does not seem to have gone to central or south Africa nor to the western hemisphere except in a tale of the Cape Verde Islanders in Massachusetts.

Herodotus tells the story in a good deal of detail, and the changes which have taken place in the twenty-four hundred years since his time consist in minor elaborations. The architect of the king's treasure house has left a stone loose in the building. As Herodotus tells it, he leaves directions to his two sons at the time of his death so that they may have free entry to the king's treasure. In some more modern versions it is the architect himself who robs the treasure house. Sometimes the theft is detected by means of a straw fire the smoke of which escapes through the secret hole. In any event, the thief is caught in a trap. In order that his identity may be concealed and that his brother can continue the thefts, he has the brother cut off his head and leave the headless body. The king wishes to identify the thief and to this end has the body carried through the streets to see if anyone will weep for it. Though the son has forewarned the family, the mother becomes importunate and insists upon the rescue of her son's body. His brother succeeds in stealing the body either, as Herodotus shows, by cleverly getting the guards drunk or else by putting on the same motley garb as the guards and thus being taken for a guard. The last attempt of the king to capture the robber is also unsuccessful. The king sends his daughter to a brothel and gives all men free access to her. She makes each of them declare his most dangerous exploit.

---

[40] A number of anecdotes concerning thieves and robbers are postponed for treatment elsewhere, since they show no such affinity to larger narrative complexes. See pp. 199ff., below.

[41] Herodotus, Book II, ch. 121.

When she learns of the theft, she is to mark the culprit with a black sign. The rascal marks all of the knights, and even the king himself, and thus escapes detection. Herodotus tells it somewhat differently. The princess is to hold tight to the hand of the robber when she discovers him. Knowing this, he takes with him the hand of a corpse, and she finds that he has escaped while she holds on to the dead man's hand. Some other versions also tell how a child is used to test guilt. The boy will hand a thief a knife. But at the proper time the rascal exchanges a toy with the child and thus escapes detection. At the end, he is always rewarded by marriage with the king's daughter.

This is one of the best examples of stability in a folktale. Nevertheless, a study of the detailed changes, especially by oral raconteurs, should be of great interest in connection with the mutual relations of literature and folklore. It would be interesting to know by what devious routes this story of Herodotus has come to be part of the repertory not only of the novelle writers of the Renaissance, but of simple story-tellers in the farthest reaches of Europe and Asia.

The interest of the teller of this tale is obviously on the side of the robber in his opposition to the king. In a tale familiar to the literature of northern Europe since the Renaissance and known orally in Germany, the Baltic states, and Hungary,[42] the king is in alliance with the robber. He joins him in disguise to rifle a bank. The robber, however, will not permit him to take more than six shillings, pointing out that the king has so many thieves. In another purely Baltic tale, The Bank Robbery (Type 951B), robbers help the king by accidentally discovering a conspiracy against him as they climb up to enter the bank.

A tale of a robber is used at least once as a framework for bringing together a group of related stories. Though the tale is undoubtedly literary, appearing as it does in written narrative collections since the twelfth century, it is nevertheless rather well known in the folklore of Ireland, Scotland, Germany, and Roumania. In this story, The Old Robber Relates Three Adventures to Free His Sons (Type 953), the captor demands that each adventure should be more frightful than the last. He tells first of all of a fearful encounter with ghostlike cats. Next comes an adventure with a one-eyed giant, such as Odysseus experienced with Polyphemus. The third adventure reminds one of Hansel and Gretel: an ogre is fooled by the substitution of a corpse for a child who is to be cooked for him. Lastly, the robber tells how he substituted himself later in order to save the child. It turns out that the rescued child of the last tale is the robber's present captor. In gratitude, he rewards the old man liberally.

Story-tellers are not always on the side of the robbers, for they realize that robber bands are often cruel and ruthless, and they may be interested

[42] The King and the Robber (Type 951A).

in the ways in which such bands are defeated. A story rather popular in northern and eastern Europe is that of The King and the Soldier (Type 952) in which the soldier is impelled to testify to the king against the crimes of his superior officer. He accompanies the king, whom he does not know, to the robbers' house and there renders them helpless by a magic spell or else succeeds in killing them and saving the life of the king. Later the king reveals himself and rewards the soldier.

Familiar to all readers of the *Arabian Nights* is the story of The Forty Thieves (Type 954). The robbers attempt to enter the house hidden in oil casks. The clever girl inside detects the plan and kills them all. This story is, of course, literary, but is occasionally heard as a folktale in all parts of Europe and sometimes elsewhere. It may not, indeed, be original with the *Arabian Nights,* since there is an ancient Egyptian tale with the same general plot.[43]

In somewhat simpler fashion, merely by cutting off their heads as they enter the house, one after the other, the hero of the story At the Robbers' House (Type 956A) gets rid of them, escapes from the hot chamber where he is confined along with many corpses, and takes away the robbers' treasure. This is not a well-known tale, though it is occasionally told all the way from Flanders to Russia.

Better known is its female counterpart, The Clever Maiden Alone at Home Kills the Robbers (Type 956B). She also cuts off their heads as they enter, one by one. But this story has a sequel, for a companion of the robbers takes revenge by appearing as a suitor for the girl. He beguiles her into the woods, where the robber band finds her. Only with great difficulty does she escape. This tale, with its greater range of interest, seems to be at home in all parts of Europe, but except for a corrupt New York State version has not been reported outside.

The girl wooed by the robber is even more familiar in the story of The Robber Bridegroom (Type 955). Though she imagines she has married a fine gentleman, she finds that she has been taken into a den of robbers. While she is hidden under the bed, she sees another girl murdered. She severs the fingers of the murdered girl and keeps them as proof of the imposition. The details of the story differ a good deal. Sometimes she finds her way, by means of ashes or peas which she has scattered, to make a path through the woods.[44]

The story has several points in common with the Bluebeard tale[45] of the girl who unwittingly marries an ogre and discovers the corpses of her sisters, and there has been some mutual influence between the two types. The Robber Bridegroom is rather popular in various countries in all parts of Europe, but seems to be quite unknown in others. The single versions in

[43] See p. 274, below.
[44] An incident already noticed in Hansel and Gretel (Type 327A).
[45] Types 311 and 312.

Armenia, India, New York State, and the Virginia mountains are the only ones thus far reported outside of Europe.

By far the chief of all folktales concerning robberies is The Master Thief (Type 1525). In one or another of its forms it appears in nearly every collection of tales from Europe and Asia and occasionally in all other parts of the world. It consists first of all of a nucleus, a well-defined series of incidents which occurs almost everywhere and which affords a clue by which even very fragmentary stories can be identified as belonging to this cycle. To this nucleus (designated as Type 1525A) other appropriate incidents are added with a good deal of freedom, though these special developments are by no means haphazard in their geographical relationship. Of this nuclear part of the tale, more than seven hundred oral versions have been noted from all over the world, and literary tellings have been common since its appearance in Pauli's Schimpf und Ernst early in the sixteenth century.

This most usual part of the tale normally begins with the return home of a prodigal son who is now a great man and who boasts of his skill as a thief. Sometimes there are brothers who have been away to learn trades, and they vie with each other in bragging about their accomplishments.[46] A neighboring earl hears about the master thief and challenges him to submit to tests. He steals the horses from under vigilant mounted horsemen, either by disguising himself as an old woman or else by skillfully inducing them to get drunk. He steals horses or cattle from their drivers when he lets loose a rabbit so that the drivers all join in the chase. A much severer test is to steal a ring from the countess's finger and a sheet from the bed in which she is sleeping. He does this by raising a corpse to the bedroom window and inducing the earl to shoot it. In order to avoid scandal, the earl goes outside and buries the body of the man whom he thinks he has killed. While this is going on, the thief enters into the dark bedroom pretending to be the husband and persuades the countess to give him the sheet, so that he can wrap up the corpse. He also persuades her that it would be the decent thing to bury him with her ring on, since he has lost his life in the attempt to get the ring. When the earl returns, they realize that they have been duped.

After these and other similar thefts, the hero is condemned to death. While he is awaiting execution, he is put in a sack. Just as in the tale of The Rich and the Poor Peasant,[47] he persuades a gullible passerby to take his place in the sack by saying that he is waiting to be taken to heaven.[48]

To this central part of the story additions may be made with considerable freedom. The cheater steals a horse by pretending to show the earl how a

---

[46] Like the skillful brothers in Types 653 and 654.

[47] Type 1535. This incident sometimes appears as an independent tale (Type 1737), though it is usually a part of one of these longer tales.

[48] A considerable variety and ingenuity is shown in the persuasive tale which the man in the sack uses to bring about this exchange of places. Instead of the expected journey to heaven, there may be almost any kind of tempting prospect held forth.

horse may be stolen but by really riding it away (Type 1525B). Or he fishes in the street and, while travelers are watching his foolish actions, his confederate steals their wagons (Type 1525C). These two latter incidents are usually inserted within the general framework of the tale. The theft of the horse is much the better known of the two. But the next series of incidents (Type 1525D) is so popular that it might well be considered an essential part of the type. It has been noted in all parts of the world and in considerably more than three hundred versions. These incidents always concern the stealing of an animal, usually an ox. One of the best known devices is the putting of shoes in the road separately. The owner of the ox passes the first by, but when later he finds the second, he leaves his ox unguarded while he returns for the first. In some versions the articles are a sword and a sheath or a knife and a fork. The ox owner may also be attracted away from his animal when the rascal apparently hangs himself in the woods or when he imitates the bellowing of cattle so that the owner leaves one ox in order to try to recover one that he has lost. More rarely in this series of incidents, the thief steals clothes by inducing the owner to take them off and go bathing. Sometimes also he scares some thieves away from their treasure by striking an ox which he himself has killed and crying out, "Those others did it."

The next two incidents to be considered are often quite independent of the central part of the master thief tale. In one of these, The Thieves and their Pupil (Type 1525E), members of the group take turns in stealing from each other. Finally the pupil surpasses them all. The last incident, a purely Baltic development, is really a combination of several other tales by which horses and money are stolen. Usually this incident is followed by the exchange of the prisoner in the sack (Type 1525F).

Stories of clever thieves are very old, and as we read literature and look into the folklore of remote parts of the world, we will find many stories of this general nature. But within the range of the European and Asiatic folktale, the story of The Master Thief is much more than a casual group of clever thefts. As a well-defined folktale, it appears to have a wide geographical distribution with clearly recognizable relationships from area to area, and a literary history going back at least to the Renaissance. Because of the interesting affinities between this tale and many other stories of thefts and because of the extremely wide circulation which this tale has experienced over the world, it would be interesting to know much more about its history and development that we do now, when no really adequate study has been devoted to it. A tale of this kind, in which incidents can be inserted rather freely, presents comparative problems which should be susceptible to analytical study with as much hope of success as any one of the two hundred and more complex tales which we have now finished reviewing.

12. ORIGIN AND HISTORY OF THE
COMPLEX TALES

NOT every complex tale known to story-tellers of the area we are considering has found a place in the discussion just concluded. But practically all of those omitted are of very limited distribution.[1] With each tale the main facts about its history and its occurrences in oral tradition have been indicated wherever conclusions seemed possible. While discussing each tale, I have had before me a summary of the scholarship which has been devoted to it and a complete list of oral versions insofar as the extensive reference books and regional surveys now available made this possible. Frequently the mere bringing together of this material was sufficient to compel conclusions about the tale which do not seem likely to need revision. But when all tales with such clear-cut histories have been considered, there remain a large number which present problems sufficient to occupy the attention of scholars for many a decade to come.

Of these complex tales, along with a few closely related simple anecdotes, we have examined somewhat over two hundred. The order in which they have been taken up has been determined by their subject matter. And that means that tales about the same kinds of characters or incidents have been brought together, often when there was no organic relationship between them and when they had little if anything in common in their origin and history. When so much remains dark about the beginnings and about the vicissitudes of so large a number of our folktales, no complete account of them can be based upon historical categories.

Nevertheless, in a very tentative way it may be of interest to see which of our tales have a history that can be proclaimed with some confidence, which of them show great probabilities of proper solution, and which of them still present difficult problems.

That many of our European and Asiatic folktales go back to a literary source is as clear as any fact of scholarship can be made. There would thus seem to be no reason to doubt that an Oriental literary text is responsible for the subsequent development of a considerable number of tales which have received oral currency in Europe and sometimes in the Orient. In the older Buddhistic sources[2] are found: Death's Messengers (Type 335); Six Go Through the Whole World (Type 513A); The Three Snake Leaves (Type

[1] An exhaustive treatment would include a considerable number of such tales of purely local development for Lithuania, for Roumania, for Russia, and for India. The material for the first three of these countries may be examined in the surveys of Balys, Schullerus, and Andrejev, respectively (see references on pp. 420f.). No adequate survey of the material for India has yet been made. I have been working upon one for some years and have reasonabl⸗ hopes of completing it.

[2] These are best represented by (1) Cowell, *The Jātaka*; (2) Chavannes, *500 Contes*.

612); The Two Travelers (Type 613); The Animal Languages (Type 670); "Think Carefully Before You Begin a Task" (Type 910C); The Brave Tailor (Type 1640); and Doctor Know-All (Type 1641). In the *Ocean of Story*, a Sanskrit collection brought together in the twelfth century but based upon much older material, there appear, as probable originals of the European oral tradition, versions of: Wise Through Experience (Type 910A); The Servant's Good Counsels (Type 910B); and Faithful John (Type 516). From other collections of literary tales originating in India appear to come: The Bridge to the Other World (Type 471); The Four Skillful Brothers (Type 653); The Wise Brothers (Type 655); and One Beggar Trusts God, the Other the King (Type 841). From various literary sources in India the incidents which make up two of our related tales have been taken and unified at some point before they entered into the oral tradition of the west.[3] These two are: The Son of the King and of the Smith (Type 920); and The King and the Peasant's Son (Type 921). Whatever may be the ultimate source of the stories in the *Thousand and One Nights*, several of our old folktales are found in that work in much the form in which these stories first reached European taletellers. Among these tales appearing in the *Arabian Nights* are: Siddhi Numan (Type 449*); Aladdin (Type 561); Open Sesame (Type 676); Luck and Wealth (Type 736); Hatch-penny (Type 745); Oft Proved Fidelity (Type 881); The Treasure of the Hanging Man (Type 910D); and The Forty Thieves (Type 954). Finally, of these tales of Oriental origin, may be mentioned one which appears in the Persian collection, *The Thousand and One Days*. This is The Prophecy (Type 930).

Similarly, an ultimate origin in European literature seems unmistakable for a dozen or more of the stories current today, whether locally or over the complete European-Asiatic area. Three of the tales which we have noticed certainly go back to Greek literature: Oedipus (Type 931) to Sophocles; Rhampsinitus (Type 950) to Herodotus; and The Wolf and the Kids (Type 123) to the Aesop collection. A fourteenth century Latin poem, the *Asinarius*, is responsible for the very few oral versions of The Ass (Type 430). Folktales have borrowed very freely from saints' legends: certainly Pride Is Punished (Type 836) is a mere oral treatment of the legend of Polycarp. The great collections of illustrative tales which in the Middle Ages went under the name of Exempla contained a considerable number of folktales. Frequently it is impossible to tell whether they may be reworkings of oral tradition, but sometimes it is quite evident that the oral tale is taken directly from the literary collection. This is clearly true of: Friends in Life and Death (Type 470); The Boy Who Learned Many Things (Type 517); The Three Languages (Type 671); The Angel and the Hermit (Type 759); and Who Ate the Lamb's Heart (Type 785). At least two tales seem to have been learned from the work of the German *Meistersinger*: The Faithful Wife (Type 888); and

[3] For a discussion of this point, see p. 160, above.

The Pound of Flesh (Type 890). Of course, both of these tales were used by Shakespeare, and that fact has doubtless been of influence on their subsequent popularity. Many stories have undoubtedly originated among the people of Italy, and it is sometimes difficult to know whether a tale recounted by those great writers of *novelle* beginning with Boccaccio was learned from the people or was invented by the author. For at least three of our folktales such literary invention by the *novella* writer seems the most reasonable hypothesis. The Wager on the Wife's Chastity (Type 882) is in Boccaccio's *Decameron*; The Luck-Bringing Shirt (Type 844) in the *Pecorone* of Ser Giovanni; and The Taming of the Shrew (Type 901) in the *Nights* of Straparola. The *Pentamerone* of Giambattista Basile of the early seventeenth century is almost completely made up of oral folktales, though transformed into an extraordinary literary style. But it is probable that he invented several tales by freely combining traditional material. Such seems to be the situation with The Forsaken Fiancée (Type 884). Finally, at least one tale given currency by the Grimms, The Two Girls, the Bear, and the Dwarf (Type 426), comes directly from a German literary collection of stories which appeared in 1818.

The fact that one may cite a literary form of a story, even a very old version, is by no means proof that we have arrived at the source of the tradition. Nothing is better authenticated in the study of traditional narrative than the fact that the literary telling of a tale may represent merely one of hundreds of examples of the story in question and have for the history of the tradition no more significance than any other one of the hundreds of variants at hand. Apuleius's telling of Cupid and Psyche and the author of Tobit's version of The Grateful Dead Man tale appear both to be rather late and somewhat aberrant forms of much older oral tales. With this warning in mind, the careful student should be slow in arriving at the conclusion that a stated literary document is the fountainhead of a particular narrative tradition. For those tales which we have just listed, the actual dependence on the literary source has seemed well established. In addition to these, there are a considerable number for which there is a well-known early literary form to which the weight of evidence would point probably, but not quite certainly, as the actual source. Some of these tales have been very popular among story-tellers, and have spread over two or more continents, and some have had only a very limited acceptance among the people. The degree of popularity and the geographical extent of the distribution is a fact which must be taken into consideration with every tale when we are trying to judge the question of its ultimate literary or oral invention. For this reason, in listing the tales with probable literary sources, it is helpful to indicate briefly what type of oral distribution each has.

At least related to the old Greek story of The Cranes of Ibycus is the tale The Sun Brings All to Light (Type 960; oral: Spain to Russia). From saints' legends at least two oral tales appear to have been taken: Hospitality Rewarded (Type 750B; oral: scattered thinly over most of Europe); and Christ and the Smith (Type 753; oral: all Europe, especially the Baltic states). Certainly influenced by some of the legends of the popes, if not directly borrowed from them, is The Dream (Type 725; oral: moderately popular in eastern Europe and the Baltic states). In addition to the folktales which we are sure have come from books of Exempla, there are several where such an origin seems likely: The King and the Robber (Type 951A; oral: Germany and the Baltic states, sporadic in Hungary and Russia); The Old Robber Relates Three Adventures (Type 953; oral: thinly scattered, Ireland to Roumania); and "We Three; For Money" (Type 1697; oral: thinly scattered over all Europe). The influence of the chivalric romance in general is seen in The Bride Won in a Tournament (Type 508) which was told in Straparola's *Nights* and received frequent literary treatment in the Middle Ages and Renaissance, but has been collected orally only in three versions in Lithuania.

The rich prose literature of medieval Iceland has in it many folktale elements, most of which doubtless go back to popular tradition. But this may not have been true in all cases: an Icelandic prose tale of 1339 seems to lie back of the oral tale Godfather Death (Type 332; oral: Iceland to Palestine, especially the Baltic states, rare in Russia). A medieval chronicle of 1175 probably forms the beginning of the tradition later carried on through French and German jestbooks and at least one English play, and connected with the name of a famous Lord Mayor of London. This is Whittington's Cat (Type 1651; oral: scattered from western Europe to Indonesia, especially popular in Finland).

The jestbooks of the Renaissance contain a number of folktales. In many cases, these were taken from older literary collections, or indeed from oral tradition. But occasionally they seem to have served as a real source for tales which now belong to the folk. Such would seem to be true of The Wishes (Type 750A; oral: popular throughout Europe, sporadic in China); The Tailor in Heaven (Type 800; oral: scattered thinly over Europe, sporadic among Buryat of Siberia); The Devil as Advocate (Type 821; oral: all Europe, especially Baltic, moderately popular); Sleeping Beauty (Type 410; oral: scattered thinly over Europe, one-third of versions Italian, based on Basile); and The Three Brothers (Type 654; oral: confined to Europe).

A German literary tale of the thirteenth century may well be the beginning of The Frog King (Type 440; oral: Germany to Russia only). The habit of writing literary folktales was carried on into the eighteenth century, both in France and in Germany. Many of these tales never assumed any oral popularity. On the other hand, The Girls Who Married Animals (Type 552), although concocted by Musäus at the end of the eighteenth century of authentic oral material, combined with an analogous tale in Basile, has since entered into the stream of oral tradition in the form he then designed. Its oral distribution shows the greatest inconsistency and indicates frequent direct use of the literary source.

For all the tales mentioned thus far in this summary there seems a strong probability of ultimate literary origin. But it cannot be too frequently repeated that the fact of the appearance of a tale in some literary document is no proof that it did not originate among the people. Oral tales have been a very fruitful source for literary story-tellers everywhere. It thus happens that frequently the literary appearance of a story only represents one of many hundreds of versions and is, of course, less important in the history of the tale than the oral variant from which the story was borrowed. It is not always easy to tell when a story belongs primarily to oral tradition and frequently the problem of priority is quite unsolvable. But a very considerable number of tales appearing in literary collections show such a preponderance of oral variants, as well as other indications of popular origin, that their literary appearance would seem to be purely incidental. There can be little doubt that they are all essentially oral, both in origin and in history.

Several such oral tales have found a place in Oriental literary collections. In the Hindu fable collection, the *Panchatantra*, occurs a good part of the tale of Luck and Intelligence (Type 945); it also occurs in recent literary form in India, but has a vigorous life in popular tradition of India and the Near East, and sporadically as far afield as Germany and the Philippines. In the *Ocean of Story*, as well as in the *Thousand and One Nights*, occur fragments of Devils Fight over Magic Objects (Type 518; oral: all Europe, western Asia, and North Africa) and of The Prince's Wings (Type 575; oral: sparingly over north and eastern Europe). In the *Ocean of Story*, likewise, there is an analogue of The Girl as Helper in the Hero's Flight (Type 313). This story does not otherwise appear in central Asia but is one of the most popular of all oral folktales in Europe and America; it is no wonder that it has been retold by such story-tellers as Straparola and Basile. Two tales popular in the tradition of the Near East appear in the Persian *Tuti Nameh*: The Grateful Animals (Type 554; oral: Europe and Asia, especially Baltic countries) and The Magic Bird-heart (Type 567; oral: eastern and southern Europe, and Persia; origin probably in Persian tradition). In an Arabic history of the ninth century appears an abbreviated version of The King and the Abbot (Type 922), though Walter Anderson has shown that the tradition is certainly oral, in spite of frequent literary treatments in Europe. Likewise, the occurrence of the story of The Monster in the Bridal Chamber (Type 507B) in the apocryphal Book of Tobit does not carry the implication that this version is the source of the tradition: it is obviously a late and considerably modified form of the story, which appears to have developed orally in the Near East.

Much more frequently have oral tales found a place in one or more European collections of literary stories. In another place more specific mention is made of popular tales embedded in the Greek or Latin classics.[3a] Sometimes these retellings represent rather faithfully what must have been the plot of one of our oral tales at the time and place it was heard, though there may be radical adaptation to literary form or fashion. Such is true of the retelling of the tale of Polyphemus (Type 1137) by Homer, of Cupid and Psyche (Type 425) by Apuleius, and of Perseus and Andromeda (a version of Type 300?) by various writers of myths.

It is sometimes difficult to tell whether such a classical story as that of Perseus is really a version of a folktale now current in Europe. There is little doubt, however, that the appearance of the story of The Dragon-Slayer (Type 300) in connection with that of The Two Brothers (Type 303) in Icelandic saga does represent an actual version of an oral tale, apparently originating in France, and now known by almost every taleteller in the world. In Icelandic saga there also appears a version of The Clever Peasant Girl (Type 875), though this does not represent its source, which is certainly oral and central European. The learning of animal speech by eating the flesh of a serpent occurs in a German and Baltic oral tale (Type 673) and also in the Siegfried story, but this is the only parallel, and the resemblance may not indicate actual relationship.

In other literary forms of the Middle Ages there occasionally appear oral tales. Geoffrey of Monmouth, in telling the story of King Lear, includes the incident of Love Like Salt (Type 923), widely known, not only through Shakespeare's treatment, but also as a part of the Cinderella cycle (Type 510). The chivalric romances, likewise, contain much that must have been taken directly from the people. Marie de France thus tells the tale of The Prince as Bird (Type 432), which, though certainly oral, has been frequently retold by both medieval and Renaissance writers. In some versions of the Tristram story occur elements of The Clever Horse (Type 531; oral: western Europe to the Philippines, origin probably India), and in an Icelandic saga of the fourteenth century there is a much clearer version. In the Fortunatus romance, which occurs in many forms, there is found a version of The Three Magic Objects and the Wonderful Fruits (Type 566), essentially west European folk tradition. The *Gesta Romanorum*, and later, Hans Sachs, have versions of The Three Doctors (Type 660), a tradition well known from Ireland to Russia. Despite the fact that the French and German fabliaux are usually literary in content, at least two oral tales are used in such collections: The Hero Catches the Princess with Her Own Words (Type 853) and King Thrushbeard (Type 900).

Though the jestbooks which were in vogue during the fifteenth and sixteenth centuries normally consist of very simple anecdotes, occasionally they included a complex folk story, like Hansel and Gretel (Type 327A); Master Pfriem (Type 801); One-Eye, Two-Eyes, Three-Eyes (Type 511); The

---

[3a] See pp. 278ff., below.

Student from Paradise (Type 1540); or The Three Lucky Brothers (Type 1650). The latter story also appears in a collection of novelle. These prose tale collections, beginning as early as Boccaccio's *Decameron,* sometimes contain stories which the author had heard, though they are usually much changed in style from what must have been the oral original. Such is true of The Smith Outwits the Devil (Type 330), and of Six Go Through the Whole World (Type 513). The latter tale appears in many other literary collections, both Oriental and European.

For the history of the folktale, two collections in the novella tradition are especially important. Insofar as they contain folktales, they are either purely oral stories or else tales of literary origin which had already become a part of the folklore of Italy. Many of these oral tales have their first literary appearance in these collections. In the *Pleasant Nights* of Straparola in the sixteenth century are versions of: The Magician and His Pupil (Type 325; apparently of oral origin in India); The Youth Who Wanted to Learn What Fear Is (Type 326); The Youth Transformed to a Horse (Type 314; one of the most popular of oral tales); Cap o' Rushes (Type 510B); The Three Golden Sons (Type 707); Our Lady's Child (Type 710); The Cat Castle (Type 545A); Puss in Boots (Type 545B); and The Lazy Boy (Type 675).

An even longer list of oral tales is found for the first time in the *Pentamerone* of Basile, 1634-36. Among them are: The Maiden in the Tower (Type 310); The Black and the White Bride (Type 403); The Three Oranges (Type 408); Little Brother and Little Sister (Type 450); The Maiden Who Seeks her Brothers (Type 451); The Spinning-Woman by the Spring (Type 480); The Three Old Women Helpers (Type 501); Dung-beetle (Type 559); The Magic Ring (Type 560); The Louse-Skin (Type 621); The Carnation (Type 652); Snow-White (Type 709); and The Good Bargain (Type 1642).

The folktale collection of Charles Perrault which appeared in 1697 is hardly to be considered as literary at all, but rather as a group of fairly faithful versions of oral tales. The later French collections of Madame D'Aulnoy, on the other hand, were definitely literary, and seldom contained any real folktales which had not already appeared in writers like Straparola or Basile. Exceptions are The Mouse as Bride (Type 402) and The Shift of Sex (Type 514).

Such are the principal collections of literary tales which have given us versions of oral stories. To complete the list, one would have to make several miscellaneous additions. The King and the Abbot (Type 922) appears in a German poem of the thirteenth century and frequently thereafter; the oral tradition of how Peter's Mother Falls from Heaven (Type 804) is given in a fifteenth century German poem; The Monster's Bride (Type 507A) appears in a sixteenth century English comedy; Bearskin (Type 361) is retold by Grimmelshausen in 1670; and Demi-coq (Type 715) is given a French name because of his appearance in a French story written in 1759.

Such is the list of those tales which, although they have appeared in one or more literary collections, seem quite certainly to be oral, both in origin and in history. Sometimes their subsequent popularity has been greatly increased by the fact that they have been charmingly retold by Basile or Perrault. Otherwise, their history is in no essential respect different from that large group of stories to which we shall now turn. These belong to the folklore of Europe and Asia, and have never had the fortune to appeal to any literary storyteller. We know them only in oral form and can therefore speak with almost complete certainty of their origin among the people. Here belong some of the most interesting of all folktales.

Most of the European stories which originated in the Orient either go back to literary sources in the East or else, in spite of their origin in popular Oriental tradition, have received literary treatment in Asia or in Europe. Such tales, of literary origin or handling, have just been discussed. There remain a few which seem to have developed orally in Asia and to have reached Europe entirely by word of mouth. Such is true of Three Hairs from the Devil's Beard (Type 461), very often told in connection with the tale of The Prophecy (Type 930). The latter story is Oriental, but is found in early Buddhistic material.[4] The widely diffused tale of The Little Red Bull (Type 511*), while showing relation to several well-known European stories, probably comes from Oriental folk tradition.

By far the largest number of purely oral European and Asiatic tales seem quite certainly to have developed in Europe. The great majority of these are confined to the European continent, but some of them are worldwide in their distribution. Examples of the latter are The Dragon-Slayer (Type 300), John the Bear (Type 301), and The Two Brothers (Type 303).[5] Some European oral tales have traveled far into the Orient: Bluebeard (Type 311); The Journey to God to Receive Reward (Type 460A); The Journey in Search of Fortune (Type 460B); The Wild Man (Type 502); The Speaking Horsehead (Type 533); and The Profitable Exchange (Type 1655). Others have gone no further than the Near East: The Princess Transformed into Deer (Type 401); The Princess on the Glass Mountain (Type 530); Strong John (Type 650); The Juniper Tree (Type 720); and The Greater Sinner (Type 756C).

A considerable number of oral stories have received very wide distribution over the entire European continent but, except for purely sporadic occurrences, they do not appear elsewhere. To this list belong: The Hunter (Type

---

[4] See pp. 139f., above.
[5] The other tales which are distributed over the world and have received literary treatment have already been discussed.

304); The Dwarf and the Giant (Type 327B); Hiding from the Devil (Type 329); The House in the Wood (Type 431); The Water of Life (Type 551); The Fisher and His Wife (Type 555); The Rabbit-herd (Type 570); The Self-righteous Hermit (Type 756A); The Devil's Contract (Type 756B); The Singing Bone (Type 780); The Peasant in Heaven (Type 802); The Birthmarks of the Princess (Type 850); The Golden Ram (Type 854); The King and the Soldier (Type 952); The Robber Bridegroom (Type 955) and The Clever Maiden Alone at Home Kills the Robbers (Type 956B).

The stories just listed are well represented in all parts of Europe, so that without special investigation it is not easy to say just where the story has developed. With a large number of tales, however, we find that, in spite of occurrences over the entire continent, their area of great popularity is clearly limited, sometimes to a single country, more often to a group of neighboring peoples. Such tales with occurrences primarily in eastern Europe are: The Princess in the Shroud (Type 307); The Faithless Sister (Type 315); and The Prince and the Arm Bands (Type 590). These last two are closely related and seem to have their center in Roumania.

General European tales most popular in eastern and northern Europe are: The Danced-Out Shoes (Type 306); Lenore (Type 365); The Helpful Horse (Type 532); and The Snares of the Evil One (Type 810).

Especially characteristic of Scandinavia and the Baltic states are: The Boy Steals the Giant's Treasure (Type 328, the English story of Jack the Giant Killer); Bear-skin (Type 361); The Man as Heater of Hell's Kettle (Type 475); The King is Betrayed (Type 505); The Spirit in the Blue Light (Type 562—popularly influenced by H. C. Andersen's treatment); The Greedy Peasant Woman (Type 751); Sin and Honor (Type 755; also very popular in Ireland); The Devil's Riddle (Type 812); The Hero Forces the Princess to Say "That is a Lie" (Type 852); The Youth Cheated in Selling Oxen (Type 1538); The Clever Boy (Type 1542); and The Man Who got a Night's Lodging (Type 1544).

Rather widespread traditions having their focus definitely in Scandinavia are: The Man from the Gallows (Type 366); The Princess Rescued from Robbers (Type 506B); The Wonder Child (Type 708); The Princess Confined in the Mound (Type 870); and The Little Goose-Girl (Type 870A).

Oral tales distributed over all Europe, but especially characteristic of the western countries, are: The Giantkiller and his Dog (Bluebeard) (Type 312); The Nix of the Mill-pond (Type 316); Little Red Riding Hood (Type 333); Bargain of the Three Brothers with the Devil (Type 360); The Healing Fruits (Type 610); and The Presents (Type 620).

Finally, at least two tales seem to be especially characteristic of British tradition: Tom-Tit-Tot (Type 500) and Out-riddling the Judge (Type 927). The special form of Type 328 known as Jack the Giant Killer and that known as Jack and the Beanstalk represent peculiar British developments.

There has been no attempt in this book to give notice to all folktales known in Europe and Asia, especially to the hundreds of oral stories which are told in only a single locality or which have never traveled far from their original home. A considerable number of such stories local to Roumania, Hungary, Wallonia, and Russia may be examined in the excellent folktale surveys of these countries.[6] Of such of them as appear in the Aarne-Thompson *Types of the Folk-Tale*, it will be noticed that a large number of the local tales are characteristic of the Baltic area. It must be borne in mind that very exhaustive lists have been made of the Finnish and Estonian tales,[7] so that these large numbers are no cause for wonder. Of these oral tales in the main part of the Aarne-Thompson index, the following seem to be confined to the Baltic states: a version of The Black and the White Bride (Type 403C); The Girl in the Form of a Wolf (Type 409); Punishment of a Bad Woman (Type 473); "Iron is More Precious than Gold" (Type 677); The Rich Man's and the Poor Man's Fortune (Type 735); The Cruel Rich Man as the Devil's Horse (Type 761); The Princess who Murdered her Child (Type 781); Solomon binds the Devil in Chains in Hell (Type 803); The Deceased Rich Man and the Devils in the Church (Type 815); The Devil as Substitute for Day Laborer at Mowing (Type 820); The Boastful Deer-slayer (Type 830); The Dishonest Priest (Type 831); The Disappointed Fisher (Type 832); How the Wicked Lord was Punished (Type 837); and The Wolves in the Stable (Type 1652).

Local to the Baltic and Scandinavian countries are[8]: a version of The Children and the Ogre (Type 327C); The Vampire (Type 363); The Prince as Serpent (Type 433); The Raven Helper (Type 553); The Magic Providing Purse (Type 564); The Magic Mill (Type 565; sporadic in Ireland, Greece, and France); Beloved of Women (Type 580); The Thieving Pot (Type 591); Fiddevav (Type 593); The Gifts of the Dwarfs (Type 611); The Beautiful and the Ugly Twin (Type 711); The Mother who Wants to Kill her Children (Type 765); the Prodigal's Return (Type 935); and At the Robbers' House (Type 956A).

A much smaller group are limited to the Baltic states and Russia: The Strong Woman as Bride (Type 519); The Man Who Flew like a Bird and Swam like a Fish (Type 665; also in Bohemia); The Punishment of Men (Type 840); The Bank Robbery (Type 951B); and Cleverness and Gullibility (Type 1539; 253 versions in Finland alone, sporadic in Greece, Turkey, and America).

Though the groups of peoples just noticed are represented by a large num-

---

[6] For Roumania, Hungary, and Wallonia, see FF Communications Nos. 78, 81, and 101 respectively. For the Russian, see Andrejev, *Ukazatel' Skazočnich Siuzhetov*.

[7] The number of purely Baltic tales would be greatly increased by inclusion of all those listed in Balys' *Motif Index*, which appeared after the Aarne-Thompson Index, and also by citing many of the "Types not Included" from the Aarne-Thompson Index.

[8] Single sporadic occurrences elsewhere are disregarded.

ber of local stories, some tales of limited dissemination occur almost everywhere. Thus The Faithless Wife (Type 315B*) belongs to the Baltic and Balkan states and Russia. Hans my Hedgehog (Type 441) is known from Norway to Hungary, but depends entirely upon the Grimm version. Born from a Fish (Type 705) seems purely Scandinavian, and four tales apparently are known only in Norway: The Animal Sons-in-law and their Magic Food (Type 552B); The King's Tasks (Type 577); The Children of the King (Type 892); and Like Wind in the Hot Sun (Type 923A). Confined to southeastern Europe is The Serpent Maiden (Type 507C). Primarily Italian, but also known in Russia, is The Wolf (Type 428). Central European, primarily German, are the three varieties of The Serpent's Crown (Types 672A, B, and C). And two tales, except for occasional appearances of the Grimm version in other countries, seem to be limited to German tradition: Jorinde and Joringel (Type 405) and The Girl as Flower (Type 407).

In the rapid summary just completed it seems clear that for most of the complex tales of the European and Asiatic areas some generalizations are safe. Though we may not be able to say just when or just where a tale originated, or whether it was first an oral story or a literary creation, the general probabilities are such as we have indicated. Many questions of detail within the limits of these probabilities will engage the efforts of future scholars.

There still remain a considerable number of these complex tales where the evidence at present available is either insufficient to lead to general conclusions or else is so overwhelming in amount that it has never yet been properly utilized for systematic investigation.

For some tales, when the data are all assembled, the question as to whether they are essentially literary or oral seems quite unsolvable without much further study. Among such tales are: The Gifts of the Little People (Type 503); The Princess Rescued from Slavery (Type 506A); The Jew Among Thorns (Type 592); Tom Thumb (Type 700); The Maiden Without Hands (Type 706); Christ and Peter in the Barn (Type 752A); The Forgotten Wind (Type 752B); The Saviour and Peter in Night-Lodgings (Type 791); The Lazy Boy and the Industrious Girl (Type 822); The Princess who Cannot Solve the Riddle (Type 851); and The Parson's Stupid Wife (Type 1750).

In another group the question as to whether the tale is essentially Oriental or European is still not satisfactorily solved: The Ogre's (Devil's) Heart in the Egg (Type 302); The Spirit in the Bottle (Type 331); The Prince as Bird (Type 432); The Man Persecuted because of his Beautiful Wife (Type 465); The Table, the Ass, and the Stick (Type 563); and "All Stick Together" (Type 571).

Finally, a half dozen stories well known over the entire world present major problems of investigation because of the great mass of materials at hand, much of it still unorganized. Each of them offers a challenge to future scholarship. These six tales are: The Man on a Quest for his Lost Wife (Type 400); Cinderella (Type 510A); The Bird, the Horse, and the Princess (Type 550); The Knapsack, the Hat, and the Horn (Type 569); The Master Thief (Type 1525); and The Rich and the Poor Peasant (Type 1535).

THE SIMPLE TALE

III

1. JESTS AND ANECDOTES

As THE extensive survey of the complex tale has shown us, many of these elaborate narratives are a constant part of the folklore of peoples scattered over two or more continents. There is no doubt that complexity of structure gives to a tale a definiteness of pattern which helps to preserve its character in the face of vast differences of time and place. But a tale need by no means be complex in order to form a strong tradition. A very considerable proportion of the legendary stories among any people is made up of simple jests and anecdotes, sometimes of human beings and sometimes of animals, and consisting of but a single narrative motif. Even in the area restricted to Europe and Asia such stories are very numerous. Each country has developed many of them which are not known outside, and everywhere new anecdotes come to life and old ones pass into forgetfulness.

It would not be a safe generalization to conclude that the simple tale is less tenacious of life than one more complex. In spite of the ephemeral quality of some and the local nature of others, there exist hundreds of simple stories which have long and interesting histories.[1]

A. TALES OF CLEVERNESS

In one way or another a large proportion of the most popular anecdotes and

---

[1] Only the better known of these jests and anecdotes are discussed here. Those interested in examining a much more complete list may consult the Aarne-Thompson *Types* and the various surveys of the tales of particular countries mentioned on pp. 419ff. A tale known only in a very few versions in a single country, as well as one belonging almost purely to literature, has not seemed pertinent for discussion here.

The arrangement of the jests and anecdotes brought together here is suggested by the scheme of the author's *Motif-Index*. For tales of one motif, such an arrangement appears more logical than that of the Aarne-Thompson *Types*. The latter work is especially well adapted to the complex tale, and has been used, at least as a general basis, for the preceding chapter.

jests are concerned with cleverness. Sometimes the interest is in the contrast between a clever and a foolish person, with the main interest in the latter. Sometimes the principal attention is given to the act of deception perpetrated by the clever man, and frequently enough, particularly in tales originating in the literature of the Orient, the story-teller seems to be concerned most of all with the display of cleverness itself. Such is true, for instance, in a group of stories concerning cleverness in the detection of truth. Literary tales of this kind are common, such as the legend of Susanna and the Elders, from the Apocrypha, and the exemplum about the false message which is sent to the thief's wife to induce her to send the stolen jewel as a bribe to the judge (J1141.4).[2] Possibly of ultimate literary origin, but now well known in the folklore of the Baltic states and even in Spain is the anecdote of the man who fishes in the street and thus arouses the curiosity of the rascal who has swindled his wife (J1149.2; Type 1382).

A clever man may sometimes find that his plans are frustrated, or even that he is liable to punishment for a crime which he did not commit, all because he has a foolish and talkative wife or son. He sometimes tells his wife about obviously impossible things, such as the catching of birds in a fish-net, so that when she tells this wild story along with the true one of his discovery of hidden treasure, no one will believe her (J1151.1.1; Type 1381). This form of the story is very popular in medieval literature and is told all over Europe and in North Africa. A number of variations on the theme were popular with the writers of jestbooks and fabliaux. A wife puts fish into a furrow and lets her husband plow them up, or a mother makes her foolish son believe that it has rained sausages. When they talk of the fish that were plowed up (J1151.1.2), or the day of the sausage rain (J1151.1.3), no one will believe them. The latter form has had some acceptance in Italian popular tales since the time of Basile. Other stories of cleverness in connection with the law courts concern repartee between the prisoner and the judge. Most of these are either purely literary, or else they form a part of long tales of cleverness, such as The Clever Peasant Girl (Type 875). One of them, which goes back to Buddhistic sources and was popular in the medieval literary collections, is also found occasionally in the folklore of peoples as widely scattered as those of Iceland and Indo-China. This story has to do with the boy who has been told by the judge that he should always kill a fly whenever he sees one. The boy obeys, and kills the fly on the judge's nose (J1193.1; Type 1586).

A very popular form of anecdote in the medieval tale collections illustrated the maxim that a rule must work both ways.[3] Generally, these tales have not been taken into folklore, although the one about the master who suggests to

[2] References of this kind consisting of a capital letter followed by a number are to the author's *Motif-Index* in which the motifs are thus numbered.

[3] See J1511 and all its subdivisions.

his servant that they will only make believe at eating and the servant's later insistence that they will only act as if they were working has some popularity in the states around the Baltic. In general, it must be said, however, that tales of cleverness have not appealed especially to the oral story-teller except when such incidents are a part of a series or of a complex tale such as The Clever Peasant Girl. If one is looking for independent stories of this kind, he will find them by the hundreds in the jestbooks of the Renaissance, the large collections of medieval exempla, and the Oriental literary works from which many of these European collections borrowed.

B. FOOLS AND NUMSKULLS

A surprisingly large number of simple tales told by unlettered men everywhere concern fools and their absurdities. This is true just as much of primitive peoples who love to see their culture heroes play the parts of buffoons[4] as it is of an older generation of British or Danish peasants who tell of the actions of the Men of Gotham or the Fools of Molbo.[5] Every generation has its new supply of such stories, though many old ones, sometimes familiar to the Egyptians or the ancient Greeks, are dressed in strange new trappings, and pass for new inventions.

Out of the large body of anecdotes based upon absurd misunderstanding there may be mentioned three which have attained considerable popularity in various folk traditions. One of these tales belongs to the general class of objects with mistaken identity (J1750-J1809). A numskull is convinced that the pumpkin which he is sitting upon is an ass's egg which he has hatched out. He believes that the rabbit which runs by is the colt (J1772.1; Type 1319). This anecdote not only appears in Turkish jestbooks, but is told all over Europe, in much of Asia, and among the mountain whites of Virginia. Similar stories tell of the servant who is sent to bring in the cows and spends the whole day trying to round up the rabbits (J1757), or about the peasant who first sees a steamship and thinks it is the devil (J1781.1; Type 1315*). Such anecdotes are probably more widespread than collections would indicate. The second of these, for example, was recorded in Virginia only a year or so ago; othewise we would probably have concluded that the tale was not known outside of Finland.

A second kind of misunderstanding may result in inappropriate and absurd actions on the part of the numskull (J1820-J1849). Best known of such stories is that of the landlubber peasants who go to visit the sea. When they see a waving flax-field, they think it is the sea and jump in to swim (J1821; Type 1290). Not so well known, but surprisingly popular for such a foolish tale,

[4] For these trickster tales, see p. 319, below.

[5] An excellent recent treatment of these stories is Christensen's *Molboernes Vise Gerninger*. For such tales in another quarter of the world, see Coster-Wijsman, *Uilespiegel-Verhalen in Indonesië*.

is the account of the fool who sees his cow chewing her cud and kills her because he thinks she is mimicking him (J1835*; Type 1211). Though this anecdote has its main popularity in the Baltic countries, it is known as far afield as India.

The fool lives in a mental world of his own, and he may endow objects or animals with any qualities that suit his passing fancy (J1850-J1909). In some of the more complex tales[6] we have seen the fool throwing money to the frogs, so that they can count it, or selling goods to animals or to a statue. Usually the subject of an independent anecdote is the numskull who feeds meat to cabbages which he imagines must be hungry (J1856.1; Type 1386). This story is very old, going back to early Buddhistic literature. Another compassionate fool fills the cracks in the ground with butter (J1871; Type 1291), or puts a cloak around a stone to keep it warm (J1873.2). Of all the anecdotes about objects or animals which are expected to go alone, the most popular is that of the numskull who lets one cheese roll down a hill, and then sends another to bring it back (J1881.1.2; Type 1291).

A much more interesting tale of this general type is The Ox as Mayor (J1882.2; Type 1675). The story consists of the strange results which happen when a peasant is persuaded to send his ox to school to learn to read. The man who is to teach the ox slaughters it, and tells the peasant that it has gone to the city and has become mayor. The peasants go to visit him, meet a man named Peter Ox, or the like, and greet him. He acknowledges the acquaintance and inherits their money. This is primarily a literary anecdote appearing in such Oriental collections as the *Thousand and One Nights* and the jests of Hodscha Nasreddin. As an oral tale it is popular only in northern Europe, though it has been recorded elsewhere all the way from France to India.

The ascribing of human characteristics to the ox is one example of the widespread misunderstanding which fools are supposed to have concerning the nature of animals. Most of such anecdotes (J1900-J1909) are purely literary, though the tale of the man who takes his cow to graze on the roof (J1904.1; Type 1210) is widely recounted in Europe, and has been heard in America. The numskull usually ties the rope to his leg as the tethered cow grazes on the roof. Of course, she falls down and drags him after.

Our proverb about hunting for a needle in a haystack probably refers to a tale of a fool who did this. For there are many stories of just such vain searches for lost objects. Best known of all such anecdotes is that about the foolish sailors who lose an object from their boat and mark the place on the boat rail to indicate where it fell, so that they can hunt for it later (J1922.1; Type 1278). This anecdote appears in Chinese Buddhistic literature and is told occasionally by people who live as far apart as England, the United States, and Indonesia.

[6] Especially Type 1642.

As a part of his general disregard for reality, the fool may overlook elementary natural laws. To the peasant story-teller, some of the most interesting of these have to do with his unsuccessful attempt to grow crops (J1932 and its subdivisions; Type 1200). The fool sometimes sows cooked grain or salt, hoping to produce more of the same. Or he sows cheese to bring forth a cow, or plants an animal tail in order to produce young animals. Most tales of this general type of absurdity seem to be literary, though they have occasional oral versions. This is true of the numskull who tries to dig up a well and take it home, or the one who digs a hole so as to have a place to throw the earth from the excavation he is making, or of the man who stands before the mirror with his eyes shut to see how he looks in his sleep (J1930-J1959). One anecdote reported from widely separated areas must be relatively recent, since it depends upon a modern invention. The fool's son, who is living in a distant city, writes his father requesting a pair of boots. A rascal persuades him that he can save time by sending them by telegraph. The father leaves them hanging on a telegraph pole, but they come into the hands of the trickster rather than the son.[7]

The essential nature of the ego has not only puzzled the great philosophers but has troubled the thinking of fools. Sometimes a man may not know himself because in his sleep his beard has been cut off or his garments have been changed, or he has been smeared with tar and feathers (J2012 and subdivisions; Type 1383). Or he may be sitting with other fools and they get their legs mixed up, so that they cannot tell whose is whose (J2021; Type 1288). To such persons counting is always a trial. One fool concludes that a member of their party is drowned because he fails to count himself (J2031; Type 1287). The difficulty is sometimes solved by the whole group sticking their noses into the sand, and then counting the holes. Such stories of absurd calculations are essentially literary, though one or another of them is occasionally found in all parts of Europe, in India, and even in European tradition in America.

Any logical arrangement of the activities of numskulls continually breaks down, since their absurdity is not confined to sensible bounds. One can only say that some fools are primarily ignorant and some primarily absent-minded. In this way it is easy to find a group whose chief failing is shortsightedness (J2050-J2199). Two well-known tales are concerned with absurd plans made by such simple souls. One of these has to do with the man and his wife who make plans for the future and eventually quarrel over the details, so that they destroy the very things they are counting on to bring them their wealth. In excitement or under the stress of other emotion, the fool breaks the jar of honey, the basket of glassware, or the eggs he is to sell, or the milkmaid tosses her head and spills her milk (J2060.1, J2061; Type 1430). These tales

---

[7] J1935.1; Type 1710*. It is reported in only a single version from Livonia, but I have heard of it as current in Spain, Italy, Lithuania, and Russia.

are very popular in Oriental and medieval literature; and they have been reported with fair frequency by folklore collectors in many parts of Europe and Asia. An Oriental literary origin would seem likely.

Much more popular as an oral tale is the story of Clever Elsie (J2063; Type 1450), who is sent to the cellar to get wine to serve her suitor. She sees the axe above her and begins weeping over the troubles she might have if she married the suitor and had a child who might come down just as the axe falls. Her foolish parents join her and, meanwhile, the suitor goes home. For a simple anecdote, this tale has received a remarkably wide oral distribution. It is probably Oriental and literary in origin.

In a world of shrewd business men, it is remarkable that more stories of foolish bargains have not been told than actually exist. Sometimes, of course, such bargains find their main interest in the sharp dealings of the trickster rather than the stupid actions of the dupe.[8] There is one well-known story, however, where the foolish man plays the leading role (J2081.1; Type 1415). He trades off his horse for a cow, his cow for a hog, and so on with ever smaller results until he has nothing left. But the story-teller does not leave him in defeat. In one way or another luck comes to his rescue. Sometimes he retrieves himself by a series of lucky bargains, but most often he is brought back to prosperity by wagering that his wife will not be angry. She continues to praise his good judgment throughout, and he thus wins back more than he ever lost. Of course, the stupid seller is not always given a last-minute rescue. No help comes to the woman who sells her cows and gets one of them back as a pledge for the unpaid purchase price (J2086; Type 1385).

A favorite theme in the literary jestbooks which is occasionally found in European oral tales is foolish acts in which the remedy is worse than the disease to be cured (J2100-J2119). Fools burn a house down in order to get rid of a cat or of insects, or they chase a rabbit on horseback and ruin the crops they are hoping to protect. Such tales have not often entered the oral tradition, and the same thing is true of the numerous stories of the fool who needlessly risks his life (J2130-J2159). Only two of such seem to be widely told, and both of them certainly go back to Oriental literary sources. One of these is about the fool who cuts off the tree limb on which he sits, and the other about the men who hang down in a chain until the top man spits on his hands and they all fall[9] (J2133.4 and J2133.5; Types 1240 and 1250).

Jestbooks record many another shortsighted act, and most of them have been heard now and again by collectors of folklore.[10] Such is the account of the man who tries to jump into his breeches, pulling on both legs at once; of the people who carry a millstone uphill so that they may roll it down; of

---

[8] For such deceptive bargains, see K100-K299, below.

[9] There is also a similar animal tale known over much of Europe about wolves who climb on top of one another to a tree, and when the lowest runs away all fall (J2133.6; Type 121).

[10] For this group of stories, see J2160-J2198.

those who do not mend the roof when it is fair weather and cannot when it rains; or of the schoolmaster who whips his pupils beforehand to keep them out of mischief. One tale of this kind is well known as an oral anecdote: that of the fool who lets the wine run in the cellar while he falls into a deep study or sometimes while he chases a dog. In the sequel he usually tries to dry up the spilled wine by pouring meal on it (J2176; Type 1387).

A frequent theme in jestbooks is the tale of the man who believes that he is dead (J2311 and subdivisions). Most frequently this is the result of a deception practiced by the wife (Type 1406). In one particular variety of this tale she lies to him and tells him that a certain pot of preserves has been poisoned. He decides to kill himself, and eats the preserves. In spite of all evidence to the contrary, he thinks himself poisoned and lies down for dead (Type 1313). Similar tales, primarily literary and seldom of interest to the unlettered story-teller, tell of how a naked person is made to believe that he is clothed, a layman that he is a monk, a well man that he is sick. One of these tales has, however, received some oral currency, that of the parson who is made to believe that he will bear a calf. The doctor makes a mistake and examine's a cow's urine instead of the man's and predicts the birth of a calf. The man is later persuaded that he has actually borne a calf (J2321.1; Type 1739).

As a part of stories concerning the saints or gods who wander on earth, we frequently find a foolish mortal attempting unsuccessfully to perform a miracle in imitation of these supernatural beings.[11] Tales of foolish imitation on a purely human level are also very popular in jestbooks and collections of medieval tales. There is, for example the anecdote about the doctor's son who has heard his father tell his patient that he has eaten too much chicken. The son wonders how the diagnosis was made, and the father tells him that as he rode up he had observed chicken feathers and had made his conclusions. The son tries the same method and sees an ass's saddle in front of a house. He diagnoses the ailment as due to the eating of ass's flesh. Another literary tale of this class, occasionally told by story-tellers, is that of the two presents to the king. A farmer takes an extraordinarily large beet as a present to the king and receives a reward. His companion is eager for an even larger reward and leads a handsome steed to the palace. The king presents him with the huge beet. Though these two tales[12] are certainly literary, one anecdote of foolish imitation has had wide acceptance both as a popular tale and, especially in English-speaking countries, as a folk ballad. A husband is scornful of his wife's labors and, at her suggestion, agrees to exchange tasks. While she succeeds with his work in the fields, he makes an utter failure in his attempt at housekeeping (J2431; Type 1408). The details of his awkwardness furnish the amusement for the story, and these may be expanded at will.

[11] See Types 531 and 753.
[12] J2412.4 and J2415.1, respectively.

The fool is frequently so literal-minded that he follows instructions even in the most inappropriate situations. The best-known tale of this kind has to do with the mother who tells her son what he should do in various circumstances (J2461 and subdivisions; Type 1696). For instance, he has tried to send a pig home alone. His mother tells him that he should have led it by a string. The next time he drags the bacon home by a string. Or he has killed a sparrow by his stupidity and has been told that he should have carried it in his hand. Accordingly, on the next trip he carries a harrow in his hand. These details are multiplied with considerable ingenuity. The story seems to go back to a Chinese Buddhistic source and appears in a number of Renaissance jestbooks. It has been collected not only all over Europe, where it appears in more than two hundred versions, but also in Indonesia, Japan, and all parts of Africa. In America it is told by the Indians of Nova Scotia and Ontario and by the French of Missouri.

What is really a somewhat specialized form of this same anecdote concerns the foolish bridegroom who follows his instructions to the letter. He is told, for example, that he should cast sheep's eyes at his bride. He buys some at the butcher shop and throws them at her. When he is told to put parsley in the soup, he throws in his dog, who happens to be named Parsley. When he is to clear out the room, he throws out all the furniture. In the end, of course, the bride becomes disgusted and leaves, but not before she has put a goat as substitute in the bed (J2462, J2465.5, K1223.1; Type 1685). Though this tale has a rather wide currency in Europe and has been found in the British tradition of Virginia, it is certainly literary in origin. Its earliest known telling is by Hienrich Bebel in his jestbook at the beginning of the sixteenth century.

Only one of the frequent literary tales of foolish extremes has become very popular in folklore. This is The Silence Wager (J2511; Type 1351). A man and his wife make a wager as to who shall speak first. They both hold out for a long time but finally the wife makes the husband so jealous that he cannot forbear scolding her, and loses the wager. This story, which depends upon a literary Buddhistic source, has been the subject of literary jests and of popular comedies and ballads. As an oral tale it is nowhere very popular, but it has been occasionally collected all the way from England to Japan.

Perhaps no peoples have been so interested in anecdotes of fools and their actions as the countries around the Baltic. Scores of other tales than those suggested here are well known in this area. In Finland, particularly, a favorite cycle of stories concerns a bungling fool who has a succession of accidents. When he goes to get a midwife, he accidentally strikes the dog dead, drowns the midwife, and kills the child (J2661.2; Type 1680). In another tale he foolishly kills his horse, and throws his axe into the lake to hit a duck. When he undresses to recover the axe, his clothes are stolen.

Then when he goes into a barrel of tar to hide, he gets covered with tar and feathers (J2661.4; Type 1681).[13]

In general, it will be noticed that while a number of stories of numskulls are handed down by tradition, either as anecdotes or as songs, they flourish most in written collections of jests. In the Middle Ages these were included in books of exempla, but beginning with the Renaissance there has been an unbroken series of literary jestbooks containing hundreds of such anecdotes. The jokes in these books may appear to be new, but they are nearly always constructed on some ancient pattern. With jests and anecdotes much more than with the serious folktale, the literary collections have directly influenced traditional story-tellers and ballad singers. This close relation between literature and folklore is nowhere better seen than in numskull tales such as those we have just noticed.

C. CONTESTS WON BY DECEPTION

The teller of popular tales does not always draw a sharp distinction between the fool and the clever man. It is not unusual to find that the numskull has suddenly acquired wisdom, so that he goes out on a successful career of cheating and deceiving. No doubt tales of clever adventurers and rascals are interesting for their own sake, but they have an added dramatic value if the successful cheater overcomes great handicaps, mental or physical. If the handicaps are mental, the success often comes from sheer luck. But if the hero is very small or weak or slow-footed he usually succeeds because he has a shrewd head on his shoulders.

Popular ever since the days of Aesop has been the story of the race between the hare and the tortoise. In its classical form it usually tells how the swift hare goes to sleep just short of his goal and permits the slow tortoise to beat him. Though this tale (K11.3) has passed on from Aesop into the folklore of most of the world, it is not nearly so popular as a similar race in which the turtle places his relatives, or at least other turtles that resemble him, at various points in the racecourse, so that the opponent always thinks the trickster is just ahead of him (K11.1; Type 1074). This story may be told either of animals or of men. Though not particularly popular anywhere in Europe, it is found from time to time all over the continent. It is especially well known in eastern Asia, in all parts of Africa, among the American Indians both North and South, among the American Negroes, and in the Portuguese tradition both of Massachusetts and Brazil.

Belonging to the same cycle, but nearly always told of a contest between two animals, is the story of how one of the contestants steals a ride on the other's back (K11.2, K25.1; Types 221, 250, 275). Sometimes the contestants are fish, sometimes birds, and sometimes other animals. This anecdote also

[13] For other anecdotes of bungling fools, see J2650-J2690.

goes back to Aesop and is known over Europe. It is a favorite in Africa and in the Negro and Indian tradition of America. It has also been reported in Indonesia.

A special form of the deceptive race has developed in eastern Europe (K11.6; Type 1072). In this tale a man challenged by an ogre to a running race persuades the ogre to race with his "little son" instead. It turns out that the little son is a rabbit. A similar ruse is used in a wrestling match in which the "grandfather" proves to be a bear (K12.2; Type 1071). In another wrestling contest, probably also eastern European in origin, but also recently collected in Virginia, the ogre squeezes the man so that his eyes bulge out. The man says that he is looking to see where to throw the ogre and thus frightens the ogre away (K12.1; Type 1070).

The story of The Brave Tailor (Type 1640) frequently contains a series of contests in throwing in which the weak hero makes the ogre believe that he can throw a prodigious distance. Sometimes he shows the ogre a bright spot on a cloud and contends that this is a golden club which he has thrown (K18.2; Type 1063). Or he throws a bird which flies out of sight and makes the ogre believe that it was a stone (K18.3; Type 1062). Both of these incidents are told as independent tales and have an extraordinary popularity in northern Europe. They have also been carried to the Philippines, to Africa, and to America. Other incidents belonging to this tale of The Brave Tailor, but also enjoying considerable popularity for their own sake, have to do with much less plausible contests. In one, the hero and the ogre try to outdo each other in pushing a hole in a tree, a hole which the hero has prepared beforehand (K61; Type 1085). In the other they are to squeeze water from a stone. The hero substitutes a cheese and deceives the ogre (K62; Type 1060). Both these anecdotes have attained extraordinary currency in northern Europe, but they are also known all over the continent, as well as in Indonesia and the western hemisphere. The incident about the cheese, which goes back to the *Panchatantra*, occurs in several hundred versions. A similar contest in biting, in which the trickster bites a nut rather than a stone (K63; Type 1061), is not nearly so popular.

This whole group of incidents which sometimes form part of the cycle of The Brave Tailor and which sometimes appear as self-sufficient anecdotes would make that tale one of the most interesting for a thorough comparative study. It would be very interesting to know with some certainty the relation between such independent incidents and a tale-type into which they may be appropriated and in which they become dependent members. But thus far no such study has been adequately carried out.

Anecdotes of various other kinds of contests are not hard to find in folktales. Sufficient to illustrate these is the contest in eating or drinking in which the trickster provides a bag for the food or a hole through which the water escapes, while the ogre eats or drinks himself to death (K81.1, K82.1; Type

1088). As independent incidents these are popular in northern Europe and are also frequently found among the North American Indians. It is not entirely certain that all of the American Indian versions are derived from the European, since the idea is so simple that independent invention is not out of the question.[14]

D. DECEPTIVE BARGAINS

The joy in a shrewd deal is by no means confined to the world of good business and does not depend upon modern capitalistic society. The principle of *caveat emptor* is only a codification of an idea already very old and very widespread. Especially if the cheater is naturally weaker or poorer than his adversary, the interest in the swindle is heightened. Several of the well-known complex folktales, such as The Rich and the Poor Peasant (Type 1535) and Cleverness and Gullibility (Type 1539),[15] are filled with sales of pseudomagic objects, false treasure, and worthless animals and services. Except as members of longer tales, these incidents do not normally have enough interest to assure them independent life. But in that group of anecdotes having to do with bargains which sound simple but become very difficult in the end there is enough real cleverness to make them popular everywhere. Such, for instance, is the tale of the deceptive crop division, sometimes told of men and sometimes of animals. Of the two who are putting in the crops, they agree that one is to have what grows above the ground and the other what grows below. The stupid person or animal chooses the tops of the root crops and the roots of all other crops (K171.1; Types 1030 and 9B). Many variations are made on this tale, though the essential idea is always the same. It may be a division of pigs with curly or straight tails where the trickster takes all the curly tails, or of animals for shearing where the trickster chooses the sheep and leaves the pigs for the dupe (K171.4, K171.5; Types 1036, 1037).

A seemingly simple agreement may lead to a kind of blackmail. Thus the trickster and his superior, usually a parson, have a quarrel over some property. They agree that the first of them to say "Good morning" the next day is to have the property. The trickster is early on the scene and witnesses the other's adultery. He may keep the property without saying "Good morning" (K176; Type 1735).

One of the oldest records of deceptive bargains in the world is that connected with the legend of Dido. In its most usual form this anecdote tells about the purchase of as much land as can be surrounded by an oxhide.

---

[14] These incidents, as well as the one in which the hero stabs a bag of prepared blood and thus persuades the ogre to stab himself (G524), are frequently a part of the cycle of The Rich and the Poor Peasant (Type 1535).

[15] For these, see pp. 165 and 166f., above.

The hide is cut into very small strips so as to include a large territory (K185 and all its subdivisions; Type 2400). The theme is subject to many variations. The boundary may be fixed by the flight of a goose, or by a race run by a supernaturally swift man. As an actual legend, such a story appears not only in Virgil, but in Herodotus, ancient Buddhistic literature, Icelandic sagas, and the *Historia* of Geoffrey of Monmouth. It is found rather infrequently as an oral tale.

If the tale of Dido is primarily a legend, the story of the strokes which were shared (K187; Type 1610) belongs to another world, that of the medieval and Renaissance literary anecdote. The boy who is going to see the king is forced to bribe the doorkeeper with an agreement to give him whatever the king promises. The only promise the king gives is a beating, and the doorkeeper must submit to the bargain. In some versions of the tale, the agreement is merely to share the profits, and these turn out to be strokes. In spite of its purely literary origin, this story is very well known in northern and eastern Europe and has been recorded in Spain and· India.

Many anecdotes of such deceptive bargains find their place in jestbooks, or in the folklore of a single country or area. Such of those as concern transactions with the devil have already been noticed in connection with one of the complex tales.[16]

The idea of a bargain of this kind appears with a slight variation in an anecdote extremely popular in northern and eastern Europe and recorded by Hans Sachs. This tells of the man who is to receive as payment all the money his hat will hold. He has a hole in his hat and the hat is over a pit (K275; Type 1130). The tale has been collected two hundred times in Finland alone.

E. THEFTS AND CHEATS

The Master Thief and The Treasure House of Rhampsinitus, two of the longer tales of robbery (Types 1525, 950), we have already noticed. There remain in addition a number of anecdotes about robbers sometimes connected with longer tales but frequently appearing as stories for their own sake. One of these has to do with the millstone or the door dropped from a tree on robbers who are counting their money below (K335.1.1; Type 1653). This anecdote is frequently joined to the story of the literal-minded woman who is told to guard the door and who takes it off and carries it with her (K1413; Type 1009). Variations (K335.1.2.1; Type 1653B and K335.1.2.2; Type 1654**) tell how the robbers are frightened away by a corpse or a sham dead man. This whole group of incidents seems to come from Buddhistic literature in India and appears frequently in fabliaux and jestbooks. But they have become well established in oral folklore in many parts of the world.

---

[16] See pp. 42ff., above.

Jestbooks have a long list of tales in which a thief presents a false order to the guardian of money or valuables. Some of these incidents appear in The Master Thief. Another of this class, well known as an independent oral tale, is the story about Long Winter (K362.1; Type 1541). A numskull has been told to keep his sausage "for the long winter." He talks about his instructions everywhere. A rascal hears this and comes to the door, introducing himself as Long Winter, and so receives the sausage. The details of the play upon words in this anecdote undergo the greatest variation, but the general idea is always the same, the trickster's taking advantage of the fool's babbling about his secret instructions.[17]

Anecdotes of the way in which a thief escapes detection assume a considerable variety of forms. In some of them, usually concerned with animal tales, the blame for the theft is fastened on a dupe. Many such incidents form a part of larger cycles, and many are purely literary and do not really belong to popular tradition at all. But some of these literary tales have their place in folklore. Such is the anecdote of the thief who steals a horse from the wagon while its owner sleeps. The thief hitches himself to the wagon and persuades the owner the next morning that he is really the horse, who has been transformed into a man overnight (K403; Type 1529). This literary tale comes from the Orient but is told in all parts of Europe and in North Africa, and has been reported from the Philippines.

We shall meet other stories of cheating and swindling when we look into the tales told about animals.

F. ESCAPE BY DECEPTION

Thieves are by no means the only persons who effect deceptive escapes from punishment or death. Most of the popular tales of this kind concern the escape of a weak but clever animal.[18] In addition to these, however, and to the many escapes from tight places by heroes of the longer fairy tales, two adventures of this kind with human actors have achieved wide currency. The first is familiar through its treatment in the *Odyssey*. As a matter of fact, in the story of Polyphemus (Type 1137) there are two escape motifs. One of these is the ruse by which the hero assumes an equivocal name, like "Noman," and thus causes a misunderstanding when his captor calls for help (K602). Afterward, it will be remembered, Odysseus escapes by concealing himself under the belly of a huge ram (K603). All of this happens after the monster has been blinded through the pretense of healing his eyesight. In most versions of the tale a glowing mass of wood is thrust into his

---

[17] For another anecdote often associated with this, see J2355. Here the fool is told that he must never serve a man with a red beard. Having heard about this, the villain dyes his beard black.

[18] For such anecdotes, see p. 217, below.

eye (K1011). This whole cycle has been thoroughly studied by Oskar Hack-man,[19] who finds the tale in greater or less completeness scattered over most parts of Europe and Asia. Aside from its literary treatment in Homer, it is in the *Arabian Nights* and in the exemplary stories of the *Dolopathos*. This tale has apparently not been reported from Africa or the Americas.

One literary anecdote of escape from punishment well known in the folklore of the Baltic states and reported also from Russia and India, con-cerns a murder committed by a numskull, who buries the body and talks about it.[20] His brothers secretly substitute a goat for the buried body and thus save him from punishment when authorities investigate his story (K661.1; Type 1600).

G. CRUEL DECEPTIONS

Objection has sometimes been raised to the teaching of the folktale to young children because of the frequent cruelty and ferocity they are likely to find in such tales. Whatever one may think of this argument, it cannot be denied that folktales everywhere are characterized by violence and suffering and sudden death. If these tales are a reflection of the simple society in which they flourish, whether in the islands of Oceania or in the fields of central Europe, just such violence is to be expected, for the stories come from people used to severe elemental conflicts in their own lives and interested in such conflicts when they hear tales of others.

Cruelty in plenty we have met already in various episodes of some of the more complex stories—Hansel burning the witch in her own fire, and the like—and in the animal tales it assumes even greater importance.[21] Some tales of cruelty tell how a victim is deceived into captivity, some of the way in which he is lured to his death or at least to serious injury of himself. A very considerable number of short anecdotes of such self-injury are very popular in Finland, Estonia, and other Baltic states, but with few or no parallels elsewhere. Several examples of these will suffice. In one of these the hero, like Odysseus, has assumed a name, "Such a one." He persuades an ogre that to improve his looks he should have his beard gilded. He covers the ogre's beard with tar and leaves him caught in the tar-kettle. The ogre wanders about everywhere with the tar-kettle inquiring, "Have you seen such a one?" (K1013.1; Type 1138). In another anecdote an ogre is tricked into eating very hot porridge and burning his throat (K1033; Type 1131). Or he is persuaded to smoke a gun instead of a tobacco pipe, or to put his fingers in the cleft of a tree in order to learn to play a fiddle, or even to allow his beard to be caught in such a cleft (K1057, K1111.0.1, K1111.1;

---

[19] *Polyphemsage.*
[20] For similar stories of talkative fools, see pp. 189f., above.
[21] For such anecdotes, see pp. 219ff., below.

Types 1157, 1159 [cf. Type 151], and 1160). Finally, one anecdote of this group characteristic of the Baltic lands has a peculiar parallel in an apparently native story of the North American Indians. The dupe is deadly afraid of thunder and has asked the trickster to tell him when it thunders. The latter deliberately deceives him, so that he is killed by a thunderstroke (K1177; Type 1148A). In the North American Indian tale the hero rides a whale across a body of water. He deceives the whale as to the nearness to shore and also as to hearing the thunder. Just as they reach shore, the whale is killed by the thunder.[22]

Medieval storybooks are filled with tales of persons who are deceived into humiliating positions. Such stories are usually purely literary and often go back to much older sources. Many of them, as we shall see later, concern exposed adultery or discomfited lovers. Such motifs are also found in complicated tales, as in the story of the boy who threatens to tell of the queen's adultery, of the king's kissing the horse's rump, or of the princess's amorous conduct, and thus receives the desired reward.[23]

A separate anecdote, sometimes about persons but more frequently about animals, tells of how a trickster makes a dupe believe that he is holding up a great rock and how he induces the dupe to take his place for a while. Sometimes he steals the dupe's goods while he is thus occupied. Sometimes the rascal pretends to be holding up the rock or the roof so that he will not have to help with the common labor. The first form of this tale is well known in Africa and America; the second in Europe, particularly the Baltic states (K1251, K1251.1; Types 1530 and 9A). A very similar tale, told in various parts of America, in Indonesia, and in Lithuania, is about how the dupe is persuaded to guard a hat supposed to cover valuable treasure. After he has guarded it for a long time and his goods have been stolen, he finds underneath only a pile of dung (K1252; Type 1528).

H. SEDUCTION AND ADULTERY

To the unlettered story-teller and listener, as well as to the writer of literary tales, there has always been a greater interest in deceptions connected with sex conduct than any other. Such deceptions may be of several kinds. They may result in seduction, in the discomfiture of unwelcome lovers, in the beguiling of cuckolded husbands, or in the discovery and punishment of adulterers by the outraged husband or by some trickster who profits by the exposure. Tales like these are very old, and they were especially popular with the writers of fabliaux, novelle, and jestbooks. A great proportion of such literary tales are never heard from popular story-tellers. But some of

[22] See Thompson, *Tales of the North American Indians*, p. 327, n. 179 (17 versions). See also p. 334, below.

[23] Types 570 and 852, pp. 154 and 156, above.

them are very well known everywhere. And many such tales have certainly been made up in entire independence of literary influences.

As a part of longer tales we have already seen a number of cases of what is essentially seduction. A girl masks as a man and wins a princess's love; or the hero frames his questions to the princess who must always answer "No" in such a way as to gain his desires; or a princess is enticed on board a merchant's ship to inspect beautiful clothes; or the garments of bathing girls are seized and held. We have also seen a young man entering the princess's room in a golden ram or hidden in a chest, or even by means of artificial wings. And we have seen the frog prince buying the right to sleep before the girl's door, at the foot of her bed, and finally in the bed itself.[24]

One of the most widely-known tales of seduction is frequently recounted as a part of the Anger Bargain cycle (Types 1000-1029). After the trickster has heaped all manner of indignities upon the master, the latter sends him into the house to bring back two articles. He meets the two daughters and calls back to the master, "Both?" "Yes, I said both," replies the master. The youth then has his will of both daughters (K1354.1; Type 1563). This anecdote is as old as the *Thousand and One Nights*, and was repeated in Renaissance jestbooks. It is a favorite in the Baltic states and has been reported in Roumania and among the French. Its appearance in three Indian tribes of North America and one of Bolivia and in Portuguese tradition in Massachusetts would suggest that not all European versions have been collected. Much less witty, but equally popular around the Baltic, is the tale of the young man who tricks a lady with a promise of a pair of beautiful shoes. The husband, however, appears before payment can be made (K1357; Type 1731).[25]

Writers of novelle and fabliaux were fond of tales of humiliated lovers. Virgil hanging in a basket below his mistress's window, or Aristotle crawling on all fours as a riding horse for his scornful lady, or the bawdy tricks recounted by Chaucer in his *Miller's Tale*—all these are a part of literature rather than of folklore.[26] On the contrary, the Oriental and Renaissance literary tale of The Entrapped Suitors (Lai l'épervier) (K1218.1; Type 1730) has attained a real popularity in the folklore of eastern Europe, and has been collected in Spain and Indonesia. The chaste wife with many suitors has them come, one at a time. As each arrives, the one before has just undressed and must hide. At the end, the husband and his guests come and chase the embarrassed suitors away.

Somewhat similar tales from fabliaux and jestbooks popular in eastern Europe but otherwise apparently unknown as folktales are two concerning

---

[24] Types 514, 851, 516, 313 and 400, 854 and 900, 882, 575, and 440, respectively.

[25] With some variation, Chaucer has used this motif for his *Shipman's Tale*. See the study by Spargo, *Shipman's Tale*, pp. 50ff.

[26] For this group of motifs, see K1210-K1239.

discovered lovers. One of them tells how a man hidden in a roof sees a girl and her lover. He becomes so interested that he falls, and they flee and leave him in possession (K1271.1.4; Type 1776). The other anecdote is only a slight variant of this. The man who has seen the intrigue from the stable roof threatens to tell about it, and the woman gives him money to keep quiet (K1271.1.4.1; Type 1360B).

In the anecdote just mentioned the situation is related by the rascal in the form of a story, so that only gradually the woman realizes that her secret is known. This conversation with a double meaning reminds one of the very well-known tale of Old Hildebrand (K1556; Type 1360C).[27] In this case the husband leaves home and, suspecting his wife, has himself carried back, where he finds her entertaining the priest. They make rhymes about the husband's absence and the good times they expect to have. From his hiding place in the basket he answers in appropriate rhymes. In his exhaustive treatment of this tale, Walter Anderson[28] carries it back to Flemish literature of the late fifteenth century and shows its subsequent treatment in songs, puppet theaters, and Russian bylini. Contrary to most anecdotes which we have noticed, this one is almost completely unknown in Finland, Estonia, and Lithuania, although it is popular in all parts of Russia, even into Siberia, and in practically every part of Europe. In America it has been reported in several places: in the English tradition of North Carolina, the Negro of Louisiana and the Bahamas, and the Portuguese of Massachusetts. The combination of literary texts with its widespread oral acceptance made this one of the best of all short anecdotes for comparative study.

In the tale cycle of Big Claus and Little Claus (Type 1535) we saw how the trickster, acting as a sham magician, discovers a woman's adultery and manages to buy the chest which contains the hidden paramour (K1574). There are a number of variations to this motif, and in several combinations they go together to make an independent anecdote (Type 1725). The trickster, having discovered the intended adultery and the prepared feast, brings it about that the food goes to the husband instead of the paramour (K1571). Sometimes he merely makes her believe that the husband is coming to punish her, and thus forces her confession (K1572). In other versions the trickster, by a ruse, sends the master running after the departing paramour (K1573). Though the master knows nothing of the adultery, the lover is thoroughly frightened and the wife confesses to the husband. Of all these incidents, the latter is by far the most popular. It appears in the *Thousand and One Nights*, in various fabliaux and jestbooks, and in the writings of Hans Sachs. It is known orally in all parts of Europe, particularly in the north. Similar tales are reported from India.

[27] This resemblance is certainly not important, and Walter Anderson is quite right in taking me to task for assigning it the number 1360C as if it were only a subdivision of 1360. Old Hildebrand has to do with a returning husband and not with an outside trickster.

[28] *Der Schwank vom alten Hildebrand.*

I. DECEPTION THROUGH BLUFFING

In contests with stronger adherents, the weak or small hero always enjoys the favor of the taleteller.[29] Not only does the unpromising man or animal use his superior cleverness in escape and even in the overcoming of the odds against him, but sometimes he is able to effect his purposes through mere deceptive boasting. The large animal or the giant is thoroughly frightened by these bluffs, and either flees or sues for peace. In one story of this kind, told sometimes of animals (Type 126*) and sometimes of a man and an ogre (Type 1149), the weak hero makes the strong one believe that he has just finished eating a large number of the latter's companions (K1715). In a variant of this episode the weak hero has a confederate, who calls out to him and says, "What, only one tiger? You promised ten." The tiger thinks he is lucky to escape alive (K1715.2). This story goes back to the *Panchatantra* and the *Sukasaptati* in India, and was a part of the *Roman de Renart* in medieval France. In Europe it seems to be primarily confined to the eastern countries, and it is a familiar anecdote in India and Indonesia. African and American Negro versions are known, as well as two in Portuguese from Massachusetts. The Indian and Indonesian versions probably depend upon the older Hindu literary collections.

Rather slight variations from this incident tell how some sheep have found a sack with a wolf's head in it. They make the wolf believe that they have killed one of his companions, and he flees in terror (K1715.3; Type 125); or how a small hero overawes an ogre by boasting about marvelous relatives. The thunder is said to be the rolling of his brother's wagon; or millstones are spoken of as pearls of the hero's mother (K1718 and subdivisions; Types 1146, 1147).

An ogre tale represented by a Middle High German poem of the end of the thirteenth century and repeated in many Renaissance jestbooks is about the bear trainer whose bear drives the ogre away. The next year the ogre inquires, "Is the big cat still living?" When he hears that it has many kittens, he is overawed and never ventures near (K1728; Type 1161). This little anecdote is extraordinarily popular in northern Europe and is known in the northern Slavic countries, but has not been reported anywhere else.

A group of short tales, some of which have attained a world-wide popularity, concerns a boast that the hero is desirous of performing a much larger task than that which the ogre has assigned. When the ogre hears the new proposal, he is frightened and runs away. When he is told to bring in a tree, the hero asks "Why not the whole forest?" (K1741.1; Type 1049); instead of shooting one or two wild boars, the boaster suggests that he shoot a thousand with one shot (K1741.2; Type 1053). Most popular of the group is that in which he is told to carry in water. He demands a bucket large enough to

[29] The whole of Chapter "L" of the *Motif-Index* is devoted to this theme.

bring in the whole well (K1741.3; Type 1049). In a similar vein are the hero's requests for a rope to pull a lake together and for one with which to haul away a warehouse (K1744, K1745; Types 1045 and 1650, 1046).

Finally, two stories of bluffing sailors should be mentioned. In one of these, a swimming match starting from the ship is held. The bluffer takes a knap-sack of provisions on his back and when his rival sees this, he gives up without starting (K1761; Type 1612). In the contest in climbing the mast, the hero falls into the rigging. "You do the same thing," he challenges. The sailors are persuaded of his expertness (K1762; Type 1611). These last two stories have very peculiar distribution. They are well known in Finland and the first has been reported from Denmark, and they have both been heard from Portuguese speakers in Massachusetts and from American Indians in New Brunswick. Further study would probably bring others to light which would clarify this strange situation.

J. IMPOSTURES

Bluffing is only one of many kinds of impositions practiced in folktales. Sometimes the assumption of a false role is a necessary part of the hero's adventures, and the listener to the story applauds the imposture. But more often the impostor is the villain of the piece and much of the interest of the story hinges upon his unmasking. These uses of impositions as a strong moti-vating force usually occur in the complex folktale, particularly the wonder tale. In shorter anecdotes deceptions of this kind are used almost entirely to produce amusing situations. One cycle of such tales is about sham church-men. The peasant who passes himself off as a clergyman sometimes betrays himself by preaching on the troubles which only the congregation could know about. Or sometimes he runs out of anything to say and keeps repeat-ing himself or saying over a few words of Latin. In the most spectacular of these anecdotes he has sawed the pulpit almost in two before ascending it; he has hardly finished predicting a great miracle when the pulpit falls down (K1961.1 and subdivisions; Type 1825ABC). These tales go back at least to the Renaissance, where they are found in many jestbooks. They are especially popular in northern and eastern Europe, and such stories are sometimes heard in France, Spain, and Italy. It would be interesting to see what, if any, effect the prevailing religion of a country has upon the popularity of these anecdotes.

The sham miracle just mentioned occurs frequently in other connections. A whole series of anecdotes tell of how a man who is standing behind a tree or a statue pretends to be God or the spirit to which a suppliant is praying. For instance, a wife prays, hoping to find out how she may fool her husband. From his hiding place he advises her to feed him well (K1971.1; Type 1380; cf. Types 1575** and 1388*). This simple incident has had a long literary history, leading back to India and coming down through Italian novelle and Turkish and Renaissance European jestbooks. Orally it is still told in India and is very popular in north Europe and in Roumania. It has not been reported from Africa or America. Many variations are rung upon the theme of the husband answering the prayer of the wife, but sometimes the role is exchanged. In one tale well known all over Europe since the Renaissance the wife behind the tree advises the husband against having his wife work (K1971.4.1; Type 1405). A third variety of this imposture tells of wives or maidens behind a tree who advise reluctant husbands or unwilling suitors (K1971.6; Type 1461*). Finally, there is the perennial old maid joke about the sexton behind the crucifix or statue who answers her prayer for a husband. Speaking as the Christ Child, he tells her that she will have no husband, but she tells the Christ Child that he knows nothing about it and that she is praying to his mother (K1971.8.1; Type 1476).

A sham miracle is used in a popular Scandinavian and Baltic story as a means of cheating an employer. Though hired to mow the grass, rascals return to their master without even having begun. When he angers them, they pronounce a curse, "May the grass grow up again." He finds it full height, and is persuaded of the miracle. In a variant of this tale, the tricksters have put a wasp nest inside of the bee-hive. The curse they utter is, "May it turn to wasps" (K1975; Type 1736).

A group of popular anecdotes tell about girls who keep up appearances so as to deceive suitors as to their desirability. Sometimes they lisp or have a speech impediment and, though they have been warned against speaking, they forget and are found out. Another boasts about how little she eats, but when the suitor sees her baking, he finds out that she eats enough. Or the mother has given the girl a new name, but the girl forgets it and does not answer when her mother calls, so that the mother must call her by the old and ugly name (K1984 and subdivisions; Types 1457, 1458, 1461). A good many variations are given this theme, which is popular over most of Europe, and which has a literary history going back at least to Hans Sachs in the sixteenth century.

In a few fairly well-known anecdotes the deception of the girl is placed in contrast to the good qualities of another who stands the severe tests she is put to by the suitor. Thus the thrifty girl makes herself a dress from the flax which the lazy one has thrown away. Or three sisters are tested by the way they trim cheese. The first eats the cheese rind and all, the second trims away much of the cheese, and the third trims it just right. Or the suitor hides a key in the flax on the spinning wheel. He finds it there the next day and realizes that the girl has done no spinning. This cycle (H381-H384; Types 1451, 1452, 1453) is popular in the Baltic states and is sometimes heard in other parts of eastern Europe.

K. FALSE ACCUSATIONS

If we take all kinds of tales, especially if we include the complex wonder tale and the literary anecdote, we should find a very large number of motifs concerning deceptions through shams. Besides the bluffs and impostures popular in oral anecdotes, we should also have found a large number of deceptions by disguise or illusion, and of tales of hypocrites; and we should meet a whole gallery of villains and traitors. These latter do not form much of a part of the repertory of jests which are preserved in oral tradition. But there does remain one series of deceptions that has attained a real popularity in folklore, though most of them are unmistakably taken from old literary collections of jokes. These are stories of false accusation.

In the wonder tale, false accusations are usually tragic in their intensity, but in short jests they may be used merely to produce a humorous situation. Such, for instance, is the tale of the priest's guest and the eaten chickens. The servant who has eaten the chickens tells the guest to flee, because the priest, who is arriving, is going to cut off his ears. Then he tells the priest that the guest has stolen two chickens. The priest runs after him and the guest makes all the speed he can (K2137; Type 1741). This medieval literary tale has been recorded over most of Europe and sporadically in other continents. It is, of course, closely related to the tale of the trickster who sends his master running after the wife's paramour (K1573), and it is often joined with that story.

A small group of tales in which the innocent are made to appear guilty secures its primary interest from its gruesomeness. In one of these, a corpse is handed around from one dupe to another. Each is accused of the murder and the trickster is paid to keep silence (K2151; Types 1536C, 1537). This well-known fabliau and medieval jest is told all over Europe and a good part of Asia, and is known in Africa and in America, both in European and American Indian tradition. In a similar tale a corpse is set up to frighten people and usually when it is knocked down, the bungler is accused of murder (K2321; Type 1536A). Of this small group, the best known in literature is undoubtedly the tale of the three hunchbacked brothers who were drowned. In this old fabliau a drunken man is employed by a woman who has accidentally killed three hunchbacked brothers to throw one of them into the river. He does so, and then she puts another out, and finally the third. The man thinks that they keep coming to life. Finally he sees the woman's hunchbacked husband and drowns him (K2322; Type 1536B). This latter story is hardly a part of oral tradition at all, but has probably been learned over and over again directly from literary collections.

L. THE BAD WIFE

In those anecdotes in which the wife hides behind a tree and deceives the gullible husband, the sympathy of the story-teller is nearly always with her, for ordinarily her cause is just. And in folktales in general the wife is likely to be the object of pity and commiseration, so that some of the most beloved characters in the wonder tales are the long-suffering and persecuted heroines. But even in these same wonder tales cruelty often shows itself most merciless in faithless sisters, mothers, and wives.[30]

In the folk anecdote, influenced perhaps by fabliaux and novelle with their medieval bias against women, the woman usually appears as wicked, overbearing, and faithless, or at best unutterably stupid.

The classical literary tale of the Widow of Ephesus (K2213.1; Type 1510) has itself never become popular among the folk, but it has given rise to a number of similar anecdotes of faithless widows. In all of these the central point is that the wife plans her new marriage on the day of the husband's funeral. In one such tale she is ready to marry the messenger who brings news of the husband's death, but the husband has only feigned death in order to test her (T231.3; Type 1350). With slight variation this tale is known in the folklore of various parts of Europe. It is the only one of the considerable cycle which has become thus popular.[31]

In the tales of King Thrushbeard and The Taming of the Shrew (Types 900, 901) we have seen how husbands have, in one way or another, brought under subjection their shrewish wives. But sometimes the wife is so evil that neither man nor devil can cure her. Thus it is in the well-known literary story of Belfagor. In its usual form, the man persuades his shrewish wife to let herself be lowered into a well. When he comes to pull her out, he raises a genie or devil, who is glad to escape from the woman. Later, when he wishes to frighten the devil, he has only to tell him that the wife has escaped (T251.1.1; Type 1164). This story goes back to India and the *Sukasaptati*, but it appears in nearly every later collection of tales down through the Renaissance, and as a folktale it has been recorded more than one hundred times in various parts of Europe.

Another literary anecdote which has been generally adopted by tellers of folktales is that of the obstinate wife. In its three forms it has essentially the same action. The husband has a long argument with his obstinate wife which ends with his throwing her into a stream. As sometimes told, the argument has been about whether something has been cut with a knife or with scissors. She gets the last word, for as she sinks under the water, she makes with her fingers the motion of shearing with scissors. Or she has called her husband a lousy-head and as she sinks she makes the sign of cracking a louse.

---

[30] See Ziegler, *Die Frau im Märchen* for a good discussion of this point.

[31] For this group of anecdotes, see T230ff., with cross references.

In a third variety the obstinate wife falls into the stream and drowns. Neighbors find him next day seeking for her upstream from the drowning place. He says that she would be too obstinate to go with the current (T255 and subdivisions; Type 1365ABC). All three of these forms appear frequently in the tale collections of the Middle Ages and all of them may still be heard in almost any part of Europe. So far as I am aware, only the variety with the sign of the shearing has been reported from America.

Evil intentions on her part are not necessary to make a wife undesirable. She can be so stupid that there is no living with her. Such is the experience of the husband who goes out on the long quest to find three persons as stupid as his wife. In one way or another, he finds them, and in comparison it turns out that his own wife is not so stupid after all (H1312.1; Type 1384). This anecdote often serves to introduce longer tales of stupid persons, but it has had a vigorous independent life. Like most jests about wives, it has a place in the older jestbooks. But this tale is also told frequently in all parts of Europe and well out into Siberia. Versions apparently based upon English originals have been found in Virginia, and close parallels exist in Africa.

In examining these tales of evil wives, one is struck not so much by the fact that some of them are told by story-tellers over a large area but that out of the scores of such anecdotes to be found in fabliaux, novelle, and books of exempla and *Schwänke* only a bare half dozen have received any general acceptance by the folk.

M. LAZINESS

In these tales of bad wives the intent is nearly always humorous, and there seems little or no tendency to wish to point a moral. The same attitude applies to tales about lazy persons. The writer of pious stories and exemplary anecdotes may try to preach a sermon on the evils of unfaithfulness or of indolence, but the story which keeps being told is the one in which these failings appear in some light that is laughable or at least mildly amusing. The most popular stories about lazy men are concerned with absurd cases of extreme laziness. Sometimes the thread that holds a series of such anecdotes together is a contest in which each person cites instances of his unwillingness to move (W111.1; Type 1950). Such contests are recounted in the *Gesta Romanorum* and in nearly all later books of anecdotes, and they appear in folktale collections from nearly all parts of Europe, though none seem to have thus far been reported outside that continent. Numerous stories are told about lazy servants. Such a one is asked whether it is raining. Instead of going out, he calls in the dog and feels of his paws. In a variant, he is to find whether there is fire in the house. He feels of the cat to see if she is warm. These two are essentially literary anecdotes. But the tale about the boy who eats his breakfast, his dinner, and his supper, one immediately after the other, and then lies down to sleep is well known all over eastern Europe (WIII.2.6; Type 1561).

As might be expected, the lazy wife does not get off unscathed, though the tales of this class show neither the originality nor the interest to be found in stories of shrews or overbearing women. Of this group, perhaps the best known, at least in eastern Europe, is the tale of the cat which is beaten for not working. During the beating the lazy wife must hold the cat, and she gets well scratched (WIII.3.2; Type 1370*).

A thorough exploration of these tales of laziness would take one through most of the literary collections of tales, both in Europe and the Orient, for many of them have considerable antiquity and have been repeated by nearly everyone who has issued a book of anecdotes.

N. DEAFNESS

By the teller of stories, physical afflictions are nearly always treated humorously. It is the shuffling gait of the crippled man or the mistaken direction taken by the blind that appeals to his sense of the ludicrous. So it is concerning those who are hard of hearing. Antti Aarne has made an interesting study of the whole group of more than a dozen anecdotes concerned with mistakes made by the deaf and near-deaf.[32] All of these he has traced back to literary sources, and many of them have never become known to the folktale teller. But several of them have attained a very considerable popularity. Among those especially beloved of the folk are the following four. In the first of these, two deaf persons meet. A inquires for his lost animals.—B talks about his work and makes a gesture.—A follows the direction of the gesture and happens to find the animals. He returns and offers an injured animal to B in thanks.—B thinks he is blamed for injuring the animal and a dispute arises which is taken to a deaf judge. The second may really be considered as a group of anecdotes, since it appears with some variation. The deaf workman keeps answering the traveler's courtesies with unsolicited remarks about his work. A third one rings various changes on the situation afforded by a buyer and a deaf seller. Usually, of course, the seller utterly disregards objections raised by the buyer, who gives in out of mere fatigue. Or the buyer promises the deaf man the payment of a beating. "Yes, it is certainly worth that," he replies. Last in this group is an anecdote in which the persons are not really deaf at all. A trickster tells each of two persons before they meet that the other is hard of hearing and must be shouted at. Such a great shouting takes place that each thinks the other out of his wits (XIII; Type 1698). That such stories still have their vitality is witnessed by their frequent occurrence in drama and the cinema.

[32] *Schwänke über schwerhörige Menschen.*

O. PARSONS

The liking of people for such a story as that of the peasant who masks as a parson and tries to preach a sermon[33] is easily understandable. In simple communities a clergyman is always a person of such outstanding respectability that if he is placed in an embarrassing position the very absurdity of the situation appeals to a sense of the ludicrous in every member of his or similar congregations. The great Danish folklore collector, Tang Kristensen, assembled in western Denmark enough of these stories to make up a very diverting volume.[34] Of course, not all anecdotes that are told of parsons are found in such a collection, for many of the old fabliaux in which the actors may belong to any trade or profession, or none at all, have frequently been retold as happening to the priest or the vicar of the local parish. But such tales aside, there are a considerable number of anecdotes which owe their point to the special position occupied in the community by the parson and the special setting afforded by church, pulpit, sermons, burials and graveyards, and, in Catholic countries, the confessional.

The fact that these tales have been so thoroughly collected in the Lutheran countries of the north may account for the presence there and the absence elsewhere of a considerable number of anecdotes. On the other hand, assiduous collection in other parts of the world, in Roman Catholic and Greek Catholic countries, for example, might bring these same anecdotes to light in other environments. In connection with one Italian priest, Arlotto, a considerable number of these jests were assembled in the Renaissance.

Some of the best known of these anecdotes which are apparently confined to the Scandinavian and Baltic states will show the general tenor of the whole collection. One group of tales tells how the parson is put to flight during his sermon. It may be that the sexton's dog steals a sausage from the preacher's pocket, or that the sexton has put a needle in the sacramental bread, so that his reverence sticks his hand; and even sometimes the sexton prepares a wasp nest for him to sit on (X411; Type 1785). Occasionally the parson wishes to vary his church service and add interest to it, as on the day in which he rides an ox into church to show how Christ rode into Jerusalem. All goes well until the sexton sticks the ox with a needle (X414; Type 1786). His sense of the dramatic sometimes proves ridiculous. Such it is when he decides to let a dove fly in the church to illustrate his sermon. Unfortunately, he finds that it has died in his pocket (X418; Type 1837). A country congregation is doubtless the scene of the accident in which the hog has been locked in the church all week by mistake. When the congregation comes, the hog runs between the parson's legs and carries him out into the churchyard (X415; Type 1838). The country preacher has other

[33] See p. 206, above.
[34] *Vore Fædres Kirketjeneste*, Aarhus, 1899.

experiences with livestock. It is told of one that he kept his fine new cow grazing in the cemetery. At a woman's funeral he is afraid the cow will break out and run away, and he keeps his eye on her so much that he makes inappropriate remarks as each spadeful of earth falls on the coffin. When at length he sees her break loose and run away, he calls out "Now she is gone to the devil," just as he lets fall the last spadeful of earth (X421; Type 1840).

One of the difficulties every clergyman has is the presentation in his sermons of difficult theological concepts and utterly unfamiliar historical characters and situations. It is no wonder that the literal-minded should sometimes make wrong interpretations. A number of such anecdotes have been collected (X435; Type 1833), some from jestbooks and some from oral story-tellers. One favorite type tells how the parson asks a rhetorical question "What says David?" The boy, thinking of a David he knows, says, "Pay your old debts." There are many variations, and not all of them very pointed. One priest has tried to explain the Doctrine of the Trinity and has illustrated his point by identifying each One of the Three with one of his cows. The boy speaks up, "The Holy Ghost has just had a calf." In a third anecdote, a boy has ridden to church with a rich man. He goes into the church and leaves his coat lying on the sled. When the parson preaches about the rich man who went to hell, the boy calls out, "Then he took my coat along."

The contrast between the spiritual devotion normally expected from the clergyman in his pulpit and the demands of ordinary life affords a basis for occasional mirth. The priest may have some business dealings with the sexton, and he may intone instructions to him as a part of the mass (X441; Type 1831). Or the parson, not unobserved, may sneak a drink of liquor or a chew of tobacco during the sermon (X445; Type 1827).

The three best known stories about clergymen are told in most parts of the world and at least two of them seem to go back to Oriental literary sources. In the first of these the parson and sexton are traveling and stay overnight at a peasant's house. In the night the parson becomes hungry and hunts some porridge in the dark, guided by a rope which the sexton has given him. He has a series of accidents because he loses his way. He spills the porridge on his host or hostess and sometimes finds himself in unseemly positions reminiscent of the two clerks in Chaucer's *Reeve's Tale* (X431; Type 1775). The second of these popular anecdotes finds the preacher back in his pulpit. During the sermon he sees an old woman weeping and believes that she is touched by his singing. When spoken to about it, she says that his voice has reminded her of the old goat which she has lost (X436; Type 1834).

Probably the most popular of all tales of parsons concerns the devil in the cemetery. A sexton hears thieves in the cemetery cracking nuts and thinks it is the devil cracking bones. With the gouty parson on his back he comes upon the thieves who, thinking it is their companion with the sheep, call out, "Is he fat?"—The sexton, dropping the parson, "Fat or lean, here he is!" (X424; Type 1791). This anecdote is certainly as old as the *Thousand and One Nights*, and appears in nearly every medieval and Renaissance tale collection. But it is widely told by oral story-tellers all over Europe and, for some reason, is about the best known of all anecdotes collected in America. It is found among the Canadian French; it has been told in the Anglo-Saxon tradition in Indiana, the Ozarks, Canada, North Carolina, and Texas; and it has been heard from Negroes in various parts of the south and the West Indies. The tale appears in two forms. In one there are sheep thieves, as in the form just given. And in another there are merely boys dividing nuts. And it is not absolutely necessary that the tale be told about a parson at all.[35]

P. LIES AND EXAGGERATIONS

The collecting of folktales from the older population centers in the United States, particularly those belonging primarily to the Anglo-Saxon tradition, has hardly begun, and much that has appeared has come out within the past five years. From what we have learned of such collections, it seems clear that only a limited group of old tales have kept on being told. Short anecdotes, like the devil in the cemetery, and animal tales of the Uncle Remus type appear everywhere. But perhaps most popular of all are what is known to American story-tellers as tall tales. Sometimes these outrageous exaggerations are original, but often they correspond rather faithfully to a well-known European form. Frequently heard on both sides of the Atlantic is the story of the man who rescues himself from a barrel by grabbing hold of a wolf's tail and being drawn out of danger (X911; Type 1875). Also popular in America as well as many parts of Europe are absurd accounts of wonderful luck in hunting (X921; Types 1890-1909). One of the best known of them tells of all the game killed by an accidental discharge of a gun. The gun, for example, kills a bird which falls on a loose limb of a tree, which falls on a bear, etc., etc. The sequence may be varied almost indefinitely. The feet of rabbits or wild ducks may freeze fast in the ice at night, or the hunter may go wading and catch his boots full of fish.[36]

The boy who was shot out of a cannon (X913; Type 1880) does not seem to be known outside of the Baltic area, but in contrast, the very popular Munchausen story of the man who falls and is buried in the earth and then goes for a spade to dig himself out (X917; Type 1882) seems to be

---

[35] For discussion of American versions, see R. S. Boggs, *Journal of American Folklore*, XLVII, 311f.

[36] For a discussion of the American versions of these tall tales, see the notes by Herbert Halpert in Richard Chase's *The Jack Tales*, pp. 198f.

quite unknown in those countries. The latter tale has been picked up over most parts of Europe and forms a part of nearly every American collection itself and then only imperfectly to the processes of folktale tradition.

Tales of lying or mere foolery are, of course, very widespread and may have the most diverse origins and histories. The nonsensical repartee in which one liar announces that the sea has burned up and the other consoles him with "Many fried fish" (X925; Type 1920A) is well known in the Baltic and in certain parts of eastern Europe and appears in at least five collections from India, but except for a single Walloon notice, does not seem to be known in western Europe or America.

A piece of nonsense known at least from the time of Straparola, and popularized by later French and Italian jestbooks, consists merely in a tale in which all kinds of animals and things are designated by senseless names (X951; Type 1940).[37] The hen is chuckie chuckie, the duck wheetie wheetie, the dog bouffie bouffie, and the like. The tale becomes, in effect, a game in identification. It is told over the most of Europe, but has not been reported outside. The fact that five English versions are known would make it seem likely that this tale might be found sometime in America, but it has apparently not been reported.

In the United States and Canada during the last fifty years one of the most interesting phenomena in the life of the backwoods and frontier, particularly among lumbermen, has been the growth of a whole cycle of tales about Paul Bunyan. The essential point about every anecdote in the cycle is the gigantic size, not only of Paul himself, but of all his animals and possessions. In spite of innovations introduced by story-tellers with original ideas and even in spite of contests held for good Paul Bunyan tales, the central core of incidents in the cycle seems to be fairly well established, and to be preserved with considerable stability. The exact history of the Paul Bunyan tradition is not clear, and we do not know to what extent analogous tales from Europe have exercised a real influence in building up this rather unified series of exaggerations.[38] But whether only chance analogues or the original of some of the Paul Bunyan incidents, there exist in Europe, in Scandinavia and Finland, a considerable series of stories of gigantic animals, buildings, and objects. Many of these are also found in the older jestbooks. There are plentiful parallels to Paul Bunyan's big ox, though probably none to the measurement between the tips of the horns by means of so and so many axe-handles *plus one plug of tobacco*. The giant kitchen can easily be paralleled, but not the waiters on roller skates. On the other hand, in spite of its long literary history as a medieval Latin poem

[37] See also: Basset, *Contes berbères*, p. 350, No. 209i; Bolte, *Zeitschrift für Volkskunde*, XXVI, 8, 370; *Béaloideas*, II, 94, 227, III 239; Jackson, *Folklore*, XLVII, 292 (1).

[38] For a good bibliography of the Paul Bunyan cycle, see Gladys J. Haney, "Paul Bunyan Twenty-Five Years After," *Journal of American Folklore*, LV (1942), 155ff. For these gigantic animals and objects, see X1021-X1049; Type 1960 and subdivisions. See p. 250, below.

and as an anecdote in jestbooks both Oriental and European, the tale of the great cabbage seems not to have become a part of the Paul Bunyan tradition. In this story one man elaborates to the best of his ability the details of the cabbage's size. His companion counters with a similar outrageous story of a huge kettle. The other asks him what use can be made of such a kettle. "Why, to put the cabbage in, of course." This anecdote has not remained merely literary, but has become a part of the repertory of story-tellers all over Europe. It has also been found in India, in Indo-China, and in the British tradition of Virginia.

That these tales of lies and exaggerations should have had great popularity in the rapid opening up of the American continent, with its incredible events of everyday life, is no cause for wonder. But it is surprising that, in spite of a continuous flow of immigrants, so many other interesting European anecdotes should have failed to find a place on American soil. It is possible that as further collecting goes on we shall find that many more of the anecdotes we have been noticing are here and have only been waiting for the collector.

However that may be, the conclusion of this survey of the better-known anecdotes current in the countries from Ireland to India does suggest that certain kinds of incidents have easily traveled across the ocean and certain kinds rarely or never. As far as Europe and Asia themselves are concerned, we see that a very large number of stories, otherwise known only through jestbooks and the like, have become a part of the store of oral anecdotes in certain countries. Particularly rich in this respect are Finland and the other Baltic states. It may well be that the relative scarcity of such anecdotes in other parts of the area is due to inadequate collection. But one gets the very definite impression, in surveying a large number of such anecdotes, that for most countries they belong to a semi-literary tradition, that they are likely to be preserved in cheap jestbooks even today, and that one is more likely to have learned his story by reading it than by hearing it.

These individual anecdotes are certainly looked upon by the story-teller in a different light from the wonder tale or, indeed, from any other complex folk story. The skillful folktale teller in such a place as Ireland or Russia is likely to be scornful of such trifles. The complexity of plot, the machinery of wonder and supernaturalism, the far-off world of the unreal—all of these seem to give value to a tale and to assist its faithful preservation over centuries of telling, even in far-separated lands. But the simple anecdote refuses to take on very definite form and texture. It has its main point with which every teller may exercise his skill. There is no special virtue attached to faithfulness of text or the maintenance of an old tradition. Of whatever ultimate origin, the anecdote is likely to be handed on from century to century and from country to country between the covers of books or pamphlets, and, with rare exceptions, as apparently in Finland, submits itself and then only imperfectly to the processes of folktale tradition.

2. ANIMAL TALES

For the teller of folktales today as in the past, and in our western culture as well as among the most primitive tribes, the world of the human and of the animal are never far apart. In all parts of the world there exist tales in which it is extremely hard to tell whether the actor is really a human being or an animal. This ambiguous concept extends even to sacred stories which make up mythologies, so that many of the deities appear one day in the image of man and the next in the guise of a beast. For people accustomed to such an equivocal conception of the main actors in their fiction, it is no wonder that a multitude of tales, many of them less serious in import than the mythologies, should show animal actors in all sorts of distinctly human situations. Sometimes folk tradition is very careful in its choice of animals, so as to make the human actions as nearly appropriate as possible. Thus, the bear is stupid, the fox sly, the rabbit swift and wily. But such careful workmanship in the composition of animal tales is not to be expected everywhere, and sometimes, because of religious associations or even from mere carelessness, the animal actions seem most inappropriate. And occasionally in the course of a long tradition the role of a particular animal completely changes. The clever fox of Europe, in the course of his long migration through Africa to Georgia, has become the dupe who lets Brer Rabbit use him as a riding horse.

As for the animal tales current in Occidental tradition, there seem to be four principal sources: (1) the literary fable collections from India; (2) the Aesop fables as they were elaborated, especially in the early Middle Ages; (3) the medieval literary animal tales brought together in the cycle of Reynard the Fox; and (4) the purely oral tradition, a very important part of which was developed in Russia and the Baltic states. The interrelation of all these streams of influence is extremely complicated, so that the writing of the history of a particular animal tale is often a matter of extraordinary difficulty. To be sure, many of the literary animal tales, particularly those known as fables, have remained entirely on the literary plane and have never become in any sense a part of the folklore of any people. For such stories, the historian needs only to make an adequate study of the appropriate documents. But a considerable number of the literary fables, and of the animal stories appearing in such a work as *Le Roman de Renart*, have been learned, in one way or another, by unlettered story-tellers and have become, in all essentials, a part of the authentic folk tradition.

For the purpose of our study of the oral folktale in Europe and Asia, we shall notice only those animal tales, of whatever ultimate source, which have thus found an actual place in folklore.

A. THE LITERARY FABLE

Of the five or six hundred fables belonging to the two literary traditions of India and of Greece,[1] fewer than fifty seem to have been recorded from oral story-tellers, and most of these are of relatively rare occurrence. Even when stories of this kind are actually taken up from unlettered persons, one must be very careful in assuming that they have had any considerable history as oral tales. The cheap fable collections have doubtless been the most important element in preserving these stories and handing them on.

If it is understood that in nearly all instances the relation of these fables to actual folklore is very limited, there can be cited as having at some time been recorded in the folklore of one or more countries the following[2]: The Animal Who Saves Himself by Making His Captor Talk (sometimes told of fox, or cock, or mouse); Fox Climbs from Pit on Wolf's Back; Wolf Descends into Well in One Bucket and Rescues Fox in Other; Fox Plays Dead and Is Thrown out of Pit; Wolf Dives into Water for Reflected Cheese; Bear Persuaded to Stick Claw into Cleft of Tree; Wolf Overeats in Cellar; Horse Kicks Wolf in Teeth; The Sick Lion; The Lion's Share; Fox Deceives Magpie Who Is Avenged by Dog; Fox and Crane Invite Each Other; Peace Among the Animals; More Cowardly than the Hare; Hare Will Not Build House in Good Weather, Cannot in Bad; Mouse Rescues Lion; Crane Pulls Bone from Wolf's Throat; Stag Admires Himself; The Cat's Only Trick; Belling the Cat; Country Mouse and City Mouse; Wolf Put Off till Children Are Baptized; Sheep Persuade Wolf to Sing and Summon Rescuers; Advice of the Fox; Ungrateful Serpent Returned to Captivity; Splinter in the Lion's Paw; Learning to Fear Men; Grateful Animals and Ungrateful Man; Cat Loses Dog's Certificate; Lean Dog Prefers Liberty to Abundant Food and Chain; Two Stubborn Goats Push Each Other into Water; Wren Elected as Bird King; Crane Flies with Fox and Lets Him Fall; Raven in Borrowed Feathers; Hunter Bends the Bow; Ape Likes Her Own Children Best; Ant and Lazy Cricket; and Little Fish Slip through the Net.

[1] A good listing of the Oriental fables will be found at several points in Chauvin's *Bibliographie des ouvrages arabes*. For the Graeco-Roman fable, see W. Wienert, *Die Typen der griechisch-römischen Fabel* (FF Communications No. 56, Helsinki, 1925).

[2] Since the fables are well known, only a brief indication of them will be given. In the order in which they appear, they bear the following numbers in *The Types of the Folk-Tale*: 6+61+122+227, 31, 32, 33, 34, 38, 41, 47B, 50, 51, 56B, 57, 60, 62, 70, 72**, 75, 76, 77, 105, 110, 112, 122A, 122C, 150, 155, 156, 157, 160, 200, 201, 202*, 221, 225, 244*, 246, 247, 249 253.

B. THE NORTHERN ANIMAL CYCLE AND REYNARD THE FOX

One of the most interesting literary products of the Middle Ages in western Europe is the collection of animal tales which eventually formed the satirical epic known from its most famous example as the *Roman de Renart*. The literary history of this group of writings is not to our purpose.[3] But no discussion of the oral tale in Europe can neglect stories with such vitality as those which are collected by the scores and sometimes hundreds in lands around the Baltic, which even seven hundred years ago were well enough known to form an animal epic and which within the past four centuries have traveled to Africa and on slave ships to all parts of the New World.

A considerable group of these tales early aroused the interest of Kaarle Krohn, and to them he applied for the first time the rigorous analytical study which has later become known as the historical-geographical method.[4] He observed that these tales still had a very vigorous life in Finland and Russia, and that most of them also formed a part of the Reynard cycle. By a close analysis of the details, he examined the question of origin and subsequent history of these stories.

He found that in practice one particular series of episodes was ordinarily handled as a unit. In this series the stupid bear or wolf is placed in opposition to the sly fox. Such an opposition Krohn does not find in the literary fables, but it is an essential part of this whole group of episodes,[5] as well as of a few related independent stories. The cycle which forms the principal part of Krohn's study usually consists of five parts, any one of which may also be found as a self-sufficient anecdote.

The fox sees a man hauling a wagon load of fish. He lies down in the road where the wagon must pass and plays dead. The man throws him onto the wagon of fish and the fox throws the fish off behind and carries them away. He tells his friend the bear about his experience. In some versions of the tale the bear tries the same trick but is caught and killed (Type 1). In others the fox suggests to the bear how he, too, may get fish, namely by fishing with his tail through a hole in the ice. He freezes fast and when he is attacked, he loses his tail (Type 2). As an independent episode, this is often used to explain why the bear has no tail. While the bear has been fishing through the ice, the fox has gone to a woman's house and told her about the bear. While she is away chasing the bear, the fox slips into the house where the woman has been churning and feasts on the milk and

---

[3] For a good discussion of the relation of the Reynard cycle to the oral animal tale and to the fables, see A. Graf, *Die Grundlagen des Reineke Fuchs* (FF Communications No. 38, Helsinki, 1921); L. Sudre, *Les sources du roman de Renart* (Paris, 1893).

[4] *Bär (Wolf) und Fuchs.*

[5] In his list of tale types Aarne had this chain of incidents in mind when he arranged his first five numbers, since the chain consists of Aarne's types 1 to 5 inclusive.

butter. When the woman returns she drives him out and beats him with the churn-dash, so that he is all covered with butter and milk. When he finds the bear, who is complaining about his misfortunes in the ice, he claims to have had an even worse time and makes the bear believe that his brains have been knocked out (Type 3). In fact, the fox is in such a poor way that he says the bear must act as his riding horse. As he is riding the bear, he sings out, "The sick is carrying the well," but misreports the song to the stupid bear. Eventually, however, the bear realizes the deception and throws him off (Type 4).[6] The fox now escapes into a hole under the roots of a tree with the bear after him. When the bear seizes him by a hind leg, the fox calls out, "Bite ahead, you are only biting the tree root." The bear lets loose and they go on their separate ways (Type 5).[7]

Although three out of five of these episodes (Types 1, 2, and 4) find a place in the medieval animal epic, Krohn brings forth convincing evidence that the whole cycle developed in the folk tradition of northern Europe. He infers from the distribution of the complete cycle, as well as of the independent parts, that the combination has existed for about a thousand years. He finds that the antagonist to the fox is the bear in western and southern Finland, and the wolf in northeast Finland. Speaking of his own study, he says,

It was clear that into Finland there came from the west Scandinavian versions, and from the east Russian versions of one and the same tale, and that Finland was not a land through which tales traveled, but was rather the final destination of two streams of tradition. . . . The most southern part of northern Europe which can be conceived of as the home of the tale of the bear and the fox is northern Germany. . . . We can conclude that in Germany the whole chain of adventures was present before the settling of the Saxons. . . . From Germany on the one hand the original form with the bear reached Scandinavia and on the other hand the form with the wolf, influenced by the fable literature and the animal epic, reached Russia.[8]

The other adventures of the fox and the wolf (or bear) more frequently appear as independent tales. In general, Krohn finds that they have much the same history as the regular cycle. In one of these episodes (Type 7) they wager as to which of them can first name three different trees. The bear names different varieties of the same tree, so that the fox wins the wager. In another (Type 8) the bear sees a magpie and envies its colors. The fox offers to paint him so that he will be even more beautiful. Following the fox's prescription, the bear lies on a haystack which the fox sets fire

---

[6] A special modification of this anecdote popular among the Negroes of the West Indies and of the United States, and also known among the Indians, tells how rabbit rides fox a-courting. He has boasted to his lady-love that the fox is his riding horse (Type 72).

[7] For a good discussion of this cycle, in the light not only of his original study but of other researches over nearly fifty years, see Krohn, *Übersicht*, pp. 18ff.

[8] Krohn, *loc. cit.*

to. The bear gets thoroughly burned. Sometimes this episode explains why the bear's fur now has a singed appearance.[9]

Neither of these two episodes entered the animal epic, but they are favorites in northern Europe. The tale of how the fox played godfather (Type 15), however, does appear in the Reynard cycle, though its origin seems to be in the northern Germanic countries. In this story the fox pretends that he has been invited to be a godfather of a newborn child. In this way he sneaks away and steals the butter or honey which he and the bear have stored in common. Each time he returns, the bear asks him the name of the child. The fox always replies in a manner suggesting the truth. For example, he says that the child's name is "Well Begun," "Half Done," or the like. When the bear realizes what has happened, they fall into a dispute as to which has stolen the provisions. The fox smears the sleeping bear with the honey or butter and thus proves that he is the thief. As those familiar with the Grimm collection will remember, the tale is frequently told of a cat and a mouse, or of a cock and a hen. Of all the stories belonging to this general cycle, this is perhaps the best known in other parts of the world than central Europe. It is to be found in most parts of Asia, all over Africa, in the Negro, the Spanish, the Portuguese, and the French traditions in America, and among the North American Indians.

In contrast to the wide popularity of the tale of the fox as godfather, the episode in *Reynard the Fox* concerning the oath on the iron (Type 44) is apparently not found outside of Russia and Yugoslavia. It usually appears as a sequel to the more popular tale. In the dispute concerning the theft of the supplies, the fox denies his guilt and swears by touching an iron trap. The bear follows his example, but hits the iron so hard that his paws are caught.

The fox's persuasive powers are shown in two more stories studied by Krohn, both of which are confined to the folklore of northern Europe. The first of these (Type 20C) begins with a cumulative tale in which the animals flee because they are afraid that the world is coming to an end or that there will be a war. Their fear has been caused by a nut which has fallen on the cock's head.[10] In their despair, they agree that they shall eat each other up. The fox persuades them that the smallest should be eaten first. Frequently as a part of this tale the fox induces the wolf to eat his own entrails (Type 21).

Some of the other episodes studied by Krohn, and having much the same history as the main cycle, are Aarne's Types 36, 37, and 43. In the first of these the fox in disguise violates the she-bear who is caught in a tree cleft. To avoid later recognition, he covers himself with soot and is mistaken for

---

[9] Similar tales concern the burning of the bear with a red hot iron (Type 152*), and the castrating of the bear (Type 153), or sometimes of the ogre (Type 1133).

[10] For further discussion of this tale, see Type 2033, p. 233, below.

the pastor. In the second of these episodes the bear searches for a nursemaid for the young bears. The fox takes service and eats the young bears up. In the third, the bear builds a house of wood and the fox one of ice. In the summer the fox tries to drive the bear out of his house.

Gerber[11] believes that the last of these tales, as, indeed, all of the incidents concerned with building or construction, belongs essentially to a series of transactions between a man and a demon or ogre.[12] He says:

> The connection between the Northern animal tale and the Norman or North-French demon tale is unmistakable, and, like the next adventure [the deceptive crop division],[13] and perhaps also the one following, is a proof of the close relations between the tales of the bear and the fox and the demon tales. The demon tale was most likely the source of the other because it is more natural. Is it in the relation between these tales that we are to seek, perhaps, the reason why the fox is called Michael with all Scandinavians?

Another story of the bear or wolf and the fox which seems to be definitely outside the cycle we have been considering is about how the bear is persuaded to bite the seemingly dead horse's tail (Type 47A). He is dragged off by the horse and the hare sees him and asks him where he is going. The hare laughs so much that he splits his lip. Sometimes in this tale the dupe is a fox. Krohn is convinced that this is not an original Bear (Wolf)-Fox tale, but that it only later passed over into this group and that finally, in the north, the characters were reversed. The latter part of the tale, about the hare, belongs to a group of legends, many of them doubtless of independent-origin in various parts of the world, which explain how the hare obtained his split lip.

Throughout the entire group of animal tales thus far discussed the dupe is sometimes the bear and sometimes the wolf, but the clever animal is almost consistently the fox. It is interesting that as these have spread from their original home, the fox has given way to the hare or the rabbit and even to the lowly spider.[14]

In addition to those animal tales studied by Krohn, several other episodes from the Reynard cycle are known in folk tradition. The simple tale of the wolf who is the guest of the dog and who drinks too much and insists on singing until he is attacked and killed (Type 100) was not only retold by fabulists in the Renaissance but is also familiar over all of Europe and in central Asia, and has even been found among the American Indians of the Southwest. Another dog story belonging to the Reynard cycle shows

---

[11] Adolph Gerber, "Great Russian Animal Tales," *Publications of the Modern Language Association of America*, VI, 55. Gerber's whole article is very valuable for its discussion of these and similar animal tales.

[12] For this group of incidents, see Types 1097 and 1030, pp. 222 and 198, above.

[13] Type 9B. Here is told of the bear and the fox the same tale as is frequently told of the man and the ogre. They raise a garden together and are allowed to choose whether they will take the crops above the ground or below the ground. See p. 198, above.

[14] See Joel Chandler Harris's Uncle Remus cycle and Beckwith, *Jamaica Anansi Stories*.

much more definite Oriental affinities, and probably origin, since it appears in the *Jātaka* and is popular today in India and surrounding countries. This is the tale of The Dog and the Sparrow (Type 248). A man has run over the dog, who is a friend of the sparrow. The sparrow takes vengeance, so that the man loses his horse, his property, and finally his life. Whatever its origin, the tale has become well known all over Europe and has been recorded among the Negroes of Jamaica.

The Reynard cycle also contains several incidents concerned with a war between groups of animals. These are not always clearly separated, but the whole series seems to come eventually from the Orient, probably from India. Sometimes there is a war between the domestic and wild animals. A cat raises her tail and the cowardly wild animals think it is a gun and flee (Type 104). Or the war may be between the birds and the quadrupeds. In this case, the fox's lifted tail is to be the signal for attack. The birds arrange for the gnat to stick the fox under the tail. He drops it, and the quadrupeds flee (Type 222). In the third anecdote, the cowardly wild animals do not even have the excuse of a war. They have never seen a cat before, and hide from her. When she shrieks, the bear falls out of the tree and breaks his backbone (Type 103). All three of these tales are very popular, especially in the Baltic states, and two of them have been recorded in various parts of America.

Finally, in the Reynard cycle, are to be mentioned the two related animal tales which have received more thorough study than any other. The first of these is sometimes not strictly an animal story, but may be concerned almost entirely with objects (Type 210); the other deals entirely with animals (Type 130). In the first, Aarne[15] conceives that the original Asiatic form tells how an egg, a scorpion, a needle, a piece of dung, and a mortar (or some other hard object) go together on a journey. They find themselves in the house of an old woman during her absence and hide themselves in various places, lying in wait to harm her. Each attacks her in his characteristic fashion and drive her forth or kill her. This form of the tale is found in India, Indonesia, Malaysia, China, and Japan, and it has spread over a good part of Europe. The corresponding tale in Europe, however, has as its actors a group of animals who hide themselves either in a wolf's den or a robber's home. The hiding and the attack on the returning owner are the same in all forms of the tale. It is the animal versions that have been most popular in Europe and that have usually been carried to America.

The objects which journey together are also found in the story of The Bean, the Straw, and the Coal (Type 295), though in quite another connection. The coal burns the straw in two and falls into the water, and the bean laughs until he splits. This tale, found in fable collections of the sixteenth century, has a peculiar oral distribution. In Europe it is known only from Germany east but is reported as very common in the West Indies and

<hr>

[15] *Tiere auf der Wanderschaft.*

is told among the American Indians in what are apparently borrowings from the French and Spanish.[16] By no means all the stories in the northern animal cycle appeared in the medieval beast epic. Indeed, the animal cycle for countries like Finland, Estonia, Lithuania, and Russia is surprisingly extensive. In addition to the stories found in other countries and in literary works, a great many have attained popularity only in a limited geographical range and have been reported in but a few versions. In spite of their geographical limitations, however, a score or more of these are so well known in their own area that they cannot be disregarded in any account of the animal tradition of Europe.[17]

C. OTHER LITERARY RELATIONS

In addition to the fable collections and the medieval animal cycle, several other important groups of literary works have told animal tales that are also known in popular tradition. The collection of Buddhist tales known as the *Jātaka*,[18] the long series of books of exempla or illustrative stories told by the medieval priests,[19] and the extensive work of the composers of new fables in the Renaissance[20] are the three most important of these.

[16] A peculiar analogue to the story of the objects traveling together is the well-known American Indian tale of Turtle's War Party. In this story the turtle recruits a war party of strange objects (knife, brush, awl, etc.) and animals. Because of their nature, the companions get into trouble. See p. 322, below. Attention may be also called at this point to an essentially literary tale of The Mouse, the Bird, and the Sausage who keep house together, each with appropriate duties, and succeed until they unwisely exchange their roles (Type 85). It is popular in Germany, perhaps from Grimm, but little known outside.

[17] The tales referred to are: The Fox Tricks the Wolf into Falling into a Pit (Type 30); The Bear Pulls Mountain Ashes Apart so that Fox's Old Mother Can Get Berries (Type 39); The Bear and the Honey (Type 49); The Contest of Frost and the Hare (Type 71); The Needle, the Glove, and the Squirrel (Type 90); The Hungry Fox Waits in Vain for the Horse's Lips (Scrotum) to Fall Off (Type 115); The Bear on the Hay-Wagon (Type 116); The Lion Frightened (Type 118); The Three Rams on the Bridge (Type 123*); The Wild Animals on the Sleigh (Type 158); Captured Wild Animals Ransom Themselves (Type 159); The Fox Eats his Fellow-lodger (Type 170); Sheep, Duck, and Cock in Peril at Sea (Type 204); Straw Threshed a Second Time (Type 206); The Council of Birds (Type 220); Wedding of the Turkey and the Peacock (Type 224); The Goose Teaches the Fox to Swim (Type 226); The Rearing of the Large-headed and Large-eyed Bird (Type 230); The Heathcock and the Bird of Passage (Type 232); The Keen Sight of the Dove and the Keen Hearing of the Frog (Type 238); The Frog Enticed out of his Hole (Type 242); The Crow Marries (Type 243*); Tame Bird and Wild Bird (Type 245); The Ant Carries a Load as Large as Himself (Type 280); and The Gnats and the Horse (Type 281*).

[18] These tales are said to consist of adventures in the former lives of the Buddha. The best introduction is to be found in Cowell's *The Jātaka*; the corresponding Chinese collection of Jātaka tales is found in Chavannes' *500 contes*.

[19] The best general introduction to exemplum literature is Welter, *L'Exemplum*. See also *Gesta Romanorum* and Crane, *Jacques de Vitry*.

[20] The most important of the Renaissance fabulists was Steinhöwel, who brought together a great mass of fables from all sources; see H. Steinhöwel, *Aesop* (ed. H. Oesterley, Tübingen, 1873). Some fables are also included in Johannes Pauli's *Schimpf und Ernst* of the early sixteenth century.

Mention has already been made of the fact that the story of the fox who succeeds in stealing the young magpies appears originally in the *Panchatantra*. It later received literary treatment in the Reynard cycle and in Hans Sachs. Alongside this purely artistic tale, and doubtless influenced by it, there developed a folktale well known in northern and eastern Europe. In this story (Type 56A) the fox threatens to push down the tree in which the magpie has its young. The crow gives good advice to the magpies and saves them. The fox avenges himself, plays dead, and catches the crow. The action in the latter part of the tale is the reverse of that in the literary fable.

Rather popular from Germany eastward is the story of the old dog as the rescuer of the child (Type 101), a story appearing in Steinhöwel's fifteenth century collection of fables. A farmer makes plans for killing a faithful old dog. The wolf has made friends with the dog, and works out a plan whereby the dog can be saved. The latter is to rescue the farmer's child from the wolf. When the wolf has permitted the plan to succeed, he wants to be allowed to steal the farmer's sheep. But the dog objects, and loses the wolf's friendship.

The medieval collections of exempla did not usually contain many animal tales except those already made familiar by fable books. One animal story, however, which seems from its distribution and general history to be essentially an oral tradition (Type 120), has found a place in Pauli's *Schimpf und Ernst* of the early sixteenth century. This tells of a wager between the fox and the hog as to which of them shall see the sunrise first. The fox places himself on a hill facing the east; the hog in a lower place facing the high trees to the west. The sun shines on the top of the trees, and the hog wins. This tale is known from Ireland to central Siberia, and has an interesting analogue in Japan.

Appearing first in the *Jātaka* and then spreading prodigiously as an oral tale is the story of the Tarbaby (Type 175). The essential point of the anecdote is that the trickster (most often the rabbit) is caught by a tarbaby (or some kind of sticky image). In a large number of cases the rabbit's enemies debate as to how he shall be punished. He agrees to various kinds of punishment, anything they suggest, but begs not to be thrown into the brier patch. Thinking to do him most injury, they throw him into the briers and he escapes (Type 1310).[21] This tale of the tarbaby has been studied very thoroughly by A. M. Espinosa, on the basis of more than 150 versions, which he has later supplemented by the addition of 115.[22] From India it seems clear that this story has reached the Negroes and Indians of America by several paths. It came from India to Africa, where it is a favorite and where it received some characteristic modifications before being

---

[21] This tale is frequently told of the turtle or crayfish who begs not to be drowned (K581.1).
[22] *Journal of American Folklore*, XLIII, 129-209 and LVI, 31ff.

taken by slaves to America. Another path was through Europe to the Hispanic peninsula and thence to American colonies. The third, but apparently very unimportant route, was directly across Europe.

In his second folktale monograph Kaarle Krohn discusses stories involving a man and a fox.[23] One of them is a definitely literary fable, The Ungrateful Serpent Returned to Captivity (Type 155). The main part of his study, however, is concerned with the tale of Bear Food (Type 154), the history of which is much more difficult to clarify. As will be seen, the story really consists of three separate episodes. A man in his anger at their laziness scolds his horses and calls them "bear food." The bear overhears and comes and demands the horses. A fox approaches and agrees to help the man from his predicament, but demands from the man geese or chickens in return for the service. The fox goes into the woods and imitates the barking of dogs, so that the bear is frightened and killed. The man now goes for the geese, but instead brings back in his bag dogs which attack the fox and chase him to his hole. Here the fox holds a conversation with his feet, his eyes, his ears, and his tail, and asks each of them how they could have helped him in his flight. The tail admits that it did not help. Thereupon the foolish fox sticks out his tail, which is seized upon by the dogs. The three parts of this story, (1) the "bear food" episode, (2) the deceptive payment given the fox, and (3) the fox's conversation with his bodily members, have not always been handled together. The first part would seem to have a more definitely literary relation than the last two. It is missing in the versions of the tale from Germany and the Romance countries, but Krohn feels that its presence in the *Roman de Renart* and in exemplum literature bespeaks its earlier presence in western Europe. He feels that the whole story is so well known over all of Europe that it is essentially a part of European folklore, though he admits the possibility that more adequate collections from India and the Orient might change his conclusions.

Almost all of the animal anecdotes thus far discussed have shown some kind of literary relationship.[24] But for animal tales there has also been a vigorous oral tradition not dependent upon literary works either as origin or as modes of dissemination. A thorough account of these purely folk stories, even in the European and Asiatic areas, would be extremely tedious, since almost every country has developed a large number of them which have not been taken over into other lands. A cursory examination of *The Types of the Folk-Tale* (especially pages 22 to 43 and 214 to 220) and of the various folktale surveys[25] will show these local tales for a number of different countries. They are particularly frequent in the Baltic states and in Russia.

[23] *Mann und Fuchs.*

[24] Of the tales discussed in Krohn's *Bär (Wolf) und Fuchs* (see pp. 219ff., above) the following types apparently do not have literary relationships; Types 3, 5, 7, 8, 21, 37, 43, 47A.

[25] For a list of these surveys, see p. 419, below.

Besides these stories of very limited distribution, there remain a number of traditional oral tales which have gained currency over a larger area.

The story told in Grimm of The She-fox's Suitors (Type 65) in which the widowed she-fox proves her faithfulness by rejecting suitors who do not resemble her deceased husband has a wide circulation in Germany and is known in Scandinavia. There are reasonably close parallels from the Gypsies and analogues apparently unrelated in various parts of Africa. A much more definite tradition appears in a story which finds its greatest concentration in Finland and Lithuania, but is also known in Hungary and among Cape Verde Islanders in Massachusetts. It tells of the dog who acts as the wolf's shoemaker (Type 102). He keeps demanding material for the shoes, so that he eventually eats up the cow, the hog, etc. which are furnished him.

Two fable-like oral tales have their greatest popularity in Scandinavia and the Baltic countries. The Norwegians are especially fond of telling how the mouse, in order to placate the cat, tells her a story. The cat answers, "Even so, I eat you up" (Type 111). In some way this story has traveled to Indonesia, where it has been reported in three versions. The anecdote in which the rat persuades the cat to wash her face before eating and thus escapes (Type 122B) has traveled from the Baltic countries in another direction: it is known in at least four different areas of Africa.

Tales of the way in which a small and weak animal overcomes a very large one occur in many parts of the world. There is probably no connection between the numerous African anecdotes of this kind and the story of The Titmouse and the Bear (Type 228) which seems to be confined to Finland and Estonia, though very popular there. In this tale the titmouse ruffles up her feathers but does not succeed in fooling her own children. In her own form, however, she flies into the bear's ear and kills him.

Mention may also be made at this place of a story obviously related to the cumulative tales soon to be discussed. In this story of The Lying Goat (Type 212) a father sends his sons, one after the other, to pasture the goat. Nevertheless, the goat always declares that he has had nothing to eat. The father angrily sends his sons from home and learns, when he himself tries to pasture the goat, that he has been deceived. This tale is popular in most parts of Europe, but has not been reported from outside.

Some of the most interesting of animal tales are sometimes not told as simple stories but may have attached to them some explanation accounting for the form or present habits of the animal. If the main purpose of such tales is this explanation, we usually consider them as origin tales, of which, as we shall see,[26] there are a large number in every country. But in some of the stories the explanatory element seems to be quite secondary to the interest of the tale itself. Such is the account of the animals as road-builders (Type 55).

[26] For a discussion of these origin tales, see pp. 303ff., 310ff., below.

The fox acts as overseer and punishes the lazy animals. The various kinds of punishment which he gives them accounts for some feature in the present-day descendant of that animal. This tale is very popular in Finland and is also widely known in Africa, and has been reported from the American Indians of the southeastern United States.[27]

Animals sometimes obtain another's characteristics by failing to return things which they have borrowed. Thus the nightingale and the blindworm used each to have one eye. The nightingale borrowed the blindworm's and refused to return it, so that she now has two and the blindworm none. The latter is always on a tree where the nightingale has her nest and in revenge bores holes in the nightingale's eggs (Type 234). This tale has been reported mainly from Germany and France, but the similar story of the way in which the jay borrows the cuckoo's skin and fails to return it (Type 235) is primarily Baltic, though analogues are known in Indonesia.

Two other tales of birds are apparently confined to Scandinavia and the Baltic countries. In the first (Type 236), the thrush teaches the dove to build small nests, so that ever afterward she has kept on doing so. In the other (Type 240), the dove and the magpie exchange their eggs, the seven dove's eggs for the two of the magpie. This accounts for the fact that the dove always lays two eggs.

Generally speaking, fish have not interested taletellers very much, though the wonder tale contains magic fishes, and the Munchausen[28] cycle has large exaggerations about great catches of fish. One origin tale (Type 252) concerning fish has acquired some popularity in Finland and Lapland. The pike races the snake to the land. The winner is to remain on land, but since the pike loses his race, he remains in the water.

When one considers all the kinds of animal tales current in the folklore of Europe and Asia, he will be impressed by the great variety of anecdotes which have been attached to animal heroes. This variety proceeds not only from the interest in the nature and qualities of actual animals, but also from the inveterate habit of making up animal tales which is common to the story-tellers of all lands. Animal stories look for their origin, therefore, not only to continuing invention stimulated by animal life, but to artistic activity extending in range from the skillful taletellers of primitive tribes to the cultivated composers of the Hindu, the classical, and the medieval fables.

[27] For a detailed analysis of this tale, see motif A2233 and subdivisions.
[28] For the magic fish, see B175; for the great catch of fish, see p. 214, above.

3. FORMULA TALES

A. TALES WITH FORMULISTIC FRAMEWORK

IN CONSIDERING the tales current in the oral tradition of Europe and Western Asia, it has been convenient to bring together three categories of narratives: (1) complex tales, (2) simple tales with human actors, and (3) simple tales with animal actors. Such a classification is simpler than the facts of the case actually warrant. It is not always possible to tell where to draw the line between simple and complex, or, indeed, between human and animal. Some tales refuse to stay within a classification, even one in which they clearly belong in their usual form.

A very special group of stories illustrates the difficulty of classifying on the basis either of complexity of plot or of the humanness of the actors. In this group of stories the form is all-important. The central situation is simple, but the formal handling of it assumes a certain complexity; and the actors are almost indifferently animals or persons. Such stories we call formula tales.[1]

Formula tales contain a minimum of actual narrative. The simple central situation serves as a basis for the working out of a narrative pattern. But the pattern so developed is interesting, not on account of what happens in the story, but on account of the exact form in which the story is narrated. Sometimes this formalism consists in a sort of framework which encloses the story and sometimes in that peculiar piling up of words which makes the cumulative tale. In any case, the effect of a formulistic story is always essentially playful, and the proper narrating of one of these tales takes on all the aspects of a game.

Certain of the countries of eastern Europe are especially fond of telling endless tales. These are usually quite simple in pattern. A situation is afforded in which a particular task must be repeated an indefinite number of times. Thousands of sheep, for example, must be put over a stream one at a time, and the narrator proceeds inexorably with his literal repetitions of the performance until his listeners can stand it no longer (Z11; Type 2300). Another kind of endless tale is the "round." Here a story proceeds to a certain point and then, in one way or another, usually by having some character tell a story, the whole tale begins over again and keeps repeating itself (Z17; Taylor, Type 2350). The round is much more common as a folksong than as a folktale. In any case, the narrative material in a prose round is likely to be of little interest or importance.

The ending of a narrative offers an opportunity for special formulistic

---

[1] For formula tales, see: *Motif-Index* Z0-Z99; Archer Taylor, "A Classification of Formula Tales," *Journal of American Folklore*, XLVI, 71ff.; Taylor, *Handwörterbuch des deutschen Märchens*, II, 164ff.

treatment. Sometimes a story-teller teases his audience by stopping just as the interest has been aroused. The ending of the tale may be similar to that of The Three Wise Men of Gotham: "If the bowl had been stronger, my tale had been longer" (Z12; Type 2250). Or the tale may be essentially a game: the teller frames his story so that a hearer is almost compelled to ask a certain question to which the story-teller returns a ridiculous answer (Z13; Type 2200). Folktale collectors have not always interested themselves in these unfinished tales and catch tales, and we cannot be sure that our knowledge of them is adequate. It would seem that the unfinished tales are well known all over Europe with an especial popularity in Hungary. Catch tales have been reported only from Flanders, but it is inconceivable that they should actually be limited to that country.[2]

B. CUMULATIVE TALES

A much more definite narrative core is found in the cumulative tale. Something of the nature of a game is also present here, since the accumulating repetitions must be recited exactly, but in the central situation many of these tales maintain their form unchanged over long periods of history and in very diverse environments. Such tales as The House that Jack Built or The Old Woman and Her Pig are so well known that no reader of the English language needs to have explained to him the way in which a simple phrase or clause is repeated over and over again, always with new additions. Most of the enjoyment, both in the telling and listening to such tales, is in the successful manipulation of the ever-growing rigmarole. The cumulative tale always gradually works up to one long final routine containing the entire sequence. The person examining cumulative tales, therefore, has only to look at this final formula to learn all that is to be learned about the whole tale.

One important group of cumulative tales has to do with the death of an animal, usually a cock or a hen. Perhaps best known of these is The Death of the Cock (Z31.2.1.1; Taylor, Type 2021A).[3] After he has choked to death, the hen goes out and seeks the aid of various objects and persons—stream, tree, pig, miller, baker, etc. This tale is very widely distributed over all of Europe and is known in India, but the problem of its ultimate origin is not easy to solve. Haavio and Wesselski, both of whom have treated the story very thoroughly, disagree as to the importance of the Oriental relationship. Not so well known, but still widely distributed in Europe and occasionally reported in America, is The Death of the Little Hen (Z31.2.2; Type 2022), a

[2] With tales of the kind we are discussing the spirit of play is so important that they are of primary interest to the student of children's games.

[3] See definitive studies on this tale by Haavio (*Kettenmärchenstudien*) and Wesselski (*Hessische Blätter für Volkskunde*, XXXII, 2ff.). They also discuss the anecdote, "What should I have said?" (Type 1696) which is really a cumulative tale as well as a story of stupidity.

tale that seems to go back to the *Panchatantra*. The hen is mourned by various objects, animals, and persons, each in a characteristic fashion: flea, door, broom, cart, ashes, tree, girl. A slight modification of this tale appears in France and Denmark, where each of the mourners for the little hen performs an action which is described by some unusual or new word. For example, the table untables itself (Z31.2.2.1; Taylor, Type 2022A). In a somewhat less popular cumulative story about the little hen's death, various animals one by one join her funeral procession. Eventually the funeral carriage breaks down, or the whole procession drowns (Z31.2.1; Type 2021).

Several cumulative tales involve the eating of an object, whether as the end result of the series of happenings or the cause of the series. Most popular of these, both in Europe and America, is The Fleeing Pancake (Z31.3.1; Type 2025), frequently known in American collections as The Gingerbread Man. A woman makes a pancake (or gingerbread man) which runs away from her. Various animals try in vain to stop it. Finally the fox eats it up. The conversation between the gingerbread man and the fox has a tendency to become formalized, much like that between Red Riding Hood and the wolf—"What makes your ears so big?", etc. Two other chains of incidents concerning the eating of an object are very similar and perhaps related. The first of these is about The Fat Cat (Z31.3.2; Type 2027). While her mistress is away the cat eats the porridge, the bowl, and the ladle. When the mistress returns, she says to the cat, "How fat you are!" The cat replies, "I ate the porridge, the bowl, and the ladle, and I will eat you." After eating the mistress, the cat likewise meets various animals. Always after the same conversation she eats them. The story ends with her finally eating too many and bursting. This is essentially a Scandinavian tale, though one version has been reported from India. The other is also well known in Scandinavia, but is found in Russia, and an analogue has been taken down in east Africa. This tale is sometimes called The Fat Troll (Z31.3.4; Type 2028), and sometimes The Fat Wolf, for the story may be told of either. A troll (or wolf) eats the watcher's five horses and finally the watcher himself. When the master goes to investigate, the troll says, "I ate the five horses, I ate the watcher, and I will eat you." After he has eaten the master, the same thing happens to the wife, the servant, the daughter, the son, and the dog—always after the same piling up of threats. When he comes to the cat, however, she scratches him open and rescues all the victims.

Much like the tale of The Fleeing Pancake is that of The Goat Who Would Not Go Home (Z31.4.1; Type 2015). One animal after another tries in vain to persuade the stubborn goat to go home. Nothing avails until a wolf (sometimes a bee) bites him and drives him home. This tale of the goat has always been especially dear to children and probably for this reason is extraordinarily popular in Europe. Except in printed children's books, however, it is not known elsewhere.

In the cumulative tales thus far mentioned the structure has been rather simple. There has been a series of events bound together by one slender thread, and the interest has usually been a conversation containing an increasing number of details. The cumulative tale reaches its most interesting development, however, when there is not merely an addition with each episode, but when every episode is dependent upon the last. Perhaps to the English-speaking world the best known of such tales is The Old Woman and Her Pig (Z41.1; Type 2030). It will be remembered that the pig will not jump over the stile so that the old woman can go home. She keeps appealing in vain for help, but the help always depends upon her getting help from someone else. She finally persuades a cow to give her milk. The final formula is: Cow give milk for cat; cat kill rat; rat gnaw rope; rope hang butcher; butcher kill ox; ox drink water; water quench fire; fire burn stick; stick beat dog; dog bite pig; pig jump over style. In the wide extent of its distribution over Europe, Asia, Africa, and America, it is natural that the details should differ a good deal. But the whole pattern is remarkably well kept. If the tale is not actually from India originally, it is at least very well known there.[4]

Whereas The Old Woman and Her Pig has had its greatest popularity with oral taletellers, the chain known as Stronger and Strongest (Z41.2; Type 2031) is essentially literary. It is found in Oriental tale collections and appears frequently in medieval literature. Though nowhere really popular, it has traveled to every continent. The chain may go in either one of two directions. It may start with God and show how he was the ultimate cause of the frostbitten foot. Or it may likewise take the cause to the little mouse who gnawed a hole in the wall. In the first, and more extensive, version, the final formula is: God how strong you are—God who sends Death, Death who kills blacksmith, blacksmith who makes knife, knife that kills steer, steer that drinks water, water that quenches fire, fire that burns stick, stick that kills cat, cat that eats mouse, mouse that perforates wall, wall that resists wind, wind that dissolves cloud, cloud that covers sun, sun that thaws frost, frost that broke my foot.

The peculiar distribution of some of these cumulative tales is nowhere better seen than in the story of The Cock's Whiskers (Z41.3; Type 2032). It is very well known in Russia and Sweden and has been reported twice from France and once from Italy. It seems not to be known anywhere else in the world—with one interesting exception, among the Zuñi of New Mexico. In Europe this tale is about a mouse who throws a nut down and hits the cock on the head. He also steals the cock's whiskers. The cock goes to get an old woman to cure him. The final formula is: Fountain give up water for forest, forest give up wood for baker, baker give up bread for dog, dog give up hairs to cure the cock. Among the Zuñi the story collector Cushing told

<hr />

[4] See Murray B. Emeneau, *Journal of American Folklore*, LVI, 272ff., who discusses twelve Indic versions of the tale.

this tale as he had learned it from Crane's Italian collection, and when he returned the next year the Indians told it to him. It had become so thoroughly adapted to Zuñi ceremonialism, however, that its original cumulative nature was hardly recognizable.

The nut hitting the cock on the head appears also as an introduction to another tale which we have already noticed (Type 20C). When the nut hits him on the head, he thinks that the world is coming to an end. He sends the hen to tell the duck, the duck to tell the goose, etc. The final formula is: Fox, who told you?—Hare.—Hare, who told you?—Goose, etc. (Z41.4; Type 2033). The animals in their fear agree that they shall eat each other up, and the fox persuades them that the smallest should be eaten first. In this story, as in several similar ones, the animals sometimes appear with queer names. The hen is henny-penny; the cock, cocky-locky; the goose, goosey-poosey, etc. (Z21.3.1). This story of the end of the world is certainly as old as the *Jātaka*. It is most popular in Scandinavia, but has been found in most parts of the world.

Much better known in popular tradition is the formula of How the Mouse Regained Its Tail (Z41.5; Taylor, Type 2034). The cat bites off the mouse's tail and will return it in exchange for milk. The mouse goes to the cow for milk, to the farmer for hay, to the butcher for meat, to the baker for bread. Other persons mentioned are the locksmith and the miner. Not only is this common all over Europe, but there are interesting analogues from all parts of Africa. Sometimes this series of adventures is joined with the anecdote of the man who permits his grain of corn to be eaten by the cock and then demands the cock as damages (Type 1655). It will be remembered that this is essentially a cumulative tale, since the hog eats the cock, the ox eats the hog, etc.

To the English-speaking reader perhaps the most familiar of all cumulative tales is The House That Jack Built (Z41.6; Type 2035), but it is not frequently told on the continent of Europe. Some analogues appear from Africa, though they are not exact. The standard form is that with which English and American readers are acquainted. Its final formula is: This is the farmer that sowed the corn, that fed the cock that crowed in the morn, that waked the priest all shaven and shorn, that married the man all tattered and torn, that kissed the maiden all forlorn, that milked the cow with the crumpled horn, that tossed the dog, that worried the cat, that caught the rat, that ate the malt that lay in the house that Jack built.

Such are the principal cumulative tales, but this list by no means exhausts the whole store of those current in one or another part of the European and Asiatic areas. There remain, for example, the German tale of Pif Paf Poltrie (Z31.1.1; Type 2019) in which the suitor is sent from one relation to the other for consent to the wedding; and the train of troubles which come from a lost horseshoe nail (Z41.9; Taylor, Type 2039).

Not all chain-tales are actually cumulative, but may consist of a simple series, verbal or actual. Such, for example, are the chains which are based upon a series of numbers, like that of the origin of chess (Z21.1; Taylor, Type 2009). The inventor asks one wheat-grain for the first square, two for the second, four for the third, eight for the fourth, etc. The amount is so large that the king cannot pay. This is essentially a literary story, as are also a group of chains concerning special meanings or objects brought into relation with the numbers one to twelve (Z21.2 and subdivisions). One of these, *Ehod mi yodea* (Taylor, Type 2010), has a long history in Hebrew ritual and frequently appears as a carol.

There remain two chain stories having to do with the houses that have burned down. One of them is a foolish tale in which the whole point is the difficulty of making a satisfactorily conservative answer. The usual formula is: My house burned down.—That is too bad.—That is not bad at all, my wife burned it down.—That is good.—That is not good, etc. (Z23.1; Type 2014). Though this story is not widely disseminated, it is apparently independent of literary tradition. In this respect it is quite the opposite from the almost purely bookish anecdote of the servant who broke the news of the fire to his master, a tale usually known as The Climax of Horrors (Z41.10; Type 2040). The details of the conversation vary much in the different tellings. The servant meets his returning master and tells him that the magpie is dead. When the master inquires why, the servant says that it had overeaten on horseflesh. As the chain proceeds, it turns out that the horses have died at the fire which burned the house. Usually the man's family has burned with the house, or other dire misfortunes have overtaken him. This story was used by the medieval priests to illustrate their sermons, and drew from it incredibly strange lessons of morality and piety.

Formula tales, especially chains and cumulative stories, though they have about them many qualities which belong to games and are therefore amusing to children and to those who never grow up, have aesthetic value of their own. Their essential formal quality is repetition, usually repetition with continuing additions. This is what students of the popular ballad call "incremental repetition," a stylistic feature which adds much to the appeal of many of our finest old ballads.

4. LEGENDS AND TRADITIONS

Thus far in the summary which we have made of the principal narratives current in the folklore of those countries extending from Ireland to India we have been dealing with fiction. Whether a story-teller has recounted the long and complicated adventures of the dragon-slayer, a joke about a stupid married couple, an anecdote of an embarrassed parson, or a shrewd trick of the fox, or has successfully threaded the mazes of a cumulative story, he is seldom under any illusions that his story refers to actual events. He knows well enough that his characters live in a world of make-believe.[1]

But that is not to say that all tales in the folklore of Europe and Asia are regarded as fiction. Simple man, though unlettered and without benefit of science and history, possesses nevertheless his own science and his own history. These have been taught him by his fathers and his neighbors. He knows how the animals acquired their present habits, why the weather behaves as it does in his country, how constellations were formed and what they mean. For each of these he has an interesting story, one that is vouched for from of old and is not open to doubt. And if his science comes thus in interesting tales, so also does his history. He knows not only famous events like Noah's flood, but also a hundred other stories which the vicissitudes of time have attached to the Biblical legend like barnacles on the ark itself.

Traditional history and traditional science of the kind here suggested seem to be a part of the folklore of peoples all over the world. But it is only in Europe and, to some extent, in western Asia that such tales are considered in a class to themselves. On the one hand stands the vast store of recognized fiction and on the other these tales which are related as undoubted facts. Most story-tellers are very clear about when they are speaking to command belief and when they are contriving a fiction.[2]

A. MYTHOLOGICAL LEGENDS

The student of popular legend and tradition cannot fail to be impressed with the fertility of imagination with which man has viewed the world around him. The simple taleteller of today, receiving much of his legendary material from an even more unlettered past, finds ready for his use a wealth of accounts, not only of the marvels of the present world and remarkable happenings of historic times, but also even of the very beginnings of the earth and the establishment of the present order of animals and men.

For all those peoples whose religious background is Christian, Mohammedan, or Jewish the legends concerning creation are normally based upon the Old Testament account.[3] But there has been no feeling that this account is so sacred that it cannot be elaborated. A very considerable number of legends have grown up around such Biblical stories as the Garden of Eden and the Flood.

[1] This remark must be taken with some caution, since there are undoubtedly story-tellers who believe in the reality of their stories. This seems to be true of certain taletellers in India, and I am informed that many story-tellers among primitive peoples do not make the distinction between fiction and history which we are accustomed to in our own culture. The remarks above are meant to describe the attitude of the normal teller of tales in the western world.

[2] For these "true tales" the English language has never devised a satisfactory term. See p. 8, above.

[3] For an excellent treatment of legends based upon the Old Testament and still current as oral tales, see Dähnhardt, Natursagen, vol. I.

When working within this Biblical tradition, the story-teller has not usually gone back to primeval chaos and divine creation, but has been content to interest himself first of all in the Garden of Eden, in man's creation, and his loss of Paradise. Well known, of course, is the fact that man was made from clay (A1241) and that the first woman was made from his rib (A1275.1). But it is more unusual to hear that Adam's body was made of eight things: his trunk from earth, his bones from stone, his veins from roots, his blood from water, his hair from grass, his thoughts from wind, and his spirit from the clouds (A1291). And it must have been a primitive misogynist who started the rumor that Eve had really been created from a dog's tail (A1224.3).

Satan consistently opposes God in his creation, but he is always unsuccessful except in his adventure with Eve. He has seen God form various animals and then breathe life into them. He tries the same thing, but his animals always remain lifeless (A1217). Another story, apparently forgetting that the devil cannot make the animals, divides the creation of all beasts between the two antagonists. The ill-disposition or unpleasantness of certain animals comes from the fact that they are the devil's creations (A1751).

The success of Satan in the Garden (A1331.1) seems to be familiar to all story-tellers, though quite generally the fruit eaten is not that of the tree of knowledge of good and evil. It was certainly an apple, as proved by the Adam's apple where it stuck in Adam's throat (A1319.1). The interest in Paradise Lost and in Adam and Eve generally ceases after they are expelled from the garden, but there have been preserved some traditions which give us a last glimpse of the first mother. She has so many children that she is ashamed when God pays her a visit. She hides some of them, and thus they fail to receive the blessing which God gives to all those who are in sight. This story is given as an explanation of superior and inferior classes of people, of downtrodden races (A1650.1), of the existence of monkeys (A1861.1), or of peoples of the underworld (F251.4).

Legends about floods appear in many parts of the world.[4] Many of these are independent growths, sometimes reminiscent of actual local catastrophes. But the most important of all flood legends is that which tells about Noah and his ark. Wherever Biblical tales have been learned, this one is sure to be popular because of its dramatic and picturesque details. Just as this legend afforded the medieval dramatist one of his best opportunities for a humorous treatment of a Biblical worthy,[5] it has given taletellers everywhere an opportunity to elaborate details afforded by the interesting situation. Perhaps most assiduous in the development of these flood legends

[4] For bibliography of flood legends, see A1010.

[5] The Play of the Flood (in The Towneley Plays, Early English Text Society, extra series, LXXI).

have been the peoples of Siberia. In areas farther away from the original home of the Noah legend missionaries have made it familiar, and it often appears along with similar tales from the local folklore. This is particularly true of the North American Indians and of the inhabitants of the Pacific islands.

The escape from the deluge in the ark (A1021), the pairs of animals preserved so that they may escape destruction (A1021.1), and the bird scouts sent out from the ark (A1021.2)—these three elements are nearly always present. The lodging of the ark on the mountain is closely paralleled by many tales in which people escape from the flood by ascending a mountain (A1022), but it is not at all certain that the Bible story is the source of these. In addition to these canonical incidents, popular imagination has supplied a number of details. A few of these will illustrate the manner in which the flood legend has been used to explain the characteristics of some animal or some other present-day situation.

It appears, for example, that the devil was in a way to be drowned and wanted a place on the ark in spite of Noah's objection. One story tells how he forbids Noah's wife to enter the ark until Noah has also invited him in (K485; Type 825). Some say that Noah loses patience and calls out, "The devil! Come in!" The devil comes in and turns himself into a mouse (C12.5.1). After the devil is in the ark as a mouse, he gnaws a hole in the bottom of the ark. Thereupon Noah asks the help of the lion. The lion sneezes, and a cat comes from the lion's nostril and eats the mouse (A1811.2). Two animals are obstreperous and suffer the consequences. The griffin refuses to go on the ark and hence is drowned and is now extinct (A2232.4), and the unicorn is thrown from the ark and suffers the same fate (A2214.3).

Such are a few of the popular variations on the Noah and Adam legends. They will serve to show the way in which popular fancy has handled the sacred writings. Besides these two groups of Bible legends are found many more, such as the Tower of Babel (C771.1) and the confusion of tongues (A1333), and many incidents concerning the childhood of Jesus.

Popular imagination, even among those people who receive their creation legends from Genesis, has many things to say about the universe, and the earth and its inhabitants. Many of these explanations seem very old, and certainly go back to a time before the present religions fixed the thinking of these peoples.

It is clear that nineteenth century scholars exaggerated beyond all reason the importance of the stars in the thinking of our early story-tellers.[6] Nevertheless, such phenomena as the Milky Way (A778), the Pleiades (A773), and the Great Bear (A771) have produced a number of legends

[6] See p. 384, below.

concerning their origin. The Milky Way is sometimes thought of as a pathway of souls, as a river, as a hunting party, or as a stitched seam in the sky; the Pleiades are nearly always imagined as seven sisters, and pretty stories are invented to tell how one of them has been lost.

Neither the sun nor the moon occupies a large place in actual legend.[7] Popular imagination has largely confined its interest in the sun to tales about how it is stolen (A721.1). Usually it is thought of as being in the possession of some monster who keeps it hidden in a box or a pot so that it is of no use to mankind. As to the moon, there are two points of interest: the figures on its surface and its monthly phases. One school of mythologists bases its theories upon the observation that the moon with these two characteristics appears to all mankind and furnishes a common object of interest everywhere. The "Man in the Moon" (A751) is not always a man, though he may well be thought of as one who has been sent there in punishment for his misdeeds. What is he doing? Some people imagine he is making a big fire, some that he is carrying buckets of water. Many others contend that we are looking at a rabbit or a frog; and the list could be greatly extended. For the phases of the moon (A755) a number of explanations are given. Most of them seem trivial, and no well recognized stories have attached themselves to this phenomenon.

The sun, the moon, and the stars, vast as these are, do not furnish a sufficiently broad scope for the folk imagination. For, outside of the earth they trod on and the heavenly bodies which they could see, our story-tellers have imagined many other realms. Some of these are a part of their regular religious conceptions: heaven, hell, and sometimes purgatory. The relation of popular conceptions of these lands of the dead to early folk thought on the one hand and to learned theological disputation on the other is a subject of much interest, but belongs essentially to the history of religions.[8]

But popular imagination has devised still other worlds. Sometimes these are thought of as above, sometimes below, and sometimes merely remote. There are frequent stories of journeys to earthly paradises on distant islands or across mystic rivers or on some inaccessible mountain (F111). The Irish have always been especially fond of stories of marvelous voyages, to the Land of Women (F112), it may be, or to the realm of youth (D1338.7), or to Avalon[9] (E481.4.1) where the dead are healed. But by no means all of the "otherworld" ideas in European folklore are Irish. Many of them

---

[7] This, in spite of the fact that some writers on mythology find practically all folktales nothing more than broken down sun myths or moon myths. See pp. 371ff. and 384, below.

[8] For some of these concepts, see the following motif numbers: A671. Hell; A692. Islands of the Blest; A661. Heaven; E481.4. Beautiful land of the dead; and E755.3. Souls in Purgatory.

[9] See A. H. Krappe, "Avallon," *Speculum*, XVIII (1943), 303-322.

are certainly Oriental,[10] and others are so widespread as to make source hunting an impossible quest. The rainbow bridge to the land of the dead (F152.1.1) is not confined to Norse mythology, and the mysterious forbidding river which one must ford in order to pass over into the evil land (F141.1.1) was traversed by many heroes before Browning sent Child Roland on his quest for the Dark Tower. Some other interesting concepts concerning the other worlds make clear enough the fact that great distances have never been a part of these popular conceptions. The lower world can be reached by descending a rope (F96) or going down a stair (F94), and a descent from the upper world may be made in the same way, not only by the angels at Bethel, but also by human heroes and heroines. On the way from the sky the rope may be too short to afford safe return.[11]

A very common legend is that of the city below the sea, a kind of submarine other-land (F133). Such legends may sometimes be based upon a real knowledge of sunken coasts, though this can be true for only a small number. Somewhat analogous to these ideas is that of the sunken continent, the Lost Atlantis (cf. Z692). But that speculation is certainly literary.

In contrast to the number of legends and traditions concerning the heavenly bodies and other worlds, the stories about the formation of the earth, its present conditions, and the establishment of its human and animal inhabitants appear in almost overwhelming numbers. Any realistic view of the available body of oral legend and tradition, whether among primitive peoples or among unlettered groups in our own culture, compels the conclusion that the taleteller's imagination has concerned itself primarily with things of this earth.

The main act of creation of the earth has not ordinarily entered into Western tradition, since that tradition has received as orthodox the explanations either of one of the great mythologies or of the Hebrew scriptures. On the other hand, there are many tales explaining the presence of particular features of landscape (A901). Certain mountains, for example, are said to be caused by stones which are dropped from a giant's clothes, or because God's sieve broke and let through large stones, or because giants hurled boulders back and forth (A965 and A966). Another large group of legends concerns indentions on rocks. These are explained as being the footprints left by some primitive man or animal, frequently by one of the gods (A972). One of the most common legends, known in the Old World, but a particular

---

[10] For an excellent discussion of the whole otherworld concept, see H. R. Patch, "Some Elements in Mediaeval Descriptions of the Otherworld," *Publications of the Modern Language Association*, XXXIII, 601-643.

[11] The rope from the sky (F51) is very popular in primitive tales. The ladder to the upper world (F52) appears more frequently in a religious context, where the upper world is usually the Christian Heaven. One of the most famous medieval books of exempla was called *Scala Celi*.

favorite of the American Indians, is that of a cliff which has served as a point from which lovers have leapt to their tragic death (A985). Sometimes, of course, this legend is merely a local story and makes no pretense of explaining the presence of a cliff.

Such are a few of the groups of explanatory legends concerning the formation of the land. As to the sea, the most puzzling feature has been the saltness of its water, and various legends have attempted to account for this. The most familiar is the tale of the stolen salt mill which will stop grinding only at the command of its master. A ship captain takes it aboard his ship, and it continues to grind salt until the ship is sunk and the whole sea has been filled with it.[12]

Legends explanatory of the weather are much more common in primitive folklore than in that of the West. There is much resemblance in these legends in all parts of the world, though the ideas are so general that no actual historic relationship between them need be assumed. The tale of Aeolus, who confines the winds in a cave (A1122) and lets them out at will appears not only in classical mythology but also in places so widely separated as Siberia, New Zealand, and California. Similarly widespread is the story of the giant bird who causes the winds by the flapping of his wings (A1125). The bird flaps too hard, and the hero cuts his wings so as to make him more moderate. This latter tale was known not only in ancient Babylonia, but in Iceland as well, and it has been reported among the North American Indians of Nova Scotia[13] and the Negroes of Georgia.

Finally, among weather legends should be mentioned those accounting for the rain and snow. Not much originality is shown in these, the most usual explanation of rain being from tears (A1131.1), or snow from the feathers or clothes of a witch (A1135.1). The latter idea appears in several forms: sometimes she is said to be picking geese and letting the feathers fall.

In relating those legends based upon the Old Testament an account has already been given of the popular traditions concerning Creation and Paradise Lost, as well as the Flood. But there are several stories about the beginnings of human life and culture which are not based upon the Scriptures. Among these are the practically world-wide myths of the theft of light (A1411), and the theft of fire (A1415). The latter is told in especially rich detail in all parts of the world. Some of the correspondences between remote versions of this legend—for example, the preservation of the fire in a hollow reed not only in the Greek myth but in tales from

---

[12] This motif appears as a part of a regular folktale, Type 565.

[13] My own investigation of the tales of the North American Indians began with just this point. In his *Algonquin Legends of New England*, Charles Godfrey Leland had called attention to the interesting parallel between this Indian tale and an Icelandic myth, and he was convinced of historic connections, probably by way of Greenland and the Eskimos. Such connection is, of course, not impossible.

Indians of California and of Bolivia—present an interesting problem of comparative folklore.

By far the largest number of explanatory legends everywhere are concerned with animals, their creation and the establishment of their special characteristics. The teller of folktales is no evolutionist. He has a tendency to explain all present-day animals in terms of the behavior of some mythical ancestor. Some act has brought about the creation of a species of animals or a change in their make-up or habits. We have already mentioned the creation of animals by God and the devil,[14] thus accounting for at least two large classes of creatures, the good and the bad. Three legends of the creation of animals (A1700 to A2199) will illustrate the whole group. The flea is created in order to give women work (A2032.2); various kinds of birds owe their origin to Pharaoh's drowned army (A1901); and the flounder with his flat side is a descendant of a fish only half eaten by the Virgin Mary (A2126).

It is with the special bodily characteristics or habits of animals that legend has mostly concerned itself. Usually, such legends assume that a change was made in an ancient animal and that this change has persisted in all its descendants. Thus in a tale we have already noted (Type 47A), the rabbit laughs at a funny sight and splits his lip so that forever after his descendants are marked by the hare-lip (A2211.2). The ant and the spider have a dispute in heaven. God decides the dispute in favor of the ant and throws the spider out. His great fall and injury account for the narrow waists of modern spiders (A2214.2). We have already learned how the bear lost his tail when his foolish ancestor fished through the ice at the fox's suggestion (Type 2). Many animals have their present colors because an ancestor got into the fire and was burned or singed (A2218), or because in some adventure he has colors spilled on him (A2219.1).

If an animal's characteristics are pleasant, or otherwise favorable, they are often ascribed to a reward given to the ancestral animal for some deed of kindness or piety. A whole series of animal characteristics are accounted for because of help given to Christ at his Crucifixion (A2221.2): the robin's red breast, the permission to flies to eat at the king's table, and the immunity of swallows' nests from destruction. On the contrary, some of the ancient animals were discourteous and were properly punished (A2231). Thus the horse, when the saint wishes to use him, always excuses himself on the ground that he is still eating. The saint curses him, "May you always be eating," and his descendants keep grazing to this day. The flounder also is punished for discourtesy. When God asks him where he is going he does not answer, but merely turns his head. Since that time all flounders have had crooked mouths.

Ancient animals were punished for various kinds of misdeeds. The Aesop

[14] P. 236, above.

fables have popularized the tales of those who make immoderate requests (A2232): the camel who asks for horns and as a punishment is given short ears, and the bees who pray for a sting but are punished by having their first sting fatal to themselves.

We have already noticed in another connection a group of tales in which animals are chastised for their refusal to help in some common task, usually the building of a road or the digging of a well (Type 55). Sometimes such tales are recounted as a part of the cycle of the fox and the wolf and the interest is in the tricks and deceptions practiced. But frequently these stories also explain the present-day characteristics of the animals concerned (A2233). Thus laziness on this occasion explains why the snake may not use the road, why the dog must remain out of doors, or why certain animals may not drink from a river or spring.

Besides rewards and punishments, many other reasons are assigned for the change from the ancient animal which is now seen in his descendants. Sometimes one animal borrows a member or quality from another and refuses to return it (A2241).[15] Sometimes a mere exchange of qualities accounts for some characteristics.[16] A considerable group of tales gives account of contests, usually races, in which the result determines the animal's form or habits.[17] Transformation of a person to an animal is sometimes cited as a reason for certain qualities which suggest human beings. Most famous of these stories is that of the shepherd who is transformed to a bird and still calls his sheep (A2261.1). This tale is used to account for various bird cries. Grimm told a pretty story of this kind about the hoopoe. In his collection is also found the explanation of the enmity existing between the cat and the dog.[18] The cat loses the dog's certificate of nobility and thus forfeits his friendship.

One remarkable thing about origin legends of this kind in countries dominated for millennia by the great historic religions is how few of them ascribe animal changes to the direct act of God. We have already seen in apocryphal accounts of creation how God and the devil both created animals,[19] and how this fact explains many present-day characteristics. It will not do to finish this account of origin legends without mention of the picturesque story of how the hog received his round snout. It seems that in the midst of the creation of the hog a great fire broke out, so that God had to leave the job half done (A2286.1.1).

Though many of these explanatory legends are told over wide areas,

---

[15] For tales of this kind concerning the nightingale and the blindworm, and also the jay and the cuckoo, see Types 234 and 235.

[16] See The Dove's Egg-substitution, Type 240.

[17] See The Pike and the Snake Race to Land (Type 252) and The Ant Carries a Load as Large as Himself (Type 280).

[18] See The Dog's Certificate (Type 200).

[19] See A1751, p. 236, above.

the relative number of them which are purely local is much greater than is true with the regular folktale. Such local legends have a great deal of interest for their own sake and for an understanding of the folklore to which they belong. But in a broad treatment of explanatory myths, it is, of course, impossible to do more than indicate the general nature of these legends in Western culture.

B. MARVELOUS BEINGS AND OBJECTS

Aside from the large number of purely imaginary beings which people the regular folktales of Europe and western Asia, and which the tellers normally recognize as unreal, there exist in every country a considerable number of such beings, human or animal in form, devoutly believed in by both storyteller and listener. It is, of course, not easy to draw a sharp line between the creatures of fiction and of actual belief. But psychologically there is a great difference, for the creatures of belief are a part of the unlettered man's view of the natural world.

Each country has its own varieties of such beliefs. Many of them are doubtless related to those of neighboring lands, but exact equations of similar imaginary creatures is usually dangerous, or at least inaccurate. Each country has its own favorite groups. The *sidhe*, or kindly fairies, of Ireland; the terrible baba yagas of Russia; the malevolent glaestigs of the Scottish Highlands; the jinns of the Near East; and the rakshasas of India—these creatures set the tone for the whole world of supernatural beings which they dominate.

In spite of these striking regional differences, there are no definite cultural boundaries, and many of the concepts relating to supernatural creatures are found with little change over whole continents, and sometimes, indeed, over the whole earth. Even when examining such widespread beliefs, however, we must always remember how hard it is to know when creatures of popular imagination merely have some feature in common and when they are actually identical.

1. *Marvelous Animals*

Perhaps the best known of all marvelous animals is the dragon (B11 and subdivisions), and there seems little doubt that for the Occident, at least, the dragon legends are organically related. But whether the fire-breathing, many-headed monster authenticated in the legend of Saint George is actually the same creature as the gigantic luck-bringing dragon of China is by no means clear. At least in Western tradition, the dragon seems to be conceived of as a kind of crocodile or alligator with something of the shape of a scorpion, or perhaps of a lizard. He seems quite generally to be a fire-breather and though sometimes he has only one head, he more usually has either three, seven, or nine. These heads have the power of growing back unless they are all cut off at once. As in Beowulf, popular fancy has very often pictured the dragon as the guardian of treasure and the devastator of a country. This seems to be a popular belief, and it is therefore no great stretch of the imagination for the teller of folktales to picture the dragon as the creature who comes to the king's court and demands human sacrifices. Such stories as The Dragon Slayer (Types 300 and 303) undoubtedly rest upon a secure basis of popular belief.

The dragon is only one of a considerable number of frightful monsters which roam the land. And the sea has also its marvelous beings, sometimes terrifying and sometimes kindly and well disposed. Proteus, the Old Man of the Sea with whom Odysseus came to grips, and Scylla and Charybdis illustrate the way in which old ideas of this kind have survived in the highly developed Greek mythology. The Sirens were dangerous, to be sure, but they were fair to look upon, and this is true also of the mermaids (B81), who inhabit not only the seas known to Greek sailors, but many more modern waters. These ladies, half woman, half fish, perhaps command as widespread a real belief as any other creatures of human fancy. There are not actually many specific tales about the adventures of mermaids, merely accounts of hundreds of people who say they have seen them. As a popular concept they have furnished subjects for art, and one of them sits, through sunshine and storm (in bronze), on a rock in the harbor of Copenhagen.

There are also mermen (B82), but so far as I know, they are never mates of the mermaid. Each of them seeks to lure a human being as spouse into the cold sea-caves. Matthew Arnold's *The Forsaken Merman* tells with inimitable charm one of the best known of all merman legends (C713): how the human wife of the merman is drawn back to earth by the sound of the church bells and how, when she has once come under their spell, he has lost her forever, and how he and their children must go back alone to their home under the waves

> Where great whales go sailing by,
> Sail and sail with unshut eye
> Around the world forever and aye.

These two inhabitants of the sea are illustrative of a very large body of tradition about water-spirits (F420 and subdivisions). Sometimes these creatures are associated with the ocean or the seas, but an even larger number inhabit lakes and streams. Greek mythology, of course, knew many such beings. But the traditions of all parts of Europe are rich with their presence. Sometimes they are not to be distinguished from fairies, and many of the beliefs about fairies are ascribed to them. Though sometimes these water-spirits have partly an animal form, they are often purely human in appearance.

To animals themselves, even when there is no touch of human physical attributes, popular fancy has ascribed many marvelous qualities. Talking beasts (B210) are a commonplace in folktales and seem to be very generally believed in. But even more widespread is the faith that certain animals have superhuman powers of perception or wisdom (B120-B169). Birds, serpents, or fishes give good advice or reveal hidden secrets. Animals may also see ghosts or spirits invisible to human eyes. Some of them may utter prophecies, and nearly all can furnish omens of good or bad luck. Very widespread is the idea that the actions of an animal may properly determine some great decision—what road to take, or where a building or a city should be founded. One group of legends, familiar to all who know the Siegfried story, tells how wisdom is acquired from some animal. Most often this takes place when the magic serpent or fish is eaten, but sometimes the animal merely teaches the human being the secrets of wisdom.[20]

Although popular beliefs have thus ascribed superhuman wisdom to some animals, there is every tendency for folk tradition to minimize the differences between man and beast.[21] Sometimes heroes may assume either quality at will, but very frequently we have tales about animals who have nothing human except certain habits and ways of thinking.

We learn nothing from popular tradition about the remarkable social arrangements in the actual lives of such creatures as ants or bees. The animal society is conceived purely in terms of the human. There are kings over each species of wild and domestic beasts (B220 and B240). Large assemblies are imagined in which the birds, and sometimes other animals, form parliaments for legislation or for the election of rulers (B230; Types 220 and 221). Chaucer's *Parlement of Foules* is only the culmination of a long line of these traditions. Saints' legends are particularly fond of stories illustrating the pious acts of religiously inclined beasts. Most picturesque of all such beliefs is that about the oxen who kneel in their stalls on Christmas Eve or who speak to each other at that time in praise of the newborn Saviour (B251.1.2). Many a skeptic has felt like the unbelieving Thomas Hardy when he went to the ox's stall on Christmas night "hoping it might be so."

Several of the folktales which we have already examined tell of regular warfare (B260) between groups of animals, the wild and domestic beasts, or the birds and quadrupeds (Types 104 and 222). Animals likewise enter into legal relationships (B270). The commonest legends of this kind concern trial and execution for crimes (B272.2 and B275.1). Of course, such proceedings were much more than mere traditions among our ancestors, and we still hold the sheep-killing dog responsible for his murders.

Most extensive of all the traditions concerning the manlike activities of animals have to do with weddings between members of different species

---

[20] See p. 260, below.

[21] For the animal hero with human characteristics, see p. 217, above.

(B280). Stories of this kind are certainly very old: they appear in early versions of the Aesop fables.[22] They were especially cultivated in the literature of the Middle Ages, often in the form of risqué songs or poems. One of the best known of American folksongs, "Frog Went a-Courting," is an elaboration of this motif.

Zoologists find many items of especial interest in the beliefs and legends that have grown up about extraordinary animal characteristics (B720-B749). These are usually mere beliefs, rather than localized stories, but over a huge portion of the world the existence of many of these phenomena are devoutly believed in. Such is the magic stone or jewel which is found in the head of a serpent, and sometimes of a dog. Sometimes such a jewel is luminous and shines with a light of its own. It is generally believed that such shining happens with a cat's eye. As for the breathing of fire, this is not confined to dragons, but is a power shared by lions, birds, or even horses.

As for extraordinary habits in animals (B750), popular fancy has never been able to reach the extremes of the medieval clerics who wrote *The Physiologus* and other bestiaries. But there is a widespread belief that snakes swallow their young to protect them, that the swan sings as she dies, that a snake will not die before sunset, that a turtle will hold with its jaws until it hears thunder, that a snake may take its tail in its mouth and roll like a wheel, that snakes milk cows at night, that a cat sucks the breath of a sleeping child, and that a salamander subsists on fire.

Aside from general beliefs, there are, of course, some specific legends about animals. One of these, for example, is about a cat whose master has been told that upon his return home he should say, "Robert is dead" (B342).[23] Robert is one of the cat's companions, and as soon as he hears this, the cat leaves for good.

2. *Other Marvelous Creatures*

In spite of the enormous variety of marvelous creatures believed in throughout the world, there are certain general concepts which are known in many lands, although these concepts vary in detail from one circle of tradition to another.

One of the most widely accepted of all such beliefs, particularly in the countries of western Europe, concerns fairies.[24] They are known by many names, the Irish *sidhe* or little folk, the English fairy or elf, and the corresponding German elf or fee. The shading off of such concepts into the French *fée* (apparently a thoroughly human woman with miraculous powers) and

---

[22] For this motif, see Type 224, p. 224, above.

[23] The same tale is told in which some kind of house spirit takes the place of the cat (F405.7).

[24] For a collection of fairy motifs, see F200 to F399. Perhaps the best general book on fairies in folklore is Hartland, *The Science of Fairy Tales* (London, 1891).

the frightful Italian *fata* brings it about that an accurate translation of folk tradition from one of these countries to the other is all but impossible. In a consideration of fairies it is perhaps easiest to think primarily of fairy beliefs of the British Isles, especially Ireland, and to realize that in other countries many of these identical beliefs are ascribed to similar, but actually different, imaginary creatures.

In contrast to most other creatures, the fairies are usually thought of as living in a land of their own, in an otherworld generally known as fairyland (F210). The Irish usually think of this world as being entered through the side of a hill or under the roots of trees. But sometimes the land is supposed to be across a body of water or even under a lake or river.

There is no agreement on the size of fairies. Between Mercutio's description of Mab, the minute queen of the fairies in *Romeo and Juliet*, and Oberon, the man-sized fairy king of *Midsummer Night's Dream* there is room for a large exercising of human imagination. It would seem that in general the Irish fairies are thought of as being much smaller than mortals. They are sometimes pictured as having bird feet and as having breasts long enough to throw over their shoulders (though these are qualities of many similar creatures). Fairies are normally invisible to the generality of men, but particular individuals may secure a magic soap or ointment which permits them to see the little folk, and it is sometimes possible to have a view of them (and of other spirits as well) by treading on someone else's foot. Various theories are advanced for the origin of fairies (F251). Some say they are the descendants of an early race of gods; others that they are the souls of the departed, particularly of unbaptized children.

Those who have seen fairies relate many interesting things about their lives. It is well known that they have rulers, Oberon, it may be, and Titania, or perhaps it is Queen Mab. One of their principal pastimes is dancing (F261), as anyone may see the next morning who observes the rings they leave on the grass. They have feasts and weddings, and they perform labor. Like the dwarfs, they may be skillful as blacksmiths (F271.3 and F451.3.4.2), and like some other creatures, they have been known to milk the farmer's cows and ride his horses sweaty at night.

The romantic imagination has long played with the idea of the fairy lover. There are many things that a young girl must not do—pluck flowers, lie under a tree, or pull nuts—or she may well be carried off by a fairy lover or elf knight. Mortal men have similar difficulties, if difficulties they are. Many is the story of the man who marries the fairy woman. Sometimes he goes to fairyland and stays with her, and sometimes he marries her and takes her to his home. In the latter case, he is always strictly forbidden to do certain things (C31), to utter her name, to see her on certain specified occasions, or to offend her in some trifle. Best known of such legends is that of Melusine (C31.1.2). This lady is not always actually a fairy, but may be a water-spirit or some related creature. In any event, the mortal husband breaks the prohibition against seeing her on a certain occasion, usually when she is transformed. When she learns that her secret has been discovered, she disappears forever.

The dealings of fairies with mortals are sometimes advantageous to people, but they are nearly always fraught with danger. In one of the common folktales (Type 503) they remove a hunchback's hump only to replace it on someone else; and they give the hero coals which turn into gold, but in the hands of the wrong man the gold will again become worthless (F344.1 and F342.1). It is dangerous to accept a gift from the fairies. This is seen in the story of The Luck of Edenhall (F348.2). Here the fairies give a cup which is to be kept in the family. When the cup is broken, bad luck descends upon the house.

Stories of changelings (F321.1) are very common all over Europe. A fairy steals a child from its cradle and leaves a fairy substitute. The changeling is usually mature and only seems to be a child. There are various ways in which he is eventually deceived into betraying his age. The problem then arises as to how he may be disposed of, and this is not easy. Sometimes the fairy does not desire a mortal child, but only to have herself assisted in childbirth by a human midwife (F372.1). The women who have actually gone to fairyland to perform this service bring eternal good luck upon themselves and their families.

Many of these legends of fairies are told also of other kinds of spirits and demons. The resemblance is especially notable in stories of water-spirits (F420) and wood-spirits (F441). We nearly always find that the female spirits have the long breasts which they can throw over their shoulders and that they have a tendency to entice mortal men. Even the trolls (F455), large and ungainly mountain creatures, dance and do skillful work as blacksmiths.

Most like the fairies, especially in the wealth of the traditions concerning them, are the dwarfs (F451). In the countries of northern Europe they are considered as spirits of the underground.[25] They are certainly more ungainly, as generally conceived, than the fairies, and are nearest in appearance to the little house-spirits which the English know as brownies (F482) and the Danes as "nisser." In his production of "Snow White"[26] Walt Disney was particularly successful in catching the traditional conception of the dwarf.

As far as legend and tale are concerned, the dwarfs seldom play a leading role. They are either subsidiary actors in a complex narrative like Snow White or The Two Girls, the Bear, and the Dwarf (Types 709 and 426), or else they are merely reported as being present or as having certain appearances or habits. Some of the latter characteristics may be mentioned. They are sometimes spoken of as having their feet twisted backward, or as having

[25] They should by no means be confused with the pygmy tradition, for the dwarf is not simply a very small person.
[26] Produced as a moving picture with the animated cartoon technique early in 1938.

bird feet; as being long bearded; as having red heads and red caps; as having
their home underground beneath the cow stable; as always turning to stone
at sunrise; and as having great fear of hymn-singing or the sound of church
bells. These last two features they share with the trolls (G304.2.5 and
G304.2.4.1). Like fairies, they seek human women as midwives; they exchange
children in the cradle; and they give perilous gifts to mortals. They sometimes act as the servants of human beings, but if a man is ever so foolish as to
pay them all he owes them, they disappear.[27]

Several other kinds of spirits are generally believed in, and some of them
have characteristic traditions. Such are the many tales of the Rübezahl (F465),
a spirit of the mountain and storm, and the beliefs in the Nightmare or Alp
(F471.1) who presses and almost strangles one in his dreams, or the Incubus
(F471.2) who consorts sexually with women in their sleep, or the Huckauf
(F472) who jumps on one's back as he walks along the road at night.
Cobolds (F481) and brownies (F482) stay close to the house but have few
distinctive traditions, unless we include as such the brewing in an eggshell
in order to drive away a cobold.[28]

If there is confusion in the concept of a dwarf, sometimes a pigmy or
thumbling and sometimes a creature of the underground, there is even a
greater variety of ideas suggested by the word giant. The term has become
confused with that of the French *ogre* and the German *Teufel*, so that mere
size is only a small consideration in a tale like Jack the Giant Killer. Giants
are even equated sometimes with the dragon concept, so that the dragon
fighter is said to go out and kill the seven-headed giant. They may, of course,
be thoroughly human, like Goliath. As far as the traditions of northern
Europe are concerned, however, neither of these concepts is valid. The giant
there is thought of as being an enormous person of human shape many times
the size of a mortal. Such giants live ordinary lives and have usual family
relationships. A huge number of stories are known about their activities,[29]
though many of these parallel the stories of fairies or dwarfs.

Polyphemus was a typical giant in this sense, for he had one eye in the
middle of his forehead (Type 1137; F531.1.1.1). Other giants are headless,
and some have shaggy hair all over their bodies, and sometimes long beards.
Some of them wade the ocean, and nearly all of them throw great rocks
around and produce changes in the landscape.[30] They have been known to
move churches or other buildings, and they are frequently said to be the
builders of certain great structures.[31] All these are rather general ideas unless
indeed it be the Polyphemus story. But there is one specific tale about the life

[27] A familiar motif in German tradition known as "Ausgelohnt" (F451.5.10.9).
[28] But this method is also used for getting rid of both changelings and dwarfs; see F481.4.
[29] For a bibliography concerning giants, see F531. Add Hottges FFC122.
[30] See A965, p. 239, above.
[31] In addition to the references in F531.6.6, see C. W. von Sydow, "Studier i Finnsägnen
och besläktade byggmästersägner," *Nordiska Museet*, 1907, pp. 65-78, 199-218; 1908. pp. 19-27.

of the giants which has had a very general appeal—"The Giant's Toy" (F531.5.3). A young giantess sees a plowman with his team. She thinks it would be fun to have such a toy, and she picks up the man and his horses and takes them to her mother. Her mother tells her, "You must take him back. He will drive us away." It is probable that the homely wisdom of the giantess who fears the conflict of brute strength with human intelligence has done most to give popularity to this pretty tale.

Two specific cycles of giant legends deserving mention are those of Gargantua in France and of Paul Bunyan in America. Readers of Rabelais are familiar with the satirical use a great author can make of such popular traditions, but they are perhaps not always aware of the extent to which such legends are actually a part of the folklore of France.[32] Whether these French traditions were preserved by the colonists in New France, or whether stories of gigantic persons reached the French Canadians from other sources there seems little doubt that these people have had much to do with the spreading of the tradition of a purely American giant, that of Paul Bunyan, the enormous woodsman.[33] In spite of all the discussion of Paul Bunyan during the last thirty years, much about the tradition of him and his enormous ox remains very dark.[34] But the popularity of this legend among lumbermen today, whatever its origin may have been, shows that the stories of giants are perennially interesting.

The giant concept is so varied in its appearances that it is hard to be sure of the role which a giant will play in popular tradition. Frequently he is thought of as a kindly helper, benevolent if slightly stupid; sometimes he is the acme of stupidity; and very often he is an ogre quite as frightful as any monster conjured up by the folk imagination. The same double nature may be found in stories of dwarfs and trolls. But about two important classes of supernatural beings there is never any ambiguity. Nothing but evil can be said for witches and their like, or for the devil. Some of the traditions of witches resemble fairy legends, but never enough to affect the essentially evil nature of the witch.

Unmistakably wicked as she is, the witch presents no clear-cut picture to the folk. Sometimes she is simply a human old woman who has, by some foul means, acquired mystic powers of evil. We hear rumors of them in Massachusetts and New York in Colonial times, and even in our own day in Pennsylvania. The three weird sisters of Macbeth are certainly superhuman

[32] P. Sébillot, *Gargantua dans les Traditions Populaires* (Paris, 1883).

[33] See p. 215, above.

[34] Students of the Paul Bunyan material are likely to take extreme positions, either saying that it is a very old popular legend among American lumbermen, or else contending that it is essentially a literary concoction of the past thirty years. As in so many such cases, the truth probably lies between these extremes. There seems to be no printed account of these legends until about thirty years ago. But they were certainly told by lumberjacks before that time, as I can testify. I heard almost the complete cycle told in the woods when I was working during the summer of 1910 in the forests of eastern Oregon near La Grande.

and belong much nearer to the world of trolls and fairies than to that of demented old women. It is this latter concept of the witch as essentially other than human that has had most appeal to the popular imagination and that seems to be implied whenever a witch is mentioned in a folktale.

As in the Macbeth legend, such witches are usually thought of as sisters, most often as three (G201). The witch may appear in almost any form, even that of an animal (G211), particularly a horse. As with some of the other creatures we have met, witches sometimes have seven heads (G215.1) or they have goose feet (G216.1). They are sometimes said to have iron members (G219.1) and are usually represented as bearded (G219.2). Being evil, the witch is opposed to Christianity and she parodies Christian expressions and religious services (G224.1). Particularly well known is the witches' sabbath (G243). In this, on certain saints' days, they meet and go through a mockery of divine service. No reader of Goethe's *Faust* can ever forget their meeting on Walpurgis Night. A few habits of witches are believed in almost everywhere they themselves are known. Such are the fact that they fly through the air on broomsticks (G242.1); that they ride on unusual animals (G241.1), a wolf, a goat, or a cat; that they have familiar spirits who serve them (G225), frequently insects or cats; that they love to steal children (G261) and to suck blood (G262.1); that, like fairies, they ride horses sweaty at night (G265.3) and make cows give bloody milk (D2083.2.1). Sometimes witches are pictured as beautiful and attractive women enticing lovers and then deserting them (G264). Such was Keats's La Belle Dame sans Merci and such, indeed, is a whole legion of Circes and Calypsos in both popular and literary tradition.

Tam o' Shanter learned much about witches in the short hour he spent in haunted Kirk Alloway, the dancing, the fiddling, and the suggestion of intimate relations with the devil (G247, G303.9.8.2, and G243.1). He, too, yielded to their female charm and forgot himself. But eventually he escaped because he knew one of the sure ways of ridding oneself of witches. They can never cross a stream, and especially if a man can induce one of them to grab his horse's tail as he crosses the bridge, he is always safe (G273.4). There are, of course, other ways of escaping from the witches which Tam did not need to employ. If he had only waited in some safe place until cock-crow (G273.3), or had even thought—good Protestant though he was—to make the sign of the cross (G273.1), all would have been well.

The most important ally of witches as a power of evil is the Devil (G303 and subdivisions). He seems to have been walking up and down on the face of the earth since long before the days of Job, and his presence is widely known, and felt, in all the lands of western civilization. There is little consistency to be looked for in such a legend. As already suggested in connection with the devil's appearance in folktales,[35] the concept seems to be an

[35] See p. 42, above.

inconsistent merging of the Biblical Satan, the general idea of evil spirits abroad, the goat-footed god Pan, or the satyrs, and sometimes the Oriental demon or "jinn." Sometimes also any ogre is spoken of as a devil, especially in German tradition.

With a figure built up from an adaptation of so many others, some of them contradictory, it is no wonder that legends about the devil should be impossible to reconcile with one another. As he appears in folktales, we have seen him enforcing bargains with those who have promised to give themselves to him at a certain time. In others, the devil is stupid, and the interest is entirely devoted to cheating him.[36] The devil sometimes is pictured as living in hell (Type 803). In at least one case he is equated with Death, and is kept magically sticking to a tree so as to keep people from dying (Type 330).

The devil, as we have seen,[37] opposed God in His creations from the first, and in the form of a snake caused the loss of paradise for mankind. Contrary, we assume, to God's intentions, he found a place on the ark and survived into the new world inaugurated by Shem, Ham, and Japheth. Sometimes he appears as the Adversary at the court of God, sometimes as Lucifer, the bearer of light. It is in the Middle Ages that the devil legends grow and proliferate. More and more in the thought of the western world there appears the antithesis between God, or Christ, and Satan. He took on during these centuries some well recognized physical characteristics: the cloven hoof, a tail, a beard, the latter always trimmed in the most stylish fashion. He often appeared as a fine gentleman, and it was only by accident that the cloven hoof or the tail betrayed him. As finally evolved into Mephistopheles, he is the essence of seductive evil, and we are far from the popular tradition of the unattractive and ogre-like demon which the devil can sometimes be.

It is easily seen, then, that devil legends are not all of one piece, so that it would be a mistake to expect the same kinds of tales in Finland and in Spain. Such differences depend not only on a fundamentally different ancient tradition, but also upon the more recently developed separation in religion.

A thorough study of devil legends would involve many things beyond our scope. Oriental demonology and, indeed, the world-wide belief in evil spirits present interesting suggestions to the student of western tradition. But the actual influence of such ideas from one culture to another is extremely difficult to trace out with any degree of certainty. Thus far no one has even attempted to give to this subject a serious scholarly investigation.

Although a complete view of all the imaginary beings in Occidental tradition would give attention to dozens of additional beliefs current in

[36] See pp. 44ff., above.
[37] See p. 236, above.

one country or another, those which have been mentioned here will serve as sufficiently typical of the traditional background from which so much of the literary and artistic life of Europe and western Asia has sprung.

3. Marvelous Objects

A very important part of this background of imagination is dependent upon the belief in magic. That the world is filled with objects which defy all the laws of nature and which obtain miraculous results without ordinary labor—such is the faith of all those who take seriously the tales of the Brothers Grimm or the properly vouched for local legends of one's own community.[38]

Aside from these magic objects familiar to everyone, even in our own culture, there appear in popular tradition a large number of extraordinary things not actually endowed with magic qualities but so far from the usual as to excite the wonder of all who hear of them. Tales of the otherworld[39] are, of course, filled with such matters, and the traditions of certain peoples are especially fond of elaborating these marvels. Readers of the *Arabian Nights* and of Irish folktales often find it difficult to follow the florid imagination of a story-teller who luxuriates in such obviously impossible conceptions (F700 to F1099).

A few typical traditions of this kind will be sufficient to bring to mind hundreds of others like them. The legends about remarkable rivers (F715), for example, show a great variety. We have them issuing from magic nuts or from pillars; we have rivers of wine, honey, blood, milk, and even of fire. There are also the well-known four rivers of paradise; rivers contained in boxes, or under a cock's wing; rivers flowing intermittently, some even observing the Sabbath. A similar variety would appear from an examination of marvelous islands, mountains, and cities. The literature of chivalry must have been a great stimulus to tales about remarkable castles (F771)—castles of gold or silver, or even of diamond, castles suspended on chains or upheld by giants or built on the sea; and most marvelous of all, a revolving castle confusing to invaders who can never find the door where they expect it. Castles or palaces may be at the world's end, or east of the sun and west of the moon; they are frequently found abandoned, or with all their inhabitants asleep; and sometimes such marvelous houses appear and disappear. Of more than one large castle or building it is a legend that there are just 365 windows and doors, one for each day in the year (F782.1).

Since we are attempting to deal with legends in which many people actually believe, we are naturally faced with the question of whether such

---

[38] For a systematic discussion of such magic objects and their uses, see Motifs D800 to D1699. Most of these have appeared at one place or another in our treatment of the complex folktale, chapter II, pp. 70ff.

[39] See p. 146, above.

stories of marvelous buildings and the like are thought of as real. No certain answer can be given, though for most taletellers they are certainly fictions. But one legend of a marvelous object which we must not fail to mention is quite certainly believed in by large numbers. This is the tale, immortalized by Hauptmann, of the sunken bell which is still heard from below the water (F993).

C. RETURN FROM THE DEAD

The same question of the reality of belief appears with especial clearness when we deal with legends concerning the return from the dead.[40] The attitude of the story-teller varies much from country to country. Tellers of popular tradition, and their listeners as well, usually make no question about the credibility of a ghost story. This is true even in those western countries most influenced by rationalistic thinking, though here the ghosts which are alleged to have appeared are usually mere spooks. The tradition of the person who returns from the realm of the dead to revisit old scenes has become much impoverished, so that we have to go to groups of people less disturbed in their ancient ways of thinking to find full-blooded ghosts. Medieval literature, in general, and the folklore of eastern Europe, not to speak of that from so-called primitive peoples, is filled with instances of dead men who appear to their friends or enemies in form and stature as they had lived. Hamlet's father is on the borderline between the two ideas: he is recognizable, but is also spectral. Sometimes, however, the ghost is little more than a living dead man in full flesh and blood pacing up and down the earth awaiting the second death when his body shall eventually disintegrate in the grave. Frightful creatures these are, often appearing as vampires living on the wholesome blood of mortals.

It is hard to tell how widespread is the faith in the possibility of raising the dead. No study has ever been made that would throw any light on beliefs of this kind at the present day in our western culture. It seems safe, however, to hazard a guess that such beliefs are very largely confined to strictly religious contexts, in which the occurrence is regarded as a definite miracle, a real interposition of power from on high. As we move eastward into Asia into other cultural patterns, and especially as we go on to Oceania or to the aborigines of the Americas or Africa, the bringing of a person back from the dead becomes much more commonplace and is easily accepted in non-sacred stories which are received as true.

Very much the same situation is found when we look into the stories of reincarnation. First of all, it is not always possible to distinguish accurately between the return from the dead in another form and the idea of ordinary transformation. As conceived by Ovid, sometimes the change of a

[40] The whole of chapter "E" of the *Motif-Index* is devoted to this subject.

person into an object or animal takes place without death and sometimes as a definite return in a new form. In present Western Culture, tales of actual reincarnation are probably nearly always thought of as unmistakable fictions, even by those who might believe in magic transformations. Of course, again, as we reach India, metempsychosis becomes for millions an object of religious faith, and this fact has made instances of reincarnation commonplace in Hindu tradition.

The very close relation of doctrines concerning future life and the next world to the whole religious belief and activity of people has profoundly affected this entire group of traditions. The pattern of organized Christian doctrine has worked for a thousand years or more to modify, and sometimes entirely to displace older concepts once universally accepted. Insofar as these survive at all, they are treated as fictions or, if not, those who believe in them are regarded as extraordinarily gullible and naïve. But the poems and tales of Europe, both literary and popular, do contain many motifs dealing with the return of the dead, and seem to indicate a much richer tradition in former times.

We have already encountered resuscitation in several of our folktales. The dead may be brought back to life by cutting off his head (E12; Type 531), by burning him (E15; Type 753), or, as with Snow White, by removing the poisoned apple from her throat (E21.1; Type 709). A magic ointment may be used (E102), or the parts of the dismembered corpse may be brought together and revived (E30; Types 303 and 720). Most popular of all in folktales is revival through the Water of Life (E80; Types 550 and 551). This water is usually found after a long quest and is powerful against both disease and death. Herbs or leaves are sometimes efficacious (E105; Type 612), or a magic fruit (E106; Type 590), or blood (E113; Type 516). In addition to these motifs peculiar to the folktale, there appear a few resuscitation tales which belong either to the world of myth or of legend. The method by which Thor, when he has killed his goats and eaten them, then reassembles their bones to bring them back to life (E32) has been employed by many other heroes in Europe and out, and the special feature of this legend, that one bone or member is missing and causes deformity in the revived animal or person (E33; Type 313), is likewise very widespread. Another tale from Norse mythology well known elsewhere is that of the warriors who fight each day and slay each other but are revived every night (E155.1).

Nearly all these stories of resuscitation appear as motifs in folktales or myths, not as actual traditions. This is also true of most of the tales of reincarnation. In folktales they are rather common, and examples will occur to almost anyone familiar with them: the little boy in The Juniper Tree (Type 720) who comes forth as a bird from the bones his sister has buried (E607.1 and E610.1.1); the appearance of Cinderella's dead mother as a cow (E611.2) or a tree growing from the grave (E631; Type 510); and the many varieties of the tale of The Singing Bone (E632; Type 780). More definitely in ballad tradition appear the twining branches which grow together from the graves of lovers (E631.0.1). We have already seen, also, how some explanatory legends have ascribed the habits of certain animals to their recollection of former existences as men (A2261.1).

On the contrary, as we have already noticed, the living tradition and active faith of nearly all countries abound in ghost legends. Not only may thousands of people be found who testify to having seen ghosts, but practices are all but universal which assume for their justification a substratum of such a belief.

There is so much variety in the general concept of ghost that one can hardly make an exact definition of it. In general, it may be said that we have legends all the way from a complete return from the dead with full human functions to the most wraithlike of spooks frightening people as they pass graveyards. We have noted that some traditions imply essentially a "living dead man," who merely wanders about waiting final death (E422). Not less complete in human functions is The Grateful Dead Man (E341) already met in a series of folktales (Types 505-508), where he returns to pay a debt of gratitude. These revenants of flesh and blood are most often malicious, and their return is usually to punish rather than to reward. The dead lover returns and takes his sweetheart behind him on horseback and attempts to carry her with him into the grave (E215).[41] The dead wife frequently returns to protest to her husband against his evil ways (E221), particularly if he has married again. Or a dead person returns to punish indignities suffered by the corpse or ghost (E235; Type 366), such as the theft of an arm or leg, or the kicking of the skull. Or, as in the Don Juan legend (E238; Type 470), the dead man is scornfully invited to dinner and then compels his host to go with him to the other world.

The dead may also return in their proper form on friendly missions. Best known of such stories, both in tales and ballads, are those concerning the return of a dead mother (E323), either to suckle her neglected baby or otherwise aid her persecuted children.[42] The dead child sometimes returns to stop the inordinate weeping of its parents (E324, E361). And sometimes conscientious dead come back to repay a money debt (E351) or to return stolen goods (E352).

Retaining some of his human characteristics, but essentially ghostlike, is the vampire (E251), who comes out of his grave at night and sucks blood (Types 307 and 363). There are many descriptions of these horrible creatures, especially in the legends of eastern Europe and of India. Elaborate means are devised for getting rid of them, the best known being the driving of a stake through the grave. Other wandering and malicious dead appear in many

---

[41] See Type 365. This tale of "Lenore" appears both as ballad and prose folktale.
[42] See Types 403, 510A, 511, and 923.

legends without the special characteristics of the vampire. They frequently make unprovoked attacks on travelers in the dark (E261), or they haunt buildings and molest those bold enough to stay in them overnight (E282-E284; Type 326).

Tales of spooks are likely to be rather vague in their outlines and frequently to be little more than instances of some popular belief or practice. There are, for example, a large number of stories about the unquiet grave (E410ff.), all telling of some reason why the dead person is unable to rest in peace. It may be because of a great sin—murder, suicide, adultery, or even, in medieval tales, the taking of usury. Particularly restless are the excommunicated or the unbaptized, or those who have not had proper funeral rites. And the murdered and the drowned are doomed for a certain period to walk the earth (E413, E414). Many special qualities are ascribed to these spectral ghosts. They are frequently invisible except to one person (E421.1.1) or to horses (E421.1.2). They are luminous (E421.3) and they cannot cast shadows (E421.2). But the wraithlike nature of these ghosts has permitted them to assume a multitude of forms in the imagination of those to whom they have appeared. Sometimes they are animals (E423), sometimes skeleton-like (E422.1.7), sometimes headless (E422.1.1), like the one which Ichabod Crane encountered.

Many are the ways in which the dead are discouraged from leaving the grave and in which they are "laid" if they become restless and wander forth (E430ff., E440ff.). All kinds of precautions are taken at funerals, the best known being to carry the coffin through a hole in the wall or to place a coin in the mouth of the corpse. Some relics of ancient sacrifice to the dead are still to be found. Many different magic objects can be carried as a protection against them, and like witches, they are thought to be powerless to cross rapid streams or to pass a crossroads. The restless ghost may sometimes be quieted by reburial or by an elaborate magic ritual, or by burning or decapitating the body. He may have to wander until some particular event takes place, or he may be only waiting for the cock to crow.

Ghosts are not always encountered by themselves. Many are the legends concerning groups of dancing ghosts (E493), of church services (E492), or processions of the dead (E491). And in addition to stories embodying these general conceptions, three of the tales concerning companies of ghosts are among the most popular in all Europe, The Wild Hunt, The Flying Dutchman, and The Sleeping Army.

The first of these, The Wild Hunt (E501), appears in the greatest variety of detail, though the central idea is always the same. It is the apparition of a hunter with a crowd of huntsmen, horses, and dogs, crossing the sky at night. Stories of this kind go back to classical antiquity, and they appear nearly all over Europe. The huntsman himself, and sometimes his companions, are identified with historic characters, sometimes even with one of the gods.

The Flying Dutchman (E511), while not nearly so well known as The Wild Hunt, has much more definite texture as a real tale. A sea captain, because of his wickedness, sails a phantom ship eternally without coming to harbor. The only variety in the different versions concerns the nature of the crime, whether it has been unusual cruelty, a pact with the devil, or defiance of a storm. The third of these legends, The Sleeping Army (E502), tells of a group of soldiers who have been killed in battle and who come forth on certain occasions from their resting place, usually in a hill or cave, and march about, restlessly haunting the old battlefield.[43]

All these, and many other traditions of the return from the dead which might be cited, imply a belief in some mysterious element which survives the death of the body, that which we ordinarily call the soul. There is every tendency for popular tradition to conceive of this element in material terms, so that the passage of soul from body at death is not only actual but visible. Sometimes it is thought of as having the form of a mouse (E731.3), or bird (E732), or butterfly (E734.1)[44] which leaves the mouth at the supreme moment. Souls are sometimes identified with the stars, and it is thought that a shooting star signifies that someone is dying (E741.1.1). And, finally, not only popular tradition, but medieval literature as well, gives us pictures of devils and angels contesting over a man's soul (E756.1). It can be little wonder that an idea so difficult for even theologians and philosophers should produce much inconsistency in the traditions of unlettered folk.

D. MARVELOUS POWERS AND OCCURRENCES

1. *Transformation and Disenchantment*

Not only in connection with ideas of the soul is popular tradition inconsistent and impossible to subject to neat labels. Tales of reincarnation and transformation, for example, are very hard to separate with any feeling of assurance. A person or animal or object changes its form and appears in a new guise, and we call that transformation; but if the living being dies between the two stages, we have reincarnation. Yet in spite of this clear theoretical distinction, we have a great interchange of motifs between these two categories.

The mythologies of all peoples are filled with metamorphoses, most of which do not imply death and return. The great role such events played in Greek myth is witnessed by Ovid's famous collection of tales gathered around this central concept. Transformation is also a commonplace assumption in folktales everywhere. Many of such motifs are frankly fictions, but a large number represent persistent beliefs and living tradition.

---

[43] For other similar tales, see D1960.1 and D1960.2, p. 265, below.
[44] Cf. the Greek ψύχη, meaning at once soul and butterfly.

One of the most picturesque of these beliefs concerns the Werewolf (D113.1.1), the man who periodically turns into a frightful wolf. In his human form the werewolf is frequently gentle and kindly, and the change of form may be involuntary. As a wolf, he often combines human mind and memory with wolflike cruelty and voracity. It is not always easy to recognize whether a man is a werewolf,[45] and thus almost anyone may be suspected. A number of stories are told as to how such recognition comes about, such as the Estonian and Finnish tale of the knife carried away by a wolf and later found in possession of a man (H132).

The first part of the werewolf story, the transformation, has many parallels. Of these, one of the most interesting is that of the Swan Knight (D536.1) in which the transformation occurs because a chain is taken off his neck. This is the Lohengrin legend, known also in the medieval romance of *Chevelere Assigne*. The recognition of the werewolf is paralleled by a widely known tale of the woman who turns into a cat and assumes witch's powers. Her husband, the miller, cuts off one of the cat's paws when she is trying to bewitch the mill at night. The next morning the woman's hand is missing and the mystery is cleared (D702.1.1).

Stories of transformation almost always imply eventual disenchantment, if not a periodic shift from one state to another. Disenchantment usually involves some kind of breaking of a magic spell. In folktales we have already noticed the efficacy of cutting off heads or even of taking off bridles, and dozens of similar means (D700-D799). But in addition to these commonplace methods—almost stock incidents in fictional folktales—there are several interesting and well defined disenchantment legends. Three of them have the central idea of disenchantment when the afflicted person succeeds in winning the love, or at least the embraces, of a normal human being. Not only in Chaucer's *Wife of Bath's Tale* and related medieval romances, but in oral tradition also, is found the motif of the Loathly Lady (D732). She can be released from the spell that puts on her a disgusting face and figure when she is actually taken to wife and embraced by a handsome man. Similar in its principal features is the tale of the White Lady or The Three Redeeming Kisses (D735.2). Here the woman can be disenchanted from her animal form if the man will kiss her three times, each time when she is in the form of a different terrifying animal. The sexes are reversed in the legend of the Hairy Anchorite (D733.1). This beast-like hermit is seduced by a beautiful woman and thereupon becomes thoroughly human and handsome.

The breaking of the enchanting spell sometimes depends upon a complicated succession of events (D791). A few examples will stand for a large variety of such traditions. The disenchanter is to take a key with his own mouth from the mouth of the enchanted woman, who is in serpent form (D759.1). Or disenchantment may happen when some superhuman task is

[45] Compare the same idea in connection with the recognition of witches, p. 251, above.

finished. Such is true of the enchanted person who appears every seven years in human form and puts one stitch in a garment. She will be delivered when the garment is finished (D791.1.2). Perhaps best known of these detailed disenchantment stories is The Deliverer in the Cradle (D791.1.3). Here it is understood that the enchanted person can only be delivered by a child rocked in a cradle from an oak sapling after the tree has grown great.

2. *Other Magic Powers*

The ability to transform and disenchant is only one of the magic powers familiar in popular tradition and folktales. The world of magic is so well established a background of such tales that frequently magic powers of all kinds are assumed without much comment, and nearly always they are only subsidiary motifs quite incidental to the main action of the tale.[46]

Out of the undistinguished mass of material of this kind a few themes are of especial interest because they have become so well known either as popular traditions or as incidents in some important literary treatment. The widespread notion that one can acquire magic wisdom from eating something, particularly from eating a part of a serpent (B161.3), like Siegfried, or like certain Irish heroes from biting upon one's own thumb (D1811.1.1); that the secret of one's strength may lie in his hair, as with Samson (D1831); and that one may acquire magic sight if only one puts the proper ointment into his eyes (D1821.4)—all these means of surpassing human limitations are common to the folklore of a good part of the world.

Witches and others who can bring about enchantments are much feared, for unwonted abilities like this may be used for harm as well as good. Hence the multitude of amulets used against the power of the Evil Eye (D2071), for it is very generally believed that certain persons can cast an evil spell on one through a malignant glance. Equally harmful are those who can shoot a person's or animal's body with small objects so that he sickens without apparent cause (D2066). And almost anyone, if he possesses the proper formulas, can, like Rossetti's "Sister Helen," make an image of an enemy and burn it or stick it full of pins and thus bring about torture or death (D2063.1.1).

All who have visited Salisbury Plain and have wondered at the enormous monoliths at Stonehenge will remember the belief that they were brought from afar through the power of Merlin. Giant rocks moved by magic power (D2136.1) are also found in Chaucer's *Franklin's Tale*, where the magician removes the stones from the coast of Brittany. Presumably these rocks were all moved in the twinkling of an eye, and such marvelous speed is a common occurrence in folk tradition (D2122). Sometimes the making of instantaneous journeys is a manifestation of unaided magic power, as when the hero is

[46] For a detailed listing of such motifs, see D1700 to D2199.

permitted to make a journey with speed as swift as thought, and sometimes it is performed through the use of seven league boots (D1521.1), or the like.[47]

3. Marvelous Occurrences

If we were examining here the interesting field of saints' legends as they appear in medieval writings or the literary tale collections of the Orient and the Near East, we should find them filled with all sorts of physical marvels, many of them magic, of course, but many of them simply miraculous and presumably due to divine intervention. Though they do not appear with such luxuriance in actual folklore, the abundant popular legends attached to this place or that show how deep-seated is the interest in such manifestations.

These often appear as incidental motifs in the background of folktales,[48] but sometimes they constitute the central interest in the narrative. Such, for example, are a considerable series of legends about churches which, for one reason or another, have sunk into the earth (F941.2). Sometimes the congregation is still heard singing from underground, or from beneath the sea which has swallowed them up. A similar tradition concerns a whole city which suddenly sinks into the ocean and which can still be seen at favorable moments beneath the waves (F944).

The reversal of the order of nature in connection with flowers and plants is a favorite theme of those interested in marvels. Biblical story, saints' legends, and wonder tales all tell of the dry rod which bursts forth into blossom (F971.1; see Type 756), and there is a well-known folktale of the rose which grows from a table or from a stone (Type 755). Even better recognized in folk tradition are the flowers or fruits which bloom or ripen in midwinter.[49] As an independent legend perhaps the best known is that of the tree which bears apples only at Christmas time. It blossoms at midnight and is full of apples by the morning (F971.5.2). This belongs to the large series of Christmas legends, partly of ecclesiastical and partly of popular origin, but now as real as any other folk traditions. Another such Christmas legend which deserves mention here is the miraculous apparition of presents on Christmas morning through the agency of Santa Claus (N816). Countries vary, of course, in the name of the benefactor, but the general legend is widespread.

Most of the marvels here discussed have lost their hold on the faith of men who have been influenced by the rise of the rationalistic spirit during recent centuries. But it is well to remember that to a large part of the world even today they are no more inexplicable than the voice which comes over the

[47] Special magic powers attributed to animals have already been noticed in other connections, see pp. 228, 245, and 260, above.

[48] For an extensive listing of such incidents, see F900 to F1099.

[49] The heroine is sent after strawberries in winter: Type 403B, and occasionally in other tales. A garden is constructed which bears in the cold weather (D1664).

radio, or the airplane which goes from continent to continent with more than seven league boots. And the most sophisticated of us have probably slipped out of bed on Christmas night with the hope that we might catch Santa Claus in the very act of coming down the chimney.

E. TREASURE TROVE

This Santa Claus legend is not so infantile as it appears. It is but a children's version of imaginings common to our humanity. In a life filled with struggle for food and shelter, with the fatigue of far travel, with the frustration that comes from thwarted ambition or disprized love, it is no wonder that in his dreams by night or his reveries by day such a creature as man should imagine conditions under which all these hardships would vanish. A magic tablecloth to supply him with food and drink, arms to defeat his enemies, carpets to carry him at will, talismans to induce love or to overcome sickness or death— the contemplation of all these has served as a drug to ease the pain of actual life. In some moods, however, these notions are sure to seem visionary and to compel a closer realization of life as it is actually lived, life in which one needs only an abundance of treasure or money to buy all that heart desires. Surely there are great hoards of treasure buried by the rich or the mighty in times of crisis and left forgotten. Why could not one, if he is clever enough, uncover such a hoard and live like a king?

Tales of the search for treasure (N500) have always been common, and they continue to flourish unabated. The interest in the gold guarded by Fafnir, or by the fire-drake in Beowulf, though the setting is of long ago and the accompanying incidents heroic, is essentially the same as that which has stirred so many, even in very recent times, to enter on futile searches in the footsteps of Coronado[50] or on beaches believed to hold the loot of Captain Kidd.

Those who have buried treasure have always seen to it that it should be hard to find, but there do exist ways of discovering it, though these methods are hard to learn about and usually even harder to carry out. Tradition seems to be clear that if one will merely go to the end of the rainbow the treasure is there (N516). Frequently a mysterious light appears to guide one (N532), though this light may well lead one astray and into great difficulties. A popular medieval legend tells of much more specific direction to treasure. A statue, or a stone, is discovered with an inscription, and sometimes a pointed finger, saying "Dig here" (N535). These are but a very few of the multitude of legends about how treasure long hidden may be discovered. Sometimes the problem of the treasure hunter is merely to find where a hoard has been recently buried and forgotten. In such case the treasure can be found only by the hand that hid it (N543.1).

[50] See J. Frank Dobie, *Coronado's Children* (Dallas, Texas, 1930).

The finding of treasure is not sufficient to assure its complete enjoyment. Very frequently there is an effective guardian over the hoard (N570), a dragon (B11.6.2) it may be, or some kind of demon, or a mysterious woman, or even a sleeping king in an underground chamber like Barbarossa. Under such circumstances the unearthing of treasure has its perils, and must be done with due ceremony (N554). Particularly are there strict rules of conduct which must be observed during the process (N553): there must be no talking, no looking around, no scolding of animals, and the greatest care against unlucky encounters and bad omens.

Even after the treasure has been successfully raised, it seldom brings the hoped-for joy. Like the Rheingold, it frequently carries with it a curse on all its possessors (N591). Or, most surprising of all, just when one thinks he is safely enriched, it turns to charcoal or shavings (N558).

F. LEGENDS OF PLACES AND PERSONS

In a somewhat systematic way, we have reviewed a number of those popular beliefs which have found a place in the traditional stories of Europe and western Asia. Nearly always the important thing about such traditions has been the underlying belief, and the exact form of the story illustrating this belief has frequently been a matter of indifference. If we think of the avowedly fictional folktale—the wonder story like The Dragon Slayer or Faithful John—as one extreme of folk tradition and actual beliefs in various supernatural manifestations as the other, we shall notice that in the accounts just reviewed of origin legends, strange animals, and marvelous manifestations, we have been moving in an area much closer to actual belief than to fiction.

But sharp lines are hard to draw; and many traditions strongly attached to particular places or persons have tendencies to wander, so that it is frequently hard to determine the original location or person about whom the legend grew up. Such stories, because of their great mobility, are often very near to fiction, though usually some effort is made at localization and at other means of suggesting that we are listening to a true tale rather than to some flight of fancy. No generalization is safe about how much actual belief is accorded legends of this kind. All depends upon the attitude of teller and hearer. But whenever there has been conscious transfer of one of these traditions from place to place or from person to person it would seem that, at least for the story-teller, we have the conscious creation of fiction.

Every country has some migratory legends of this kind, so that a listing of all of them would be unduly tedious. In addition to these tales of limited area, however, there are a considerable number known pretty well throughout the western world. Some of them have remained on the purely oral level, and some have taken their place in literature, although unmistakably popular in origin.

This literary development of a very widely known mythological concept is clearly seen in the last chapter of the Arthur legend, where it is confidently asserted that the great king will one day return in the hour of his people's need (A580). This belief is usually held concerning some god or demigod whose second coming is awaited by the faithful. It is found in most parts of the world, and is not peculiar to any one of the great religions.

Of the localized legends about animals, two have had extensive migrations. To Romulus and Remus, the founders of Rome, have long been attached the story of how they were suckled by the she-wolf (B535). But the animal nurse is not always a wolf, and she is found ministering to children almost anywhere. The same type of popularity is accorded to the legend of Llewellyn and his Dog (B331.2) in which the master returns and finds that the child who has been trusted to the dog is covered with blood. He thereupon kills the dog, only to find that the blood has come from a snake which threatened the child's life and which the faithful dog has killed.[51] This tale keeps being reported from various parts of the world as an actual happening, and it may, of course, depend in last resort upon a real event.

Tales of magic have not usually resulted in well-formed traditions that persist in all details. We hear much about witches in general and about magic powers, and we have already noticed a few cases, like the moving of the rocks at Stonehenge, in which a magic act is attached to a well-known historical or legendary character. There are, to be sure, a series of literary legends concerning Virgil as a magician (D1711.2), and a similar series concerning Solomon (D1711.1), though none of these has ever been adopted by the oral story-teller. Much nearer to real folklore is the Pied Piper of Hamelin (D1427.1), the tale of the magician who, in revenge for the failure of the city to pay him when he has piped away its rats, uses his pipe to entice all the children into a cave and underground. This tale has traveled so that Hamelin is but one of several cities which have their Pied Pipers. More definitely attached to a particular place is the story of Bishop Hatto and the Mouse Tower (Q415.2), familiar to all who have made the trip by steamer up the Rhine. The Bishop is punished for his hardheartedness by being devoured by swarms of mice or, as it is sometimes told, of rats.

In another connection we have noticed the story of The Sleeping Army[52] which is only waiting to come back from the dead at the moment of supreme need. Hardly to be distinguished from this legend is that usually known as

---

[51] It is hard to know whether this is a purely literary tradition or not. Certainly it has a long literary history, both in the European Middle Ages and in the older Oriental collections. But it has had a vigorous life in the oral folklore of India; cf. M. B. Emeneau, *Journal of American Oriental Society*, LXI (1941), 1-17 and LXII (1942), 339-341.

[52] See E502, p. 258, above; cf. also N570, p. 263, above.

Kyffhäuser (D1960.2) from the mountain in which the aged Barbarossa sits through the ages surrounded by his men. Whether this is death or magic sleep, his beard has grown through the table (F545.1.3) from long sitting and he, too, will not stir except to rescue his folk when they need him most. This story of the sleeping king belongs, of course, definitely to medieval historical legend. But the related tale of The Seven Sleepers (D1960.1) is much older and is connected with the early days of the struggling Christian Church. The legend of these pious young men who awake in their cave after a sleep of many years is attached to the city of Ephesus. But there have been a series of analogous tales extending over the centuries to Rip Van Winkle and beyond.

However prominent a part of folk thought the idea of tabu is, it has not formed the central motif of many definite legends. To be sure, the Biblical tradition of Lot's wife looking back and being turned into the pillar of salt (C961.1) has appealed to the popular imagination and is generally known and frequently told. One prominent historical tradition, that of Lady Godiva and Peeping Tom, does rest upon the enormity of violating an express prohibition (C312.1.2). This legend, it will be remembered, is attached to the city of Coventry in late Anglo-Saxon times. In order to free the townspeople of a grievous tax, Lady Godiva agrees to ride the full length of the city nude, and clothed only in her long hair (F555.3.1). The citizens are all commanded to shut their windows and stay indoors and all obey except one. Peeping Tom is stricken with blindness because of his disobedience (C943).

Several marvelous legends, told of ancient Greek gods or heroes, have lived on and are met even today in unexpected quarters. Such, for instance, is the group of legends around King Midas: the person with the ass's ears (F511.2.2); the magic reed which grows from the hole where the king has whispered his secret and which spreads the secret to the rest of the world (D1316.5); the king's barber who discovers the monstrous ears and who lets the world know (N465); and especially King Midas's power to turn all things into gold, and his distress when his wish is fulfilled (J2072.1).

The myth of Orpheus and his descent to the world of the dead to bring back his wife (F81.1) lived on into the Middle Ages, both in the literary romance and the popular ballad. There has been a transfer of the action from the world of the dead to the land of the fairies and, although the name of Orpheus has been retained, some of the details have dropped out, such as the marvelous harping and the prohibition against looking at the wife on the way out and the consequent failure of the mission. The general outlines of this story with its journey to the otherworld to bring back the dear departed is of such universal interest that we might well expect to find parallels where there is little likelihood of actual contact. It is, however, surprising to learn that the analogous tale among the North American Indians nearly always contains the prohibition about conduct on the return journey and in many cases the disastrous violation of this tabu.[53] All evidence, however, would indicate that, in spite of the resemblances, the so-called American Indian "Orpheus myth" is an independent growth.

Readers of Herodotus find one of the chief interests in his accounts of marvels and of other incredible traditions. Whatever may be his value as sober history, he is an excellent source for the legends and traditions of the Mediterranean world in his day. Some of his stories have worked themselves into the regular folktale repertories of many parts of Europe,[54] sometimes constituting complete tales and sometimes only subsidiary motifs. It is in the latter use that his legend of The Ring of Polycrates (N211.1) survives in modern folklore. The ring which the ruler has thrown into the sea is found the next day in a fish which is being prepared for his table. This motif fits into stories about lost magic objects or about the marvelous accomplishment of impossible tasks.[55]

Biblical legend, especially explanatory tales, are an important element in the folklore of Europe and a large part of Asia.[56] Such traditions are by no means confined to accounts of origins. A number of the well-known Bible stories, such as Ruth, Susanna and the Elders (J1153.1), Daniel in the Lions' Den, Jonah in the belly of the Fish (F911.4), and the like, keep being told with no substantial change. But certain of the biblical worthies have attracted to themselves appropriate legends not authorized by Scripture. Some of these have been propagated primarily through literary collections, Jewish[57] and others, though they have received a certain amount of acceptance in actual folklore. Solomon's wisdom, for example, is illustrated not only by the authorized story of the quarrel of the two women over the child and his offer to cut the infant in two and divide him (J1171.1), but also by much elaboration of detail concerning the visit of the Queen of Sheba. Perhaps most interesting of these is the account of the riddles which she propounds and which he always answers correctly (H540.2.1).[58] Likewise, the contest of wits between king and servant, frequent in European tales, is often ascribed to Solomon and his man Marcolf (H561.3; Type 921). Indeed, almost any legend dealing with a wise king may enter into the Solomon cycle. Such, for instance, is the story of the hidden old man whose wisdom

---

[53] See A. H. Gayton, "The Orpheus Myth in North America," *Journal of American Folk-Lore*, XLVIII (1935), 263ff. See also p. 351, below.

[54] See, for example, Type 950. Cf. W. Aly, *Volksmärchen, Sage und Novelle bei Herodot und seinen Zeitgenossen* (Göttingen, 1921).

[55] See, for example, Types 554 and 560.

[56] See pp. 235ff., above

[57] Good collections of such Jewish material may be found in: M. J. bin Gorion, *Der Born Judas: Legenden, Märchen und Erzählungen* (6 v., Leipzig, 1918ff.); M. Gaster, *The Exempla of the Rabbis* (London and Leipzig, 1924); and L. Ginzberg, *The Legends of the Jews* (tr. Paul Radin; 7 v., Philadelphia, 1910ff.).

[58] Some of these have worked themselves into the folktale of The Clever Peasant Girl, Type 875.

saves the kingdom. In the famine, all of the old men are ordered to be killed. But one man hides his old father and when all goes wrong in the hands of the young rulers, the old man comes to the rescue (J151.1).[59] To Solomon is also ascribed the tale of The Widow's Meal (J355.1). The king upbraids the wind for blowing away a poor widow's last cup of meal. But when he finds that the wind has saved a ship full of people by that very act, he acknowledges, in all humility, the superior wisdom of God.

The Bible contains several incidents parallel to motifs well known in other connections in European and Asiatic folklore. The exact relation between these traditions and the Scriptures is not always clear, for we do not know certainly which is dependent upon the other. In the story of Moses, for example, we learn that he was abandoned in a basket of rushes (L111.2.1); and the same general legend is attached to Cyrus, to Beowulf, and to many less known heroes. The adventures of Joseph, likewise, contain incidents paralleled not only in folktales[60] and in classical Greek literature, but also in miscellaneous popular legends. The prophecy of future greatness coming from a dream (M312.0.1), and the vain attempt to get rid of the youth who has had the dream (M370) are found in several folktales. The same general pattern also occurs in the story of Oedipus, though here the infant is exposed (M371) in order to avoid the carrying out of the predicted murder of his father and marriage to his mother. All of these motifs concerning the avoidance of fate have been rather freely used as traditional themes. Joseph's experience in Egypt with Potiphar's wife (K2111) is paralleled not only in the legend of Bellerophon, in the *Iliad*, but also in the old Egyptian story of The Two Brothers.[61] Similar tales of temptresses and false accusations are found in many traditions, some certainly not directly dependent upon the Joseph story.

Such are some of the legends of classical antiquity and of Biblical or Apocryphal literature which have lived on through the centuries. There are, of course a legion of anecdotes about historical characters which have been repeated in many literary collections but have in no sense become a part of popular legend. Such is true of the stories about Socrates and Xantippe, and about Diogenes. One tale about the painter Zeuxis (also told of Apelles) came to be ascribed to various artists of the Renaissance. Two artists compete in the painting of realistic pictures. The first paints a mare so realistic as to deceive a stallion, whereupon the second paints a curtain which deceives the first artist. Variations in details appear: sometimes a fly is painted on the nose of some figure in the painting and the other artist involuntarily tries to drive the fly away (H504.1).

A widely known legend connecting the ancient and modern worlds is

---

[59] See also Type 920, p. 159, above, and H561.5, p. 277, below.
[60] Particularly Type 930.
[61] See p. 275, below.

that of the Wandering Jew (Q502.1), the blasphemer punished with inability to die and restlessly going from place to place from the days of Christ down to our own. This is but the best known of a number of medieval legends directed against the Jews. Another is the persistent tale of a Christian child killed to furnish blood for a Jewish rite (V361). This legend is best known in connection with Hugh of Lincoln, and is familiar to all readers of Chaucer's *Prioress's Tale*.

Popular stories concerning kings and their adventures were particularly common in the Middle Ages, and many of these have become truly traditional. Of the boyhood of a number of future kings the story is told of how the child first learns of his illegitimacy when he is taunted by his playmates (T646). Sometimes an earlier chapter in his adventures has told of how a royal lover has left with a peasant girl certain tokens to be given to their child if it should turn out to be a son (T645). In perhaps the most famous of such tales, Sohrab and Rustem (N731.2), we have an example of another widespread tradition. Unaware of each other's identity, the father and son engage in mortal combat and the son is killed, to the everlasting grief of the father.

Kings are so in the habit of assuming command that they sometimes lose all humility and need to be given a lesson. King Alfred in disguise is beaten by the peasant for letting the cakes burn (P15.1), and the same tale has been repeated with variations about other royal figures. Much beloved also have been the stories of Canute and of Robert of Sicily. The former is said to have placed his throne on the beach and to have vainly forbidden the tides to rise and surround it (L414). Robert of Sicily comes out of his bath to find that an angel in his form has taken his place and that he himself is regarded as an impostor. He is repulsed on all sides and thoroughly humiliated until he repents of his haughty conduct (L411). The latter tale seems to go back to an Oriental original but has become very definitely related to the figure of King Robert.

Some royal legends have attached themselves to the popes. One of these, known also in folktales (Type 671) and in Oriental and classical tradition, is associated with Gerbert, whose election to the papacy is said to have been decided by the lighting of a bird. In similar tales horses or elephants determine the choice of ruler, and sometimes the future pope's candle lights itself (H41.3).[62]

Of the hundreds of saints' legends current in the Middle Ages,[63] only a

---

[62] For these legends of popes, see J. J. I. von Döllinger, *Die Papst-Fabeln des Mittelalters* (2nd ed., Stuttgart, 1890). Another interesting papal legend is that of Pope Joan, the woman in disguise who is supposed to have served as pope (K1961.2.1).

[63] The literature of saints' legends is very extensive. A good introduction to the general subject is found in G. H. Gerould, *Saints' Legends*. The most important compendium of such legends is the *Legenda Aurea* of Jacobus a Voragine, which has appeared in many editions. Definitive treatment is found in the enormous collection known as *Acta Sanctorum*

relatively few have become popular in Protestant countries. But even there one finds repeated stories of Saint Peter and the Lord wandering on earth.[64] A pious tale appearing in the Grimm collection (No. 205) and known over a good part of Europe tells of the holy man who dies as an unknown pilgrim in his own father's house (K1815.1.1), a legend certainly related to that of Saint Alexis. But much more familiar, even if not always known in all its details, is the story of Saint Christopher, who carries an unknown child on his shoulders across a stream. In spite of the fact that the child grows miraculously heavier on his shoulders, he bears him to the other bank. He finds that he has been carrying the Christ Child and for his faithfulness receives an eternal reward (Q25).

Ecclesiastical legend has furnished stories not only of saints and holy men, but also of their opposites, sometimes merely exemplars of wicked lives and sometimes persons actively in league with the devil. A monstrous tale of punishment meted out to those who sit in judgment is that of the woman who has three hundred sixty-five children (L435.2.1). In her self-righteousness she has unmercifully condemned a girl who has a bastard child. Whether or not the unusual number has been influenced by the length of the year and has some appropriate symbolic meaning, the tale was widely known in the Middle Ages.

In the story of The Devil's Contract (Type 756B) it will be remembered that even before his birth the parents have promised their son to the devil.[65] A form of this motif especially popular in medieval romances and Renaissance chapbooks is known as *Robert the Devil* (S223.0.1). Perhaps the most skillful use of this legend appears in the romance of *Sir Gowther*. Here a childless wife, having despaired of help from heaven, at last invokes the devil to give her a child, even if he is like the devil himself. Her wish is fulfilled. In a blasphemous parody of the Annunciation the devil appears to her and tells her that she shall have such a son. The child kills his nurses and commits unnamable crimes. Eventually he is converted and does severe penance before he is rescued from the dominion of the adversary.

Gowther, or Robert the Devil, was not himself to blame for his demonic association, since the fault lay entirely with his mother. But sometimes it is said that a man has deliberately, at an age of discretion, sold himself into the devil's power for a sufficient consideration (M211). So it was with Theophilus, and so, of course, with Faust. The details of this bargain and the dealings between man and the evil one have interested not only men like Goethe and Marlowe but many more humble bearers of tradition since the Middle Ages.

---

which has been appearing for the last three centuries under the editorship of the Bollandist Society of Brussels.

[64] See p. 150, above.

[65] For the sale or promise of children to the devil or an ogre, see S220ff.

A favorite type of legend has always been that dealing with narrow escapes. Sometimes these concern the mere escape from captivity of persons and their pursuit, such as the legend, attributed to various heroes, of the spider who spins her web over the hole in which the fugitive is hiding and thus throws his pursuers off the track (B523.1). It is also about flight from personal danger that another ancient and widely known anecdote is told, the escape by reversing the shoes on the horse or the ox (K534). This anecdote appears in the Buddhistic legends of China, in Greek antiquity, in Icelandic saga, in Scottish ballads, and in folk legends from northern Europe to Central Africa.

A third story concerning escape from captivity lacks the happy ending. This is the tale of the noble lady who pleads for the release of her husband (or sometimes her brother) and eventually agrees in return for the promise of release to sacrifice her honor to his captor. But she is shamefully betrayed, for the lord refuses to carry out his bargain (K1353). This tale is recounted of various women with the setting of the action usually in Italy and in the Renaissance. It is still popular as an Italian folksong.

The most interesting legends concerning warfare usually have to do with famous sieges. The events connected with military attack and defense are in general so alike that anecdotes of this kind are easily taken up and are likely to travel from place to place, however definitely they may at first have been localized. One of these legends favors the attackers. It is said that in a certain siege of Cirencester the surrounding army attached flaming articles to the feet of birds so that when they flew into the city they set it on fire (K2351.1). The interest in the attackers is also seen in the legend, used so effectively by Shakespeare in *Macbeth*, of Burnam Wood which comes to Dunsinane (K1872.1). The army cuts boughs and carries them so that the whole wood seems to be on the march. As used in connection with the prophecy of disaster when the wood shall come to Dunsinane, the stratagem is doubly impressive.

Finally, any consideration of legends of besieged cities must include that tale of wifely devotion usually known as The Women of Weinsberg (J1545.4.1). The conqueror of the city gives each woman permission as she leaves the town to carry out her dearest possession. Much to the surprise of the general, they take out their sleeping husbands.[66]

As we have been viewing legends of various cities and persons, it has been obvious how strong is the tendency for such material to make new attachments which may even drive out all memory of the original person or place. It has been perfectly clear to the tradition of the last century and a half that it was Marie Antoinette who, when told that the people had no bread to eat, said, "Let them eat cake" (J2227). Yet this very legend was sufficiently alive to be recorded in a sixteenth century jestbook. Whatever may have been Marie Antoinette's failings, it is not likely that this cruel remark was hers.

[66] For a similar ruse otherwise employed see Type 875.

Popular legend in Europe and Asia covers an enormous area not only with regard to the material handled, but also to the form in which it is transmitted and the audiences for which it is designed. It is by no means all of one piece. Some of it is essentially mythology, some less pretentious origin legend, some local history, some an embodiment of supernatural belief; and some assumes such definitive narrative form that it differs little from the complex folktale. Probably from no point of view could a logical justification for bringing all of this material together be made. But it has been at least convenient to pass in rapid survey the principal classes of narrative which have not formed themselves into regular folktales, either complex or simple. Whatever may be the heterogeneous origin of the varied literary forms in which they appear or the present-day acceptance of these legends, they do all have in common their connection with the world of fact, at least as conceived in the mind of the teller of the story. As fantastic as some of this material is, it is related as an object of belief and its effect, in contrast with that of the ordinary folktale, is the effect of history, rather than of fiction.

THE FOLKTALE IN ANCIENT
LITERATURE

IV

WE SHALL never know just what tales were told around the campfires by the hosts drawn up before Troy or by the sailors who brought the Queen of Sheba to Solomon's court. The slaves who built the Pyramids doubtless stole time from their tasks to listen to stories, and priests and wise men of that age certainly entertained nobles and kings with real or imagined adventures. This we have a right to assume if the ancients were like other men. But nearly all direct account of this activity has vanished with the centuries.

And yet we are not utterly ignorant of the folktales of antiquity. In two ways we learn not only of their existence, but something of their place in the life of the age, and often have a clear enough indication of the action of the stories themselves. Frequently in ancient literature mention is made of tales which were current among the people of the time. Moreover, in a large number of the literary monuments of the ancient world appear stories undoubtedly based on current tradition.

Johannes Bolte has assembled about thirty-five passages from the literature of Greece and Rome[1] which show the use of the folktale among those peoples. References begin with Aristophanes' *Wasps* of 422 B.C. In a number of these we see clearly enough that these tales resembled in many ways the folktales current today in Europe. They told of fairies and monsters and marvels. A frequent term used for them is "old women's stories," and authors keep referring to the telling of these tales to children.

Many of these oral folktales we find embedded in some literary classic to which it has been adapted both in form and spirit. Where oral tales are thus found we always have two possibilities. (1) The ancient classic is the original

[1] Bolte-Polívka, IV, 40-94.

from which the present day oral forms have been borrowed, or (2) the story in the ancient classic is merely one version (perhaps with literary elaboration) of a widespread oral tale already in existence.

Though there can be no doubt that some ancient stories—particularly the Aesopic fables—are purely literary in origin, the probability of an oral tradition back of many of the best known of the classic tales is very strong. Such of these as have been subjected to comparative study show that the literary retelling by the ancient author is chiefly valuable not for furnishing the original of the story but for showing the way in which traditional material has been adapted to different religious or literary patterns. Particularly interesting is the elaboration of such tales or motifs under the influence of religious cults and their assimilation into a well-integrated system of mythology.

1. ANCIENT EGYPTIAN

FROM ancient Egypt we have several collections of tales which have been preserved on papyri.[2] These show rather clearly a traditional background in many respects resembling that found in the oral literature of present-day Europe and western Asia. Most of them are obviously the work of priests, and the tales probably fail in two ways to give us a true indication of the exact content or style of an oral narrative of that era. Generally the stories are not well integrated and suggest that the writer had a very imperfect understanding of the action. The tales are given a definitely Egyptian setting and are closely related not only to the known history and geography of Egypt but to its religious conceptions and practices as well. On the other hand, they are so clearly related to folk tradition outside of Egypt that they are valuable indications of the antiquity of many of our oral motifs and even of complete tale types.

The earliest of these surviving Egyptian tales, dating from about 2000-1700 B.C., is that of the Shipwrecked Man. An Egyptian sailing in the Red Sea is shipwrecked, and he alone of all on the ship escapes drowning. He is cast up on a lonely island which is inhabited by a king of the spirits in the form of a serpent. The latter receives him kindly and succeeds after four months in having a passing ship rescue him, but meantime tells him of his own misfortunes and predicts that his days are numbered and that the island will sink into the sea. Mention is also made (without explanation) of an earthly maiden who had formerly lived on the island but had perished along with the family of the king of the spirits. The story is so confused that it seems hardly possible that the man who wrote it in its present form understood its motivation. The hero is said to have been in great fear before the giant serpent, who is so kind to him. The role of the maiden is left unex-

---

[2] See G. Maspéro, *Les contes populaires de l'Egypte ancienne* (Paris, 1882); W. M. F. Petrie, *Egyptian Tales* (2 vols., London, 1899).

plained and undeveloped. Are we dealing with the tale of an ogre and the rescue of a girl, as in the folktale of today? Whatever may be the answer to these speculations, the tale seems to point unmistakably to the existence of folktales much like our own in Egypt by 2000 B.C. Aside from a fragmentary story of a shepherd and a kind of fairy woman who keeps enticing him, nothing except this tale remains from this important era of Egyptian literature.

For the period around 1700 B.C. there exists one manuscript containing folktales. Though there are only three stories, they give the student of the folktale important information. For one thing we are told that Cheops, the builder of the great pyramid caused folktales to be told to him; and we are thus able to get our first historic view of story-telling as a human activity five thousand years ago. Moreover, the stories in the collection seem to contain very old tradition, since one of them explains the supernatural origin of three kings of the fifth dynasty, about a thousand years before the tale was written. Two of the stories are little more than accounts of magicians and their deeds —the magic creation of a giant crocodile to punish adultery, and the magic recovery of a lost ornament from the river—, but the third is much like a modern wonder tale. A magician who eats and drinks enormously makes slain animals live but refuses to obey the king when he is commanded to try his powers on a human being. The king commands him to find "the castles of the god Thoth." These (whatever they may be), the magician says, can be found in a chest in the temple of the sun god at Heliopolis, but can be obtained only by the eldest son of a priestess of the god Rē of Sachebu who is pregnant with three children of that god. The story now goes over to the adventures of that woman. The children became the first three kings of the fifth dynasty.

The best-known Egyptian folktales come to us from the New Kingdom (about 1600 to 1000 B.C.). One is a tale of military strategy containing two well-known motifs. The opposing leader is deceived by the Egyptian general, who pretends to be willing to betray his army and who thus gets the enemy general into his tent and so much off his guard that he is easily overcome. The next day he pretends to send hundreds of sacks into the city as presents, but the sacks contain soldiers who overcome the city (the Trojan Horse motif, K754.1). Another fragment dealing with historic characters tells how the cries of the hippopotamuses of Egypt keep people awake 600 miles away (B741.2). This motif appears later in other parts of the world with the expected changes of place.

Another story from this period of the New Kingdom is about The Enchanted Prince. At the prince's birth it is prophesied that he will meet his death from a serpent, a crocodile, or a dog (M341.2.4.1). To forestall this fate he is confined to his tower (M372). When he grows up, however, he sets out on adventures and finds a king who will give his daughter in marriage to the suitor who can reach the princess's chamber, seventy ells above the ground.[3] Though the youth has introduced himself as the son of an army officer, the king is eventually informed of his identity and the marriage takes place. In later parts of the story the princess saves his life from a snake and he himself escapes from a crocodile. The tale breaks off without coming to the expected conclusion—his death in some way through the toy dog which he has kept. This tale as a whole has no exact modern parallels, though it contains several widely known motifs.

Better known is The Two Brothers, discovered in 1852 in a papyrus dating from about 1250 B.C. and once belonging to King Seti II. The story is given in great detail and is much like a modern folktale. There are two brothers. The elder, Anup, is married; the younger, Batu, lives in his house. The wife tries in vain to seduce Batu and then accuses him before her husband. Anup believes her and takes his knife and waits behind the stable door so as to kill his brother when he returns in the evening. But Batu, being warned by his cow, who speaks to him in human voice, flees and as he flees he calls for help to the sun god Rē. The god creates behind him a stream full of crocodiles, so that Anup cannot reach him. At sunrise Batu reveals to his brother the falseness of his wife and departs. He goes into the valley of cedars and hides his heart in a cedar flower. The nine gods give him the most beautiful of maidens, but the seven Hathors prophesy an evil end for her. The river carries a lock of her hair to Pharaoh, who is so taken with its perfume that he will not rest until he has her as wife. The thankless woman reveals the secret of her first husband and has the cedar flower cut down in which his heart is hidden. Then Batu falls down dead. But his elder brother sees that his beer foams up and he knows that his brother is in distress. He sets forth, finds the body and, after a long search, discovers the heart and places it in water and gives it to Batu to drink. The dead brother comes to life and begins to plan revenge. He turns himself into a bull, has his brother take him to the king's court and talks to the faithless wife. She has the bull killed but from two drops of his blood grow two peach trees. When the woman has these cut down, a splinter flies into her mouth and from this she bears a child, who is none other than Batu. He grows up as son of Pharaoh and succeeds him to the throne. Then he has the woman slain and calls his brother to share the kingdom with him.

Though this tale has some resemblance to the present day European story of The Two Brothers, the plot is essentially different and they probably do not have direct connection. C. W. von Sydow sees in it a corruption of an original Indo-European myth and finds parallels in Eastern Europe and Asia.[4] But whether it is organically connected with any of the current tale types, it has many motifs that are a part of the common store of such tales:

---

[3] A motif very close to the central theme of The Princess on the Glass Mountain, Type 530.
[4] "Den fornegyptiska Sagan om de två Bröderna," *Yearbook of the New Society of Letters at Lund*, 1930, pp. 53-89.

Potiphar's wife (K2111); advice from speaking cow (B211); obstacle flight (the river separating the fugitive from his pursuer) (D672); separable soul (E710); evil prophecy (M340); love through sight of hair of unknown woman (T11.4.1); betrayal of husband's secret by his wife (K2213.4); life token: foaming beer (E761.6.4); resuscitation by replacing heart (E30); repeated reincarnation (E670); person transforms self, is swallowed and reborn in new form (E607.2). It is of great interest to the student of oral fiction to know that at least these themes were already developed as early as the thirteenth century before Christ.

Some indications of the presence of the oral tale in the later pre-Christian centuries are found in illustrations on papyrus, many of which have not been published.[5] From these and from a few scattered texts we can conclude that the ancient Egyptians had a good number of animal tales, some of them, but not all, related to the Aesop fables.

Herodotus, writing in the middle of the fifth century B.C., has an interesting section on Egypt and recounts several stories he has heard there. One that is still told is The Treasure House of Rhampsinitus (Type 950)—the story of the architect who has left a stone loose in the treasury, of how the treasury is robbed and the thief escapes detection. Herodotus is skeptical of the truth of the story, but this fact has not kept it from surviving the vicissitudes of twenty-four centuries.

2. BABYLONIAN AND ASSYRIAN

HISTORIC records from the valley of the Tigris and Euphrates do not go back so far as those from the valley of the Nile, but even so they carry us into the past for a good five thousand years. From the ancient period with its interplay of Accadian, Sumerian, Chaldean, Assyrian, and Babylonian there remain an abundance of cuneiform writings, most of them from the latter part of the period. The texts consist largely of legal documents, business accounts, and religious writings.

It is the latter which interests the student of the folktale, for though we may be reasonably sure that the illiterate masses told and enjoyed stories during all these centuries and long before, these oral tales have left not a trace behind. But it may well be that nevertheless some reflection of this old folklore is to be found in the mythological texts which have come down to us. These stories, obviously written by a priesthood and in a style far removed from that of the story-teller of the folk, contain many motifs familiar to all students of the folktale, and they thus bear witness to the early development of many of these narrative themes.

Most interesting of these old stories is the epic of Gilgamesh,[6] dating in its

[5] *Handwörterbuch des deutschen Märchens*, I, 36; Bolte-Polívka, IV, 100.
[6] For a list of Gilgamesh studies, see Bolte-Polívka, IV, 102, n. 1.

present form from about 650 B.C., but certainly going back to at least 2000 B.C. This epic contains the adventures of a strong hero (F610) and his friend; the death of the friend and the visit of Gilgamesh to the world of the dead (F81; E481.1) to interview the ghost. This world of the dead is found under the sea (F133) and is guarded by monsters (cf. F152.0.1). The reason for the visit to the otherworld is to learn from the dead the solution of certain riddles (cf. H1292). In the garden of the gods (A151.2) which he finds on the way, the trees bear jewels instead of fruit (F811.2.2). He is carried over into the world of the dead by a boatman (A672.1). In the lower world he obtains possession of a life-giving plant (D1346.5), but a serpent steals it back from him (cf. G303.3.3.15), so that never again will man be able to overcome death (cf. A1335).

In a kind of beast fable from the same early period, the tale of Etana,[7] appear several motifs familiar in folklore all over the world, though there is certainly no necessity to suppose direct influence of this old tale on the folklore of modern Europe. The serpent complains to the sun god that the eagle has descended upon its young and has eaten them. On the advice of the god, the serpent hides in the carcass of an ox (K751.1) so that when the eagle flies down to eat of the carcass, the serpent catches him and breaks his wings. Later, however, when the hero Etana finds that his wife is about to die in childbirth, he frees and heals the eagle so that the great bird can carry him to heaven (B552; F62) where he may secure a marvelous healing plant (D1500.1.4). The eagle carries Etana so high that the earth seems no larger than a cake and the sea looks the size of a breadbasket. Before they reach the throne of Ishtar the eagle falls exhausted to the depth below.

Even more famous than the descent of Gilgamesh to the lower world is the myth of the descent of the goddess Ishtar (F85), but it is a question whether this myth is in any wise based upon an older popular tradition. As the goddess goes to the lower world of the dead she must pass a series of watchmen, and each of them demands of her a garment until, on her arrival in the otherworld, she is completely unveiled. Eventually, on her return, she receives back her garments one by one.

In addition to these three important myths, the folklorist is interested in a very old flood legend, parallel in many respects to the story of Noah. It seems to have influenced the Biblical tale, if not actually to be its original.[8] Finally, he will discover that the very famous story of wise Achikar (H561.5)[9] goes back to a papyrus text of about 420 B.C. referring to the minister of the Assyrian king Asarhaddon. This is the tale of the wise counselor who when

---

[7] See Johnston, "Assyrian and Babylonian Beast Fables," *The American Journal of Semitic Languages*, XXVIII (1912), 81-100.

[8] See p. 236, above. For a discussion of the mutual relations of these flood legends, see S. H. Langdon, *Semitic Mythology* (Boston, 1931), pp. 206-233.

[9] See also J151.1. For a bibliography of the Achikar material, see, in addition to these motif numbers, Bolte-Polívka, IV, 104, n. 2.

he is condemned to death successfully hides and then, when the land is in peril, appears and saves it.

3. ANCIENT GREEK

FROM ancient Greece we have an abundance of literary records of almost every kind, but not a single attempt to preserve for us an authentic folktale as known and told by the ordinary Greek. The situation is much the same as with Biblical tradition:[10] there is much evidence of the presence of many of our best-known folktale motifs and sometimes indication that many of the more elaborate narratives were known in much the form familiar to us in present-day folklore. But both in the Bible and in Greek literature these narratives are lifted from their natural homely surroundings and are made to serve the purposes sometimes of the writer of sacred books, sometimes of the epic poet, and sometimes even of the dramatist.

From casual references scattered throughout Greek literature we may be sure that something very close to the folktale as known among the peasantry of modern Europe was a part of the entertainment not only of children but of adults.[11] They are frequently spoken of as "old wives' tales," and as filled with all kinds of marvels, including a large array of frightful animals and ogres.

Much more about the real nature of the ancient Greek folktales can be inferred from the way in which they are handled in Greek literature. In spite of the fact that they are often adapted to an entirely different literary medium, it is frequently easy to recognize close analogies to modern folktales.[12] Sometimes, of course, the literary form may be the original from which a modern folktale has been developed, but a thorough study of the individual cases tends to show that normally the story as it appears in Greek literature is merely the adaptation of a popular Greek form of a folktale already well established in the world.[13]

There is much folktale material in Homer. Besides the Polyphemus episode, the whole series of adventures which Odysseus relates to the Phaeacians is laid in a world of wonders characteristic of the popular tale. Such are the

[10] Many of these Biblical traditions have already been mentioned: The Garden of Eden, The Flood, and various explanatory legends (pp. 235ff.), Ruth, Susanna, Daniel, Jonah, Solomon, Moses, and Joseph (pp. 266ff.). For the Apochryphal story of Tobit, see Type 507B, above. For references to later Jewish legends, essentially literary, see p. 266, above.

[11] Ample evidence on this point has been assembled; see Bolte-Polívka, IV, 41ff.

[12] In his *Griechische und albanesische Märchen* (Leipzig, 1864), von Hahn classifies modern folktales on the basis of their resemblance to ancient Greek myths. The comparisons are often interesting, but the kind of direct relationship which he assumes is in most cases certainly not actual.

[13] Mention has already been made of the story of Oedipus (Type 931), of Rhampsinitus (Type 950), of The Wolf and the Kids (Type 123), coming respectively from Sophocles, Herodotus, Aesop, and Homer.

harpies (B52); the sirens (B53); the enchantress Circe, who transforms his men (G263.1); the journey to the world of the dead (F81); the successive transformations of Proteus, the old man of the sea (G311); and the lotus flower that causes his companions to forget the homeward way (D1365.1.1). The *Iliad*, too, has its folktale motifs. For such, certainly, is Achilles' horse which speaks and advises him (B211.3); the war between the pygmies and the cranes (F535.5.1); and especially the tale of Bellerophon, containing as it does the motif of the hero falsely accused by the queen of attempting her honor (the Potiphar's wife motif, K2111), the letter sent to a neighboring king ordering the hero's execution (Uriah letter motif, K978), and the winning of a princess as a reward for overcoming monsters (T68).

In the myths which arose around the figure of Heracles we have many analogies to modern tales of the deeds of the strong man (Type 650). By his precocious strength, manifested already in the cradle, he overcomes the marvelous serpent, and later performs the whole series of "labors" in which he overcomes monsters, secures the golden apples, strikes off the hydra's nine heads, and brings Cerberus from hell. Some of these deeds are paralleled in the legend of Theseus, who also performs great feats of strength. Particularly like adventures in folktales is the defeat of the minotaur in King Minos's labyrinth where Theseus is helped by the king's daughter Ariadne (G530.2). Another widely used motif in the Theseus story is the substitution of the sails on the ship, the color of which was to announce the good or bad news from the voyage (Z130.1).

On the legend of Perseus, Hartland wrote a three-volume study[14] in which he made comparisons with folktales in all parts of the world, as well as with many primitive customs and beliefs. He equated this legend with the present-day folktale of The Dragon Slayer and its related tale, The Two Brothers (Types 300 and 303). It cannot be assumed that the modern tale was definitely built upon the Perseus tradition, though no one would deny that there is a relationship of some kind between them, for certainly the Greek legend of Perseus has many analogies to these tales and others in modern folklore. The supernatural birth of the hero (T511), his abandonment and persecution along with his mother (S301), the theft of the single eye belonging to the Phorcides (K333.2), the overcoming of Medusa in spite of her power of turning people to stone through her glance (D581), and, finally, the winning of the princess Andromeda as a prize for defeating the sea monster to whom she was to be sacrificed (T68.1), all show us that we are here very close to a narrative form and to narrative material familiar to us in the modern folktale of the European peasant.

A considerable series of folktale motifs appears in the tale of the Argonauts.[15] Phrixos and Helle flee from the persecutions of their stepmother, as

[14] *The Legend of Perseus.*
[15] See Apollonius Rhodius, *Argonautica.*

in several modern tales (cf. Type 450). We also find a goddess appearing to Jason in the winter in the form of an old woman so as to put his kindness to a test. Like Saint Christopher with the Christ Child, he puts her on his shoulders and carries her across the stream.[16] In Jason's fellow voyagers is to be found a good example of a very popular motif, that of the extraordinary companions.[17] In a part of the Argonauts story, that dealing with Jason and Medea, we have many interesting parallels to one of the most widespread of modern European tales, The Girl as Helper on the Hero's Flight (Type 313). As in that tale, Medea, through her magic power, helps Jason perform the impossible tasks which have been assigned by her father. The lovers flee and throw behind themselves obstacles to delay pursuit. In this case the obstacles are not magic; for Medea throws, one by one, the members of her slain brother, Apsyrtos into the sea. Later Jason abandons Medea for another wife. The obstacle flight (D672) and the forgotten fiancée (D2003) of the modern folktale are at least clearly suggested by this train of incidents.[18]

In two Greek tales we have the incident of the bride being given to the winner of a race. King Oenomaos tries to discourage the suitors of his daughter Hippodamia by himself challenging them to a race (H331.5.2) and displaying before his palace many poles, each bearing the head of an unsuccessful contender (H901.1). Both of these motifs are found in modern tales (particularly Type 329), as well as in literary treatments both Oriental and western.[19] The other suitor race in which Atalanta, the athletic maiden, is tricked by the hero into stopping for the apples which he throws (H331.5.1.1), seems not to have entered modern folklore in just that form.

Such are only the most striking of the tales in classical Greek literature which show motifs familiar in modern folklore. A search through the entire field of ancient literature and art would certainly double the number of such motifs. Bolte calls attention to various sources in which are found: the escape by exchanging caps on the heads of the ogre's children (K1611); the learning of animal languages by having one's ears licked by a snake (B165.1.1); the identification of the heroine by her lost slipper (H36.1); the fool who tries to count the waves of the sea (cf. J311.1); the coin which keeps returning to the owner (Type 745; D1602.11, cf. N211); magic wishing rings (D1470.1.15); magic seats which hold one fast (D1413.5); and magic self-supplying tables (D1472.1.7).[20] In addition to these, we have already noticed several legends attached to the names of particular persons, real or

---

[16] We have here an analogue not only to the Christopher story (Q25), but also to the much more general series of tales in which the gods or saints visit mortals in disguise (K1811).

[17] Cf. Types 513 and 514. These men, each endowed with some remarkable power (supernatural sight, hearing, speed, or the like), appear not only in modern folklore, but in the older written literature of such widely divergent places as Wales and India.

[18] For a good discussion of these relations, see Sven Liljeblad, "Argonauterna och sagorna om flykten från trollet," Saga och Sed, 1935, pp. 29 ff.

[19] For a good discussion of this motif, see Bolte-Polívka, III, 368.

[20] See Bolte-Polívka, IV, 113 ff.

fictional. Such are the stories about King Midas, about Orpheus and his descent to Hades, and about the Ring of Polycrates.[21]

The Greeks doubtless had many popular stories about animals. Most of these found their way into the cycle of Aesopic fables and early received literary form. In this way they were carried over into the Middle Ages, and many of them entered so thoroughly into the stream of oral folklore that their literary source has been forgotten.[22]

4. LATIN

THESE old stories of the Greeks are frequently best known to the modern world through their appearance in Ovid's *Metamorphoses*. This gifted writer of the very beginning of the Christian era and end of the old brought together a great variety of stories out of the old mythology. Many of these have familiar folktale motifs, and all of them contain marvels of a kind; for the general principle determining his choice of stories is the presence of some transformation which accounts for present-day conditions in the lives of animals or men.[23] Yet with all this affinity to folk belief, Ovid is far removed in his narrative manner from the traditional folktale. He has taken old myths, themselves perhaps sophisticated reworkings of older folklore, and has brought them back into a new secular atmosphere even farther removed from what they must once have been.

Nor can real folktales be found in Virgil. The visit to the lower world in the sixth book of the *Aeneid* is little more than an imitation of a similar journey in the *Odyssey*. If Virgil knew about story-telling among Italian shepherds of his day, he gives no sign of it in his *Eclogues*.

We must come down a full century after these Augustan writers before we find the track of a real folktale, and then Latin literature does give us one beautiful example of a story widely known in present-day folklore. This is the tale of Cupid and Psyche, which appears in the *Metamorphoses* of Apuleius, who wrote in the early part of the second century of our era. This tale appears in a framework of adventures which itself is common in folklore. The hero is transformed into an ass, but keeps his human intelligence, and has many interesting and exciting adventures before he is finally restored.[24] Among other things, he hears an old woman tell the tale of Cupid and Psyche —how Venus is incensed at the beauty and fame of Psyche, how she brings a curse upon the marriage of her son Cupid to the girl, and of how, after long wandering, the couple are reunited.[25] The tale has most of the elements of

---

[21] For these, see pp. 265f., above.
[22] For the literary fable, see p. 218, above.
[23] For a discussion of tales of this kind, see p. 242, above.
[24] Cf. Type 567 for a similar transformation.
[25] See Type 425A, pp. 98ff., above.

the present-day folk story: the jealous sisters, the prohibition against seeing the miraculous husband, the dripping candle, the tasks which must be performed by the heroine, and the helpers she meets on the way. But this whole folk story is taken over into the atmosphere of ancient mythology so that, if we did not have our analogues in the folklore of today, we might never guess that we have here what certainly appears to be a real tale of the Italian and Greek countryside under Marcus Aurelius. It is an interesting question whether just this process of transformation of authentic folktales into myths through the efforts of priests and poets may not have been of prime importance in the development of the great mythologies.

However this may be, Apuleius was certainly familiar with the folk tradition, and bears witness to the existence of at least one highly developed tale in his generation. For the later centuries of the ancient Roman Empire, however, we have nothing more of the kind. It is only with the rise of the power of the Christian church and the growth of its legends of saints and martyrs that we again begin to see signs in literature of the presence of old and persistent narrative tradition among the common folk.

It is not the purpose of this study to enter into a discussion of the great literary collections of tales. Much of the narrative activity among the learned of the Middle Ages can be fairly well guessed by the contents of various kinds of written tale compilations. Some of these go back to the Orient, such as the various derivatives of the *Panchatantra*, the cycle of the *Seven Sages*, and some of the material we now know in the *Thousand and One Nights*. Many Oriental themes also appear elsewhere, mingled with strictly western material. Some of the special literary forms of the Middle Ages particularly adapted to the use of folklore were the saints' legends; the exempla, used by priests for illustrations of their sermons; the fabliaux; the novelle; and the somewhat later jestbooks.

Not only many influences of the folktale, but also occasionally actual versions of such tales appear in some of the earlier medieval literary classics written in the vernacular. From this point of view particularly interesting to the folktale student are the Old English poem of Beowulf, many of the Icelandic sagas, and a considerable number of the medieval romances, particularly the so-called Breton Lais. But in all these literary treatments, folktales are merely taken as bases for artistic reworking, now in one narrative style and now in another. This attitude towards the folktale persists even in such a good collection of authentic popular tales as Basile's in the seventeenth century, and gave way to faithful recording of the actual words of the traditional story-teller only about a hundred years ago.

EUROPEAN-ASIATIC FOLKTALES

IN OTHER CONTINENTS

V

Much of the movement of folktales within the area from the Atlantic to the Bay of Bengal has certainly been gradual, extending over centuries of time and thousands of miles. In ordinary times of peace and plenty, the movement was doubtless so slow as sometimes to be almost imperceptible. But when famine or war caused great disturbances of populations, the tales of the people followed them into new areas.

Since the unprecedented shift of peoples beginning in the fifteenth century by the entry of Europeans into Africa and the discovery of America, the folktales of the Old World have made long jumps and find themselves in many alien environments and often in strange enough company. Sometimes these tales have merely remained a part of the tradition of old world descendants in new lands; and sometimes these stories have been so thoroughly taken over by the natives of Africa or the New World that they often seem, on first sight, to be merely a part of the native tradition.

1. INDONESIA

The penetration of these tales into the islands lying southeast of Asia has been going on for a very long time and has been dependent upon the spread of religions, Buddhist and Mohammedan, as well as upon actual migration. A very considerable number of folktales has certainly traveled from India to the islands of Sumatra, Java, and Borneo, and to the Celebes and the Philippines. All these islands, and hundreds of others in the area, have a considerable uniformity in native tradition. Sometimes they have made over the tales which they have borrowed from the west into the regular native pattern, but most often the tales have remained foreign, exotic.

Much folklore has appeared from these islands within very recent years, but even so the very excellent synoptic study made nearly twenty years ago by Jan de Vries[1] will serve as a good indication of the degree to which such borrowed tales were even then known and recognized. Something over a hundred, or about one-seventh of the traditional tales current in western Asia and Europe have been reported from Indonesia. It is not certain that all of these have actually entered into the folklore, because some of them are taken from ancient priestly manuscripts—a good indication of the importance of religion in transplanting these tales from India and countries farther west.

It is natural that these Indonesian tales should show a greater resemblance to those of India than to those of European countries. The old literary Hindu collections and the Buddhist writings are the direct source of a considerable number of stories in Java, Sumatra, and Borneo. In the Philippine Islands, however, the question of foreign influences is less simple. In addition to the unmistakable contact with India and especially with the religions of India from an early time, the Filipinos have had four centuries of association with Spanish culture and with Christianity. This latter has affected their folklore very considerably, as contrasted with the Dutch islands where European influence is decidedly less. Indonesia is of course exceptional as compared to the larger Oceanic area, for almost none of this material we are considering has entered into the folklore of Micronesia, Melanesia, or Polynesia. It is therefore of interest to the student of the folktale to see just which tales have been taken over by the East Indians and which of them appear to be particularly popular. A tabulation of these is given at the end of this chapter.

2. AFRICA

THE Sahara Desert has always served as a great dividing line for the cultures of the African continent. North of the desert, from Egypt to the Atlantic Ocean, the contact with European and Moslem culture has been intimate and continuous. As far as the folktale, at least, is concerned, that whole stretch of land is properly to be considered as a southern fringe of the European and Asiatic area. South of the Sahara, however, though there are intrusions from Europe and Asia, folk traditions are essentially native. The great majority of their tales have certainly had their origin on the soil of central or southern Africa.

The extent to which these tales are purely African differs greatly from tribe to tribe and especially from one culture area to another. Where there has been little direct contact with the Asiatics or Europeans, contamination is negligible, but it increases in direct proportion to outside contacts. In east

[1] *Volksverhalen.*

Africa, especially that part lying close to Arabia and even further south, there is ample evidence of long association with Asiatic Moslems, even when the native populations have not embraced Mohammedanism. In contrast to this very old intrusion of outside tradition, the taking over of tales from Europe has occurred only during the last two or three centuries with the gradual penetration of the Western Powers into Africa. Some of this may have taken place rather early in the development of the American slave trade, since there are unmistakable signs of European tales which have been brought to America by slaves, probably during the eighteenth century.

An analysis of the occurrence of European and Asiatic tales in central and south Africa shows a considerable difference in the interest various tribes have had in stories which have come to them from outside. In some, the folk tradition is very little affected; in others, the material from outside actually overbalances the native. Of the tales which have been brought in, some are found once or twice but have never made much of a place for themselves, while others have spread over the whole continent. Some of these tales which have great popularity in Africa have certainly come directly or indirectly from India. Such are The Tarbaby (Type 175), The Animal Languages (Type 670), The Four Skillful Brothers (Type 653), and probably The Table, The Ass, and The Stick (Type 563). A larger number seem clearly to have arrived from Europe: The Theft of Butter (Honey) by Playing God-father (Type 15); The Fox as Nursemaid for the Bear (Type 37); The Wolf Flees from the Wolf Head (Type 125); Red Ridinghood (Type 333); The Quest for the Lost Wife (Type 400); The Black and the White Bride (Type 403); The Cat as Helper (Puss in Boots) (Type 545); Race with Relatives in Line (Type 1074); Ogre Kills Own Children: Substitutes in Bed (Type 1119); The Rich and the Poor Peasant (Type 1535); and The Eaten Grain and Cock as Damages (Type 1655). The Aesop tradition seems to be almost entirely lacking. Biting the Foot (Type 5), while it belongs to that tradition, probably came to the Africans from Northern Europe.

The tales just listed are very popular, not one of them appearing in Africa in fewer than ten versions. Their conformity to the European or Asiatic type is unmistakable, and we are sure that for at least this many stories there has been a widespread borrowing from the other continents. For a few very widely distributed African tales, the situation is not quite so clear. The story is told with some difference from the European or Asiatic analogue, and there is at least a possibility that we are dealing with a closely parallel narrative rather than an actual borrowing. Doubtful cases of this kind are represented by The Animals Build a Road (Type 55); The Princess Who Murdered Her Child (Type 781); Attempted Murder with Hatchet (Type 1115); Crayfish as Tailor Drowned (Type 1310); Holding Up the Rock (Type 1530); and Lending and Repaying, Progressive Bargains (Type 2034C).

These are only the most popular of the foreign tales in Africa. When we consider all of the borrowings which have thus far been reported, we find a total of 119 of the 718 types listed in the Aarne-Thompson catalogue. Perhaps most popular are the animal tales, a goodly number of which have become familiar to us in a later stage of development in the American Negro Uncle Remus cycle. But we also find a considerable group of the typical wonder tales such as Cinderella, Puss in Boots, The Two Travelers, and, strangely enough, six black adaptions of Snow White.

There are, of course, certain types of European stories not likely to appeal to such an alien culture, with different social conventions and life experiences. We seek in vain for tales based primarily upon the typical religious organization in Europe. But these fields of very special interest are strictly limited, and the African finds enjoyment in nearly every kind of European folktale. He may do some queer things with them and change them around so that little more than a skeleton of the original remains and so that it takes the expert eye to discover that they are not actually native. On the other hand he may take the tale over completely with all its foreign trappings, and it may remain as completely exotic as the railroad train or the airplane.

3. NORTH AMERICAN INDIAN

WHAT has been said of the African tales applies in large degree to those which have been borrowed by the North American Indians. We are dealing in the latter case entirely with contacts established within the past four centuries. The areas within which these contacts have taken place can be rather easily defined. Certainly most important for the dissemination of foreign tales among the Indians has been the presence of the French in all parts of Canada and, to a lesser degree, in various sections of western America. The Spanish from Mexico and New Mexico have also brought a considerable number of European stories into circulation among the Indians of the southwest. There has been some borrowing and lending between Negroes and the southeastern tribes. These are the main routes by which European stories have come to the American Indian.

The negative side of this picture is quite as interesting as the positive. Unless our collectors have been very negligent, we seem to be forced to the conclusion that that group which was to become dominant in Canada and the United States, and which carried the British tradition to this country, has contributed nothing to the folklore of the American Indians. Many things help to explain this, but the most important fact is that the British never fraternized with the natives, and particularly did not intermarry with them as did Frenchmen or Spaniards. There has apparently been a slight impact of Scandinavian tradition on the tribes of western Canada, and there is the bare possibility that some folktale motifs came to the eastern Indians from Iceland through the Eskimos.[2]

As far as the animal tales are concerned, they appear among the Canadian and southwestern Indians almost without change in the form in which they were learned from the French or the Spanish. The Tarbaby (Type 175), which is found in at least 23 American Indian versions, has been frequently borrowed from Negroes and then further spread by the Indians themselves. When we come to the regular wonder tales, we find that some of them are much more popular among American natives than they are in Africa. Particularly beloved are a few of the most complicated of such stories. For instance, there are at least 14 tales of The Dragon-Slayer (Type 300), 16 of The Three Stolen Princesses (Type 301), 33 of The Girl as Helper in the Hero's Flight (Type 313), 15 of The Youth Transformed to a Horse (Type 314), and 29 of The Quest for the Lost Wife (Type 400). Taken all in all, these American Indian borrowings involve at least 104 out of the 718 of the Aarne-Thompson types.

Just as is true in Africa, the degree of adaptation to the native lore differs profoundly as we go from tribe to tribe. Particularly among the eastern tribes where there has been long contact, the French tales have suffered little change. The opposite extreme is found in some of the Pueblo stories where an almost complete adaptation has been made to local religious and mythological patterns. A study of these European tales as taken over by our native Americans is interesting not only for showing exactly how much of the foreign folklore has been borrowed, but for the light it throws on the general problem of tale migration. We see here the results of varying attitudes between members of simpler and more complex cultures, the freedom of movement where there is easy fraternization and intermarriage and the exactly opposite effect produced by the lack of these.

The Indonesians, the Africans, and the North American Indians have been chosen to illustrate the way in which European tales have traveled to other cultures and have adapted themselves there with more or less success. These areas, of course, do not exhaust the possibilities for this type of study, since some tales have penetrated into Oceania, into northeast Siberia, and into the native folklore of Latin America.[3]

A general view of the dissemination of European tales in these three major areas can be had from the table appearing at the end of this chapter.

---

[2] This discussion of American Indian tales is based in the first instance on my *European Tales Among the North American Indians*. This has been supplemented by more recent, unpublished studies by my students.

[3] It is not the purpose of this chapter to discuss the tales of Europeans and their descendants in such countries as America or South Africa. This is essentially European folklore without adaptation. There is a good deal of such material, and it has normally been indicated in the discussion of particular tales.

For the Indonesian, the figures in De Vries's study mentioned earlier[4] have been used as a basis. For the African, the material is taken from an unpublished study of Dr. May A. Klipple[5] which covered the literature up to the date of writing. The American Indian figures are not quite so recent, since my study of this subject has not been brought down further than about 1930. It is certain that the list of these borrowings could be considerably increased from the literature of the last fifteen years.

NUMBER OF BORROWINGS OF EUROPEAN-ASIATIC TALES BY
INDONESIANS, AFRICANS, AND AMERICAN INDIANS

Type		Indo-nesian	Afri-can	American Indian
1.	The Theft of Fish		5	7
2.	Tail-Fisher		3	13
4.	Carrying the Sham-Sick Trickster		5	
5.	Biting the Foot	13	16	
6.	Inquiring about the Wind		2	
7.	Calling of Three Tree Names		1	
8.	The Painting	2	7	
9A.	The Unjust Partner: Bear Threshes		7	
9B.	The Unjust Partner: Corn and Chaff Crop Division			2
15.	Theft of Butter (Honey) by Playing Godfather		13	2
21.	Eating His Own Entrails	1	1	
30.	Fox Tricks Wolf into Falling into a Pit		1	
31.	Fox Climbs from Pit on Wolf's Back	15		
33.	Fox Plays Dead and is Thrown out of Pit and Escapes	20	5	
36.	Fox in Disguise Violates the She-Bear	1		
37.	Fox as Nursemaid for Bear	7	30	
38.	Claw in Split Tree	11	2	
47A.	Fox Hangs by Teeth to Horse's Tail		2	1
49.	Bear and the Honey			2
50.	Sick Lion	1		
55.	Animals Build a Road		18	1
56.	Fox Steals Young Magpies		7	
60.	Fox and Crane			3
62.	Peace Among Animals			1
72.	Rabbit Rides Fox a-Courting	1	6	7
73.	Blinding the Guard		2	2

[4] *Volksverhalen uit Oost Indië.*
[5] "African Folktales with Foreign Analogues," doctor's dissertation, Indiana University, 1938.

NUMBER OF BORROWINGS OF EUROPEAN-ASIATIC TALES BY
INDONESIANS, AFRICANS, AND AMERICAN INDIANS

Type		Indo-nesian	Afri-can	American Indian
100.	Wolf as Dog's Guest Sings			1
101.	Old Dog as Rescuer of Child			1
104.	Cowardly Duelers			3
105.	Cat's Only Trick		2	
111.	Cat and Mouse Converse	3		
122A.	Wolf Seeks Breakfast		2	
122B.	Cat Washes Face before Eating		5	
123.	Wolf and Kids			1
125.	Wolf Flees from Wolf-Head		12	
130.	Animals in Night Quarters			1
154.	"Bear-Food"		6	1
155.	Ungrateful Serpent Returned to Captivity	12		
156.	Splinter in Bear's Paw		1	
157.	Learning to Fear Men		1	1
175.	Tarbaby and Rabbit	2	39	23
210.	Cock, Hen, etc. on Journey	10		
221.	Election of Bird King	2		
222.	War of Birds and Quadrupeds		4	
225.	Crane Teaches Fox to Fly	4	3	43?
228.	Titmouse Tries to be Big as Bear	1	8	
235.	Jay Borrows Cuckoo's Skin	3		
248.	Dog and Sparrow	1		
249.	Ant and Cricket			3
275.	Race of Fox and Crayfish	26		1
295.	Bean, Straw, and Coal			3
300.	Dragon-Slayer	1		14
301.	Three Stolen Princesses			16
302.	Ogre's Heart in Egg	2		1
303.	Twins or Blood-Brothers	3		3
307.	Princess in the Shroud		2	
311.	Rescue by Sister (Girls in Sacks)		5	1
313.	Girl as Helper in Hero's Flight		2	33
314.	Youth Transformed to Horse (Goldener)	24	4	15
325.	Magician and Pupil	1		
326.	Learning What Fear Is			2
327A.	Hansel and Gretel	6	8	10
327B.	Dwarf and Giant	3		
327C.	Devil Carries Hero in Sack		9	6?
328.	Boy Steals Giant's Treasure			6
331.	Spirit in Bottle			1
333.	Red Ridinghood; Six Little Goats		16	
400.	Quest for Lost Wife	37	11	29

NUMBER OF BORROWINGS OF EUROPEAN-ASIATIC TALES BY
INDONESIANS, AFRICANS, AND AMERICAN INDIANS

Type		Indo-nesian	Afri-can	American Indian
401.	Princess Transformed into Deer		1	
402.	Mouse (Cat, etc.) as Bride	1		
403.	Black and White Bride	1	15	6
408.	Three Oranges		1	
425.	Search for Lost Husband (Cupid and Psyche)	5	5	1
432.	Prince as Bird		1	
450.	Little Brother and Little Sister		3	
451.	Maiden Who Seeks her Brothers			1
461.	Three Hairs from Devil's Beard	17	1	1
471.	Bridge to Other World	1	1	1
480.	Spinning Woman by the Spring	6		3
506.	Rescued Princess: Grateful Dead	6		1
507.	Monster's Bride: Grateful Dead			1
510A.	Cinderella	2	3	4
510B.	Cap o' Rushes		2	1
511.	One-Eye, Two-Eyes, Three-Eyes	3		
513.	The Helpers (Extraordinary Companions)		2	3
514.	Shift of Sex	1		
516.	Faithful John		1	
518.	Devils Fight over Magic Objects		2	
531.	Clever Horse		3	2
533.	Speaking Horse-head		6	
545.	Cat as Helper (Puss in Boots)	2	10	
550.	Bird, Horse, and Princess	4	4	
551.	Sons on Quest for Remedy		4	
552A.	Three Animal Brothers-in-Law			1
554.	Grateful Animals	11		
555.	Fisher and His Wife	5		
559.	Dungbeetle		1	4
560.	Magic Ring	36	8	2
561.	Aladdin	1		2
563.	Table, Ass, and Stick	7	14	4
566.	Three Magic Objects and Wonderful Fruits	2		1
567.	Magic Bird-heart	13	1	1
569.	Knapsack, Hat, and Horn	5		5
570.	Rabbit-herd	1	1	
571.	"All Stick Together"		1	
590.	Prince and Arm Bands			1
592.	Jew Among Thorns	1		
612.	Three Snake-Leaves	2		
613.	Two Travelers		5	1

NUMBER OF BORROWINGS OF EUROPEAN-ASIATIC TALES BY
INDONESIANS, AFRICANS, AND AMERICAN INDIANS

Type		Indo-nesian	Afri-can	American Indian
621.	Louse-Skin	3		
650.	Strong John	27	3	4
653.	Four Skillful Brothers	8	12	
655.	Wise Brothers	1	2	
670.	Animal Languages	6	23	
671.	Three Languages		2	
675.	Lazy Boy	2		
676.	Open Sesame	1	9	
700.	Tom Thumb		5	1
706.	Maiden Without Hands		6	2
707.	Three Golden Sons		8	1
709.	Snow White		6	
750.	The Wishes: Hospitality Rewarded	1	1	3
780.	Singing Bone		8	
781.	Princess Who Murdered her Child		12	
785.	Who Ate the Lamb's Heart?	1		
851.	Princess who Cannot Solve Riddle	3	2	
852.	Princess Forced to Say, "That is a Lie."	1	2	
853.	Princess Caught with her own Words		2	
854.	Golden Ram			1
875.	Clever Peasant Girl	3	3	
882.	Wager on Wife's Chastity	2		
900.	King Thrushbeard		1?	
901.	Taming of the Shrew			1
910.	The Good Precepts		2	
921.	King and Peasant's Son	1	2	
922.	King and Abbot	1		
923.	Love Like Salt		1	
930.	Prophecy for Poor Boy		1	1
931.	Oedipus	1		
935.	Prodigal's Return			1
945.	Luck and Intelligence	8	1	
950.	Rhampsinitus	1		
1000.	Anger Bargain	5		2
1004.	Hogs in Mud, Sheep in Air	2	3	4
1012.	Cleaning the Child	1		
1015.	Whetting the Knife	2		
1030.	Crop Division	1		
1031.	Roof as Threshing Flail			2
1060.	Squeezing the Stone	1	1	1
1061.	Biting the Stone		1	1
1062.	Throwing the Stone	1		1

NUMBER OF BORROWINGS OF EUROPEAN-ASIATIC TALES BY
INDONESIANS, AFRICANS, AND AMERICAN INDIANS

Type		Indo-nesian	Afri-can	American Indian
1063.	Throwing Contest with Golden Club			1
1074.	Race with Relatives in Line	6	38	12
1085.	Pushing Hole in a Tree			1
1088.	Eating Contest: Food in Bag			20
1115.	Attempted Murder with Hatchet		10	
1119.	Ogre Kills Own Children: Substitutes in Bed		14	5
1149.	Children Desire Ogre's Flesh	10	4	
1157.	Gun as Tobacco Pipe		1	
1200.	Sowing of Salt		1	
1250.	Bringing Water from Well: Human Chain		1	2
1260.	Porridge in Ice Hole	1		
1276.	Rowing without Going Forward	4		
1278.	Bell Falls into Sea: Mark on Boat	2		
1310.	Crayfish as Tailor: Drowned	18	22	31
1319.	Pumpkin as Ass's Egg, Rabbit as Colt			1
1350.	Loving Wife: Man Feigns Death		1?	
1360C.	Old Hildebrand			1
1380.	Faithless Wife: Husband Feigns Blindness		1	
1384.	Quest for Person Stupid as Wife		2	
1386.	Meat as Food for Cabbage	7		
1415.	Lucky Hans	2		1
1430.	Man and Wife Build Air Castles	7	1	
1525.	Master Thief	2		6
1528.	Holding Down the Hat	2		1
1530.	Holding up the Rock		11	3
1535.	Rich and Poor Peasant	10	16	11
1537.	Corpse Killed Five Times	3		2
1539.	Cleverness and Gullibility	7		3
1540.	Student from Paradise (Paris)	3		
1541.	For the Long Winter			2
1542.	The Clever Boy: Fooling-Sticks			8
1563.	"Both?"			3
1585.	Lawyer's Mad Client			1
1590.	Trespasser's Defense			1
1610.	To Divide Presents and Strokes		2	
1611.	Contest in Climbing Mast			1
1612.	Contest in Swimming			1
1640.	Brave Tailor	3		4
1641.	Doctor Know-All	21	3	
1642.	The Good Bargain: Money to Frogs			4

NUMBER OF BORROWINGS OF EUROPEAN-ASIATIC TALES BY
INDONESIANS, AFRICANS, AND AMERICAN INDIANS

Type		Indo-nesian	Afri-can	American Indian
1651.	Whittington's Cat	2	2	
1653.	Robbers under Tree	2	1	5
1655.	Eaten Grain and Cock as Damages		10	1
1685.	Foolish Bridegroom	6	1	
1696.	"What Should I Have Said?"	6	4	2
1698A.	Search for Lost Animal: Deaf Persons	1		
1698B.	Travelers Ask the Way: Deaf Peasant		1	
1730.	Three Suitors Visit Chaste Wife	2	3	
1737.	Parson in Sack to Heaven		1	
1775.	Hungry Parson			3
1920A.	Lying Contest: "Sea Burns"	1		
1930.	Schlaraffenland		3	
2028.	Troll (Wolf) Cut Open		1	
2030.	Old Woman and Pig	2	4	
2031.	Frost-bitten Foot	4	3	
2033.	Nut Hits Cock's Head		3	
2034C.	Lending and Repaying, Progressive Bargains		22	
2035.	House that Jack Built		4	
2400.	Ground Measured with Horse's Skin			1

PART THREE

The Folktale in a Primitive
Culture---North American Indian

THE NORTH AMERICAN
INDIAN TALES

❚

OF ALL groups of peoples outside our own Western civilization, none have been so thoroughly studied as the North American Indians. From the first arrival of white men in the days of the Discovery, the native inhabitants excited the curiosity of European conquerors and settlers. For the Mayas, Aztecs, and other Indians of Middle America European records go back to the early sixteenth century. Frequent notices of the Pueblo tribes of our Southwest also occur in Spanish records of that century. And for the tribes of the eastern seaboard accounts begin almost with the date of the first white settlement. Especially important in this respect are the *Jesuit Relations*, voluminous papers covering the efforts of the Jesuit fathers, largely during the second quarter of the seventeenth century, to convert the Algonquins and Iroquois to Christianity.

These early records tell us a great deal about the legendary history of the Indians, about their practices and beliefs, and there are even some vestiges of pre-Columbian literature.[1] The early Spanish accounts do not permit us to hazard much of a guess about what kind of tales were currently told by the natives they were describing. Some of the Jesuit Fathers in Canada, however, interested themselves greatly in listening to such stories. They were, of course, much concerned to learn exactly what kinds of error they must combat in their attempt to convert these simple folk. But their curiosity went far beyond this immediate need, and they recorded a number of stories merely because they were interesting.

With the activities of the Jesuit Fathers, the collecting of American Indian

[1] For a gathering together of such material, see D. G. Brinton, *Library of Aboriginal American Literature* (6 vols., Philadelphia, 1882-85 [especially vols. 1 and 6]).

tales began. Not much more was to be done for two centuries, though the writers of the Romantic Movement talked much about "the noble Indian" and speculated about his philosophy. It was not until the time of Henry Rowe Schoolcraft that any serious efforts were made to learn about Indian tales. During the 1830's, and for more than a decade afterward, this talented man took advantage of his position as Indian Agent among the Ojibwas to make an extensive record of their life and legends. He knew his Indians thoroughly and spoke their language, but his work is marred by two great defects. He has included legends from other tribes and he has reconstructed many of the tales according to his own romantic notions.[2] In spite of these limitations, however, Schoolcraft exerted a powerful influence on the study of American Indian tales. Hardly was his work published before it engaged the interest of the most popular American poet then writing, and in the guise of Longfellow's *Hiawatha* the Ojibwa tales collected by Schoolcraft became a part of American literature.

Schoolcraft had many followers—Indian agents, doctors, missionaries and teachers who heard tales which interested them and who refurbished them for a generation of romantic readers. But it was not until the last quarter of the nineteenth century that we begin to receive faithful recordings of American Indian tales. With the development of the Bureau of American Ethnology and the influence of such scientists as J. W. Powell there begin to appear an increasing number of first-rate collections, some of them even accompanied by the original text. By the time the last frontier disappeared in the 1880's, a generation of scholars was preparing itself for a thorough investigation of the life of the aboriginal peoples.

Many men have contributed to the vast accumulation of works on the North American Indian which have appeared within the past half century. Not only through his own labors but through that of his many distinguished disciples, Franz Boas made a colossal contribution to the study of every aspect of aboriginal American life.[3] Not least important in these studies have been voluminous collections of folktales from every quarter of the continent. From him and from his contemporaries at Harvard, Yale, Columbia, Pennsylvania, Chicago, Washington, and California, and in the Bureau of Ethnology and the Field Museum—to mention only a few of the obvious sources—we now possess faithful recordings of native tales in such quantity that for a large number of representative tribes we can be reasonably sure that we now have something approaching the complete repertory of narrative material. Many of these collections are accompanied by linguistic texts, so that it is possible to

---

[2] For an account of Schoolcraft and his work, see Chase S. Osborn and Stellanova Osborn, *Schoolcraft, Longfellow, Hiawatha* (Lancaster, Penn., 1942).

[3] For a discussion of Boas's work, see *Journal of American Folklore*, LVII, No. 1 (1944 [Boas Memorial Number]).

use them for the study of narrative style. Both in respect to the faithfulness of recording and to the relative number of texts available to the student, we are better prepared for a study of the North American Indian tale than for even those of Europe and the Near East.[4]

This vast amount of material offers ample opportunity for the student of folktale dissemination, of narrative style, of cultural adaptations, and of individual differences in narrators. But the mere bulk of available texts is such as to make a comprehensive study all but impossible. Most students have wisely confined their efforts to a single area or to a single aspect of the general subject. When, therefore, one attempts to discuss in somewhat general terms the folktales of the North American Indians, he must be continually aware of the debt he owes to many specialists, as well as of the frequent danger that his generalizations may be premature or ill-informed. Nevertheless, it does not seem to be too early a stage in the investigation of American Indian tales to examine some results already certainly attained and to suggest others of which we are not so sure.

When one begins to read folktale collections from various parts of the continent he is impressed with the great variety of narrative current within this large area. The kinds of stories which fill Rasmussen's large collection from Greenland seem to belong to a different world from the tales of California or the Southwest. And this first impression is confirmed by further study. For in spite of detailed resemblances and even identities in the incidents of their folktales, there are important and essential differences as one moves from area to area. These differences concern not only the presence of tales specially characteristic of each area and found seldom or never elsewhere, but also the peculiar treatment which may be given to all narratives, even those brought in from a distance. The tribes in a particular region may, for some reason, prefer to confine themselves to tales of a certain kind, and this preference determines the repertory of the tribal story-tellers.

A close examination of American Indian stories would probably bring to light a large number of these regions in which there have been developed a common type of narrative. Generally, such geographical units correspond to what anthropologists call "culture areas." Such areas can, of course, never be exact, since the boundaries determined by the distribution of one element of culture will seldom correspond exactly with those based upon another equally important element. But the general centers of such areas are usually clear enough, and the tribes representative of the typical culture are so distinctive that there is usually little practical difficulty in describing the principal differentiations of culture areas.

[4] For a rather complete bibliography of the North American Indian tale down to 1926, see Thompson, *Tales of the North American Indians* (Cambridge, Mass., 1929), pp. 368ff. Some important subsequent works will be mentioned in our later discussion.

On the basis of general culture, therefore, it is practicable to divide the North American Indians into a series of areas.[5]

1. *Eskimo.* Extending from East Greenland to the northeast corner of Siberia are the Eskimos. They are scattered over large distances, but they have a remarkably uniform culture, dependent upon their living in an arctic climate and on the shores of frozen seas. They are never found more than a few miles from a coast.

2. *Mackenzie.* Meeting the Eskimos at the mouth of the Mackenzie River and extending far to the south into Alberta and Saskatchewan is a group usually designated by the name of the Mackenzie River along which they live.

3. *Plateau.* From the eastern wall of the Rocky Mountains to the Cascades on the west, and from British Columbia to Northern Nevada is a fairly unified culture.

4. *North Pacific.* From the coast of southern Alaska southward almost to the boundary of California a large group of peoples, many of them linguistically unrelated, have developed common traits. Details vary, especially as one approaches the southern or eastern limits, but the interest in salmon fishing, in the multiform uses of the giant cedar trees, and in the tales of totemistic culture heroes such as Raven, Mink, or Bluejay persists throughout this region.

5. *California.* The state of California constitutes a well-defined aboriginal area of culture. The tribes are usually very small, and most of them have apparently always been so. Linguistically they show great diversity, though some of them belong to language families very large and important outside of the California area.

6. *Plains.* The Indian culture most familiar to white readers is that of the Plains, with its tipis, its beadwork, its elaborate featherdresses, its horsemen, and in an older day, its buffalo herds. As a boundary, the Rocky Mountains and eastern Nevada serve as a western limit; south it extends to the New Mexico line and well over into Texas. On the east the demarcation between this area and the Central Woodlands is vague and perhaps impossible to establish. In some respects the Plains culture is found as far east as the Mississippi River, in others it seems to be coterminous with the treeless prairie. To the north it reaches far into Canada. The part of this area lying west of the Rockies is spoken of specifically as "Basin."

[5] The areas used as a basis of this discussion are those proposed by Clark Wissler many years ago (*American Anthropologist*, new series, XVI, 447ff.). Later I used the Wissler map as a basis for my annotations in *Tales of the North American Indians*, pp. 271ff. As a result of recent study, some suggestions for modification of these areas, particularly the mutual relations of Plains and Woodland areas have been made, but even if they are found to be valid, they would have no practical effect upon such a study as we are making here. Even if the boundary between Plains and Woodland is vague or nonexistent, no harm is done in treating separately the material on opposite sides of even an arbitrary geographical line.

7. *Central Woodland.* Culturally all the tribes east of the uncertain line we have just suggested and south to Tennessee and North Carolina have much in common. It is convenient, however, to treat them as three subareas. The first of these, the Central Woodland, has very vague boundaries. The term is usually applied to the Indians of the Great Lakes region, but logically it is also used for the whole Woodland area except the next two to be mentioned.

8. *Northeast Woodland.* The tribes of New England, the Maritime provinces, and Quebec are so characteristic in culture that they constitute a distinct subarea.

9. *Iroquois.* Forming a cultural island in the midst of the other Woodlands groups (who nearly all belong to the Algonquian linguistic family) are the Iroquois of the Lake Ontario region, especially of New York State. They speak Iroquoian tongues, and they show many unusual and characteristic traits. Perhaps chief of these was their practically unique ability to organize themselves for political and military purposes.

10. *Southeast.* Perhaps least well studied of all our native tribes are those which originally occupied the Southern States east of the Mississippi. Most of them were moved at an early time into the Indian Territory, and the best modern studies have had to be made in Oklahoma, far from their original home. But such tribes as the Cherokee, the Yuchi, and the Choctaw still have interesting traditions.

11. *Southwest.* There remain the natives of New Mexico and Arizona. In contrast to the Southeastern tribes, these peoples, with few exceptions, occupy their old home. They easily divide themselves into two groups, on the one hand the Pueblo tribes who occupy permanent villages, many of them centuries old; and on the other the Navaho and Apache, who avoid permanent habitation. Within this Southwestern area are found some of the most interesting of aboriginal cultures, notably the Zuñi, the Hopi, and the Navaho.

Such are the principal groupings of American Indian tribes which the student of folktales, as well as the ethnologist, finds significant for his studies.

When one begins a penetrating examination of American Indian tales he soon sees that the areal boundaries we have just outlined, while in many ways important as points of reference, have seldom acted as real barriers in the path of a tale as it travels from its original home. There has been a large amount of borrowing and lending, not only within culture areas, but from one to the other, sometimes across the whole continent. The association of the American Indian tribes has covered a long period and it has been accompanied by much shifting about of peoples, by much trade and commerce, and by much intertribal war. Tales, like other elements of culture, have been exchanged, so that in addition to regional patterns, there has developed a very considerable common store of narrative material which may be heard wherever North American Indians are found.

This common material is of two general kinds: specific tales and general narrative patterns. Of the specific tales we shall see later that a larger number than might well be imagined are told over the whole continent. With all of them the plot outline is relatively clear and firm, and there is seldom ground for doubt as to whether we are actually dealing with a particular tale. On the other hand, there exist certain narrative patterns, such as creation myths and trickster tales, which are very vague and constitute little more than a framework into which a series of small incidents may be fitted.

CREATION MYTHS

THE folklorist who has been primarily interested in the historic Western cultures is likely to think of folktales and myths as being essentially different both in narrative content and in their significance to the people who tell them. Though this differentiation has some validity for such peoples as the Greeks and Hindus,[1] it breaks down almost completely for the North American Indians. Most groups will, indeed, recognize a difference between tales which belong to the present world and those which are supposed to have happened in a previous one, and in some tribes there are found myths explaining the origin of certain rituals and known in detail only to the initiated or to the priesthood. But these classes of tales flow freely into one another. Insofar as the differentiation exists in the minds of tellers, it seldom seems to be important. Collectors of American Indian tales betray this indifference, since they publish their collections sometimes as "tales," sometimes as "myths," and sometimes merely as "traditions."

Nevertheless, though sharp distinctions from other tales cannot be maintained, most of the tribes do tell stories about their beginnings, and sometimes about superior beings; and these it is convenient to speak of as "creation myths." Such myths differ a good deal in various parts of the continent. Sometimes, but rarely, a real attempt is given to account for creation; but more often these origin tales are nothing more than reports of important changes taking place in an already existing world. These changes may involve the creation of the present earth, or particular features of it, or even of the heavenly bodies; and, more frequently, the creation and conditioning of men and animals.

1. THE SOUTHWEST

ABOUT the nearest approach to the true creation myth in aboriginal North America is found in a sacred story of the Zuñi of New Mexico. It was taken

[1] For a discussion of this point, see p. 389, below.

down by Cushing many years ago and, with some different phraseology, by Mrs. Stevenson, but later students of Zuñi religion[2] find the account considerably colored by monotheistic ideas in the collectors. It is certainly true, however, that in broad outline the tale is an important part of Zuñi ceremonial. Cushing's account begins with the creator Awonawilona who alone has being. He "thought outward in space, whereby mists of increase, steams potent of growth, were evolved and uplifted. Thus, by means of his innate knowledge, the All-container made himself in person and form of the Sun whom we hold to be our father and who thus came to exist and appear." The Sun Father rubs his skin and makes balls of his cuticle. This he casts upon the waters and from it there are created Earth Mother and Sky Father. From the cohabitation of these two there comes forth all life on the earth. The Earth Mother thereupon repulses the Sky Father and ever after he guards the sky and she the earth. The Earth Mother afterwards creates all the landmarks of the earth and the clouds and rains. The Sky Father creates the stars.[3]

This is the bare outline of the Zuñi creation myth. Zuñi ceremonial is responsible for a considerable development of this myth in its later stages, for we have accounts of the emergence of the tribe from one world to another, and of the origin of many features of their religion.

In a study of this Zuñi origin myth Mrs. Parsons[4] finds a number of motifs some of which are common to other tribes: hierarchy of worlds (A651), origin of death (A1335), lizard-hand (A1311.1), brother and sister incest (T415), land of the dead (E481), distribution of tribes (A1620), birth from foam (T547.1), and twins visit sun-father (A515.1.1). Most of these ideas are found in parts of America far distant from the Zuñi, as well as in the neighboring peoples. But there is, nevertheless, a considerable resemblance in the basic pattern of the creation myths for the whole southwestern area. The emergence of the tribe from one or more lower worlds, the great attention to the origin of ceremonials, the creation from the creator's or culture hero's cuticle, the frequency of twin heroes, and the overcoming of primeval monsters—these are found over the whole area. The close relation of the creation legend to their elaborate ceremonialism is such a characteristic feature of the myths of this area that they stand out in clear distinction from all other parts of the continent.

2. CALIFORNIA

To THE creation myths of the southwestern area, filled as they usually are with a reasonably logical account of the emergence of the tribe from lower

[2] Ruth Benedict, *Zuni Mythology*, I, 256, 276.
[3] Thompson, *Tales of the North American Indians*, p. 17, and n. 36. For the entire section on American Indian tales the references will be to this work, abbreviated as *Tales*. Extensive bibliographies are there given which are unnecessary to repeat here.
[4] *Journal of American Folklore*, XXXVI, 131ff.

worlds and closely related to religion and ceremonialism, those of California afford a considerable contrast. In a large number of tribes of the state it is impossible to find a coherent creation myth. But where these do appear they all have certain features in common. Very usual is the idea that the culture hero, be he of human or animal shape, finds himself alone, or with a single companion, floating about in a boat or on a raft in a chaos of primeval water. The culture hero, or creator, sends animals to dive for earth and when one finally succeeds, he creates the present earth from the bit of soil thus secured. After the earth is created the culture hero sometimes creates a second culture hero (frequently Coyote, who is conceived of having both human and animal form) or another human hero. Coyote proceeds to create man, from clay or wood, and gives life to him. Later he creates the animals and arranges all the affairs of the earth as they now are.[5]

Much variation will, of course, be found, and very frequently the myths begin with the assumption that the earth is already in existence and proceed with the adventures of Coyote. Within the framework of this type-myth there is room for a considerable variety of motifs, most of which are also known in other parts of America. Especially prominent in California are the tales of the theft of fire, light, the sun, and the like (A1415, A1411, A721.1). Much attention is given to the establishment of topographical features of the earth (A900ff.) and to the regulation of human existence and human characteristics (A1200ff.). Such motifs are the origin of death (A1335), the lizard hand (A1311.1), determination of seasons (A1150ff.), and the establishment of marriage (A1555). The myths of the tribes of the extreme south of the state have many things in common with those of the southwestern area, particularly the concept of Sky Father and Earth Mother (A625), and the migration legend.

3. ESKIMO

THE basic myth of the Eskimo is very simple and only serves to account for their goddess of the underworld. There is no attempt at explaining original creation, and practically no special creations are mentioned. This myth, known throughout the Eskimo world, is called "Sedna."[6] Sedna is a girl who has refused all her suitors, but she eventually is enticed into marriage by a bird (or sometimes a dog). The bird takes her to his own land, and only then does she realize that the life of birds is different from that of human beings, and she is much distressed. She gives birth to bird (or dog) children. Her father comes across the sea to the bird country to rescue her. He kills the bird husband and takes his daughter and her children into his boat. On the return a storm comes up and the father feels

---

[5] See *Tales*, pp. 24, 30, and n. 47. For a good recent comparative study of the creation myths of north-central California, see Gayton and Newman, *Yokuts and Western Mono Myths*.

[6] *Tales*, p. 3, No. 1, n. 2 (A315.1).

that a sacrifice is called for. He throws the daughter overboard and when she clings to the boat, he cuts off her fingers. These fingers fall into the water and become the various kinds of fish. Sedna sinks in the ocean and becomes the goddess of the lower world.

Within this pattern there is not the room for a multitude of miscellaneous motifs which is usually found in American Indian creation myths. There are, however, independent tales, rather incoherent, telling of the origin of man, of thunder, lightning, and rain, and of day and night. In addition, one widespread story tells the reason for the pursuit of the sun by the moon. This happens because a brother visits his sister secretly at night. She identifies him by painting his back with her hands. She then cuts off her breasts and gives them to him, and in her anger she ascends to the sky. He follows, and continues to chase her. They are the sun and moon.[7]

4. NORTHEAST WOODLAND

The tribes of the Maritime Provinces and New England possess a common store of sacred legends. They are not truly creation myths, though many of them account for specific origins. The central characters of these sacred legends is Glooscap.[8] Of all American Indian culture heroes, there seems to be about him the least suggestion that he is at once human and animal. For although his animal nature is unmistakable, his activities are always essentially those of a man. We learn of how his wanderings are responsible for various features of landscape (A901), of his taming of the winds (A532), and securing water and food from those who hold it back (A1111, A1421). At the end of his career he departs for the west and takes up his abode in another world, where he is making arrows in preparation for the great battle at the last day. An interesting account is given of the visit made to him by some men who succeed in passing the barriers of the otherworld. He agrees to fulfill for each of them a single request.[9] In fulfilling these he actually satisfies only the man who has made a very modest demand. But the one who asks for eternal life is turned into a stone,[10] and the promise literally fulfilled. Many miscellaneous incidents connected with the Glooscap story are found in other parts of America, particularly from the Great Lakes eastward.

[7] Brother and sister incest, *Tales*, n. 8 (T415); telltale hand mark, *Tales*, n. 7 (H58); pursuit of sun by moon, *Tales*, n. 9 (T415); sun sister and moon brother, *Tales*, n. 6 (A736.1).
[8] *Tales*, p. 5, No. 3, n. 10.
[9] Deity grants requests to visitors: *Tales*, n. 17 (A575).
[10] Request for immortality punished: *Tales*, n. 18 (Q338.1).

5. IROQUOIS

OVER the whole of the area inhabited by the Iroquois of New York State and Ontario and among the Algonquian tribes immediately to the north and to the south there is found a rather consistent myth accounting for the creation of the present earth and its inhabitants.[11] This myth begins with the assumption of an upper world and a vast expanse of water below. The daughter of the Sky Chief is taken ill, and he receives advice that he must have her lie beside a certain great tree. Though this tree has been furnishing the food for the upper world people, the chief has been advised to have it dug up. An angry man shoves the girl into the hole thus opened in the sky.[12] She falls down, but the waterfowls, seeing her, fly up and catch her, so that she is eased down to the surface of the water. They persuade the great Turtle to receive her. But it finally has to be decided where she will rest permanently. Therefore from the back of the Turtle·animals are sent to dive for earth. All fail except the toad, who brings back some soil.[13] From this the earth is made, resting on the back of the Turtle. The story now proceeds with the adventures of the daughter of the woman who fell. This girl, in spite of warning against exposure to the wind, is impregnated by the West Wind.[14] She gives birth to twins, who, while still in her womb, quarrel as to which shall be born first.[15] These twins, one good and one bad, are the culture heroes of the Iroquois. Many of the detailed points of their mythology concern the deeds of these boys. In comparison with the basic creation myths of other areas, the Iroquois is well integrated and frequently told with a good deal of narrative interest. Most of the incidents are found elsewhere, the only things especially characteristc of this myth being the fall from the sky and the earth resting on the turtle's back. Even the twins quarreling before birth is a characteristic common to the Iroquois and the tribes farther west as far as the Lake Superior region.

6. CENTRAL WOODLAND

BY FAR the best known of all American Indian creation myths is that made famous by Longfellow's *Hiawatha*.[16] Actually, the hero of these legends was not Hiawatha (who was a historical Iroquois leader of the sixteenth century), but Manabozho.[17] His name varies slightly as one moves from the Menomini of central Wisconsin around to the west and north of Lake

---

[11] *Tales*, p. 14, No. 5, n. 27 (A21.1).
[12] Sky window: *Tales*, n. 28 (F56).
[13] Earth diver: *Tales*, n. 30 (A812).
[14] *Tales*, n. 21 (T524).
[15] Twins quarrel before birth: *Tales*, n. 33 (T575.1.3).
[16] For some discussion of Longfellow's use of these legends, see pp. 298, 318.
[17] *Tales*, p. 8, No. 4, n. 20.

Superior and even over to the east of Lake Huron. But over this entire area the basic legend is rather consistent. It has a few points in common with the Iroquois.

Indeed, the beginning of the myth is identical with the latter. An old woman warns her daughter against facing south as she digs potatoes. She disobeys, and is impregnated by the wind. Here, too, the twins speak to each other in their mother's womb.[18] When they are born, however, they are not opponents, but are friendly. They are evidently thought of as human and animal at the same time. In their animal form they are the White Rabbit and the Wolf. The more important of the two is Manabozho, the Rabbit. He lives with his old grandmother, Nokomis.

This account of the birth and boyhood of the Culture Hero is not made very consistent with certain other of the creation myth motifs, such as the diving for earth (A812) and the creation of man (A1200ff.). The earth diving usually takes place in the waters of a flood, and is merely one of the experiences of the Culture Hero rather than a primary act of creation. A large part of the Manabozho myth is occupied with his taming of monsters (A531) and his bringing of culture to his people (A541). Very prominent is the story of his wolf brother who is drowned by evil manitous as he crosses the lake on the ice. As a result of Manabozho's lamentations which call his wolf brother back to earth there is formed the Grand Medicine Lodge. In the end, Manabozho takes his departure for the west (A561), and there is sometimes a hint that he may eventually return (A580).

Possibly because of its central location, this myth includes a very large number of the incidents common to the creation legends of other areas. The contests of heat and cold (D2144.2), the existence of the creator's grandmother (A31), the pursuit of the sun by the moon (A735), the theft of summer (A1151) and of fire (A1415), the origin of corn (A2611.1), and the regulation of the winds (A1120ff.)—all these are very widely known. In some ways this myth shows close relationship to the Iroquois and Eastern Woodland legends, but in one respect at least it differs from them and fits into the western pattern: the Culture Hero also appears in the quite opposite role of trickster and fool. In this he is like Coyote of the west rather than Glooscap of the east.

7. NORTH PACIFIC COAST

On the North Pacific Coast there is not, strictly speaking, any creation myth. But various incidents usually connected with such a myth are made a part of the legend of the Culture Hero. This Culture Hero is conceived of in animal form, though the nature of the adventures shows that he is at the same time given human characteristics. From southern Vancouver

[18] Cf. footnotes 14 and 15, above, for Iroquois parallel.

Island northward the animal form he assumes is that of Raven; in the tribes around the Gulf of Georgia he is Mink; and for the most of those of the Washington and Oregon coast he is Blue Jay. But the general plan of the basic myth seems to be fairly constant, although in many tribes, probably because of inadequate collection, the outlines are very obscure.

This myth has been studied with extraordinary thoroughness by Boas.[19] All the varieties of the legend begin with the birth of a child, either from supernatural conception or from an adulterous connection. It proceeds to the adventures of that boy, who has supernatural growth (T615). As a young man he seduces his uncle's wife (or in some tales the daughter of the Sky Chief) and by this misdeed brings on a flood (A1018). To escape from the flood, the boy flies to the sky. His child drops from the sky onto drifting kelp. This child is found and adopted by a chief. The child will not eat, but he is instructed in the use of food, and becomes so voracious that it is hard to keep him in provisions. This child is Raven, and the various adventures of the Culture Hero are ascribed to him.

This outline is highly schematic and there is much confusion in the various accounts. The myth continues with a series of thefts carried on by Raven—fire, sunlight, water, animals, and the like (A1415, A721.1, A1111, A1421). Having secured all of these necessities for mankind, Raven travels about and transforms animals and objects so that they have their present characteristics. Many of these transformer tales are nothing more than stories of deception, and sometimes show the cleverness of the transformer, and sometimes display only his stupidity.

The best examples of the Raven story as a creation myth are found in the more northerly tribes, the Tsimshian and the Tlinkit, though even there it is not entirely consistent. The general pattern fades out in the tribes of Oregon.

8. OTHER AREAS

THE seven myth patterns just reviewed stand out rather clearly in North American mythology. For the remaining general culture areas the picture is much more confused. Many of the individual mythical incidents which we have already met are found everywhere, but there is no well-conceived central myth around which such incidents cluster, as they do with the Manabozho or Raven cycle. The creation incidents of the Mackenzie River area and of the Plateau show very close relation to those of the North Pacific Coast. In the large Plains area there is a considerable variety of legend having to do with creation. Much of it belongs to the cycle of Coyote, the trickster hero, which extends over the entire west of the continent. As among the southwestern tribes, some of the Plains people relate

[19] *Tsimshian Mythology*, pp. 565ff.

their mythology directly to their ceremonialism; so that among certain Siouan tribes, for example, many myths explain the origin of the sun dance.

There is likewise no unified pattern for the Southeastern tribes. For most of them the record is not very complete, but even for the Cherokee, whose myths have been well collected, we have merely a collection of motifs, all of them widely known, but no well integrated myth.

9. MYTH MOTIFS

THE larger myth patterns which have just been passed in review, while they show distinctive features in their general plans, are naturally all concerned with a similar type of material and contain many details common to the tribes of a large part of the continent. Most of these myths, either expressly or by implication, tell of the origin of the earth, of the establishment of its first peoples, of the Culture Hero and his deeds, of the establishment of human culture, and of a liveable environment. Most of them give some incidental information about the origin and characteristics of animals.

In many ways a study of these individual incidents in the mythological tales of the North American Indians is more important as an indication of the dissemination of these ideas than the basic patterns which serve as frameworks for them. Many tribes do not arrange their mythical material in such patterns. Particularly the peoples of the central plains, the southeastern states, and the Plateau and Basin areas are likely to handle each mythical incident as a tale unto itself. Many of these are the same incidents as have a definite place in one of the larger cycles, such as that of the Zuñi or the North Pacific Coast.

Of these separate mythical incidents several are concerned with the Creator, who is usually not to be distinguished from the Culture Hero. A very peculiar motif already noted in the Glooscap and Manabozho legends is that of the Creator's grandmother.[20] The Culture Hero, or even the Creator, is represented as living with his grandmother. This is a constant feature of the Northeast Woodland myths and is a necessary part of the Iroquois and Central Woodland. But it is also found in California often enough to show that it is well established there.

As to the principal work of the Culture Hero, the motifs are so general as to suggest that they have no necessary connection with each other. Nearly all the mythologies tell of the way in which various experiences of his result in changes in the contour of the land, the piling up of mountains, the locating of rivers or lakes, and the establishment of the shore line (A920ff.). Concerning the end of his career, however, several rather more definite motifs appear. Perhaps they are most clearly stated in the Glooscap story of the Northeast. At the end of his labors he departs for the west,

[20] *Tales*, n. 13 (A31).

and he is expected to return eventually to help his people.[21] The departure
for the west is common in the Manabozho story of the Central Woodlands
and is also known on the North Pacific coast and in California. The expected
return of the Culture Hero is likewise a part of the Manabozho story, and
is well recognized among both the Plateau and Southwestern tribes.

An orderly, systematic arrangement is not to be expected in any except
the most philosophical of mythologies. Sometimes we find the Creator living
in a world before he has created it, and sometimes we are told of a primeval
water presumably covering a not-yet-created earth. This latter conception is
present in almost every American Indian creation story, with the probable
exception of the Eskimo.[22] It is on such a body of primeval water that the
Creator, sometimes with a companion, finds himself floating about on a boat
or raft. He sends various animals down to the bottom of the water to try to
find some earth. One after another, they float back dead and unsuccessful.
Finally, one of them—usually the muskrat—comes back with a bit of soil
between his paws. The Creator takes this soil and works with it so that it
expands and becomes the earth floating upon the original flood. This episode
of the earth diver[23] is sometimes illogically connected with the story of the
flood which destroys the earth, a widespread deluge tale resembling in many
ways the story of Noah.[24] In one or other of these forms the diving for earth
appears frequently in all sections of the continent except for the Southwestern area. It is so evenly distributed that its center of distribution is hard
to determine, though the majority of versions thus far noted have come
from the Plains. The Southwestern tribes nearly all tell of the primeval
water, but their creation proceeds in another direction from that given in
the myths of the rest of the continent.

These tribes are much more interested in tales of the emergence of their people from below the present earth. Frequently they give accounts of as many
as three or four such progressions from one world to another. This obviously
implies a series of worlds, one above the other, and sometimes a series of
separate creations in which an unsatisfactory creation is destroyed and another made to take its place.[25] Characteristic of the Southwest and California
is the tale of the original World Parents. The earth and the sky were once
joined together, the earth being the mother and the sky the father of mankind.[26] In the course of time it is possible, in one way or another, to push the

[21] Tales, notes 11, 11a, (A561, A580).
[22] Tales, n. 29 (A810).
[23] Tales, n. 30 (A812).
[24] For these deluge myths among the American Indians, see p. 313, below.
[25] For the Hierarchy of Worlds, which appears practically over the whole continent, see
Tales, n. 58 (A651). The story of the series of emergencies is confined to the Southwest.
The series of creations (A636) appears in four areas, apparently unconnected with one
another: Central California, Arizona, the southern Plains, and southern Michigan. The last
of these is probably influenced by the Biblical account of Paradise Lost.
[26] Tales, n. 37 (A625); Raising of the Sky (A625.2).

sky up and thus make room for the existence of mankind. A similar concept, but apparently quite unconnected with these legends, is that of the Earth Mother,[27] known to the tribes of Washington and British Columbia.

It has already been noted that many tribes represent the earth as floating around on a primeval water. But other suggestions for its support appear in various parts of the continent. The Iroquois and the Northeast Woodland peoples tell about the turtle who holds the earth on his back.[28] Much more widespread, however, is the belief that it is supported by a great post; usually it is thought that a beaver is gnawing at this post and that when he cuts through it the world will come to an end.[29] A few peoples mention the support of the earth on a man's shoulders.[30] One of the items in several California and Southwestern tales concerns the establishment of columns to support the earth at each of the four cardinal directions.[31] A similar tale is told in the Southeast.

The interest of the North American Indians in the stars and other heavenly bodies seems not to be nearly so great as some writers on mythology would have us expect.[32] There are explanations of the existence of certain groups of stars, such as the Pleiades,[33] but usually these are rather incidental conclusions to tales of various kinds in which, at the end, certain fugitives rise in the air and become stars. Such tales are found all over the continent, but many of them certainly have nothing to do with one another. The same may be said of various explanations of the Man in the Moon.[34]

The teachings of American Indian mythology concerning the Creator and the establishment of the universe, particularly of the earth, are, for the great majority of the tribes, fragmentary and meager and such explanations are often entirely lacking. But when we come to the beginning of mankind, of the establishment of his relationships with the world, nearly every people contributes a store of interesting tales.

In such stories the Culture Hero is usually not thought of as the original Creator, though sometimes he is instrumental in the creation of man. The latter incident, of course, is almost a necessary part of any creation legend, and its presence in tales all over the continent only sometimes indicates direct relationship. There is in southern California and the Southwest a definite tradition of the creation of man from the rubbings of skin of the Creator. When we find him made from clay, as in some California tales and

---

[27] *Tales*, n. 37a (A401).

[28] *Tales*, n. 31 (A815).

[29] A843. This has been reported from the Mackenzie, Plateau, North Pacific, California, and Plains areas.

[30] For this Atlas motif, see *Tales*, n. 56b (A842). It appears in the Mackenzie district, the North Pacific, and California.

[31] *Tales*, n. 56 (A841). For the World Tree of the Iroquois myth, see p. 307, above.

[32] See p. 384, below.

[33] *Tales*, n. 71 (A773). For the Escape to the Stars, see n. 71a (A761).

[34] *Tales*, n. 69 (A751). For the pursuit of the sun by the moon, see p. 308, above.

sporadically in the Middle West, a suspicion of Biblical influence is justified. Only among the Navaho do we find him made from ears of corn.[35]

As Professor Waterman pointed out in his essay on "The Explanatory Element in North American Mythology,"[36] there are hundreds of explanations of natural phenomena scattered through the tales of these peoples. But in most cases such explanations are merely incidental and are not used with any consistency as a part of the tale. Thus we have frequent stories of the origin of certain lakes, usually because of some adventure of the Culture Hero or Transformer. Such stories, especially among tribes distant from one another, are usually quite independent. Three tales of this kind may be mentioned as an illustration of this point. Practically all over the country are to be heard Indian legends of a cliff marking the place where despairing lovers have jumped to their death. Likewise, nearly everywhere one can hear stories of markings on rocks which have been left by the Culture Hero in his wanderings. I was recently shown some of these by an Ojibwa near Sault Sainte Marie. He was convinced that they had been made by Manabozho. Somewhat more localized is the story of the Bridge of the Gods, which explains the great rocks in the Columbia River at The Dalles.[37]

Although the idea of a series of creations is confined to a relatively few tribes, mainly in the Southwest,[38] the simpler concept of the destruction of the world by flood or fire and then its renewal is found almost everywhere. As for the stories of deluges, it is often extremely hard to tell whether we are dealing with an aboriginal idea or with some modification of the tale of Noah as learned from missionaries or other Europeans. Of the flood tales which have the appearance of being aboriginal there are good examples in every part of the continent. Sometimes these are obviously related to each other, and sometimes they are clearly independent stories, perhaps frequently the reflection of some actual catastrophe.[39] Interesting causes for these floods are sometimes related. Rather widespread is the notion that the flood is caused by tears, often those of a disappointed suitor. This concept is found with great frequency among the Plateau tribes and on the North Pacific Coast, and even over into Siberia. Its distribution shows that this is a very definite tradition, obviously disseminated from some center, probably the North Pacific Coast. Another definite tradition, this time extending all the way from California to Nova Scotia, is about a monster who drinks up a lake and then when he is killed and his belly pierced causes the flood.

Rather general over the western half of the continent is the idea that the

---

[35] Man from rubbings of skin, A1263.3; from clay, A1241; from ears of corn, A1255.2.
[36] *Journal of American Folklore*, XXVII, 1ff.
[37] A985, A972, and A986, respectively.
[38] See p. 311, above.
[39] Deluge, *Tales*, n. 57 (A1010); Noah's flood (A1021); flood from tears, *Tales*, n. 57b (A1012); flood from tears of disappointed suitor, *Tales*, n. 70 (A1012.3*); flood from belly, *Tales*, n. 57c (A1013).

world is destroyed by a conflagration.[40] Sometimes this happens by accident, much like a forest fire; and sometimes it is the deliberate work of the Culture Hero or Trickster.

Occasionally a similar destruction of the earth or its inhabitants takes place as the result of the poor regulation of the sun. Such is the tale of The Man Who Acted as the Sun, well known on the North Pacific Coast. Like Phaethon in Greek mythology, this hero is permitted by his father the Sun to carry the sun. He almost burns up the earth and has to be rescued.[41]

No very consistent ideas concerning the renewal of the earth after the destruction by fire or flood are to be looked for in these myths. Often, as we have already noticed, there is the diving for earth, as in the original creation, and sometimes there is the foundation of a new race from a single surviving couple.[42] Even better known is the tale of The Sun Snarer.[43] A young man is angered because the sun has burnt his robe. He makes a snare (usually from his sister's pubic hair) and catches the sun. Because the sun is held back, everything is burning up and there is desperate need for the snare to be broken. Many animals try to release the sun, but only the mouse succeeds. This tale is especially interesting because of its relatively long recorded history and its definite area of distribution. It seems to have originated in the Lake Superior region, but was reported as early as the 1630's by the Jesuit Fathers among the Algonquin tribe to the east of Lake Huron.

An important part of the mythical tales of nearly every American Indian tribe has to do with the changes which must be made before the earth is fit for human habitation. It appears that there was not originally any set length for the night and day, or for the various seasons of the year. A good deal of ingenuity has been used in explaining why it is that we have the proper alternation of light and darkness. Such tales have been reported from every area except the Pacific Coast, but the details differ considerably.[44]

There is a much greater wealth of legend concerning the determination of the seasons. Sometimes this is in the form of a debate in which the winner is allowed to prescribe the length of summer and winter. Such tales are known

[40] *Tales*, n. 57d (A1030).

[41] *Tales*, n. 66 (A724.1.1). In the neighboring Plateau region there is a group of tales in which animals have a contest as to who shall act as the sun. The results are sometimes similar. In another tale known to the Shoshonean tribes Cottontail, the rabbit, makes war on the sun, shoots it and sets the world on fire. In this story Cottontail is a combination of culture hero and trickster. See Lowie, *Journal of American Folklore*, XXXVII, 142, No. 15.

[42] The latter idea may well be taken from the Bible story. For California and Basin references, see Gayton and Newman, *Yokuts and Western Mono Myths*, p. 91. Similar Biblical influence is probably to be found in the idea of a great battle at the end of the world, which we have seen in the story of Glooscap (p. 306, above).

[43] *Tales*, p. 42, No. 15, n. 65 (A728.1). This story has been very thoroughly studied by Katharine Luomala (*Oceanic, American Indian, and African Myths of Snaring the Sun* [Bernice P. Bishop Museum, Bulletin No. 168, ii, Honolulu, 1940]). She compares the American Indian tale with certain Polynesian and African analogues and concludes that they represent three separate traditions.

[44] *Tales*, n. 62 (A1172).

everywhere, but are particularly popular among the western tribes.[45] In addition to accounts of a debate as a means of determining the seasons, there are three other well-known tales. A very pretty story known on the North Pacific Coast and among neighboring Plateau tribes is that of the Marriage of the North and South. When the son and daughter of these great natural forces become man and wife, they regulate the succession of heat and cold. Among the more eastern tribes the tale of the Theft of the Seasons is popular. Usually the story is much like that of the Theft of Fire, and the thief is usually represented as a bird or animal. Most often the season which has to be brought back is summer. Though this tale is most at home in the Great Lakes region, it has been reported from the Plateau and from California. The third of these tales is very popular on the North Pacific Coast, but apparently unknown elsewhere. This is the war which the Culture Hero wages upon the south wind.[46] He always succeeds in overcoming the wind and regulating it properly. The particular wind in question depends upon the actual weather conditions of the tribe concerned, since some of them call it the east wind, some the west, etc.

In this tale the conquest of the wind is for the purpose of adjusting the length of the seasons. But frequently the wind is merely too strong, or out of control, and the purpose of the Culture Hero is to see that it is so regulated as to be beneficial to the race. Well known in the Northeastern tribes is the tale of the giant bird the flapping of whose wings causes the wind. Glooscap overcomes him and breaks his wing. This causes a great calm and only when the bird's wing is healed, though made much smaller, do the winds blow just right, neither too hard nor too lightly.[47] In California and Southern Oregon there are stories of the way in which the winds are confined in a cave and released, and also tales of conflicts between the north and south wind.[48]

Almost all over the continent are stories in which there is the establishment of the winds at the four quarters of the earth. This seems usually to be merely to afford a neat arrangement of affairs, and sometimes to be arranged for ceremonial purposes.[49] Frequently it is related, especially among the Southwestern tribes, to an elaborate color symbolism.

Summer weather was not the only good thing secured for man by means of theft. One of the important functions of many of the American Indian Culture Heroes is the stealing of light, or fire, or water, or game supply from some monster who keeps them from men. The analogy with similar stories in other parts of the world is striking, but actual borrowing seems unlikely.

[45] *Tales*, n. 60 (A1150). Theft of the seasons, *Tales*, n. 60a (A1151); marriage of the north and south, *Tales*, n. 61 (A1153).

[46] Boas, *Tsimshian Mythology*, pp. 658ff.

[47] *Tales*, n. 74 (A1125).

[48] Cave of winds (A1122); contest of winds (Modoc), J. Curtin, *Myths of the Modocs* (Boston, 1912), pp. 76ff.; bag of winds, *Tales*, n. 72 (C322.1).

[49] A1127 and A1182.

The basic concept of a conflict between a beneficent Culture Hero and opposing powers—whether they be thought of as the forces of nature or as animal or man-like ogres—is general enough to arise anywhere.

The Theft of Light[50] occurs all over America, but is most persistent as a legend on the Pacific Coast. The earth is in complete darkness, but the Culture Hero hears a rumor that a certain monster has in his possession a vessel or basket containing light. Usually in his animal form, and frequently accompanied by helpers, he goes to the monster's house and succeeds in stealing the light. On his return he releases it so that it scatters over the earth. Details of the way in which the theft is accomplished vary a good deal from place to place, but in all the stories the monster's attention is drawn away while the light is stolen. One method of accomplishing this is so extraordinary that it shows rather conclusively by its presence all over America that these tales of the Theft of Light form a real traditional unit. The Culture Hero turns himself into a stick, or otherwise transforms himself, so that he is swallowed by the ogre's daughter and reborn.[51] As the young child of the house he runs away with the light.

This same motif frequently occurs in the myths of the Theft of Fire.[52] Indeed, the two legends are usually parallel in all respects, and one of them normally appears as little more than a repetition of the other. But many tribes tell only of the theft of fire, and that motif is one of the most popular of all occurring in American Indian tales. It seems to be lacking, however, among the Iroquois and the Northeastern tribes. Any connection with the Prometheus myth seems highly unlikely, though at least two California tribes tell that the fire was carried from the monster in a reed or flute[53]—a striking parallel to the flute of Greek mythology. There are, of course, many myths of the origin, rather than the theft, of fire, but these show great variety and certainly represent no single tradition.[54]

Two other stories of thefts have a wide currency. It is said that all the water is held back by a monster, often a giant frog, and that the hero succeeds in defeating the monster and releasing the water. The distribution of this myth is very peculiar. It is found in numerous versions along the North Pacific Coast and on the North Atlantic, and has been reported occasionally from the Plateau regions close to the Pacific Coast, and from Siberia. Otherwise it does not seem to be known. A modification on the North Pacific Coast refers to the rescue of the ocean tides from the monster who controls them, so that they are now properly regulated.[55] The analogous story of the

[50] Tales, n. 42 (A1411).
[51] Tales, n. 44 (A1411.2).
[52] Tales, n. 63 (A1415).
[53] Tales, n. 64 (A1415.1).
[54] A1414. For a general discussion of this problem, see J. G. Frazer, Myths of the Origin of Fire (London, 1930).
[55] Tales, notes 76 and 76a (A1111).

Release of the Wild Animals is very popular in every area. All the game animals are kept in one place, frequently in a cave, until they are finally released and made available for mankind.[56] Sometimes the food obtained is not game animals, but rather vegetables, tobacco, nuts, or the like.

A considerable part of all creation myths is concerned with the ordering of human life after the initial act of the creation of man. The newly created human being is often thought of as imperfectly formed, with only rudimentary limbs and features. In a widespread but rather pointless California tale it is said that at first people had solid hands, like the paws of a coyote, but that the lizard decreed that they should ever after have hands like hers.[57] Far better known is the idea that original man was not properly provided with sexual organs. Many stories, most of them probably independent, account for the way in which this need was supplied, and for initiation into sexual intercourse.[58]

Did the first tribes or first families all speak the same language? American Indians, like the ancient Hebrews, generally believe that their own language was the original, and many of them have accounts, sometimes strangely similar to the Biblical story, of the way in which they came to speak their present tongues. This tale of the Confusion of Tongues[59] is especially popular in all of the western areas, but is not unknown among the Iroquois and the Northeastern tribes.

Having given man his present form and arranged for his life on earth, the Culture Hero is faced with the problem of whether there shall be any end to it. Shall his people live forever, or shall there be death? In some tales he does not even know what death is, but has to learn it in some extraordinary way. It is frequently in his form as a trickster or mischief-maker that the Culture Hero, often by the mere drawing of lots, decrees that man shall die. This general tale is popular everywhere. An interesting sequel appears all over the western half of the continent. After the Culture Hero has thus instituted death, his own child dies and he mourns in vain.[60]

In the myth patterns which we have examined, and in the separate mythical motifs as well, we have usually been able to discern definite areas of distribution for the various traditions. But we have already noted several general concepts widely distributed over the continent but differing from each other in details. It is, of course, from the small details of the action that we detect identity between two traditions. And when these are lacking we must at least entertain the possibility of completely independent origin. Such an independent growth seems to be the logical explanation for the

[56] *Tales*, n. 75 (A1421).
[57] *Tales*, n. 59 (A1311.1).
[58] *Tales*, n. 59a (A1313.3).
[59] *Tales*, n. 53 (A1333).
[60] Origin of death, *Tales*, n. 51 (A1335); originator of death first sufferer, *Tales*, n. 52 (K1681).

scores of stories explaining the form or characteristics of animals or plants and of peculiar social organizations within tribes. Some of the most interesting of the myths of such peoples as the Navaho and Zuñi concern the origin of ceremonials, but they are highly individualized, and even such tales from neighboring tribes show more differences than similarities. Equally inconclusive for the study of myth dissemination are the tales accounting for the present distribution of tribes. Tales of the Origin of Corn show much variety in the west, but a fairly unified myth with this explanation is told in the Central and Eastern Woodlands and among the Iroquois, and with some modifications in the Southeast. A long-haired maiden, the Corn Deity, appears to the hero and asks that she be slain and her body be dragged over the ground. From those places where it was dragged there springs forth the corn plant with its tassels and silks as a reminder of her flowing hair.[61]

[61] *Tales*, n. 77 (A2611.1). Longfellow makes effective use of this tale in his Hiawatha.

THE TRICKSTER CYCLE

UNDOUBTEDLY the most characteristic feature of the tales of the North American Indians is the popularity of trickster stories. We cannot speak of a definite, all-inclusive trickster tale, or even with any strictness of a trickster cycle. Nevertheless, there does exist over the western two-thirds of the continent a considerable body of widely known anecdotes told in various areas as the adventures of different tricksters. Best known of all of these is Coyote, familiar to the tribes of California, the Southwest, the Plateau, and the Plains. On the North Pacific Coast the Trickster is also the Transformer—Raven or Mink or Blue Jay. Variations on the trickster's name are frequent in the Plains, where he appears as Old Man (Blackfoot and Crow), Nihansan (Arapaho), Inktomi (Siouan tribes), or Sitkonski (Assiniboin). In the Central Woodlands the adventures are usually ascribed to Manabozho or Wiskedjak (sometimes written Whiskey Jack).

Coyote, the North Pacific Coast Transformers, Old Man, and Manabozho all appear in other tales as the serious Culture Hero, and in some cases the Creator himself. This double concept seems characteristic of this whole Western area. In the eastern part of the country there are incidents similar to those in the trickster tales of the west, but there is little tendency to bring into the serious activities of such a character as Glooscap any element of buffoonery.

The adventures of the Trickster, even when considered by themselves, are inconsistent. Part are the result of his stupidity, and about an equal number show him overcoming his enemies through cleverness. Such a trickster as Coyote, therefore, may appear in any one of three roles: the beneficent Culture Hero, the clever deceiver, or the numskull. As we look at these incidents, we find that this mixture of concept is continually present, so that any series of adventures is likely to be a succession of clever tricks and foolish mishaps.

1. CENTRAL WOODLAND

THE group of trickster tales maintaining the clearest order and most logical relationship to each other is that told in the Central Woodland area about the Culture Hero Manabozho. The more serious tales of this hero seem to be confined to very special occasions, so that normally when one asks for Manabozho tales, he hears only anecdotes illustrative of the hero's foolishness or cleverness.[1]

Perhaps most popular of all are his adventures with the ducks. One of these stories tells about how he dives under the ducks and ties their legs together. They all rise at once and carry him high in the air until the string finally breaks and he falls headlong. In another encounter with the ducks he is much more successful. He goes singing and attracts the ducks about him. He persuades them to join him in a dance. He is to drum and they are to sing as loud as they can while they dance about and keep their eyes closed. One after another, he kills the ducks, until finally one of them discovers the trick. It is sometimes said that the bird who betrays Manabozho is later punished. This, for example, is the reason why the helldiver is red-eyed and tailless to this day. Having killed his ducks, he takes them out to a sandbar and buries them, some with their heads out, and some with their feet sticking out. He builds a fire and, being tired, stretches himself on the ground with his back to the fire to go to sleep. He speaks to his buttocks and says, "You watch the birds and awaken me if anyone comes near them." While he is asleep some people come along and pull all of his ducks out of the sand, but carefully replace the heads and feet, so that when he awakes he finds that he has been robbed. He complains bitterly to the bodily member which he has assigned as his watchman. Some tales say that he burned or scratched his flesh so much in this adventure that we still see the injured flesh as gum on trees.

It is on another occasion that his absurd sympathies bring about the loss of his feast. When he hears two trees scraping together in the wind, he feels sorry for them, or at least dislikes the noise, and climbs the trees to see if he can help. He gets caught between the limbs, and has to watch intruders eat up his feast. At last he frees himself, but there is nothing left to eat. He does find a buffalo skull, and he turns himself into an ant so as to enter the skull and feast on the brains. His ant's meal finished, he turns himself into a man, but he finds that his head is inside the skull and he cannot see. He wanders about blindly and feels his way. When he comes to trees, he asks them who they are and they always answer him. Thus he always knows about where he is. He eventually comes to a lake

[1] *Tales*, n. 79; Thompson, *Publications of the Modern Language Association of America*, XXXVII, 130ff.

and swims across, breaking the skull when he lands violently on a rock. On one occasion Manabozho persuades the buzzard to take him for a ride through the air. In spite of all of his efforts to hold on, the buzzard is able to shake him loose, so that he falls from a great height. When he recovers from his shock he notices the buzzard above gloating over the trick he has played. He turns himself into a dead deer and deceives the buzzard, who comes to eat and sinks his head far into the carcass. Some say that the buzzard was killed and some that he was merely punished by having a featherless head and by being made to eat stinking food.[2]

These are about all the motifs that assume a definite order in the trickster tales. Many of these are very widespread and occur frequently outside this particular cycle. The dancing ducks, for example, appear all over the country except on the Pacific coast and are most popular of all in the Plains. The loss of his feast while he is asleep and the use of some bodily member as a magic watchman are almost inevitable sequels to the hood-winked dancers. The explanation of the gum on trees appears frequently both in the Great Lakes region and in the Plains. The creaking limbs, the adventure with the buffalo skull, and the help of trees likewise have a large distribution throughout the whole Central Woodland, Plains, and Plateau areas. The carrying of the trickster either by a great bird or by a number of birds is known over the whole continent, but is most popular in the Plains. The idea of transforming himself in order to catch an enemy belongs not only to this cycle, but to several others. In the Central Woodland the most popular form of transformation is to a tree.

2. PLAINS

IT WILL easily be seen that there is no sharp line of demarcation between the trickster tales of the Great Lakes region and of the Plains, and that many of these incidents appear also in the Plateau and the Southwest. Of those which appear to have their greatest popularity in the Plains, a number illustrate the cleverness of the Trickster either in the cheating or the destruction of his enemies or the killing of game. One well-known tale combines cleverness with wanton cruelty. The Trickster (usually thought of in his animal form) is left at home as a guardian of their children by other animals. In the absence of their mothers, he kills the children and cooks them, and when the mothers return, they eat their own children without

[2] Hoodwinked dancers, Tales, n. 82 (K826); sleeping trickster's feast stolen, Tales, n. 84 (J2173.1); buttocks watcher, Tales, n. 83 (D1610.6.3); trickster's burnt or scratched flesh becomes gum on trees, Tales, n. 109-1 (A2731.1); creaking limbs, Tales, n. 85 (J1872); trickster puts on buffalo skull, Tales, n. 86 (J2131.5.1); blinded trickster directed by trees, Tales, n. 86a (D1313.4); transformation to kill enemies, Tales, n. 26 (D651.1); trickster carried by bird and dropped, Tales, n. 80 (K1041).

realizing it. A good part of the story is usually concerned with the tricks used by the rascal to effect his escape.[3]

Three incidents relating to the capture of game are extraordinarily popular in the Plains, but also well known elsewhere. The tricking of birds into a bag is a motif shared with eastern tribes; the enticing of animals over a precipice, with all the western areas; and the feigning of death in order to catch game, with peoples of every area. The latter motif is so general that it need not indicate borrowing.[4] Much less well known, and confined entirely to the Plains and Central Woodland, are the stories of how the trickster, out of pure mischief, pollutes the nest and the young birds while the old bird is away; and of how he tells lies to the various fishes and causes them to fight each other.[5]

The trickster is sometimes a mere swindler, as when he uses his power of transformation to help him in begging. He repeatedly asks for food, each time in a different guise. With some variation this incident is known both on the Plains and in California. Two tales tell how he wins races by foul means. In one of them, confined apparently to the Plains and the Southwest, he feigns lameness and thus receives a handicap in the race. He then returns and eats up the food which has been put aside as the prize. In the other tale, popular everywhere from the Great Lakes westward, he stations his relatives along the race course and they keep substituting for him without detection. The latter tale is, of course, almost worldwide, and it may be a borrowing from the Europeans or the Negroes.[6]

One of the most popular trickster tales in the Plains and in all the neighboring areas, is Big Turtle's War Party.[7] The adventures in this tale are always ascribed to the turtle, although he is not ordinarily considered as a trickster. As the turtle starts out on his war party he asks various swift animals and birds whether they can run and keep up with him on the war party. Neither the coyote nor the fox nor the hawk nor the rabbit are swift enough for him. But the flint knife, the hairbrush, and the awl, in spite of their inability to run, are chosen to go with him. He sends these companions one by one into the enemy's camp. The knife cuts the man's fingers and is thrown away. When he comes back and reports his misfortunes, the brush is sent. It pulls a girl's hair, and later the awl pricks a woman's finger. His companions having failed, the turtle himself goes into the camp. The people capture him and decide to punish him. As they pro-

[3] *Tales*, n. 97 (K931). This does not seem to be connected with the analogous European tale.

[4] Birds enticed into bag, *Tales*, n. 82a (K711.0.1); animals enticed over precipice, *Tales*, n. 91 (K894.1); game caught by feigned death, *Tales*, n. 88 (K751).

[5] *Tales*, n. 109a (K932) and n. 109j (K1084.1).

[6] Protean beggar, *Tales*, n. 117d (D611); trickster's race: feigned lameness, *Tales*, n. 90 (K11.5); trickster's race: relative helpers (K11.1), see Boas, *Kutenai Tales* (Bulletin of the Bureau of American Ethnology, LIX), 307. He cites fifteen versions.

[7] *Tales*, p. 75, No. 38, n. 108 (F1025.2).

pose various punishments, he always seems to be willing to undergo them but begs them not to throw him into the water. He thus cheats them into sending him back to his real home.

The first part of this tale has some interesting affinities with a European story, The Bean, the Straw, and the Coal,[8] but the present tale is so well known over the whole of the continent and has such characteristic details that borrowing is unlikely. The second part, the drowning punishment for the turtle,[9] is told over a good part of the world, usually without specific connection with the present tale.

Many are the amorous adventures ascribed to the American Indian trickster. Most of these are rather widely distributed, and it is not always easy to tell where the center of dissemination for each motif is to be found. All over the Plains, for example, is heard the story of The False Bridegroom, the Trickster who poses as a man of great magic powers and boasts particularly of his ability to produce treasure.[10] Under this pretense, he marries various girls, but he is unmasked at a dance where the girls learn that he is an impostor. With slight variations this tale appears over the whole continent except on the northeast and northwest coasts. Even more widespread and popular is the tale of the Lecherous Father. The Trickster seduces his own daughter when he feigns death and returns in disguise.[11] This story has been subjected to excellent analytical study by Miss Henrietta Schmerler who finds it most at home in the western part of the Plains area. Aside from these two well constructed tales, there occur among many western tribes frequent anecdotes of transformations effected by the trickster in order to seduce women.[12]

The Plains Indians are also fond of telling about the foolish or stupid adventures of their Trickster. Very popular is the tale of The Offended Rolling Stone,[13] a story also current on the Plateau and in the Southwest, and with analogues elsewhere. Like the European fool who gives food to the cabbages, this Indian dupe leaves his blanket with a great stone to keep it warm. Repenting later, he goes back and gets his blanket. The stone is offended and chases him. It is only through the aid of various kindly animals that he is able to destroy the stone and escape. Even more popular in the whole west, and known in Siberia, on the Atlantic Coast, and even in South America, is the foolish tale of the Eye-Juggler. This Trickster has

---

[8] See Motif F1025.1, p. 223, above.

[9] Motif K581.1, pp. 223, 225, above.

[10] Jewels from spittle, Tales, n. 190 (D1454.3).

[11] There is also a rather popular Plains and California tale of a son-in-law who tricks his mother-in-law into sleeping with him, usually when they are camping together on a trip, Tales, n. 109s (T417).

[12] False Bridegroom, Tales, p. 124, No. 49, n. 189 (K1915); Lecherous father, Tales, n. 109p (T411.1.2, cf. K1325), see Schmerler, Journal of American Folklore, XLIV, 196ff.; transformation to seduce women, Tales, n. 109v (D658).

[13] Tales, p. 64, No. 30, n. 96 (C91.1).

been given the power of throwing his eyes into the air and replacing them successfully. But he must not do this beyond a specified number of times. He pays no attention to the restriction, and loses his eyes. Most tribes tell how he finally secures the eyes of some animal as a substitute for those which he has lost. Very similar, and with much the same distribution, is the story of the Sharpened Leg. He is given power of sharpening his leg and sticking it into trees, but he must do this no more than four times. Because of his disobedience, he is left with his leg sticking in a tree. The stories do not usually provide for his rescue.[14]

Of other Plains tales of the trickster's foolishness, the best known in the rest of the country is that telling how he dives for reflected food. A few of these may be borrowings from the Aesop fable, but certainly most of the versions are native. Common to the Plains and the Central and Northeast Woodland tribes is the tale of how the dupe eats scratchberries, or other fruit which causes unbearable itching. Or they may tell of how he overeats on medicines that physic him. Two anecdotes about equally popular in the Plains and Lake areas relate how he steals a magic robe, or a pair of moccasins, which always immediately return to the owner, and how he joins the waving bulrushes in a dance, and dances with them until he falls from exhaustion.[15]

3. PLATEAU

As FAR as tales of a trickster are concerned, the tribes of the Plateau area do not show any great differentiation from the Plains peoples to the east and south and from their neighbors on the North Pacific coast. Most of the trickster incidents known in the areas adjacent to them appear also, at least occasionally, in Plateau tales. In respect to the distribution of trickster incidents, therefore, the Plateau tribes are essentially transitional. As they approach surrounding areas, their trickster tales imperceptibly yield to outside influences.

Coyote is the trickster throughout the whole area. Among the tribes of British Columbia he becomes identified with the Transformer, and his adventures are often identical with those of Raven or Mink or Blue Jay of their coast neighbors. Several trickster incidents are perhaps better known among these tribes than elsewhere. A favorite motif is the transformation of Coyote into a dish so that he may receive the food which people place on it. This incident is heard elsewhere, but only rarely. Likewise chiefly popular in the Plateau, though several times reported from the Pueblo area and

---

[14] Eye-juggler, *Tales*, n. 92 (J2423); sharpened leg, *Tales*, n. 95 (J2424). For some other tales of using a magic power too often, see *Tales*, n. 93 (C762.1).

[15] Diving for reflected food, *Tales*, n. 81 (J1791.3); eating scratchberries, *Tales*, n. 109k (J2134.1); eating medicines, *Tales*, n. 109h (J2134.2); self-returning robe, *Tales*, n. 109i (D1602.3); dancing bulrushes, *Tales*, n. 109dd (J1883).

from Siberia, is the contest between Coyote and the cannibal. In a series of adventures Coyote bluffs him into believing that it is he rather than the cannibal himself who eats human flesh.[16]

The interest in Coyote in these two tales, as well as in many others common to neighboring peoples, lies in his cleverness as a cheater. The Plateau tribes are also fond of him as a buffoon. They share with the California area the anecdote in which the overcurious Trickster borrows a rattle from the fox and wears it. This causes him to be caught in the brush and almost killed. In a story known also in the Mackenzie area and Siberia the Trickster succeeds in killing a good supply of birds only to have them revive and fly away as he is about to pick them up.[17]

In the well organized and popular story of Coyote and Porcupine the trickster appears only in the second episode, and then in an ambiguous position. He is both cheater and dupe. This tale, related almost everywhere throughout the Plains and Plateau and at least occasionally in California and the Southwest, relates first of all how the tricky porcupine persuades buffalo to carry him across a river, but on the way he climbs into buffalo's paunch and kills him. As porcupine is rejoicing over his prize, Coyote arrives and challenges porcupine to a jumping game. Coyote cheats and wins the game, so that porcupine is left without his feast and very angry. Porcupine now visits Coyote's home and kills his children. He sets their bodies up so that when Coyote comes home he knocks them over and realizes that Porcupine has had the last word.[18]

4. NORTH PACIFIC COAST

ON THE North Pacific coast the trickster tales are usually associated with the Culture Hero, though this is not universally true. These peoples relate a good many of the anecdotes we have already encountered from the Central Woodlands westward. They seem to be particularly concerned with incidents illustrative of the Trickster's gluttony and lust.

A tale of rather unusual distribution is that of The Deceived Blind Men. It is very popular on the North Pacific Coast, and in the Plateau and Central Woodland areas, but occurs only sporadically in the Plains, in California, and among the Iroquois. The Trickster finds that two blind men (or women) live together and cooperate in keeping house. They have lines leading to the water. The trickster covets their food supply. He changes the lines so that the partner who is sent for water finds himself in the bushes. The other partner tries it, and this time the lines are back and he

---

[16] Trickster becomes a dish, *Tales*, p. 68, No. 33, notes 100 and 117c (D251, D657); Coyote proves himself a cannibal, *Tales*, p. 70, No. 34, n. 102 (K1721).

[17] Coyote wears fox's rattle, *Tales*, n. 109bb (J2136.1); killed game revives, *Tales*, n. 109e (E161).

[18] *Tales*, notes 104, 105 (K952.1, K17, K2152).

finds water. This brings about a quarrel, and meantime the Trickster steals the provisions. The resemblance of this tale to the Greek myth of the Phorcidae is striking, but the two tales are certainly independent.[19]

Most of the anecdotes of the Trickster's gluttony are much simpler, but even these simple incidents are known not only on the coast, but also both in the Plateau area and in Siberia. In some stories the Trickster shams death so that he may eat the grave offerings. Sometimes he poses as a helper for women and eats all their provisions. And sometimes, in one way or another, he frightens people from their food and eats it himself.[20]

Of the amorous adventures of the Trickster, three are of very frequent occurrence with the coast tribes.[21] Often here and on the Plateau, and occasionally in California and Siberia, the trickster poses as a doctor in order to seduce women. One particular form of this motif involves incest, like the story of the lecherous father already discussed. In this story a brother, lusting after his sister, brings it about that she burns her groins. He suggests a remedy, usually that she sit upon a certain plant. This tale has been borrowed by the Plateau and Mackenzie tribes. Both of these stories just mentioned are thoroughly realistic, but the most characteristic of all the tales of the lecherous Trickster, and popular from the Great Lakes westward, is fantastic in the extreme. He attempts magically to have intercourse with a woman on the opposite side of a stream. In many versions this gets him into great trouble, since a fish bites off his member and reduces it to normal size.[22]

Aside from these two main motives for the action of the trickster, there appear some, on the North Pacific Coast, as elsewhere, designed to illustrate his cleverness but not for these specific ends. For instance, in a tale popular here, but also current in all parts of the continent, the trickster passes himself off as a woman and marries a man. The whole purpose of this trick is to embarrass the dupe. Much more definitely characteristic of the North Pacific Coast, and probably all originating there, are tales of how the hero kills a monster by throwing hot stones into his throat; of how he transforms himself into a fish so that he may steal a valuable harpoon or fishhook; and of how he makes an artificial whale as a stratagem. In the latter case, the image of the whale comes to life and affords its maker protection.[23]

On the whole, the trickster tales of the North Pacific Coast tend to emphasize his cleverness, rather than his stupidity. Nevertheless, some of

[19] *Tales*, n. 89 (K333).

[20] *Tales*, notes 109d, 109c, 109b (K1867, K1983, K335).

[21] Usually told of a woman rather than the male trickster is the story of feigning death in order to meet the paramour in the grave-box, *Tales*, n. 109t (K1538). It is found both in the North Pacific and Plateau areas.

[22] *Tales*, notes 109r, 109q, 109u (K1315.2, K1315.2.1, K1391).

[23] Trickster poses as woman and marries man. *Tales*, n. 109n (K1321.3); monster killed by throwing hot stones into throat, *Tales*, n. 167 (K951.1); stolen harpoon, *Tales*, n. 109x (D657); artificial whale, *Tales*, n. 287j (K922).

the stories of buffoonery current among the Central Woodland and Plains tribes are occasionally repeated here, and several such motifs common to the whole western half of the continent are particularly popular. For some reason, stories about the trickster's diving for reflections in the water—the image of his enemy, or of a woman—or of his shooting at a reflection, though also widely known elsewhere, are favorites in this area. Of course, there are some tales of the Trickster's misfortunes which seem to be purely local, or at most to be known in a few adjacent tribes. An example is the anecdote about how he tries to steal bait from fishhooks and is caught and injured.[24]

Perhaps best known of all tales of the Trickster's foolish actions is that generally known as The Bungling Host. Though perhaps more versions appear on the North Pacific Coast than elsewhere, the tale is current in one form or another in every culture area on the continent except the Eskimo, and is even known in Siberia. The trickster visits various animals, each of whom displays his peculiar powers (often magical) of securing food. The trickster returns the invitation and tries to produce food in the same way. He always fails, and usually has a very narrow escape from death. The details as to how his hosts produce the food show a good deal of variety. Sometimes the host lets oil drop out of his hands, or birds produce food by their song, or salmon eggs by striking their ankles, or an animal cuts off its own hands or feet and serves them for dinner. Sometimes the animals stab or shoot themselves, or they transform wood into meat, or they kill their own children, and later revive them. The details of this story are so specific that a good comparative study of it is valuable for an understanding of tale dissemination over the continent.[25]

Usually associated with the Trickster cycle is the story of how Beaver and Porcupine trick each other.[26] Implicit in the story is the idea that Porcupine has magic control over the cold.[27] Beaver carries Porcupine to the center of the lake and leaves him there where he cannot swim home. Porcupine causes the lake to freeze and escapes on the ice. Later he retaliates by taking Beaver to the top of a tree and leaving him there. Though best known on the Pacific Coast, this story is told throughout the west.

Finally, there should be mentioned a few motifs hardly constituting independent anecdotes. There are frequent stories, both in this area and elsewhere, of the captive who tricks his captor into giving him a long

---

[24] Diving for reflected enemy, *Tales*, n. 270a (J1791.5); diving for reflected woman, *Tales*, n. 270b (J1791.6); shooting at enemy's reflection in water, *Tales*, n. 270c (J1791.5.1); trickster caught on fishhook, *Tales*, n. 109y (J2136.2), with an analogue both in Mackenzie area and in Siberia.

[25] *Tales*, n. 103 (J2425). For detailed study, see Boas, *Tsimshian Mythology*, pp. 694ff. For other tales of death through foolish imitation, see *Tales*, n. 271b (J2401).

[26] Beaver and Porcupine, *Tales*, p. 75, No. 37, n. 106 (K896.1).

[27] *Tales*, n. 107 (D2144.1.1).

respite, so that he is able to escape. This incident may occur almost anywhere. Much more characteristic of American Indian tales is a story rather widely distributed of how a man eats himself up or gradually dismembers himself until there is nothing left.[28]

A careful analysis of all trickster tales would find many examples of magic. Particularly frequent as a means of extricating the trickster from a difficult position is the motif of the talking excrements. The Trickster is given magic advice by his excrements or private parts. A similar European motif where the talking magic objects delay the pursuer is probably not related to this.[29]

Trickster tales exist all over America and not only in the four areas just discussed. But these seem to be the principal centers of interest in such stories and most incidents of this kind are found somewhere in these areas. Some additions would, of course, result from a detailed treatment of others, particularly of California and the Southwest.

[28] *Tales*, notes 109m, 109cc (F1035, K550).
[29] *Tales*, notes 83c, 83a, 83b (D1312.1.1, D1610.6, D1610.6.2).

TEST AND HERO TALES

IV

OVER practically the whole continent a considerable portion of the tales of the North American Indians are concerned with the exploits of heroes who overcome seemingly invincible adversaries. Frequently, as in familiar European tales, the hero is deliberately sent out with the idea of having him killed, though sometimes the principal motive seems to be merely to subject him to a series of very difficult tests.

There are a relatively few general patterns for these tales. As one moves from one culture area to the next, the nature of the person assigning the tests changes, as does the reason for the assignment and the nature of the hero himself. And in certain areas there is actually no test, but the hero undertakes to overcome monsters and other adversaries of his own volition. But while there is a rather clear-cut difference in the various frameworks in which these adventures appear, the individual motifs belonging to tales of this kind do not confine themselves strictly to these basic plots. They move rather freely from one to another, and many of them occur over a good part of the continent. It will be convenient, therefore, to consider a series of these hero and test tales, and in that way acquaint ourselves with the principal motifs. It will then be possible to give some consideration to the widespread use of some of these incidents and perhaps to arrive at a succinct statement about the areas of distribution both of the larger patterns and of the detailed adventures.

1. NORTH PACIFIC COAST

SOME of the most interesting tales involving the test theme are found on the North Pacific Coast. Typical of a story current over the whole area is the Bella Coola tale, The Sun Tests his Son-in-law.[1] As in practically all North Pacific

[1] *Tales*, p. 78, No. 39, n. 111 (H310).

tales of this kind, the story begins with describing the supernatural birth of the hero. In this case a child is found inside a salmon. He is adopted, but on one occasion a tabu is broken and he dies. His body is placed in the river, and there he is resuscitated by the salmon and taken to their country. He eventually returns to the home of his adopted human mother, but he is caught in his salmon form and eaten. He returns to life, however, when his bones and intestines are thrown in the river.

Our twice-resuscitated hero ascends into the upper world on a pile of eagles' down. At the house of the sun an old woman gives him a bladder containing a cold wind, and by the use of this he is able to save himself from the excessive heat of the sun's presence. He is imprisoned in an underground house and a fire is built around him. But the cold wind again saves him, and the sun's daughters find him alive. The sun realizes that he is a suitor for his daughters and determines to kill him. The sun now sends his four daughters off to the mountainside in the form of mountain goats, and then he sends the young man out to hunt them. He exchanges arrows with the hero so that when the young man shoots he finds that he has only arrows made with blunt points of coal. He fails to kill the mountain goats, and they rush upon him and push him down the steep mountain. But when he has fallen about half way, he transforms himself into a ball of birds' down. He makes his way back to the house of the sun, gets his own arrows, and kills the goats. He cuts off their feet and takes them back to the sun to prove his success. When he learns that he has killed the sun's daughters, he repents, reassembles their members, and throws the bodies into the river, so that they are restored to life. The sun now agrees that the youth is to marry two of his daughters, but he continues to subject him to dangerous tests. He first takes the youth to raise the trap of his salmon weir, but really throws him into the water and tries to drown him. The boy merely turns himself into a salmon and escapes. The next day the sun proposes that they split wood. As they are traveling in a canoe, the sun drops his hammer and commands it to fall sideways. He then requests his son-in-law to dive for it. As soon as the boy has dived, the sun causes the sea to freeze over. The boy, nevertheless, turns himself into a fish and finds a crack from which he escapes. He returns with the hammer and warns the sun to stop persecuting him. The sun now asks for a certain bird. The boy gets the bird, but tells the bird about his troubles with the sun. The next morning the sun finds that the bird has blinded him and is afraid to start on his daily course. The youth heals the blinded sun with magic water, and he and his father-in-law are reconciled. Eventually the hero and his wife return to the lower world on a ball of eagles' down.

This common North Pacific pattern exemplifies many separate motifs. In the preliminary part of the tale there is a story of a door which tries to bite everybody who enters. By skillfully jumping through, the hero escapes this snapping door. Several times in the tale occurs the motif of resuscitation by assembling the members of the body, and sometimes by throwing them in the water. Also in the earlier part of the narrative we learn of the supernatural growth of the hero and also of his adventures with the dangerous woman who kills all her husbands by means of her toothed vagina. Repeatedly we have the transformation to reach a difficult place, and here we have a good example of a heat test in which burning is magically evaded. Parallel tales from the North Pacific tell of attempts to kill the hero by smoke, by burning food, or by the swallowing of red-hot stones. The substituted arrows, the pushing of the hero over the precipice, the sun father-in-law—all are common throughout the North Pacific. The hero is sent at the end for the dangerous bird. Many other tales tell of searches for other ferocious animals, and it is not uncommon for these captured animals to avenge themselves on the man who has sent the hero to capture them.[2]

The test stories on the Northwest Coast are very widespread and popular. In his comparative study of this group of tales,[3] Boas deals with forty-five versions which had been recorded from the coast tribes. Many of the incidents are used in these tales without much regard to the general framework of the whole story. This framework may be that which we have just outlined and may concern the tests imposed by a supernatural father-in-law: thirty of Boas's versions are of this kind.

In another rather popular introduction to the test episodes it is a jealous uncle who tries to make away with his nephew.[4] A typical version is that of the Kodiak Islanders. An unnatural uncle always kills his nephews shortly after their birth. On the advice of the uncle's wife, the mother of the boy conceals the sex of her newly-born child and thus deceives the uncle. The hero is brought up as a girl. When he is grown, the uncle discovers the deception and demands that the boy be sent to him. Before going, the boy takes along with him three objects which have been playthings of his brothers. These are a knife, some eagle down, and a sour cranberry. The uncle takes the boy into the forest to get wood. He arranges it so that the boy is caught in the cleft of a tree when he is sent in to bring out a wedge. By means of the magic cranberry the boy opens the cleft and escapes. The second time he is taken out by his uncle they hunt ducks and eggs, but really the uncle pushes him over a precipice. By using the eagle down, the boy floats easily through the air to the ground below. The next time, the boy is sent to capture a giant clam. He is swallowed by the clam, but, by using his knife, he cuts the clam from within and escapes. He is next put into a box and set adrift on the ocean. The box finally floats ashore, where he is rescued by the chief's

[2] A resumé of these motifs will be made at the end of our discussion of the various patterns of hero tales. Those just mentioned are covered by *Tales*, notes 112 to 126, inclusive.
[3] *Tsimshian Mythology*, pp. 794ff.
[4] *Tales*, n. 127. Somewhat similar test stories of jealous uncles trying to destroy their nephews are found among the Eskimo, the Iroquois, and in one instance among the Biloxi of Mississippi.

daughters. He finds he is in the Eagle country, and he marries the Eagle chief's elder daughter. The boy now has the power to turn himself at will into an eagle. All he needs to do is to put on an eagle skin and feathers.

He now plans revenge on his uncle. He brings a large whale and leaves it on the beach near his home. His uncle claims the whale and refuses to let his parents have their share. The youth as eagle swoops low and, after three warnings, takes the uncle in his talons and flies off with him. He tells the uncle who he is and why he is taking revenge. He then lets him fall from a great height into the sea.

Not all these details occur in other stories of cruel uncles, since the incidents in this cycle and in that of the tests given by the sun father-in-law exchange with a good deal of freedom. This tale has, however, introduced the following motifs characteristic of test stories: boy passes as girl to avoid decree of death on males; wedge test; clam test; and abandonment in boat.[5]

Among the tribes of the lower Columbia river and of the Washington coast there occurs a test story differing essentially from all others on the continent. Elsewhere the dangerous adventures are imposed at the instance of someone who wishes to get rid of the hero, or else they are voluntarily undertaken by a hero who wishes to overcome monsters threatening the life or happiness of his people. In this Northwest Coast tale, however, the hero and his companions merely go on adventures—much like medieval knights—and as soon as they have escaped from one peril, deliberately seek another. Typical is the version from the Quinault.[6] Blue Jay and four companions mistreat Grouse, so that he plans to take revenge on them. Grouse makes an artificial seal, and when Blue Jay and his companions harpoon it, the seal carries them far out over the ocean. They eventually get loose, and after a long time and the loss of one of their number, they reach the shore, but find themselves in a strange village. Here they are challenged to a contest in climbing a smooth pole. Blue Jay wins this contest, and they go on to another village, where they are challenged to a diving match. Blue Jay wins this match by trickery, coming up for breath under some brush without being discovered. At the next village they are challenged to go into a sweathouse to see who can stand the most heat. Two of Blue Jay's companions make a tunnel so that they can reach water and refresh themselves while their rival contestants are baking in the sweathouse. At the next village they are challenged to sit up for five days and nights without sleeping. In this contest all their opponents drop off to sleep the fourth day. The companions leave pieces of old wood with phosphorescent spots on them, so that people will think these are their eyes shining. When their hosts see that they have been deceived, they pursue in canoes. The companions use their magic powers and create a storm and fog so that they are able to reach home.

⁵ *Tales*, notes 128 to 131.
⁶ *Tales*, p. 93, No. 41, n. 133

In addition to the climbing, diving, and waking contests of this Quinault tale,[7] several other contests appear in parallel stories of neighboring tribes: shooting, whaling, and gambling matches, as well as escapes from ferocious animals which guard doors and from attempts at murder by poisonous food, smoke, and a snapping door.

2. CENTRAL WOODLAND

THE testing of sons-in-law is by no means confined to the west coast, but such tales are present in practically every area. A good example of such a story from the Central Woodlands may be cited from the Timagami Ojibwa of western Ontario.[8] The father-in-law is represented as the regular trickster, Wemicus. He has always succeeded in killing off his sons-in-law. The hero is warned by his wife that her father will try to kill him. They go hunting together, and the old man attempts to burn the youth's moccasins while he sleeps. The hero sees this, and succeeds in exchanging them, so that it is the father-in-law who finds himself barefooted. Shortly afterwards the old man takes the youth tobogganing on the snow. He has arranged so that the boy will land in the midst of some poisonous snakes. The young man's wife has given him some magic tobacco, and this protects him from the snakes. His wife now warns him that her father has poisonous lizards in his hair instead of lice. When the old man asks the boy to pick the lice from his head, he takes some cranberries and cracks them instead. He has no sooner escaped from this peril than he is compelled by the old man to go with him to a rocky island for gulls' eggs. The young man is abandoned on the island, but he succeeds in killing the ferocious gulls, and he is able by putting on the gulls' wings to fly back home across the lake. The old man now tells the youth to go with him to cut down a tree. He tries by magic to have the tree fall on the boy, but, as usual, the young man turns the trick, and the tree falls on the father-in-law. But the old man is a manitou and, of course, is not killed. The last episode of the tale concerns a challenge to a boat race. The old man puts a large sail on his boat, but the youth professes to be afraid to do so on his. He encourages the old man to put on too much sail, so that the boat is overturned. When the youth comes up to the capsized boat, he sees a huge pike, and realizes that his father-in-law has been transformed. This, concludes the tale, is the origin of the pike.

Several of the motifs in this father-in-law story are very widespread: the help from the ogre's child or wife and the deception by the lousing of an ogre. Others are largely confined to this particular area, especially the burning of the ogre's moccasins, the toboggan test, and the marooned egg-gatherer.[9]

[7] *Tales*, notes 134 to 137. For a much more complete account of all these motifs in North Pacific tales, see the tabulations in Boas, *Tsimshian Mythology*, pp. 814-16.
[8] *Tales*, p. 113, No. 46, n. 170.
[9] For these motifs, see *Tales*, notes 171 to 175.

In the Central Woodland area these motifs do not always concern a malevolent father-in-law. Some of them occur in the tale of The Jealous Father.[10] A man with two wives has a son by the elder. He suspects the son of intimacy with his younger wife,[11] and determines to get rid of him. As in the tale we have just noticed, the father takes him to an island to hunt eggs. When he is abandoned on the island the boy is approached by a walrus who agrees to take him to the mainland. The walrus asks the boy if the sky is clear. The boy lies and says that it is, though the clouds are thick. The walrus tells him that he cannot stand thunder and that if it should thunder, he would have to go down under the water. The boy keeps deceiving the walrus until he arrives at shallow water, where the walrus is killed by a thunderbolt.[12] The walrus has been magically provided by the boy's mother, and the magic storm raised by the father. Throughout the tale there is a contest in magic between the two parents. The boy's helpers are always provided by the mother and their opponents by the father. The boy is advised by a friendly old woman. But the next old women he sees have sharp dagger-like elbows. When they try to kill him, however, he tricks them into killing each other. He next has to pass a place guarded by ferocious dogs. On the advice of the old woman, he digs a tunnel and thus escapes. At the end of the tale the youth and the old man have a contest in magic in which the boy sets the surrounding country on fire and burns up his father. By magic, he and his mother escape and fly away together as birds.[13]

3. IROQUOIS

As WE move from the Great Lakes area to the Iroquois tribes of New York State, we find that the test theme is still an important part of the folklore. Many of the incidents found elsewhere appear here. As far as general pattern is concerned, the scheme is usually very simple, and permits a great variety of detailed treatment. In one group of stories we have a close parallel to the North Pacific tale of the jealous uncle.[14] In another, the tests are assigned by the hero's mother-in-law, who dreams (or feigns to dream) the various perilous missions she sends him on.[15] In these Iroquois tales, in spite of their

[10] *Tales*, n. 177 (S11). This Cree story has very few exact parallels, but the general situation of a jealous father subjecting the son to perils occurs rather widely. For a special Plateau and North Pacific handling of the situation, see the tale of The Arrow Chain, p. 349, below.

[11] This is probably the Potiphar's wife motif in which the woman falsely accuses the young man. See *Tales*, n. 178 (K2111). The motif is popular in the Plains and among the Central Woodland, but is also found in all parts of the continent.

[12] This motif, usually known as the Whale-boat, is found throughout all the northern areas from Nova Scotia to Siberia. It is particularly popular in the northeast, and occurs in many connections. There are also European analogues. See *Tales*, n. 179 (R245).

[13] For motifs in this story, see *Tales*, notes 178 to 182. The old woman adviser and the sharp-elbowed women are widespread tale elements.

[14] See p. 329, above. For Iroquois versions, see *Tales*, n. 127.

[15] Tales, n. 191g. These four Seneca versions are largely repetitions of one another.

length, there are usually a very few tests related in great detail and with tedious iteration.

4. CALIFORNIA

IN A tale seemingly confined to California, and well exemplified among the Hupa,[16] a girl is forbidden by her grandmother to dig any kind of roots that have two stocks. The girl disobeys and digs up such a root, which changes into a child who calls her "mother." She refuses to acknowledge him, and the boy is brought up by the girl's grandmother. When he grows up, the young man sees his mother coming back bringing acorns. She has said to herself, "If he will bring acorns from the place I bring them, and if he will kill a white deer, I will call him my son." The young man goes to the tree for acorns and climbs it, and the tree grows with him to the sky. In the upper world he has adventures with three girls, and he also kills a deer and brings it and the acorns he has gathered to his mother. She acknowledges him as her son. The grandmother now equips him with a bow and arrow, a shinny stick, and some sweathouse wood, and he goes on his adventures. He arrives at the home of the immortals at the edge of the world toward the east. Here he undergoes various tests. He must secure enough sweathouse wood to care for ten sweathouses. By magically increasing that which the grandmother has given him, he is able to do this. He also engages in a shinny match which he wins on account of the shinny stick which he has concealed. His winning of the various games of shinny is given as an explanation for the shape of certain animals' faces. After winning a shooting match with his miraculous bow, he goes back home to his mother and grandmother. As many nights as it seemed to him that he had been away, so many years had he actually been absent.[17]

Except for the peculiar type of supernatural birth and the incident concerning the sweathouse, all parts of this California tale are found elsewhere. Even the birth of the boy from the plant dug from the ground has at least some interesting parallels in the tales of the Plains where we have children born from blood-clots or from splinters which have been stuck in a man's foot.[18]

5. PLAINS

ONE of the most popular tales of the Plains area is that of Blood-Clot-Boy.[19] A young man abuses his father-in-law and makes life miserable for him. He refuses to let him have any meat from the buffalo which they kill. One day

---

[16] *Tales*, p. 97, No. 42, n. 139.

[17] The idea that years appear as days occurs in tales all over the continent. See *Tales*, n. 143 (D2011).

[18] For Splinter-Foot-Girl, see p. 358, below.

[19] *Tales*, p. 108, No. 45, n. 165 (T541.1.1). Some twenty versions have been reported from the Plains, and there are somewhat remote analogues in other areas.

the old man sees a clot of blood in the trail and takes it home, thinking that he can make some soup. When the pot begins to boil, he and his wife hear a child crying. They look into the pot and see that there is a boy baby. They hide the boy from the son-in-law, and that night the baby sleeps with the old man and asks to be held against each of the lodgepoles in succession. When this has been done, the baby has become a full-grown man. He tells the old people that he has come down from the upper world to help them. The next day the boy kills the cruel son-in-law and the old man's two elder daughters who have helped him. The kindly younger daughter he leaves in charge of the old people while he goes on adventures. He first overcomes some bears who are depriving the people of all the best meat. He kills them by throwing hot stones down their throats. He releases all of the bears' prisoners and gives their booty to the tribe. He next has similar adventures with a savage snake who takes all of the people's meat. He finds the snake asleep with his head lying on the lap of a beautiful woman. In spite of her warning, he cuts off the snake's head. He again sets out and although he has been cautioned to keep on the south side of the road, he pays no attention, and he is sucked by a great windstorm into the mouth of a giant fish. Inside the fish he finds many people, some of them still alive. He leads them in a dance and jumps up and down until the knife on his head strikes the fish's heart. He then cuts his way out between the ribs of the fish. His next adventure is with a woman who wrestles and throws her victim on to large knives hidden in straw on the ground. He succeeds in throwing her upon the knives. The last adventure is with a woman who challenges people to swing with her. He feigns ignorance as to how the swinging is to be done and when she is showing him he cuts the swing, and she drops to her death. After Blood-Clot-Boy has rid the world of all the monsters, he is killed and appears in the sky as a star.

Several motifs in this tale are of widespread occurrence and find their places in other stories than that of Blood-Clot-Boy. The old man abused by his son-in-law, the kindly youngest daughter, the growth of the baby to manhood in a single night, and the overcoming of monsters who are depriving the people of food, the killing of the giant fish from within, the attempt to kill the hero by knives on the ground and by letting him fall from a swing—all of these are known in other tales of the Plains, and some of them appear all over the continent. Nevertheless, the general pattern of the story is clear-cut and has a very definite distribution.

Another interesting type of hero tale is usually known as Lodge-Boy and Thrown-Away. It is most popular in the Plains but, in contrast to Blood-Clot-Boy, there are versions all the way from the Iroquois to the Pacific Coast. The details of the beginning of the story vary considerably, though the general plot is clear. In her husband's absence, a pregnant woman is killed. The slayer takes twin boys from her body,[20] leaves one inside the

<hr/>

[20] Motif T584.2.

lodge and throws the other into the bushes. The father returns and cares for the boy who has been left in the lodge. Eventually, as he is growing up, Lodge-Boy discovers his wild brother who has been thrown into the bushes. With difficulty, he captures the wild boy and magically restores his human qualities. Afterwards the two boys are brought up together.

When they are grown, the twin boys go on adventures. They are continually warned by their father against going in certain directions, but this only shows them where danger is to be found, and they always disobey. They first visit their mother's grave and by frightening the corpse, bring her back to life. They meet and defeat a series of monsters. The first of these is an old woman who has a pot that draws into its boiling water whatever she points it toward. The boys find her asleep and turn her own pot against her. They next encounter the giant serpent that sucks everything into its belly and, like Blood-Clot-Boy, they cut its heart and liberate themselves and others. They also escape from some trees that swoop down upon passers-by; from poisonous snakes which enter the rectum while one is asleep; from a monster who pushes people over a precipice; from a man who wears moccasins of fire and is able to defeat his enemies by surrounding them with burning grass or trees; and, finally, from a murderous otter in a lake, whom they kill by throwing hot stones into his mouth.[21]

Particularly popular over the whole Plains and Plateau areas is the story usually known as Dirty-Boy.[22] The outline of the story is simple. A supernatural being assumes a humble disguise. There is to be an open contest with the prize to be marriage to the chief's daughter. The loathly boy actually wins the contest, but an impostor claims the prize. The truth is eventually discovered, and the loathly bridegroom assumes his original form and marries the chief's daughter. There is some variety in the description of the contest or contests.[23] The most usual are a competition in shooting an eagle and in trapping. The unpromising hero is assisted by his grandmother, who sees that he has fair play. The chief is not willing to give his daughter at the end of the first contest, but does so after the second. The chief sends his three daughters and commands them to marry Dirty-Boy. Only the youngest goes on to him and cares for him. At the end of three days he transforms himself and his surroundings and magically beautifies his wife.

[21] *Tales*, p. 104, No. 44, n. 152. The interesting parallel between the adventures of Lodge-Boy and Thrown-Away and the medieval romance of Valentine and Orson, both concerned with twin heroes, one brought up at home and the other abandoned at birth, is certainly nothing more than a coincidence. That the American Indians should have known the chivalric romance is almost inconceivable, since it has never been told by Europeans as a folktale.

[22] *Tales*, p. 120, No. 48, n. 183 (L112.4).

[23] *Tales*, notes 183 to 188, inclusive.

The central idea of this may be the contests engaged in, but sometimes the emphasis is on the loathly-bridegroom motif, or at least on the success of the unpromising hero. These latter motifs[24] are very widespread among the American Indians, as they are in many other parts of the world. Tales containing them are often quite unrelated to each other, since they fit easily into all kinds of romantic stories. Among the American Indians they are frequently found outside the strict hero and test cycle.

6. SOUTHWEST

AMONG the tribes of the Southwest many details from hero stories of neighboring areas are often found adapted to a different general plot. For example, the adventures of heroic twins may be a part of the sacred legend, and the twins may be demigods. The attack upon malevolent persons holding back food or other supplies from the tribe is usually thought of by these people as a part of the origin legend and sometimes as having occurred in a previous world. It is entirely possible that some of the incidents in the hero tales of the Plains and Plateau are taken from these sacred stories of the Southwest, but in most cases the evidence seems to show a primary development of the motif in the Plains or Plateau and only an accommodation of these essentially secular motifs to the highly developed mythologies of the New Mexican and Arizona tribes.

This is not to say that the regular hero tale does not exist in the Southwest. A very good example of such a story, popular among the Apaches and Navahos, is The Attack on the Giant Elk.[25] With slight modifications, this story is also known by the tribes of the Basin, and the Plateau, and even by some of the Mackenzie River area. The hero is frequently supernatural and may be spoken of as the son of the Sun. He grows to manhood in a few days and is ready to go out on adventures. His grandmother furnishes him with weapons and tells him about various monsters who are preying upon the people. The first of these is a giant elk. On his way to the elk he finds a lizard, who lets him masquerade in his coat. In the form of the lizard, he approaches the elk. A gopher offers to help him by digging a tunnel under the elk. The gopher also succeeds in gnawing off the hair from around the heart of the elk. The hero shoots the elk through the heart, but has a hard time escaping through the tunnel. Before he dies, the elk succeeds in plowing up the tunnel—and thus making our present mountains. The hero makes a coat from the elk's hide and rewards his friends the gopher and the lizard with the front and hind quarters. He returns home in triumph with the antlers, and there he finds that his grandmother has

---

[24] Male Cinderella, *Tales*, n. 185 (L10); Loathly Bridegroom, *Tales*, n. 188 (D733).
[25] *Tales*, p. 101, No. 43, n. 144.

watched his progress by means of a roll of cedar bark which has risen or sunk to indicate whether he was in danger.

The hero next attacks a giant eagle. He dresses himself in his hard elkskin garment and lies down as if dead below the cliff where the eagle has her nest. The eagle carries him to her nest in her talons, and leaves him for the eaglets to eat. With his giant elk antlers he is able to kill both the male and female eagles as they return bearing human victims to their nest. He also strikes the young eagles with the antlers and thus brings it about that they may never grow any larger. He is finally helped from the eagle's nest by a bat who has a magic basket made of a spider web. By strictly obeying the command not to open his eyes on the way down, he reaches home safely.

In general lines, this is the form of the tale as known by the Apaches, but most of these incidents belong together in all versions. The second half of the story, the giant bird who carries the hero to the cliff, the killing of the bird and the escape by help of the bat, is well known independently throughout the Plains, Plateau, and Mackenzie areas.[26] In the episode of the attack on the elk the motif of the help which the hero receives from the gopher who gnaws the hair away from the monster's heart is identical with one that occurs in the Plains story of Splinter-Foot-Girl.[27]

7. TEST-THEME MOTIFS

ALTHOUGH the best known of the stories of heroes and their tests are those which have just been outlined, it would be a mistake to assume that there are no others. Many divergent patterns are found everywhere, often quite unknown beyond the tribe or possibly its near neighbors. But the independence of such tales is often only apparent: the component motifs are frequently the same as appear in other stories among distant tribes. For this reason, the student of American Indian tales who is interested in the dissemination of material over the continent cannot confine himself to studies of larger patterns. He will often find very significant distributions of particular details. Frequently the more minute and seemingly meaningless the motif, the more important it is for showing actual relationships. Lowie long ago showed the value of the present cycle of stories for such a comparative motif study.[28]

A résumé of the motifs occurring in test and hero tales will serve to illustrate the way in which certain incidents are dependent upon particular plot structures and certain others may occur in a variety of tales. We shall pass in review many of the incidents already met in the stories just examined,

---

[26] *Tales*, n. 151 (B31.1) and subdivisions. There are other tales of giant birds in California and the Northeast. The giant Thunderbird appears all over the continent.

[27] *Tales*, n. 147. See p. 358, below.

[28] "The Test-theme in North American Mythology," *Journal of American Folklore*, XXI, 97.

and see something of their distribution and popularity. Of first interest in such tales are the circumstances of the hero's birth and childhood, and then the various causes assigned for his setting forth on adventures. Even more important for this study will be those motifs dealing with the quests, the dangerous tests and adversaries, and the difficult contests he experiences. Finally, there are certain striking auxiliary incidents related to the tests and their outcome.

The general idea of the miraculous birth of the hero is so common all over the continent that a listing of occurrences is of no especial value. On the other hand, the particular way in which the hero is conceived or brought forth is frequently distinctive enough to furnish the basis for interesting studies of motif distribution. Conception from rain falling on a woman seems to be confined to Southwestern legend; but pregnancy from eating is known to practically all tribes except those of the Southwest. Pregnancy from some casual contact with a man occurs most frequently in the North Pacific area, but also in the Plains and Plateau. In the California tale of Dug from Ground we find a child coming up like a plant. Also in California and the Southwest are stories of a child who is born in a jug. That a hero is the result of a very short pregnancy, and usually a growth to manhood in a few days is an idea common to the whole continent. The removal of the hero from the body of the dead mother, which we met in Lodge-Boy and Thrown-Away, is also found outside this tale cycle. It is most popular in the Plains, and is well represented in all areas, with the possible exception of the Southwest and California. The birth of a child from a clot of blood seems to occur only in the Blood-Clot-Boy tale; and similarly, the birth from a splinter wound in the story of Splinter-Foot-Girl, but there are similar tales from the North Pacific Coast telling of birth from tears or from other secretions of the body. Most frequently this is from mucus of the nose.[29]

Since the heroes of most of these adventures are likely to have a very short boyhood, little is usually told about it. Sometimes there are remarkable resemblances to such heroes of chivalry as Percival, particularly in the way in which the youth learns to shoot and to use weapons in spite of the care of his grandmother or guardian. The series of adventures comes to a climax when he is forbidden to go in certain directions lest he meet with danger. This only spurs him on to disobey. Each time when he returns successful, the same kind of warning is given in vain. This motif, usually known as the Dreadnaught incident, is a regular part of Lodge-Boy and

---

[29] For motifs covered by this section, see, in general, *Motif-Index*, T500-T599. The annotations in *Tales* are as follows: conception from rain, n. 166g; from eating, n. 166h; from casual contact with man, n. 166f; Dug from Ground, n. 139; child born in jug, n. 166c; short pregnancy, n. 116; supernatural growth, n. 112; child removed from dead mother, n. 166l; Blood-Clot-Boy, n. 165; Splinter-Foot-Girl, n. 228; birth from wound, n. 229; birth from tears, n. 166a; from secretions of body, n. 166b; from mucus, n. 269.

Thrown-Away and of Blood-Clot-Boy, both of which we have seen are primarily tales of the Plains. But this motif is also known in other connections all over the continent, and is especially popular among the Iroquois and in California and the Southwest. It is frequently connected with the tale of the twin adventurers, as it is in Lodge-Boy and Thrown-Away.[30] Belonging also to the youth of the hero, but to an earlier stage, is an incident occurring in The Jealous Uncle.[31] In this tale the boy passes himself off as a girl so that he may escape from the uncle who kills all his nephews. Though this incident is especially popular only on the North Pacific Coast, it occurs also in the Plains and on the Plateau. There are, of course, interesting European analogues.

A valuable comparative study can be made of the detailed incidents in the central adventures of the hero cycle. Only a few points can be summarized here. Dangerous quests of some kind are found in every culture area. The most popular kind of quest is that after dangerous animals which may be expected to kill the hero. This general concept is found everywhere, but one special variation is confined to the North Pacific Coast: the captured animals or persons avenge themselves on the man who sent the hero to capture them. Besides these dangerous quests, some American Indian tales, apparently without European influence, have the hero seek for what is impossible or absurd. Especially striking because of the European parallel is his search for berries in winter, a motif known both on the North Pacific Coast and in the Plains.[32]

In these hero tales the most usual incidents concern various kinds of perils or dangers which threaten the life of the hero. Practically all of them have been encountered in one or other of the tales of this cycle. A summary of their distribution follows:[33]

Whole continent: heat test (n. 120, H1511); vagina dentata (n. 115, F547.1.1); cliff ogre (n. 163, G321); guardian animals evaded (n. 113a, B576.1.1); sucking monster, (notes 158 and 159, G332 and K952); swinging contest (n. 169, K1618).

Best known on North Pacific Coast; also found in neighboring areas: spine test (n. 168, H1531); poisoned food test (n. 140, H1515); wedge test (n. 129, H1532); abandonment in boat (n. 131, S141); drowning test (n. 124, H1538); precipice test (n. 122, H1535); climbing match (n. 135, K15); shooting contest (n. 142, K31); diving match (n. 136, K16.1).

Practically confined to North Pacific Coast: swallowing red-hot stones (n. 120c, H1511.1); burning food test (n. 120b, H1511.2); snapping door (n. 113,

[30] Dreadnaughts, Tales, n. 156 (Z211); twin adventurers, Tales, n. 155 (T685).
[31] See p. 331, above. For this motif, see Tales, n. 128 (K514).
[32] Quest for dangerous animals, Tales, n. 126 (H1360); captured animals avenge themselves, Tales, n. 126a (Q385); impossible quests, Tales, n. 126b (H1010); berries in winter, Tales, n. 126c (H1023.3).
[33] Note references in this summary are to Tales.

K736); clam test (n. 130, H1521); harpooning contest (n. 134, K33); waking contest (n. 137, H1450.1).

Common to the Plateau and North Pacific Coast: smoke test (n. 120a, H1511.3); substituted arrows (n. 121, K1617).

Common to Plateau and Plains (scarce): wrestling contest (n. 137a, K12).

California and neighboring areas (all rather scarce): tree-pulling contest (n. 191f, K46); shinny match (n. 141, K23); eating contest (n. 137b, K81).

Apparently confined to the Plains: fire moccasins (n. 164, G345); rectum snakes (n. 161, G328); killing trees threaten hero (n. 160, H1522); pot-tilter (n. 157, G331).

Central Woodland: toboggan test (n. 173, H1536).

Most popular in Central Woodland; known over entire continent: sharp-elbowed women (n. 181, G341); marooned egg-gatherer (n. 175, K1616.1); ogre's own moccasins burned (n. 172, K1615).

Peculiar distributions: smoking test—Northeast Woodland, Southwest (n. 191d, H1511.4); burr-women: hero takes old woman on his back and she sticks there magically—Plains, Central Woodland, Iroquois (n. 191e, G311).

In the course of their adventures the heroes of this cycle of tales sometimes use supernatural or magic powers. They are frequently able to travel by some magic means.[34] The hundred league stride of European tales is not frequent, though something very much like it occurs in a Seneca tale. In most parts of the continent we hear of ways in which a road may be magically contracted, and even better known is the magic arrow which the hero shoots and always manages to keep ahead of, or the magic ball which carries its owner with it. The Iroquois tell tales of magic journeys under ground or through the air, and these are not unknown elsewhere.

It frequently falls to the lot of the hero to resuscitate those whom he has rescued. Most popular of all means used for this end is the assembling of the members of the slaughtered person's body.[35] This practically world-wide motif is nearly always accompanied by some magic[36] in addition to the mere assembling—playing or singing of music, the breathing on the corpse, or the frightening of the dead person. All of these are widely distributed. One peculiar motif found all over America, as well as elsewhere, is frequently attached to these tales of resuscitation. When the victim comes to life, the first thing he says is, "How long I have slept!"[37]

Another world-wide motif occurring in these and sometimes in other American Indian tales is the life token.[38] When the hero sets out on adventures, he leaves some magic object behind him which indicates whether he is safe or not. It may be a plant that fades, or some liquid which boils

[34] See Tales, n. 145 and subdivisions (D2120).
[35] Tales, n. 114 (E30).
[36] Tales, n. 153 and subdivisions (E50).
[37] Tales, n. 154 (E175).
[38] Tales, n. 149 (E761).

when he is in danger. There seems no reason to look for outside influence on the dozens of occurrences of this incident in purely American Indian tales, though it also occurs in many tales obviously borrowed as a whole from the Europeans.

When the hero is sent to encounter some monstrous animal or ogre he is sometimes swallowed, and succeeds in killing the monster from within, as in the tale of Blood-Clot-Boy.[39] This incident occurs all over the continent and in many connections. Nearly always the hero thereby rescues a large number of victims who have been swallowed by the monster. A very peculiar incident in this connection is known on the North Pacific Coast and also in Siberia. As a result of being swallowed by the monster, the victims become bald.

We have found the hero receiving help from both persons and animals. In some cases the idea is so general as to make it unnecessary to look for direct influences. Such is true with the large number of instances where the hero is helped by the ogre's wife or child.[40] It is also doubtful whether the old women advisers, appearing in several North Pacific Coast tales and occasionally as far east as the Great Lakes, represent a unified tradition.[41] The mouse or weasel, or other rodent, who helps the hero by gnawing, appears in two regular tales, The Attack on the Giant Elk and The Sun Snarer,[42] but it is also occasionally attached to other tales. One very peculiar example of animal help has a definite distribution in the southwest and in southern California. The hero is compelled to smoke a fatal pipe, but he carries a friendly insect on his head who substitutes in smoking the pipe.[43]

In the accomplishment of his trials, the hero sometimes resorts to trickery. Some of the deceptions he practices are also found in the trickster cycle, but some are especially characteristic of the hero tale. Almost everywhere are found stories of the defeat of a monster by lousing his head. Sometimes the purpose of the lousing is to put him to sleep; at others, the ogre asks for the treatment, and the hero deceives him by cracking cranberries in his teeth.[44] European analogues probably have no relation to the incident in this cycle. The same is true of the trick whereby the hero avoids eating poisoned food or human flesh by dropping the meat into a bag.[45] More remotely resembling one of the European animal tales is the ruse whereby the hero feigns death, and by the use of juice or some other liquid makes him think that his blood and brains are oozing out.[46]

---

[39] See p. 335, above. *Tales*, n. 159 and subdivisions (F910).
[40] *Tales*, n. 171 (G530).
[41] *Tales*, n. 180 (N825.3).
[42] See pp. 314, 338, above.
[43] *Tales*, n. 191c (K528.1).
[44] *Tales*, n. 174. Lousing to produce sleep, D1962.2; cracking the cranberries, K611.1.
[45] *Tales*, n. 191b (K81). It appears practically over the whole continent.
[46] *Tales*, n. 191a (K522.1). Known over the entire continent. For the European form, see p. 220, above.

Finally, in a motif apparently confined to the Plains, the hero uses what is essentially a hypnotic spell. He overcomes the dangerous snakes by singing songs to them that will put them to sleep. The form and wording of these songs have recently been the subject of a very interesting study by Lowie.[47]

It will be seen that the hero cycle is least developed in the Southeast, in the Northeast Woodland, and among the Eskimo. But even in those areas, some of the individual incidents occur, and even some complete tales resembling the more fully developed hero and test stories. It is clear from our study, however, that the most vigorous growth of this cycle has been on the North Pacific Coast, in the Plains, and in the Great Lakes region.

[47] *Tales*, n. 162 (D1962.4.1). R. L. Lowie, *Studies in Plains Indian Folklore* (University of California Publications in American Archaeology and Ethnology XL [1], 1-28).

JOURNEYS TO THE OTHER WORLD

V

A CLEARCUT distinction between events of this world and of others is not usually found in American Indian tales. In the Iroquois myth of origins we begin in an upper world and come down to the waters of this, and in the typical Southwestern story of beginnings we proceed through a series of worlds, one above another. Sometimes these worlds are thought of as the home of divine beings, and sometimes they are vaguely connected with such bodies as the sun and the moon. They may be reached by stretching trees, by a magic chain of arrows, by crossing a tempestuous river or sea, by descending underground, or merely by uttering a wish. Many of these tales remind one of European stories—of Jack and the Beanstalk, or of Orpheus and Eurydice. But there is little doubt that the American Indian myths of this group have developed independently. Each has a well-defined distribution quite different from those borrowed from the Europeans.

In many ways the most interesting of all North American Indian tales, The Star Husband,[1] is thus laid in two worlds. In spite of all the variations of this tale, its central episode is everywhere the same. A mortal girl finds herself in the upper world. There she takes the Star as husband. He forbids her to dig in a certain place, and when she disobeys, she sees her old home below and is seized with longing to return. Secretly, often with supernatural help, she prepares a rope and descends on it. This much of the plot shows a unified tradition in all the eighty-five or ninety versions of this story which have been noted. But, within the area of its distribution, the tale has assumed several well-defined types by means of variation in the introduction

[1] *Tales*, pp. 126, 128, Nos. 50, 51, n. 193. A detailed study of this tale, or group of tales, was made by the late Mrs. Edith Gore Campbell, and is in an unpublished manuscript in the Indiana University Library. It is hoped that, properly revised to include recent additions, this manuscript may be published.

and in the sequel. In one form or another the story is known from the Micmacs in Nova Scotia to southern Alaska; it extends on the Pacific Coast as far south as central California; it is extraordinarily popular through the Plains; and it even has two versions in the Southeastern area. A detailed examination of the story shows three easily distinguished types.

The first of these is the simplest, and looks as if it may have been the original form from which the other two have branched off in different directions. Two girls are sleeping under the open sky and make wishes that they may marry certain stars. In the morning they find themselves in the upper world. One of the girls is disappointed, and when she breaks the prohibition against digging and sees her old home, she makes a rope and succeeds in returning. In this basic story there are some inconsistencies. Two girls go to the upper world, and only one returns. In about one-third of the versions belonging otherwise to this simple form, only one girl is involved. This variety of the tale, which we may call Type I, is widely distributed in some twenty-five versions. It is popular in southern British Columbia, in the northern Plateau, and among the tribes of Washington. There are scattered variants in all parts of the Plains, and it is known as far to the southeast as the Koasati of Alabama. One California story is a mixture of this and the next variety to be considered.

The second group of Star Husband tales would seem to be a special development among the Plains tribes. Although an actual majority of all Star Husband tales are of this kind, Type II is not found outside of the Plains area. There it appears side by side with Type I. A sky man selects a wife from among the earth people. In the form of a beautiful porcupine, he decoys her up a tree which stretches with them to the sky. In the upper world they are married, and she gives birth to a son, Star Boy. She breaks the prohibition against digging, sees her old home below, and prepares a rope. She descends with her son, but finds that the rope is too short. The husband sees her dangling on the rope and sends a stone below with instructions to kill the woman but to spare the boy. This happens. The boy is rescued and cared for, and he becomes the hero of a series of tales similar to those of Lodge-Boy and Thrown-Away.

A careful study of all the details of this characteristically Plains type verifies the impression that this is a special development of the simpler tale (Type I)—a development which has achieved a great popularity in the Plains. The elaborations differentiating this form from the simpler have usually been worked out so as to produce a logically consistent narrative, but sometimes the influence of Type I has produced peculiar inconsistencies. In Type II, for example, the sky husband makes a choice of an earth woman for his wife before he ever descends and assumes the form of a porcupine. Four-fifths of the variants have this consistent motivation for the union of the earth woman and the star. But one-fifth, either through mere lack of skill by the narrator or because Type I served as an actual original of Type II, tell also of the wish uttered by the girl for union with the star. The experiences of the wife in the sky world are much more numerous in this type than in the simpler. Often these experiences have no plot significance, but seem to be added merely for their own interest. They are usually closely allied to the customs and culture of the Plains, and are often used as an explanation of Plains ceremonial.

The third special form assumed by the Star Husband tale is extremely interesting on account of its wide and yet quite clear-cut distribution, and its uniformity of structure. It seems to be about as well known in Nova Scotia as in northern British Columbia. Between these two extremes as the horns of a crescent, the area of its distribution is almost entirely within Canada. The only exception is in the center of the area, where the tale appears as far south as northern Minnesota. It is in the northern Plains that this type is found alongside the simpler Type I.

The beginning of this story is identical with Type I. There are two girls who wish for star husbands. They find themselves the next morning in the upper world. The two girls escape together and descend on a rope. It is only at this point that the special characteristics of this northern type appear. For always the two girls in their descent lodge in the top of a tree and do not know how to get down. They have usually broken some tabu, such as opening their eyes on the descent, and it is for this reason that they fail to reach the ground. While the girls are in the tree, a trickster comes along and attempts to seduce them. They deceive him so that he helps them down. Later they pretend to have forgotten something and by this ruse escape from him. This trickster incident would not seem to be of great narrative interest, and yet it is remarkably uniform from ocean to ocean. This special form of the tale apparently developed in the center of its present area of distribution and from there spread in both directions.

In this Star Husband tale, then, it would look as if we have one rather simple basic story now represented by Type I, which developed probably in the western Plains. Two special elaborations then seem to have occurred, one of them in the central part of the Plains area, and especially adapted to Plains ritual and to the Plains hero cycle. This form appears not to have traveled very far. The second variation, as we have just pointed out, may well have taken place in the northern Plains. This time the narrative seems to have traveled with the greatest mobility.

The motifs constituting the tale of the Star Husband are, for the most part, characteristic of this story and are not found elsewhere. The tree that stretches to the sky, however, is by no means uncommon. We shall find it later in the tale of The Stretching Tree,[2] and it appears also in other tales, particularly in certain origin legends. As a part of the Star Husband, it

[2] See p. 348, below. See also *Tales*, n. 200 (D482).

belongs only in the Plains. The idea of a woman in the upper world being forbidden to dig in a certain place and, as a result of her disobedience, opening up a hole through which she sees the lower world—a motif usually known as Sky Window—we have already met in the Iroquois origin myth,[3] and it is found in tales all over the continent, as well as among the tribes of northeastern Siberia.[4] The rope from the sky is also found everywhere and in a number of contexts. Sometimes the rope is prepared by the spider, though most frequently that type of rope is used for descent from a cliff.[5]

The tree which stretches to the sky is the essential part of a tale rather well known throughout the Plateau, the California, and North Pacific areas.[6] A father is jealous of his son, and while the son is climbing a tree, the father uses his magic and causes the tree to stretch to the sky. Meantime the father runs away with the son's wife (or wives). The young man finally gets the help of the spider, who weaves a rope for him so that he can descend. He returns and takes vengeance on his father. In some versions it is clear that the son goes into the upper world; in others he appears merely to have stayed in the top of the tree.

Much more interesting because of its peculiar introductory motif and its greater wealth of detail is the story of The Arrow Chain.[7] It is well known within a relatively small area: the coastal and Plateau tribes of British Columbia, Washington, and northern Idaho. The versions show considerable uniformity, even at the edges of this area. The hero makes a huge quantity of arrows which he shoots toward the sky, one after the other, so rapidly that they form a chain. Upon this chain, which magically turns into a ladder, he ascends into the upper world. For the ascent, he takes along plants which magically furnish him with food. When he reaches the upper world, he finds that it is summer there. He lies down to sleep, and a girl wakes him and takes him to her grandmother. The old woman produces food by magic and gives him a spruce cone, a rose bush, a piece of "devil's club," and a small piece of whetstone to take with him. He wishes to find a companion who has been taken to the upper world and who, he learns, is at the house of the Moon. He rescues his friend from imprisonment, and leaves the magic spruce cone to answer for him while he escapes. They flee together. As the Moon approaches them in pursuit, he throws behind the piece of devil's club and this makes a huge thicket of devil's club in the Moon's pathway. Similarly, the rose bush makes a thicket of roses, and the whetstone becomes a great mountain. The boys escape and reach the old

[3] See p. 307, above.
[4] *Tales*, n. 28 (F56). For the digging tabu, see *Tales*, n. 197 (C523).
[5] Sky rope, *Tales*, n. 48 (F51); spider-web sky rope, *Tales*, n. 201 (F51.1.1). For the descent from a cliff on such a rope, see p. 339, above.
[6] The Stretching Tree, *Tales*, p. 130, No. 52, n. 199 (D482, K1113).
[7] *Tales*, p. 131, No. 53, n. 202.

woman's house. She tells them to lie down at the place where they have arrived in the upper world and to concentrate their thoughts on their old playground below. Though they fail once and find themselves back at the old woman's house, they succeed at the second trial and awake lying on the earth at the foot of the ladder. They find that their parents are celebrating a death feast for them. They do not immediately show themselves, but they do make themselves known to a child and one of them sends in a part of his garment. His mother recognizes this, and there is a happy reunion.

This is the form of the tale known among the Tlingit, and is the most northern version. The others are like it except that sometimes there is much more attention given to fights and wars made on the sky people, and to the difficulty of escape from the upper world. Some of the separate motifs are much better known than the complete tale. For example, the ascent to the upper world on the arrow chain occurs in the Plateau and North Pacific areas thirty or forty times, though this tale has not been reported more than about ten. The arrow chain motif is also known in Siberia, and has a very interesting analogue, probably quite independent, in Melanesia. The ladder to the upper world, as given in the version we have here, is not very common. It seems to be a quite separate tradition from the well-known rainbow bridge to the other world.[8]

The escape from the ogre by means of throwing magic objects behind is one of the best known folktale motifs in the world. We have already noticed it in connection with Old World tales,[9] but it appears on the American continent also in scores of versions, not only in European borrowings, but in tales like the present where it seems to be quite free from such influences. It is known both in Siberia and in South America, and the theory seems not unreasonable that it came to America from Asia a long time ago. If this be true, we find the same motif in European tales and in aboriginal tales of the same tribe, the former having arrived from the east and the latter from the west, so that the motif has made a complete circuit of the globe.[10]

An upper world journey is the culminating point of a tale current around the Great Lakes and in the neighboring parts of the Plains. There is considerable variety to the half a dozen versions we know, though the general outline is clear enough. It consists of a quest for a supernatural wife who has been lost—a quest which leads at the end to the ascent into some kind of upper world. The close resemblance of some of the versions

[8] Ascent on arrow chain, Tales, n. 203 (F53); ladder to upper world, Tales, n. 204 (F52); rainbow bridge to other world, Tales, n. 204a (F152.1.1). The rainbow bridge is most popular in the Southwest, but is also found in California and among the Iroquois, and sporadically elsewhere. The Bridge Bifrost of Norse mythology is an interesting analogue.

[9] See p. 60, above.

[10] Tales, n. 205 (D672).

to European tales, especially the Cupid and Psyche story (Type 425A) and the Swan Maiden (Type 400), is so striking that we cannot be quite sure whether this actually is an aboriginal tale. Its most complete version is found among the Plains Cree.

The title of the Cree tale, Mudjukiwis,[11] has a familiar sound to all readers of Longfellow's *Hiawatha*. Ten brothers, the eldest of them being named Mudjikiwis, keep house together. When they return from the hunt, they find that their house has been mysteriously put in order. They take turns in remaining home to investigate the mystery. One of the brothers succeeds in finding a girl who has been hiding from them. He marries her, and she remains as housekeeper for the brothers. Mudjikiwis, the eldest brother, becomes jealous, and tries to win the girl from his brother. When she rejects him, he shoots her and goes back home. When her husband misses her and follows her, she tells him that she is supernatural and that after four days if he will come for her, he can find her. He becomes impatient and comes for her on the third day. She therefore disappears, leaving bloody tracks behind her. Her husband now undertakes a long quest to recover her. It is from this point on that the tale follows very closely the European story of the lost Swan Maiden. He encounters a mysterious old woman helper, who has an inexhaustible meat pot the size of a thimble. She informs him that his wife is one of ten daughters of the supernatural people in the sky. From this old woman he is sent on in turn to three others, each older than the last. They give him magic objects to help him climb into the upper world. By means of these objects, and by the power of transformation which they give him, he succeeds in overcoming all the perils of the journey and reaching the upper world. He finds that there is to be a contest to see who is to marry his wife. He wins the contest, and takes back not only his own wife, but her nine sisters for his nine brothers.

If this is actually an aboriginal tale, it is one of the most elaborately developed of any thus far reported. But the combination of the lost supernatural wife, the difficult quest for her, the succession of old woman helpers, the climbing of a slippery mountain into the upper world, the arrival there just as the wife is about to marry another—all these are so close to the Swan Maiden tale that we surely have at least a considerable amount of contamination.

Some of the special motifs in this tale are clearly enough established in American Indian tradition. The mysterious housekeeper occurs not only here, but all over the continent. It is implied, though not clearly stated, that the husband here is forbidden cohabitation with his wife for a definite number of days and that the misfortune comes because he violates this tabu. This marriage regulation appears occasionally in every area, and the same is true of the inexhaustible food supply and the compressible objects

---

[11] *Tales*, p. 135, No. 45, n. 206.

which the hero encounters in possession of the old women. After the hero has reached the upper world, he finds that his wife has already borne him a son. Various rivals claim to be the father, and the choice is left to the baby, who magically picks out his own father. This motif has probably been brought over into one or two versions of the present tale from other stories well known in the Plains, the Plateau, and particularly the North Pacific Coast area.[12]

Visits to the lower world do not occur in many American Indian tales. But there is one series of stories, many of them certainly belonging to a single tradition, in which such a journey is the central motif. The lower world in this story is always the abode of the dead. We have here a most interesting parallel to the Greek myth of Orpheus and Eurydice.[13] The details vary, but the main plot in all parts of the country is the same. A man's wife or close relative dies. He follows her to the world of the dead, and gets permission to bring her back. But there is nearly always some condition attached to this unusual favor by the rulers of the dead. This condition may be, like the classical myth, not to look at the wife, not to touch her, not to let her out of a bag, or not to be too hasty. Out of some forty versions, only three tell of the successful return of the wife. It is clear that, in the regular American Indian pattern, she remains in the world of the dead.

This tale is concentrated on the eastern and western sides of the continent, and is almost completely lacking among the central and northern tribes. From her study of the tale, Gayton concludes, "The forms of the Orpheus story surveyed above, typical for various areas in North America, clearly indicate two facts: that the plot, using the term in its widest sense to include motivation, incidents, and succession of incidents, has been maintained with remarkable consistency throughout its wide distribution, and that it is thoroughly integrated with cultural forms." The relation of this story to the religious concepts of the various tribes where it is told is especially interesting, since the story frequently gives us the clearest picture we have of the current conception of the abiding place and condition of the dead.[14]

The tribes of the North Pacific Coast are particularly fond of tales involving journeys to unusual places, not only to the lower or upper worlds

[12] Mysterious housekeeper, *Tales*, n. 207 (N831.1); nuptial tabu, *Tales*, n. 209 (C117); inexhaustible food supply, *Tales*, n. 210 (D1652.1); compressible objects, *Tales*, n. 210a (D491); succession of helpers, *Tales*, n. 211 (H1235); father test, *Tales*, n. 212 (H481).

[13] *Tales*, p. 215, No. 55, n. 215 (F81.1). A comparative study of the various "Orpheus" tales in North America was made in 1927 by Mrs. Gretchen Dye Meyncke as a Master's essay in Indiana University. The unpublished manuscript is in the Indiana University library. Quite independent of this is the study by A. H. Gayton, "The Orpheus Myth in North America," *Journal of American Folklore*, XLVIII (1935), 263ff. The results of the two studies are in general agreement. For European analogues, see p. 265, above.

[14] For other occurrences of some of the motifs in the Orpheus tale, see *Tales*, notes 216 and 217, with subdivisions. These motifs are: visit to the land of the dead, F81; metempsychosis, E600; looking tabu, C300; tabu: profanely calling on spirit, C10; tabu: drinking, C250; tabu: eating in otherworld, C211.

or to the kingdom of animals, but also to more unusual imaginary realms. There is, for example, a story of considerable popularity which recounts the visit of the hero to a land where everything is shadows and echoes. In this land of Chief Echo the people are invisible and live on the odors of food. Dishes and other objects seem to move of themselves, but are actually handled by invisible people. Thinking that he is not watched, the hero attempts to steal meat from the Chief's house, but he gets punished and injures his ankle. In the sequel, he arrives at the house of Pitch and has an adventure in which he takes his host fishing in a boat. When he becomes hot in the sun, Pitch melts away and spreads over the sides of the halibut they have caught. This is why the halibut is black on one side.[15]

[15] *Tales*, pp. 148, 199, Nos. 56 and 77, notes 219, 285. The idea of shadow people is also found in other areas; see *Tales*, n. 221 (E482). Analogous to the death of Pitch is a tale known from the Great Lakes to Siberia in which a trickster creates men from his excrements, but at the crucial point, they melt in the sun, *Tales*, n. 286 (J2186).

ANIMAL WIVES AND HUSBANDS

VI

IN FOLKTALES everywhere the human world and the animal world lie close together, and we easily move from one to the other, hardly noticing when the transition is made. In the European nursery tales, the wolf talks to Red Ridinghood, the cat and dog help the hero recover magic objects, or the frog marries the princess. To be sure, in the latter case, the frog is really an enchanted prince, and in this way the European tale recognizes that the animal actor is not really an animal. In tales of American Indians, however, and, indeed, of primitive peoples everywhere, the marriage of human beings to actual animals is of very frequent occurrence. A few of the best known of such American Indian stories will serve to illustrate the general type. They are most popular among the Eskimo, on the North Pacific Coast, and among the Plains tribes.

An interesting Eskimo tale of animal marriages is The Fox-Woman.[1] It has not been reported often, but its presence in various parts of the Eskimo area, as well as in Siberia, is clear enough. A tale almost identical is known in Japan.[2] A man finds his house put in order by a mysterious housekeeper. He discovers that the housekeeper is sometimes a woman and sometimes a fox. They marry and are happy until one day he makes mention of her origin as a fox, and she leaves him in anger. A number of the individual motifs in this tale occur in popular tradition everywhere, and they are naturally found all over America.[3] The relation of our Eskimo story to the Japanese analogue is not at all clear.

In the whole length of the Eskimo area from Greenland to Siberia appears the tale of the Eagle and Whale Husbands.[4] Two young girls playing

[1] *Tales*, p. 161, No. 61, n. 233 (B651, N831).

[2] See MacCulloch, *The Childhood of Fiction*, p. 261, n. 1.

[3] Mysterious housekeeper, see p. 351, above. Tabu: offending animal wife, *Tales*, n. 223 (C35); offended supernatural wife, *Tales*, n. 223a (C31); origin tabu, *Tales*, n. 234 (C441); transformation by putting on skin, *Tales*, n, 132 (D531).

[4] *Tales*, p. 160, No. 60, n. 231,

together make wishes, one that she shall have an eagle for her husband, the other, a whale. Their wishes are fulfilled, and one of the girls is carried to the eagles' country at the top of a cliff. She eventually pieces together a long rope and escapes. The other girl is carried by the whale to the bottom of the sea. Here she is unhappy, since she is tied to her place by a rope and must keep picking the lice from the whale's body. Her brothers succeed in rescuing her by means of a magic boat. The whale gives chase, but she throws various garments behind the boat which detain him long enough to let them reach home.

This story has some resemblance in its introduction to the tale of the Star Husband,[5] where the girls wish that they might be married to the two stars which they see in the sky. Actual relationship between the tales, however, seems unlikely. The escape of the girl and her brothers from the whale has parallels, not only in the ancient Greek myth of Apsyrtos, but also on all parts of the American continent and in Siberia.[6]

Another tale of a whale husband[7] is popular on the North Pacific Coast. A man fishing for halibut catches a strange fish which his wife cleans and cuts up. She washes her hands in the sea and is pulled below by a killer whale who takes her down to his home under the sea. The husband follows her and, with the help of Shark, finds that she is working as a slave in the killer whale's house. Shark by trickery extinguishes the light in killer whale's house and steals the woman back for her husband. In some parallels to this story the animal husband is some other kind of sea beast, and the idea that she is actually kept as the wife is made clearer. There are also parallels on the North Pacific Coast and in the Plateau area, in which the woman is stolen by a bear,[8] and also a number of other stories of persons who go to the kingdom of the fishes, or to some other world under the water.[9] Finally, it may be mentioned that the trick of stealing a woman by extinguishing the light or fire where she is kept is known not only on the North Pacific Coast, but in Siberia.[10]

Especially characteristic of the tribes of British Columbia, both Coast and Plateau, is the tale of The Youth Who Joined the Deer.[11] He finds himself mysteriously in an underground kingdom of the deer. The deer are represented as human in form most of the time. He temporarily becomes a deer, and marries there. He finds it hard to accustom himself to the new habits, but eventually does so. They visit the young man's relatives and

---

[5] See pp. 345ff., above.
[6] Obstacle flight—Atalanta type. Objects are thrown back which the pursuer stops to pick up while the fugitive escapes, *Tales*, n. 232 (R231).
[7] The Woman Stolen by Killer Whales, *Tales*, p. 162, No. 62, n. 235.
[8] *Tales*, n. 235, paragraphs 2 and 3.
[9] *Tales*, notes 236 and 236a (B223, F133).
[10] *Tales*, n. 237 (R31).
[11] *Tales*, p. 169, No. 66, n. 252.

magically provide deer for their eating. It is only necessary to throw the bones of the eaten deer into the water, and the deer come back to life (E32).

Tales somewhat analogous to this may be found all over the continent. But the details differ in many points. The general idea of an underground animal kingdom[12] is even more popular in the Plains than it is farther west. The particular story of the young man's experiences among the deer has some characteristics not usually present in American Indian animal tales. Even while transformed to a deer, the young man keeps his human way of thinking. The psychological conflicts implied in the situation are clearly developed. This is especially marked in the hero's adjustment to the sexual cycle and habits of his new companions.

Almost entirely confined to the tribes of the Great Plains is the story of The Piqued Buffalo Wife.[13] A man marries a buffalo cow who becomes a woman and bears him a child. The man also has a human wife who slightingly refers to the buffalo wife's origin or who offends her in some other way. The woman and her child return to the buffalo herd and become buffaloes. The husband goes in search of them. The old buffalo agrees to return them if he is able to pick them out from all the others of the herd. His buffalo child prearranges a signal, so that he chooses correctly and recovers them.[14]

It is not usual for a tale to be current both on the North Pacific Coast and among the Eskimo, but the story of The Dog Husband[15] is an exception. It has a very clear-cut distribution: the western plains and the Mackenzie tribes form the eastern boundary, and northern California the southern. Within these limits, the tale is told in almost every tribe to the west and north. In the Eskimo area, there is frequently amalgamation with the myth of Sedna,[16] for sometimes this girl marries a dog rather than a bird. Among the Plateau and North Pacific Coast tribes, on the other hand, there is considerable confusion between this tale and that of The Deserted Children. In all the stories, a girl is visited by an unknown lover who has the form of a dog by day and a man by night.[17] When, in due time, she gives birth to dog children, the tribe feels itself disgraced and deserts her. She is befriended by Crow, who hides some fire for her in a clam shell. When the dog children grow up, she destroys their dog skins and changes the boys into human form. The boys become prosperous, while at the same time the tribe who has deserted them is at the point of starvation.

[12] *Tales*, n. 253 (F127).

[13] *Tales*, p. 150, No. 57, n. 222.

[14] The offended supernatural wife (C31) is well known in European folklore as well as in the tale of The Fox-Woman, p. 353, above. The picking out of the transformed wife and child from identical companions is also found in Europe (H161).

[15] *Tales*, p. 167, No. 65, n. 247.

[16] See p. 305, above.

[17] *Tales*, n. 248 (D621.1). The interesting parallel in the story of Cupid and Psyche (Type 425A) will occur to everyone.

The friendly Crow visits the deserted daughter and her children and takes home some meat for her own children. When the starving tribe discover the meat, they are glad to return and be reconciled with the girl they have deserted.

The last part of the tale, the accidental discovery of the deserted daughter's good fortune, particularly by means of food carried to the starving tribe, is very popular on the North Pacific Coast, not only in this story, but in that of The Deserted Children.[18] Likewise, the disenchantment of the dog children by destroying their animal skin is a widespread motif, known all over America and parallel to a well-known incident in the tale of Cupid and Psyche and of The Swan Maiden.[19]

It is difficult to tell exactly whether the tradition of The Dog Husband has spread from the Eskimo southward or vice versa. The uncertain evidence would seem to favor the latter. A reasonable hypothesis suggests an origin on the North Pacific Coast. As taken over by the Eskimo, the tale joins quite another cycle. But the southern form of the story is likewise usually joined to The Deserted Children, though the interrelations of that tale and The Dog Husband have not been adequately explored. A thoroughgoing study of this group of stories would be interesting.

The relations of the girl and the dog in the story we have just considered are always conceived of as essentially those of husband and wife. We are interested in their family and only incidentally in their sexual associations. On the other hand, a considerable group of stories, known over the entire American Indian area, but especially popular among Plains tribes, finds its chief interest in the clandestine sexual relations of a woman with some animal. These various tales have much in common, but several of them have rather well-developed and characteristic plots. One of these is the Plains story of The Rolling Head.[20] A husband discovers that his wife has been leaving the camp to commit adultery with a snake. He kills the snake and punishes the wife. In some versions he serves the snake or the snake's privates to the wife, so that she eats it unawares. In other versions, particularly those of the Plains, he also kills the wife and cuts off her head. The head rolls after the man and his family, and they escape only with the greatest difficulty.

The essential part of this tale seems to be the adultery and the punishment. The story of the rolling head, which is here worked in as a part of the punishment, is also known in other contexts over a large part of the continent.[21] This incident would seem to be simple enough to be told for its own sake by any people who will make the preliminary assumption of the power of such a head to roll independently. The incident has, however, served the pur-

[18] *Tales*, notes 250 (S361) and 251 (N732.2). See p. 361, below.
[19] Types 425A and 400, respectively. For American Indian references, see *Tales*, n. 249 (D721.3).
[20] *Tales*, p. 163, No. 63, n. 238.
[21] *Tales*, n. 238a (R261.1).

poses of various folklore theorists who wish to find some hidden "meaning" in the tale. The psychoanalyst finds that it is the result of a nightmare (though whether the nightmare was only experienced by the first teller, whoever he was, or must be re-experienced by every other teller is never clear); to others it seems plain that the rolling head is nothing but the moon, or even possibly the sun.[22]

In most of the Plateau and North Pacific versions of the tale of the woman with the snake paramour, she is made to eat unwittingly from some member of her murdered lover. This incident has world-wide analogues. In Europe it is normally the lover's heart which is served to the woman.[23] But this may well be only a chivalric refinement. In America the incident is found everywhere except possibly in California and in the Southwest.

In certain versions which contain the rolling head motif the children finally escape and are in danger of being destitute. One of the girls, however, finds that she has the power of killing deer merely by looking at them. Such a death-giving glance[24] occurs frequently in other stories, particularly of the Southwest and of the Plains. But it is also known in most parts of the continent, as is also the related incident of death by pointing.

Similar in its general plan is another Plains tale, usually referred to as The Bear-Woman.[25] In this story the woman's paramour is a bear. The husband eventually discovers the situation and kills the bear lover. The woman thereupon turns into a bear and attacks her family. They flee, and delay her pursuit by throwing magic objects behind themselves. They find that the bear-woman is invulnerable except for a single spot. They are able to discover this spot and eventually they kill her. The introduction to the tale varies from place to place. Most usual is the form we have given. But in many of the versions from the Plateau tribes the woman is kidnapped by a bear. In still other variants, we begin with the incest of a brother and sister: when the girl is scolded, she turns into a bear. The attack on the family, the Achilles-heel motif, and the obstacle flight (D672) are very regular, regardless of which introduction may be used. The tale as a whole is most popular in the Plains, but is known from the North Pacific Coast to the Iroquois tribes of New York State.

Miscellaneous tales of bear paramours are popular in all parts of the continent.[26] There are also other appearances of the person who can be wounded in only one place, of the person possessed of a soul which can be separated

---

[22] For an example of this species of reasoning and the airy heights to which it may lead one, see A. K. Coomaraswamy, "Sir Gawain and the Green Knight: Indra and Namuci," *Speculum,* XIX (January, 1944), 104-125. Such scholars have little interest in tales as actually told, or in discovering where particular tales have come from.

[23] *Tales,* n. 241 (Q478.1).

[24] *Tales,* n. 242 (D2061.2.1). Death by pointing, *Tales,* n. 242a (D2061.2.3).

[25] *Tales,* p. 164, No. 64, n. 244.

[26] *Tales,* n. 245 (B611.1). More of these tales appear around the Great Lakes than elsewhere. For a related Plains tale of a woman with a stallion as paramour, see n. 254a (B611.3).

from his body, and of bodily members which rejoin the body and bring the owner back to life. All these motifs occur over the entire continent, and they all have analogues in European folklore.[27]

Finally, among the tales of the marriage of a woman to an animal, the tribes of the Plains tell a story of Splinter-Foot-Girl.[28] Its beginning reminds one of Blood-Clot-Boy,[29] for the heroine, like him, is born of the blood from a wound. A group of young men are living alone and one of them wounds himself with a splinter. From this splinter wound in his foot a girl is born, and she is kept by the young men, who adopt her as a sister. When she grows up, a buffalo bull in the neighborhood demands her in marriage, and when he is refused, he carries her off. The young men now get the help of their friends, the mole and the badger.[30] They rescue the girl, and flee with her. When the buffalo husband pursues, they take refuge in a tall tree[31] which the buffalo tries in vain to break down. The story as a whole is almost confined to the Plains area. Sometimes instead of the buffalo, it is a round rock which demands the girl in marriage. A third variation, also characteristic of the Plains, tells how a girl is stolen away by a buffalo. The rescue party finds that she is being made into a ring by the buffalo, so that they can play their "ring and javelin" game. When the rescue party tells the ring that they are friends, the ring rolls to them and they carry it off. Sometimes the ring is given to the eagle, so as to escape the buffaloes more easily. The girl eventually assumes her own form.[32]

Besides these rather well-developed stories of the marriage of human beings to animals, there are hundreds of anecdotes in which similar relations are implied. American Indian tales are particularly rich in the stories of trickster heroes who are conceived of sometimes as men and sometimes as animals. When tales are told of the experiences of such heroes with women, there is usually some ambiguity as to whether the story-teller is thinking of a human-animal relationship or not. From the stories which we have just examined, however, it is clear that American Indians tell many tales in which this relationship is definitely set forth.

[27] *Tales*, notes 246, 246a, and 246b, respectively (Z311, E710, and E78~`
[28] *Tales*, p. 341, No. 59, n. 228.
[29] *Tales*, n. 229; see p. 335, above.
[30] *Tales*, n. 147 (B431); see p. 338, above.
[31] *Tales*, n. 230 (R311).
[32] *Tales*, n. 228a (R11.1, D263, B550).

MISCELLANEOUS AMERICAN
INDIAN TALES

VII

Though most of the main classes of North American Indian tales have now been noticed, it would be a mistake to assume that we have reviewed all the important stories which they tell. Every area has its own specially developed tale cycles,[1] some of which have entered in a minor way into the folklore of their neighbors, and some of which have remained entirely within the area.[2] Moreover, there are a small number of stories of much more than local distribution which belong in subject matter to none of the categories we have discussed.

Such, for instance, are four tales current on the North Pacific Coast. One of them tells the story of the proud princess who scorns her lover after she has induced him to disfigure himself. He journeys to the supernatural people, is magically beautified, and, on his return, humiliates her. Of two cannibal tales, one is distinctly reminiscent of Hansel and Gretel. Children are abducted by a giantess. A boy, born from the mucus of his mother's nose, has miraculous growth and goes in search of his brothers and sisters. He finds the children seated on the floor, and a woman rooted to the floor. The latter warns him of the cannibal giantess. He and all the captives flee and take refuge in a tree. The fugitives are betrayed by their reflections in the water. The giantess asks the hero how he happens to be so beautiful. He tells her that his head has been pressed between stones, and thus per-

---

[1] For the general nature of these areal differences, see pp. 299ff., above.
[2] Good discussions of such local tales are to be found in Gayton and Newman, *Yokuts and Western Mono Myths* (Central California); Benedict, *Zuni Mythology* and M. E. Opler, *Myths and Tales of the Chiricahua Apache Indians* (Southwestern tribes); Boas, *Tsimshian Mythology* (North Pacific Coast and Plateau tribes); and J. Curtin and J. N. B. Hewitt, *Seneca Myths and Fictions* (Iroquois tribes).

suades her to submit to the same treatment. Even though he has killed her, she revives, because she has a soul outside her body. In spite of this, however, the fugitives escape. In the other cannibal story, especially popular in the North Pacific Coast and Plain areas, the monster is overcome and burned in a fire. The ashes from this fire turn into mosquitoes. Also worthy of mention from the North Pacific Coast is the story of the blind man whose wife always aims his arrow for him. She always says that he has missed his aim, but she herself eats the slain animals. His sight is miraculously restored, and he avenges his ill treatment.[3]

Widely distributed over the continent but especially throughout the west is the story of The Deserted Children.[4] In the latter half it is identical with a group of versions of The Dog Husband.[5] The tale begins with the abandonment of a group of children by the tribe who find it difficult to provide food for everyone. The children come to an old woman, who kills all of them except a boy and a girl. By various pretexts, the girl saves herself and succeeds in fleeing with her brother. Behind her she leaves magic objects which answer in her place when the old woman talks to her. The story up to this point has many resemblances to the Hansel and Gretel cycle (Type 327). But the incidents in the rest of the story show more relation to other aboriginal tales than to European tradition. The children are carried across the stream on a water monster whom they deceive first by a pretended lousing of his head and secondly concerning the nearness to the shore and whether they have heard thunder. The lightning actually strikes the monster and kills him, but the children are near enough to the shore to save themselves. Later they come across a crane who lets them cross on his leg. The old woman asks the crane's help, but he refuses or else pretends to help her and shakes her off into the water. When the children return to the camp, they are not welcome and are tied to a tree. Through the help of a friendly animal, they are rescued and given fire. The boy is able to kill game by glancing at it, and the girl likewise performs magic feats by means of her glance. The children prosper and have much food, while the camp which has moved away is at the point of starvation. As in the Dog Husband

---

[3] The Princess Who Rejected her Cousin, *Tales*, p. 178, No. 68, n. 256; The Child and the Cannibal, *Tales*, p. 190, No. 71, n. 268; The Cannibal Who Was Burned, *Tales*, p. 193, No. 72, n. 274; and The Deceived Blind Man, *Tales*, p. 195, No. 74, n. 278. A few interesting motifs belonging to these four tales, with note numbers referring to Thompson's *Tales*, are: magic beautification, n. 259 (D1860); resuscitation (various methods), notes 260, 261, and 273 (E0-E199); magic beautification by dismemberment and resuscitation, n. 258; healing water shown by animals, n. 279 (B512); water of life, n. 279a (E80); water of life and death, n. 279b (E82); magic self-boiling kettle, n. 257 (D1601.10.3); years thought days, n. 143 (D2011); looking tabu, n. 217 (C300ff.); local winter, n. 61c (D2145.1.1); insects from burnt monster's body, n. 275 (A2001); false beauty-doctor, n. 271 (K1013); and children kidnapped in basket deceive kidnapper and escape, n. 268a (K526).

[4] *Tales*, p. 174, No. 67, n. 255 (S301, S362).

[5] See p. 355, above.

tale, the visiting friendly animal discovers their prosperity and eventually the repentant camp returns and begs the children for food.[6]

The escape across the river on the crane's leg is a regular feature of Bear-Woman and Deer-Woman,[7] a tale especially popular in California and well known in the Plateau and North Pacific areas. The bear and the deer let their children play together. One day the bear kills the deer while the children are away, and throws her into the fire. Her eyes burst with the heat, and the deer's children realize that their mother has been killed. Later they avenge themselves by playing a game with bear's children in which they smother all of them in a hollow log. The mother bear is deceived into eating her own children. When she discovers the trick, she pursues the deer's children. They escape from her across a river with the help of a crane who lands them safely on the other side. He drowns the grizzly by shaking her off into the water.

The bursting eyes of the mother who is burned remind one of a similar incident in a California story usually known as The Loon Woman, or The Girl Who Married Her Brother.[8] One of the brothers in a large family is kept concealed by his parents. His sister discovers a hair and has a longing for the person to whom the hair may belong. It is discovered that the owner is the hidden brother. She insists upon his going away with her. But when she attempts to commit incest with him, he flees and returns to his family. Usually she has magically hastened the coming of night and he has taken extraordinary precautions to prevent the accomplishment of incest. He leaves a log behind him in the bed to deceive her. When he returns home, the family realize that they must flee. They make a "sky basket" and ascend to the sky so as to escape the great fire which they realize she will kindle. The family is warned that they must not look down to the earth. Because one of their members does so, they all fall into the great fire. As they burn, their hearts burst out and are gathered together by the daughter (Loon Woman), who strings them about her neck. This explains why the loon appears to have a necklace to this day. There are various ways in which this story may end, but usually the impious sister is killed and her victims resuscitated. Though this tale as a whole is practically confined to California, the elements appear in many parts of America, and some of them are world-wide.[9]

[6] Three of the motifs in The Deserted Children have already been found in tales previously discussed: deception by lousing, Tales, n. 174, p. 343, above; whale-boat, Tales, n. 179, p. 334, above; and death-giving glance, Tales, n. 242, p. 357, above. They are all well known throughout the continent. The escape across the river by means of the crane's leg (crane-bridge), Tales, n. 227 (R246), occurs regularly in this tale and in Bear-Woman and Deer-Woman, the next story to be noticed. It is a popular motif in every culture area on the continent.

[7] Tales, p. 153, No. 58, n. 226 (G61).

[8] Tales, p. 196, No. 75, n. 280. For a definitive study of this tale, see D. Demetracopoulou, "The Loon Woman Myth," Journal of American Folklore, XLVI, 101-128.

[9] Lover identified by hair floating in water, Tales, n. 281 (H75.1) (well known in European tales); magic objects talk and delay pursuer, Tales, n. 196 (D1611); sky basket, Tales, n. 283 (F51.2); Achilles heel (vulnerability in one place alone), Tales, n. 246 (Z311).

The jealousy between a mother and daughter, or between an old woman and a young one, is the motivating force of two closely related stories very popular in the Plains and among other central tribes. In one of them, The Fatal Swing,[10] the old woman who covets her daughter's husband induces the young woman to swing out over a pool of water. She causes the swing to break, and the girl falls into the water. Here she is taken by a water monster, but she is allowed to return to the surface four times to suckle her baby. Through supernatural help, the husband is able to rescue her on her last appearance.[11]

In a closely related tale,[12] the jealous elder woman takes the younger into the woods, kills her, and dresses in the younger woman's skin. She is able to deceive the younger woman's husband until the skin begins to decay. She is discovered and punished, and the husband succeeds in bringing his real wife back from the dead. The outline of this tale is gruesome enough, but it is rather popular and is frequently very well told. Especially elaborated are the devices by which the older woman leads the younger farther and farther into the woods. Other features well developed are the discovery of the deception and the resuscitating of the dead wife.

In general, the folklore of the Southwestern tribes has maintained considerable independence from that of the neighboring Plains and Plateau. But even here there is no real lack of such borrowings. One example of a tale which Southwestern tribes have apparently taken over from the Plateau is that of The Conquering Gambler,[13] in which we see how a bankrupt gambler acquires supernatural power and wins back even more than he has lost. This story appears over the entire western half of the continent.[14]

The tales just passed in review will indicate something of the wealth of narrative interest in the stories of the North American Indians, and will give some idea of the folktale among other primitive groups, such as those in Oceania and Africa. A different emphasis on particular narrative elements from that found in European tales is to be expected. But the actual range of material is by no means narrow. Though these aboriginal tales are frequently available to us only in outline, we know from many which have been faithfully recorded that the narrative style and the development of situation and character frequently show a considerable cultivation of the

[10] *Tales*, p. 184, No. 69, n. 262.

[11] A close analogue to an incident in several European tales, in which the wife returns from below the water three times to suckle her child. The hero must disenchant her on her third appearance. Cf. Type 403. For American Indian analogues, see *Tales*, n. 263.

[12] The Skin-Shifting Old Woman, *Tales*, p. 186, No. 70, n. 265. Similar tales are found in most parts of the continent. For other stories of disguised flayers, see *Tales*, notes 267 and 267a.

[13] *Tales*, p. 194, No. 73, n. 276.

[14] In these gambling stories we frequently hear of a man wagering his own life; see *Tales*, n. 277.

story-teller's craft. These American Indian tales are worthy of study as the most important literary expression of this large group of aboriginal peoples. Not only do these stories exemplify for us the problems of invention, dissemination, growth, and decay of popular tradition, but they also give us opportunity for basic studies in the narrative art proper to the oral tale.

≫ PART FOUR ≪

Studying the Folktale

THEORIES OF THE FOLKTALE

OUR rapid review of folk narrative in various parts of the world and in different cultural levels makes certain facts in regard to this material clear enough. No one will doubt that we are dealing everywhere with essentially the same human activity, and that the interest in a story is practically universal. Moreover the actual subject matter of folktales shows many striking resemblances from age to age and from land to land. And although the patterns differ somewhat, there is a tendency for the tales to range themselves into certain well-recognized formal groups, depending on style, purpose, or occasion for which they are used.

The attempt to understand such obvious facts as these confronts the student of the folktale with his most challenging problems. Assiduous collecting of stories throughout the world and skillful analyzing and cataloguing make the material to be explained more and more accessible and capable of study. Besides the mere description of it, however, the scholar is interested in explaining it. He wants to know not only *what* but *how* and *why*.

For more than a century the folktale has engaged the attention of a number of keen thinkers, so that in that time a considerable body of theoretical discussion has been written. It will be noted that these men are not all treating the same problems and that what most interests one may enter but slightly into the speculations of another. Before examining these theories, therefore, it may be well to suggest a few of the general questions concerning the tale, so that the whole subject can be kept in mind, even though only one aspect is being considered at the moment. These problems may be stated as follows:

1. *Origin of folktales.* How did the custom of telling stories begin and what is the origin of the particular tales we now have?

2. *Meaning of folktales.* Do tales mean just what they say, or do they have a hidden significance?

3. *Dissemination of folktales.* A study of tale collections shows clearly that many tales are widely distributed over the globe. What is the nature of this distribution, how did it occur, and why?

4. *Variations in folktales.* Each version of an oral folktale is different from any other. What is the nature and cause of these differences?

5. *Relation of different forms of the folktale: Märchen,* myth, *Sage,* hero tale, and the like.

Other questions are, of course, touched on but most of the discussion has concerned these five points. Usually a position assumed for one of these questions logically necessitates certain conclusions as to one or more of the others. It will help much, as we review some of these opinions, if the mutual relationship of all these problems is remembered.

The first serious consideration of any of these questions appeared in the second edition of the Grimms' *Kinder- und Hausmärchen* in 1819. These scholars had apparently given little thought to the international aspect of folktales when they issued their first edition, but in the meantime similar tales had been published from other countries, especially Serbia, and had raised the whole question of how these resemblances and identical plots could be explained. The final statement of the theories of the Grimms was made by Wilhelm Grimm in 1856.[1]

> The resemblance existing between the stories not only of nations widely removed from each other by time and distance, but also between those which lie near together, consists partly in the underlying idea and the delineation of particular characters and partly in the weaving together and unraveling of incidents. There are, however, some situations which are so simple and natural that they reappear everywhere, just as there are thoughts which seem to present themselves of their own accord, so that it is quite possible that the same or very similar stories may have sprung up in the most different countries quite independently of each other. Such stories may be compared with the isolated words which are produced in nearly or entirely identical form in languages which have no connection with each other, by the mere imitation of natural sounds. We do meet with stories of this kind in which the resemblance can be attributed to accident, but in most cases the common root-thought will by the peculiar and frequently unexpected, nay, even arbitrary treatment, have received a form which quite precludes all acceptation of the idea of a merely apparent relationship. I will give some examples. Nothing can be more natural than to make the fulfilment of a request depend on the performance of some very difficult tasks; but when the tasks are the strangest imaginable, as they are in *The Peasant's Wise Daughter* (No. 94), and when moreover they coincide, this can no longer be a chance agreement. That in cases of difficulty an umpire should be called in, is a thing which is clear to all, but that in every place it is exactly three persons who are quarrelling, that

---

[1] *Kinder- und Hausmärchen* (Reklam, Leipzig, 1856), III, 427ff. Translation: Margaret Hunt, *Grimm's Household Tales* (London, 1884), II, 575ff.

they are beings endowed with higher powers, that it is an inheritance which is to be divided between them, that this should consist of three magic things, and that finally the man who is summoned to make the division should craftily cheat the owners out of them (a man must use the rare opportunities which present themselves if he wants to win away from the dwarfs or kobolds their magic treasures), proves the connection between the traditions. This common source is like a well, the depth of which no one knows but from which each draws according to his need.

I do not deny the possibility, nor in particular instances the probability, of a story's passing over from one people to another, and then firmly rooting itself on the foreign soil, for the *Siegfriedslied* penetrated to the most remote north in the very earliest time, and became indigenous there. But one or two solitary exceptions cannot explain the wide propagation of the property common to all; do not the selfsame stories crop up again in places most widely remote from each other, like a spring which forces its way up in spots which lie far apart? And just as wherever the eye can pierce we find the domestic animals, grain, fields, and kitchen-utensils, household-furniture, arms—in fact, all the things without which social life would be impossible—so do we also find sagas and stories—the dew which waters poetry—corresponding with each other in this striking and yet independent manner. They are just as much a necessity of existence as these things, for only where avarice and the jarring wheels of machinery benumb every other thought can anyone imagine it possible to live without them. Wherever assured and well-established order and usages prevail, wherever the connection between human sentiment and surrounding nature is felt, and the past is not torn asunder from the present, these stories are still to be found. I have picked up the best of these from peasants, and I know that this book has been read by them with the greatest delight, indeed I might say that it has been bought up by them, and that even Germans who have long been living far away from their fatherland in Pennsylvania have shown interest in it. May we not liken the sudden springing up of the Saga to the stream of a wandering tribe pouring itself into one uninhabited tract of land after another and filling it? How can we explain the fact of a story in a lonely mountain village in Hesse resembling one in India, Greece, or Servia?

[Many examples of motifs that have a common character and appear everywhere as common property.] Fragments of a belief dating back to the most ancient times, in which spiritual things are expressed in a figurative manner, are common to all stories. The mythic element resembles small pieces of a shattered jewel which are lying strewn on the ground all overgrown with grass and flowers, and can only be discovered by the most far-seeing eye. Their significance has long been lost, but it is still felt and imparts value to the story, while satisfying the natural pleasure in the wonderful. They are never the iridescence of an empty fancy. The farther we go back, the more the mythical element expands: indeed it seems to have formed the only subject of the oldest fictions. . . . In proportion as gentler and more humane manners develop themselves and the sensuous richness of fiction increases, the mythical element retires into the background and begins to shroud itself in the mists of distance, which weaken the distinctness of the outlines but enhance the charm of the fiction.

We shall be asked where the outermost lines of common property in stories begin, and how the degrees of affinity are gradated. The outermost lines are coterminous with those of the great race which is commonly called Indo-Germanic, and the relationship draws itself in constantly narrowing circles round the settlements of the Germans, somewhat in the same ratio as that in which we detect the common or special property in the languages of the individual nations which belong to it. If we find among the Arabians some stories which are allied to the Germans, this may be explained by the fact the *Thousand and One Nights* where they appear, is derived from an Indian source, as Schlegel has justly maintained. However accurate the boundaries here given may be at present, it may be necessary to enlarge them if other sources become open to us, for we see with amazement in such of the stories of the Negroes of Bornu, and the Bechuanas (a wandering tribe in South Africa) as we have become acquainted with, an undeniable connection with the German ones, while at the same time their peculiar composition distinguishes them from these. On the other hand, I have found no such decided resemblance, at least no resemblance extending to mere trifles, in the North American stories. Tibetan stories exhibit some points of contact and so do Finnish; we see a visible relationship in the Indian and the Persian, and a decisive one in the Slav. . . . In the next place there is a very strong similarity between our stories and those of the Romance nations; this may be satisfactorily explained by the connection which has at all times existed between the two races and the intercourse which took place between them even at an early period. . . . It is my belief that our German stories do not belong to the Northern and Southern parts of our fatherland alone, but that they are the absolutely common property of the nearly-related Dutch, English, and Scandinavians. . . .

It will be seen that Grimm is here speaking of the folktale in a very general sense, not specifically of the wonder-story. He puts forward two ideas which were to secure general acceptance for a long time: (1) the circle of those tales which show close resemblances is coterminous with the Indo-European language family and these tales are doubtless inheritances from a common Indo-European antiquity; (2) the tales are broken-down myths and are to be understood only by a proper interpretation of the myths from which they came. These pronouncements give expression to what is generally known as (1) the Indo-European theory, (2) the broken-down myth theory.

He also suggests, but does not develop, certain other ideas which were later to be stressed by other scholars. Such are the "situations so simple and natural that they reappear everywhere," which he thinks not very common. He also admits borrowing from one people by another but feels that this is exceptional. These two principles were to become the foundations of folktale scholarship a half century later, whereas Grimm's main contentions were gradually to lose the support of nearly all scholars.

Grimm's theory that the folktales with common incidents are primarily Indo-European was a natural result of the great interest in comparative philology in the early part of the nineteenth century. With the awareness of the importance of Sanskrit which came about toward the close of the eighteenth century, many European scholars interested themselves in the problem of reconstructing the parent speech from which descended most of the languages from India to Ireland.[2] Though many details remained unsolved, the general principles were rather clear by the middle of the nineteenth century, and the various subdivisions were well established. It was generally agreed that if there was a parent speech there must have been a unified group of people who used this speech, the primitive Indo-European stock. But where these people lived before they separated on their wanderings to India or Europe was a problem that these scholars—and, for that matter, later ones—failed to solve. Most of them seemed to feel that this original homeland was somewhere in western Asia and that it was in the highlands. They were at least sure that their Indo-European ancestors were shepherds.

The approach to this problem, which would seem to present-day scholars primarily a matter of archeological and ethnological investigation, was made exclusively through the study of comparative philology. The newly discovered relationship of words was for those men the key to unlock the mysteries of the past. In the *Rig-Veda* they could go back thirty-five hundred years—and that was far enough to give real indication as to the life of the Indo-Europeans. They did not take into consideration that the *Rig-Veda* was a Sanskrit work of a highly developed priesthood, who evidently delighted in expressing everything metaphorically. From this extraordinary work of the ancient priests of India, they proceeded to the theory that the original Indo-Europeans in their daily life used just such expressions with hidden meanings. And in this way had arisen the Indo-European myths and tales. Their real original meanings had become obscured if not lost, and it was the business of the scholar, through use of the *Rig-Veda* and his own philological skill, to restore these meanings.

Such was the goal of the students of "comparative mythology." In the course of a half century they evolved a system that grew ever more complex. Proceeding from a few major premises, which they seem to have found entirely by introspection, they built up a structure so fantastic that the modern reader who ventures to examine it begins to doubt his own sanity. The only way to give an idea of their work is to quote from some of the members of the school. Though they did not all agree in every detail, the

---

[2] For a good discussion of this movement see J. W. Spargo, *Linguistic Science in the Nineteenth Century* (Cambridge, Mass., 1931).

general method will be seen well enough in the work of Max Müller, Angelo de Gubernatis, John Fiske, and Sir George Cox.[3]

The members of the school did not believe that the resemblances in folktales and myths come from borrowing. They were rather an inheritance from a common Indo-European past. "The real evidence," says Cox, "points only to that fountain of mythical language from which have flowed all the streams of Aryan epic poetry, streams so varied in their character yet agreeing so closely in their elements. The substantial identity of stories told in Italy, Norway, and India can but prove that the treasure-house of mythology was more abundantly filled before the dispersion of the Aryan tribes than we had taken it to be."

Andrew Lang's satirical summary of Cox's general theory does not make it more fantastic than does Cox's own verbose treatment[4]:

> In the beginning of things, or as near the beginning as he can go, Sir George finds men characterised by "the selfishness and violence, the cruelty and slavishness of savages." Yet these cruel and violent savages had the most exquisitely poetical, tender, and sympathetic way of regarding the external world (Mythol. Ar. i. 39), "Deep is the tenderness with which they describe the deaths of the sun-stricken dew, the brief career of the short-lived sun, and the agony of the Earth-mother mourning for her summer child." Not only did early man cherish these passionate sympathies with the fortunes of the sun and the dew, but he cherished them almost to the exclusion of emotions perhaps more obvious and natural as we moderns hold. Man did not get used to the dawn; he was always afraid that the sun had sunk to rise no more, "years might pass, or ages, before his rising again would establish even the weakest analogy." Early man was apparently much more difficult to satisfy with analogies than modern mythologists are. After the sun had set and risen with his accustomed regularity, "perhaps for ages," "man would mourn for his death as for the loss of one who might never return."
>
> While man was thus morbidly anxious for the welfare of the sun, and tearfully concerned about the misfortunes of the dew, he had, as we have seen, the moral qualities of the savage. He had also the intellectual confusion, the perplexed philosophy of the contemporary savage. Mr. Tylor, Mr. Im Thurn, Mr. Herbert Spencer, and most scientific writers on the subject, have observed that savages draw no hard and fast line between themselves and the animal or even the inanimate world. To the mind of the savage all things organic or inorganic appear to live and to be capable of conscious movement and even of speech. All the world is made in the savage's own image. Sir George Cox's early man was in this savage intellectual condition. "He had life, and therefore all things else must have life also. The sun, the moon, the stars, the ground on which he trod, the clouds, storms, and light-

[3] Max Müller, *Chips from a German Workshop* (New York, 1881); Angelo de Gubernatis, *Zoological Mythology* (London, 1872); John Fiske, *Myths and Myth-Makers* (Boston, 1872), and Sir George Cox, *Mythology of the Aryan Nations* (London, 1870).
[4] Lang in Margaret Hunt, *Grimm's Household Tales,* I, xx.

nings were all living beings: could he help thinking that, like himself, they were conscious beings also? . . ."

We now approach another influence on mythology, the influence of language. While man was in the condition of mind already described by Sir George Cox, he would use "a thousand phrases to describe the actions of the beneficent or consuming sun, of the gentle or awful night, of the playful or furious wind, and every word or phrase became the germ of a new story, *as soon as the mind* lost its hold on the original force of the name." Now the mind was always losing its hold on the original force of the name, and the result would be a constant metamorphosis of the remark made about a natural phenomenon, into a myth about something denoted by a term which had ceased to possess any meaning. These myths, caused by forgetfulness of the meaning of words (as we understand our author), were of the *secondary* class, and a third class came into existence through folk-etymologies, as they are called, popular guesses at the derivations of words. We have now briefly stated Sir George Cox's theory of the origins of myths, and of the mental condition and habits through which myths were evolved. But how does this theory explain the origin of Household Tales?

This question ought to lead us to our third problem, what are the relations of Household Tales to the higher mythologies? But it may suffice to say here that in Sir George Cox's opinion, most of the Household Tales are, in origin, myths of the phenomena of day and night.

Some of the applications of these theories we may well see from quotations from Angelo de Gubernatis' *Zoölogical Mythology*.

The aurora, as the first of those who appear every day in the eastern sky, as the first to know the break of day, is naturally represented as one of the swiftest among those who are the guests of the sun-prince during the night; and like her cows, which do not cover themselves with dust (this being an attribute which, in the Indian faith, distinguishes the gods from mortals, for the former walk in the heavens, and the latter upon earth), she, in her onward flight, leaves no footsteps behind her. The word *apâd* (*pad* and *pada*, being synonymous) may, indeed, mean not only she who has no feet, but also she who has no footsteps (that is, what is the measure of the foot), or, again, she who has no slippers, the aurora having, as appears, lost them; for the prince Mitras, while following the beautiful young girl, finds a slipper which shows her footstep, the measure of her foot, a foot so small, that no other woman has a foot like it, an almost unfindable, almost imperceptible foot, which brings us back again to the idea of her who has no feet. The legend of the lost slipper, and of the prince who tried to find the foot predestined to wear it, the central interest in the popular story of Cinderella, seems to me to repose entirely upon the double meaning of the word *apâd*, *i.e.*, who has no feet, or what is the measure of the foot, which may be either the footstep or the slipper; often, moreover, in the story of Cinderella, the prince cannot overtake the fugitive, because a chariot bears her away. . . . (I, 30 f.)

The same phenomenon, a divorce of husband from wife, or a separation of brother and sister, or the flight of a sister from her brother, or again, that of a daughter from her father, presents itself twice every day (and every year) in the sky. Sometimes, on the other hand, it is a witch, or the monster of nocturnal darkness, who takes the place of the radiant bride, or the aurora, near the sun; and in that case the aurora, the beauteous bride, is spirited away into a wood to be killed or thrown into the sea, from both of which predicaments, however, she always escapes. Sometimes the witch of night throws the brother and sister, the mother and son, the sun and the aurora, together into the waves of the sea, whence they both escape again, to reappear in the morning. . . . (I, 40)

The aurora is a cow; this cow has horns; her horns are radiant and golden. When the cow aurora comes forth, all that falls from her horns brings good luck; . . . (I, 51)

The aurora who possesses the pearl becomes she who is rich in pearls, and herself a source of pearls; but the pearl, as we have already seen, is not only the sun, it is also the moon. The moon is the friend of the aurora; she comforts her in the evening under her persecutions; she loads her with presents during the night, accompanies and guides her, and helps her to find her husband. . . . (I, 55 f.)

As the genealogy of the gods and heroes is infinite, so is there an infinite number of forms assumed by the same myth and of the names assumed by the same hero. Each day gave birth in the heavens to a new hero and a new monster, who exterminate each other, and afterwards revive in an aspect more or less glorious, according as their names were more or less fortunate. It is for the same reason that the sons always recognize their fathers without having once seen them or even heard them spoken of; they recognise themselves in their fathers. . . . (I, 83 f.)

The solar hero comes out of his difficulties and triumphs over his enemies, not only by force of arms, but by his innate strength and prowess. This extraordinary strength, by which he is borne along, and which renders him irresistible, is the wind. . . . (I, 105)

The girl who has been married to a monster, whom she flees from to follow a handsome young lover, who arriving at the banks of a river, despoils her of her riches, leaves her naked and passes over to the other side, after which she resigns herself to her fate and resolves to return to her husband the monster, represents the evening aurora, who flees before the monster of night to follow her lover the sun, who, in the morning, after adorning himself with her splendour, leaves her on the shore of the gloomy ocean and runs away, the aurora being thereupon obliged in the evening to re-unite herself to her husband the monster (I, 122).

Gubernatis makes some interesting if absurd interpretations of particular folktales. The first is Type 1540, the joke about the student who tells a woman that he comes from Paris. She understands him to say "Paradise" and gives him money and goods to give to her husband. Gubernatis bases his discussion on the Kalmuck version in *Siddhi-Kür*.

Another beautiful myth of analogous import occurs again in the eighth story. A woodman and a painter envy each other; the painter makes the king believe that the woodman's father, who is in heaven, has written ordering his son to repair to paradise, in order to build him a temple, and to take the route that the painter shall indicate. The king orders the woodman to set out for paradise. The painter prepares a funeral pyre, by way of exit; from this the woodman succeeds in escaping, and going back to the king, he tells him that he has been to paradise, and presents a letter which his father has given him, ordering the painter to come by the same road, and paint the temple. The king requires the summons to be obeyed, and the perfidious painter perishes in the flames. The morning sun emerges safe and sound from the flames of the morning aurora; the evening sun passes through those flames, and dies (I, 130).

It would seem that the absurdities of such interpretations should have been sufficiently obvious to their inventors. But two generations of scholars vied with one another in spinning fancies of this kind. It was only in the 1870's that common sense began to assert itself. The trenchant wit of Andrew Lang made clear enough to everyone the ridiculous conclusions of the mythological school. In a more serious vein he sums up his conclusions thus[5]:

> On the whole, then, the student of *Märchen* must avoid two common errors. He must not regard modern interpolations as part of the mythical essence of a story. He must not hurry to explain every incident as a reference to the natural phenomena of Dawn, Sunset, Wind, Storm, and the like. The points which are so commonly interpreted thus, are sometimes modern interpolations; more frequently they are relics of ancient customs of which the mythologist never heard, or survivals from an archaic mental condition into which he has never inquired.

Though some teachers of Greek and Latin mythology in the schools still tell their students the "interpretations" which their teachers had in turn learned from *their* teachers of the 1870's, the general absurdity of the whole doctrine has long been recognized by all serious scholars in the field. This change of opinion is due not only to this devastating criticism of Lang but also to certain other satirical attacks. Among the latter the best known is Gaidoz's *jeu d'esprit*, "Comme quoi M. Max Müller n'a jamais existé: étude de mythologie comparée,"[6] in which, by using the approved methods of comparative mythology he disposes of the great scholar Max Müller, and shows that he himself is nothing but a myth.

While one school of research was exploring the *Rig-Veda* and its influence on the folktale, another, which entirely rejected both the general Indo-European and the mythological theories, was also, from another point of

[5] *Op. cit.*, I, xviii.
[6] *Mélusine*, II, 73.

view, finding India the fountainhead of folktale tradition. The leader of this school was Theodor Benfey.

As early as 1838 Loiseleur Deslongchamps[7] had suggested that the originals of the European folktales were probably to be found in India, but it was Benfey who took this suggestion and advanced it to a dogma. Though in several of his earlier studies he had put forward this idea, it was expressed with especial clearness and authority in the Introduction to his edition of the *Panchatantra* in 1859. This doctrine was so important for the scholarship of the next two generations that it calls for a translation of the whole passage.[8]

As far as the sources and the dissemination of the stories contained in the *Panchatantra* are concerned, it is clear that in general most of the animal fables originated in the occident and are in greater or less degree transformations of the so-called Aesop fables. Nevertheless, some of them give the impression of having an origin in India, for as in the case of the great mass of Indic stories as a whole, the freedom with which the borrowed material has been handled as well as many other considerations indicate that the Hindus, even before their acquaintance with the animal fables of Aesop which they received from the Greeks, had invented their own compositions of a similar kind, and a great many of them at that. The difference between their conceptions and those of the Aesop fables consisted in general in the fact that whereas the Aesopic writer had his animals act in accordance with their own characteristics, the Indic fable treated the animals without regard to their special nature, as if they were merely men masked in animal form. Furthermore, to these may be added, for one thing, the essentially—and in India exclusively—didactic nature of the animal fable, and for another the prevalent Hindu belief in the transmigration of souls.

Folktales on the other hand, and especially *Märchen* show that they were originally from India; and, what is still more important, it is with these tales that the Hindus—although in a large measure only at a later time —have, so to speak, paid back over and over again the debt incurred by the borrowing of the animal tales from the Occident. My investigations in the field of fables, *Märchen*, and tales of the Orient and Occident have brought me to the conviction that few fables, but a great number of *Märchen* and other folktales have spread outward from India almost over the entire world. As far as the time of this dissemination is concerned, comparatively few had wandered toward the west before about the tenth century after Christ, and these (except for the stories made known through translations of the groundwork of the *Panchatantra* or *Kalilah and Dimnah*) only through oral tradition occasioned by the meeting of travelers, merchants, and the like.

With the tenth century, however, there began with the continued attacks and conquests of the Islamites in India an ever-increasing acquaintance with India. From that point on the oral tradition became less important than the

[7] *Essai sur les fables indiennes* (Paris, 1838).

[8] T. Benfey, *Pantschatantra: Fünf Bücher indischer Fabeln, Märchen, und Erzählungen* (2 vols., Leipzig, 1859).

written. The narrative works of India were now translated into Persian and Arabic, and sometimes the works themselves and sometimes only the contents were scattered in a relatively short time over the realm of the Islamites in Asia, Africa, and Europe, and, because of the frequent intercourse of these peoples with Christians, also throughout the Christian Occident. In the latter respect the chief points of contact were the Byzantine Empire, Italy, and Spain.

In still greater numbers and in part even earlier, the already mentioned three classes of Hindu compositions spread to those districts to the east and north of India. From our investigations comes a conviction that these compositions found their principal expression in Buddhist literature. With this literature, from about the first century after Christ, as long as China remained in close contact with Buddhist India, they penetrated without interruption into China, and the striking discovery of Stan. Julian, which we have already mentioned, shows that the Chinese feel a strong sympathy for just this side of Buddhism and considered it worth their while to make special collections of the various compositions found in the Buddhist traditions.

In the same way as they had spread to China they also reached Tibet. As long as the latter received its religious concepts from China, these came from China, but after Tibet was in immediate contact with India they came from India.

From the Tibetans they finally came along with Buddhism to the Mongols, and of these people we know with the utmost certainty that they took over the tales of India into their own language—to be sure, with many changes and modifications, concerning the details of which we cannot yet give any more definite account. In addition to the Mongolian reworking of the *Vetalapanchavimcati*, and of the *Vikramacharitra*, it may be remarked that it has become certain that the third tale collection, the *Sukasaptati*, was also familiar to the Mongols. Now, the Mongols for almost two hundred years were in power in Europe and in this way opened up a wide gate for the intrusion of Indic conceptions into Europe.

Thus it is on the one hand the Islamites, and on the other the Buddhists who have brought about the diffusion of the folktales of India over almost the whole world. But how easily such compositions spread abroad, with what pleasure and passion they are heard and repeated, everyone knows from his own experience. . . . Because of their inner excellence the tales from India seem to have absorbed whatever similar ideas already existed among the various people to whom they came. Individual traits, however, could hardly have been preserved in the rapid adaptations of material of such alien nationality. For the transformations which tales experience, especially as they are disseminated orally, are, aside from an adaptation to a different nationality, almost entirely a kaleidoscopic confusion of forms, traits, and motifs which were originally separated. To the same cause is due their great numbers; though this is, as a matter of fact, only apparent, for in reality the great mass of them, especially the European folktales, reduce themselves to a by no means considerable number of fundamental forms, out of which with greater or less luck and skill they have been multiplied, through the activity partly of the folk and partly of individuals.

The literary vehicle was primarily the *Tuti Nameh*, Arabic, and very probably Jewish writings. Alongside of these ran oral traditions, especially in the Slavic lands. In the literature of Europe the narratives appear above all in Boccaccio, the *Märchen* in Straparola. From literature they were taken over by the people, and having been changed by them they went again into literature, again to the folk, etc. and assumed, especially because of this alternate activity of national and individual spirit, that character of national truth and individual unity which gives to not a few of them such great poetic value.

This point of view concerning the origin and history of concepts of this kind, which are found outside India among cultivated peoples or among those who are in closest contact with them, is a question of fact which will not receive its full settlement until all or at least the greater part of these conceptions are traced back to their source in India. This work is only begun in the following Introduction; by far the greater part of my results will appear in further investigations which will be devoted to the editing and investigating the other narrative collections of India. As everyone will realize, these studies necessitate a multitude of comparisons and not seldom a consideration of dry details of development. These, however, will be enlivened or at least be made readable because of the mixing in of many unknown or little known tales and *Märchen*. Nevertheless, I feel that I can hardly hope to reach my goal—namely, the winning of a wider circle to my opinion—unless I encounter a certain measure of good will on the part of my readers. Perhaps this may be accorded me more readily if it is remembered that the introduction of these cheerful conceptions into the midst of, and in opposition to, the ascetic direction of the Middle Ages was by no means of small importance. Their sensuality, even if occasionally somewhat lascivious, helped not a little to bring literature back to its straight path, that is, to nature, so that almost immediately after their reception in Europe they resulted in Boccaccio's *Decameron* and Don Manuel's *Conde Lucanor*—those flowerings of medieval prose which still stand almost unrivaled in Italy and Spain. Finally, it is the *Märchen* we have spoken of which create the inexhaustible, ever-bubbling fountain at which all the people, high and low, but especially those who have no other springs of spiritual enjoyment, continually refresh themselves anew.

Benfey thus sees the origin of folktales, except the Aesop fables, in India, and thinks the spread westward had taken place through three channels: (1) a certain number by oral tradition before the tenth century; (2) after the tenth century by literary tradition along the lines of Islamic influence, particularly through Byzantium, Italy, and Spain; (3) Buddhistic material through China and Tibet (or directly) to the Mongols and from them to Europe. Important as literary vehicles were the Persian *Tuti Nameh,* Arabic, and probably Jewish writings. Oral tradition also assisted in spreading the tales, especially in Slavic countries.

The elaborate comparative notes made by Benfey for each of the stories in the *Panchatantra* gave convincing scholarly weight to his opinions and for at least a generation directed the research of many folktale scholars into the channels he had indicated. A period of intensive comparative studies of tale collections began, which resulted in the real beginning of the structure of modern folktale scholarship. The underlying hypothesis of these studies posited India as the fountain from which the European tales had all flowed, but whether their labors actually pointed to that conclusion or not, the vast collections of analogues brought together under this stimulus was a permanent gain.

After Benfey himself the most important scholar engaged in such researches was Reinhold Köhler, Librarian of the Ducal Library at Weimar. For many years he published annotations of the chief collections of European tales as they appeared[9] and more and more, through the accumulation of these facts, the mutual relationship of the various tales and motifs were clarified. These studies did not by any means all lead back to India, and though they established India's importance for European tales, they also showed that Benfey had overstated his case.

Köhler was primarily an annotater and appears not to have concerned himself much about general theories as to the origin of European tales. Much more of a real proponent of Benfey's basic ideas was Emmanuel Cosquin, who published a distinguished series of monographs over a period of thirty years beginning around 1890.[10] He studied scores of tales and motifs, always with emphasis on the relation to analogues from India, which he was convinced represented the source. His studies usually do not consider a sufficient number of versions of the tales in question to arrive at a real conclusion, but they indicate a remarkable advance in our knowledge of many stories, and they furnish a foundation for more definitive work by future scholars.

Cosquin modified the Benfey theory in two respects. He became convinced that Benfey was mistaken as to the important role he had assigned the Mongols in the dissemination of stories over Europe. He was also impressed by collections of Egyptian folktales which were too early for the borrowing from India as described by Benfey. India may not have originated all the tales, thought Cosquin, but it has nevertheless served as the great reservoir into which tales of diverse origins have flowed and from which they flow out in turn over the earth.

The Indianist theory of Benfey is not utterly dead today, but with the passing of Cosquin in 1921 it lost its last apologist. Most modern folktale scholars are convinced that India was important as a source of many stories, but that it was only one of several great centers of invention and dissemination.

To this Indianist theory as well as to the mythological theory Andrew

---

[9] These were assembled and edited by Johannes Bolte under the title of *Kleinere Schriften*.
[10] These are to be found for the most part in *Revue des traditions populaires*. Two collections of these studies are: *Etudes folkloriques* and *Contes indiens*. See also the notes to his *Contes populaires de Lorraine*.

Lang was perhaps the most skillful opponent. He began pointing out the significance in the light of this theory of the discovery of the Egyptian folktales dating from the thirteenth century B.C., as well as of the tales mentioned in Herodotus and Homer. These facts made Lang disbelieve in the primary importance of India for the history of the tale.

As for his positive ideas about the origin of tales, he called attention to the many primitive ideas in modern folktales and put forward the opinion that the presence of these traits showed that the tales are survivals from a very ancient time. It is often said that Lang was a believer in "polygenesis," or the theory that resemblances in stories are due to independent invention in many places, since they are made up of beliefs, customs, etc. which are common to peoples of the same stages of culture. This position has then been criticized because it is based on the presupposition of a parallel development of culture everywhere, a parallelism which would manifest itself in analogous tales. Though it is possible to find adherents of such an extreme doctrine of "polygenesis," it is certain that Lang did not believe in it.

Lang was, indeed, so eminently reasonable in his attitude that the summary of his conclusions gives expression, perhaps better than in any other way to the position folktale scholarship had reached by the end of the nineteenth century, and from which, with only slight modifications, it has moved on into the twentieth. This statement deserves quoting at some length.[11]

Coming from childhood into the light of common day, I found certain theories of popular tales chiefly current. They were regarded as the *detritus* of Myths, the last echo of stories of Gods and Heroes, surviving among the people. These myths, again, were explained, by the schools of Schwartz, Kuhn, Max Müller, as myths either of storm, thunder, and lightning, or of the Sun and Dawn. Further, the myths, and also the tales, were believed to be essentially and exclusively Aryan, parts of the common Aryan heritage, brought from the cradle of the Aryan race. The solar and the elemental theories of the origin of myths, and of their *detritus*, popular tales, did not convince me. The linguistic processes by which words and phrases of forgotten meaning developed into the myths, did not seem to me to be satisfactory solutions. I observed that tales similar to the Aryan in incident and plot existed in non-Aryan countries—Africa, Samoa, New Guinea, North and Central America, Finland, among the Samoyed, and so forth. As it was then denied that tales were lent and borrowed, from people to people, I looked for an explanation of the similarities. The same stories were not likely to be evolved among peoples who did, and people who did not, speak an Aryan language, if language misunderstood was the source of tales. I also reached the conclusion that, when similar incidents and plot occurred in a Greek heroic myth (say the Argonautic Legend or the *Odyssey*) and in popular tales current in Finland, Samoa, Zululand, the tales are not the *detritus* of the heroic myth, but the epic legend, as of Jason or Odysseus, is an artistic and literary modification

[11] Introduction to Cox, *Cinderella*, pp. xi ff.

of the more ancient tale. The characters of the *tale* are usually anonymous, and the places are vague and nameless. The characters of the *epic* are named, they are national heroes; the events are localised; they occur in Greece, Colchis, and so forth. So I concluded that the *donnée* was ancient and popular, the epic was comparatively recent and artistic. Next I observed that the tales generally contained, while the epics usually discarded, many barbaric incidents, such as cannibalism, magic, talking animals. Further, I perceived that the tales varied in "culture" with the civilisation of the people who told them. Among savages, say Bushmen, or in a higher grade Zulus, the characters were far more frequently *animals* than in European *märchen*. The girl who answers to Medea is not the daughter of a wizard king, but the wife of an elephant. The same peculiarity marks savage religious myths. The gods are beasts or birds. These facts led me to suppose that the tales were very ancient, and had been handed down, with a gradual refining, from ages of savagery to ages of civilisation. But the peasant class which retains the tales has been so conservative and unaltered, that many of the wilder features of the original tale (discarded in early artistic and national epic) linger on in *Märchen*. Thus, in most peasant versions of the *Cinderella* theme, the wonder-working character is a beast, a sheep in Scotland; sometimes that beast has been the heroine's mother. In our usual *Cinderella*, derived from Perrault's version (1697), the wonder-working character is a fairy godmother. Thus I seemed to detect a process of genealogy like this:

Original Tale, probably of Savage Origin

Popular Tale of Peasants

Ancient Literary Heroic Myth (Homer, Cyclic Poems, *Argonautica*, Lays of Sigurd, *Nibelungenlied*, Perseus Myth, etc.)	Modern Literary Version (Perrault)

Discovering an apparent process of refinement and elaboration, and behind that ideas very barbaric, I examined the more peculiar incidents of popular tales. Talking beasts are common, beasts acting as men are common: no less common, among savages, is the frame of mind in which practically no distinction is taken between gods, beasts, and men. The more barbaric the people, the more this lack of distinction marks their usages, ritual, myth, and tales. Of magic and cannibalism it is needless to speak. The more civilised the people, the less of these elements appears in their ritual, usage, and myth: most survives in their popular tales, and even in these it is gradually mitigated. My conclusion was that the tales dated from an age of savage fancy. . . .

I have frequently shown the many ways in which a tale, once conceived, might be diffused or transmitted. . . . On the other hand, I have frequently said that, given a similar state of taste and fancy, similar beliefs, similar circumstances, a *similar* tale might conceivably be independently evolved in regions remote from each other. We know that similar patterns, similar art (compare Aztec and Mycenaean pottery in the British Museum), have thus been independently evolved; so have similar cosmic myths, similar fables, similar riddles, similar proverbs, similar customs and institutions.

The interest which Lang had in primitive man is natural because of the remarkable work done by the English school of anthropologists during the second half of the nineteenth century. Under the leadership of E. B. Tylor the study of primitive peoples had come to occupy the attention of a very able group of scholars who began to investigate special aspects of human behavior in the light of the accumulating mass of data being reported from all over the world. The concept of organic evolution in the realm of biology was still but new and had not worked itself properly into the general thinking of scholars. Where it was accepted at all, it was likely to be applied too far.

All sorts of illogical practices and beliefs were found over the world not only among primitive peoples but among the most enlightened, and these were brought together and compared. In such a work as Frazer's twelve-volume *Golden Bough* a remarkable collection of these data are displayed in a logical sequence that seems to present a picture of the thinking and acting of man in his more primitive stages. But remarkable as the assemblage of material is, the conclusions to be drawn are not nearly so certain as Frazer indicates. Story motifs, practices, and beliefs are shown which are practically identical among the American Indians, the natives of Australia, and those of South Africa. The assumption is that all peoples have gone through the same stages of culture in a direct line of evolution and that in each stage they react to the world and express themselves in the same way. In higher stages there may be survivals of the earlier stages. Thus among European peasants many illogical things are found that go back to a time when they were objects of belief or actual practice.

These two theories, namely, of the direct and parallel evolution of cultures and of survivals in culture, caused such folklorists as MacCulloch[12] to study folktales primarily as products of primitive culture and as filled with motifs going back to a remote period in Europe and Asia when they were believed; and they assembled parallels among primitive peoples. The findings of such scholars as Frazer and MacCulloch are of the utmost interest, but they overlook two considerations, so important as to take away much of the value of their work. One is that culture is a matter of historical development for each people, and is subjected to all sorts of special influences internal and external, so that except in the vaguest and most general sense, parallelism between differing ones, especially if they are far removed, is an unjustified assumption.

---

[12] *The Childhood of Fiction* (London, 1905).

Such studies also underestimate the role which diffusion of the elements of tribal life has played, and they pay scant attention to the great community of interest among peoples within particular "culture areas."

In their studies of the folktale, the English anthropologists had the virtue of catholicity of interest. They concerned themselves with all sorts of motifs common to European tales and those of primitive peoples and they were sensible of the fact that many tales belonged to particular areas and had limited distribution. But the dissemination of complete tale types, and consequently of all the component motifs, seemed to them not nearly so significant as the establishing of the primitive nature of the motifs themselves.

This interest in the motifs, rather than in complete tales, is, in fact, characteristic of all those scholars who seek to find some general principle by which to explain the origin of tale-telling as a human activity. The motifs are simple and it is therefore much easier to make simple explanations of them than if one has to explain a whole tale which consists of a complex of motifs. The same simple motif may arise independently in different places, or it may be carried from place to place. It is therefore possible to assemble hundreds or even thousands of instances of the same motif from all parts of the earth, and this fact has been used by scholars to establish the most diverse and mutually exclusive explanations of the origin of tale-telling. Each group has interested itself in particular kinds of material and the scholars representing each have usually neglected everything that does not fit itself into their theories.

The Indo-European mythological method of explaining the origin of stories and myths was generally discredited by the end of the nineteenth century, but it did not put an end to the use of similar reasoning on the part of certain anthropologists who now adapted it to the tales of the whole world. It was early applied to American Indian myths by Brinton, who saw sun gods in the Iroquois and Ojibwa heroes.[13] A whole school of writers[14] has engaged in the study of "comparative mythology" which attempts to show that mythological stories (and this seems to mean practically all folktales) of all peoples are essentially the same because these stories are saying exactly the same things, though in diverse ways. The most complete exposition of this theory is perhaps that of Ehrenreich.[15]

This scholar agrees that folktales have been disseminated from certain centers, but he feels that even a complete understanding of such dissemination is only the beginning of the scholar's real task. For a full understanding of the tales scattered over the globe we need to examine the "inner relationship,"

[13] D. G. Brinton, *American Hero Myths* (Philadelphia, 1882), *Myths of the New World* (New York and London, 1868), *passim*.

[14] A good idea of their work can be had from the files of *Mythologische Bibliothek* (Leipzig, 1907-1916).

[15] Paul Ehrenreich, *Die allgemeine Mythologie und ihre ethnologischen Grundlagen* (Leipzig, 1910).

that is the *meaning* of the contents. "Every natural phenomenon," he says,[16] "produces by psychological necessity definite forms of expression which arise in part from apperception and in part from association." Thus the observation of the eclipse of the sun by the moon may, through association and analogy, find expression in a number of ways; for example (1) the swallowing of a hero; (2) the hero's fight with a monster; (3) jumping of the moon-being into a fire-pit (a bath of rejuvenation, etc.); (4) being cooked in a vessel (the last visible crescent of the moon is conceived of as a vessel); (5) copulation (incest of the sun and the moon). In other places Ehrenreich finds the crescent moon to be a snake. The waxing and waning of the moon, he asserts, may suggest the following—and many other—motifs: (1) blackening (of some person or animal); (2) three-day hiding or absence; (3) cutting off a head with a sickle; (4) substitutions; (5) disguises. Ehrenreich says that his study is based upon the "undeniable" parallel development of all cultures. The same natural phenomena must produce the same mythical expression, and hence there is a myth-making process subject to definite laws.

For a study of this kind one needs the simplest and most transparent form of the myth, a form which Ehrenreich calls the *naturmythologisches Märchen*. "These primary forms, or *Urmären*, relate simply what is seen and in a fanciful manner bring detailed points of the impressions and appearances into causal relationship through human likenesses." From this first stage the development is by definite psychological laws (mainly association) working irrespective of time and place, not merely on the gifted individual but on the mass of people.

The most important of those natural phenomena which form a common basis for ideas all over the world are the sun, the moon, certain stars and constellations. Of these Ehrenreich considers the moon most important.

This "astral" mythology can, of course, be nothing more than a hypothesis to explain striking analogues in tales. But it is never stated as a simple hypothesis. Like the weather-mythology of Müller and Gubernatis, it depends on assumptions that are never proved. We have no assurance, nor does it even seem likely, that most primitive peoples really concern themselves much with the heavenly bodies. The analogies between actual motifs and these astral phenomena are based on the most tenuous suggestions and are probably not valid even for one people, though they are stated as dogmas and applied to the whole world.

Another school of mythologists and folklorists is particularly impressed with the prevalence of certain patterns of thought in widely separated places. Examples of such concepts are twin heroes or twin gods who go on adventures together. In his *Cult of the Heavenly Twins* and his *Boanerges*[17]

---

[16] P. 34.
[17] Cambridge [England], 1906, 1913.

Rendel Harris studies such story cycles and thinks he finds in these elementary concepts the key that unlocks all the difficulties of myth and folktale. This method of study shows the same weaknesses in the field of folk narrative as Frazer's *Golden Bough* in the larger world of custom and belief. Resemblances from far and near are assembled without adequate consideration of the probability or improbability of their being actually connected in human tradition. Intermediate peoples without these concepts are disregarded, so that no rational conclusions as to the actual relation between two similar but widely separated motifs can be reached.

Any careful student of such incidents soon learns that logical relationship does not necessitate organic connection and that identical simple ideas arise over and over. It is not necessary to strain for an explanation either by proposing dubious routes of diffusion or by asserting a mystical theory by which all men through a necessity of some kind make up tales of twin gods. If men tell tales at all they must sometimes hit upon the same motifs. And no copyright office even today prevents this.

The value of scholars of the type of Harris and Frazer consists primarily in their bringing to our attention a huge number of interesting similarities in narrative pattern. Even if we do not see the same significance in these resemblances which they do, we must at least realize that they have posed a large number of important questions for future students of comparative mythology and folklore.

Interest in the origin of many of the motifs of modern folktales as survivals from the life and experiences of primitive peoples was especially strong among anthropologists and folklorists of a generation ago. Obsolete customs and beliefs of all kinds and their appearance in European tales were studied not only by Lang, MacCulloch, and Hartland, but by such German scholars as Friedrich von der Leyen.[18] The latter paid special attention to the likelihood that dreams originally gave rise to many of the incidents now found in folktales. This theory had been stated in extreme form by Ludwig Laistner in his *Das Rätsel der Sphinx*,[19] where he held that dreams and their meaning were the clue for an understanding of all folktales, legends, and traditions. Von der Leyen recognizes that some ancient dreams may have brought about certain incidents—flight from ogres, attempts to perform impossible tasks and many others—but he is rightly sceptical of any wholesale application of the theory.

Laistner was most concerned with the dream of fear or distress. The Freudians have also done much "interpreting" of folktales as expression of dreams of suppressed desires. Neither of these groups have been realistic in their approach to the problem of folktale origins. With no knowledge of when or where or by whom a tale or an incident was first told they proceed

[18] *Das Märchen* (3rd ed., Leipzig, 1925).
[19] Berlin, 1889.

to dogmatize as to the exact circumstance that gave rise to it. Such speculations can be of little aid to an understanding of either the beginning or
development of the folktale. At most their proponents point out mere possibilities, even though they usually assert them as established facts.[20]

Another particular feature of primitive life has been stressed by Saintyves,[21]
who studies the well-known tales of Perrault's collection and thinks that he
has discovered the ultimate origin of each. These eleven tales he arranges in
three classes, but all of them, he is convinced, show their origin in some kind
of ancient ritual. Saintyves is careful to show for each of the tales the
absurdities of previous interpretations by the mythological school of folklorists, but the explanations which he substitutes have seemed to most
judicious scholars to be not less fantastic than those he seeks to replace. Five
of the tales (Red Ridinghood, Les fées, Sleeping Beauty, Cinderella, and Cap
o' Rushes), he says, have their origin in a ritual celebrating the seasons; four
(Petit Poucet, Bluebeard, Riquet à la Houpe, and Puss in Boots) go back to
initiation ceremonies; and in two (Patient Griselda and The Foolish Wishes)
he sees the remains of medieval sermons.

The utilitarian character of tales, especially as they relate to the institution
of totemism and totemistic rites is developed by Arnold van Gennep in his
very important work La formation des légendes.[22] Basing his findings on a
wide knowledge of anthropology, particularly of the Australian natives, van
Gennep attempts to arrive at some general conclusions about how tales are
formed. He is entirely unimpressed with the explanations of the Ehrenreich
school and in his discussion of legends of the heavenly bodies and the stars
he points out what a small part such legends actually play in the tales
of primitive peoples. Very important among all such tribes, however, are
animal tales. These, he thinks, are of great interest to the tribe—because of
the importance of totem animals and of rites connected with the totem. The
recitation of myths and legends in primitive and ancient society was an
indispensable rite. It was of practical importance in furthering the efficacy of
the ceremony.

Primitive myths and tales, he contends, always taught a lesson of conduct
or they were helpful to the tribe in bringing about ends which were desired.
On the primitive level the same thing may be in one place a myth (which,
according to van Gennep, is a tale having direct relation to a rite), a legend,
or a tale. These are always localized and individualized; the unlocalized tale
(Märchen) is a later development. From a utilitarian point of view, the
genres of folktale proceed from myths and legends, which are of most practical value, to the fairy tales and novelle, which are of least. The legend may

---

[20] For examples of such speculations, see p. 99 f.
[21] P. Saintyves [pseud. of É. Nourry], Les contes de Perrault et les recits parallèles (Paris,
1923), pp. xvii ff.
[22] Paris, 1910.

explain a duty, the myth help with a rite. Intermediate are animal tales, and fables, which teach lessons.

Van Gennep's very illuminating discussion of the development of mythologies and heroic legends is well documented and does not depend on any theories of parallelism or any mystical interpretations of heavenly phenomena. It recognizes the cosmological significance of more developed mythologies, but sees in them an elaboration under the influence of cults and priests.

Van Gennep's interest in totemism has undoubtedly caused him to give it a larger place in his treatment of the origin of tales than it merits. But one feels that he has his feet on the ground and that in so far as he goes he is a safe guide.

In agreement in many ways with van Gennep is Hans Naumann, who has presented his views in a series of essays entitled *Primitive Gemeinschafts-kultur*.[23] He feels that the various forms of the folktale—myth, legend, hero tale, *Märchen*—are in their broad scope nearly the same. "They are, though by no means always very old, often made up in their fundamental motifs of narrative material which belongs to primitive man. They differ from each other above all in the manner in which they are definitely related to time and place or attached to a definite human, historic, or divine personality."[24] The differences in the forms of the tale are stylistic and are not based on deep psychological facts. All of them are founded on primitive beliefs which have at the same time been expressed in religious rites. Hence we find many traces of religious rites in folktales—sometimes almost hidden from view.

This last idea brings us around to a point which is so much insisted on that it seems central to Naumann's treatment. Primitive religious rites are most concerned with avoiding the malevolent return of the dead—not a "soul" but a dead man who still has it in his power to do harm. A great number of folk stories either contain some disguised ritual for avoidance of the dead or else they reflect the primitive belief concerning the dead. Hence the motif of the obstacle flight, in which magic objects are thrown back to retard or block off the ogre in pursuit, he says, is based on such a ritualistic procedure used to prevent the return of the dead. This ritual being universal, the tale motif is also universal.

From the belief about and fear of the dead among primitive men have come all sorts of ogre stories. The ogre is nothing but the dead, who has been variously imagined by different people. Whenever we have an ogre and a hero overcoming the ogre we have the dead and the protector against the dead. Fairies, dwarfs, nixes, brownies, and all ogres of any kind come from the belief in the living dead. Naumann brings together a huge number of tales of the Bluebeard and of the Hansel and Gretel types and, though he

[23] Jena, 1921.
[24] P. 61.

admits certain of them are borrowed from others, in general he insists that they are all the natural expression of the fear of the dead and of the desire to overcome their power.

Both Naumann and van Gennep are impressed by certain widespread beliefs and practices of primitive man. Each has taken one feature of primitive religion and has found it the most important psychological fact in the life of all primitive men. From these beliefs and practices they have attempted to explain the origin of certain identical tales in various parts of the world. They are both interested, therefore, in supporting the independent origin of analogous stories—that is, the theory of polygenesis of motifs—though neither denies diffusion.

The fundamental weakness of both theories is the assumption of much greater uniformity among primitive peoples than probably exists in fact. When we look at primitive society through one pair of glasses we see nothing but the interest in the totem animal and its relation to the tribe. The other glasses show the tribe living in continual fear of the return of dead men and expressing this fear by the invention of all sorts of supernatural creatures. No doubt both of these conditions can be found, but they are probably not both as important for the origin of folk narrative as the respective authors think.

One must not try to explain everything in primitive life by one simple formula—whether it be totemism, fear of the dead, or obsession with stars or dawn maidens. Doubtless certain motifs go back to each of these sources, and in spite of the emphasis of the studies of van Gennep and Naumann it is clear that these scholars recognize that this is true. But with them as indeed with Cox, Gubernatis, Ehrenreich, and all those who try to explain tales from one characteristic of primitive man, the reader is continually being persuaded that he has at last reached the exclusive fountainhead of all folk narrative.

Anthropological research for the past half century has resulted in a widespread and justified skepticism regarding the validity of most generalizations about primitive man. We are more and more aware that in spite of many resemblances in the culture of peoples outside the circles of modern civilized man, many of these resemblances are not real identities either from the psychological or historic point of view. Often they are merely the lack of certain elements of our civilization—a lack which they naturally share in common. Closer acquaintance brings knowledge of difference as well as of likeness. Better awareness of the geographical and historical factors makes us see a particular culture surrounded by others and being continually influenced by its neighbors. The statement, "Primitive man believes so and so" or "Primitive man acts thus and thus," ceases to carry the conviction which it did in the early days of Tylor's *Primitive Culture*.

The complex nature of the problem of the distribution of all culture traits, including folktales, has been widely recognized of late years by many anthropologists and folklorists. Particularly has the intensive study of the American Indian tale during the last half century made it possible to speak of "primitive" tales with a knowledge of the facts impossible to scholars of an earlier generation. In the Pacific area also Malinowski[25] has clarified for us the myth-making process of a group of Melanesians whom he has studied with extraordinary intensity. Though Malinowski has a tendency to treat the tales of his Trobriand Islanders as if they had grown up entirely uninfluenced by stories of the rest of the world, he demonstrates beyond all doubt the fact that tales and myths are an extremely important element in the culture of an isolated island group. They are much more than mere entertainment: they are a part of the primitive man's science, medicine, religion, law, and agriculture. Malinowski's findings give no comfort to those who look for hidden meanings or fantastic origins for the folktale.

With all his qualities of thoroughness and clear-headed interpretation, Malinowski seems provincial in his point of view. The study of a world-wide phenomenon like the tale or the myth can hardly be made in total disregard of all places other than a single group of islands.

A proper grasp of the larger bearings of his study of primitive narrative is always shown in the work of Franz Boas.[26] He had the advantage of knowing exhaustively the tales of one tribe, the Kwakiutl, and he studied the relation of these tales to their life and culture. But he also knew the folklore of the rest of America, and in a measure, of the whole world. As far as folktales on the primitive level are concerned, he has perhaps uttered the final words of wisdom.

For one thing, he is convinced that no study of the origin of myths can be undertaken without a knowledge of the modern history of myths. Before one can speculate about what must have happened in far-off times and places, he should find what actually happens today in a particular tribe. "We have no reason," says he, "to believe that the myth-making processes of the last ten thousand years differed materially from modern myth-making processes" (p. 404).

Boas also minimizes the distinction between folktale and myth. "The facts that are brought out most clearly from a careful analysis of myths and folk-tales of an area like the northwest coast of America are that the contents of folk-tales and myths are largely the same, that the data show a continual flow of material from mythology to folk-tale and *vice-versa*, and that neither group can claim priority. We furthermore observe that contents and form of mythology and folk-tales are determined by the conditions that determined early literary art" (p. 405). In both cases he is convinced that the origins of the narrative are due to the play of the imagination with the events of

[25] Bronislaw Malinowski, *Myth in Primitive Psychology* (New York, 1926).
[26] *Race, Language, and Culture* (New York, 1940).

human life. But this play of the imagination in man is rather limited, so that there is every tendency to operate with an old stock of imaginative happenings rather than to invent new ones (p. 406).

Boas is convinced that mythologies did not begin with the simple observation of natural phenomena. He recognizes that these have a part now in many myths, but he is certain that it would be a mistake to interpret any specific myth as being due to such observations. The growth of myths and tales is extremely complex, and there have been all kinds of disintegration and accretion of foreign materials. The original form of any particular myth may be quite impossible to discover. And there is certainly no one explanation which will afford an easy answer to the general problem (p. 429).

Boas has some valuable observations concerning the relation of tale-types and motifs. Except in the European area where the tale-types have been rather clearly evolved, he finds that it is the individual motif which forms the object of dissemination and borrowing. Among most peoples these motifs combine rather freely. The forming of them into permanent clusters occurs among primitive peoples, but much more rarely than among Europeans. The individual motifs are likely to be much less realistic than the general plot of the tale, which is usually based upon the experiences of ordinary life (p. 399).

Finally, Boas was much interested in the study of style in folktales, and the relation of stylistic qualities to the tribe, and to the function of the particular tale in the life of the people. He recognized that this study was just beginning, and it is a fact that most of the actual efforts in this direction have been made by later scholars whom he has influenced.

By no means all the theoretical treatment which men have devoted to the folktale has been touched on in the preceding pages, for many points are brought up elsewhere in connection with appropriate aspects of the subject. Considerations of various folktale forms appear as introductions to the detailed factual discussion of each of these genres.[27] Specific problems of dissemination, collecting, and style are most conveniently handled in connection with the pertinent chapters on "The Life History of a Folktale," "Collecting Folktales," and "The Folktale as Living Art."[28]

[27] Pp. 21, 188, 217, and 234.
[28] Pp. 428, 406, and 449.

INTERNATIONAL ORGANIZATION
OF FOLKTALE STUDY

In the last years of the nineteenth century the study of the folktale, as well as of all other aspects of folklore, began a period of vigorous activity. We have seen something of the mingled success and failure of the earlier students in this new field. They were pioneers opening up a virgin land where there had been no boundaries surveyed and where there were no prospectors to guide them. Is it any wonder that sometimes their newly found riches proved to be fool's gold and that in their eagerness to grasp everything at once they sometimes came forth empty-handed? Wilhelm Grimm, Benfey, Max Müller, and Andrew Lang had all essayed to answer the fundamental questions as to the nature of the folktale, its origin and distribution, and though representatives of each school still labored and wrote, it was clear that these nineteenth century scholars had been premature in their dogmatisms.

Not enough was known about the folktale or any part of popular tradition in the nineteenth century to permit the arrival at safe conclusions. The collected material was still scanty, especially among primitive peoples, and yet on this inadequate basis scholars with great names had ventured to generalize. Even if they did state their opinions as opinions and not as dogmas, the weight of their names soon caused their younger disciples to overstep the caution of their leaders. Thus a large part of the intellectual effort being devoted to the study of folk tradition was leading in divergent directions because it was based upon different assumptions.

And these assumptions were not really axiomatic, but, as later scholarship has shown, extremely dubious. One group of students was staking everything on the analogy between the development of the Indo-European languages and that of Indo-European folktales and took it for granted that inheritance from a common (linguistically determined) ancestry is the explanation for similarities in folktales. Another assumption (often by the same group of scholars) was that men in an early state of culture were greatly concerned with the behavior of the heavenly bodies, and the various aspects of the weather—so much so that if we could only penetrate the mystery we would find that all (or most) stories were originally about these cosmic forces and only later had degenerated into the stories we now have. The Indianists were tracing almost everything back to India, and the English Anthropologists were doing remarkable work under the inspiration of a new assumption: the parallel development of culture all over the world. None of these four important ideas, so widely taken for granted, had really been submitted to an unbiased study. As we are now aware, not one of the assumptions was safe.

It is small wonder then that among the students of the folktale the judicious should have grieved and aspired to the establishment of a solid foundation for their studies. Beginning about 1880 more and more of the efforts of such scholars were directed toward the assembling of trustworthy material and the unprejudiced empirical study of what was already available.

Folklore journals multiplied and with them the collecting and studying of tales flourished. Between 1878 and 1890 nearly every country in Europe started one of these periodicals, and in 1888 one was also founded in America.[1]

This activity in publishing was one expression of the zeal of a new generation of folklorists in many lands. A few of these men wrote their names large in the annals of folktale study and became of international importance.

In France three scholars of that generation emerge in a retrospect of fifty years. Being the good Frenchmen they were, they did not always agree, but each in his own way helped produce a golden age of folklore study in France. H. Gaidoz (1842-1932), the editor of *Mélusine*, encouraged collecting and wrote many critical articles, but his greatest service to the cause of folktale study was the devastating satire by which he laughed the mythological interpretation of folktales out of court. We have seen how he used the methods of these mythologists and proved thereby that Max Müller and his activities at Oxford were not real, that the great Max himself was but a nature myth, as were also Oxford and the German home from which he came.[2] This bit of laughter was all that was needed to show the insubstantial base on which the speculations of the whole school was founded. Though not without remote

---

[1] A few of these journals (many of them still appearing) were: French: *Mélusine* (1878), *Revue des traditions populaires* (1886), and *La tradition* (1887); German: *Am Urdhsbrunnen* (1881), *Zeitschrift für Volkskunde* (edited by Veckenstedt) (1888), *Am Urquell* (1890), and *Zeitschrift des Vereins für Volkskunde* (1891); England: *Folk-Lore Record* (1878), followed successively by *Folk-Lore Journal* (1883), and *Folk-Lore* (1890); Denmark: *Dania* (1890); Italy: *Archivio per lo Studio delle Tradizioni Popolari* (1882); United States: *Journal of American Folk-Lore* (1888). There were also journals in Greece, Bohemia, Poland, and Russia, and many local periodicals.

[2] See p. 375, above.

influence on some modern theorists, the old idea of the tale as a disintegrated myth of the weather or the dawn or the heavenly bodies and only to be understood by the methods of comparative philology—this was discredited and the sane study of the folktale was relieved of a great incubus.

The most important organizer of folklore studies in France in the closing years of the century was Paul Sébillot (1846-1918), editor of the *Revue des traditions populaires*. During the thirty years of its existence this journal was the principal organ for the publication of tales collected in all parts of France and for some of the most important scholarly articles from the pen of Sébillot himself and numerous colleagues, especially Cosquin. Sébillot was an indefatigable collector of tales and other folklore from Brittany. It is largely through his stimulus that other sections of France were represented by volumes of *contes populaires*, accurately taken from the people themselves—such, for example, as those of Bladé for Gascony and Luzel for Lower Brittany.

The third of these French scholars was Emmanuel Cosquin (1841-1921). His activity started before the death of the Grimms, who encouraged him in his ambitions to collect folktales. In 1876 he began to issue tales from Lorraine and finally published his *Contes populaires de Lorraine* in 1887. This work has generally been accepted as the representative French collection, occupying much the same position for France as the Grimms' *Household Tales* do for Germany. At the time of their appearance, his comparative notes to the stories were the most extensive available, and they are still valuable. Cosquin was a follower of Benfey and felt that his principal goal was to discover the original of his stories and motifs in India, but he did not let this bias prevent him from pursuing his researches wherever they led him. In his many special studies[3]—some of them of great value—he modified his position from time to time as the facts before him dictated. Thus he acknowledged the priority of Egyptian tales to those of India, but as we have already shown,[4] felt that India had, nevertheless, acted as a great reservoir of ancient tales.

Though Cosquin and Sébillot continued to work well into the new century, the study of folktales in France languished, largely because of the influence wielded by Joseph Bédier, whose *Les fabliaux*[5] appeared in 1893. This convincing rebuttal of the mythological, the Indianist, and the Anthropological theories of the origin of the folktale was accompanied by a skeptical attitude toward the value of recording and analyzing large numbers of variants of tales. Whether or not the subsequent dearth of interest in the folktale was entirely because of this agnostic influence, it is true that after the

[3] These studies have been collected in two volumes, *Etudes folkloriques* (1922) and *Les contes indiens et l'occident* (1922). Acting on the suggestion contained in the latter that Cosquin's papers had been deposited in the Institut Catholique in Paris, I went through this manuscript material in 1927 but found that everything of value had been published.

[4] See p. 379, above.

[5] For further discussion see p. 50, above.

death of Sébillot and Cosquin practically no one in France except Arnold van Gennep[6] interested himself in the study of popular tradition. Even the active new generation of folklorists which arose in France around 1930 and succeeded in establishing an official department and museum and acted as host to the International Folklore Congress of 1937 has been mainly interested in other aspects of folklore than the *conte populaire*.

The end of the nineteenth century was also a high point in British folklore, though much of the work now seems somewhat antiquated, since it was so thoroughly committed to the anthropological interpretation of all popular tradition as "survivals in culture." This point of view we have seen expressed by Andrew Lang (1844-1912), who was a canny enough Scot to see that not all folktale parallels could be so explained. His adherents, especially such men as J. A. MacCulloch (1868-   ) have continued to present this polygenetic theory.[7] Not all folklorists of the 1890's were of this persuasion, however, for several of the studies which paved the way for later systematic treatments of diffusion appeared then. The International Folklore Congress held in London in 1891 afforded an excellent symposium, where adherents of various schools met and presented their points of view.[8] English scholars became acutely aware of work being done on the continent, and for some years their journal, *Folk-Lore*, maintained an unusually high standard. Joseph Jacobs (1854-1916) and Lang issued many books of folktales[9] which, although entirely secondary, stirred the English public with interest in traditional stories. Jacobs prepared a list of incidents in folktales[10] which was widely discussed, though little used. Marian Emily Roalfe Cox (1860-1916) and E. Sidney Hartland (1848-1927) made monumental studies of single folktale cycles, she with her *Cinderella*[11] and he with his *Legend of Perseus*.[12] These were the first folktale monographs based upon a reasonably adequate number of versions. With these two works it would seem that England was in a position to lead subsequent research in the folktale. But this promise has not been fulfilled, and the leadership has been in other hands.

The energetic collecting of all kinds of folklore in Denmark by Svend Grundtvig in the middle of the nineteenth century and later by E. Tang Kristensen and H. F. Feilberg culminated in the organization of the Dansk Folkemindesamling in 1904 under the leadership of Axel Olrik. He was an able and enthusiastic executive and a scholar with a broad factual knowledge and a philosophical temperament. Perhaps aside from making the Danish

[6] See p. 386, above.

[7] See p. 385, above.

[8] See *International Folk-Lore Congress, 1891* (London, 1892).

[9] Joseph Jacobs, *English Fairy Tales, More English Fairy Tales, Celtic Fairy Tales, Indian Fairy Tales;* Andrew Lang, *The Blue Fairy Book,* followed by those of other colors.

[10] See p. 414, below.

[11] Publication of the Folk-Lore Society, No. 31 (London, 1893).

[12] *The Legend of Perseus* (3 vols., London, 1894 ff.). See also his *The Science of Fairy Tales* (London, 1891).

folklore collection a model for the rest of the world, Olrik's greatest contribution was his work concerning the "epic laws," a study of what happens to tales or songs as they are handed about by word of mouth.[13] Besides these services Olrik was a potent force in uniting the efforts of folklorists over the world and bringing them into close friendly relations. His death in the ripeness of his activity was mourned as a personal loss by his colleagues in a dozen countries.[14]

In the wake of the Indianist theory promulgated by Theodor Benfey, a large amount of first-rate comparative study of tales was done in Germany, much of it devoted to proving Benfey's contention. An assiduous search for parallels of plot or motif began. As we have already seen, the most important of such annotaters was Reinhold Köhler (1830-1892), the librarian of the Ducal Library at Weimar. Hardly an important collection of tales appeared without being followed shortly afterward by exhaustive comparative notes by Köhler.

These annotations were to be carried on in a new generation by Johannes Bolte (1858-1937), the greatest student of the folktale in Germany, if not in the world. In his earlier years he made extensive comparative notes to many of the sixteenth century German jestbooks and collected Köhler's learned articles (with valuable additions of his own) in a three volume work.[15] He edited the *Zeitschrift des Vereins für Volkskunde* for the last half of his life and kept his readers informed of all new folklore works and movements. But his greatest service, the result of thirty years of untold labor, was the five volumes of notes to Grimms' *Household Tales* which he issued with the cooperation of Georg Polívka of Prague.[16] Except for the Slavic lands, Polívka's contribution, the work was nearly all Bolte's. It is the foundation stone for all comparative study of the European folktale.

Besides doing his own work, Bolte was a great stimulus to German folklore scholarship. He was unusually helpful to younger students and his encouragement played a large part in the development of a brilliant group of folklorists in Germany.

In spite of Bolte's interest in the folktale in all parts of the world, his German colleagues have had a tendency to confine their interest to tales or motifs which are at least important in Germany. On the other hand, the greatest impetus for the truly international study of folklore—especially of the folktale—has come from Finland.

In many ways the most important cultural event in the life of the Finnish

---

[13] See pp. 455 ff., below.

[14] It was my rare privilege in 1926 to make a third with Kaarle Krohn and Johannes Bolte in their visit to Olrik's grave. The sincere emotion shown by these men and their conversation at the time form the basis for my remarks on Olrik.

[15] Reinhold Köhler, *Kleinere Schriften* (ed. by Johannes Bolte, Weimar, 1898-1900).

[16] J. Bolte und G. Polívka, *Anmerkungen zu den Kinder- und Hausmärchen der Brüder Grimm* (5 vols., Leipzig, 1913-31).

people was the appearance in 1835 of the national epic, the *Kalevala*.[17] This poem was based on very extensive collections of heroic ballads made by the author, Elias Lönnrot, who arranged them in sequence and welded them into an artistic whole. The heroic past thus far preserved only through the prodigious memory of humble singers now became a possession of the whole people, and these legends henceforth were a rallying point for all those forces working toward political freedom and Finnish nationalism. The interest in all kinds of folklore became intense and gave rise to a phenomenal activity in its collection and preservation.

Elias Lönnrot's ablest disciple was Julius Krohn, who pursued a lifelong study of the songs belonging to the Kalevala cycle. He perfected a technique for a comparison of all versions with a view to determining the life history of each of the heroic songs. This method depended primarily upon an analysis of the songs into motifs and a study of the distribution of each motif, so as to see in which geographical direction a tradition had moved, and what changes it had undergone in the process.

It was Julius Krohn's son, Kaarle Krohn (1863-1933) who first applied this historical-geographical method to the study of the folktale. In his doctoral dissertation in 1886 he investigated a group of animal tales especially well-known in Finnish tradition[18] and in 1891 followed this with a second monograph dealing with the cycle of the man and the fox.[19] For these studies he acquainted himself with folktales from all parts of the world and he became convinced that an adequate investigation of tales must have a world-wide scope. Moreover, his experience with the historical-geographical technique, which he had modified and adapted to the study of the tale, convinced him that there was no short road to the truth about the origin and history of the folktale as a whole. Only by special studies of each story, based always on as large a number of versions as possible, could one hope to approach a real knowledge of the facts.

Such a conviction might well have discouraged even a courageous scholar. To Krohn it was a challenge. The tales of the world must be collected as soon as possible; they must be arranged and be made available. An adequate technique for study must be developed; each of the hundreds of tale types must be submitted to exhaustive study—and in the end the results of these studies synthesized into adequate generalizations.

This program would naturally demand wholehearted cooperation by scholars of all lands, who were willing to work together even if they did not always completely agree on all details of a plan. Krohn was unusually successful in enlisting the labors of men from other communities as well as in infecting his own disciples with his zeal. For forty years folktale students

[17] English translations by Kirby and by Crawford.
[18] *Bär (Wolf) und Fuchs* (Helsingfors, 1883).
[19] *Mann und Fuchs* (Helsingfors, 1891).

from all parts of Europe, as well as from America, made the pilgrimage to Helsinki to enjoy his companionship and to benefit from his ripe scholarship.

He always kept the entire program before him. He encouraged collecting wherever he could. He labored over systems of classifying tales and assisted his disciple Antti Aarne, who issued the index he approved,[20] and he eventually arranged for its revision. Aarne shortly issued a catalogue of Finnish tales as a model for the score of other such catalogues which Krohn encouraged, and for which he arranged publication. His earlier description of the historical-geographical method was elaborated by Aarne and later by Krohn himself; and Aarne produced a series of studies using this technique. Twenty or thirty similar monographs appeared from scholars in many countries, all using the same basic methods. Finally at the end of his life, and as a mark of the half century since his first trip to collect tales, he brought all these results together in the synthesis for which he had so long planned.[21]

This fifty-year work, it must be stressed, was not wholly Krohn's: it was a large cooperative task that extended over Europe and into America. But Krohn's leadership and the generosity of the Finnish State in its financial support of the program stimulated other scholars in their tasks and carried on the active study of the folktale even through the days of the first World War.

A great practical help in this plan for cooperation was the establishment in about 1907 of the international organization of folklore scholars under the neutral title of FF—Folklore Fellows, Fédération des Folkloristes, Folkloristischer Forscherbund, etc., according to the language of the country concerned. This was really only a loose organization without officers or an official list of members, but it served nevertheless as a center of reference for folklore scholars throughout the world. At first there were local sections in various countries, but only for a time. The principal function of FF has been to furnish an international body to sponsor the outstanding series of monographs which Krohn began to issue in 1907 under the title of *FF Communications*. These publications, by far the most important in the field of international folklore, now extend to more than 125 numbers, most of them full-length volumes.

The *FF Communications* have published most of the tale catalogues, two versions of the folktale classification, several motif-indexes, and a long series of monographs on particular stories. It has not confined itself to the

[20] *Verzeichnis der Märchentypen* (FF Communications, No. 3, Helsinki, 1910). My revision appeared under the title *The Types of the Folktale* (FF Communications, No. 74, Helsinki, 1928).

[21] *Übersicht über einige Resultate der Märchenforschung.* All the studies there referred to will be detailed in subsequent chapters.

tale, but has also issued many valuable studies in other branches of folklore —notably Krohn's series of *Kalevalastudien*.

One of the principal reasons for the devising of the folktale classification which Krohn promoted was the desirability of making generally available the growing wealth of traditional narrative in various folklore archives. Hitherto such material had been almost useless not only because it was in manuscript but also was often in languages and dialects unknown to the general world of scholars. It was of the highest importance, therefore, that by a systematic series of surveys based on a uniform system the scholar should be informed in some detail of the content of these collections and be afforded an easy means of securing access to such items as interested him. In the thirty years since the first index was issued this goal has largely been reached, for practically all the archives have been indexed by the Aarne system, although some of these surveys remain unpublished. It is nearly always possible today for a student interested in investigating a particular tale to discover the manuscript versions either in printed catalogues or, in times of peace, by writing to the archive, and to have such items copied, and if desirable translated, at a reasonable cost.

The growth of these folklore archives has been rapid in the past half century, especially in northern Europe. In Helsinki the Finnish collection dates back to Lönnrot's time and has had a constant growth. Every year new manuscripts of tradition come in and find their place in the files beside the yellowing notebooks which furnished the songs for the Kalevala. Of folktales alone the collection possesses upward of fifty thousand.

In Estonia a similar collection of manuscript was formed under the leadership of J. Hurt and M. J. Eisen and continued by Walter Anderson and Oskar Loorits. For some years the entire collection was in Helsinki, and while it was there an index of the folktales in it was published by Aarne.

The Lithuanian archive has achieved a huge size in recent years and is being made available in a series of surveys by the director, J. Balys. The inconvenience of the fact that these appear in Lithuanian is only partially mitigated by the short summaries in English.

In Sweden the archives are scattered in four centers, Uppsala, Stockholm, Gothenburg, and Lund. They are excellently arranged and competently manned—in many ways serving as models[22] to other countries. Their archivists have devised an elaborate system of questionnaires which direct the efforts of a large number of workers all over Sweden.

The Dansk Folkemindesamling in Copenhagen has already been mentioned in connection with its founder Axel Olrik. It occupies quarters in the Royal Library and is supported by the state. It is particularly rich in older manuscript material which it is gradually publishing. The tales in this

---

[22] The entire personnel of the Irish Folklore Commission has been trained in the archives at Uppsala and Lund.

collection are arranged by a system devised by Svend Grundtvig, but there is also a cross-index to the usual Aarne classification.

In Norway the state folklore archives at Oslo are in charge of R. Th. Christiansen, one of the ablest of folktale scholars. Under his direction a large part of the material is being issued in the series *Norsk Folkminnelag*. Christiansen's survey of the Norwegian folktales is perhaps the most thorough that has appeared from any country.[23]

Though an archive of German folksong has been maintained at Freiburg im Breisgau for many years, it is only recently that a central collection of Märchen has been instituted in Berlin. Here are brought together not only a very fine library but also much manuscript material, particularly the papers of the tireless Mecklenburg folklorist, Richard Wossidlo. The newness of the establishment and the outbreak of the recent war have made it difficult to know just how it will fit into the general program of international folktale study.

The new Département et Musée National des Arts et Traditions Populaires in Paris received a considerable stimulus from the International Folklore Congress which it sponsored during the Paris Exposition of 1937. It has undertaken a survey of the French *contes populaires*, and though it has few of them in manuscript, it seemed to be in a fair way to begin systematic collecting at the outbreak of the war in 1939.

By far the most spectacular achievement in the field of the folktale in recent years has been that of the Irish Folklore Commission under the leadership of Seamus O'Duilearga. A huge program of recording tales by means of trained collectors has resulted in the accumulation of well over a million pages of manuscript, mainly from the Gaelic-speaking districts. The cataloguing is an enormous task, but the energy and skill of Séan O'Sullivan, the archivist, brings it ever nearer to completion. The journal *Béaloideas* published by the Folklore of Ireland Society is essentially the organ of the Commission.

There are, in addition to these large public archives, a number of private collections of tales and smaller public archives that are available to the serious student.[24] In Russia a number of institutions have interested themselves in such collections, though their material has been practically unavailable to other scholars.[25] And in the United States the American Folksong Archive in the Library of Congress is being expanded so as to embrace other aspects of folklore, including the popular tale.

For organizing the cooperative study of folktales the archives just dis-

---

[23] The index appearing as FF Communications No. 46 is only a summary in English of the much more elaborate Norwegian original: *Norske Eventyr* (Kristiania, 1921).

[24] Some account of these may be found in various numbers of the periodicals *Folk* and *Folk-Liv*.

[25] For an account of this Russian activity, see D. K. Zelenin, *Folk-Liv*, 1938, pp. 218 ff. and M. Schlauch, *Science and Society*, VIII (1944), pp. 205-222.

cussed have been invaluable, but their services would have been minor if there had not been an able group of scholars to make use of them and to promote in other ways the whole study of the tale on a comparative basis.

If the folktale has during the last half century come to be looked on as a world-wide phenomenon, it is primarily because great numbers of tales of primitive peoples have been made available. Best of all are the collections from the North American Indians. Though many individuals and institutions have participated in the enormous amount of field work involved, the principal impetus to the prosecution of this large and well-conceived program came from Franz Boas, who devoted a long life to the cause of anthropology in America. He was always scrupulous in his own collecting of texts and thus set a high standard which characterized a large part of the efforts of his disciples and colleagues. He also carried out some extensive studies of the distribution of types and motifs and encouraged others in similar undertakings.[26]

Though it represents no such thoroughgoing program of collecting and comparison as that realized by the students of the American Indian, the remarkable series of African tales issued by Leo Frobenius under the title of *Atlantis*[27] has made easily accessible the tales of a number of tribes, mostly between the Sahara and the Congo.

The bibliography of such a field as folklore is very extensive. Even to keep abreast of the literature currently appearing is almost impossible without some special help. A number of journals from time to time undertook an annual bibliography, but they all lapsed until the establishment of the annual *Volkskundliche Bibliographie*[28] under the editorship of Édouard Hoffmann-Krayer and later of Paul Geiger. This invaluable work, which has appeared for about twenty years, has had many collaborators and has steadily become more comprehensive. A very valuable part of the recent numbers has been the excellent bibliography of folklore of North and South America prepared by Ralph S. Boggs.[29]

Much of the cooperative effort of German-speaking folklorists in recent years has gone toward the preparation of encyclopedias. The first to be undertaken was the *Handwörterbuch des deutschen Aberglaubens*[30] under the editorship of Hanns Bächtold-Stäubli of Basel. The articles cover not only German superstition but many aspects of folklore on a world-wide scale, and represent the work of the leading specialists of Europe and America. After this encyclopedia was well along, another, the *Handwörter-*

---

[26] For further account of these American Indian collections, see p. ooo, below. A bibliography of the material up to 1926 appears in Thompson, *Tales of the North American Indians* (Cambridge, Mass., 1929).

[27] *Atlantis: Volksmärchen Afrikas.*

[28] *Volkskundliche Bibliographie für das Jahr 1917* (etc.) (Berlin).

[29] See also his *Bibliography of Latin American Folklore* (Washington, 1940).

[30] Berlin and Leipzig, 1927-37.

buch des deutschen Märchens,[31] was begun under the general editorship of Johannes Bolte but under the actual direction of Lutz Mackensen, formerly of Greifswald and later of Riga. Thus far this work has reached only the end of its second volume, about one-third of the whole, but many of the articles represent the ripest scholarship of the best students of the folktale. Tale types, motifs, stylistic and formulistic features, theories, collectors—in short, everything connected with traditional narrative, not only in Germany but everywhere, finds its place here. It is a pity that a reference work so indispensable to folktale scholars should have been interrupted in 1936 by preparation for war. It can only be hoped that some day the project can be completed.

One difficulty with the study of folktales is the assembling of the material for easy study. A good library of traditional narrative must have at least several thousand volumes, many of them old and long out of print. In order to make more easily available a good selection of tales from over the world, Friedrich von der Leyen has edited his series of *Märchen der Weltliteratur.*[32] These thirty or more volumes often contain the best collection from the people concerned and in any case are a great boon to the scholar of limited means. In France two series with a similar purpose are the *Collection de chansons et de contes populaires*[33] and *Les littératures populaires des toutes les nations.*[34] All these series are attractive, the German volumes being bound in special designs characteristic of the various peoples treated.

In the promotion of international folktale study, especially as conceived by Krohn, a leading role has been played by Walter Anderson. This cosmopolitan scholar is of German descent but he began his career in Russia where he issued his first folktale studies from the University of Kasan. He escaped from Russia at the time of the Bolshevik revolution and eventually became established at Dorpat in Estonia as Professor of Folklore. He has issued several of the most thorough monographic studies of a folktale[35] and has striven constantly to improve the technique developed by Krohn and Aarne. He has been convinced of the fundamental soundness of the historic-geographic method and has not hesitated to defend it when it has been attacked.[36] Anderson's knowledge of the tale is probably unsurpassed, certainly in respect to the Baltic and Slavic fields, and he has been generous in helping other scholars, particularly young students, in discovering elusive material. His own standards of scholarship are very exacting, so that slipshod work by others is not likely to escape his caustic censure.

[31] Berlin and Leipzig, 1930-36.
[32] Jena, 1915-38.
[33] Paris, 1881-1930. 46 vols.
[34] Paris, 1881-1903. 47 vols.; new series, Paris, 1931-33, 3 vols.
[35] His first appeared in Russian and are difficult of access. His two most important later studies are *Kaiser und Abt* and *Das Märchen vom alten Hildebrand.*
[36] See pp. 436ff., below.

The excellent catalogue of Norse tales prepared by Reidar Th. Christiansen has already been mentioned. This is, however, but one of the services of Christiansen in the cause of comparative folktale study. He has written several monographs on tales, has for many years conducted the Norsk Folkminnesamling, and has interested himself in cultural relations of peoples of all of northern Europe. In recent years he has given much assistance to the Irish Folklore Commission toward the arranging of the Gaelic tales. Christiansen is an accomplished linguist, being at home in languages so far apart as Irish and Finnish.

The only Dutchman who has taken an important part in comparative folktale study is Jan de Vries of Leiden. Besides his studies in Norse mythology and the popular ballad, he has produced two books important for the tale. In one[37] he has brought together representative stories from Indonesia with a thorough analysis and study of their types and motifs, thus opening up for the non-specialist the folktales of a large and little known area. The other work is his monograph on The Clever Peasant Daughter, one of the most ambitious of the studies thus far made by the historic-geographic method.[38] Besides his writings De Vries has been influential in the practical organization of the efforts of folklore scholars. In 1937 he was elected president of the International Association for European Ethnology and Folklore and also of the International Folklore Congress at Paris.

In discussing the Irish Folklore Commission mention has been made of the leadership of Seamus O'Duilearga (James Delargy). Though he has a passionate interest in the tales of his own people, he has himself traveled so widely and informed himself so thoroughly in the best scholarship of all countries that his remarkable Irish collections are being properly integrated in the whole field of folktale study. O'Duilearga's infectious enthusiasm for the lowly folk who tell him stories, and his generous and hearty spirit have made him friends everywhere, but especially among folktale scholars of all countries. He recently had a most enthusiastic reception in America, where he helped make many scholars conscious for the first time not alone of the human interest in peasant taletellers but also of the important scholarly problems of the folktale.

O'Duilearga is one of the considerable number of the present generation of folklorists who take pleasure in acknowledging their indebtedness to C. W. von Sydow, professor at Lund and director of the Lund folklore archives. Von Sydow is an experienced collector and has done field work not only in Sweden but in Ireland, where his influence went far in the establishing of the Folklore Commission. He has written many monographs on tales and has directed a large number of others. He does not easily fit into any established school of folklorists, for he is an original thinker who

---

[37] *Volksverhalen uit Oost Indië.*
[38] *Die Märchen von klugen Rätsellösern*

has a tendency to form independent theories. Some of these, for example, his doctrine of *oiƙotypes*, his criticisms of the historic-geographic method, his revival, with modifications, of Grimm's Indo-European theory, and his proposals for new terminology have been very stimulating not only to his disciples but to all who study the tale.[39] In spite of his disagreement in detail with some of his principal colleagues, he has been a great force for international cooperation in the study of the tale. He has helped with the work of the Folklore Fellows, has busied himself with large schemes for the manifolding of tale collections, and has taken a leading part in international folklore congresses.

Finally, among those who have helped in the international study of the folktale may be mentioned several American students. The influence of Francis James Child (1825-1896), the great ballad student, made Harvard University at the end of the last century the unrivaled center in America for the study of folklore. George Lyman Kittredge, one of the chief of American scholars, ably carried on the Child tradition. The remarkable folklore library at Harvard has been another reason for a considerable series of studies made there in the folktale—studies many of which have been of real importance in the large international program of research.

Archer Taylor, a student of Kittredge's, was the first American folklorist of the present generation to make contact with European scholars. For many years he has been on the editorial board of FF Communications and his advice has been widely sought on all matters of international cooperation in this field. He is among those who have journeyed to Finland, where twice he spent months with Krohn. On one of these occasions he made a historic-geographic study of a northern tale and on the other he used the same method for the study of a ballad.[40]

Taylor has had a group of able disciples, the most active of whom is Ralph S. Boggs, whose *Index of Spanish Tales*[41] established him as a thorough folklorist. In later years he has become a skilled bibliographer and is an authority on the folklore of Latin America. He is the chief mover in the development of pan-American folklore study and in that interest has made three extensive trips and has secured the cooperation of leading scholars of the whole hemisphere.

As a pupil of Kittredge the present author also became interested in the comparative study of the tale. *European Tales among the North American Indians*[42] was a treatment of dissemination of elements that were clearly foreign and was logically followed by *Tales of the North American In-*

---

[39] All of these points are discussed elsewhere in this book. See pp. 440f.

[40] *The Black Ox* (FF Communications, No. 70, Helsinki, 1927) and *Edward and Sven i Rosengård* (Chicago, 1931).

[41] FF Communications, No. 90 (Helsinki, 1930).

[42] Colorado College Publications, Vol. II (Colorado Springs, 1919).

dians[43] where the native incidents were handled. The revision of Aarne's type-index and the larger *Motif-Index of Folk-Literature*[44] have been helpful in organizing large bodies of material for subsequent investigation.

The more comprehensive study of folktales as planned by Krohn has in one way or another been promoted by these men. They have, of course, worked with a considerable degree of independence but they were contributing to the main program that is to take the study of oral narrative from a purely speculative stage to one where results are based upon ascertained facts. These men have generally maintained contact by correspondence and by visits and they have profited by discussions of common problems.

It was the feeling of a need for something more than occasional letters and trips that occasioned the calling of a Congress for the Study of the Folktale at Lund in Sweden in November of 1935.[45] The meeting was sponsored by the Royal Gustav Adolf Akademi för Folklivforskning, and was in general charge of C. W. von Sydow. Among the folktale scholars present at the regular sessions were Martti Haavio of Helsinki; Uno Harva of Turku (Åbo), present editor of FF Communications; Walter Anderson and Oskar Loorits of Estonia; Sven Liljeblad and W. Liungman of Sweden; Hans Ellekilde (Olrik's successor) and his assistant Inger Boberg, of Copenhagen and also Arthur Christensen; R. Th. Christiansen and Knut Liestøl of Norway; Lutz Mackensen and Elisabeth Hartmann of Germany; Seamus O'Duilearga of Ireland; and Stith Thompson from America.

The importance of the Congress was more in the bringing of these men together for informal talks than for the actual discussions, though these were interesting. It was an opportunity to debate issues and to seek to determine where the studies as a whole were leading. Plans for certain cooperative ventures were broached and some received the approval of the Congress. An expansion of the Congress into an International Association for European Ethnology and Folklore was approved, and the first meeting in Edinburgh in 1937 was arranged for. A quarterly journal entitled *Folk* was founded and eventually placed under the editorship of Jan de Vries. This was later (1938) merged with a similar journal sponsored by the Gustav Adolf Akademi called *Folk-Liv*.

The meeting two years later at Edinburgh brought most of these scholars together again for a pleasant week of companionship and work.[46] Some practical plans were made and committees appointed and many papers were read, but the importance of these international meetings was rather in the individual visiting and private discussions. They were also important for

[43] Cambridge, Mass., 1929.

[44] For a discussion of these indexes see Chapter IV, below.

[45] For a full account of this congress see *Saga och Sed* (annual publication of the Gustav Adolf Akademi för Folklivsforskning), 1935, pp. 71ff.

[46] An account of the Edinburgh meeting is in *Folk-Liv*, 1938, pp. 109ff.

stimulating general interest in the folktale. It is largely due to urgings voiced in these congresses that two large publication projects are being sponsored. In Sweden the rarer printed books and manuscripts of tales, especially the great tale collections of Hyltén-Cavallius which have lain unpublished for three quarters of a century have begun to be issued by the Gustav Adolf Akademi,[47] and in Scotland a similar manuscript of the tales of the Western Highlands made by Francis Campbell of Islay in the 1850's was undertaken by the Scottish Anthropological and Folklore Society.[48]

Shortly after the Edinburgh Congress there occurred the Premier Congrès International de Folklore in Paris.[49] The other congresses had been confined to Northern Europe and America, but the one in Paris had representatives from many other countries. Actually the folktale section was a small part of the whole, but it gave occasion for another assembling and for a week of companionship. The two congresses arranged to merge and appointed committees for such merging, and also a general executive committee to arrange a meeting in Stockholm in 1940.

But by 1940 there was little thought in Europe of the international organization of folktale scholarship.[50]

---

[47] These have appeared under the title of *Svenska Sagor och Sägner*, Stockholm, 1938—.

[48] Only one volume has thus far appeared under the title *More West Highland Tales* (edited by J. G. McKay, Edinburgh, 1940).

[49] See *Travaux du Ier Congrès International de Folklore* (Tours, 1938).

[50] (June 1946) Since the writing of this account the great war has come to an end. After a year of readjustment something of the situation of folktale study in the postwar world begins to clarify. Less actual disruption by the war appears than might be expected. In spite of hostilities or precarious neutrality, the archives and the scholars connected with them have either maintained their activity or have resumed it in Finland, Norway, Sweden, Denmark, Ireland, and France. The German folktale archive, though moved about, seems to be intact at Marburg. Two important archives have in large part been lost. Oscar Loorits escaped with only a fragment of the Estonian material and is now in Sweden and Jonas Balys was likewise able to carry but a small part of the rich Lithuanian material when he escaped into Germany. Rather fewer deaths than normal seem to have occurred among the leading folktale scholars. Several European specialists are in America but expect to return home soon—Inger Boberg of Denmark, Ariane de Felice of France, and Sven Liljeblad of Sweden. Finally, it is encouraging to know that FF Communications, in spite of all hardships in Finland, has maintained publication uninterrupted and has now issued its 134th number. Swedish publication of *Svenska Sagor och Sägner* has also continued into the sixth or seventh volume.

COLLECTING FOLKTALES

The most fundamental of all aspects of folktale study is the adequate collecting of the stories. For more than a century scholars have recognized the ideal of accurate recording of tales from as many sources as possible, and in the more and more systematic researches of the past generation there has been increasing interest in promoting field work and insistence that it be skillfully and faithfully carried out. Collecting, classifying, cataloguing, studying by a comparative method, and synthesizing all the results—such is now the goal of all folklorists, whether or not they have come under the direct influence of Kaarle Krohn. But all these activities depend on the first; for no valid studies can be based upon meager or untrustworthy collections.

Though this attitude toward faithful recording of tradition is now so generally accepted by all scholars as to be almost axiomatic, it is not very old, but has gradually developed since the early nineteenth century. Not until there arose an interest in a serious investigation of stories as an important part of human culture could such a feeling exist. For in all the earlier presentations of traditional material the principal motive was to give the reader what would entertain him. The story heard at first hand or more remotely from the unlettered teller was only a frame within which the author employed his own narrative skill. Thus, many of our well-known tales appear in the most diverse literary treatments. Polyphemus is worked into the Homeric epic.[1] Cupid and Psyche becomes an episode in a long satirical prose work, Apuleius's *The Golden Ass*.[2] The Prince as Bird is retold by Marie de France in her octosyllabic couplets[3] and brought into the general circle of chivalric romance. Many oral jests were worked over into

---

[1] See p. 278.
[2] See p. 281.
[3] See p. 103.

poetic form and made into fabliaux,[4] and traditional animal tales were given a satirical twist in the *Roman de Renart*.[5] With Straparola[6] and Boccaccio fairy tales take on the guise of Italian novelle.

Even in Basile, where the collection consists entirely of folktales, they are retold in a baroque style, far removed from any conceivable traditional form. Throughout the eighteenth century in Europe, after the Galland translation in 1704 made the *Arabian Nights* popular, folktales were given an Oriental or pseudo-Oriental flavor. And the story collections direct from Arabia and India[7] were conscious and sophisticated literary works. Until the nineteenth century we have only the slightest indication as to what the traditional oral folktale actually sounded like. We know that even the Grimms, who took down their stories as they heard them, had no scruples against reworking them from edition to edition.[8] But by 1840 or thereabouts a number of scholars were making serious attempts to publish authentic oral texts, and since that time there has been an increasing effort to furnish records that are faithful not only to all details of the action but to the narrative style as well.

Some of the most successful collections of folktales in Europe were made in the middle and late nineteenth century. Afanasief in Russia, Hyltén-Cavallius in Sweden, Asbjørnson and Moe in Norway, Grundtvig and Kristensen in Denmark, Campbell of Islay in the Scottish Highlands, Patrick Kennedy in Ireland, Cosquin and Sébillot in France—these are but the best known of a large group who established an ideal of careful workmanship in the recording of folktales.[9] They had to find their own methods of procedure, and each in his own way was eminently successful. It is a pity that we have so little indication as to how these men worked, for the best sort of training to anyone aspiring to gather tales would be to follow one of these great folklorists on his daily rounds and observe how he solved the difficult problems he met.

Though organization on a large scale is possible, the actual collecting of folktales is essentially an individual activity. Its success depends on the skill and tact of the lone worker.

The first of the problems he meets is the discovery of the persons who can tell folktales. It is not easy to know just where these informants are to be found, for conditions vary from place to place. A large number of the tales in Grimm came from educated persons of the Grimms' own social circle, who told the tales as they remembered them from childhood, when

---

[4] See p. 282.

[5] See A. Graf, *Die Grundlagen des Reineke Fuchs* (FF Communications No. 38, Helsinki, 1921).

[6] For titles of the collections mentioned here and in the next paragraph, see p. 467 ff.

[7] See pp. 15, 17.

[8] See Bolte-Polívka, IV, 418 ff., especially p. 453.

[9] For full titles, see p. 467 ff.

they had heard them from a nurse.[10] For uncontaminated oral tradition, these are probably not as good sources as the nurse herself would have been. Stylistically there was every chance that passing literary modes should exert their influence. Some collectors have successfully used school children as informants,[11] but more often children have been of value merely in bringing to light the narrative talent of some older person from whom they received the tale in the first place.

Elderly or at least middle-aged persons have nearly always yielded the best folktales. Assuming that they are interested in learning stories—and if they are not, they will probably never learn to tell them well—they have had a long life in which to acquire a repertoire and to improve their style of delivery. Both men and women may generally be expected to know stories, but there is frequently a local custom that relegates all taletelling to one or other of the sexes. In Ireland the actual delivery of the stories seems to be a prerogative of the men, though women certainly know them and teach them to their children.[12] On the other hand, the tales reported from East Prussia were taken down from women, though this may be because the collector of the latter stories is a woman.[13]

Among some peoples the tales are largely in the hands of special groups of professional or semi-professional standing. Whether these persons are priests, shamans, initiates, or members of a craft of story-tellers, it is necessary to discover them and to induce them to perform.

It is not always easy to secure tales even after the proper person has been found. Most collectors have learned by experience to overcome this diffidence, but it takes tact and patience. Whether money should be offered depends on local custom, often hard to discover. With some primitive peoples a regular scale of pay may be agreed upon. But in any case presents are always welcome. Food, drink, or tobacco, or articles of clothing help smooth the way to that good will which is necessary for successful results.

Even with the best will, however, a story-teller may feel that he has nothing worth giving. He will deny that he knows any stories at all. If the collector can tell tales himself, it is often possible to produce the proper atmosphere. He must realize that the old man or woman knows nothing of distinctions which he takes for granted and that it will not do to go about asking for "Märchen" or "myths." If he knows something of what kind of tales he may expect to find, he can of course suggest stories about this or that, but he is sure to get much that is of little value for his purpose. And

[10] See Bolte-Polívka, IV, 419 ff.

[11] See, for example, W. Anderson, *Novelline popopari Sammarinesi* (2 parts, Dorpat, 1927-29).

[12] The remarks on Irish collecting are based on information received during my visit to Ireland in 1937. See Thompson, "Folktale Collecting in Ireland," *Southern Folklore Quarterly*, II (June, 1938), 53 ff.

[13] See p. 411, below.

he must accept it all without question. For any intimation of disapproval will put an end to all spontaneous story-telling. The collector must inure himself to recording material which he does not want in the hope of getting what he is seeking. Only tact and the power of suggestion will reduce this lost motion, and even that will not completely prevent it.[14]

The difficulty of taking an oral form and transferring it to written shows itself very clearly in the attempt to record a tale when it is being told. Perhaps the most usual manner of doing this is to write down the story while the raconteur tells it slowly and pauses. Even with the use of frequent abbreviations such recording slows the narrative so much that many story-tellers are loath to tell the tale at full length, for they can hardly imagine writing down a complete folktale. Or else a teller with an animated style, especially a rapid speaker, feels himself hampered, and does scant justice to himself or his audience. It is remarkable that in spite of these handicaps some of the greatest tale collectors have succeeded by using this method.

Shorthand is a logical answer to the need for a means of rapid recording. But only a few collectors of stories can handle it, and this method seems to have been little tried. Krohn employed it on his field trips[15] and Wisser had his son take down a few tales for him in this way.[16] Perhaps more tales have been recorded stenographically than is generally believed, but it seems certain that no really adequate use has been made of this method.

An increasingly important adjunct of field work in the folktale is the phonographic recorder. If the story-teller can be taught to use it without self-consciousness, it gives the most accurate record, for it can preserve every word and intonation, and the speaker can talk as rapidly as he wishes. Most collectors find little difficulty in teaching their informants to use the machine. After they have once heard their own story played back to them and their neighbors, no further stimulation is usually necessary. The collector must then beware lest he waste his records with all kinds of trivialities and spend too much time at entertaining the group with repeatedly playing them back.[17]

Properly used, phonographic recording produces entirely satisfactory results for the collector of tales. In practice there are fewer difficulties than might be imagined. Not only can speakers become accustomed to using the

---

[14] It would seem, all things considered, that a collector is better prepared for his task if he is acquainted with the tales already collected from the people among whom he is working or from their neighbors. But he must beware of letting this knowledge influence his record. It should help him lead out his informant by inquiring for something the latter may not have thought of.

[15] Krohn, *Übersicht*, p. 3.

[16] W. Wisser, *Auf der Märchensuche* (Hamburg, n.d. [1926?]), p. 13.

[17] Original records should be played as little as possible, since they wear down easily. Copies should be made of those that need to be played much. The Irish Folklore Commission keeps only a selection of their records after they have been transcribed and pares the rest so that they can be used again.

machine, but the very novelty of the experience is likely to bring to light other tellers who are eager to hear their own tales and are pleased that these are being preserved as something of permanent worth. The machines are rather expensive and the equipment is heavy. But ordinarily some library or university can be found to furnish the recording machine, and the weight is not beyond the strength of most men.

Mechanical recording is especially valuable for securing texts from native languages which the collector may not speak fluently. The difficulty is in transcribing and translating the record. Though this is primarily a problem of language, it affects the work of the folklorist, for everywhere among primitive groups he may receive texts in a language which he knows but imperfectly. Not only must the text be faithfully transcribed but the translation must be accurate. For this purpose a bilingual native can be of most help, for he can give loose translation which the student can later check in detail.

Anthropologists who do much field work seem agreed that texts taken in the native languages represent the real tradition in the tribe better than those taken in one of the world languages from bilingual informants.[18] For the study of narrative style this is undoubtedly true and this fact makes it very desirable that recording be done in native texts as often as possible. But for a knowledge of the material of the tales and the relation of that material to neighboring or remote peoples, texts taken in broken English (or another world language) are also valuable. A large number of the tales we have at present were taken down from a bilingual speaker. An interpreter is also frequently used with good results.

Whether tales are taken down in longhand or in shorthand, on paper or on records, in native texts or in a world language, success depends primarily on the skill and judgment of the collector. He must be able to meet his informants easily and with no feeling of awkwardness. He must have a genuine interest in their lives and in understanding of their pleasures and their difficulties. He need not, of course, be one of them, for some of the best collectors have been university professors or public school teachers. Physicians and lawyers and clergymen have also been successful, for such men meet story-tellers easily and habitually.

Where tale collecting is done on a large scale by central bureaus it has usually been found best to depend on residents of the community for the recording. The Swedish archives have a large number of correspondents from the various neighborhoods over the country. To these, instructions are sent periodically and a close check is kept on their activity. They are paid according to their experience and the value of their services.[19]

[18] See, for example, F. Boas in discussing my selection of texts for *Tales of the North American Indians* (*Journal of American Folklore*, XLIII, 224).
[19] The remarks on the Swedish archives are based on visits in 1935 and 1937 and especially on information given by Sven Liljeblad.

Perhaps the most systematic collecting of tales now being carried on is directed by the Irish Folklore Commission in Dublin.[20] Eight or ten full-time collectors are employed. These are usually school teachers who are on temporary leave from their regular work and are kept on their usual salaries. Each of them has a definite territory which he cultivates intensively. He takes down tales on cylinder records, transcribes them at home and sends the record and transcription to the Commission at Dublin. Besides these full-time workers, there are about a hundred fifty part-time helpers. The Director of the Commission makes personal visits to all these collectors, often going with them on their visits. Much of the success of the Commission comes from the fact that the Director is known and liked by hundreds of the *shanachies*, who will do all in their power to please him. Recently all the school children in Ireland have been asked to bring in folktales as part of their regular work in English composition. They tell where the tale came from and thus have brought to the attention of the regular collectors the taletelling abilities of many persons not known about before. The Commission has now over a million pages of these tales from school children in addition to their more valuable half million pages of carefully recorded texts. These are all being catalogued, but unfortunately for the world at large, the texts are nearly all in Gaelic.

It is strange that so few collectors have thought it worth while to give an account of their experiences and to describe their methods. The most that one is usually able to find is the names of informants and some indication as to sex, age, and occupation. And yet the few who have discussed their adventures in tale collecting have shown that the search for the folktale may be filled with all kinds of interesting encounters which others enjoy hearing about. A book filled with great human interest as well as with much practical guidance to the tale collector is Wilhelm Wisser's *Auf der Märchensuche*[21] which gives an almost day by day account of his twenty years of hearing and recording stories in Holstein. We become acquainted with a great range of real characters, many of them extraordinarily picturesque and striking, and the whole work, though written as a simple account of daily activity, gives us an authentic picture of life among people for whom the folktale is still a vivid memory, if no longer a living art.

Another very valuable account of tale collecting is that of Hertha Grudde who tells how she collected her Low German tales in East Prussia.[22] Her account does not cover the same extent as Wisser's, either in territory or in time. But it goes into much greater detail as to the methods used to discover the women story-tellers (for hers are all women), to overcome their shyness

---

[20] See note 12, above.

[21] See note 16, above.

[22] Hertha Grudde, *Wie ich meine "Plattdeutschen Volksmärchen aus Ostpreussen" aufschrieb* (FF Communications No. 102, Helsinki, 1932).

and their fear that they were being held up to ridicule. She describes the successful system of abbreviation which she worked out—essentially a system of shorthand—and the great improvement it made in her recording.

Mark Azadovsky has given some account of the individuals from whom he collected in Siberia and he cites other Russian writers who have given facts about their informants.[23] The Russians are especially interested in the tale as a social phenomenon and thus give emphasis to the individual and the environment from which folk stories are recorded.

The Irish collectors all keep diaries, and it is hoped that some of these may eventually be published, for they should be extraordinarily interesting and very helpful to all who wish to learn to collect tales.

It is also greatly to be hoped that some of the anthropologists will share with us more of their experiences in recording the tales of primitive peoples than they have thus far done. The tales they collect are of the first value. But we should also like to go with the field worker on his interesting quest so that we may meet his native friends and sit with him as he collects their stories.

[23] M. Azadovsky, *Eine sibirische Märchenerzählerin* (FF Communications, No. 68, Helsinki, 1926). See pp. 451ff., below. Another good account of story-tellers is found in Angelika Merkelbach-Pinck, "Wanderung der Märchen im deutschsprachingen Lothringen," *Travaux du I*ᵉʳ *Congrès International de Folklore*, pp. 137ff.

CLASSIFYING FOLK NARRATIVE

$$IV$$

BEFORE it can become an object of serious and well-considered study, every branch of knowledge needs to be classified. There was a time when geology and botany consisted of random collections of facts and hastily constructed theories. It was only when this anecdotal stage gave way to systematic classification that real progress was made toward a thorough method of study.

With the folktale the long lack of analysis and orderly arrangement led to much confused discussion and was at least partly responsible for a good deal of the premature and ill considered theorizing characteristic of many nineteenth century folklorists. The materials with which the student of traditional narrative deals is so enormous in its bulk, so varied in its form, so widely distributed geographically and historically that an actual firsthand acquaintance with it all is beyond one man's powers. Yet though his personal journey of inspection through this vast domain can cover but a small district, he needs an adequate map to give him proper orientation in respect to the whole. It is only when he is thoroughly aware that the subject of his research is essentially world-wide that the man who deals with the folktale can avoid a narrow parochialism that exaggerates the importance of the folklore of his particular land or that founds all-embracing theories on the special habits of expression of a small portion of mankind.

The student of local or national tradition needs comprehensive classifications as a stimulus toward widening horizons, but the scholar of the opposite type needs it even more to keep him from aimless wandering. He cannot go far without the help of the classifier and the cataloguer.

The chief practical use that is always made of scientific classifications is for listing and cataloguing. Biologists have long since labeled their flora and fauna by a universal system and by using this method have published

---

[1] Some parts of this chapter are taken with little change from my article, "Purpose and Importance of an Index of Types and Motifs," *Folk-Liv*, 1938, pp. 103-108.

thousands of inventories of the animal and plant life of all parts of the world. In like manner it should be possible to make available for study the entire body of collected folk-narrative in the world. This is best done by exhaustive catalogues covering particular countries or areas. For such catalogues there must be classifications that are reasonably logical and reasonably complete, that are applicable to the material everywhere, and that are not too cumbersome to be easily learned and used.

The need for such an arrangement of narrative has been realized for a long time, and several endeavors have been made to devise systems. The first attempt at a logical ordering of folktales was made in 1864 by J. G. von Hahn in the notes to his *Griechische und albanesische Märchen*.[2] His system has for us now only a historical interest, for it was grounded on a relatively small number of tales and it was too much concerned with correlating modern folktales with Greek myths. From a practical point of view his greatest weakness was his complete disregard of the fundamental difference between the tale type and the separate motifs of which it is composed.

As a result of these difficulties Hahn's system was never used and most folklorists continued to refer to tales by well-known names, such as Cinderella, Cupid and Psyche, Snow White, or Jack and the Beanstalk or else by the purely accidental numbers they bore in great collections, such as the Grimms' *Household Tales*. In the course of time such annotaters as Köhler gave currency to a large number of apt phrases descriptive of incidents in tales and of other motifs. Though books using such lists usually have an alphabetical index, it is helpful only to the person who happens to know the style of catchword or title employed and is thoroughly familiar with the language used. Nevertheless these three forms of reference, the well-known title, the Grimm number, and the motif catchword, have continued in use down to the present time and for casual reference have done good service. Köhler's and Cosquin's works, all of Bolte's, including the *Anmerkungen* to Grimm, and the *Handwörterbuch des deutschen Märchens* depend for their usefulness upon such alphabetical lists. The invaluable motif-references collected over a long lifetime by the Danish scholar H. F. Feilberg are similarly arranged, both in his dictionary of the Jutish dialect,[3] and his manuscript card catalogue in Copenhagen.[4]

A serious attempt to construct a comprehensive list of catchwords—naturally from the point of view of the English language—was made by Joseph Jacobs, and presented at the International Folklore Congress in London in 1891. It marked no real progress toward a classification, for it was merely an alphabetical list of motifs and types indiscriminately mixed.

[2] Two vols., Leipzig, 1864; new edition, München, 1918.
[3] *Bidrag til en Ordbog over Jyske Almuesmål* (4 vols., København, 1886-1914).
[4] See H. Ellekilde, *Nachschlagregister zu Feilberg* (FF Communications, No. 85, Helsinki, 1929).

The terms, many of them already in general use, were perhaps given a wider currency by Jacobs' work, but that is all.

These alphabetical lists which we have mentioned were confined almost exclusively to Europe and the Near East, and no convenient means of reference existed for primitive peoples. It is natural that the energetic collectors of American Indian tales should have found need for something of the kind. The beginning was made by Robert H. Lowie and Alfred L. Kroeber, who issued lists in 1908.[5] These were later (1916) used and expanded in the masterly study of *Tsimshian Mythology* by Franz Boas, and have been added to continually by such collectors as Elsie Clews Parsons. For the American Indian field such catchwords have proved convenient; but their use is strictly limited geographically, and like all of the other alphabetical lists, they confuse tale types and the smaller motifs.

For a systematic classification of folk narrative a clear differentiation between type and motif is necessary, for the problems of arrangement are essentially different in the two fields. Such a study as Miss Cox's *Cinderella* shows clearly how a complete tale (the type) is made up of a number of motifs in a relatively fixed order and combination. An example will be her analysis of Grimm's version of Cinderella:

> Ill-treated heroine (by step-mother and step-sisters)—Hearth-abode—Gifts chosen by three daughters from father. Heroine chooses hazel-branch, and plants it on mother's grave.—Help at grave—Task (grain sorting)—Task-performing animals (birds)—Transformed mother help (bird on tree)—Magic dresses—Meeting-place (ball)—Three-fold flight—Heroine hides (1) in pear-tree, (2) in pigeon-house, which are cut down by father—Pitch-trap—Lost shoe —Shoe marriage test—Mutilated feet—False brides—Animal witness (birds) —Happy marriage—Villain Nemesis.[6]

A type is a traditional tale that has an independent existence. It may be told as a complete narrative and does not depend for its meaning on any other tale. It may indeed happen to be told with another tale, but the fact that it may appear alone attests its independence. It may consist of only one motif or of many. Most animal tales and jokes and anecdotes are types of one motif. The ordinary *Märchen* (tales like Cinderella or Snow White) are types consisting of many of them.

A *motif* is the smallest element in a tale having a power to persist in tradition. In order to have this power it must have something unusual and striking about it. Most motifs fall into three classes. First are the actors in a tale—gods, or unusual animals, or marvelous creatures like witches, ogres, or fairies, or even conventionalized human characters like the favorite youngest child or the cruel stepmother. Second come certain items in the background of the action—magic objects, unusual customs, strange beliefs,

---

[5] *Journal of American Folklore*, XXI (1908), 24-27, 222.
[6] Cox, *Cinderella*, p. 17, No. 37.

and the like. In the third place there are single incidents—and these comprise the great majority of motifs. It is this last class that can have an independent existence and that may therefore serve as true tale-types. By far the largest number of traditional types consist of these single motifs.

For the purpose of furnishing a basis for the survey of traditional narrative in an area having a large common store of tales a type-index is necessary; the principal use of a motif-index is to display identity or similarity in the tale elements in all parts of the world so that they can be conveniently studied. A type-index implies that all versions of a type have a genetic relationship; a motif-index makes no such assumption.

It has been pointed out in the discussion of his plan for regional folktale surveys[7] that Kaarle Krohn recognized the prior necessity of a comprehensive folktale classification. The preparation of this work was entrusted to Antti Aarne, who had the constant advice of Krohn and the help of Oskar Hackman of Helsinki, Axel Olrik of Copenhagen, Johannes Bolte of Berlin, and C. W. von Sydow of Lund. The general purpose and plan may be described in Aarne's own words:

> The difficulties with which the student of comparative folk literature must contend in the collecting of material are undoubtedly greatest in the special field of the folk-tale. This circumstance has induced the Folk-Lore Fellows to set as their first goal the preparation of catalogues of tales. A list of Finnish folk-tales, the preparation of which has been entrusted to the undersigned, is to open the series of these catalogues. The rich treasure of tales which is found in possession of the Finnish Literary Society, and the contents of which for linguistic reasons have up to the present remained for the greater part unknown to foreign scholars, will no longer be shut up in this way and will be made available for use.
>
> Yet this first catalogue has necessitated certain preliminary work. There has existed no system that arranged the various types to be found in the variegated multitude of folk-tales and united them into a well-ordered whole. Hence it was desirable to work out such a systematic catalogue of types as would serve the purpose. The need of a common system of classification which should meet so far as possible the demands of the various countries has been felt for a long time. Such a system, to be sure, has its significance in so far as it arranges and classifies folk-tales, but its importance is primarily practical. How much would it facilitate the work of the collector of tales if all the collections of folk-tales thus far printed should be arranged according to the same system. The scholar would be in a position to discover in a moment the material for which he has need in any collection, whereas at present he is compelled to look through the entire work if he wishes to acquaint himself with the contents. For each editor has arranged his collection according to his own judgment, which in only a few instances has been guided by a deeper knowledge of the subject. Material that belongs together or is closely

[7] See pp. 396 ff., above

related is often found scattered here and there. If now the classification of types issued by the Folk-Lore Fellows, in their collections and catalogues to appear in the future, should come into general use, the collecting of material would thereby be made very much easier.[8]

Aarne was careful to disclaim any pretension to completeness. He used as a foundation the huge manuscript collection of tales at Helsinki, the Grundtvig material at Copenhagen and the Grimms' *Household Tales*. Even from these he made a few omissions when he felt that he was not dealing with a real folktale, and he added a few numbers from other sources. He realized that his classification was tentative and that it was reasonably complete only for northern Europe. He felt certain that it would be expanded in the future and with that in mind left many numbers open for new types. Though the index consisted of but 540 items, the system of numbers extends to 1940.

A clear-cut difference between type and motif distinguishes the *Verzeichnis der Märchentypen* from all previous lists. As Aarne says,

> So far as possible a complete narrative has served as a basis for each type. It might also naturally be conceivable to work out a classification of separate episodes and motifs, yet this would have necessitated such a cutting into pieces of all complete folk-tales that the scholar would be able to make a much more limited use of the classification. Nevertheless in some instances one is compelled to depart from the method decided upon. The separate tales belonging to the cycle of the stupid ogre are told by the people in such varied combinations that the necessity presented itself of handling each episode under its own number. In part, the same method had to be followed in connection with the animal tales and the humorous anecdotes. All of this has given rise to a certain inconsistency, but looked at from the standpoint of practical usefulness, which is the chief goal set up in the construction of the system of classification, this procedure has seemed most advisable. Otherwise, the information given to the scholar by a catalogue of tales based upon a system of types would in certain places seem entirely too general. Moreover, it is to be noted that the separate stories which generally appear as parts of a longer narrative are occasionally found by themselves, and then in any case merit an independent place.[9]

An examination of the index reveals the fact that somewhat more than half of the types included consist of a single narrative motif. For such tales the problem of classification is relatively simple, since only one item needs to be considered. The really difficult problem is a logical arrangement of the more than two hundred fifty complex types. Each of these is made up of a whole group of motifs and the question is continually presenting itself as to which of these motifs shall be used as the basis of classification. For example, is it the nature of the principal actor, or some striking external

[8] *Types*, pp. 8f.
[9] *Types*, pp. 10f.

accessory of the tale (such as a magic object), or the central event of the action itself which seems most important? It will be seen that in various parts of the type-index Aarne has used each of these methods, according to which seemed most applicable to the group of tales in question. Theoretical consistency has made way for practical convenience.

Aarne's general system is clearly stated in the Introduction to his Index:

> Taken as a whole, the tales are divided for the purpose of classification into three principal groups: animal tales, regular folk-tales, and humorous tales. For the animal tales, the smaller groups are differentiated according to the kind of animals playing a part in the story; and in each of these groups again the tales dealing with the same animal are placed together. Thus, for example, the group of wild animals begins with the favorite of folk-tales, the sly fox. Wherever animals belonging to different groups appear in a tale, the decision as to the place to be assigned the tale has been determined by the question as to which animal plays the leading role in the action. Thus, to cite an example, the tale "More Timid than the Hare" is not ranged with the stories of the fox but with the group, "Other Wild Animals," since the hare is here the principal character; likewise "The Dog and the Sparrow" (Type 248) is among the tales of birds and not in the group, "Domestic Animals."
>
> The largest group of tales, ordinary folk-tales, is divided into magic or wonder tales, religious stories, romantic stories, and those dealing with the stupid ogre. In the tales of magic is always found some supernatural factor, and generally likewise in the religious; whereas the romantic stories move entirely within the bounds of possibility. For the tales of the stupid ogre it has been difficult to find a satisfactory place in the classification. They are really wonder-tales and as such should be placed along with other wonder-tales, but since, on the other hand, in their character and nature they resemble the humorous tales, they have been placed as the last group of the regular folk-tales, next to the humorous anecdotes. In the arranging of the tales of magic into subdivisions, the persistence of the element of wonder, of the supernatural becomes clear. Thus these groups stand out: the supernatural adversary, in which group cross-reference is made to the closely-related ogre tales; the supernatural husband or wife; the supernatural task; the supernatural helper; the supernatural object; supernatural knowledge or power; and, lastly, a group in which some other supernatural element enters. These groups are again, in so far as possible, separated in accordance with their contents into new subdivisions; just as has also been done with the religious and romantic tales.
>
> Sometimes it happens that the same tale can be assigned to two different groups. In company with a supernatural adversary or helper, for example, a magic object may appear. The issue as to position is decided in accordance with which factor is most important for the action of the tale; but in addition the tale in question is also recorded in parentheses in the second position, with a note as to the place assigned it in the classification. . . .
>
> The third group of tales, jokes and anecdotes (*Schwänke*), will doubtless receive with the passage of time more additional numbers than the animal

tales or the ordinary folk-tales; for these humorous tales originate more easily among the people than other kinds. As the first subdivision of the jokes and anecdotes, the classification shows the numskull stories, which are arranged in accordance with whether they deal with farming, herding, fishing, hunting, building, preparing food, or other similar processes. The next part deals with "married couples," with a "woman" or with a "man." In the last-named, most numerous group, are further divisions into tales of the clever man, of lucky accidents, of the stupid man, and of the parson. In stories of the parson, he is usually treated as a fool, and especially often by the sexton, a fact which has been considered in arranging the tales of parsons. The last group of jokes and anecdotes forms the "Tales of Lying," which differentiate themselves into hunting tales, accounts of enormous animals, objects, etc.[10]

At the time of its appearance the *Verzeichnis der Märchentypen* received practically no notice, and it was only after Aarne had given an object lesson of its use in his catalogue of Finnish tales and Oskar Hackman in his index of the Finnish-Swedish types that students of the folktale realized its value.[11] These surveys were the beginning of a series that has continued ever since. In spite of the World War, eight of them appeared before Aarne's death in 1923, covering, in addition to the two areas just mentioned, Estonia, Norway, Lapland, Flanders, Bohemia, and Livonia. Though each of the scholars who have prepared surveys proposed numerous additions, they found the general plan of the classification entirely satisfactory as a basis for their work.[12]

By 1924 the many additional types which had been suggested made the time seem ripe for the revision of the *Verzeichnis*, to which Aarne had looked forward. But this great Finnish scholar died too soon to carry out the plan, and Professor Krohn invited the present writer to undertake it. During the academic year 1926-27 the revision and expansion of the Index was finished[13] and was published in 1928 under the title *The Types of the Folk-Tale*.

[10] *Types*, pp. 12-14.

[11] The slowness with which the Aarne index came into use is illustrated by the fact that although it was issued in 1910 and although I was in great need of just such an index for work on my dissertation at Harvard University from 1912 to 1914, it entirely escaped my attention and no one there seems to have heard of it for several years thereafter.

[12] These surveys were: A. Aarne, *Finnische Märchenvarianten* (FF Communications, Nos. 5 and 33) and *Estnische Märchen- und Sagenvarianten* (FF Communications, No. 25); O. Hackman, *Katalog der Märchen der finländischen Schweden* (FF Communications, No. 6); J. Qvigstad, *Lappische Märchen- und Sagenvarianten* (FF Communications, No. 60); R. Th. Christiansen, *The Norwegian Fairytales, a Short Summary* (FF Communications, No. 46 [an abstract of *Norske Eventyr*, Kristiania, 1921]); M. de Meyer, *Les Contes Populaires de la Flandre* (FF Communications, No. 37); O. Loorits, *Livische Märchen- und Sagenvarianten* (FF Communications, No. 66); V. Tille, *Verzeichnis der Böhmischen Märchen* (FF Communications, No. 34), having its own peculiar arrangement, but with cross-references to Aarne's list.

[13] My work on the index during this year's sojourn in Europe was greatly encouraged and aided by a number of able folklorists whom I then met for the first time. I had the good fortune at the very beginning of my stay to meet Krohn and Bolte together in Copenhagen

The revision was much more than a translation of Aarne into English with certain additional items. Although none of the new types which had appeared in the various surveys were omitted, a number of them were rejected from the main index, as having only local interest and were relegated to a supplementary list. Aarne's general scheme was not disturbed, and all of his type-numbers were retained. Additions were made from French folktales and from well-known literary stories which have become a part of popular tradition. The original index was baffling to all but very expert students of the tale because of the brevity of the description given each type and because of the lack of guidance as to where the tale could be found.[14]

Usually the exact original text of Aarne's statement was retained but was followed by such elaboration as seemed desirable. In complex tales this addition consisted in a detailed generalized statement of the type, and an analysis into constituent motifs.[15] For such statements great help was found in the Bolte-Polívka *Anmerkungen* and in Christiansen's *Norske Eventyr*, both of which had appeared subsequent to Aarne's list. Various monographs on tales also helped formulate these statements.

Instead of the occasional bibliographical references in the *Verzeichnis*, the revision attempted to list not only the Grimm and Grundtvig numbers but also all studies of the tale, great and small, especially those in Bolte-Polívka or in FF Communications. Indications were given as to which of the regional surveys contain the type and frequent references to American Indian or African versions were added.

Since the appearance of this revision the preparation of tale surveys has continued. The Russian index[16] which came out almost immediately afterwards made some last-minute changes in accordance with the new edition. In FF Communications have appeared surveys of Roumanian, Hungarian, Icelandic, Spanish, and Walloon folktales.[17] Published elsewhere have been

---

and to talk over plans. Arnold van Gennep in Paris, Edouard Hoffmann-Krayer and Hanns Bächtold-Stäubli in Basel, John Meier in Freiburg-im-Breisgau, Eugen Fehrle in Heidelberg, Hans Naumann in Frankfurt, Hugo Hepding in Giessen, and Jan de Vries in Leiden were all cordial and helpful. Most of the work was done in Paris, but it was completed during a two months' stay in Copenhagen, where the invaluable collections of the Dansk Folkmindesamling were available. Hans Ellekilde, the *arkivar*, gave me constant aid, and Ferdinand Ohrt and Arthur Christensen of Copenhagen, C. W. von Sydow of Lund, and R. Th. Christiansen of Oslo all helped make the stay in Scandinavia invaluable. Finally a week in Helsinki with Professor Krohn not only brought a pleasant climax to the year but cleared up many difficulties which could be solved in no other way.

[14] A few of the types could be found and explained only after a search of the Danish MSS in Copenhagen and the Finnish in Helsinki.

[15] Numbers were inserted throughout, referring to the *Motif-Index of Folk-Literature*, then in preparation.

[16] A. N. Andrejev, *Ukazatel' Skazočnich Sjuzhetov po Systeme Aarne* (Gosud. russ. geogr. obščestvo, otd. etnogr. skazočnaya komissiya, Leningrad, 1929).

[17] A. Schullerus, *Verzeichnis der rumänischen Märchen* (FF Communications, No. 78); H. Honti, *Verzeichnis der publizierten ungarischen Märchen* (FF Communications, No. 81); E.

lists from Prussia and Lithuania.[18] Besides this a number of tale collections have appeared with an index after the Aarne classification.[19] Several surveys are finished but unpublished.[20]

One of the changes made in the revision was the addition of formulistic tales—particularly cumulative stories. A notable improvement in that part of the index has been made by Archer Taylor who revised that section in 1933.[21]

A problem discussed at the Congress for the Study of the Folktale at Lund in 1935 was the further revision of the Type-Index. It was agreed that such a revision must be made and that it must be greatly strengthened by an adequate consideration of material from southern and eastern Europe from the Moslem countries, and from India. A series of special studies of the tales of this part of the world is necessary before a revision can be adequately carried out.[22]

Though the Aarne index has been generally accepted, it is natural that there should have been criticisms of detail. Some of these are theoretical and are not directed toward an actual change in the classification,[23] though they do bring to light useful relationships between types widely separated in the Index. Others suggest more accurate subdivision at various points.[24]

Ol. Sveinsson, *Verzeichnis isländischer Märchenvarianten* (FF Communications, No. 83); R. S. Boggs, *Index of Spanish Folktales* (FF Communications, No. 90); G. Laport, *Les contes populaires Wallons* (FF Communications, No. 101).

[18] Karl Plenzat, *Die ost- und westpreussischen Märchen und Schwänke nach Typen geordnet* (Königsberg, 1927); J. Balys, *Motif-Index of Lithuanian Folktales* (Kaunas, 1936).

[19] In FF Communications No. 10, Aarne published a concordance between his index and several important collections, viz. Grundtvig's classification of Danish tales in the Dansk Folkemindesamling; Grimm's *Kinder- und Hausmärchen*; Gonzenbach's *Sicilianische Märchen*; Afanasief's *Narodnie Russkie Skazki*; and Hahn's *Griechische und albanesische Märchen*. Among other works which have appeared with an index according to the Aarne classification are: N. M. Penzer, *The Pentamerone of Basile;* J. G. McKay. *More West Highland Tales;* Jan de Vries, *Volksverhalen uit Oost Indië;* and M. Azadovsky, *Russkaya Skazka* (Moskva, 1930).

[20] Three manuscripts in the Indiana University Library contain such surveys: Latin American tales by Cecelia Dean, African tales by May A. Klipple, and European tales among the North American Indians by Llora B. Lydy. In the University of Chicago Library is a type-index of the collection of exempla, *Scala Celi,* by Luella Carter. In addition there are, of course, card indexes of the various folktale archives which use the Aarne classification; see pp. 398f.

[21] A. Taylor, "A Classification of Formula Tales," *Journal of American Folk-Lore,* XLVI, 77ff.

[22] Since my acceptance at Lund of the responsibility for this revision I have undertaken an analysis of the oral tales of India and, with the cooperation of a group of American Orientalists, also of the great written collections of Indic fiction. In view of the undoubted importance of India in the history of the tale, such a preliminary study seems essential.

[23] For example, the rearrangement suggested in M. Ziegler, *Die Frau im Märchen.* Some pertinent suggestions from the point of view of the Spanish folktale is in A. M. Espinosa's article, "La Clasificación de los Cuentos Populares," *Boletín de la Academia Española,* XXI (Madrid, 1934), 175-208.

[24] Especially R. S. Boggs, in his *Index of Spanish Folktales* (FF Communications, No. 90), introduced additional subdivisions and has also provided a valuable alphabetical index which is much fuller than that in the Aarne-Thompson.

A question sometimes broached concerns the desirability and possibility of extending the index of types to embrace the whole world. Of course in so far as the European and West Asiatic tales are found among distant peoples, the present index is usable and has been successfully employed, for example, for African, Indonesian, and North American Indian tales.[25] But the native cycles of tales, such as we have examined in Part III of this volume, would probably not easily fit into the Aarne classification. Shall separate type lists be undertaken for each of these great areas or should a serious attempt be made at a radical expansion of the present classification?[26] Though some students of primitive tales feel that no such type-lists are necessary, there would seem little doubt that sooner or later they will be attempted.[27]

In his introduction to the *Verzeichnis* Aarne had mentioned the possibility that one might also make an index of particular motifs. But except in so far as many of the types in his index and all the *Sagen* in the special catalogue he made of these[28] consist of but a single incident, he did not himself undertake this task. Up to the time he made this suggestion there existed only alphabetical lists in which motifs and types were indiscriminately mixed, and these inventories were usually very limited in their geographical scope. Nothing on a world-wide scale had been undertaken, and no attempt had been made to arrange motifs in any logical order.

Even the classification proposed by Arthur Christensen in 1925[29] was based upon a very restricted group of literary tale and fable collections and its arrangement, though interesting, depended upon considerations entirely too theoretical to permit of its successful use by others. His divisions into "éléments de relation," "motifs," "accessoires épiques," "thème," "motifs sans thème," "motifs a thèmes faibles," etc. left a large number of miscellaneous items that could be handled only by an alphabetical index. Christensen's classification was really only a sketch and made no effort to list more than a relatively small number of motifs to illustrate the different categories proposed.

Nor was the broad division of motifs suggested by Albert Wesselski[30] of real help for a comprehensive arrangement. He divided the motifs of folktales, novelle, and myths into "Mythenmotive," "Gemeinschaftsmotive,"

[25] For the African and North American Indian tales, see note 20 above. For Indonesian, see DeVries, *Volksverhalen*. See also pp. 283f., above.

[26] In DeVries's notes to his Indonesian tales (*Volksverhalen*) he has successfully employed a greatly expanded form of the Aarne index.

[27] Something of a beginning of a list for American aborigines can be seen in the notes to my *Tales of the North American Indians*.

[28] *Verzeichnis der finnischen Ursprungssagen und ihrer Varianten* (FF Communications, No. 8, Hamina, 1912).

[29] *Motif et Thème* (FF Communications, No. 59, Helsinki, 1925).

[30] *Märchen des Mittelalters*, p. 17.

and "Kulturmotive," and on a basis of this distinction discussed the difference between the narrative forms. But he gave only samples of each class and was not concerned with the question of a general index.

The present writer became interested in the problem of classifying the elements of tales many years before he actually undertook it. As a necessary part of several of his early studies, particularly his doctoral dissertation on *European Tales among the North American Indians*, he began the accumulation of references to incidents and other traits in tales both European and American Indian. All the lists then in existence were copied, each item on a separate card, and additions grew at such a rate that a tentative arrangement of the material became imperative. With the new notes made available by the publication of the Bolte-Polívka *Anmerkungen* and with those resulting from further reading in the American Indian field, the tentative arrangement had to be modified again and again. When in 1922 the author decided to undertake a study of the incidents in American Indian tales which were not obvious borrowings from Europe, he became convinced that all such studies must await an adequate classification of motifs.

A tentative draft was first worked out, based upon the notes which had already been taken. This first form, extending only to some four hundred pages, revealed a number of weaknesses of detail in the classification and demonstrated that in order to be of real value the Index must be based on as extensive a foundation as possible. It was this conviction that delayed the work so much, for the program of reading and note-taking determined on in 1923 was so extensive that actual writing did not begin until five years later.[31] Publication began in 1932 and was completed in 1936.

This is not a proper place to discuss in detail the works covered as a basis for the *Motif-Index*. The ideal was to bring together narrative elements from as many different fields of traditional fiction as possible. Tales and myths from primitive peoples everywhere, European and Oriental stories and ballads, local and explanatory legends, the well-known mythological cycles, literary collections like the *Panchatantra* and the *Thousand and One Nights*, fabliaux, exempla, jestbooks—all such works were explored and analyzed. Folklore journals of all kinds, and all books with comparative studies of tales or incidents—Bolte-Polívka, the files of FF Communications, Cosquin's works, and the like—these all swelled the accumulations with the fruit of other men's labors.

The *Motif-Index* thus attempts to bring together material from everywhere and arrange it by a logical system. It makes no assumption that items listed next to each other have any genetic relationship, but only that they belong in neighboring logical categories. The classification is for the

---

[31] Work was interrupted for the preparation of *Tales of the North American Indians*, in which were published all my notes in that field. In this way it was possible to avoid overloading the Motif-Index with these references. The revision of *The Types of the Folk-Tale* was also made during these years.

practical purpose of arranging and assorting narrative material so that it can be easily found. In that respect it most resembles a library classification, where books good and bad, old and new, large and small appear together on the shelves: all that matters is that the items belong to the same division and subdivision of human knowledge. The general scheme finally adopted is thus described in the Introduction of the *Motif-Index*:

> In a very general fashion the groups may be said to progress from the mythological and the supernatural toward the realistic and even the humorous. But no such progress is to be observed in all parts of the index: the last half is nearly all realistic.
>
> In Chapter A are handled motifs having to do with creation and with the nature of the world: creators, gods, and demigods; the creation and nature of the universe, and especially of the earth; the beginnings of life; the creation and establishment of the animal and vegetable world.
>
> Chapter B is concerned with animals. Not all tales in which animals figure are placed here, for most frequently it is the action and not the particular actor that is significant in such stories. In Chapter B, on the contrary, appear animals that are in some way remarkable as such: mythical animals like the dragon, magic animals like the truth-telling bird, animals with human traits, animal kingdoms, weddings, and the like. Then there are the many helpful or grateful beasts, marriages of animals to human beings, and other fanciful ideas about animals.
>
> Just as the motifs in Chapter B suggest some possible relation to the savage institution of totemism, those in Chapter C are based upon the primitive idea of tabu. Forbidden things of all kinds are here listed, as well as the opposite of that concept, the unique compulsion.
>
> The most extensive group is that devoted to magic (Chapter D). The divisions are quite simple: transformation and disenchantment, magic objects and their employment, magic powers and other manifestations.
>
> The motifs listed in Chapter E concern ideas about the dead—resuscitation, ghosts, and reincarnation—as well as ideas concerning the nature of the soul.
>
> Aside from magic and the return of the dead, traditional literature records many marvels: journeys to other worlds; extraordinary creatures such as fairies, spirits, and demons; wondrous places, such as castles in the sea; and marvelous persons and events. These form Chapter F.
>
> Because of the prominence of dreadful beings, such as ogres, witches, and the like, these have been given a special division, G. It will be seen that there is naturally much relation between Chapter E, F, and G; for example, between ogres and evil spirits, or between fairies and witches or ghosts. These relationships are noted by means of cross references.
>
> Beginning with Chapter H, the purely supernatural assumes a minor importance, though it is still present. Chapter H has been formed gradually from three separate divisions in the original plan. These, however, are all comprehended under the term "Tests." Tales of recognition are really tests of identity; riddles and the like, tests of cleverness; and tasks and quests, tests of prowess. In addition are to be found sundry tests of character and other qualities.

Chapter J was likewise originally three chapters—Wisdom, Cleverness, Foolishness. Their fundamental unity is apparent: the motivation is always mental. The first part (Wisdom) consists in large part of fable material. The tales of cleverness and of stupidity come in large measure from jestbooks.

In the motifs in Chapter J the attention is directed primarily to the mental quality of the character. In K, on the contrary, primary importance is given to action. A very large part of narrative literature deals with deceptions. The work of thieves and rascals, deceptive captures and escapes, seductions, adultery, disguises, and illusions constitute one of the most extensive chapters in the classification.

The rest of the work is made up of smaller chapters. In "L" appear such reversals of fortune as the success of the unpromising child or the downfall of the proud. "M" deals with such definite ordaining of the future as irrevocable judgments, bargains, promises, and oaths. In "N" the large part that luck plays in narrative is shown. Tales of gambling, and of the favors and evil gifts of the Goddess Fortuna appear here.

Chapter P concerns the social system. Not all tales about kings and princes belong here, but only such motifs as rest upon some feature of the social order: customs concerning kings, or the relation of the social ranks and the professions, or anything noteworthy in the administration of such activities as law or army. A very great number of cross-references appear in this chapter.

In "Q" are recorded rewards and punishments, in "R" motifs concerning captives and fugitives, and in "S" instances of great cruelty. In "T" are treated together the motifs dealing with sex, though there are, of course, many other parts of the index where such motifs are also of interest. Here particularly come wooing, marriage, married life, and the birth of children, as well as sundry types of sexual relations.

In Chapter U are gathered a small number of motifs, mostly from fable literature, that are of a homiletic tendency. A tale is told with the sole purpose of showing the nature of life. "Thus goes the world" is the text of such tales.

Many incidents depend upon religious differences or upon certain objects of religious worship. These motifs make up Chapter V. In "W" stories designed to illustrate traits of character are classified. The last of the systematic divisions, "X", contains incidents whose purpose is entirely humorous. Many cross-references to merry tales listed elsewhere are, of course, given.

At the end, in Chapter Z, appear several small classifications which hardly deserve a chapter each. In the future should other small classifications seem desirable, they can easily be added as new parts of Chapter Z.

A numbering system was devised, remotely similar to that used by the Library of Congress, so that the Index can be indefinitely expanded at any point. Every motif has a number indicating its place in the classification. The details of the system are not difficult. Chapters (indicated by capital letters) are divided into large groups, usually of 100 numbers, and these in turn into tens, etc.

An attempt was made to furnish some bibliographical help with each motif, so that the work would have value as a general reference book on folk narrative. In this respect it supplements the Aarne-Thompson *Types of the Folk-Tale*.

Relationship between the *Type-Index* and the *Motif-Index* has been close in many ways. Although the motif classification had not been entirely completed at the time of the revision of the Aarne *Verzeichnis*, the numbers were inserted at the proper place in the motif-analyses of the various types.[32] In the *Motif-Index* also, care was taken to make note of the appearance of the motif in the various tale-types.

It would seem that careful analysis of stories into motifs and proper cross-indexing would teach much about the nature of these narrative elements. Do some of them owe their existence to a particular story and belong nowhere else? Do some combine freely everywhere? Are some isolated, living an independent life as a single-motif tale-type?

Much improvement in folktale surveys of various areas would now seem possible by the use of a combination of the two indexes. By furnishing a motif-analysis of each type the author could not only indicate its presence but also state the exact form in which it appears.[33] He could thus give a full and accurate account of the tales of an area.

Use is being made of the *Motif-Index* mainly for two purposes. Several works containing many motifs have special indexes based on this classification. Such are Penzer's edition of *The Pentamerone of Basile*, McKay's *More West Highland Tales*, and Carrière's *French Folklore from Missouri*, and the author's *Tales of the North American Indians*. The *Handwörterbuch des deutschen Märchens* carries the appropriate motif-numbers in its margins.

A considerable program of surveying narrative material which has little relation to the *Types of the Folk-Tale* is now under way, and for these the *Motif-Index* appears to serve as a satisfactory basis. D. P. Rotunda's *Motif-Index of the Italian Novella*[34] illustrates its use with these literary tales. The fabliau, the Irish mythological and heroic texts, some of the medieval romantic cycles, the Icelandic Fornaldersögur, Renaissance jest books, and African tales are all being worked on and may be expected without great delay. All of these studies naturally furnish new motifs, which it is hoped will all be embodied in an eventual new edition of the *Motif-Index*.

No differentiation is made in the classification as to the literary *genre* to which a particular item may belong. Not only *Märchen*, but also *Sagen*, fables, jests, exempla, myths, and *novelle* have furnished these motifs. For the student investigating one of these special forms it is convenient to have together all the incidents belonging to that form. For this reason,

---

[32] A few numbers, thus prematurely announced, proved impossible to retain, but on the whole the references are correct.

[33] I am attempting such an analysis of the oral tales of India.

[34] Indiana University Publications, Folklore Series. No. 2 (Bloomington, 1942).

special check-lists of motifs for each of these large fields have been prepared and are being used. It would seem possible that as such lists are perfected they may serve as quite satisfactory classifications for each of these forms, since stories of these categories for the most part consist of single motifs.

It is, of course, clear that the main purpose of the classification of traditional narrative, whether by type or motif, is to furnish an exact style of reference, whether it be for analytical study or for the making of accurate inventories of large bodies of material. If the two indexes can in this way promote accuracy of terminology and can act as keys to unlock large inaccessible stores of traditional fiction, they will have fulfilled their purpose.

THE LIFE HISTORY OF A FOLKTALE

V

THE recording and publishing of folktales, the classifying, and the arranging of them in archives and surveys have demanded the labor of many men and women of the most varied interests. It is not therefore to be expected that they have all worked toward a well-defined goal or that they would agree even in general terms on the end to be attained by their efforts. Especially divergent in their attitude toward their work are the collectors of folktales. Some, of course, are anthropologists or trained folklorists, but perhaps the greater number are teachers, doctors, clergymen, missionaries, or travelers, who have labored for the mere love of the harvest they were gathering. They have recognized the worth of these old traditions, have found them interesting and often beautiful things in themselves, and have been impelled to recover them before it is too late. They have felt no need of a remoter reason for their efforts.

But the comparative student of the folktale sees that, in addition to the intrinsic interest which every story has as a means of entertainment or for giving aesthetic pleasure, it presents a challenging problem in social history and at the same time furnishes help toward the solution of that very problem. The story which the collector has just recorded from the lips of the old peasant was not original with this aged man but was learned, perhaps in his youth, from someone else. The teller prides himself in preserving it as an ancient tradition. It is not his, but belongs to his people and is as much a part of them as any of their customs or beliefs could be. Though the naïve collector may not realize it, the scholar knows that the folktale he reads in a book or manuscript has probably had a long life and that the version before him is merely one of the many, many retellings of the story in many lands since it was first told and started on its long journey.

But even if a particular telling of a story is no more than one of many scores or hundreds of variants, it plays its due part when the scholar follows the urgings of his curiosity and begins to study the tale in its entirety. If he should be interested in an analysis of the devices of narrative style in the various literary and oral tellings of the story he must, of course, make a careful examination of individual versions.[1] These variants are also especially important for the proper reconstruction of the entire life history of the tale—and the more of them the historian of the story has to work with the better for his results.

It is primarily to furnish a basis for these historic investigations of tales that the great collections have been gathered in archives, that classifications and surveys and indexes have been prepared, and that comparative notes have been published. All these labors are but preliminary to the actual researches for which they must furnish the data.

Some attempt at the study of particular tales was made in a small way by Wilhelm Grimm and published in his notes to his *Household Tales*.[2] But the first important investigations on a factual historical basis were undertaken by Theodor Benfey,[3] under the conviction that such studies would demonstrate the fact that the origin of European folktales was in India. In respect to the tales which he treated he made a good case for the theory.

Benfey's monographs, as well as those of Cosquin,[4] who followed in his footsteps, show that these authors were interested in the tale as it appears in written documents and were but mildly concerned with its oral history. The more thorough student of the folktale, however, must not only be a master of the technique proper to the study of the mutual relation of manuscripts and books, but must also be prepared to deal with a tradition when it is supported only by the memories of oral tellers and hearers.

The two kinds of study are not alike. With the literary tradition we have a given number of manuscripts and books. Our task is to see their relations to one another. The essential process of this tradition has always been that of reading and copying (with or without change). By a knowledge of the dates of the documents and a careful examination of their contents the scholar tries to work out a "stemma," or genealogical tree, showing what manuscript, either existent or hypothetical, formed the basis of the tradition; then which manuscripts were copies or adaptations of this; and then which came from these secondary documents, etc. However complicated the "stemma" may be, the tradition is always direct from written page to written page.

With the oral folktale the situation is quite different. The story is not fixed in writing, but is dependent upon human memory for its preservation.

---

[1] In the next chapter some remarks are made about stylistic studies. Their validity depends above all on the faithfulness of the recording.

[2] *Kinder- und Hausmärchen* (3d edition, Göttingen, 1856), vol. III (new ed. Reclam); English translation by Margaret Hunt (London, 1884).

[3] Collected in his *Kleinere Schriften*.

[4] *Etudes folkloriques* and *Les contes indiens et l'occident*.

At first sight the multitude of versions of a well-known folktale show such variety that one is inclined to feel that he is moving in an absolutely lawless realm. It seems that the kaleidoscopic changes from tale to tale are the merest workings of chance. No wonder that such scholars as Joseph Bédier[5] have insisted on the futility of the attempt to see any order in the confusion.

But this state of anarchy is only apparent. Even a superficial examination of the versions of a tale will show that on the whole those which have been recovered from the same district show more resemblances in detail than those which come from a distance. Some causes have been at work to produce this result and though they may not be easy to discover and define exactly, they are very real. The problem is complicated, to be sure; for with the oral tale many factors influence the course of tradition, not only geographical and historical, but sociological and psychological as well.

The most serious attempt to perfect a technique for the study of the folktale has been that made by Kaarle Krohn and known as the historic-geographic method,[6] or in deference to its origin, the Finnish method. Though this scheme has, as we shall see, been subjected to some adverse criticism, it has been employed in a number of excellent studies, the general validity of which can hardly be doubted, and the method has been continually improved. No one who really knows about the behavior of oral tales can take exception to the careful analysis which is the foundation of the technique. The historic-geographic method is so important in the study of the folktale that it must be considered in some detail.

The goal toward which a student using this method strives is nothing less than a complete life history of a particular tale. He hopes by proper analysis of the versions, by a consideration of all historical and geographical factors, and by the application of some well-recognized facts about oral transmission to arrive at something approaching the original form of the tale and to be able to make a plausible explanation of the changes the story has suffered in order to produce all the different versions. This study should also give indications as to the time and place of its origin and the course of its dissemination.

His first problem is that of assembling the variants on which his study is to be based. By using the notes in Bolte-Polívka,[7] the various folktale surveys, and all other bibliographical sources available, he extends his list as much as possible. But he needs more than mere references; he must use the tales themselves. Finding them is a major task, involving not only visits

[5] See p. 393.
[6] Good discussions of the method are given in: A. Aarne, *Leitfaden der vergleichenden Märchenforschung* and K. Krohn, *Die folkloristische Arbeitsmethode.*
[7] See p. 395, above.

to great folktale libraries but much correspondence with archives[8] and individuals in order to obtain manuscript recordings. The utmost diligence is necessary, for, generally speaking, the larger number of versions studied the safer are the conclusions.

In some cases scholars have brought together from five hundred to a thousand. It is convenient to have them in complete form, or at least in a full summary, since frequently a seemingly insignificant detail may have an important bearing on a problem in hand. The next step after assembling the variants is labeling and arranging them. All are marked by date and place of recording. The literary versions are placed in chronological order, and the oral in geographic.

The FF Communications uses a conventional method of marking these oral versions. Each country is given an abbreviation, and after the first listing of the versions with all bibliographical detail, each can be referred to by this abbreviation. The symbol for Norwegian, for example, is GN. If there are nine tales from Norway, they are cited as GN1, GN2, . . . GN9. The seventh Norwegian tale can always be referred to as GN7. The abbreviations were first announced in German and hence are not always immediately apparent to the reader of English. The first element is the initial of the linguistic group the country belongs to, and the second is the country itself. A list of the most frequently used abbreviations follows:

GN	= Norwegian	RR	= Roumanian
GD	= Danish	SR	= Russian
GS	= Swedish	SRW	= White Russian
GSF	= Finnish-Swedish	SRK	= Little Russian
GI	= Icelandic	SČ	= Czechoslovak
GG	= German	SP	= Polish
GH	= Dutch (Holland)	SB	= Bulgarian
GV	= Flemish (Vlämisch)	SS	= Serbocroatian
GE	= English	FF	= Finnish
CS	= Highland Scottish	FL	= Lappish
CI	= Irish	FE	= Estonian
CB	= Breton	FLiv	= Livonian
CW	= Welsh	FM	= Hungarian (Magyar)
RF	= French	RFAm	= American French
RS	= Spanish	GEAm	= American English
RP	= Portuguese	RSAm	= American Spanish
RI	= Italian	RPAm	= Brazilian Portuguese

Such an arrangement of the versions of a folktale—several hundred it may be—facilitates a rapid geographic and historical survey of any trait of the tale and provides a means for exact, though highly abbreviated, reference.

---

[8] For an account of these archives and individuals, see pp. 398ff., above.

After this thorough preparation of the foundations of the study, the next step is an analysis of the tale itself into its principal traits. This process can best be seen by citing an actual example. One of the most thorough studies employing this technique is Walter Anderson's *Kaiser und Abt.* This story is well known in English tradition through the ballad "King John and the Bishop."[9] The king tells the abbot that unless within three days he can answer the three questions which the king will ask him, he will lose his life. A shepherd disguises as the abbot and answers the questions. The ending of the story varies greatly in different versions.

Anderson finds that the details of his story concern (1) the persons involved, (2) the riddles, and (3) other details of the narrative. His traits then are:

I. *The persons involved—*
   (a) Number of persons involved
   (b) The question-giver
   (c) The questioned
   (d) The answer-giver
II. *The riddles*
   (a) The number of questions
   (b) The actual riddles and their answers
     A. How high is heaven?
     B. How deep is the sea?
     C. How much water is in the sea?
     ....
     Q. What am I thinking?
III. *Other details of the narrative*
   (a) Reason for propounding the riddles
   (b) Time limit for answering the questions
   (c) Penalty for failure to answer the questions
   (d) Physical resemblance of questioned and answer-giver
   (e) How substitution is carried out
   (f) End result of the action

It will be seen that this is not a breaking of a tale up into its motifs, but rather an analysis so arranged as to display all possibilities of variation in the versions. The next stage, the listing of these possibilities, can only be done by exploring the tales themselves and noting the way in which each handles the item in question. The trait marked I b (the question-giver) is thus treated by Anderson:

Emperor (Russian Tsar, Turkish Sultan or Calif): Rom Weltchr., Jan

---

[9] F. J. Child, *English and Scottish Popular Ballads*, X, 410, No. 45. For a discussion of this story see p. 159, above.

v. Hollant, Gesta Rom., Fastnachtsp . . . ,[10] GG 32, 44, 45, 48, 54, 55, GV 1, 2, 4-7, GD 22, GN 1, Lit. 1, SR 1-9, (10), 11-20, 23, 24, (25), SRW 1-5, SU 1, 3-7, 9, 10, 13, SP 2, 3, SC 1, SS 3-7. . . . (121 variants=25.5% of the whole).

King: (listed in the same way) (254 variants=53.6% of the whole).

President: . . . (11 variants=2.3% of the whole).

And so on, through Pope, Bishop, other high churchman, Priest, Vizier, Nobleman, Professor, Wise man, Gypsy, and finally "Trait is lacking." The latter point is important for the percent count.

After such a listing of versions the scholar is ready to study his results. He finds a monarch as the question-giver in the overwhelming majority of the versions (81.4%), so that this would undoubtedly seem to be the original form of the tale. Mere majorities of course are not conclusive, but serve as only one type of evidence. The versions having the exceptional handlings of the trait must be looked over separately as a group not only from the chronological point of view but also the geographic to see whether perhaps some of the less popular forms may have had definite historical or geographical limits to their appearance.

Each of the traits of the story must be studied in this way. By counting frequency of occurrence of each possible handling of the trait, by considering for each the historical and geographical elements involved, the scholar tries to see just what has been the history of each of these elements of the tale. Often these facts make such a convincing accumulation of evidence that there can be little doubt as to the form the element in question had in the original tale. But the historian of the story must consider all of his data, for he is interested in all the developments of the narrative, and not merely in tracing its origin.

In studying the data assembled for each one of the traits, the scholar must carefully judge of the relative value of percentage counts, breadth of distribution, age, etc., in the history of the item. Aarne has discussed several of these considerations which are important for determining whether a particular trait belonged to the original form of the tale, the archetype.[11] Each trait should be tested for: (1) its relative frequency of occurrence (the percentage count illustrated above), (2) the extent of its distribution, (3) its agreement with the complete type in the direction of its dissemination (where the latter is certain), (4) its presence in well-preserved versions (more important than if it is in confused variants), (5) striking qualities in the trait itself that would make it easily remembered, (6) naturalness in the trait in contrast to unnaturalness in others, (7) its essential place in the action of the story, so that without it the plot would not hold together, (8) its presence in one tale only (this is more likely to show that it is original than if it also belonged in other tales), (9) the possibility of other forms of

---

[10] These first abbreviations refer to literary versions.
[11] *Leitfaden*, p. 41.

the trait having easily developed from it. Such a test should ordinarily result in an indication as to which forms belonged to the archetype and which developed later.

If the evidence from a study of the various traits is clear and unambiguous, the scholar may attempt the construction of an archetype immediately by combining all the details that are shown to be original. But it is not often that the survey of all the parts permits so easy a solution of the problem. The most that can be done at this stage is usually a *trial archetype* which will be subject to correction as the study proceeds.

The detailed display of the variants which the scholar has now before him will allow him to examine historical and geographical elements with an ease not otherwise possible. For example, it may be noticed that one of the traits which is not important for its actual number of occurrences is found in all the older literary versions. Are there also other traits that belong just to these? Perhaps these versions have enough in common to compel the grouping of them as a special development of the tale. Perhaps because of their age these versions may be near to the real archetype. Or again an item may have a definitely limited area of occurrence, e.g., the Baltic countries. This suggests that all the tales of that area should be subjected to a special analysis to discover whether a special Baltic subtype may have been developed. If it seems so, then an attempt should be made to determine its original form and to see whether all the Baltic tales belong to it or whether some quite clearly belong to other secondary developments. In this way it will generally happen that a number of subtypes each with its geographic center will be discovered.

When the original forms of all these special developments have been worked out, they can be studied together to see what light they throw on the ultimate archetype which could produce them all. Such a study will also probably reveal geographic groupings that point clearly to the place of origin of the story. It may indicate the relation of the whole tradition to early written forms and thus furnish some idea as to the period at which the tale was first told.

In his *Leitfaden der vergleichenden Märchenforschung*, Antti Aarne wrote an excellent practical guide for studying tales by the historic-geographic method, and he practiced his preaching by producing a group of researches by this technique.[12] In discussing the place of origin of tales,[13] he pointed out that it is not always possible to find the place where a tale was invented, and that the most that can be expected is some such general indication as southwestern Asia, the Balkans, northern Africa, Asia Minor, and the like. The fairy tale in particular (unlike the local legend) is seldom concerned with definite places, so that the actual texts are not likely to be

[12] See p. 444, below.
[13] *Leitfaden*, p. 48.

very helpful. Aarne suggests an examination of all the older literary versions to see if perhaps they may all point in the same direction. But he warned the student that literary texts have often been copied far from the place of origin. Better evidence for the center of dissemination comes from a consideration of the whole geographic distribution and particularly the frequency and popularity of the tale in certain places. Once in a while a necessary trait in the tale may place its origin in a particular climate: the story of the bear who froze his tail in the ice could not have originated in the tropics.

The possibility of discovering that a dated literary document represents an early or late form of a tale and thereby of getting an indication of the age has already been suggested. It is clear to any student of the tale of Cupid and Psyche that the version of Apuleius told in the second century after Christ is a much more highly developed form of the tale than that current in much of Europe today. The date of the archetype must therefore be well before the Christian era. The same is true of the story of Tobit and the Grateful Dead Man. It appears in the Apocryphal book of Tobit about the beginning of our era, but this version has suffered changes that indicate a much earlier date of origin.

These are some indications as to the way the student proceeds to interpret the data he has so conveniently arranged. If he succeeds in avoiding the many pitfalls awaiting him and always uses good judgment he should have arrived at a close approximation of the archetype of the story he is studying. His task has not been unlike that of the student of Indo-European languages who has worked out the theoretical Indo-European form for a word. He has constructed this by first studying the word in each of the Germanic languages and, by the application of general laws of change, positing a primitive Germanic form which would normally produce these words. In like manner he works out theoretical constructions for primitive Celtic, primitive Slavic, etc. Then from all these primitive forms for the main branches of the language family he arrives at a hypothetical word which could serve as the common ancestor of them all. This method of working back to primitive local forms and from them to an ultimate archetype is applicable not only to language but also to traditional narrative.

It must not be supposed, however, that the actual behavior of the two kinds of material is alike. For the dissemination of tales is not greatly hindered by language frontiers, and individuals learn foreign tales much more readily than they learn new languages. From wide experience with studying oral tradition Aarne and Anderson have laid down some principles that the student should keep in mind as he examines the way the archetype he has established suffers modification. While the kinds of change listed by Aarne[14] would seem to be obvious to anyone who has even a moderate

[14] *Leitfaden*, pp. 23 ff.

acquaintance with folktale diffusion, they are convenient as continual reminders while the scholar is trying to account for the variations which he finds. A brief statement of these kinds of change will be sufficient:

1. Forgetting a detail, especially an unimportant one. This is perhaps the most frequent cause of modifications in stories.

2. Adding a detail not originally present. Most often this may be a motif from another tale, though sometimes it is pure invention. The beginning and end of a story are especially subject to such accretions.

3. Stringing two or more tales together. Short tales of animals or ogres and tricks of rascals are particularly liable to this experience.

4. The multiplication of details—usually by three.

5. Repetition of an incident which occurs but once in the original tale. Sometimes this may not be an actual repetition but merely an analogy to something in the same or some other story.

6. Specialization of a general trait (a sparrow instead of a bird) or the generalizing of a special (a bird instead of a sparrow).

7. Material from another tale may be substituted, particularly at the end of the story.

8. Exchange of roles, often of opposing characters: the clever fox and stupid bear may change places.

9. Animal tales may have human characters replace the animals.

10. Human tales may have animal characters replace men and women.

11. Likewise animals and ogres or demons may be shifted.

12. A tale may be told in the first person as if the teller were one of the characters.

13. One change in a tale will force others to be made to maintain consistency.

14. As a tale wanders it adapts itself to its new environment: unfamiliar customs or objects may be replaced by familiar. Princes and princesses become chiefs' sons and daughters in American Indian versions.

15. Likewise obsolete traits may be replaced by modern. The hero takes the train to go on his adventures.

These are some changes which experienced students of folktale dissemination actually encounter. They are in no sense "laws" of oral transmission, since in the case of perfect transmission not one of them would be effective. But an oral tale lives on the lips of its tellers and like all living things is continually subject to change. An understanding of the processes listed above will help clarify the relation between the archetype and the multiform versions that have developed from it.

To these general observations of Aarne's on modifications in tales, Walter Anderson has, as a result of his exhaustive study of "The Emperor and the Abbot," added some conclusions on the nature of oral tradition.[15]

---

[15] *Kaiser und Abt*, pp. 397 ff.

These concern (a) the law of self-correction in folk-narrative, (b) the formation of special redactions of a tale, (c) the direction of dissemination of folktales.

The Law of Self-Correction. The examination of all the versions of a tale impresses one with the remarkable stability of the essential story in the midst of continually shifting details. Anderson feels that this stability is not primarily due to the prodigious memory of the unlettered story-teller, for stories are not repeated verbatim and no two recovered from oral telling are exactly alike. The stability is rather due to the fact that (1) each teller of a tale (or jest, legend, etc.) has heard it from his informant not once but often; (2) that, as a rule, he has heard it not from one single person but from a whole group of persons and often in differing versions. Intelligent hearers often correct careless tellers and in that way bring the tale back nearer to the regular tradition. The hearer of many versions of a tale naturally constructs a kind of standard form as a composite of what he has heard, and thus keeps the tale from going off at purely fortuitous tangents. If he has heard a tale in two widely different versions he is likely to keep them separate and tell them without contamination.

It is the gifted raconteur who is important for the stability of a tale. Any narrative which has had life enough to survive for a long time must have about it a certain logical and artistic unity which the bungler will often violate but which the skillful teller will appreciate and make fullest use of. His version will, of course, be popular and will exert great influence toward retaining all the vital parts of the story.

Formation of Special Redactions of a Tale. The first time a change of detail is made in a story it is undoubtedly a mistake, an error of memory. But sometimes the change thus made is pleasing to the listeners and is repeated. If it is popular enough, it replaces the original trait and hence the original exception becomes the rule. A new form of the tale has thus arisen and will be diffused from the center of its origin in the same way as the original tale from its center. Often the old and new forms may live on side by side.

It may happen on occasion that one of these new forms may spread over the whole territory of the original tale and replace it. Such an event Anderson calls a revolution in the history of the story. In The Emperor and the Abbot he notes three such fundamental changes, (1) about 1300, in which there is a change in two of the characters, one of the riddles and the ending; (2) about 1500, in which there is a change in one of the riddles; (3) about 1700, in which the inscription on the abbot's house "I have no sorrows" becomes general.

In spite of the emergence of local redactions or even of revolutions, some vestiges of the original form of the tale will in all probability persist. They may be found, of course, in some of the earlier literary variants but even in the popular tradition they may have lived on in company with newer versions. Since the tale has been diffused from an original center and the local redactions from other centers (normally within the territory of the original diffusion) there is a good chance that versions close to the archetype may be found on the periphery of the area of total distribution. If these peripheral forms are really close to each other and especially if they correspond to old literary versions, the case for their validity as older strata is strong. But one must be on guard lest he give too much weight in this respect to chance variations on the outskirts of the area over which the tale has spread.

Direction of Dissemination of Tales. Anderson is persuaded that stories usually proceed from culturally higher to culturally lower peoples. This principle is naturally hard to apply in a place like Europe with so many claimants for leadership, but even there it may be something of a guide in particular instances. Certainly, there is no doubt of the direction of transmission in the case of European settlers in America and the native tribes. About fifty European tales are current among the American Indians and not one tale has been borrowed in exchange.[16] The only way to test Anderson's contention in Europe would be to take obvious examples of simple cultures next to more highly developed ones; for instance, the Lapps and the Norwegians. Anderson himself cites the Finns who have received their stories from the Russians and the Swedes. If the principle is really valid we may ask whether tales must keep running down hill culturally until they are to be found only in the lower ranges. This doubtless would be an overstatement of Anderson's position.

As for actual routes of travel, tales follow the paths of most important cultural intercourse. They will do this over huge stretches of water often with more ease than they will invade a neighboring country of alien culture. And they will often follow a direct water route rather than an indirect one by land. Many tales have thus gone from Germany immediately to Sweden without touching Denmark.

All kinds of borders, Anderson shows, hinder the course of tradition somewhat—physical, political, linguistic, cultural, and religious. Very interesting situations happen where there is a conflict between these borders. Anderson cites the Walloon tales which belong politically with the Flemish and linguistically with the French. The cultural boundaries undoubtedly form the strongest barriers in the path of a traditional narrative. The linguistic frontier is rendered much less formidable by the almost universal bilingualism at the borders.[17]

In so far as Asiatic tales entered Europe, there were, as Aarne points out,[18]

---

[16] See Thompson, *European Tales among the North American Indians.*

[17] How much more important is the cultural rather than the linguistic boundary for the dissemination of tales I learned from my first attempt at making comparative studies of American Indian stories. At first I arranged them by linguistic families with disappointing results. As soon as I made the arrangement on a geographic principle and according to general culture areas the relationships stood out clearly.

[18] *Leitfaden,* p. 51.

two main routes which they took. The first was from southwestern Asia through the Balkans or through north Africa into southern Europe. The other was between the Orient and Russia by way of Siberia and the Caucasus. Especially often on the latter route the course of the tradition was eastward from Russia. One good way to determine the direction in which a tale is moving is to study the versions in two adjacent countries. But the sparseness of the collections for the Near East very seriously limits such investigation.

The historic-geographic method, it will be seen, is essentially a technique for the study of the dissemination of oral tales. It cannot be successfully employed unless the tale is present in a relatively large number of versions— the more the better—and unless the tale has enough complexity to permit a breaking up into separate traits which can be studied independently. Aarne therefore did not feel that the study could go further back than the archetype to an investigation of the motifs out of which it was composed. The motifs themselves are usually simple and cannot be broken up for analytical study.

While this contention of Aarne's is undoubtedly true, his general thesis concerning motifs seems unsatisfactory.[19] He says that originally every motif was a part of a particular tale and that although it frequently appeared in other types, it had been borrowed from the tale where it originally belonged. This statement entirely overlooks the fact that many narrative motifs (simple incidents having a single point) exist as independent narratives. Actually more than half the tale-types in Aarne's list are nothing more than independent motifs. Moreover there are among those motifs which serve as background or as characters in tale-types many which are merely the result of beliefs or customs of the people among whom the story first developed. Cruel stepmothers, tabu, magic, talking animals, ogres, witches, fairies, dwarfs—these were a common stock in trade of characters and setting that the taleteller used at will. That this primitive element in folktales has been overstressed by some anthropologists should not cause us to lose sight of its real importance. These motifs of the common life and thought of primitive peoples are likely to arise independently in many places. They furnish important parts for folktales, but before they can serve as such they need to be utilized by the composer of a tale. He brings them together into a narrative and artistic unity. He doubtless invents motifs to give interest to his story, but he also uses much from the common store.

Aarne's conclusion that motifs cannot be investigated by the historic-geographic method must be accepted with reservations. All depends upon how simple the motif is. For instance, the Obstacle Flight[20] (a fugitive throws magic objects behind him which become great obstacles and delay the pursuer) is a motif in a number of tales. It does not exist independently as a

[19] *Leitfaden*, p. 16.
[20] See Aarne, *Magische Flucht*. Cf. p. 60, above.

story, but is always a trait of some complex narrative. Yet Aarne has himself written a monograph on this incident. Variations can be found in the following items: (1) the fugitive, (2) the number of objects thrown, (3) the various objects thrown, (4) the various obstacles produced, (5) the pursuer, (6) the tale-types with which it is associated, (7) its combination with certain related motifs, e.g., Transformed Fugitives. Where there is variation, there is the possibility of study by this method. This principle applies to local traditions (*Sagen*) and all other single-incident tales.

Neither of these objections to Aarne's idea about motifs affects in any way the validity of the historic-geographic method as applied to story types; but they rather suggest an even wider applicability. More fundamental objections, however, have been raised, especially by C. W. von Sydow of Lund and Albert Wesselski of Prague. Neither of these scholars, it would seem, objects to the thorough preparation of the material with a display of all the known literary and oral forms, so that one can secure a comprehensive view of the whole tradition. But from quite different angles they have objected to the interpretation given to the material thus assembled.

The wave-like diffusion of tales from an original center and similar wave-like movements from where new redactions set up other centers—such is the fundamental assumption for the study of oral tales by the methods of Aarne and Anderson. The gradual and rather even spread of these tales is not actually a necessary part of their theory, and Anderson is careful to specify the various kinds of barriers to this diffusion. But von Sydow feels[21] that the practitioners of the technique have conducted their studies too much on the assumption that tales spread slowly from one community to the next, mile by mile, over an entire province, then a whole state and perhaps, at long last, the whole world. He feels that there are actually more long jumps in the process than usually thought. Written versions, travelers, soldiers, etc. have, as Anderson also points out, carried the tale long distances, and after its establishment in various countries it has produced new redactions. It is with these special local developments that von Sydow is particularly interested. In certain countries (or certain racial or political groups which are notably conscious of themselves as units) there are special forms of each tale which von Sydow calls *oikotypes*. These are types which are "at home" in one country and are felt as alien elsewhere. They have normally been inherited from a distant past—if wonder tales, from a common Indo-European antiquity—and have not been borrowed from abroad. Modifications coming from other *oikotypes* are grudgingly adopted.

One of the facts contributing to the relative stability of the *oikotypes* is the rareness of persons who are good enough raconteurs to take a tale to a new environment and successfully launch it into the current of a new tradition.

---

[21] A good summary of his ideas is found in his article, "Om traditionsspridning" (*Scandia*, Nov. 1932, pp. 320-344).

If it is a tale they already know, in their own *oikotype*, the strangers are likely to make it conform to what is already familiar. And at any rate these active tradition bearers are infrequent.

So far as one can judge, von Sydow feels that most of the modifications of tales have taken place through the mobility of gifted taletellers rather than through the gradual spread from community to neighboring community. The inherited *oikotype*, of certain extensive unified areas, is for him the most important consideration in the study of the tale. Most students have difficulty in distinguishing these *oikotypes* from the special redactions which Aarne and Anderson have shown in tales studied by the historic-geographic method. The validity of the *oikotype* idea can be shown only by a thoroughgoing study of a number of tale-types with particular attention to the geographic area of each of the local subtypes. Only if it should happen that these special developments coincide geographically with great consistency would one be justified in defining general *oikotype* areas. No such comprehensive study has been carried out and the demarcation of these areas remains a matter of dogma rather than of empirical investigation.

Albert Wesselski's objections[22] are on other grounds entirely. He is so convinced of the importance of the written versions of tales that he entirely mistrusts the study of oral tradition. He feels certain that the written tales or the published version of oral tales have carried these stories to those who now repeat them. The only method of study is the comparison of written documents. All that oral tradition does is to cause a story to disintegrate.

Wesselski was an able scholar and a formidable debater. His knowledge of the novella, the Renaissance jestbook, the exemplum, and the fabliau was perhaps unsurpassed, but he had little or no real appreciation of the nature of oral tradition. He seemed to feel that if he had shown that the Grimms, for example, had reworked their stories and had actually taken many from literature,[23] he had thereby discredited the whole idea that tales really do live in the memories of people and are handed down by word of mouth. Anderson has given a convincing refutation to Wesselski's one-sided treatment of the folktale.[24] Instead of inevitable disintegration of oral tales, his long and rich experience has shown them undergoing continual correction which keeps them from losing their original unity and interest.

In spite of Wesselski's insistence to the contrary, the practitioners of the historic-geographic method have given much attention to the written versions of the tales they have studied. One has only to look at Anderson's *Kaiser und Abt* to see that he has used 161 literary versions out of the total of 571 and he has actually found some of these literary versions of greatest

---

[22] See particularly his *Versuch einer Theorie des Märchens.*

[23] See, for instance, his article, "Die Formen des volkstümlichen Erzählguts," in Spamer's *Die Deutsche Volkskunde* (Leipzig, 1934), I, 216 ff.

[24] W. Anderson, *Zu Albert Wesselskis Angriffen auf die finnische folkloristische Arbeitsmethode* (*Commentationes Archivi Traditionum Popularium Estoniae*, Tartu [Dorpat], 1935).

use to him in establishing his archetype. Anderson makes a very careful study of just which of the oral variants show influence of the written. These are by no means so many as Wesselski would suppose.

The question raised by Wesselski is of the highest importance for folktale research. The relation to each other of the two kinds of tradition—written and oral—is very complicated and demands more study than has been given to it. More real analyses of the mutual influence must be made. It would be enlightening to know just how many of the oral versions of such tales as appear in the *Pentamerone* or in Perrault show unmistakable signs of influence from these collections. Wesselski doubtless overestimates the importance of the relationship, but it must not be forgotten or neglected by students of the tale.

The necessity of conducting at once a study in literary relationships and in the course of oral tradition makes the investigation of an important tale with distribution in Europe and Asia one of the most complicated pieces of research imaginable. The student of such tales must often feel how much easier would be his task if he either had no oral versions at all or if they were all oral. If he could actually have a story of which there were absolutely no literary variants, could he not tell how valid is the purely oral side of the historic-geographic technique? It is in this respect that tales of such peoples as the North American Indian offer excellent opportunities for study. Some of them, e.g. "The Star Husband," are distributed over nearly the whole continent and appear in several definite local developments. These tales are sufficiently complicated to offer the variation necessary for thorough studies. There are perhaps twenty or thirty American Indian stories which could be studied in this way. Those which have been investigated thus far would seem to confirm the general validity of the historic-geographic method.

The criticisms directed toward this technique have all helped to improve it. Particularly the emphasis on the importance of literary variants and on the establishment of special local forms as preliminary to the construction of the ultimate archetype have served to meet the most serious criticisms. Though much good folktale study was done before the method was developed, it represents a real advance; and it seems certain that future research will strive to keep improving the technique, but not to dispense with it or replace it.

The comparative studies of folktales made before the elaboration of the historic-geographic method were likely to be weak in one of two directions. Such works as Miss Cox's *Cinderella* were thorough in their assembling of versions and in the analysis into traits, but no attempt was made to interpret the data thus assembled. Others discussed origins and distribution with an inadequate assembling of variants. Not only is this true of such studies as those of Benfey and Cosquin, who were interested primarily in literary tradition and especially that coming from India, but even the monumental work by Hartland on *The Legend of Perseus.*

Nor have all treatments of tales in the past thirty years adhered strictly to this technique. C. W. von Sydow and his students[25] have usually modified the studies in two directions. They have examined groups of tales together to establish or disprove organic relation and have been interested in special investigations of *oikotypes* rather than the attempt to establish an ultimate archetype. These studies are based upon the assumption that the *oikotypes* characteristic of particular areas have been due to inheritance from a hoary antiquity rather than to dissemination from an original center.

Certain other monographs on the tale have likewise suffered from a too doctrinaire approach, but from different points of view. One cannot help feeling that such is true, for example, of Tegethoff's study of Cupid and Psyche.[26] It is an excellent analytical treatment, but its interpretations of the composition of the original because of dream experiences is hardly convincing. Much less satisfactory is Böklen's handling of the Snow White tale.[27] His collection of versions is insufficient and his methods of interpretation are unsystematic and arbitrary. One would like to see Snow White really studied by a thorough technique.[28]

Of course, not all the important monographs on folktales in the past generation purporting to use the historic-geographic method have employed it in its entirety. But more and more they have been characterized by the essential aims of that method. Documentation by as complete a collection of variants as possible and analysis detail by detail of the stories have come to be widely accepted as prime requisites of a good study of the life history of a folktale. And the great majority of outstanding treatises have followed very closely the technique worked out by Krohn and Aarne and developed by Walter Anderson.

In 1886 Krohn published his first study concerning a whole group of tales of the bear and the fox.[29] Here the method was applied for the first time to the tale. He followed this work shortly afterward by a monograph on two stories involving a man and a fox.[30] In both these studies he considers both literary and oral versions. Thus from the first he and his students have recognized the importance of written forms of the folktale.

For about fifteen years Antti Aarne produced a series of remarkable treatments of folk stories. As a result of his labors we now have definitive

[25] For example, Sven Liljeblad in his *Tobiasgeschichte,* Elisabeth Hartmann in her *Die Trollvorstellungen in den Sagen und Märchen der skandinavischen Völker* (Stuttgart-Berlin, 1936) and Inger M. Boberg in her *Sagnet om den Store Pans Død* (København, 1934) and her "Prinsessen på Glasbjærget," *Danske Studier,* 1928, pp. 16-53.

[26] *Studien zum Märchentypus von Amor und Psyche.*

[27] *Sneewittchenstudien* (Leipzig, 1915).

[28] Similarly unsatisfactory because not really carried out is Holmström, *Studier över svanjungfrumotivet* (Types 400, 465).

[29] *Bär (Wolf) und Fuchs* (Types 1, 2, 3, 4, 5, 15, 36, 37, 47).

[30] *Mann und Fuchs* (Types 154, 155).

studies of sixteen tale-types[31]: Type 130, The Animals in Night Quarters; Types 313, 314, The Magic Flight; Types 460, 461, The Rich Man and his Son-in-Law; Type 560, The Magic Ring; Type 561, Aladdin; Type 562, The Spirit in the Blue Light; Type 563, The Table, the Ass, and the Stick; Type 564, The Magic Providing Purse; Type 565, The Magic Mill; Type 566, The Three Magic Objects and the Wonderful Fruits; Type 567, The Magic Bird Heart; Type 670, The Man Who Understood Animal Languages and his Curious Wife; Type 1540, The Student from Paradise; Type 1698, Deaf Persons and Their Foolish Answers. Some of these, especially the tales of the Aladdin and Fortunatus cycle, are among the best known of *Märchen*.

Walter Anderson's handling of the Emperor and the Abbot[32] (Type 922) has been discussed in some detail already. It is probably the most exhaustive study ever made of a folktale. Some years after its appearance he issued an investigation of the widely known jest, Old Hildebrand[33] (Type 1360C).

Not many men are able to produce more than one or two studies in a lifetime when these must be so thoroughly worked out as the historic-geographic method demands. Some of the best monographs now to be mentioned represent almost the only work of this kind in the author's life. Oskar Hackman studied the Polyphemus story in literature and popular tradition and treated certain related tales of the stupid ogre.[34] Hackman, who helped so much with the work of the Finnish school, had accumulated before his death the material for a definitive study of the whole stupid ogre cycle. His material has never been used and its only practical value was for his classification of the ogre material, which appears as Nos. 1000-1199 in the Aarne *Verzeichnis der Märchentypen*.

N. P. Andrejev of Leningrad, in addition to his working out the survey of Russian tales mentioned elsewhere, wrote monographs on two related religious legends in popular tradition: Type 756B, The Legend of Robber Madej (or the Devil's Contract); and Type 756C, The Greater Sinner.[35] Jan de Vries of Leiden in his study of The Clever Peasant Daughter explored all the related stories of clever riddle solvers (Types 875 and 921).[36] His monograph called forth some destructive and some constructive

[31] *Tiere auf der Wanderschaft* (Type 130); *Magische Flucht* (Types 313, 314); *Reiche Mann und sein Schwiegersohn* (Types 460, 461); *Vergleichende Märchenforschungen* (Types 560, 561, 562, 566, 567); *Die Zaubergaben* (Types 563, 564, 565); *Der tiersprachenkundige Mann und seine neugierige Frau* (Type 670); *Mann aus dem Paradiese* (Type 1540); and *Schwänke über schwerhörige Menschen* (Type 1698).

[32] *Kaiser und Abt.*

[33] *Der Schwank vom alten Hildebrand.*

[34] *Die Polyphemsage in der Volksüberlieferung* (Types 1135-1137) and *En finländsk-svensk saga av österopeiskt ursprung* (Särtryck ur Brages Årsskrift IV, Helsingfors, 1910) (Types 1045, 1071-2).

[35] *Die Legende vom Räuber Madej* and *Die Legende von den zwei Erzsündern.*

[36] *Die Märchen von klugen Rätsellösern.*

criticism from Albert Wesselski.[37] Some other important studies are: Lutz
Mackensen's treatment of the story of the Singing Bone (Type 780),[38] of
especial interest to English-speaking students because this is the well-known
English and Scottish ballad of the Two Sisters (Child No. 10); Ernst
Philippson's study of King Thrushbeard[39] (Type 900); R. Th. Christiansen's
work on the Two Travelers[40] (Type 613); E. Rösch's Faithful John[41]
(Type 516); Archer Taylor's The Black Ox (Motifs D2121.8 and D2122.3);
Kurt Ranke's The Two Brothers[42] (Type 303); R. S. Bogg's study of
The Half-Chick Tale (Type 715); Axel Olrik's articles on Little Red Riding
Hood and related tales[43] (Types 123, 333); Waldermar Liungman's elaborate
study of the Scandinavian story of the Princess in the Earth Mound (Type
870) and of the Little Goose Girl[44] (Type 870A); and A. M. Espinosa's
monograph on The Tarbaby[45] (Type 175).

Several rather elaborate treatments have been given to *Sagen* or legendary
material. Valerie Höttges made a comparative study of The Giant's Toy[46]
(Motif F531.5.3) and C. W. von Sydow of the Masterbuilder legend[47]—
the giant who built the cathedral and was cheated (Motif F531.6.6). F.
Paudler has brought together tales explaining why we no longer kill off old
people[48] (Motif J121), and Inger M. Boberg has written a monograph on
The Death of Pan[49] (Motif F442.9).

Three authors have produced important studies on the two tales about
Spinning Women (Types 500, 501). Edward Clodd[50] was interested primarily in pointing out the primitive elements in the stories; Georg Polívka[51]
and C. W. von Sydow[52] were more concerned with them merely as narratives.

The historic-geographic technique has been applied to the study of

[37] *Der Knabenkönig und das kluge Mädchen.*
[38] *Der singende Knochen.*
[39] *Der Märchentypus von König Drosselbart.*
[40] *The Tale of the Two Travellers.*
[41] *Der getreue Johannes.*
[42] *Die zwei Brüder.*
[43] "Den lille Rødhatte og andre æventyr om mennesker, der bliver slugt levende," *Natur og Mennesket,* 1894, pp. 24-39; 1895, pp. 187-204= *Folkelige Afhandlinger,* I (1919), 140 ff.
[44] *En traditionsstudie över sagan om prinsessan i jordkulan* and *Två Folkminnesunder-sökningar.*
[45] "Notes on the Origin and History of the Tarbaby Story," *Journal of American Folklore,* XLIII, 129-209, LVI, 31-37.
[46] *Die Sage vom Riesenspielzeug* (Jena, 1931).
[47] "Studier i Finnsägnen och besläktade byggmästersägner," *Nordiska Museet,* 1907, pp. 54-78, 199-218; 1908, pp. 19-27.
[48] *Die Volkserzählungen von der Abschaffung der Altentötung.* (FF Communications No. 121, Helsinki, 1937 [Grimm No. 78; Motif J121]).
[49] *Sagnet om den store Pans Død* (København, 1934 [Motif F442.1]).
[50] *Tom Tit Tot, an Essay on Savage Philosophy in Folktale* (London, 1898).
[51] "Tom Tit Tot: zur vergleichenden Märchenkunde," *Zeitschrift des Vereins für Volks-kunde,* X, 254-72, 325, 382-96, 438-9.
[52] *Två spinnsagor* (Types 500, 501).

cumulative tales by Martti Haavio,[53] who has written on Types 1696 (What Should I have Done?) and 2021 (The Cock and the Hen). His latter study called forth a monograph by Albert Wesselski,[54] who also treated other cumulative stories.

Serious investigations of folktales have not been confined to Old World themes. Some of the American Indian stories are especially well adapted to comparative study, because of their relative stability and wide dissemination. A very remarkable comparison of the whole mythology of one tribe with its neighbors is seen in Franz Boas's *Tsimshian Mythology*. R. H. Lowie's "Test-Theme in North American Mythology" treated a group of related tales. Gladys Reichard has made tabulations of several types but did not attempt much interpretation of her data.[55] In the last few years Ann Gayton has investigated the Orpheus tales in America,[56] Henrietta Schmerler the tale of the Lecherous Father,[57] and Dorothy Demetracopoulou the California story of Loon Woman.[58] Covering the world from America through Oceania to Africa, Katherine Luomala has recently examined all versions of the Sun-snare[59] in these three areas, and finds that they are really three separate traditions.[60]

This account has doubtless overlooked some important studies, but even so it gives some indication of the great amount of interest in the investigation of individual folktales within the past generation. The fact that generalizations must await the accumulation of many of these monographs seems to have been widely recognized. Are there any tentative conclusions that we may already draw from these investigations?

On the fiftieth anniversary of his first field trip to collect tales, Kaarle Krohn issued his *Übersicht* giving some results of *Märchenforschung* during the past half century. The studies he reviews are largely confined to Europe and Asia. He summarizes the conclusions of each and sometimes criticizes them. At the end he tries to bring together some results.[61]

"For whatever kinds of folktales we may be handling," he says, "two centers of dissemination in historic times are clearly distinguishable: India and Western Europe. If a tale originated in India, its wanderings can, as

---

[53] *Kettenmärchenstudien* (Types 1696, 2021).

[54] *Das Märlein vom Tode des Hühnchens und andere Kettenmärlein* (Hessische Blätter für Volkskunde, XXXII, Geissen, 1933).

[55] Lowie, *Journal of American Folklore*, XXI, 95ff.; Reichard, *ibid.*, XXXIV, 269ff.

[56] *Journal of American Folklore*, XLVIII, 263ff.

[57] *Ibid.*, XLIV, 196ff.

[58] *Ibid.*, XLVI, 101.

[59] "Oceanic, American Indian, and African Myths of Snaring the Sun," *Bernice P. Bishop Museum, Bulletin* No. 168 (Honolulu, 1940).

[60] Several unpublished studies of American Indian tales have been made by the historic-geographic method. In the Indiana University Library are such studies of The Star Husband, The Dog Husband, and The Son-in-Law Tests.

[61] P. 169.

a rule, be shown to proceed in the direction of the general stream of culture from Asia to Europe. The spread of the West European tales in the opposite direction has reached only to those parts of Asia which have come under Russian control. These centers of dissemination, however, have not been the only ones. In Asia Minor and in Eastern and Northern Europe new tales have occasionally developed along with stories which have come from outside. Moreover the West European tales have not arisen without material and formal influence of those from India. The immediate or indirect dependence of European folktales on those of India does not, however, solve the question of the original home. Not only the ancient Egyptian fragments but the ancient Babylonian as well raise the question of these respective areas as original centers for the distribution of tales. These possibilities must, so far as possible, be looked into by future scholarship."

It is clear that much still remains to be learned about the life history of folktales. Most of the effort we have been discussing has gone toward a clarification of the origin and dissemination of particular folktales and eventually toward the discovery of certain general facts that will apply to large groups of stories. We may in this way learn something of the affinities of these groups—whether, for example, one people prefers wonder tales, another witty anecdotes, another local legends, and the like. When many more tales have been studied analytically and without a previously formed theory, it may be possible actually to gauge the importance of language boundaries and also of language families in the history of the folktale. Will the facts, for instance, indicate any real correlation between the great Indo-European family and the kinds of tales current in particular countries?

The question of narrative style in traditional stories has hardly been systematically touched. Are tales in India and the Near East less unified in plot and less definitely fixed in form than those in western Europe? Casual observation would suggest this, but a thorough study might show this to be a mistake. If it is true, does it indicate that tales are still living organisms in the east and that in the west they have crystallized into definite form and lost their vitality? Or does it mean that a unified folktale goes to pieces as it travels from Europe eastwards? Stylistic investigations combined with the study of dissemination of certain stories may clarify such points in the general history of traditional narrative.

Historic-geographic studies are concerned primarily with the content of tales. The results of these researches show that though the form may keep changing, the plot of the tale persists. If this is really true, the finely drawn distinctions between the genre of folk tradition—for example, between *Märchen* and *Sage* or Hero Tale—have little importance for the history of a particular tale. But such distinctions may be of great interest in themselves. The typical western European folktale as it appears in Grimm or Cosquin has a characteristic style. What are the historic and geographic limits of that style? If we are to confine a term like *Märchen* to versions of a tale conforming to this style, we are always faced with the question, when is a particular tale a *Märchen* and when is it not? And what changes of structure or plot, if any, are to be explained by the fact that one variant is and another is not, on stylistic grounds, a *Märchen*? It should be possible to make an objective study of such a question and perhaps clarify thinking on the whole problem of the nature of *Märchen*. Certainly Wesselski, who thinks of it as a relatively late and sophisticated form (perhaps not older than the Renaissance), and von Sydow, who considers it an inheritance from a common Indo-European antiquity, are not talking about the same thing. The future should bring forth a number of investigations of dissemination with adequate attention to structure as well as to content.

When the folklorist has done his best to discover all the facts about the life history of the tale, there may be room for the psychologist and the sociologist and the anthropologist. Up to the present time, however, the work of these scientists has been made less valuable for the understanding of folk narrative than it might be because these facts about the tale have been little known. When the original form of a story has been approximated with some degree of certainty by a study of all the available variants, the psychologist may well speculate on the psychological principles at work in the formation of this archetype, and when he knows exactly what changes have taken place from version to version, he can try to assign reasons for these changes. The material is all before him, and for many tales is neatly and accurately arranged. Do the data thus provided show that Aarne's general principles of oral change are valid? The reason the folklorist has not found psychologists very helpful is that many of the latter either have been quite ignorant of methods for the study of oral tradition or they have made no use of them. It is to be hoped that speculations on the origin of particular stories will no longer be based on recent and often untypical versions[62] and that studies of remembering and forgetting will, in addition to practical experiment,[63] consider all the data now available as to the changes actually made in stories as they travel from teller to hearer.

The folktale is an important part of the cultural history of the race. The anthropologist and all students of human institutions should be able to use the growing mass of life histories of various tales to clarify their own findings. The greater the number of the stories which they understand thoroughly, the clearer and more accurate becomes their view of the entire intellectual and aesthetic life of man.

---

[62] Most studies of the psychoanalytical school have this failing.
[63] For example, F. C. Bartlett, *Remembering* (Cambridge [England], 1932).

THE FOLKTALE AS LIVING ART

VI

For a large proportion of the world's inhabitants the traditional tale is even today one of the principal forms of entertainment. Books, the cinema, and the radio have not yet changed age-old habits among people essentially out of the reach of these modernizing agencies. Hundreds of millions in India and China, in fact nearly the whole native population of Asia, and of the entire continent of Africa except recent colonies; the natives of Australia and New Zealand and of all the Pacific Islands; the Indians of North and South America—all of these still depend on the song, the dance, and the folktale for their amusement and their aesthetic expression. And there are still parts of Europe and groups among those peoples sharing European culture where the oral tale lives on actively in spite of education and books. But here it is primarily a peasant activity, and has largely ceased to interest the other social and intellectual classes.

Whether among the peasants of western Ireland or among the natives of Lapland, India, or Alaska, folktales are much more than a casual part of the life of those who tell them and hear them. Even where the reciting of tales is to be expected of everyone, there is every effort to make a story interesting and pleasing to the audience. And where taletelling is the function of a chosen few, professional or semiprofessional, it is cultivated as a serious art. Voice, gesture, and narrative effects are carefully studied and practiced. The man who excels is rewarded with the esteem of his fellows and with much coveted prestige.

The exact nature of these effects of voice, gesture, and narrative art have not yet received adequate study. Only the *Märchen*, which in its present characteristic form is confined within relatively narrow limits both of age and geographic territory, has been accorded real attention by students of literary style. The whole world of primitive tales, and the local and historic legends, jests, and anecdotes of all peoples challenge the folklorist to try to understand the nature and practice of oral narrative art.

Such studies cannot be based on casually selected texts, for if these have not been recorded exactly as heard, they are of as little value for stylistic analysis as a corrupt literary text would be. Unfortunately for the serious student, many folktale collectors have been primarily interested in making the stories they publish attractive to the persons who might buy their books. And this public, whether of children or of adults, is generally not responsive to the same kinds of effects as the audience for whom the tales were originally meant. Hence the collector revises the tales according to his own fancy or taste. Even with the Grimm collection, we have seen that there was a reworking of the material from edition to edition. The study of these texts is, therefore, of importance only as showing us the literary skill of the Grimms and their idea of what a properly told folktale should sound like.

One cannot be too insistent upon this matter of accuracy of text if one is to study the form of the folktale. If a story has been recorded in a native text and is accompanied by a close translation, it is likely to be rather accurate, since a skillful collector can usually train informants to tell tales slowly enough to record them. Best of all, of course, is phonographic recording, for we have seen that Irish *shanachies* at least speak without self-consciousness into the machine, especially if they have an audience present. Voice modulations and arrangement of words are thus preserved with absolute accuracy.

If the proper narrative style for the oral stories is to be investigated it must be judged by its successes rather than by its failures. Among many peoples, at least, taletelling is a consciously acquired and practiced art, and it is obviously foolish to study this technique in the hands of bunglers. Only the best efforts of raconteurs most successful with their own audiences can form a basis for a study of style which will tell us anything of value.

That the narrative details of an oral story in any particular community are relatively fixed is clear to any student of the distribution of tales. Is the form of the narrative similarly stable, and is there an attempt to hand it on exactly as learned? How much liberty does the taleteller feel justified in taking with his stylistic effects? The answer would seem to be that the skillful raconteur usually handles his material very freely, but within traditional limits. There are certain commonplaces of event or background or of word order so traditional that they are an indispensable part of the manner of the story-teller. If he is gifted, he has a command of all these old, well-tried devices and he adds thereto his individual genius and often the genius of the man or men from whom he learned his art.

The various kinds of folktales have their own effects. The *Märchen*, or wonder tale, is perhaps the richest in its special devices for seizing and holding the interest of the listener. But the jest, the romantic tale, the animal story, the fable—all of these may be told well or poorly. In most of the world the taleteller does not draw a fine line between these narrative forms but carries over his general narrative manner from one to the other. One must be on his guard lest after a study of narrative style in the tales of Western Europe he try to apply the same rules to the rest of the world. Although most peoples and groups have wonder tales, with subject matter analogous in many respects to the European nursery story, the manner of telling is likely to vary greatly from one place to another. Even in Europe there is not nearly so much uniformity of style as one would gather from some studies which have been made.

The scholar must realize that he is dealing with a folk art and that if the unlettered story-teller and his audience have little regard for distinctions that may seem to him important, they may well insist upon their own distinctions which may seem quite arbitrary and illogical. Irish *shanachies*, for example, will shift without notice from the fairy tale to a pious story, a saints' legend, or an account of the warlike deeds of the O'Flahertys. But they seem to feel that explanatory or local legends belong to a different order of story-telling. They will tell them if called on, but as an artistic medium such tales are not to be taken very seriously.

Russian folklorists have given special attention to individual differences in taletellers. In many of their collections the tales told by each informant are grouped together, along with an account of his life and social background. These Russians, of course, are aware of the value of their stories for comparative folklore, and usually call attention to this in their notes, but their main interest is in the folktale as an element in the social life of the people. The individual teller of tales and his relation to his friends and neighbors is therefore of prime importance to these writers.

The most illuminating treatment of these individual story-tellers—certainly the best available to those who do not read Russian—is Mark Azadovsky's *Eine Sibirische Märchenerzählerin*.[1] After giving a clear account of the work of Russian folklorists and their studies of the sociological background of the folktale—all of which has been practically a closed book to Western scholars—he discusses his own experience with taletellers in Siberia. On the Lena River, where Azadovsky collected most of his stories, a very special combination of social groups is present. Not only are there the regular long-established inhabitants but a considerable group of persons deported from Russia who have served prison sentences. Some of these settle down and some become vagabonds. Because of this situation tales are brought into this region from all parts of Russia. Moreover, the rather primitive conditions of life make these people depend on their own resources. At the work of building boats, or on hunting and trapping expeditions, or felling timber the story-teller is in great demand.

Vagabonds often use their narrative ability to secure food and lodging. One of the frequent tricks of these wanderers is to string out their stories to an inordinate length so that they will last till dinnertime or bedtime.

[1] FF Communications No. 68. Helsinki, 1926.

Sometimes, indeed, the scheme of Scheherazade is successfully employed and the hearer left in suspense until the next day. Such story-tellers have learned how to elaborate their tales to an extraordinary degree. They keep the old general patterns, but their special treatment is all in the direction of expansion. Azadovsky finds that in a place where the folktale is still as vital as it is on the Lena it is by no means narrated in a stereotyped style. He illustrates his point by giving account of three raconteurs who handle the same stories in ways essentially different (p. 31).

"These particular qualities of the folktale, namely, a multitude of motifs and episodes, and the presence of smutty, indecent elements are characteristic of all the tales of the story-teller Ananyev from the village of Anga. Especially characteristic is the dragging of the obscene into the tale. Generally such a story is complete and unified in construction. At the center there is a satisfactory subject, and details proper to this subject are brought together and worked out. The tales of Ananyev have an additional character. With him the obscene constitutes a part of nearly every story. At those points where another man would content himself with a light wink or where a slight suggestion would be sufficient, Ananyev begins with the wink and proceeds from it to a long-winded, detailed risqué episode. One might well consider this an individual preference of the story-teller, but from my observation it is clear that such tales, or rather such ways of telling tales, are by no means rare on the Lena. Apparently we are here dealing with an established tradition, with a regular style, with a special school of narration."

"Among the many men and women whom I have had the opportunity to hear tell stories," says Azadovsky (p. 36), "there may be distinguished three principal types. A representative of the first type is the miller Ananyev, already mentioned, in the formal structure of whose tales is so clearly and fully expressed the life of the exile class. As an example of the second type the seventy-five year old Medvidev will serve. He is an unusually gifted raconteur, and for him the exact repetition of the story and all its details is of great importance. He tells everything without hurry, at the same time elaborating every detail and taking care with the proper effect to be produced. He did not tell many tales, only four in all, but his texts were so inclusive and extensive that they covered as many pages as ten of those told by Vinokurova.

"For such a story-teller the careful retention of the traditional form of the tale—that which can be called the folktale canon—is characteristic. He gives in full all beginning and end formulas, the obligatory epic threefold repetition, etc. With such men the subject is generally unified and not split up, and very seldom is there found such grouping and binding together of subjects as, for example, in the case of Ananyev....

"Vinokurova occupies a very special position. Although her tales and those of Ananyev have sprung from the same soil and are almost equally permeated with the same Siberian local color, it is hard to find story-tellers more different than these two. To the comparatively orderless but rich tales of Ananyev, full of many subjects, and rich in added episodes and details, there stand in sharp contrast those of Vinokurova, meager in details, unified, and self-sufficient."

The author spends many pages describing the art of this remarkable woman. She is not much concerned with the tricks of *Märchen* style, its formulas and repetitions. She often summarizes events rather than narrating them at length and she is not always careful to preserve the traditional story intact. With these negative qualities it would hardly seem possible that she should be a great narrator. Her power lies in two directions. She visualizes her characters so that they take on life. The supernatural is so minimized that even in that realm ordinary human life is imagined. Her realization of the dramatic situation comes from her interest in the background and the psychology of the action. She fills the tale with homely details of life as she has known it as servant girl and as housewife. Her knowledge of the experiences of the exiles in prison and in their later life crops out in many a scene. She thinks of every important episode dramatically and describes all the psychological reactions. In short, for her the folktale is a form of living art and she puts into the telling of it all her knowledge of life and understanding of human nature. Perhaps this is as far as such a traditional form can be modified by the individual taleteller without changing its entire nature and becoming creative literature.

Among some primitive groups a careful distinction is made as to the kinds of tales proper for certain occasions. Some may be told by women, some by men only, some by initiates. Among some American Indians they may be told only in the winter. All these varying conditions can be studied only by an actual examination of the practices for each people. No sweeping generalizations are possible.

Perhaps nowhere is the variation in these conditions so great as it is in the position that the story-teller occupies among his fellows. We see something of these differences in the accounts collectors have given of their experiences in recording tales. Some have found that they were likely to hear them from almost anyone, and that hardly a person in the group was so obscure that he would not have at least a few stories that he could tell. Here the art was all but universal. With other groups, even in Europe, the cultivation of the skill is generally confined to men or to women, and even where there is no sex division it is often true that men specialize in one kind of tale and leave others for women. Some collectors have found interesting stylistic differences in the stories told by men and by women.[2]

---

[2] See A. Merkelbach-Pinck, "Wanderung der Märchen im deutschsprachigen Lothringen," *Travaux du I*ᵉʳ *Congrès International de Folklore*, pp. 137-140.

Many and varied are the conditions favorable to the telling and hearing of folktales. In Europe they were once as important in the life of the court as among the common peoples. Kings had their story-tellers and gave them rewards and honor.[3] Even outside of courts many men, especially in the Orient, have made a profession of telling tales and have thus earned their living. The coffeehouse is a favorite place for these Oriental raconteurs, but many other places and occasions have been used by other tellers of folktales to carry on their art. By the fireside in the evening after work the peasant loves to hear stories—and even uses them, like a young child, to go to sleep by. During working hours also the story-teller has been important in the spinning room and in the nursery; and all over the world the rest periods of shepherds, woodchoppers, fishermen, sailors, and soldiers have been favorite times for listening to tales.

Actual professionalism in taletelling seems to be relatively rare. But something approaching it is found among the most diverse peoples, both European peasants and primitive natives. Gifted individuals are likely to cultivate the art and to become known for their ability. They acquire a great popularity and prestige and are jealous of their reputation. Rivals spur them on to greater feats of memory and to a more finished artistic production. Their repertories grow yearly and, however they may earn their daily bread, they give more and more of their attention to their interesting avocation.

No better place to observe such gifted artists can be found than in western Ireland. It was the writer's privilege several years ago to hear some of the best of these *shanachies*.[4] They were all men, and most of them far advanced in years—though there were some younger men and even one small boy who was learning the art. They lived lives of great deprivation and frequently of suffering, but they delighted in carrying themselves and their listeners off into a world of imagination or adventure in which they escaped utterly from their present existence. The best of these old men could tell fifty to a hundred full-length fairy tales, any one of which takes at least a half hour for the telling.

The sense of rivalry is strong with these *shanachies*. The best way to get one of them started with telling a particular tale is to remark that a certain rival has told it well. He will then insist that you have never heard the story really told as it should be, and he then proceeds to demonstrate. Often these story-tellers meet and have what is essentially a competition. At funeral wakes the night is whiled away by tales told now by one, now by another of the gifted *shanachies*.

Such artistic performances by these men are not a casual thing either to them or to their audiences. When the rumor goes about a village that one

[3] For a good discussion of the conditions of taletelling see Bolte-Polívka, IV, 5-9.
[4] For a fuller account, see my "Folktale Collecting in Ireland," *Southern Folklore Quarterly*, II, 53 ff.

of them is in action a crowd of interested listeners will always gather and give absorbed attention. They have doubtless heard the tale he is telling, but they love to hear it repeated, and especially with such elaboration as the skillful raconteur is sure to give the story. These men will tell you that they learned the tale many years ago from a certain man—"the greatest story-teller in all Ireland." But they have not merely learned the story, they have worked it up with all the care that a great actor gives to the interpretation of a role, so that each man delivers his story with his own characteristic manner of voice, gesture, and literary style. The actual material of the tale alone remains intact, and this is carefully checked by the presence of many who have heard it from others.

Ireland has preserved this custom of telling and listening to folktales better than most countries of western Europe, and it probably gives us a chance to observe the process in the same kind of social setting that was very common a thousand years ago and before. Much the same situation can still be found in Russia and in some of the other lands of eastern Europe, though women seem to play a larger part as taletellers there than in Ireland.[5] All through these countries the folktale is still one of the important means of entertainment for those who are still largely untouched by books, the moving picture, or the radio.

As we have seen in an earlier chapter, primitive men also delight in folktales. They too have their masters of the craft, though in many tribes almost everyone will be able to tell stories acceptably. It would be interesting to know whether or not the narrative technique is better in those tribes where the tales are largely in the hands of skilled raconteurs, but no serious study of this question seems to have been made. Unfortunately, it is entirely possible that many of our tale collections are based upon versions recovered from very indifferent story-tellers, and that the tales are therefore not representative of the best narrative art the tribe could produce. This fact, it may be added, is usually not the fault of the collector. He is often taking his text from one of the few survivors of a once flourishing people, whose good narrators are all gone. And even when this is not the case it is often hard to discover the best informant.

Whether stories are told by a special group trained for that purpose or by an average member of the social group, there are certain qualities of style which are found very generally valid for all oral narrative. These have been studied with some care by Axel Olrik,[6] who based his findings largely on

<hr/>

[5] For a good account of individual Russian story-tellers, with pictures of each, see Azadovsky, *Russkaya Skazka*.

[6] "Folkedigtningens Episke Love," in A. Olrik, *Folkelige Afhandlinger* (Kjøbenhavn, 1919), pp. 177 ff. (= *Nordisk Tidskrift*, 1908, pp. 547-554); cf. "Episke Love i Folkedigtningen," *Danske Studier*, 1908, pp. 69-89, and, more in detail, *Nogle Grundsætninger for Sagnforskning* (Kjøbenhavn, 1921).

European material. These qualities are, however, by no means confined to Europe, but with the smallest exceptions can be paralleled everywhere.

"Everyone who deals with folk-literature," says Olrik, "has had the experience that when he reads compositions from widely different peoples he has a feeling of recognition, even when the particular group and its world of folktales has thus far been unknown to him." He is here referring not so much to the general resemblance everywhere among primitive and unlettered peoples in their ideas, their naïve explanations of nature and the like, but rather to certain kinds of details in the structure of stories that seem to be characteristic of all oral traditional narrative.

No matter what the genre—tale, myth, hero story, ballad, or local legend —there is so great a stylistic resemblance in all narrative which comes from the folk and which is carried on by word of mouth and by the power of memory that Olrik feels that certain "epic laws" may be enunciated. These principles limit the freedom of folk narrative to an extent quite unknown in written literature.

1. A tale does not begin with the most important part of the action and it does not end abruptly. There is a leisurely introduction; and the story proceeds beyond the climax to a point of rest or stability.

2. Repetition is everywhere present, not only to give a story suspense but also to fill it out and afford it body. This repetition is mostly threefold, though in some countries, because of their religious symbolism, it may be fourfold.

3. Generally there are but two persons in a scene at one time. Even if there are more, only two of them are active simultaneously.

4. Contrasting characters encounter each other—hero and villain, good and bad.

5. If two persons appear in the same role, they are represented as small or weak. They are often twins and when they become powerful they may become antagonists.

6. The weakest or the worst in a group turns out to be the best. The youngest brother or sister is normally the victor.

7. The characterization is simple. Only such qualities as directly affect the story are mentioned: no hint is given that the persons in the tale have any life outside.

8. The plot is simple, never complex. One story is told at a time. The carrying along of two or more subplots is a sure sign of sophisticated literature.

9. Everything is handled as simply as possible. Things of the same kind are described as nearly alike as possible, and no attempt is made to secure variety.

These principles laid down by Olrik are for the most part obvious to any reader of folktales, no matter of what kind or from what part of the world.

Some of them, of course, are also valid for all narrative art, even the most highly developed, as well as for the art peculiar to the oral tale.

Such principles as Olrik enunciates have their value primarily in directing attention to qualities that differentiate all kinds of oral tales from the literary tale. But there is also need of careful study of the special qualities of each of the various kinds of oral tale and of the narrative art of different parts of the world. Only with the rather long wonder story—that is, the *Märchen*, the fairy tale, the romantic story, the hero legend—has much been done in the study of either structure or literary style.

Some students have investigated in considerable detail the appearance of certain kinds of characters in the European folktale, especially in the stories of certain countries. The German *Märchen* has in this way received considerable attention. Though such studies as those of Petsch on the formulas and on the dialogue[7] are based largely on German versions, they are applicable in greater or less degree to the whole *Märchen* tradition of western Asia and Europe. These studies of form suggest the desirability of many others which will determine the geographical and historical limits of these special *Märchen* characteristics. Much remains to be discovered about these traditional narrative traits.

Some beginning of investigations that may clarify differences in oral narrative styles of various peoples has been made, but hardly more than a beginning. A. von Löwis of Menar's discussion of the hero in Russian and German folktales[8] points the way for many other possible comparisons that will allow us to speak with much more certainty of regional styles in folktales. For the whole world of primitive peoples, nothing comparable has been undertaken.

In spite of the relatively small attention which scholars have given to the study of style in folktales, it must be remembered that those accustomed to listen to them are by no means indifferent to the manner in which a tale is told. The good raconteur remembers not only all the details of the plot and characterization but also all the traditional stylistic traits, and his audience appreciates them.

The beginnings of the fairy tale with its "Once upon a time" and the various end formulas such as "they lived happily ever after" are always expected. But even more elaborate formulas are much appreciated. Bolte has assembled a large collection of these.[9] The beginning of the tale may have a much expanded development of the idea of "once upon a time." A Russian tale thus begins, "In the olden times when God's world was still full of wood spirits, witches, and nymphs, when rivers of milk still flowed,

[7] R. Petsch, *Formelhafte Schlüsse im Volksmärchen* (Berlin, 1900), and "Dialog," *Handwörterbuch des deutschen Märchens*, I, 384 ff.

[8] *Der Held im deutschen und russischen Märchen* (Jena, 1912).

[9] For a good treatment of this subject see Bolte-Polívka, IV, 10 f.

when the banks of streams were made of porridge and baked partridges flew over the fields." For these introductions the Russian tales are especially noteworthy. In the midst of a story a teller may heighten interest by directly addressing his hearers—"Now, what do you think he found there?"

The end formulas have received detailed study[10] and show more variety than the beginning. These go all the way from the simple "Now it is finished" to more unusual conclusions with the imitation of the crowing of a cock, a final rhyme, good wishes (with or without a request for pay), the request to another to tell a tale, or a remark about where the tale was learned, so as to give it proper authority. Especially well-liked are formulistic descriptions of the happy marriage at the end. A good example is found in one of Seumas MacManus's Donegal tales[11]:

> The marriage lasted nine days and nine nights. There were nine hundred fiddlers, nine hundred fluters, and nine hundred pipers, and the last day and night of the wedding were better than the first.

Often the teller represents himself as being present at the wedding. Such a sharing in the delights of the happy lovers will not be strange to any addict of the older cinema who remembers the long fade-outs with the lovers embracing in the light of the setting sun.

Cumulative stories like The Old Woman and Her Pig or The House That Jack Built are entirely formulistic, and their chief joy to the listener is to hear the repetition of the whole series of items, always with the addition of a new one. The tale is like a game in which the hearers follow the story-teller with interest through his complicated maze.

Among some groups rhyming stanzas or couplets are frequently found in the tale. Sometimes these are well-motivated, in that they represent the singing of a person or a bird. Such is the song of the little bird in Grimm's tale of The Juniper Tree[12]—a song immortalized by Goethe, who has Marguerite sing it in prison. This song is repeated a number of times in this Märchen, and serves to make popular one of the most repelling of the tales. Even where no song is represented there are frequently rhyming phrases. Thus if the story-teller wishes to say that the hero went to the other world, he may speak of the land where the wind never blew and the cock never crew. Frequently such rhymes show the obvious influence of the popular ballad.

An interesting formulistic feature of Gaelic tales is the "run." This is a recurring prose pattern conventionally used to describe some series of events in a tale, such as the fights of the hero with various adversaries. When the story-teller gets to these points he changes his style of speech and recites

[10] Bolte-Polívka, IV, 24 ff.
[11] *Donegal Fairy Stories*, pp. 31-55.
[12] Grimm No. 47.

the rigmarole as fast as he can speak. Such runs occur in the story from Donegal already cited. Every fight is thus described:

> And if his fights before had been hard, this one was harder and greater and more terrible than the others put together. They made the hard ground into soft, and the soft into spring wells; they made the rocks into pebbles, and the pebbles into gravel, and the gravel fell over the country like hailstones. All the birds of the air from the lower end of the world to the upper end of the world, and all the wild beasts and tame from the four ends of the earth, came flocking to see the fight.

The audience looks forward to these points in the tale and delights in having them over and over again. A study of these "runs" in Gaelic tales with special attention to their effect on the listeners and to the original or traditional character of the runs themselves would be interesting.

It will be seen that our sketchy discussion of the problems of style in the oral folktale is not so much an account of scholarly accomplishments as suggestions for future labors. And we are faced with the same situation when we encounter the question of the stylistic interaction between the literary and the oral folktale. How much influence, for example, was exerted on Basile by the actual form of the tales when he reworked them in the high-flown style of the *Pentamerone*? Perhaps we shall never know, for we have no tales accurately recorded from seventeenth century Naples. With the style of Perrault the problem seems more approachable, for the authentic French oral collections which we possess offer at least a fair indication of a traditional oral style that may be compared with the literary reworking of the tales.

Perrault seems much nearer to the people than his Italian predecessors Straparola or Basile and indeed than anyone who published folktales until the nineteenth century. The whole race of authors of *Contes des fées* in the eighteenth century were far removed from any contact with the folk background of such of their tales as were of popular origin. The German Romanticists were almost equally alien to the authentic oral style, until we come to the Grimm *Kinder- und Hausmärchen* in 1812. With the latter we have a very conscious effort to give the effect of oral folktale style, if not actually to record it. And since the Grimms composed their stories under the immediate influence of the actual folktale, their stories have had the fortune to be generally accepted as models of this kind of story-telling. The Grimm tales have been learned not only in Germany but also in other countries, and there is no doubt of the influence of their style on many tellers of folktales.

The amount of this influence has, however, undoubtedly been exaggerated even for Germany. How much these great collections may have actually affected the general manner of story-telling in the past century should not be beyond discovery by the scholar with patience, skill, and literary feeling. It would be possible, for example, to establish, by a historic-geographic investigation of the material of the tales, which versions of Cinderella, if any, seem to be borrowed directly from Basile, Perrault, and Grimm, and then to see to what extent the stylistic qualities were also taken over.

Such a study would, however, offer its difficulties. It is not likely that any systematic method for the comparison of narrative styles will be worked out which will not depend overmuch on the mere subjective reaction of the critic. And yet some approach to an objective comparison can undoubtedly be made, and the procedure for such studies may well be expected to improve.

The folktale has been utilized not only by the authors of story collections such as Basile's *Pentamerone,* but also by dramatists, artists, and musicians. Even in Elizabethan times Peele wrote his *Old Wives' Tale* about folktale themes. It was, however, only with the appearance of the Grimm collection in Germany that the *Märchen* began to be much utilized by writers and artists.[13]

Illustrated editions of individual tales or small groups began about 1840 and have continued in an unbroken line down to the present time. Not only the Grimm tales but such literary reworkings as those of Hans Christian Andersen have received frequent illustration. An exhibit of these pictures would show all the pictorial styles of the past century. Among the most interesting recent publications is the remarkable set of woodcuts illustrating a Hungarian collection.[14]

The dramatists have found the Grimm collection of tales a mine which they have eagerly worked. Bolte and Polívka[15] list more than a hundred and fifty German dramatizations of these stories besides some outside of Germany. Certain of the tales such as Cinderella, Red Ridinghood, Snow White, Sleeping Beauty, Puss in Boots, and Rumpelstilzchen are favorites, but many more, perhaps thirty or forty, have appeared at one time or another on the stage.[16]

Marionettes offer an excellent medium for the artistic presentation of folktales, with their world of unreality. The State Library in Berlin has manuscripts of puppet plays for at least ten of the tales of Grimm,[17] and these are still being given by companies in Europe and America.

Several *Märchen* and legends have received musical treatment. Since about 1830 there have been over forty operas based on the Grimm collec-

---

[13] For an account of the *Märchen* in art, see Bolte-Polívka, IV, 482.
[14] G. Ortutay, and G. Buday, *Nyíri és Rétközi Parasztmesék* (Budapest, n.d.).
[15] IV, 483 ff.
[16] *Ibid.,* IV, 483 n. 2.
[17] *Ibid.,* IV, 483.

tion.[18] The favorite subject has been Sleeping Beauty, but perhaps the most famous single one of these operas has been Humperdinck's "Hansel and Gretel." The number of choral works on these subjects is also large, not fewer than thirty-five having appeared in Germany alone before 1900. Among other musical treatments may be mentioned "The Sorcerer's Apprentice" by Paul Dukas.

The cinema, especially the animated cartoon, is perhaps the most successful of all mediums for the presentation of the fairy tale. Creatures of the folk imagination can be constructed with ease and given lifelike qualities. Undoubtedly the best of these performances up to the present time is the Walt Disney production of Snow White and the Seven Dwarfs.[19] Many adults who had long ago dropped their interest in the fairy tale unexpectedly found great pleasure in this old product of the folk imagination.

Children, of course, were very fond of it, for in our civilization it is primarily the young child who carries on the interest in the folktale. In spite of the efforts of certain educators, these tales continue to be told in the nursery and later to be read in easy retellings. In fact, this situation is so well recognized that publishers and libraries are likely to class all folktales as juvenile literature. As a practical measure this attitude is justified, for adults in a world of books have given up these old stories as childish things. The folktale has gone the way of the bow and arrow.

And yet we have seen that once everywhere these tales were not considered childish. They have been one of the chief forms of entertainment for all members of society, young and old. Even today in remote corners of our western world, and everywhere among primitive men, folktales serve to give artistic expression to the imagination and to bring amusement and excitement to monotonous lives. They will long continue to be one of the chief means of furnishing education and solace to unlettered men and women.

[18] *Ibid.*, IV, 486 and n. 1.
[19] See p. 123, above.

APPENDIX A

IMPORTANT WORKS ON THE FOLKTALE

For folklore journals, see p. 392; for regional surveys of folktales, see pp. 419ff; for monographs on folktales in addition to those given below, see pp. 444ff.

Aarne, Antti. Leitfaden der vergleichenden Märchenforschung. FF Communications No. 13. Hamina, 1913.

———. Die magische Flucht: eine Märchenstudie. FF Communications No. 92. Helsinki, 1930.

———. Der Mann aus dem Paradiese in der Literatur und im Volksmunde. FF Communications No. 22. Helsinki, 1915.

———. Der reiche Mann und sein Schwiegersohn. FF Communications No. 23. Helsinki, 1916.

———. Schwänke über schwerhörige Menschen. FF Communications No. 20. Hamina, 1914.

———. Die Tiere auf der Wanderschaft. FF Communcations No. 11. Hamina, 1913.

———. Der tiersprachenkundige Mann und seine neugierige Frau. FF Communications No. 15. Hamina, 1914.

———. Vergleichende Märchenforschungen. Mémoires de la Société Finno-Ougrienne, XXV. Helsingfors, 1908.

———. Verzeichnis der Märchentypen. FF Communcations No. 3. Helsinki, 1910. See Thompson, S., below.

———. Die Zaubergaben. Journal de la Société Finno-Ougrienne, XXVII. Helsinki. 1911.

Anderson, Walter. Kaiser und Abt. FF Communications No. 42. Helsinki, 1923.

———. Der Schwank vom alten Hildebrand: eine vergleichende Studie. Dorpat, 1931.

Andrejev, N. P. Die Legende vom Räuber Madej. FF Communications No. 69. Helsinki, 1927.

———. Die Legende von den zwei Erzsündern. FF Communications No. 54. Helsinki, 1924.

Arfert, P. Das Motiv von der unterschobenen Braut. Rostock, 1897.

Azadovsky, Mark, Eine sibirische Märchenerzählerin. FF Communications No. 68. Helsinki, 1926.

Basset, René. Mille et un contes, récits et légendes arabes. 3 vols. Paris, 1925-27.

Beckwith, Martha W. Jamaica Anansi Stories. Memoirs of the American Folklore Society, XVII. New York, 1924.

Bédier, Joseph. Les Fabliaux. 2d ed. Paris, 1893.

Benedict, Ruth. Zuni Mythology. 2 vols. New York, 1935.

Benfey, Theodor. Kleinere Schriften zur Märchenforschung. Berlin, 1894.

———. Pantschatantra: fünf Bücher indischer Fablen, Märchen, und Erzählungen. 2 vols. Leipzig, 1859.

Boas, Franz. Race, Language, and Culture. New York, 1940.

———. Tsimshian Mythology. Report of the Bureau of American Ethnology No. 31. Washington, 1916.

Boggs, Ralph S. The Half-chick Tale in Spain and France. FF Communications No. 111. Helsinki, 1933.

Böklen, Ernst. Sneewittchenstudien. Mythologische Bibliothek, III and VII. Leipzig, 1910 and 1915.

Bolte, Pauli. See Pauli.

Bolte-Polívka = Johannes Bolte and Georg Polívka. Anmerkungen zu den Kinder- und Hausmärchen der Brüder Grimm. 5 vols. Leipzig, 1913-32.

Campbell, Killis, ed. The Seven Sages of Rome. Boston, 1907.

Carrière, Missouri = Joseph M. Carrière. Tales from the French Folk-Lore of Missouri. Evanston and Chicago, 1937.

Chase, Richard. The Jack Tales. Boston, 1943.

Chauvin, Victor C. Bibliographie des ouvrages arabes publiés dans l'Europe chretienne de 1810 à 1885. 12 vols. Liège, 1892-1905.

Chavannes, Edouard. Cinq cent contes et apologues extraits du Tripitaka chinois. 4 vols. Paris, 1910-34.

Child, Francis James, ed. The English and Scottish Popular Ballads. 10 vols. Boston, 1882-98.

Christensen, Arthur. Molboernes Vise Gerninger, København, 1939.

Christiansen, R. Th. The Tale of the Two Travelers, or The Blinded Man. FF Communications No. 24. Helsinki, 1916.

Cosquin, E. Les contes indiens et l'occident. Paris, 1922.

———. Contes populaires de Lorraine. 2 vols. Paris, 1887.

———. Etudes folkloriques. Paris, 1922.

Coster-Wijsman, L. M. Uilespiegel-Verhalen in Indonesië. Santpoort, Netherlands, 1929.

Cowell, E. B. (and others), eds. The Jātaka or Stories of the Buddha's Former Births. 6 vols. Cambridge, 1895-1914.

Cox, Marian Roalfe. Cinderella. Publications of the Folk-Lore Society, No. 31. London, 1893.

Crane, Thomas F. The Exempla of Jacques de Vitry. Publications of the Folk-Lore Society, No. 26. London, 1890.

Dähnhardt, Oskar. Natursagen. 4 vols. Leipzig and Berlin, 1907-1912.

DeVries, Jan. Die Märchen von klugen Rätsellösern. FF Communications No. 73. Helsinki, 1928.

———. Volksverhalen uit Oost-Indië. 2 vols. Zutphen, 1925-28.

Feilberg, H. F. Bidrag til en Ordbog over Jyske Almuesmål. 4 vols. København, 1886-1914.

Frazer, J. G. The Golden Bough. 3rd ed. 12 vols. London, 1907-15.

Frobenius, Leo. Atlantis: Volksdichtung und Volksmärchen Afrikas. 12 vols. Jena, 1921-28.

Gardner, Emelyn E. Folklore from the Schoharie Hills, New York. Ann Arbor (Mich.), 1937.

Gaster, Moses. Studies and Texts in Folklore, Magic, Medieval Romance, Hebrew Apocrypha and Samaritan Archaeology, 3 vols. London, 1925-28.

Gayton, A. H. and Stanley S. Newman. Yokuts and Western Mono Myths. Berkeley, 1940.

Gerould, Gordon H. The Grateful Dead. Publications of the Folk-Lore Society, No. 60. London, 1908.

———. Saints' Legends. Boston, 1916.

Gesta Romanorum. Edited by H. Oesterley. Berlin, 1872. English translation by C. Swan. London, 1888.

Grimm, J. and W. Kinder- und Hausmärchen. Reklam, Leipzig, 1856. Many editions. Translated by Margaret Hunt under title Household Tales. London, 1884.

Haavio, Martti. Kettenmärchenstudien. FF Communications Nos. 89 and 99. Helsinki, 1929 and 1932.

Hackman, O. Die Polyphemsage in der Volksüberlieferung. Helsingfors, 1904.

Hahn, J. G. von. Griechische und albanesische Märchen. 2 vols. Leipzig, 1864; new ed., München, 1918.

Handwörterbuch des deutschen Märchens. Edited by Johannes Bolte and Lutz Mackensen. Berlin and Leipzig, 1930—.

Hartland, E. S. The Legend of Perseus. 3 vols. The Grimm Library Nos. 2, 3, and 5. London, 1894-96.

———. The Science of Fairy Tales. London, 1891.

Holmström, Helge. Studier över Svanjungfrumotivet i Volundarkvida och annorstädes. Malmö, 1919.

Hunt. See Grimm.

Jameson, R. D. Three Lectures on Chinese Folklore. Peiping, 1932.

Köhler, Reinhold. Aufsätze über Märchen und Volkslieder. Berlin, 1894.

———. Kleinere Schriften (ed. J. Bolte). 3 vols. Weimar, 1898-1900.

Krappe, Alexander H. The Science of Folklore. London, 1930.

Krohn, Kaarle. Bär (Wolf) und Fuchs: eine nordische Tiermärchenkette. Journal de la Société Finno-Ougrienne, No. 6. Helsingfors, 1889.

———. Die folkloristische Arbeitsmethode. Oslo, 1926.

———. Mann und Fuchs: drei vergleichende Märchenstudien. Commentationes variae in memoriam actorum CCL annorum edidit universitas Helsingforsiensis, Nos. 3 and 4. Helsingfors, 1891.

———. Übersicht über einige Resultate der Märchenforschung. FF Communications No. 96. Helsinki, 1931.

Leyen, Friedrich von der. Das Märchen. 3d ed. Leipzig, 1925.

Liljeblad, Sven. Die Tobiasgeschichte und andere Märchen von toten Helfern. Lund, 1927.

Liungman, Waldemar. En traditionsstudie över sagan om Prinsessan i Jordkulan. Göteborg, 1925.

———. Två Folkminnesundersökningar. Göteborg, 1925.

Lowie, Robert H. "The Test Theme in North American Mythology," Journal of American Folklore, XXI (1908), 97.

MacCulloch, J. A. The Childhood of Fiction. London, 1905.

Mackenson, Lutz. Der singende Knochen. FF Communications No. 49. Helsinki, 1923.

Motif-Index. See Thompson, S.

Naumann, Hans. Primitive Gemeinschaftskultur. Jena, 1921.

Olrik, Axel. Folkelige Afhandlinger. Kjøbenhavn, 1919.

Ocean of Story = Penzer, Norman M. The Ocean of Story, being C. H. Tawney's translation of Somadeva's Kathā Sarit Sāgara. 10 vols. London, 1924-28.

Panzer, F. Beowulf (Studien zur germanischen Sagengeschichte No. 1). München, 1910.

Pauli, Johannes. Schimpf und Ernst, ed. Johannes Bolte. 2 vols. Berlin, 1924.

Penzer, N. M. The Pentamerone of Giambattista Basile. Translated from the Italian of Benedetto Croce. 2 vols. London, 1932.

Philippson, Ernst. Der Märchentypus von König Drosselbart. FF Communications No. 50. Greifswald, 1923.

Ranke, Kurt. Die Zwei Brüder: eine Studie zur vergleichenden Märchenforschung. FF Communications No. 114. Helsinki, 1934.

Rösch, E. Der getreue Johannes. FF Communications No. 77. Helsinki, 1928.

Steinhöwel, H. Aesop (ed. H. Oesterley). Tübingen, 1873.

Straparola, G. F. Le piacevoli notti, ed. G. Rua, 2 vols. Bologna, 1899-1908.

Sydow, C. W. von. Två spinnsagor: en studie i jämförande folksagoforskning. Stockholm, 1909.

Tales. See Thompson, S.

Taylor, Archer. The Black Ox. FF Communications No. 70. Helsinki, 1927.

Tegethoff, Ernst. Studien zum Märchentypus von Amor und Psyche. Bonn und Leipzig, 1922.

Thompson, Stith. European Tales among the North American Indians. Colorado College Publications, No. 2. Colorado Springs, 1919.

————. Motif-Index = Motif-Index of Folk-Literature: a classification of narrative elements in folktales, ballads, myths, fables, mediaeval romances, exempla, fabliaux, jest-books, and local legends. 6 vols. FF Communications Nos. 106-109, 116, 117. Helsinki, 1932-36. [Also Indiana University Studies Nos. 96-97, 100, 101, 105-106, 108-110, 111-112. Bloomington, Indiana, 1932-36.]

————. Tales = Tales of the North American Indians. Cambridge, Mass., 1929.

————. Types = The Types of the Folk-Tale: Antti Aarne's Verzeichnis der Märchentypen translated and enlarged. FF Communications No. 74. Helsinki, 1928.

Travaux du Ier Congrès International de Folklore. Tours, 1938.

Types. See Thompson, S.

Welter, J.-Th. L'Exemplum dans la littérature religieuse et didactique du moyen âge. Paris-Toulouse, 1927.

Wesselski, Albert. Märchen des Mittelalters. Berlin, 1925.

————. Der Knabenkönig und das kluge Mädchen. Prag, 1929.

————. Die Schwänke und Schnurren des Pfarrers Arlotto. 2 vols. Berlin, 1910.

————. Versuch = Albert Wesselski. Versuch einer Theorie des Märchens. Reichenberg i. B., 1931.

Ziegler, M. Die Frau im Märchen. Leipzig, 1937.

APPENDIX B

PRINCIPAL COLLECTIONS OF FOLKTALES

Only books of collections are normally listed here. Many more are found in the various folklore journals. See p. 392, above.
Three invaluable series of folktale collections are: *Märchen der Weltliteratur* (ed. F. von der Leyen, Jena, 1915-38); *Collection de chansons et de contes populaires* (46 vols., Paris, 1881-1930); *Les littératures populaires des toutes les nations* (47 vols., Paris, 1881-1903; new series, 3 vols., Paris, 1931-33). Many individual items from these series appear in the following list.

EUROPE

ENGLAND. S. O. Addy. Household Tales, Collected in the Counties of York, Lincoln, Derby and Nottingham. London, 1895.—J. O. Halliwell. Popular Rhymes and Nursery Tales. London, 1849.—E. S. Hartland. English Fairy and Folk Tales. London, 1890.—Joseph Jacobs. English Fairy Tales. London, 1890; More English Fairy Tales. London, 1893.—Andrew Lang. The Blue Fairy Book. London, 1889; The Red Fairy Book. London, 1890.
SCOTLAND. F. J. Campbell. Popular Tales of the West Highlands. 4 vols. Edinburgh, 1860.—Joseph Jacobs. Celtic Fairy Tales. London, 1892; More Celtic Fairy Tales. London, 1894.—J. MacDougall. Folk and Hero Tales. London, 1891.—J. G. McKay. More West Highland Tales. Edinburgh and London, 1940.
IRELAND. Jeremiah Curtin. Hero Tales of Ireland. London, 1894; Myths and Folklore of Ireland. Boston, 1890; Irish Folk-Tales (ed. S. O'Duilearga). Dublin, 1943.—Douglas Hyde. Beside the Fire. London, 1890.—Joseph Jacobs. Celtic Fairy Tales. London, 1892; More Celtic Fairy Tales. London, 1894.—Patrick Kennedy. The Fireside Stories of Ireland. Dublin, 1870; Legendary Fictions of the Irish Celts. London, 1866.—William Larminie. West Irish Folk Tales and Romances. London, 1893.—S. MacManus. Donegal Fairy Stories. New York, 1919.—W. B. Yeats. Irish Fairy and Folk Tales. London, 1892.
ICELAND. J. Arnason. Icelandic Legends (tr. G. Powell and E. Magnusson). London, 1864.—Hans and Ida Naumann. Isländische Volksmärchen. Jena, 1923.—J. C. Poestion. Isländische Märchen. Wien, 1884.—Adeline Ritterhaus. Die neuisländischen Volksmärchen. Halle, 1902.
NORWAY. P. Chr. Asbjörnsen. Norske huldreeventyr og folkesagn. 2 vols. Kristiania, 1845-48, 1859-66, 1870.—P. Chr. Asbjörnsen og J. Moe. Norske Folkeeventyr. 2 vols. Kristiania, 1842, 1871.—G. W. Dasent. Popular Tales from the Norse. Edinburgh, 1858, 3d ed., 1877; Tales from the Fjeld. London and New York, 1896.—H. and J. Gade. Norwegian Fairy Tales. New York, 1924.

468 →»» APPENDIX

DENMARK. Hans Christian Andersen. Eventyr fortalte for børn. 1st ed., Kjøbenhavn, 1835. Many editions and translations.—Svend Grundtvig. Danske Folkeæventyr, efter utrykte Kilder. 3 vols. Kjøbenhavn, 1876, 1878, 1884. (Partial translation: J. Mulley. Fairy Tales from Afar. London, n.d.; and Danish Fairy Tales. New York, 1919).—E. T. Kristensen. Æventyr fra Jylland. 4 vols. København, 1881-97; Danske Dyrefabler og Kjæderemser. Kolding, 1896; Danske Skjæmtesagn, samlede af Folkemunde. Aarhus, 1900; Fra Mildebo, jyske Folkeæventyr. Aarhus, 1898; Molbo- og Aggerbohistorier. 2 vols. Viborg, 1892, Aarhus, 1903; Vore Fædres Kirketjeneste, belyst ved Exempler optegnede efter Folkemunde. Aarhus, 1879.

SWEDEN. A. Bondeson. Svenska folksagor. Stockholm, 1882.—N. G. Djurklou, Sagor och äfventyr berättade på svenska landsmål. Stockholm, 1883.— G. O. Hyltén-Cavallius and G. Stephens. Svenska Folksagor och Äfventyr. Stockholm, 1844-1849. Jöran Sahlgren and Sven Liljeblad. Svenska Sagor och Sägner. 3 vols. Stockholm, 1937-39.—Eva Wigström. Skånska visor. sagor och sägner. Lund, 1880.

FRANCE. J. F. Bladé. Contes populaires de la Gascogne. 3 vols. Paris, 1886. —Emmanuel Cosquin. Contes populaires de Lorraine. Paris, 1886.—F. M. Luzel. Contes populaires de Basse-Bretagne. 3 vols. Paris, 1887.—E. W. Rinder. The Shadow of Arvor: Legendary Romances and Folk-Tales of Brittany. Edinburgh, n.d.—P. Sébillot. Contes de terre et de mer. Paris, 1883; Contes des landes et des grèves. Rennes, 1900; Contes populaires de la Haute-Bretagne. 3 vols. Paris, 1880-82.—Arnold van Gennep. Legendes populaires et chansons de geste en Savoie. Paris, 1910.

SPAIN. Fernan Caballero. Cuentos y poesias populares andaluces. Sevilla, 1859, Leipzig, 1866. (Translation: J. H. Ingram. Spanish Fairy Tales. New York, 1920.)—E. S. Eells. Tales of Enchantment from Spain. New York, 1920.— A. M. Espinosa. Cuentos populares españoles. 3 vols. Stanford University, Calif., 1923-26.—F. Maspons y Labrós. Lo rondallayre. 3 vols. Barcelona, 1871-74.— H. A. Reed. Spanish Legends and Traditions. London, 1914.

PORTUGAL. Th. Braga. Contos tradicionaes do povo Portuguez. 2 vols. Porto, 1883.—F. A. Coelho. Contos nacionaes. Lisboa, 1882; Contos populares portuguezes. Lisboa, 1879.—Z. Consiglieri-Pedroso. Contos populares Portuguezes. Lisboa, 1910; Portuguese Folk-Tales. (Translated by H. Monteiro). London, 1882.

ITALY. Rennaissance forms of Italian tales are reflected in the well-known works of Straparola and Basile.—Walter Anderson. Novelline popolari sammarinesi. 2 vols. Dorpat, 1927-29.—T. F. Crane. Italian Popular Tales. Boston, 1885.—D. Comparetti. Novalline popolari italiane. Torino, 1875.—G. Finamore. Tradizioni popolari abruzzesi. 2 vols. Lanciano, 1882-86.—L. Gonzenbach. Sicilianische Märchen. Leipzig, 1870.—A. de Gubernatis. Novelline de Santo-Stefano di Calcinaja. Roma, 1894.—G. Pitrè. Novelle popolare toscane. Firenze, 1885.— G. Schneller. Märchen und Sagen aus Wälschtirol. Innsbruck, 1867.—J. Visentini. Fiabe popolari mantovane. Torino, 1879.

CORSICA. F. Ortoli. Les contes populaires de l'île de Corse. Paris, 1883.

MALTA. Bertha Ilg. Maltesische Märchen und Schwänke aus dem Volksmunde gesammelt. 2 vols. Leipzig, 1906.—H. Stumme. Maltesische Märchen, Gedichte und Rätsel in deutscher Übersetzung. Leipzig, 1904.

ROUMANIA. Ion Creangă. Contes populaire de Roumanie. Paris, 1931.—M. Gaster. Rumanian Bird and Beast Stories. London, 1915.—Mite Kremnitz. Rumänische Märchen. Leipzig, 1882.—L. Săinénu. Basmele române. Bucuresci, 1895.—Arthur and Albert Schott. Walachische Märchen. Stuttgart, 1845.

GERMANY. P. Behrend. Märchenschatz: Märchen in Westpreussen gesammelt und nach dem Volksmunde wiedergegeben. Danzig, 1908.—Wilh. Busch. Ut ôler Welt: Volksmärchen, Sagen, Volkslieder und Reime gesammelt. München, 1910.—J. and W. Grimm. Kinder- und Hausmärchen. 1812 and later editions. (Translation: Margaret Hunt. Grimm's Household Tales. London, 1884, new ed., New York, 1944.)—Joseph Haltrich. Deutsche Volksmärchen aus dem Sachsenlande in Siebenbürgen. Berlin, 1856.—G. Henssen. Volksmärchen aus Rheinland und Westfalen. Wuppertal-Elberfeld, 1932.—G. Jungbauer. Böhmerwald-Märchen. Jena, 1924.—O. Knoop. Volkssagen, Erzählungen, Aberglauben, Gebräuche und Märchen aus dem östlichen Hinterpommern. Posen, 1885.—Adalbert Kuhn. Sagen, Gebräuche und Märchen aus Westfalen. 2 vols. Leipzig, 1859.—Adalbert Kuhn und Wilhelm Schwartz. Norddeutsche Sagen, Märchen und Gebräuche. Leipzig, 1848.—R. Künau. Schlesische Volksmärchen. Breslau, 1907.—Elisabeth Lemke. Volkstümliches aus Ostpreussen. 3 vols. Mohrungen, 1884, 1887, Allenstein, 1899.—Ernst Meier. Deutsche Volksmärchen aus Schwaben. Stuttgart, 1852.—G. F. Meyer. Plattdeutsche Volksmärchen und Schwänke. Neumünster, 1925.—Müllenhoff, Karl. Sagen, Märchen und Lieder der Herzogtümer Schleswig, Holstein und Lauenburg. Kiel, 1845, new ed. Schleswig, 1921.—W. E. Peuckert. Schlesiens deutsche Märchen. Breslau, 1932.—Heinrich Pröhle. Kinder- und Volksmärchen. Leipzig, 1853; Märchen für die Jugend. Halle, 1854.—G. Schambach und Wilhelm Müller. Niedersächsische Sagen und Märchen. Göttingen, 1855.—Wilhelm Wisser. Plattdeutsche Volksmärchen. 2 vols. Jena, 1914 and 1922; Volksmärchen aus dem östlichen Holstein. Kiel, 1899-1903; Wat Grotmoder vertellt, ostholsteinische Volksmärchen. 3 vols. Jena, 1904-1909.—J. W. Wolf. Deutsche Hausmärchen. Göttingen, 1851. (Translation: R. H. Mackenzie. Fairy Tales Collected in the Odenwald. London, 1857.); Deutsche Märchen und Sagen. Leipzig, 1845.—P. Zaunert. Deutsche Märchen seit Grimm. Jena, 1912-23.

SWITZERLAND. W. E. Griffis. Swiss Fairy Tales. New York, 1920.—J. Jegerlehner. Sagen und Märchen aus dem Oberwallis. Basel, 1913; Sagen aus dem Unterwallis. Basel, 1909; Was die Sennen erzählen: Märchen und Sagen aus dem Wallis. Bern, 1906, 3rd ed., 1908, 1921.—S. Singer. Schweizer Märchen. 2 vols. Bern, 1903-1906.—O. Sutermeister. Kinder- und Hausmärchen aus der Schweiz. Aarau, 1869.

AUSTRIA. Th. Vernaleken. Osterreichische Kinder- und Hausmärchen. Wien, 1864.—P. Zaunert. Deutsche Märchen aus dem Donaulande. Jena, 1926.—I. V. und Joseph Zingerle. Kinder- und Hausmärchen aus Tirol. Innsbruck, 1852.

GREECE, ALBANIA, and MACEDONIA. E. H. Carnoy and J. Nicolaïdes. Traditions populaires de l'Asie Mineure. Paris, 1889.—R. M. Dawkins. Modern Greek in Asia Minor. Cambridge, 1916.—L. M. J. Garnett. Greek Folk Poesy. 2 vols. (vol. 2: Folk-Prose). London, 1896.—E. M. Geldart. Folk-lore of Modern Greece. London, 1884.—G. Georgeakis et L. Pineau. Le folklore de Lesbos. Paris, 1894.—J. G. v. Hahn. Griechische und albanesische Märchen. 2 vols.

Leipzig, 1864.—E. Legrand. Recueil de contes populaires grecs. Paris, 1881.—
Bernhard Schmidt. Griechische Märchen, Sagen und Volkslieder gesammelt,
übersetzt und erläutert. Leipzig, 1877.—G. F. Abbott. Macedonian Folklore.
Cambridge, 1903.—A. Dozon. Manuel de la langue chkipe. Paris, 1878.—J. G.
v. Hahn. Albanesische Studien. Jena, 1859.

SLAVIC COUNTRIES (GENERAL COLLECTIONS). Alexander Chodzko.
Contes des paysans et des pâtres slaves. Paris, 1864 (tr. in part by Emily J.
Harding. London, 1896).—C. F. Cogswell. Siberian and other Folk-Tales. Lon-
don, 1925.—F. S. Krauss. Tausend Sagen und Märchen der Südslaven. Leipzig,
1914.—Louis Paul Marie Léger. Contes populaires slaves. Paris, 1882.—John T.
Naaké. Slavonic Fairy Tales. London, 1874.—W. W. Strickland. Panslavonic
Folklore. New York, 1930.—A. H. Wratislaw. Sixty Folk-Tales from Exclusively
Slavonic Sources. London, 1889.

RUSSIA. A. N. Afanasief. Narodnye Russkie Skazki. 3 vols. Moskva,
1936-40.—M. Azadovsky. Russkaya Skazka. 2 vols. Moskva, 1931-32.—M. A.
Biggs. Polish Fairy Tales [really White Russian]. London, 1920.—R. N. Bain.
Russian Fairy Tales from the Skazki of Polevoi. 3d ed. London, 1901.—J. Curtin.
Myths and Folk Tales of the Russians, Western Slavs and Magyars. Boston,
1903.—L. A. Magnus. Russian Folk Tales. London, 1917.—W. R. Ralston.
Russian Folk-Tales (translation of tales from the collections of Afanasief and
others). London, 1873.—Ivan Rudčenko. Narodnyja južnorusskija skazki. Kiev,
1870.—R. Jakobson. Russian Folk Tales. New York, 1945.

CAUCASUS. A. Dirr. Kaukasische Märchen. Jena, 1920.—M. Wardrop.
Georgian Folk Tales. London, 1894.

SERBO-CROATIA. Vuk S. Karadzic. Volksmärchen der Serben, translated
by Wilhelmine Karadzic. Berlin, 1854.—C. Mijatovics. Serbian Folklore. London,
1874.

CZECHOSLOVAKIA. Jos. Baudiš. Czech Folk Tales. London, 1917.—
Parker Fillmore. Czechoslovak Fairy Tales. New York, 1919.—Šárka B.
Hrbkova. Czechoslovak Stories. New York, 1920.—Alfred Waldau. Böhmisches
Märchenbuch. Prag, 1860.—Jos. Wenzig. Westslavischer Märchenschatz. Leipzig,
1857.

LITHUANIA and LATVIA. M. Boehm. Lettische Schwänke und verwandte
Volksüberlieferungen. Reval, 1911.—M. Boehm and F. Specht. Lettisch-litauische
Volksmärchen. Jena, 1924.—A. Leskien and K. Brugmann. Litauische Volks-
lieder und Märchen. Strassburg, 1882.—A. Schleicher. Litauische Märchen,
Sprichworte, Rätsel und Lieder. Weimar, 1857.

FINLAND. K. Krohn. Soumalaisia kansansatuja. 2 vols. Helsinki, 1886-93.—
A. v. Löwis of Menar. Finnische und estnische Volksmärchen. Jena, 1922.—E.
Schreck. Finnische Märchen. Weimar, 1887.

ESTONIA. H. Jannsen. Märchen und Sagen des estnischen Volkes. 2 vols.
Dorpat, 1881, Riga und Leipzig, 1888.—O. Kallas. Achtzig Märchen der Ljut-
ziner Esten. Dorpat, 1900.—Fr. R. Kreutzwald. Ehstnische Märchen, aus dem
Ehstn. übs. v. F. Löwe. 2 vols. Halle, 1869 and Dorpat, 1881.—A. v. Löwis of
Menar. Finnische und estnische Volksmärchen. Jena, 1922.

LAPLAND. J. C. Poestion. Lappländische Märchen. Wien, 1886.—J. Qvigstad.
Lappiske eventyr og sagn. 4 vols. Oslo, 1927-29.

HUNGARY. W. Henry Jones and Lewis L. Kropf. The Folktales of the Magyars. London, 1889.—Elisabet Róna-Sklarek. Ungarische Volksmärchen. Leipzig, 1909.—G. Stier. Ungarische Sagen und Märchen aus der Erdelyischen. Berlin, 1850.

YIDDISH. J. L. Cahan. Yiddish Folk-Tales. New York, 1931.—Gerald Friedlander. Jewish Folk-Tales. London, 1917.

BASQUE. M. Monteiro. Legends and Popular Tales of the Basque People. New York, 1887.—W. Webster. Basque Legends. London, 1877, 1879.

GYPSY. F. H. Groome. Gypsy Folktales. London, 1899.—H. v. Wlislocki. Märchen und Sagen der transsilvanischen Zigeuner. Berlin, 1886.

AFRICA

GENERAL COLLECTIONS. Alice Werner. African Mythology. Mythology of All Races, vol. VII. Boston, 1925.

ARABS OF NORTH AFRICA. Yacoub Artin-Pacha. Contes populaires du Soudan égyptien. Paris, 1909; Contes populaires de la vallée du Nil. Paris, 1895.—René Basset. Contes populaires d'Afrique. Paris, 1903.—J. Desparmet. Contes populaires sur les ogres, recueillis à Blida. 2 vols. Paris, 1909-10.—Leo Frobenius. Atlantis, vols. I-III. Jena, 1921-22.—F. K. Green. Modern Arabic Stories. London, 1893.—E. Littmann. Modern Arabic Tales. Leyden, 1905.—G. Spitta-Bey. Contes arabes modernes. Leyden, 1883.—H. Stumme. Märchen aus Tripolis. Leipzig, 1898; Tunisische Märchen. 2 vols. Leipzig, 1893.

BERBER. René Basset. Contes populaires berbères. 2 vols. Paris, 1887-97.—Françoise Légey. Contes et légendes populaires du Maroc. Paris, 1926.—J. Rivière. Recueil de contes populaires de la Kabylie du Djurdjura. Paris, 1882.

NORTHEAST AFRICA. Leo Frobenius. Atlantis, vol. IV. Jena, 1923.—Charles Victor Monteil. Contes soudanais. Paris, 1905.

HOTTENTOT. W. H. I. Bleek. Reynard the Fox in South Africa. London, 1864.

BUSHMAN. W. H. I. Bleek and L. C. Lloyd. Specimens of Bushman Folklore. London, 1911.

EAST AFRICAN CATTLE AREA. G. W. Bateman. Zanzibar Tales. Chicago, 1901.—Rosetta Gage Baskerville. The Flame Tree and other Folk-Lore Stories from Uganda. London, 1925; The King of the Snakes and other Folk-Lore Stories from Uganda. London, 1922.—E. J. Bourhill and J. B. Drake. Fairy Tales from South Africa. London, 1908.—C. Callaway. Nursery Tales, Traditions and Histories of the Zulus. Natal, 1868.—Clement M. Doke. Lamba Folk-Lore. Memoirs of the American Folklore Society, XX. New York, 1927.—J. R. Fell. Folk Tales of the Batonga and Other Sayings. London, 1923.—H. Fuchs. Sagen, Mythen und Sitten der Masai. Jena, 1910.—Bruno Gutmann. Volksbuch der Wadschagga. Leipzig, 1914.—A. C. Hollis. The Masai, their Language and Folk-Lore. Oxford, 1905; The Nandi, their Language and Folk-Lore. Oxford, 1909.—J. A. Honeÿ, South-African Folk-Tales. New York, 1910.—E. Jacottet. The Treasury of Basuto Lore. London, 1908.—H. A. Junod. Les chants et les contes des Ba-Ronga de la baie de Delagoa. Lausanne, 1897; Nouveaux contes Ronga. Neufchatel, 1898.—R. S. Rattray. Some Folk-Lore, Stories and Songs in

Chinyanja. London, 1907.—E. W. Smith and A. Dale. The Ila-Speaking People of Northern Rhodesia. London, 1920.—E. Steere. Swahili Tales. London, 1870, 1889.—G. M. Theal. Kaffir Folk-Lore. London, 1886; The Yellow- and Dark-Skinned People of Africa South of the Zambesi. London, 1910.—J. Torrend. Specimens of Bantu Folk-Lore from Northern Rhodesia. London, 1920.—Alice Werner. Myths and Legends of the Bantu. London, 1933.—Diedrich Westermann. The Shilluk People, Their Language and Folklore. Philadelphia, 1912. CONGO. W. H. Barker and C. Sinclair. West African Folk Tales. London, 1917.—R. E. Dennett. Notes of the Folk-Lore of the Fjort, French-Congo. London, 1898.—George W. Ellis. Negro Culture in West Africa. New York, 1914.— Leo Frobenius. Atlantis, vol. XII. Jena, 1928.—Wilhelm Lederbogen. Kameruner Märchen. Berlin, 1901.—R. H. Nassau. Where Animals Talk. Boston, 1912. GUINEA COAST SUB-AREA. F. M. Cronise and H. W. Ward. Cunnie Rabbit, Mr. Spider and the Other Beef. London, 1903.—H. Chatelain. Folk-Tales of Angola. Boston, 1894.—E. Dayrell. Folk Stories from Southern Nigeria, West Africa. London, 1910.—A. B. Ellis. The Ewe-Speaking Peoples. London, 1890; The Tshi-Speaking Peoples of the Gold Coast. London, 1887; The Yoruba-Speaking Peoples of the Slave Coast of West Africa. London, 1894.—Leo Frobenius. Atlantis, vols. V-XI. Jena, 1921-25.—M. I. Ogumefu. Yoruba Legends. London, 1929.—R. Sutherland Rattray. Akan-Ashanti Folk Tales. Oxford, 1930.— P. A. Talbot. In the Shadow of the Bush. New York, 1912.—Northcote W. Thomas. Anthropological Report on the Edo-Speaking Peoples of Nigeria. London, 1910; Anthropological Report on Sierra Leone. London, 1916.—René Trautmann. La littérature populaire à la côte des esclaves. Paris, 1927. EAST HORN. Leo Reinisch. Die Saho-Sprache. 2 vols. Wien, 1889, 1890. WESTERN SUDAN. L.-J.-B. Berenger-Feraud. Recueil de contes populaires de la Sénégambie. Paris, 1879.—Victor François Equilbecq. Contes indigènes de l'Ouest-Africain Français. 3 vols. Paris, 1913-16.—R. Sutherland Rattray Hausa Folk-Lore Customs, Proverbs, etc. 2 vols. Oxford, 1913.—Moussa Travélé. Proverbes et contes bambara. Paris, 1923.—A. J. N. Tremearne. Hausa Superstitions and Customs. London, 1913; Hausa Folk-Tales. London, 1914.—Frantz de Zeltner. Contes du Sénégal et du Niger. Paris, 1913. THE ISLANDS. G. Ferrand. Contes populaires malgaches. Paris, 1893.—Ch. Renel. Contes de Madagascar. 2 vols. Paris, 1910.—C. Baissac. Folklore de l'île Maurice. Paris, 1888.—Elsie Clews Parsons. Folklore from the Cape Verde Islands. Memoirs of the American Folklore Society, No. 15. New York, 1923.

ASIA

TURKEY. R. Nisbet Bain. Turkish Fairy Tales. London, 1901 (partial translation of Kúnos' Turkish collection, first published in Hungarian).—L. M. J. Garnett. The Women of Turkey and their Folklore. 2 vols. London, 1890-91.— Friedrich Giese. Türkische Märchen. Jena, 1925.—I. Kúnos. Türkische Volksmärchen aus Stambul. Leiden, 1905.—J. Nicolaïdes. Contes licencieux de Constantinople et de l'Asie mineure. Paris, 1906.

TURKO-TATARS OF SOUTH SIBERIA. W. Radloff. Proben der Volksliteratur der türkischen Stämme. 6 vols. St. Petersburg, 1866-86.

ARMENIA. E. H. Carnoy et J. Nicolaïdes. Traditions populaires de l'Asie mineure. Paris, 1889.—H. v. Wlislocki, Märchen und Sagen der Bukowinaer und Siebenbürger Armenier. Hamburg, 1891.
ARABIA, SYRIA, MESOPOTAMIA. A. Jahn. Die Mehri-Sprache in Südarabien. Wien, 1902.—M. Lidzbarski. Geschichten und Lieder aus den neuaramäischen Handschriften zu Berlin. Weimar, 1896.—D. H. Müller. Mehriund Hadrami-Texte. Wien, 1909; Die Mehri- und Soqotri-Sprache. 3 vols. Wien, 1902-07.—E. Prym and A. Socin. Der neuaramäische Dialekt des Tûr Abdîn. 2 vols. Göttingen, 1881.—E. S. Stevens. Folk-Tales of Iraq. Oxford and London, 1931.
PERSIA. A. Christensen. Contes persans en langue populaire. København, 1918.—D. L. R. and E. O. Lorrimer. Persian Tales. London, 1919.
TIBET. W. F. O'Connor. Folk-Tales from Tibet. London, 1906.—W. R. Ralston. Tibetan Tales, derived from Indian Sources. London, 1884, 1906, 1926.—A. Shelton. Tibetan Folk Tales. New York, 1925.
MONGOLS AND OTHER PEOPLES OF NORTH ASIA. C. F. Coxwell. Siberian and Other Folk-Tales. London, 1925.—B. Julg. Kalmükische Märchen. Die Märchen des Siddhi-Kür oder Erzählungen eines verzauberten Toten. Leipzig, 1866; Mongolische Märchen: die neun Nachtrags-Erzählungen des Siddhi-Kür und die Geschichte des Ardschi-Bordschi-Chan. Innsbruck, 1868.—R. H. Busk. Sagas from the Far East. London, 1873 (translation of B. Julg).
NORTHEAST ASIA. Waldemar Bogoras. Chuckchee Mythology. Jesup North Pacific Expedition, VIII. Leiden and New York, 1913; Tales of the Yukaghir, Lamut, and Russianized Natives of Eastern Siberia. Anthropological Papers of the American Museum of Natural History, XX. New York, 1918.—Waldemar Jochelson. The Koryak. Jesup North Pacific Expedition, vol. VI. Leiden and New York, 1908.
INDIA. P. O. Bodding. Santal Folk Tales. 2 vols. Oslo, 1925-27.—C. H. Bompas. Folktales of the Santal Parganas. London, 1909.—F. B. Bradley-Birt. Bengal Fairy Tales. London, 1920.—A. Campbell. Santal Folk Tales. London, 1892.—Lal Behari Day. Folk-Tales of Bengal. London, 1883.—A. E. Dracott. Simla Village Tales. London, 1906.—Murray B. Emeneau. Kota Texts. Berkeley, 1944.—M. Frere. Old Deccan Days. London, 1868.—J. Jacobs. Indian Fairy Tales. London, 1894.—H. Kingscote and N. Sastri. Tales of the Sun, or Folklore of Southern India. London, 1890.—J. H. Knowles. Folk-Tales of Kashmir. London, 1888-1893.—W. McCulloch. Bengali Household Tales. London, 1912.—H. Parker. Village Folk-Tales of Ceylon. 4 vols. London, 1910-15.—Natêsa Sastri. Folklore of Southern India. 3 vols. Bombay, 1884-1888; Indian Folk Tales. Madras, 1908.— F. A. Steele. Tales of the Panjab. London, 1894.—F. A. Steele and R. C. Temple. Wide-awake Stories, a Collection of Tales told in the Panjab and Kashmir. Bombay, 1884.—M. Stokes. Indian Fairy Tales. Calcutta and London, 1879, 1880.— Ch. Swynnerton. Romantic Tales from the Panjab with Indian Nights' Entertainments. New ed., London, 1908.
FARTHER INDIA. S. W. Cocks. Tales and Legends of Ancient Burma. Bombay, 1918.—A. LeClère. Cambodge, contes et légendes. Paris, 1895.—A. Landes. Contes et légendes annamites. Saïgon, 1886.
CHINA. Wolfram Eberhard. Chinese Fairy Tales and Folk Tales. London,

1937.—H. A. Giles. Strange Stories from a Chinese Studio. London, 1880, 1909, 1916.—E. T. C. Werner. Myths and Legends of China. London, 1923.—R. Wilhelm. Chinesische Volksmärchen. Jena, 1914, 1921.
KOREA. H. N. Allen. Korean Tales. New York, 1889.—J. S. Gale. Korean Folk Tales. London, 1913.—W. E. Griffis. Korean Fairy Tales. London, 1923.
JAPAN. D. Brauns. Japanische Märchen und Sagen. Leipzig, 1885.—W. E. Griffis. Japanese Fairy Tales. London, 1923; Japanese Fairy World. London, 1887.—E. R. Miller. Japanese Fairy Tales. Tokyo, 1889.—A. B. Mitford. Tales of Old Japan. 2 vols. London, 1871.
AINU. J. Batchelor. The Ainu and their Folk-Lore. London, 1901.—B. H. Chamberlain. Aino Folk-Tales. London, 1888.

AUSTRALIA AND OCEANIA

GENERAL. Roland B. Dixon. Oceanic Mythology. Boston, 1916.—P. Hambruch. Südseemärchen aus Australien, Neu-Guinea, Fidji, Karolinen, Samoa, Tonga, Hawaii, Neu-Seeland u. a. Jena, 1916.
INDONESIA (GENERAL). Jan de Vries. Volksverhalen uit Oost-Indië. 2 vols. Zutphen, 1925-28.—W. Skeat. Fables and Folk Tales from an Eastern Forest. Cambridge, 1901.
INDONESIA (BORNEO). Charles Hose and William McDougall. The Pagan Tribes of Borneo. London, 1912.—H. Ling Roth. Th᷄ Natives of Sarawak and British North Borneo. London, 1896.
INDONESIA (PHILIPPINES). Fay Cooper Cole. Traditions of the Tinguan, a Study in Filippine Folk-Lore. Chicago, 1915.—Mabel Cook Cole. Philippine Folk Tales. Chicago, 1916.—Dean S. Fansler. Filipino Popular Tales. Memoirs of the American Folklore Society, XII. New York, 1921.
AUSTRALIA. A. W. Howitt. The Native Tribes of South-West Australia. London, 1904.—Mrs. K. L. Parker. Australian Legendary Tales. London, 1897; More Australian Legendary Tales. London, 1898.—B. Spencer and F. J. Gillen. The Arunda. London, 1927; Native Tribes of the Northern Territory of Australia. London, 1914; The Native Tribes of Central Australia. London, 1899; The Northern Tribes of Central Australia. London, 1904.—Arnold van Gennep. Mythes et légendes d'Australie, études d'éthnographie et de sociologie. Paris, 1906.
MELANESIA. R. H. Codrington. The Melanesians. Oxford, 1891.—L. Fison. Tales from Old Fiji. London, 1904.—W. W. Gill. Myths and Songs from the South Pacific. London, 1876.—A. Ker. Papuan Fairy Tales. London, 1910.—G. Landtman. The Folk-Tales of the Kiwai Papuans. Helsingfors, 1919.—G. C. Wheeler. Mono-Alu Folklore. London, 1926.
POLYNESIA. Martha W. Beckwith. Hawaiian Mythology. New Haven, 1940. —K. M. Clark. Maori Tales and Legends. London, 1896.—Edward W. Gifford. Tongan Myths and Tales. Bishop Museum Bulletin, No. 8. Honolulu, 1924.—G. Grey. Polynesian Mythology and Ancient Traditional History of the New Zealand Race. Auckland, 1885, London, 1907.—William Hyde Rice. Hawaiian Legends. Bishop Museum Bulletin, No. 3. Honolulu, 1923.—J. F. Stimson. The Legends of Maui and Tahaki. Bishop Museum Bulletin, No. 127. Honolulu,

1934.—Th. G. Thrum. Hawaiian Folk Tales. Chicago, 1912.—W. D. Westervelt. Legends of Old Honolulu. London, 1915.—Ch. A. Wilson. Legends and Mysteries of the Maori. London, 1932.

AMERICA
NORTH AMERICAN INDIAN

Some of the best collections of American Indian tales are found in the *Journal of American Folklore*. They are not here listed in detail.

Most American Indian tales have appeared in certain series of learned publications. A list of abbreviations by which they are referred to in the following bibliography is here given:

BAM   Bulletin of the American Museum of Natural History, New York
BBAE   Bulletin of the Bureau of American Ethnology
CI   Publications of the Carnegie Institution
CU   Columbia University Contributions to Anthropology
FM   Field Museum of Natural History, Anthropological Series
GSCan   Geological Survey of Canada, Anthropological Series
JE   Publications of the Jesup North Pacific Expedition
MAFLS Memoirs of the American Folk-Lore Society
PaAM   Anthropological Papers of the American Museum of Natural History, New York
PAES   Publications of the American Ethnological Society
RBAE   Report of the Bureau of American Ethnology
UCal   University of California Publications in American Archaelogy and Ethnology
UPa   University of Pennsylvania, The University Museum Anthropological Publications
UWash University of Washington Publications in Anthropology

GENERAL. Edward S. Curtis. The North American Indian. 20 vols. Cambridge, Mass., 1908-30.—Stith Thompson. Tales of the North American Indians. Cambridge, 1929.

ESKIMO. Franz Boas. The Central Eskimo. RBAE, VI. Washington, 1888; The Eskimo of Baffin Land and Hudson Bay. BAM, XV. New York, 1901.—Diamond Jenness. Notes and Traditions from Northern Alaska, the Mackenzie Delta, and Coronation Gulf. Report of the Canadian Arctic Expedition, Southern Party, 1913-16, XIII. Ottawa, 1924.—Edward William Nelson. The Eskimo about Bering Strait. RBAE, XVIII. Washington, 1899.—K. Rasmussen. Eskimo Folk Tales. London, 1921; Myter og sagn fra Grønland. 3 vols. Kjøbenhavn, 1921-25.—H. Rink. Tales and Traditions of the Eskimo. Edinburgh, 1875.

MACKENZIE. J. W. Chapman. Ten'a Texts and Tales from Anvik, Alaska. PAES, VI. Leyden, 1914.—Pliny Earle Goddard. The Beaver Indians. PaAM, X. New York, 1916; Chipewyan Texts. PaAM, X. New York, 1912.—Robert H. Lowie. Chipewyan Tales. PaAM, X. New York, 1912.—Émile Petitot. Traditions indiennes du Canada nord-ouest. Paris, 1886.

PLATEAU. Franz Boas. Folk-Tales of Salishan and Sahaptin Tribes. MAFLS,

XI. New York, 1917; Kutenai Tales. RBAE, LIX. Washington, 1918.—Livingston Farrand. Traditions of the Chilcotin Indians. JE, II. New York, 1909.—Archie Phinney. Nez Percé Texts. CU, XXV. New York, 1934.—Edward Sapir. Wishram Texts, together with Wasco Tales and Myths, collected by Jeremiah Curtin and edited by Edward Sapir. PAES, II. Leyden, 1909.—James A. Teit. Mythology of the Thompson River Indians. JE, VIII. New York, 1912; The Shuswap. JE, II. New York, 1900-09; Traditions of the Thompson River Indians. MAFLS, VI. Boston, 1898.

NORTH PACIFIC. Thelma Adamson. Folk-Tales of the Coast Salish. MAFLS, XXVII. New York, 1934.—Arthur C. Ballard. Mythology of Southern Puget Sound. UWash, III. Seattle, 1929; Some Tales of the Southern Puget Sound Salish. UWash, II, Seattle, 1927.—Manuel J. Andrade. Quileute Texts. CU, XII. New York, 1931.—Franz Boas. Bella Bella Tales. MAFLS, XXV. New York, 1932; Bella Bella Texts. CU, V. New York, 1928; Chinook Texts. RBAE, XX. Washington, 1894; Kathlamet Texts. RBAE, XXVI. Washington, 1901; Kwakiutl Tales, CU, II. New York, 1910; Kwakiutl Tales, New Series. CU, XXVI. New York, 1935; The Mythology of the Bella Coola Indians. JE, I. New York, 1898; Tsimshian Mythology. RBAE, XXXI. Washington, 1916.— Franz Boas and George Hunt. Kwakiutl Texts. JE, III and X. New York, 1905-06.—James Deans. Tales from the Totems of the Hidery. Chicago, 1899.—Livingston Farrand. Traditions of the Quinault Indians. JE, II. New York, 1909.—Leo J. Frachtenberg. Alsea Texts and Myths. BBAE, LXVII. Washington, 1920; Coos Texts. CU, I. New York, 1913; Lower Umpqua Texts. CU, IV. New York, 1914.— Erna Gunther. Klallam Folk Tales. UWash, I. Seattle, 1925.—Melville Jacobs. Coos Myth Texts. UWash, VIII. Seattle, 1940; Northwest Sahaptin Texts. UWash, II; CU, XIX. Seattle and New York, 1929.—John R. Swanton. Haida Texts and Myths. BBAE, XXIX. Washington, 1905; Haida Texts, Masset Dialect. JE, X. Leiden and New York, 1908; Tlingit Myths and Texts. BBAE, XXXIX. Washington, 1909.

CALIFORNIA. S. A. Barrett. Pomo Myths. Bulletin of the Public Museum of Milwaukee, XV. Milwaukee, 1933.—Jeremiah Curtin. Creation Myths of Primitive America. Boston, 1898; Myths of the Modocs. Boston, 1912.—Grace Dangberg. Washo Texts. UCal, XXII. Berkeley, 1927.—Roland B. Dixon. The Chimariko Indians and Language. UCal, V. Berkeley, 1907-10; Maidu Myths. BAM, XVII. New York, 1905; Maidu Texts. PAES, IV. Leyden, 1912.—Cora DuBois and Dorothy Demetracopoulou. Wintu Myths. UCal, XXVIII. Berkeley, 1931.—A. H. Gayton and Stanley S. Newman. Yokuts and Western Mono Myths. Berkeley, 1940.—Pliny Earle Goddard. Chilula Texts. UCal, X. Berkeley, 1914; Hupa Texts. UCal, I. Berkeley, 1904; Kato Texts. UCal, V. Berkeley, 1909.—Edward Winslow Gifford. Miwok Myths. UCal, XII. Berkeley, 1917.— J. P. Harrington. Karuk Indian Texts. BBAE, CVII. Washington, 1932.—Alfred L. Kroeber. Indian Myths of South Central California. UCal, IV. Berkeley, 1907; Yuki Myths. Anthropos, XXVII. Wien, 1932.—Clinton Hart Merriam. The Dawn of the World: Myths and Weird Tales Told by the Mewan Indians of California. Cleveland, 1910.—Paul Radin. Wappo Texts—first series. UCal, XIX. Berkeley, 1914.—Edward Sapir. Takelma Texts. UPa, II. Philadelphia, 1909; Yana Texts, together with Yana Myths collected by Roland B. Dixon. UCal, IX.

Berkeley, 1910.—Julian H. Steward. Myths of the Owens Valley Paiute. UCal, XXXIV. Berkeley, 1936.

PLAINS. Martha Warren Beckwith. Mandan-Hidatsa Myths and Ceremonies. MAFLS, XXXII. New York, 1938.—Leonard Bloomfield. Plains Cree Texts. PAES, XVI. New York, 1934; Sacred Stories of the Sweetgrass Cree. National Museum of Canada, Anthropological Series, XI. Ottawa, 1930.—Ella Deloria. Dakota Texts. PAES, XIV. New York, 1932.—George Amos Dorsey. Traditions of the Caddo. CI, XLI. Washington, 1905; Traditions of the Osage. FM, VII. Chicago, 1904; Traditions of the Skidi Pawnee. MAFLS, VIII. Boston and New York, 1904; The Cheyenne. FM, IX. Chicago, 1905; The Mythology of the Wichita. CI, XXI. Washington, 1904; The Pawnee: Mythology, part I. CI, LIX. Washington, 1906; Traditions of the Arikara. CI, XVII. Washington, 1904.— George Amos Dorsey and Alfred L. Kroeber. Traditions of the Arapaho. FM, V. Chicago, 1903.—James Owen Dorsey. The Thegiha Language. Washington, 1890.—George Bird Grinnell. Blackfoot Lodge Tales. New York, 1892; Pawnee Hero Stories and Folk-Tales. New York, 1889.—Pliny Earle Goddard. Sarsi Texts. UCal, XI. Berkeley, 1915.—Alfred L. Kroeber. Gros Ventre Myths and Tales. PaAM, I. New York, 1908.—Robert H. Lowie. The Assiniboine. PaAM, IV. New York, 1910; Myths and Traditions of the Crow Indians. PaAM, XXV. New York, 1918; The Northern Shoshone. PaAM, II. New York, 1909.—Walter McClintock. The Old North Trail, or life, legends and religion of the Blackfeet Indians. London, 1910.—Edward Sapir. The Southern Paiute. American Academy of Arts and Sciences, Proceedings, LXV. Boston, 1930-31.—Stephen Chapman Simms. Traditions of the Crows. FM, II. Chicago, 1903.—C. C. Uhlenbeck. Original Blackfoot Texts. Verhandelinger der Koninklijke Akademie van Wetenschappen te Amsterdam, XII, XIV. Amsterdam, 1911, 1912.—Clark Wissler and D. C. Duvall. Mythology of the Blackfoot Indians. PaAM, II. New York, 1909.

CENTRAL WOODLAND. Leonard Bloomfield. Menomini Texts. PAES, XII. New York, 1928.—J. P. B. de Josselin de Jong. Original Odjibwe-texts, with English translation, notes, and vocabulary. Leipzig and Berlin, 1913.—Walter James Hoffman. The Menomini Indians. RBAE, XIV. Washington, 1896.— William Jones. Fox Texts. PAES, I. Leyden, 1907.—William Jones and Truman Michelson. Ojibwa Texts. PAES, VII. 2 vols. New York, 1919.—Pàul Radin. Some Myths of the Ojibwa of Southeast Ontario. GSCan, II. Ottawa, 1914.— Henry Rowe Schoolcraft. Algic Researches. New York, 1839; The Myth of Hiawatha. London, 1856.—Alanson Skinner and John V. Satterlee. Folklore of the Menomini Indians. PaAM, XIII. New York, 1915.—Frank G. Speck. Myths and Folk-lore of the Timiskaming Algonquin and Timagami Ojibwa. GSCan, IX. Ottawa, 1915.

IROQUOIS. C. Marius Barbeau. Huron and Wyandot Mythology. GSCan, XI. Ottawa, 1915.—Mrs. Harriet Maxwell Clarke Converse. Myths and Legends of the New York State Iroquois. Albany, 1908.—Jeremiah Curtin. Seneca Indian Myths. Boston, 1923.—Jeremiah Curtin and J. N. B. Hewitt. Seneca Myths and Fictions. RBAE, XXXII. Washington, 1918.

NORTHEAST WOODLAND. Charles Godfrey Leland. The Algonquin Legends of New England. Boston, 1885.—William H. Mechling. Malecite Tales.

GSCan, IV. Ottawa, 1914.—Silas T. Rand. Legends of the Micmacs. New York, 1894.—John Dyneley Prince. Passamaquoddy Texts. PAES, X. New York, 1921. SOUTHEAST. J. Mooney. Myths of the Cherokee. RBAE, XIX. Washington, 1900.—Frank G. Speck. Catawba Texts. CU, XXIV. New York, 1934.—Günter Wagner. Yuchi Tales. PAES, XIII. New York, 1931.

SOUTHWEST. Ruth Benedict. Zuni Mythology. New York, 1935.—Franz Boas. Keresan Texts. PAES, VIII. New York, 1928.—Ruth Bunzel. Zuñi Texts. PAES, XV. New York, 1933.—F. H. Cushing. Zuñi Folk Tales. New York, 1901.— Pliny Earle Goddard. Jicarilla Apache Texts. PaAM, VIII. New York, 1911; Myths and Tales of the San Carlos Apache. PaAM, XXIV. New York, 1920; Myths and Tales from the White Mountain Apache. PaAM, XXIV. New York, 1920; Navaho Texts. PaAM, XXXIV. New York, 1934.—Harry Hoijer. Chiricahua and Mescalero Apache Texts. University of Chicago Publications in Anthropology, Linguistic Series. Chicago, 1938.—Washington Matthews. Navaho Legends. MAFLS, V. Boston, 1897.—Morris E. Opler. Myths and Legends of the Chiricahua Apache Indians. MAFLS, XXXVII. New York, 1942; Myths and Legends of the Lipan Apache Indians. MAFLS, XXXVI. New York, 1940; Myths and Tales of the Jicarilla Apache Indians. MAFLS, XXXI. New York, 1938.—Elsie Clews Parsons. Taos Tales. MAFLS, XXXIV. New York, 1940; Tewa Tales. MAFLS, XIX. New York, 1926.—Frank Russell. The Pima Indians. RBAE, XXVI. Washington, 1908.—Henry R. Voth. The Traditions of the Hopi. Chicago, 1905.

OTHER AMERICAN GROUPS

SOUTH AMERICAN INDIAN. Gustavo Barroso. Mythes, contes et légendes des Indiens: folk-lore brésilien. Paris, 1930.—W. H. Brett. Legends and Myths of the Aboriginal Indians of British Guiana. London, 1880.—P. Ehrenreich. Die Mythen und Legenden der südamerikanischen Urvölker und ihre Beziehungen zu denen Nordamerikas und der alten Welt. Berlin, 1905.—Th. Koch-Grünberg. Indianermärchen aus Südamerika. Jena, 1921.—R. Lenz. Araukanische Märchen und Erzählungen. Valparaiso, 1896.—Walter E. Roth. Animism and Folk-lore of the Guiana Indians. RBAE, XXX. Washington, 1915.—K. von den Steinen. Unter den Naturvölkern Zentral-Brasiliens. Berlin, 1894.—A good summary in H. B. Alexander. Latin American Mythology. Boston, 1920.

BRITISH TRADITION. Richard Chase. The Jack Tales. Boston, 1943.— Emelyn E. Gardner. Folklore from the Schoharie Hills, New York. Ann Arbor, 1937.—Harold W. Thompson. Body, Boots, and Britches. Philadelphia, 1940.

FRENCH TRADITION. C. Marius Barbeau. Contes populaires canadiens. Journal of American Folklore, XXIX, 1; XXX, 1; XXXII, 90.—Joseph M. Carrière. Tales from the French Folk-Lore of Missouri. Evanston and Chicago, 1937.—Alcée Fortier. Louisiana Folk-Tales. MAFLS, II. Boston, 1895.—G. Lanctot. Contes populaires canadiens. Journal of American Folklore, XXXVI, 201; XXXIX, 371.

SPANISH TRADITION—(NEW MEXICO). José Manuel Espinosa. Spanish Folk-Tales from New Mexico. New York, 1937.—Juan B. Rael. Cuentos Españoles de Colorado y de Nuevo Méjico. Journal of American Folklore, LII, 227 ff.; LV, 1 ff.—(MEXICO). Alfredo Ibarra. Cuentos y Leyendas de Mexico.

Mexico, 1941.—Paul Radin and A. M. Espinosa. Folklore de Oaxaca. New York, 1917.—(PUERTO RICO). Maria Cadilla de Martinez. Raices de la Tierra. Arecibo (Puerto Rico), 1941.—Rafael Ramírez de Arellano. Folklore portar-riqueño. Madrid, 1928.—(CHILE). Ramon A. Laval. Cuentos populares en Chile. Santiago, 1923; Leyendas y cuentos populares recogidos en Carahue. Santiago, 1920; Cuentos de Pedro Urdemales. Santiago, 1925.
PORTUGUESE TRADITION. Basilio de Magalhães. O Folk-lore no Brasil. Rio de Janeiro, 1928.—S. Roméro. Contos populares do Brasil. Lisboa, 1885.
AMERICAN NEGRO. Manuel J. Andrade. Folk-Lore from the Dominican Republic. MAFLS, XXIII. New York, 1930.—Martha Warren Beckwith. Jamaica Anansi Stories. MAFLS, XVII. New York, 1924.—A. M. H. Christensen. Afro-American Folk Lore. Boston, 1892.—Suzanne Comhaire-Sylvain. Les contes haïtiens. Wetteren (Belgique) and Port-au-Prince (Haïti), 1937.—Charles L. Edwards. Bahama Songs and Stories. MAFLS, III. Boston, 1895.—Arthur H. Fauset. Folklore from Nova Scotia. New York, 1931.—J. C. Harris. Nights with Uncle Remus. Boston and New York, 1911; Uncle Remus, His Songs and His Sayings. New York and London, 1915; Uncle Remus and His Friends. Boston and New York, 1892.—C. F. Hartt. Amazonian Tortoise Myths. Rio de Janeiro, 1875.—M. J. and F. S. Herskovits. Suriname Folk-Lore. CU, XXVII. New York, 1936.—C. C. Jones, Jr. Negro Myths from the Georgia Coast. Boston and New York, 1888.—W. Jekyll. Jamaican Song and Story. London, 1907.—Mary P. Milne-Horne. Mamma's Black Nurse Stories. Edinburgh, 1890.—Mary A. Owen. Voodoo Tales. New York, 1893.—Elsie Clews Parsons. Folk-lore of the Antilles, French and English. MAFLS, XXVI. 3 vols., New York, 1933, 1936, 1943; Folk-Lore of the Sea Islands, South Carolina. MAFLS, XVI. New York, 1923; Folk-Tales of Andros Island, Bahamas. MAFLS, XIII. New York, 1918.—Pamela Coleman Smith. Annancy Stories. New York, 1899.—A. J. de Souza Carniero. Os Mitos Africanos no Brasil. São Paulo, 1937.—Herman van Capelle. Mythen en Sagen uit West-Indië. Zutphen, 1926.

INDEX OF TALE TYPES

Arranged according to the Aarne-Thompson **Types of the Folk-Tale.** Italicized pages refer to principal discussion. See also lists on pp. 285-293.

I. ANIMAL TALES

1-99. Wild Animals

1. The theft of fish, 219f., 443
2. The tail-fisher, 219f., 241, 443
3. Sham blood and brains, 220, 226, 443
4. Carrying the sham-sick trickster, 220, 443
5. Biting the foot, 220, 226, 443
6. Inquiry about the direction of the wind, 218
7. The calling of three tree names, 220, 226
8. The painting, 220, 226
9A. In the stable the bear threshes, 202
9B. In the division of the crop the fox takes the corn, the bear the more bulky chaff, 198, 222
15. The theft of butter (honey) by playing godfather, 221, 443
20C. The animals flee in fear of the end of the world or of a war, 221
21. Eating his own entrails, 221, 226
30. The fox tricks the wolf into falling into a pit, 224
31. The fox climbs from the pit on the wolf's back, 218
32. The wolf descends into the well in one bucket and rescues the fox in the other, 218
33. The fox plays dead and is thrown out of the pit and escapes, 218
34. The wolf dives into the water for reflected cheese, 218
36. The fox in disguise violates the she-bear, 221, 443
37. Fox as nursemaid for bear, 221, 226, 443
38. Claw in split tree, 218
39. The bear pulls mountain ashes apart so that the fox's old mother can get berries, 224
41. The wolf overeats in the cellar, 218
43. The bear builds a house of wood; the fox of ice, 221, 226
44. The oath on the iron, 221
47A. The fox (bear, etc.) hangs by his teeth to the horse's tail: hare's lip, 222, 226, 241, 443
47B. The horse kicks the wolf in the teeth, 218
49. The bear and the honey, 224
50. The sick lion, 218
51. The lion's share, 218
55. The animals build a road, 227, 242

56A. The fox threatens to push down the tree, 225
56B. The fox persuades the magpies to bring their young into his house, 218
57. The raven with cheese in his mouth, 218
60. Fox and crane invite each other, 218
61. The fox persuades the cock to crow with closed eyes, 218
62. Peace among the animals—the fox and the cock, 218
65. The she-fox's suitors, 227
70. More cowardly than the hare, 218
71. Contest of frost and the hare, 224
72. Rabbit rides fox a-courting, 220
72**. In winter the hare says, "If it were warm, I should build a house," 218
75. The help of the weak, 218
76. The wolf and the crane, 218
77. The stag admires himself in a spring, 218
85. The mouse, the bird, and the sausage, 224
90. The needle, the glove, and the squirrel, 224

100-149. Wild Animals and Domestic Animals

100. The wolf as the dog's guest sings, 222
101. The old dog as rescuer of the child (sheep), 225
102. The dog as wolf's shoemaker, 227
103. The wild animals hide from the unfamiliar animal, 223
104. The cowardly duelers, 223, 245
105. The cat's only trick, 218
110. Belling the cat, 218
111. The cat and the mouse converse, 227
112. Country mouse visits city mouse, 218
115. The hungry fox waits in vain for the horse's lips (scrotum) to fall off, 224
116. The bear on the hay-wagon, 224
118. The lion frightened by the horse, 224
120. The first to see the sunrise, 225
121. Wolves climb on top of one another to tree, 193
122. The wolf loses his prey, 218
122A. The wolf (fox) seeks breakfast, 218
122B. The rat persuades the cat to wash her face before eating, 227
122C. The sheep persuades the wolf to sing, 218

II. ORDINARY FOLKTALES

300-749. A. Tales of Magic

400-459. Supernatural or Enchanted Husband (Wife) or Other Relatives

460-499. Superhuman Tasks

500-559. Supernatural Helpers

850-999. C. Novelle (Romantic tales)

1000-1199. D. Tales of the Stupid Ogre

III. JOKES AND ANECDOTES

1200-1349. Numskull Stories

1350-1439. Stories about Married Couples

1440-1524. Stories about a Woman (Girl)

1525-1874. Stories about a Man (Boy)

INDEX OF MOTIFS

Arranged according to Thompson, **Motif-Index of Folk-Literature.**
Only motifs actually referred to by number are listed here.

A. MYTHOLOGICAL MOTIFS

A0-A99. Creator

A21.1. Male and female creators, 307
A31. Creator's grandmother, 308, 310

A100-A499. Gods

A151.2. Garden of the gods, 277
A401. Mother Earth, 312

A500-A599. Demigods and Culture Heroes

A515.1.1. Twin culture heroes, 304
A531. Culture hero (demigod) overcomes monsters, 308
A532. Culture hero tames winds in caves, 306
A541. Culture hero teaches arts and crafts, 308
A561. Divinity's departure for the west, 308, 311
A575. Departed deity grants requests to visitors, 306
A580. Culture hero's (divinity's) expected return, 264, 308, 311

A600-A899. Cosmogony and Cosmology

A625. World parents: sky father and earth mother, 305, 311
A625.2. Raising of the sky, 311
A636. New creation shouted away, 311
A651. Hierarchy of worlds, 304, 311
A661. Heaven, 238
A671. Hell, 238
A672.1. Ferryman on river in lower world, 277
A692. Islands of the blessed, 238f.
A721.1. Theft of sun, 238, 305, 309
A724.1.1.Phaëthon, 314
A728.1. Sun-snarer: burnt mantle, 314, 446
A735. Pursuit of sun by moon, 308
A736.1. Sun sister and moon brother, 306
A751. Man in the moon, 238, 312
A755. Causes of moon's phases, 238
A761. Ascent to stars, 312
A771. Origin of Great Bear, 237
A773. Origin of Pleiades, 237, 312
A778. Origin of Milky Way, 237

A810. Primeval water, 311
A812. Earth Diver, 307f., 311
A815. Earth from turtle's back, 312
A841. Four world-columns, 312
A842. Atlas, 312
A843. Earth supported on post, 312

A900-A999. Topographical Features of the Earth

A901. Topographical features caused by experiences of primitive hero (demigod, deity), 239, 306
A920. Origin of the seas, 310
A965. Mountains from stones dropped, 239, 249
A966. Mountains and hills from stones thrown by giant at church, 239
A972. Indentions on rocks from prints left by man (beast), 239, 313
A985. Cliff from lovers' leap, 240, 313
A986. Bridge of the gods, 313

A1000-A1099. World Calamities

A1010. Deluge, 236, 313
A1012. Flood from tears, 313
A1013. Flood from belly, 313
A1018. Flood as punishment, 309
A1021. Deluge: escape in boat, 237, 313
A1021.1. Pairs of animals in ark, 237
A1021.2. Bird scouts sent out from ark, 237
A1022. Escape from deluge on mountain, 237
A1030. World-fire, 314

A1100-A1199. Establishment of Natural Order

A1111. Impounded water, 306, 309, 316
A1120. Establishment of present order: winds, 308
A1122. Cave of winds, 240, 315
A1125. Winds caused by flapping wings, 240, 315
A1127. Winds of the four quarters established, 315
A1131.1. Rain from tears, 240
A1135.1. Snow from feathers, 240
A1150. Determination of seasons, 305, 315
A1151. Theft of the seasons, 308, 315

E. THE DEAD

F. MARVELS

G. OGRES

H. TESTS

H382.1. Bride test: key in flax reveals laziness, 207
H383.1.1. Bride test: bread-making, 207
H384.1. Bride test: kindness—father-in-law disguised as beggar, 207
H481. Infant picks out his unknown father, 351

H500-H899. Tests of Cleverness

H504.1. Contest in life-like painting, 267
H530. Riddles, 163
H540.2.1. Queen of Sheba propounds riddles to Solomon, 266
H561.3. Solomon and Marcolf, 266
H561.5. King and clever minister, 267, 277
H592.1. Love like salt, 128
H601. Wise carving of the fowl, 159

H900-H1199. Tests of Prowess: Tasks

H901.1. Heads placed on stakes for failure in performance in task, 106, 280
H1010. Impossible tasks, 341
H1023.3. Task: bringing berries in winter, 341
H1050. Paradoxical tasks, 159

H1200-H1399. Tests of Prowess: Quests

H1212.1. Quest assigned because of feigned dream, 234
H1235. Succession of helpers on quest, 351
H1292. Answers found in otherworld to questions propounded on way, 277
H1312.1. Quest for three persons as stupid as his wife, 210
H1360. Quest for dangerous animals, 341

H1400-H1599. Other Tests

H1450.1. Waking contest, 342
H1511. Heat test, 341
H1511.1. Heat test: swallowing red hot stones, 341
H1511.2. Burning food test, 341
H1511.3. Smoke test, 342
H1511.4. Task: stealing ring from finger, 342
H1515. Poisoned food test, 341
H1521. Clam test, 342
H1522. Killing trees threaten hero, 342
H1531. Spine test, 341
H1532. Wedge test, 341
H1535. Precipice test, 341
H1536. Toboggan test, 333, 342
H1538. Drowning test, 341

J. THE WISE AND THE FOOLISH

J0-J199. Acquisition and Possession of Wisdom (Knowledge)

J21. Counsels proved wise by experience, 165
J121. Ungrateful son reproved by naïve action of his own son: preparing for old age, 445
J151.1. Wisdom of hidden old man saves kingdom, 267, 277

J200-1099. Wise and Unwise Conduct

J355.1. The widow's meal, 267

J1100-J1699. Cleverness

J1141.4. Confession induced by bringing unjust action against accused, 189
J1149.2. Cheater discovered by fishing in the street, 189
J1151.1.1. Talkative wife discredited, 189
J1151.1.2. Husband discredited by absurd truth, 189
J1151.1.3. The sausage rain, 189
J1153.1. Susanna and the Elders, 266
J1171.1. Solomon's judgment: the divided child, 266
J1191. Reductio ad absurdum of judgment, 159
J1193.1. Killing the fly on the judge's nose, 189
J1511. The rule must work both ways, 189
J1545.4.1. The besieged women's dearest possession, 270

J1700-J2799. Fools (and Other Unwise Persons)

J1750-J1809. One thing mistaken for another, 180
J1757. Rabbit thought to be cow, 190
J1772.1. Pumpkin thought to be ass's egg, 190
J1781.1. Steamship thought to be the devil, 190
J1791.3. Diving for cheese, 324
J1791.5. Diving for reflected enemy, 327
J1791.6. Diving for reflection of beautiful woman, 327
J1820. Inappropriate action from misunderstanding, 190
J1821. Swimming (fishing) in the flax field, 190
J1850. Gift or sale to animal (or object), 191
J1856.1. Meat fed to cabbages, 191
J1871. Filling cracks with butter, 191
J1872. Creaking limbs, 321
J1881.1.2. One cheese sent after another, 191
J1882.2. The ass as mayor, 191
J1883. Trickster joins bullrushes in a dance, 324
J1900. Absurd disregard or ignorance of animal's nature or habits, 191
J1904.1. Cow taken to roof to graze, 191
J1922.1. Marking the place on the boat, 191
J1930. Absurd disregard of natural laws, 192
J1932. Absurd practices connected with crops, 192

K. DECEPTIONS

K0-K99. Contests Won by Deception

K100-K299. Deceptive Bargains

M. ORDAINING THE FUTURE

N. CHANCE AND FATE

P. SOCIETY

Q. REWARDS AND PUNISHMENTS

R. CAPTIVES AND FUGITIVES

S. UNNATURAL CRUELTY

T. SEX

T11.4.1. Love through sight of hair of unknown princess, 276
T68. Princess offered as prize, 279
T230. Faithlessness in marriage, 209
T231. The faithless widow, 209
T251.1.1. Belfagor (devil frightened by shrewish wife), 209
T255. The obstinate wife, 210
T411.1. Lecherous father, 323
T415. Brother-sister incest, 304, 306
T417. Son-in-law seduces mother-in-law, 323
T500. Conception and birth, 340
T511. Conception from eating, 279, 340
T522. Conception from falling rain, 340
T524. Conception from wind, 307
T531. Conception from casual contact with man, 340
T540. Miraculous birth, 86, 340
T541.1.1. Birth from blood-clot, 335, 340
T541.2. Birth from wound, 340, 358

T541.3. Birth from tears, 340
T541.8. Birth from secretions of the body, 340
T541.8.2. Birth from mucus, 340
T545. Birth from ground, 335, 340
T547.1. Birth from seafoam, 304
T561. Child born in jug, 340
T573. Short pregnancy, 340
T575.1.3. Twins quarrel before birth, 307
T584.2. Child removed from body of dead mother, 336, 340
T612. Child born of slain mother cares for self during infancy, 337
T615. Supernatural growth, 309, 340
T645. Paramour leaves token with girl to give their son, 268
T646. Illegitimate child taunted by playmates, 268
T685.1. Twin adventurers, 341

V. RELIGION

V361. Christian child killed to furnish blood for Jewish rite, 268

W. TRAITS OF CHARACTER

W111.1. Contest in laziness, 210
W111.2.6. Boy eats breakfast, dinner, and supper, one immediately after other, 211

W111.3.2. Cat beaten for not working (lazy wife), 211

X. HUMOR

X111. Deaf men and their answers, 211
X411. Parson put to flight during his sermon, 212
X414. Parson rides ox into church, 212
X415. The hog in church, 212
X418. Parson lets dove fly in church, 212
X421. At the blessing of the grave the parson's ox breaks loose, 213
X424. The devil in the cemetery, 214
X431. Hungry parson and porridge pot, 213
X435. The boy applies the sermon, 213
X436. Parson sings like a goat, 213

X441. Parson and sexton at mass, 213
X445. Parson refreshes himself during sermon, 213
X900. Humor of lies and exaggerations, 157
X911. Man in barrel grabs wolf by tail, 214
X913. Boy shot from cannon, 214
X917. Man goes for spade to dig self out of earth, 214
X921. The wonderful hunt, 214
X925. Lie: sea has burned up, 215
X951. The extraordinary names, 215
X1020. Exaggerations, 215

Z. MISCELLANEOUS GROUPS OF MOTIFS

Z0-Z99. Formulas

Z11. Endless tales, 229
Z12. Unfinished tales, 230
Z13. Catch tales, 230
Z17. Rounds, 229
Z20. Cumulative tales, 234
Z21.1. Origin of chess, 234
Z21.2. Ehod mi yodea, 234
Z21.3.1. The animals with queer names, 233

Z23.1. The house is burned down, 234
Z31.1.1. Pif Paf Poltrie, 233
Z31.2.1. Funeral procession of the hen, 231
Z31.2.1.1. Death of the cock, 230
Z31.2.2. Death of the little hen, 230
Z31.2.2.1. Same: described with unusual words, 231
Z31.3.1. The fleeing pancake (gingerbread man), 231

Z100-Z199. Symbolism

Z200-Z299. Heroes

Z300-Z399. Unique Exceptions

GENERAL INDEX